The Hapsburg Monarchy

1867-1914

The
HAPSBURG
MONARCHY
1867-1914

Arthur J. May

**PROFESSOR OF HISTORY IN THE
UNIVERSITY OF ROCHESTER**

The Norton Library
W · W · NORTON & COMPANY · INC ·
NEW YORK

To H. J. M.

Books That Live
The Norton imprint on a book means that in the publisher's
estimation it is a book not for a single season but for the years.
W. W. Norton & Company, Inc.

PRINTED IN THE UNITED STATES OF AMERICA

1 2 3 4 5 6 7 8 9 0

Preface

IN A MEMORABLE PHRASE, WHICH HAS FIRMLY ROOTED ITSELF IN the soil of history, David Lloyd George alluded to the Hapsburg Monarchy as "that ramshackle realm." As clichés go, that one is not without superficial merit. For within this venerable state, smaller in area than Texas, a mélange of languages, traditions, and creeds nourished almost as many species of nationalism—which are the despair of the historian.

It was a herculean assignment to keep the centrifugal forces of nationalism from splitting the Hapsburg patrimony asunder. In the end the smash-up came by reason of World War I, whether "inevitably" or no may emerge from another study, now in preparation, covering the span from Sarajevo to the Treaties of St. Germain and Trianon.

Inside the Hapsburg boundaries wide disparities prevailed in economic conditions, social habits, and standards of culture. It was a far cry indeed from cosmopolitan and cultivated Vienna, for instance, to the remote and backward hamlets of the Ukrainian east. From this polyglot Monarchy, moreover, came the largest body of emigrants to the United States in the early twentieth century. Acquaintance which the writer had as a boy with human fragments of that movement, who settled in bleak anthracite communities of Pennsylvania, first excited his curiosity about the strange and seemingly far-off lands from which they had emigrated.

How the extraordinary and amorphous Hapsburg Monarchy came into being is sketched at the beginning of this study. Then the evolution of the two partners, Austria and Hungary, has been traced, period by period, from the epochal *Ausgleich* of 1867 to the eve of World War I. Paralleling the record in domestic affairs are summaries of the vital role of the Dual Monarchy in the anarchical diplomacy of very modern Europe. It is hoped, however, that excessive consideration has not been devoted to political affairs and the power of the State.

Social, economic, and cultural developments have been comprehensively surveyed and, at appropriate places, the cultural attainments of the smaller nationalities have been woven into the narrative. Various projects for remodeling the Monarchy, none of which, alas, was put to performance, and the bonds that held the disparate peoples together in an era of rampant nationalism have been appraised in the concluding chapter.

It would be arrant dogmatism to assert that every puzzle in the realm of the Hapsburgs has been unraveled in these pages. Many problems remain obscure, awaiting the patient toil of dedicated historical spadeworkers.

Unpublished evidence has been drawn, in my investigations, from official treasure houses, political mainly, in Vienna, London, and Washington. For contemporary flavor, heavy reliance has been placed upon the *Neue Freie Presse,* the great middle-of-the-way German newspaper, which sometimes spoke the mind of Hapsburg officialdom, and the *Arbeiter Zeitung,* the leading organ of democratic Socialism.

And yet to a considerable extent, this study represents a synthesis of a broad range of monographic researches and larger works of scholarship. To get "the feel" of the Hapsburg lands and peoples, so invaluable for faithful historical reconstruction, the writer has four times visited the countries formerly embraced in the Monarchy and has wandered over large sections of them.

Nearly every page reflects gleanings from the labors and learning of scholars in many countries. Very special debts have been scantily acknowledged in footnotes. Considerations of cost, regretably, compelled me to pare the bibliography to the bone; little more than a sampling of the works laid under tribute appears at the end of the book. Half a dozen studies which were published too recently for use are appended.

No scholar can ever adequately discharge debts of gratitude and esteem to individuals who have personally contributed in one way and another to his studies. It will not be invidious, however, to record my exceptional obligations to the late Professor Dr. Alfred F. Pribram and the late Professor Dr. Ludwig Bittner of Vienna, men of radically different mold, and to Professor R. W. Seton-Watson of the University of London. Professor Sidney B. Fay of Harvard, with characteristic generosity, offered suggestions for improvement of the manuscript.

The faculty committee on publications of the University of Rochester—Professor Emeritus John R. Slater, Professors Kathrine Koller and Dexter Perkins, and Mr. John R. Russell—painstakingly read the manuscript. A liberal grant from the Board of Trustees of the University has made publication possible. Miss Marjorie Gilles of Rochester has cheerfully borne most of the heat and burden of typing the manuscript.

My heaviest and happiest debt is hinted at in the dedication.

The University of Rochester   Arthur J. May
Christmas 1950

Contents

The Hapsburg Monarchy

1867-1914

CHAPTER ONE

THE REALM OF THE HAPSBURGS

On december 2, 1848, francis joseph, a slim, lithe youth, was crowned emperor of Austria. For the high and exacting responsibilities of ruling a realm composed of a mélange of "races," languages, customs, and creeds without close parallel in the world, the new sovereign was wretchedly prepared. His equipment in political philosophy was meager and old-fashioned, for it was grounded on the antiquated precept that monarchs were chosen of God to bring happiness to their subjects, with the help of very human bureaucrats. That conservative doctrine had served the Hapsburgs not too badly in the past; it would be a sound guide for the future.

From the throne Francis Joseph looked out upon a veritable sea of troubles. Across his many-tongued realm the ancient bonds of loyalty, of obedience, of discipline seemingly had snapped. Hungary had rebelled; the Italian provinces had rebelled; Bohemia had rebelled; Germans had rebelled. Citizens of Vienna, reputedly gay and nonchalant, had chased away old Prince Metternich, who for two generations had powerfully directed the destinies of Europe and, to a lesser extent, the affairs of Austria. The Minister of War, Count Latour, popularly detested as a symbol of stagnation and reaction, had been barbarously murdered, and Vienna's academic youth, intoxicated with the enthusiasms of the great French Revolution, had perished on barricades fighting for broader freedoms.

Confronting the untried, serious-minded lad of eighteen, then, was an exceedingly complex political situation which might well have daunted a far more mature and fundamentally wiser mind.

II

The evolution of the realm over which Francis Joseph was summoned to rule is surely one of the amazing oddities of European history. Power had grown up without a national foundation. The Hapsburg empire of 1848 consisted of a grotesque collection of odds and ends—Austria proper, the core of the realm, Hungary, Bohemia, parts of Italy and Poland—which by some of the strangest of political whims had fallen into the possession of a certain dynasty, the Hapsburg. European states of that heterogeneous character had existed before, to be sure, such as the Burgundian kingdom of the fifteenth century, but their annals had been short and none too sweet.

The original nucleus of the Hapsburg Monarchy belonged to the far-ranging dominion of Charlemagne; indeed, the very name Austria derives from the circumstance that the region was an eastern rampart of the Carolingian realm, set up to guard against marauding tribesmen to the East.[1] It was *Marca Orientalis,* the eastern mark, the Oesterreich, or in its Latin form, Austria. This particular Austria was not unique, for other areas in Europe were similarly labeled; in fact, Austria was a term often employed whenever a region was partitioned into eastern and western sections, but only for that Austria south of the Danube and beyond the Enns did the designation stick.

Earlier peopled by Celts, whom the Romans had subdued just before the dawn of the Christian era, and by Mongolian Avars, the region was occupied by German colonists after Charlemagne's conquests.[2] But Frankish lordship over Austria was rudely abbreviated. Crude barbarians relentlessly harried the eastern mark, chief among them the plundering pagan Magyars, soon to be considered, who in 907 totally destroyed this outpost of Charlemagne's. From the beginning Austria served as a meeting place and a battleground of Slavs, Germans, and Magyars, and that it continued to be until the downfall of the Monarchy in 1918.

It was Otto the Great, refounder of the German empire as the Holy Roman Empire (962), who recreated Austria as a bulwark against external aggression. To the Babenberg family, whose ancestral lands lay in the German Main valley, the Austrian mark, which covered merely the area round the present city of Vienna, was assigned (976) on feudal tenure. By successive Babenberg rulers the feudatory was expanded piece by piece, until it exceeded in strength all other German states, Bohemia alone excepted. It was entirely fitting that the Roman-German emperor should raise the master of Austria to the dignity of duke (1156) and allow him considerable autonomy. Styria and much of "Upper Austria" accrued to the Babenbergs by inheritance (1192) and part of Carniola to the south by purchase (1229).

Now it was that medieval Austria reached the zenith of its prosperity and power, the golden epoch falling in the reign of Leopold VI, who died in 1230, the contemporary of such renowned figures as Pope Innocent III, Richard the Lion-Hearted, and the famed Philip Augustus of France. Vienna, which was selected as the seat of the government in 1146, developed into one of the most affluent of German communities; well located to profit by the trade of middle Europe, Vienna benefited, along with the rest of the duchy, from the stimulus to commerce during the Crusades. As early as 1189, Vienna secured a formal charter granting the municipality judicial, administrative, and commercial rights and regulating the operations of foreign merchants. Early in the thirteenth century, stout fortifications were raised round Vienna, financed, tradition asserts, with the ransom paid for the release of Richard the Lion-Hearted, who had unluckily fallen into the toils of the Austrian duke.

Surpassing wealth made Vienna an oasis for the cultivation of the higher living. There and at other points in the duchy, monastic houses of several Christian orders were erected and generously endowed—isles of enlightenment in a sea of general ignorance. Not until 1469, however, was Vienna raised to a bishopric, and to an archbishopric only in 1722. Much energy the quarrelsome Babenberg dukes expended in warfare with neighboring "Bohemians" and Magyars. Magyar warriors pushed into Austria in 1246, and, though the invader was defeated, the Austrian duke, Frederick II, suffered a mortal wound. With his death the male line of the Babenbergs became extinct; poets and monastic chroniclers bewailed the passing of this bellicose feudalist and for generations the anniversary of his death was the occasion for popular lamentations.

Over the succession to the Austrian duchy fighting at once broke out, for the pope had assigned the region to a noble from Baden, while the Roman-German emperor had given it to a Bavarian. But with the approval of bishops and leading nobles Ottokar II of Bohemia (c. 1230–1278) was elected duke and he consolidated his position by wedding the sister of the last Babenberg. By force of arms he firmly joined Styria to his domain, and by inheritance Carinthia and a bit of Carniola.

Since Ottokar had succeeded his father as king of Bohemia, he stood forth as the mightiest prince of the holy German empire. Ambition spurred him to seek the office of German emperor, but the imperial electors instead conferred (1273) the crown upon Count Rudolph of Hapsburg (1218–1291), the strongest feudalist of southwestern Germany, esteemed for his prudence and his genius in avoiding controversy with the papacy. Ottokar declined to recognize Rudolph and refused to yield up the Austrian territories which the Hapsburg claimed, but in the warfare that ensued Ottokar was worsted and obliged to cede the Austrian lands to Rudolph. Renewal of the fighting cost Ottokar his life, and his grand design of a great middle Danubian realm, governed from Bohemia, collapsed. Rudolph of Hapsburg beat down the feudal resistance to his rule and in 1282—one of the more important dates in Austrian history—he proclaimed the newly acquired territories as a hereditary possession of the House of Hapsburg.[3]

Once the Austrian duchy had passed to the Hapsburgs, it remained in their name until 1918. Rudolph invested his son Albert as duke and actual sovereign of the possession and thenceforth House of Austria and House of Hapsburg were identical.

In spite of struggles for the gilded German imperial crown and family bickerings, Hapsburg dukes gradually added a batch of adjoining feudatories to their inheritance. Of those gains, that of most of the Tyrol, acquired in 1363, which brought the duchy into geographical alignment with the peninsula of Italy, had the most considerable significance. At that point the Hapsburg domain was essentially the same as the territory of the Austrian republic created in 1919. Italian cultural influences, architectural especially, now enriched the land and lives of Hapsburg subjects.

High-spirited, ambitious Duke Rudolph IV (1358–1365) devised stratagems to link Bohemia and Hungary to his possessions, and dreamed of liberating his territory from the German empire. Documents that he produced to fortify his pretensions were pronounced spurious by the scholar Petrarch. Rudolph sponsored the founding of the University of Vienna, financed the enlargement of the cathedral church of the capital, and generously encouraged commercial enterprise. A chronicler of the day recorded that if Rudolph had not died prematurely he would "either have raised Austria to the stars or led it to the deepest degradation." To the Hapsburg lands part of Istria, at the head of the Adriatic, was annexed in 1374, and eight years later the serviceable port of Trieste voluntarily united with Austria to escape the servitude of Venice.

When, in 1438, Duke Albert V was chosen German emperor, Hapsburg prestige rose higher, and by marrying the heiress of the kingdoms of Hungary and Bohemia Albert V became titular sovereign of those states as well, thus realizing an old ambition of his family. But his authority over Bohemia was never more than nominal, and both kingdoms soon slipped from the Hapsburg grasp. Albert perished on his way to do battle with the onrushing Turks, and during the reign of his son Ladislas V (the Posthumous), the once extensive family holdings dwindled to tiny dimensions. Uprisings on all sides stripped him of power and at his death the bond with Bohemia and Hungary was rent asunder. Even Austria itself was parceled out among his relatives.

Albert V's uncle, chosen German king and Roman emperor (1452) as Frederick III (1415–1493), obtained the archduchy of Austria and from this time onward until the formal extinction of the Roman-German empire in 1806, except for a short interlude in the eighteenth century, the imperial German crown was worn by a Hapsburg. Quarreling between Frederick III and other legatees was constant; civil war, *jacqueries*, gangs of brigands ravaged the countryside and paralyzed trade and industry. Nonetheless, in this time of troubles, Frederick III contrived to extend his territory, picking up a section of Istria and the seaport of Fiume (1471).

Dynastic rivalry between Frederick III and the celebrated king of Hungary, Matthias I (1440–1490) or Corvinus, produced almost endless war. Vienna passed under the control of the Hungarian in 1485, as did much of the rest of Hapsburg Austria. These successes whetted Matthias' ambition to obtain the Holy Roman crown and to bring the whole middle Danube under his sway, but gout carried him off before his purposes were fulfilled.

Frederick III, who had retired from public life (1486) in favor of his son, Maximilian I (1459–1519), soon followed Matthias to the grave. In spite of multiplied misfortunes, in spite of expulsion from his own capital, Frederick III clung fantastically to the belief that his family was destined for world mastery. That conviction he reinforced by arranging (1477) a match between his heir, Maximilian, and Mary, wealthy heiress of Burgundy, which brought to the Hapsburgs the fat province of Flanders and parcels of modern France. Frederick's soaring confidence in the mission of the Hapsburgs was expressed in the letters AEIOU, which he inscribed in books and had cut on public buildings; in his own words they meant "Alles Erdreich ist Oesterreich Untertan" (Austriae est imperare orbi universo; "To Austria is the whole world subject"). In spite of his faults, errors of omission and commission, Frederick III had nonetheless defended the imperial prerogatives and prepared the way for the later eminence of the imperial Austrian line.

Spoken of sometimes as the second founder of the Hapsburg fortunes, Maximilian I cherished exalted personal ambitions, and even thought at one time of seeking the papal tiara. While he reigned, the Burgundian properties of his wife, Mary, the districts of Görz and Gradisca, and Tyrolese parcels were added to the family holdings. Aspiring to the kingship of Hungary, Maximilian struck a bargain with the reigning Hungarian sovereign which would net him the crown if the latter died without male issue. That contract, fresh evidence of Hapsburg covetousness for Hungary, signified that the future of the dynasty lay chiefly to the East, where a formidable menace not alone to Austria, but to Christendom entire, had arisen in the terrifying advance of the fanatical Moslem Turks.[4]

III

At the dawn of the modern age the Austria of Maximilian I was a well-knit state and a not inconsiderable factor in the high politics of Europe—a state far removed from the diminutive Carolingian border dependency on the south bank of the Danube and east of the Enns. Strategic location, inherent strength, and Hapsburg ascendancy in "Germany" presaged Austrian prominence in European affairs and implicated her in the tangled international involvements of modern times.

By political astuteness, profitable alliances, lucky inheritances, and a succession of enterprising marriages, the Hapsburgs had built up a splendid power, and the end was not yet. The witticism coined by the droll Hungarian, Matthias Corvinus,

> Bella gerant alii! Tu, felix Austria, nube;
> Nam quae Mars aliis, dat tibi regna Venus,
> (Let other powers make war! Thou, happy Austria, marry;
> For Venus will give you those realms which usually Mars bestows),

aptly hit off an astute and fashionable way in which wings were built on to the House of Hapsburg.

By marrying Mary of Burgundy, Maximilian I had done well for himself and he managed even better for his son, Philip, and his grandson, Ferdinand. The first took to wife Joan, heiress of Spain, which put the Hapsburgs in a position to lord it over a world-wide empire upon which the sun never set. Charles V, the offspring of this marriage, exercised authority over more territory, in fact, than any other European sovereign before or since: Flanders, the Netherlands, Franche Comté, the Spanish kingdom together with Naples, Sicily and Sardinia, the vast overseas dominions of Spain, and, momentarily, the Austrian lands of the Hapsburgs too.

For Ferdinand, Maximilian contrived a marriage with Anna, daughter of Ladislas, king of Bohemia and Hungary. If good fortune attended the Hapsburgs, these lands would fall into the voracious family basket. Fundamentally, the matrimonial stratagems of Maximilian were inspired by dynastic traditions and ambitions, but he was also animated by a loftier motive—the desire to unite the Christian powers for defense against the infidel Turk.

For all his political activity—and he was indefatigable, fought wars incessantly, lived in the saddle—Maximilian I took time and had the inclination to befriend and patronize culture and letters, after the manner of Renaissance princes. Scholars and artists such as Conrad Peutinger, Augsburg humanist and student of Roman antiquities, and Albrecht Dürer he reckoned among his friends; Dürer drew illustrations for books that the emperor wrote. All manner of painters, engravers, and sculptors were beneficiaries of Maximilian's fostering care; and other Hapsburg princes and the nobility too fostered cosmopolitan tastes in art and architecture and collected rich treasures of painting, later the pride of a great empire.

At Maximilian's death in 1519, Charles V was chosen Roman-German emperor, but he established himself in Spain, bestowing his Austrian lands upon his brother, Archduke Ferdinand. It was in the year 1526 that the Hapsburg Monarchy really came into being. Ferdinand then obtained the ancient crowns of Bohemia and Hungary, which radically transformed the character of the Hapsburg realm. Up to that point Austria had been pretty thoroughly German, despite the presence of enclaves of Slavs; thenceforth Austria was an extremely polyglot realm, whose sovereigns, preoccupied with the responsibilities of non-German peoples, failed to maintain lordship over German Europe.

IV

Before the merger with Austria in 1526, Bohemia and Hungary were kingdoms with brilliant pasts, national heroes, unique traditions and customs, and distinctive dominant tongues. Each of them merits a few explanatory comments of a historical character.

At the time that Hapsburg authority was established, the kingdom of Bohemia, comprising the provinces of Bohemia, Moravia, and Silesia, was inhabited by men who were chiefly Czech in speech and sentiment, but contained a considerable admixture of Germans. Here was a classic arena of linguistic and nationalistic antagonisms. Learned scholars, ethnologists, philologists, historians, have engaged in interminable and acrimonious controversy as to the relative proportions of the two nationalities in Bohemia and the comparative merits of the contributions each made to the fair name of the kingdom.

It would appear that as long ago as the eighth century B.C. Bohemia had an ethnologically mixed character. Celtic folk doubtless were the first inhabitants in historic times and, by reason of invasions, Slavic-speaking people assumed importance in the final centuries of the pre-Christian era. But German clansmen meanwhile had established settlements and impressed upon the region a pattern of living, an outlook, that was clearly German. After about 500 A.D., migrations of Germans westward reopened Bohemia to Slav occupation and it took on a heavily Slavic complexion, the Slavs of the area coming to be called Czechs.

Dubious legend has it that Bohemia figured conspicuously in an early medieval confederacy, at whose head stood Moravia, which effectively resisted conquest by the masterful Charlemagne. To escape subjugation by the fierce Magyars, who had overwhelmed Moravia, Bohemia commended itself to a German king early in the tenth century, pledging to pay tribute, without, however, sacrificing its political identity, it seems.

After the Magyar invasions had been stopped, Bohemia itself pursued an expansionist career, overpowering and retaining the northern section of Moravia, while the southern district, whose people were Slovak Slavs, kinsmen of the Czechs, passed by conquest to the Magyars. In the centuries that followed, Bohemia underwent a process of Germanization; native nobles frequently intermarried with Germans; priests moving in from Germany carried with them German ways and manners, and the German tongue vied with Latin as the speech of the cultured. Traders, craftsmen, and peas-

ants, moreover, attracted from Germany to counterbalance the local aristocracy, reinforced the German element in Bohemia, and where these newcomers took root their descendants lived until 1945. By cession of Poland in
1335 the heavily German duchy of Silesia was linked to the historic provinces of Bohemia and Moravia.

Political power in the Bohemian state was shared by the king with a
feudal assembly or diet, composed of great nobles, knights, and clergy. Upon
the extinction of the native dynasty (the Přemyslide) in 1306, foreigners were
chosen by the diet to wear the royal crown. Charles I (1346–1378), Roman-
German emperor as well as Bohemian king, temporarily retarded the Germanizing drift, and his reign, blessed by material and cultural progress, is
spoken of by German and Czech alike as the golden age.

Prague, the Bohemian capital, grew into the most prosperous city of central Europe, and the royal university, founded in 1348 with papal sanction
and richly endowed by monarch, nobles, and prelates, was esteemed as the
finest institution of the highest learning beyond the Alps. The international
composition of the student body reflected the belief that rival national cultures in Bohemia would blend into a cosmopolitan community, but that expectation scarcely outlived Charles I.

Czech aversion to German priests and townsmen and German ways and
manners in general found fierce, open expression in the Hussite wars, half
religious, half political in inspiration, of the early fifteenth century. Professor John Huss, spiritual son of John Wycliffe and one of Martin Luther's
spiritual fathers, the preëminent hero of the Czech nation, roused his countrymen against their German neighbors, dwelling upon the financial exactions of "foreign" laymen and churchmen. Primitive passions thus and then
whipped up never wholly died away. Huss's death in 1415, as a heretic, at
the instance of the Council of Constance, set a martyr's halo on his head
and gave a decided impetus to Czech nationalism and incipient Protestantism.[5]

A furious German crusade against heresy and heretics in Bohemia caused
widespread devastation and untold suffering on both sides, leaving imperishable memories of a German-Czech feud which historians of a later age
revived and romanticized. For a time the Hussite warfare halted the Germanization of Bohemia, but upon its close the tide of German immigration
set in anew.

As sovereign, the diet of Bohemia in 1471 chose Ladislas II, a prince of
Poland, and subsequently the crown of Hungary was likewise conferred
upon him. It was his son and heir who perished at Mohács in 1526, an event
that was the prelude to Hapsburg lordship over the Bohemian kingdom.

V

Of all the themes worthy of investigation, the study of the origins of national groupings ranks among the most challenging, and not the least interesting is the investigation of the beginnings of the Magyars.[6] Their language classifies them with the Finno-Ugrian family. Once upon a time this people possessed Turki physical features and even nowadays the high flat cheekbones of the Asiatic nomad occasionally distinguish their descendants, though intermarriage with other stocks has radically modified the physical appearance of the mass of the Magyars. Among the aristocracy, blood mixture was even more extensive than among commoners.

From the wastes of western Asia the Magyars marched across Russia late in the ninth century, pushed beyond the Carpathians, displacing the Avars there residing, and absorbed the tattered remnants of the Huns. On into the valley of the Danube the fearless, ferocious Magyar warriors galloped, conquering Slavs who lived in their path and driving a wedge into the body of middle European Slavdom which exists to this hour. The accepted date for the foundation of the Magyar state on the Danube is 896.

From that base Magyar invaders terrorized surrounding peoples, earning for themselves an enduring reputation for savagery and inhumanity; it is said that they were called Hungarians because of their appetite for human prey. Not far from Augsburg in 955 they were decisively whipped by the levies of Emperor Otto the Great and obliged to be content with a share of the fat and fertile Danubian plain. Shortly, under the leadership of the fabulous King Stephen, the Magyars entered the Roman Catholic communion, becoming beneficiaries of and participants in the more orderly and civilized ways of Christendom. From Rome in 1001 came papal sanction for a free and independent Magyar kingdom, and the sanctified King Stephen has been venerated above all the heroes of the Magyar nation.

With the history of Hungary as a potent medieval state there is no need to deal here, but a few central threads in the skein, which have had lasting importance, deserve attention. First of all, the boundaries of the kingdom were rounded out by the seizure of adjoining regions. At the outset of the twelfth century, a Magyar monarch, having overpowered the Slav-peopled kingdom of Croatia, which included coastal Dalmatia, installed himself as sovereign of Croatia under terms which ever since have been a gushing well of debate and dispute. According to the Magyar interpretation, Croatia was annexed as a conquered country, while Croat scholars contended that their kingdom voluntarily united with Hungary as an allied nation and that each partner was autonomous, the two being linked by a common ruler. Certain it is that in the early period of the union Croatian legal customs were perpetuated and Magyars were forbidden to acquire landed property.

Northern Hungary, the dwelling place of the Slovaks, was fully incorporated in the Magyar state before the thirteenth century had closed. For the sake of convenience this area may be called Slovakia, though prior to 1939 there never was an independent Slovak state, nor a region officially designated as Slovakia. Ethnically akin to the Czechs, the Slovaks wrote in the Czech language, and no literature in Slovak dialects appeared before the advent of the Jesuits in the era of the Counter Reformation; for public business Latin was ordinarily used in Slovakia. Such towns as existed were largely dominated by German immigrants and the Slovaks in the main were unlettered, submissive serfs, subject to haughty Magyar overlords.

Almost simultaneously with Slovakia, Transylvania to the east was absorbed into the Magyar kingdom. Once a part of the old Roman empire, Transylvania was settled by Rumanians, by Magyar colonists in favored valleys, and by "Saxons" imported from Germany as frontier guardsmen and "scientific" farmers.

Just before the middle of the thirteenth century, Mongol marauders out of Asia ruthlessly pillaged and might utterly have wrecked the Magyar kingdom, had they not been withdrawn, haunted, perhaps, by fear of starvation in a land which they had despoiled. Following the Mongol evacuation, Rumanian peasants trekked into Transylvania, as did Balkan refugees, Serbs principally, fleeing before the oncoming Turks; and some Serbs took up land in the Banat of Temesvár, which the Magyars had annexed in the eleventh century. Moreover, after 1382, Hungary embraced a region to the south and west of the Carpathians, sometimes spoken of as Ruthenia or Carpatho-Russia, and peopled by Ruthenes or Ukrainians.[7]

As conquerors the Magyars had entered the Danubian valley and as conquerors they remained, haughtily lording it over the subjugated. Rather like the Chinese, the Magyars believed that the rest of humanity possessed little that had value; for "foreigners" their contempt was boundless, as is illustrated by the adage, "Extra Hungariam non est vita, et si est vita, non est ita" (Outside of Hungary nothing exists, or if anything does exist, it is not comparable to what we have). According to national law, all descendants of the original Magyar invaders were equals; they formed the "nation" and jealously they guarded their special privileges, such as exemption from taxation. In time, social differentiation separated the wealthier Magyar nobles from the lesser gentry.

Aside from territorial expansion, the evolution of the Hungarian constitutional structure in the medieval epoch has had enduring significance. From the king in 1222, the nobility exacted the famous *Aurea Bulla,* or Golden Bull, the Magyar counterpart of England's Magna Charta, which, while reaffirming traditional liberties, transformed what had been an autocratic regime into an aristocratic one. In the Golden Bull it was forbidden the king to imprison a noble without legal warrant or to levy taxes on the nobility and the churchmen. All freemen, all the nobles, were allowed to participate in the election of the ruler, which meant a wider franchise than prevailed in England before 1832, and under certain conditions the nobility might lawfully resist the crown, even to the point of taking up arms. A national assembly comprising nobles, ecclesiastics, and representatives of counties and towns was to be convened annually, though the "third estate" had relatively little weight since the vote of its delegates was equal only to that of the aristocracy of a single county. Yet to the towns, many of whose citizens were Germans invited in by kings, extensive privileges were granted, such as the rights of refusing admission to "foreigners" and of conducting business on their own terms.

The Hungarian county system, inaugurated in the tenth century and managed by the local gentry, attained lasting importance in Magyar constitutionalism. Each county boasted a council or assembly which sent deputies to the royal diet with precise instructions on how to vote; and the assemblies passed and enforced local legislation, maintained courts of justice, and chose officials to administer finance and command the military forces. Against arbitrary acts by the crown, the county assemblies possessed two potent weapons, which they did not hesitate to unsheathe: refusal to collect taxes or to furnish soldiers, and refusal to execute royal decrees that the high-spirited gentry held to be unconstitutional.

The third memorable fact about pre-Hapsburg Hungary was its service as the shield of western Christendom against the Turks. Toward the close of the fourteenth century the Ottoman peril first loomed upon the Magyar horizon, in an hour when the kingdom was tormented by internal dissension arising out of struggles for the crown, a kind of political football after the ending of the original Arpád dynasty in 1301. Chief figure in the resistance to Turkish invasion was John Hunyádi (c. 1387–1456), whose troops not only drove the enemy back into the Balkans but themselves pressed deep into that troublesome peninsula. Hungary's independence was thus assured and Hunyádi deserved and received international acclaim as the bright and flashing sword of Christendom.

The Magyar gentry, grown weary of kings imported from abroad, now chose Hunyádi's son, Matthias I, or Corvinus (1458–1490), as their ruler. While he reigned, Hungary attained the peak of its brilliance, the final epoch of prosperity and grandeur as an independent state, and Corvinus has been honored as one of the greatest of the nation's heroes and one of the most accomplished of European monarchs.

An illustrious statesman, and a canny diplomatist, Corvinus was also an energetic warrior doing battle with Turkey and Poland, with Bohemia and Austria. For a time conquered Vienna, as has been observed, served him as capital. Sometimes likened to Bonaparte for his versatility and attainments, Corvinus established a reputation for honesty, fidelity, and probity which made him an ideal figure for patriotic emulation. Yet in military campaigns against his Christian neighbors, he squandered Hungarian resources, which might have been better employed in a full-bodied assault upon the Turks.[8]

Upon the death of Corvinus, the Magyar oligarchs bestowed the crown of St. Stephen on Ladislas II of Bohemia, who was succeeded by his ill-starred son, Louis II (1506–1526).

VI

Suleiman the Magnificent, most masterful of Ottoman sultans, undertook in 1526 the crowning campaign of his career.[9] In August of that year his armies annihilated the flower of the Hungarian forces and of the national leadership on the historic plain of Mohács, on the west bank of the Danube, rather more than a hundred miles south of Budapest. The young and frivolous king, Louis II, fleeing from the scene of carnage, was accidentally drowned in a small stream. That twin disaster heralded the beginning of Turkish domination over much of Hungary, and facilitated the merger of Hungary, as well as of Bohemia, for Louis II was sovereign there too, with Austria.

Archduke Ferdinand of Austria (1519–1564), brother-in-law of the childless Louis II, claimed the crowns of Hungary and Bohemia, both by treaty and by right of his wife. The assemblies of the two kingdoms eventually ratified the claim by naming him king, though entering reservations intended to safeguard the independence and national liberties of their countries. It was the stark menace of Turkish conquest, the mutual need for self-preservation, that brought to pass the association of Austria, Hungary, and Bohemia, each with prized traditions, under the single ruling house of Hapsburg.

Irresistibly the Turkish flood rolled along the broad valley of the Danube, and in 1529 it lapped at the very walls of Vienna. But there Suleiman and his hosts were brought face to face with the first power able to arrest their progress—the triune Hapsburg realm. Defeated, the invader was compelled to drop back into Hungary, and more than a century elapsed before Turkish mastery over Hungary was fully broken. The kingdom of St. Stephen in fact dissolved into three fragments: Transylvania, the central part of the state, and Hapsburg or "Royal" Hungary. Transylvania, where native Magyar princes held sway under Turkish suzerainty, gained full independence for a time, only to fall wholly under the Moslem scimitar again. There much of the Magyar heritage in politics and culture was perpetuated; there benevolent religious toleration prevailed; there the Reformation carried hosts into the Calvinistic worship.

Over the central Hungarian plain, meantime, Turkish control was absolute, exercised through a pasha residing in Buda, and part of Croatia and the Banat, too, were administered by agents of the sultan. Many Magyar residents, nobles and commoners, fled or were enslaved or slain, and peasants were introduced from the Balkans to till the vacant soil. The third section of the kingdom, the western borderlands and Slovakia, Hapsburg arms managed to recover, though annual tribute had to be paid to the Turkish sultan for almost a century. Into this "Royal Hungary" Germanizing influences penetrated, which the enfeebled Magyar gentry combatted as best they could.

Much of the international politics of southeastern Europe in the seventeenth century centered upon the struggle between Hapsburg and Turk, between Cross and Crescent, for supremacy on the lower Danube and the Sava. Toward the end of the century the Turks renewed their pressure westward and in 1683 encamped themselves for two months outside of imperial Vienna, utterly destroying the suburbs. Then an international army, Polish chivalry marshaled by King John Sobieski and imperial German troops, relieved the beleaguered Danubian capital and possibly saved Christendom from conquest by the infidel.

From 1683 onward the record of Turkey in Europe is a bleak story of decay and retreat, with Austria as the principal, but by no means the only, beneficiary. When, in 1687, Buda was delivered from the Turk, a fraction of the Magyar diet out of gratitude renounced the historic right of resistance to the monarch and recognized the hereditary right of the Hapsburgs in the male line to the crown of St. Stephen, thus abandoning the century-old principle of an elective kingship. It was prescribed, however, that before taking the crown a new ruler would have to confirm all "customs, privileges, and prerogatives" of the Magyar "nation."

Hapsburg soldiers in time expelled the Turks from Hungary (except the Banat), from Croatia, and from Transylvania. The decisive battle, curiously, was fought at Mohács (1687), the site of the Turkish triumph of 1526; and in the peace of Carlowitz of 1699, Turkey formally acknowledged Hapsburg sovereignty over Hungary. Then on into the Balkans Austrian armies marched, and in 1717 that dashing cavalier, Prince Eugene of Savoy, greatest of Hapsburg captains, captured Belgrade and pushed down the Morava valley. In the Treaty of Passarowitz (1718) the sultan ceded to Austria the Banat, strips of Walachia and Bosnia, and a small Serb state which encircled Belgrade. Those gains gave Austria a splendid position in Danubian Europe and afforded a rare opportunity for further expansion southward, but the chance was lost when Hapsburg energies were largely diverted elsewhere.

Austria was soon forced to relinquish its Balkan winnings to the Ottoman empire, so that the Danube and the Sava formed the frontier between the two rival powers and faiths.

It was a melancholy Hungary indeed that the Hapsburgs reclaimed from the Turk, a land gravely depopulated, fearfully wasted during the long warfare, and left exceedingly poor. Hapsburg sovereigns assigned vast tracts of Hungarian soil to their noble followers and invited fresh companies of immigrants to settle in the country; Serbs, in particular, seeking escape from Moslem servitude, swarmed into the southern districts. As soldiers and as tillers of the soil, they received a cordial welcome, but feudal standards of life and labor and Roman Catholic proselytism soon caused many Serbs to return to Turkish-ruled lands.

As a protective bastion against Turkey a military frontier was erected along the Hungarian border and behind it Yugoslavs and Rumanians or Vlachs permanently settled. Elsewhere on the reconquered Hungarian territory also foreigners were allowed to establish homes, Germans, Rumanians, and others. It has been estimated that in 1720 the authentic Magyar element in Hungary represented only 45 percent of the population and it fell below that figure in the course of the eighteenth century.[10] To the Magyar mind the purpose of the Hapsburg in planting outsiders in the country was to dilute if not to extinguish Magyar national sentiments. There is validity to that interpretation, though economic urgencies and military requirements seem to have counted for more than purely political considerations.

The recovery of Hungary from the Turks was achieved under circumstances peculiarly advantageous for the House of Hapsburg, then at the apogee of its strength. Although the continuity of Hungary's constitutional rights was unimpaired, and the county governments and historic privileges of the nobility were preserved, strong Austrian monarchs bent the Magyars to their sovereign will. Charles VI, for example, induced the Hungarian diet (1723) to ratify the Pragmatic Sanction which recognized, *inter alia,* that the crown of St. Stephen might be worn by a woman, should the male line of Hapsburgs die out, and reaffirmed the indivisibility of the Austrian and Hungarian kingdoms. To this Pragmatic Sanction we shall later recur.

VII

While the Hapsburgs were contesting with Turkey for lordship on the Danube, they were likewise warring upon that collective religious heresy with political and social implications and complications called Protestantism. For the Austrian rulers, dynastic interests, the fundamental instinct to preserve their realm, combined with religious convictions to make them warm champions of Catholicism and zealous partisans of the Counter Reformation.

With remarkable speed, Protestantism had swept over the Hapsburg lands.

Criticisms of Mother Church similar to those voiced so fervently by Luther were heard in Austria proper, and defections from Catholicism were large. Bohemia's virile Hussite heritage made that region peculiarly susceptible to the new religious teaching, and Magyar churchmen, after the military disaster at Mohács, were impotent to combat religious heterodoxy. Wherefore, Lutheranism, Calvinism, and the Anabaptists, rebels as well as heretics, captured the allegiance of multitudes of Hapsburg subjects. Attendance on Catholic services dropped precipitately and ecclesiastical fees dwindled away; in a span of twenty years, only two students in the theological faculty of Vienna fulfilled the requirements for the priesthood! Protestant doctrines were preached even in Vienna's cathedral and the Hapsburg court chapel. By the middle of the sixteenth century a majority of the inhabitants in the Hapsburg realm, not excluding the great noble families, had embraced the reformed faith in one variety or another, and it seemed only a matter of time until all would go over to new versions of the old religion.

But three agencies chiefly checked the spread of Protestantism and brought back most of the subjects of the Hapsburgs, though by no means all, to the Roman communion: the reformation within Catholicism prescribed by the Council of Trent; the zeal of the militant Jesuits, who as teachers, preachers, and confessors were singularly successful among the nobility; and recourse to the sword by the Vienna government. The appeal to force against religious dissidents reached a terrible climax in the Thirty Years' War, which originated in Bohemia.

It was indeed in the kingdom of Bohemia that Protestantism won its largest successes. Over two-thirds of the families, Czechs in much higher proportion than Germans, went over to the reformed conception of Christianity; and from a reluctant emperor, the diet secured (1609) freedom of conscience for Bohemia. But that was merely a truce, a truce endangered when it appeared that Ferdinand II (1618–1637) would presently ascend the throne. Strictly authoritarian in his political philosophy and staunchly Catholic, Ferdinand has been called the "beau ideal of the Counter Reformation." Resentment in Bohemia against alien and Germanizing influences, which was ever present, rose again to high passion.

Insurrection against Austria began in 1618, when noble rebels of Bohemia dramatically hurled three Hapsburg partisans out of the windows of the gloomy Hradčany royal palace of Prague. Next, the diet voted the deposition of Emperor Ferdinand II and chose a German as Bohemian king, Frederick of the Palatinate, the chief of the Union of German Calvinists. It was romantically imagined that this young prince would be able to enlist military help from his father-in-law, King James I of England.

Without a large army of his own, Ferdinand appealed to the Catholic League of Germany for assistance and it readily responded. Against that

force the undisciplined coalition of Bohemians and Rhenish Calvinists offered only feeble opposition and was ignominiously routed in the Battle
of the White Mountain just outside of Prague in 1620. That crushing defeat,
occurring in the very year that the Pilgrim Fathers landed in the New
World, cost Bohemia and the Czechs much of their independence, which
three centuries later descendants of the Pilgrims were to aid in recovering.

Austria treated Bohemia as a conquered province, making the crown
hereditary in the house of Hapsburg and giving the emperor full authority,
except in the raising of taxes, a right retained by the emasculated Bohemian
diet. German was declared an official language alongside of Czech, and Catholicism was ordained as the only lawful creed of Bohemia; Jesuit fathers
took charge of Prague University and other educational institutions.

Gradually Protestantism was stamped out in Bohemia, and the insurgent
local nobility, whether Czech or German, were killed, or emigrated or forfeited their properties to the crown. These estates were then parceled out
among loyal partisans of the emperor, Germans and other foreigners. Thenceforth, into the twentieth century, the upper and landed class of Bohemia was
preponderantly German in speech and sentiment, while commoners were
largely Czech. Small wonder that Czech patriots, generation after generation, were wont to speak of the Battle of the White Mountain as "our recent
disaster."

To guard and consolidate the interests of the Monarchy and of Catholicism, Ferdinand II dispatched the famous commander, Wallenstein (Vald-
stejn), against the armies of Gustavus Adolphus, the Swedish sword of
Protestantism, which had marched into central Europe. Campaigns of ruinous destruction, attended by an almost incredible sacrifice of life, ensued;
Silesia, for instance, lost probably three-quarters of its inhabitants and in
the province of Bohemia the depopulation was about as heavy.

At the Peace of Westphalia of 1648, which formally ended the Thirty
Years' War, the Hapsburgs transferred certain of their old Rhineland holdings to France and, except in name, the Roman-German empire virtually
ceased to exist. Nonetheless, the Hapsburg bearer of the imperial title still
carried some weight in German affairs, though Hapsburg ardor for expansion was thereafter less concerned with "Germany" than with lands to the
south, the Italian peninsula and the lower Danube valley.

Upon the conclusion of the prolonged warfare with Turkey and in central Europe, Austria witnessed a wonderful outburst of building; Italian
artists and architects swarmed northward once more and imparted their
methods and principles to native designers and builders. Monumental structures in the baroque style, ornate and pretentious, were raised in Prague,
in Salzburg, and, above all, in Vienna. There the imperial palace, the *Hofburg,* was enlarged, and the chancellery or *Ballhaus,* the votive Karlskirche,

the elaborate imperial château of Schönbrunn, and mansions for the aristocracy, conspicuously the Belvedere castle for Prince Eugene of Savoy, were erected.

All in all, Vienna rivaled Paris among the modern cities of Europe. And across the Hapsburg realm, churches and monasteries, ruined by warfare, were rehabilitated and new ones were constructed, such as the immense Benedictine establishment at Melk on the Danube.

VIII

Into the complicated maze of diplomatic Machiavellism, blatant power politics, and armed strife which engaged the Hapsburg Monarchy in the eighteenth century there is no necessity to enter. Suffice it to say that Austria picked up the Spanish Netherlands, essentially present-day Belgium, early in the century and held it as a sort of continental colony until 1797; and the richest provinces of Italy, Tuscany, most of Lombardy, Naples, Parma, and Sardinia were acquired, though the last three soon were lost to other sovereignties.

Of peculiar significance in the constitutional evolution of the Hapsburg state was the Pragmatic Sanction promulgated finally in 1724. Without a male heir, Emperor Charles VI (1711–1740), solicited the approval of the local assemblies for his eldest daughter, Maria Theresa, as his successor. The formal document, known as the Pragmatic Sanction, specified that the possessions of the Hapsburg house, however obtained, should never be separated. This has been called the first fundamental law of the Hapsburg Monarchy. To this the assemblies assented, although Bohemia and Hungary made it clear that if the Hapsburg line petered out, they might select a new dynasty.

In time, radical and acrimoniously debated differences arose over the precise nature of the Hungarian acceptance of the Pragmatic Sanction. In the opinion of Magyar legalists Hungary preserved her independent identity and was linked to Austria solely by the bond of a common sovereign, though as Hapsburg partisans interpreted the contract Hungary was nothing more than a constituent member of the Monarchy. The circumstance that after the Pragmatic Sanction Austria treated Hungary as a foreign country in respect to tariffs tended to bolster up the Hungarian interpretation. Croatia approved the Pragmatic Sanction on its own account, but later the local diet referred to the Magyar acceptance as binding and its own action as simply an expression of fidelity to the crown. Lawyers with keen minds and sharp pens, both serviceable in constitutional casuistry, were subsequently to contend that the original assent of Croatia symbolized that kingdom's independence of Hungary.

The accession of Maria Theresa to the Hapsburg throne in 1740 inspired Frederick II of Prussia, who, like his fellow monarchs, had solemnly endorsed the Pragmatic Sanction, to lay claim to the industrially rich and heavily German-inhabited province of Silesia, part of the lands of the Bohemian crown. An appeal to arms to decide the issue opened the first military chapter in the prolonged contest between Hohenzollern Prussia and Hapsburg Austria for supremacy in central Europe, a struggle that closed only in 1866. The armies of Frederick seized most of Silesia and held on permanently, despite repeated and valiant Austrian attempts to repossess it; and it was this choice territorial morsel, with its iron resources and manufactures, which largely enabled Prussia to claim a place among the first powers of Europe.

Throughout the arduous tussles with Prussia, subject peoples of the Hapsburgs were generally faithful to the dynasty, loyal defenders of the supranational realm. To curry favor in Bohemia, Maria Theresa was crowned with the ancient crown of the kingdom, but bit by bit she whittled away the limited rights of the local diet and merged the administrative institutions with those of Austria proper.[11]

Without the devoted support of Hungary it is doubtful whether the Hapsburg state could have sustained the struggle with Prussia at all. Magyar oligarchs, though chafing under the infringement of their medieval rights, rallied behind the crown when Maria Theresa confirmed their liberties, including exemption from taxation, and declared Fiume to be a "corpus separatum" of the crown of St. Stephen. Yet, bent as she was upon unifying the Monarchy, the queen placed Hungarian state finances more thoroughly under the direction of Vienna and invested royal lieutenants with part of the authority of the old county assemblies.

Affluent Magyar grandees were assigned posts in the imperial service at Vienna, married German wives, and became markedly "Austro-German" in outlook. But the lesser Magyar gentry stubbornly held to the national language and literature, the national customs and costumes, to be preserved at all costs, along with inherited political institutions, from imperial encroachment.

Compensation, in a sense, for the loss of the greater part of Silesia accrued to Austria in the form of a section of Poland. Sharing with Russia and Prussia in the first partition of that country in 1772, Austria gained the province of Galicia (or, more accurately, Galicia, Lodomeria, and the county of Zips), inhabited by Poles and Ruthenians or Ukrainians. In 1795 another chunk of Poland, which included the cities of Cracow and Lublin, passed into the Hapsburg orbit. Austria also laid claim to northern Moldavia, a Turkish property, to the southeast of Galicia, in which Russia had an interest, and which was peopled by a heterogeneous peasantry, mostly Ruthenians and Rumanians. Under pressure from Vienna, the Porte relinquished sovereignty, and the area entered (1777) the polyglot Hapsburg realm as the Bucovina.

Joseph II (1780–1790), who had been coregent with his mother and succeeded her on the throne, belongs near the top of the benevolent autocrats of the age. He carried forward the work of monarchical centralization which Maria Theresa had started.[12] Influenced by the philosophy of the "Enlightenment" and utterly contemptuous of traditions and conventions, he ordained that German should be the official language of the realm save for Galicia and the Italian provinces. No friend of organized Christianity, this innovating, doctrinaire experimentalist proclaimed freedom of worship, suppressed monasteries by the dozen, and deprived foreign-born bishops of their properties. Thus he established a tradition of anticlericalism in Austria, which never wholly died away, and many an Austro-German of the next century was accustomed to refer to his political creed as "Josefinismus," which he appealed to whenever clericalism had to be combatted or the leadership of the German element in the monarchy seemed to be endangered.

For the welfare of commoners Joseph II displayed a deep and abiding concern, and for their benefit he published many humanitarian measures. On his command, for instance, the peasantry was liberated from serfage, the penal code was humanized, punishment of alleged witches was stopped, and discriminations against Jews were relaxed.

Reforms are seldom popular with those whose interests and convictions are or seem to be adversely affected, and it was thus in the realm of Joseph II. His innovations roused violent hostility in conservative and conventional circles. Proudly conservative Magyar aristocrats, enraged by religious and social changes, were further embittered by the refusal of Joseph II to take the royal coronation oath or to convoke the Hungarian diet. Similar discontent and antidynastic rumblings prevailed among big landowners in Bohemia, in Galicia, and in Lombardy. And in every province militant Catholic clericalism raised the battle cry that "religious toleration is the parent of dissension."

Just before "the revolutionary emperor" died, rebellion broke out in the Austrian Netherlands, diplomatic relations with Prussia were strained almost to the point of rupture, and Hapsburg troops were actually at war with Turkey. The economic life of the realm, moreover, was well-nigh prostrate.

Zeal for reform had inspired the ambitious monarch to try to accomplish too much too quickly, and to his contemporaries his short reign must have seemed a mere parenthesis, a weird political monstrosity. For his tomb, Joseph II composed his own epitaph: "Here lies Joseph II, who was unfortunate in all his enterprises."

His brother, the new ruler, Leopold II (1790–1792), radically reversed state policies, repealed reforms right and left, remanded the peasants to bondage, restored Catholic privileges, and endeavored to appease national minorities. The Hungarian assembly, for one thing, was called together, and it clearly and cleverly reasserted the liberties and constitutional rights of the Magyar nation.

"Hungary," the law of the diet read, "together with the parts thereunto annexed, is a free kingdom and independent as regards the whole form of government . . . [it] is possessed of its own separate existence and must consequently be governed and ruled by its hereditary king, crowned according to law." At the same time Hungarian lordship over Croatia was reaffirmed, for the Croatian diet at Agram formally resolved that affairs of concern to both kingdoms should be regulated at Budapest; only domestic matters—not defined with precision—remained within the competence of the Croatian assembly. Taken together, these measures attested that the Magyar governing elements, which had been on the defensive ever since the catastrophe at Mohács, had assumed the initiative, and they held it through the succeeding century.

Prudence and wisdom characterized Leopold II's dealings with Bohemia. He convoked the diet, listened to local grievances, agreed to modest political changes, and had himself formally crowned as king. At Prague he attended theatrical performances in the Czech language, and heard a scholarly lecture in Czech on the importance of the Hapsburg Slavs. While Leopold reigned, the growth of the Czech intelligentsia was fostered by the establishment of a chair in the Czech language at the University and by the building of Czech gymnasia in Prague.

IX

Like the rest of Europe, the Monarchy of the Hapsburgs was stirred to the depths by the French Revolution and the ambitions of Napoleon Bonaparte. Lust for territorial aggrandizement, dynastic ties with the French queen, Marie Antoinette, daughter of Empress Maria Theresa, dread of the repercussions that the French revolutionary ideology would have upon its own repressed and nationally diversified subjects, the upthrust of patriotic sentiments among the Austro-Germans—these varied interests and impulses made the House of Hapsburg the implacable foe of revolutionary and Napoleonic France.

Warfare with France started in 1792 and persisted with interruptions until the fallen Bonaparte as an abject prisoner was shipped to a desolate isle in the southern reaches of the Atlantic. More than once in the interval Hapsburg arms tasted defeat, more than once the French adventurer dictated humiliating terms of peace to the venerable Hapsburg state. And to Napoleon, Emperor Francis I (1792–1835)[13] offered up his daughter, Marie Louise, as a matrimonial sacrifice quite in conformity with the cherished maxim of the dynasty: "Bella gerant alii! Tu, felix Austria, nube."

Hapsburg soldiers, it is true, inflicted a major defeat upon the French at

Aspern, close by Vienna (1809); the army was commanded by Archduke Charles, whose military prestige rivals that of Prince Eugene of Savoy in Austrian annals. Both heroes on prancing chargers adorn the *Heldenplatz* in the heart of Vienna. The commander of the allied troops which administered a catastrophic whipping to Napoleon at Leipzig in 1813 was the Austrian Field Marshal Charles Schwarzenberg, who is remembered in another of Vienna's equestrian monuments.

Not to be outshone by the parvenu Bonaparte, who had been crowned as French emperor in 1804, Francis I proclaimed himself Austrian emperor in the same year and bestowed upon the realm of the Hapsburgs the title of Empire of Austria. Magyar and Czech spokesmen promptly repudiated this innovation, for it implied, or seemed to imply, the loss of the independent integrity jealously claimed for Hungary and Bohemia. In 1806 the moribund Holy Roman Empire, whose headship had for almost four centuries been virtually hereditary in the Hapsburg family, was unceremoniously laid in the grave.

Territorial permutations and combinations which crowded the Napoleonic epoch entailed very considerable alterations in the Hapsburg map, mostly impermanent. At the international congress that wrote settlements of peace after the Napoleonic warfare, convened significantly in Vienna, and presided over by the suave Austrian foreign minister and later chancellor, Count Clemens Metternich, the House of Hapsburg achieved impressive territorial gains. But it was obliged to renounce title to the southern Netherlands, modern Belgium, and small holdings along the Rhine.[14]

By the Treaty of Vienna, Dalmatia, western Istria, scattered islands in the Adriatic, which were formerly possessions of the Venetian republic, Venetia itself, and the adjoining province of Lombardy, passed under the Austrian scepter. Inasmuch as members of the Hapsburg dynasty held the thrones of Tuscany, Parma, and Modena, and since Austrian influence in the Papal state and in the kingdom of the Two Sicilies was extensive, the Italian peninsula had much the appearance of an appendage to the Austrian empire. Polish Galicia, less actually of the Polish kingdom than had belonged to Austria before the advent of Napoleon but still a large area, was assigned to the Hapsburgs. And the tiny republic of Cracow, the sole free fragment of Poland left by the peacemakers of 1815, was ultimately absorbed by Austria in 1846 with the sanction of Prussia and Russia, partners in the Polish partition.

As a substitute for the discarded Holy Roman Empire, statesmen at the Congress of Vienna invented the loose German Confederation which embraced all of German Europe and that part of the Hapsburg realm which had belonged to the Holy Roman Empire; and Austria was given the presidency of the diet of the confederation in perpetuity. Acceptance of that responsibility signified the Austrian intention to play a leading part in German affairs of the future as it had in the past. In fact, in Germany and in Italy the Austrian government was constrained to balk, if possible, territorial unification and liberalizing tendencies as essential for the preservation of the many-tongued Hapsburg realm itself.

x

In the forepart of the nineteenth century, Francis I (1792-1835), the dry, bureaucratic, and reactionary Austrian emperor, and his faithful servant, Metternich, were devoted to the conservative pattern, to the maintenance of the territorial *status quo,* to the Germanization of subject peoples, and to patriarchal autocracy. The emperor's political philosophy was crystallized in the injunction, "Govern and change nothing." To these gentlemen, the radical ideas unloosed by the French Revolution and given wide currency by the charioteers of Bonaparte were anathema, charged with dynamite, to be repressed at all costs. "My realm," remarked Francis I to a Russian diplomatist, "resembles a worm-eaten house. If one part is removed one can not tell how much will fall," and that line of logic was never absent from the calculations of the directors of Hapsburg policies. Such schooling as was made available served as a facile instrument for indoctrinating pupils with a sense of allegiance to the *status quo*.[15]

Able men, the Rhineland-born chancellor Metternich excepted, Francis I distrusted and kept in subordination. And Metternich's weight in domestic affairs was limited, though he is erroneously supposed to have been omnipotent. As he himself candidly acknowledged, "J'ai gouverné l'Europe quelquefois, l'Autriche jamais." Elaborate and closely reasoned recommendations which the chancellor sponsored for modest reforms in government were carefully pigeonholed, though he saw to it that every province had an assembly to scrutinize projects of law and tax proposals. By means of the bureaucratic trinity, police, espionage, and rigorous censorship, the masters of Austria attempted to hold the realm in a strait jacket.[16]

Ferdinand I, who succeeded to the throne in 1835, was genial and benevolent-minded enough, but otherwise he was ill-endowed, and a victim of epilepsy. He was, in fact, little more than a head upon which to rest, one after another, the varied crowns of the dynasty. State affairs were actually directed by a council of three men, Metternich among them, who quarreled among themselves to the detriment of imperial well-being.

Try as they would, the ruling authorities could not curb the centrifugal dynamics of nationalism, nor stifle the notion of popular participation in government which the French Revolution had brought to the fore. All across the realm nationalist movements gathered force in the early decades of the nineteenth century, and they were not only a challenge to dynastic authoritarianism but positively dangerous for the unity of the Hapsburg state. Provincial assemblies served as forums in which to voice dissatisfaction with prevailing arrangements and to agitate on behalf of the natural rights of men. Intellectuals of many kinds and all tongues inveighed heatedly against the rigors of the censorship. True, laws regulating the importation of foreign books were relaxed in the 1840's, but restrictions on periodicals and newspapers stood unchanged.

Industrialism, in the meantime, the supreme revolutionizing force of the nineteenth century, had started to transform the economy of the empire, or rather of sections of it. The laying down of railways in the thirties and forties symbolized the dawning of the new machine age in the old state. With machinofacture both the middle class and the industrial working class grew larger; both were restive under the existing political and social order; both were touched by the revolutionary ideology of 1789.

Even in the countryside open discontent with anachronistic customs and institutions displayed itself. Protests over the bondage of serfdom and demands for reformation in landholding were frequent and loud in Austria proper and in Bohemia, while a murderous *jacquerie* of Ruthenian laborers against their Polish masters in Galicia in 1846 strikingly testified to the prevalence of deep-seated grievances with the *status quo*.[17]

XI

Throughout the Napoleonic era Hungary was no less loyal to the Hapsburg crown than in the trying years of Maria Theresa's reign. True, a secret society of intellectuals inspired by French revolutionary principles was organized, but its membership was small and its life short. Magyar chiefs would have nothing to do with a shimmering overture made by Bonaparte, which would have given Hungary independence. Rather the military requisitions of the crown, which drained the land of men and goods, were dutifully met in spite of the fact that the national constitution was suspended and the royal diet not assembled between 1811 and 1825.

These infringements upon tradition fostered a Hungarian national revival which, in some of its manifestations, was definitely anti-Hapsburg. Men of letters in this Augustan age of Magyar literature encouraged the use of the mother tongue and propagated nationalistic and even separatist sentiments. The establishment of a Hungarian academy of science and of a national theater were concrete signs of the Magyar cultural renaissance. When, on the urgings of Prince Metternich, the diet was at last restored, law upon law was passed with the object of making Magyar the language of all the peoples of Hungary.

Nationalistically minded men—for the aristocrats, Count Stephen Széchényi, coiner of the optimistic watchword, "prefer to think not that

Hungary has been but that Hungary shall be," and for the bourgeoisie, Louis Kossuth,[18] ambitious lawyer, sonorous orator, and author of impassioned editorials—summoned their fellows to struggle for a reordering of the connection with Austria. Between the two men little love was lost, for the former was narrowly conservative, while Kossuth thought along more dramatic and revolutionary lines. Apart from these, there was a company of "moderate liberals," keenly concerned about Hungarian liberties. Their favorite representative was Francis Deák, a hardheaded, judicially minded country gentleman.

Even as Magyar nationalism waxed more militant, so stirrings among subject Hungarian minorities betokened strife with the dominant grouping. Flame kindled flame. Measures of Magyarization provoked shrill outcries from minority spokesmen. Croat and Slovak authors, particularly, stimulated interest in politics and some sense of national consciousness among their countrymen. In keeping with the old maxim of "divide and rule," officials in Vienna did not hesitate to promote minority nationalisms, as weapons to counteract antimonarchical feelings in Magyar circles.

Czech national patriotism flamed up under the leadership of an active galaxy of scholars and writers. Outstanding was Francis Palacký (1798–1876), a romantically patriotic historian, who in a monumental *History of Bohemia from its Legendary Origins to 1526,* the first volume of which was printed in 1836 and the last forty years later, idealized the past glories of the Czechs and recalled the illustrious achievements of the forefathers, notably in the epoch of Hussitism. As a democrat in political outlook, deeply imbued with the French principles of 1789, and as a politician keenly interested in the recovery of the "just rights" of Bohemia, Palacký exploited his erudition to kindle hopes for the Czech future.[19]

The *Society of the Bohemian Museum,* founded in 1827, one division of which published works on Czech medievalism, significantly encouraged the growth of a distinct national consciousness. Essentially, the Czech national resurgence was a bourgeois phenomenon, though it attracted the patronage of some of the wealthy Bohemian landed proprietors; as yet the mass of the Czech population was little touched by national emotions.

XII

Political, social, and economic forces, inimical to the settled Hapsburg order of things, which had been slowly gathering momentum for half a century and more, burst into a revolutionary unheaval in 1848. It was a year of widespread revolt in Europe. Starting in southern Italy, the flame of insurgency spread to France, destroying the government there, and raced across the continent, shaking the Hapsburg monarchy to its very foundations.[20] In Vienna, rebellious university students, bourgeoisie, and industrial workers, helpfully abetted by highly placed personal enemies of Prince Metternich, drove the venerable and cynical chancellor into exile. And twice the revolutionaries obliged the imperial court to seek sanctuary in a more serene environment than the imperial capital.

On the demand of the rebels, the Vienna government granted liberty of the press, which invited the publication of scores of "radical" papers, and promised to publish a constitution, and indeed did so. But the insurgent triumph lasted only a brief time, for thundering imperial cannon soon blasted away the dreams of reforming liberalism. Presently the incompetent Emperor Ferdinand relinquished the throne to his boyish nephew, Francis Joseph, who was to preside over the monarchy until 1916.

As one chapter in the revolutionary tumult, middle-class Germans and Czechs in Bohemia combined momentarily to gain Bohemian rights, but the unity was short-lived. At Prague in June of 1848 a Pan-Slav congress, attended by Hapsburg and Russian Slavs and a sprinkling of Slavs from European Turkey, was called together. Resolutions affirming the solidarity of Slavdom were adopted and pledges were taken to work together for the advancement of Slav interests. The idea of reconstructing the Hapsburg state along federal lines was earnestly discussed.

That the Czech leaders had no desire to see the Hapsburg state destroyed was illustrated by the unforgettable utterance of Palacký: "If the Austrian Monarchy did not exist, it would be necessary to create it quickly, in the interest of Europe and of humanity." Nevertheless, the Czechs insisted on the integrity of their own nationality. When Palacký was invited to the Frankfurt Parliament, which had been called to draft a new constitution for the German Confederation, he replied: "I am not a German, but a Bohemian, belonging to the Slav race [sic!] . . . My nation is certainly a small one, but it has always maintained its historic individuality."

Believing that the time was ripe for the establishment of a free state, Czech extremists in Prague broke out in rebellion. That furnished Austrian authorities with reason to bombard the city, disperse the Pan-Slav congress, and cancel a tentative pledge to unite the lands of the Bohemian crown.

Off to the south, delirious patriotic risings occurred in Austria's Italian provinces of Lombardy and Venetia and in adjacent principalities. At first, Austrian garrisons were compelled to give way, but reinforcements were thrown in and after hard fighting they quelled the disorders, though rebels in Venice defiantly and heroically held out until August of 1849.

To Field Marshal Radetzky and his triumphant soldiers, Grillparzer, the foremost Austrian poet of the time, addressed an oft-quoted refrain: "In deinem Lager ist Oesterreich. Wir Andern sind einzelne Trümmer" (Thy camp alone preserves Austria. We are but scattered fragments). Vienna liberalism branded the author of this paean to military might as the songster of reaction, but conservatives rejoiced, for Grillparzer had crystallized a naked truth for them; that is, the imperial army was one of the stoutest bulwarks of the polyglot realm and thus it remained. Had the armed forces been won over, the uprisings of 1848 would probably have succeeded, but so long as military discipline and troop loyalty prevailed, revolution was almost bound to fail.

It was from Hungary that the most serious challenge to the integrity of the Danubian Monarchy came in the mid-century revolutions. Magyar "radicals," with the irrepressible Kossuth at their head, demanded wide-ranging change in the constitutional bonds with Austria, while more sober elements merely asked for the restoration of what they regarded as their country's rights. The Vienna government, plagued by revolts on every hand, temporized by granting Hungary an entirely separate ministry responsible to the national diet, which would have full jurisdiction over the political affairs of the kingdom.

Measures of serf emancipation enacted by the Hungarian parliament, similar to laws passed in Austria, completed the legal liberation of the country-folk from the bondage in which they had long been enchained. Freedom of the press and of conscience were promised and the nobility was deprived of the ancient privilege of exemption from taxes. Hungary, it appeared, had been liberalized, and had virtually separated itself from the lordship of Vienna.

In the turbulence of revolution, the Magyars endeavored to consolidate their hold upon Transylvania and Croatia. The former was declared an integral part of the Magyar state, and a kindred destiny for Croatia was frankly indicated. That program, with its implication of even more thoroughgoing Magyarization, combined with the intrigues of Hapsburg agents, roused subject minorities, except the Germans in the Banat, against the ruling Magyars. Civil war broke loose in which cruel inhumanities were perpetrated by both sides and have never since been fully forgotten. An Austrian army, supplemented by Croatian troops under a Hungarophobe Croat, Jelačič, expelled the Hungarian government from Buda. Thereupon the rebel chieftain, Kossuth, solemnly proclaimed the deposition of the Hapsburgs and declared the independence of Hungary (April 1849).

Those revolutionary acts, along with the reverberations which the central European insurgencies were having upon his own repressed subjects, caused the Russian Tsar, Nicholas I, self-styled policeman of Europe, to intervene in Hungary, as he was invited to do by Francis Joseph. Muscovite troops poured across the Carpathians and in short order drowned the Magyar rebellion in blood, something proud Magyars were never to forget. Insurgent leaders were scattered to the four winds, and the Russian commander, Prince Paskevitch, laid conquered Hungary at the feet of Vienna. Forthwith the constitutional liberties of Hungary were rescinded and the country was degraded to the rank of a mere province of Austria.

In the meantime, in July of 1848, a parliament representative of the Hapsburg lands, except Hungary and the Italian provinces, had been convened in Vienna. That body liberated the small peasant from the last remnants of feudal servitude, and plans were considered to provide the freedmen with soil of their own. Apart from that epochal social reform little of moment was accomplished, though Palacký presented an interesting project for the federalization of the Monarchy on an essentially nationalist basis. But the ministry would not hear of it. The emperor published (1849) a moderately progressive and centralistic constitution for the Monarchy which was never put into operation, and was in fact formally cancelled in 1851.

XIII

After the revolutionary fires had been quenched, the Hapsburg Monarchy entered upon an era of arbitrary and despotic absolutism. On the revocation of the Constitution of 1849, a Council of State was created to study legislative proposals and to render advice to the crown. But real political power resided in an authoritarian ministry, whose prominent spirits were the prime minister, Prince Felix Schwarzenberg, a hard-working dictator and a firm believer in force as an instrument of government, and the quondam Viennese liberal, Alexander Bach, minister of justice and later of the interior. The mother of Emperor Francis Joseph, the strong-willed Archduchess Sophia, exerted effective pressure upon her young and inexperienced son. Upon Schwarzenberg's death (1852), the emperor personally assumed the presidency of the ministry. Committees of consultation representing the several social classes in the monarchy superseded the old provincial diets.[21]

Throughout the Bach regime, as the 1850's are sometimes labeled, the reorganized and much enlarged Austrian bureaucracy, backed by the military forces, administered the Hapsburg realm with a rod of iron. Officials, though usually conscientious and with some sense of social justice, were arbitrary in conduct and many of them were ignorant of the language of the district in which they were stationed. Reaction against the surge of revolution reached flood tide in a treaty concluded in 1855 with the Vatican. Thereby Catholicism was freed from state control to a degree unapproached since the seventeenth century, and far-reaching authority over educational institutions and partial censorship over publication were assigned to the church hierarchy. Priest and dogma, as Austrian liberals hurriedly pointed out, were allied with corporal and bayonet in upholding monarchical authoritarianism.

Bohemia was crushed under the Bach regimentation. With might and main Austro-German bureaucrats strove to suppress the Czech language and

to suffocate the budding nationalist revival. Palacký was kept under close
police surveillance and his ally, the journalist, Karel Havliček, was hounded
to an early grave. At the same time Czech soldiers were sent to hold down
the lid in other provinces, which earned them the hatred of Vienna progressives, while Magyars spoke of Czechs as either thieves or musicians.

Cruelty and terror were invoked to cow proud and rebellious Magyar
spirits, and as penalties for the insurrection the constitution of 1848 was
withdrawn, the county assemblies were dissolved, and Croatia (with Fiume)
and Transylvania were detached from Hungary. Administrative officials of
foreign origins, many among them Czechs and Poles, governed the land
with scant regard for Magyar susceptibilities.

XIV

Before very long, in 1859, Austria became involved in war with the Italian
kingdom of Sardinia, to which the France of Napoleon III was allied. Defeat in that struggle cost Austria the province of Lombardy, though it retained Venetia, and presently Hapsburg princes were expelled from Tuscany,
Modena, and Parma. Those principalities, with Lombardy, merged with
Sardinia to form the new kingdom of Italy.

Defeat in the War of 1859 dramatized the bankruptcy of Hapsburg absolutism. Commanders had shown themselves incompetent, little reliance
could be placed on troops recruited in Hungary, and imperial finances were
in a parlous condition.[22] That Austrian political institutions imperatively required overhauling was apparent to all but the willfully blind. But should
reorganization proceed along centralistic or federalistic or other lines? As
the prelude to a remodeling of the realm, the discredited Bach was removed
from office, and to the Council of State were appointed representatives of the
component parts of the realm. Most of the Magyar appointees, however,
indignantly declined to take their seats.

Francis Joseph, anxious to appease the Magyars, therefore restored the
county governments and named General Benedek, a popular Protestant
Magyar, as governor of the kingdom. These conciliatory gestures satisfied
some of the feudally minded aristocrats but the Magyar country gentry and
middle-class folk insisted upon representative parliamentary institutions.
And in that demand they had the backing of the great "liberal" press of
Vienna.

Financial stress combined with pressure for popular participation in government impelled Francis Joseph along the thorny and distasteful path of
constitutionalism. In October of 1860, an imperial diploma was published,
setting up a central or federal parliament, whose deputies would be chosen
by provincial assemblies to be revived throughout the realm. The imperial
legislature would have competence in matters of finance, currency, tariffs,

and the fighting services; but almost all other public affairs would be decided by the local assemblies. Hungary's constitutional regime as it existed in 1847 would be revived.

This October Diploma elicited little approval in Hungary, except among the court aristocrats, because it called for a central law-making body and denied the ministerial responsibility and other rights of the constitution of 1848. To anticlerical German liberals and others who opposed federalization of the realm the constitution was totally unacceptable; they were aggrieved because the constitutional proposals went too far, imperiling, as they thought, the integrity and international prestige of the Monarchy, while Magyar "liberals" were incensed because the constitution had not gone far enough.

Invoking a right of ancient lineage, the Hungarian county councils refused to vote the raising of recruits or the collection of taxes. Riotous excesses that occurred might well have cycled into another general insurrection, if large bodies of troops had not been on the scene. Hungarian disaffection naturally aggravated the already grave financial plight of the Monarchy.

Since Magyar resistance and German liberal antipathy had effectively nullified the October Diploma, Francis Joseph entrusted the task of working out a substitute scheme to Anton von Schmerling (1805–1893), minister of the interior. Schmerling had himself participated in the liberal movement and in fact had quit Schwarzenberg's cabinet in protest over authoritarian measures. Instead of federalism, he believed in a highly centralized government, and that philosophy he incorporated in the February (1861) Patent, which created a bicameral legislature for the entire Monarchy. To the central legislature were assigned somewhat broader powers than had been envisaged in the October Diploma; on the other hand, the local assemblies were allotted little power beyond sending deputies to the imperial parliament.

These assemblies, the Patent prescribed, would be chosen by four categories of electors (or curiae), to wit: large landlords, chambers of commerce, townsmen, and peasants. The right to vote in the last two classes was restricted to men who paid at least ten gulden in taxes, and seats were distributed in such fashion as to discriminate against the peasantry. To illustrate, the assembly of Bohemia would contain seventy deputies of the landed grandees—under four hundred in all—and eighty-seven men from the towns and chambers of commerce, but only seventy-nine from the countryside. And since the Bohemian town population was heavily German while the rustics were largely Czech, the franchise was weighted against the latter nationality. These franchise prescriptions of 1861 were perpetuated in the Austrian constitution of 1867 and the class or curia system stood firm until 1907.

Magyar public men would have nothing to do with a constitution that created a central or monarchical parliament; the Hungarian diet was dismissed and authoritarianism resurrected. Similar treatment was meted out to Croatia. On the other hand, Schmerling persuaded the diet of Transylvania to send delegates to Vienna.

When the central parliament met, advocates of centralism clashed violently with the friends of federalism and extensive autonomy for the provinces. Lined up in the centralist bloc were German liberals, German landowners from Bohemia, Ruthenians, and a few Italian deputies; standing against them were Czechs, Slovenes, most of the Italians, and German clericals and conservatives. Polish delegates oscillated uneasily between the two factions, for while they were not unsympathetic to a central parliament, they wanted broad autonomous rights for their Galician diet.

After the ministry declined to accede to the Polish claims, the Poles quit the parliament and the Czechs lingered only long enough to protest that the February constitution transgressed the inalienable rights of the kingdom of Bohemia. With the withdrawal of these two Slav groups, not more than a rump assembly remained, mostly German liberals, to deliberate on state business in "Schmerling's theater."

All the debate about constitutional rights, fundamental human liberties, and the like stirred representatives of smaller national groups to seek safeguards for their interests. Ruthenians, for example, demanded that Galicia should be partitioned into two districts, one Ruthenian, one Polish; Slovenes called for a separate Slovenian diet; and Serbs and Slovaks put in pleas for guaranteed rights inside Hungary.

Inasmuch as Magyar obduracy had balked the Schmerling program for a unified Monarchy, Francis Joseph requested moderate Magyar politicians to specify the terms on which they would coöperate with the crown. In their name, Deák, who detested the wild enthusiasms of the Kossuth independence faction, declared that if the Hungarian constitution of 1848 were reinstated, a compromise might be worked out whereby the Monarchy would form a unit in international and military affairs, but which would leave Austria and Hungary autonomous in domestic affairs. In other words, Deák recommended a dualistic scheme in contrast to the centralism espoused by Austro-Germans or the federalism so popular among the Slavs and the Clericals.

Presently Francis Joseph suspended the February constitution and appointed a new cabinet headed by Count Richard Belcredi (1823–1902), a Bohemian aristocrat, to formulate yet another governmental pattern. Negotiations with the Magyars were proceeding smoothly, as is later explained, only to be interrupted in the summer of 1866 by war with Prussia in which Austria was quickly defeated. Thereafter a constitutional settlement between the crown and the Magyar moderates, spoken of as the *Ausgleich* or compromise of 1867, was hammered out. The Hapsburg realm now entered upon a new epoch in its long and checkered career.

‡ CHAPTER TWO ‡

GOVERNMENTS OF THE DUAL MONARCHY

At four in the morning of June 8, 1867, Budapest echoed with twenty-one cannon shots proclaiming the dawning of the day on which Francis Joseph would be crowned king of Hungary. This ceremony would be the outward and visible sign of reconciliation between ruler and ruled. Not all the Magyars shared the jubilation, and there was some uneasiness in high places lest dissenters might mar the harmony of the coronation festivities; but actually they passed off without untoward incident.

Never had the Hungarian capital witnessed a more brilliant spectacle. Houses were garishly decorated with the recently proscribed Hungarian tricolor, and crowds lined the streets to watch the coronation procession and to testify to their satisfaction that the stubborn struggle for constitutional rights had ended successfully. First in the grand parade rode over six hundred horsemen, representing the fifty-two Hungarian counties, each in the peculiar costume of his district; then two hundred magnates in gorgeous medieval apparel, seated on gaily caparisoned horses, and followed by foot servants almost as luxuriously dressed as their masters. The king, in full coronation robes and wearing the sword and the crown of St. Stephen, was surrounded by the greatest dignitaries of the Hungarian court and a score of prelates in their richest vestments. Arrived at the parish church in Pest, the king dismounted, stepped upon a platform, and holding a crucifix in his left hand, raised three fingers of his right hand and swore to uphold the Hungarian constitution and to preserve the territorial integrity of the country.

That done, the ruler remounted, galloped up coronation hill, pulled his sword from its scabbard, thrust it in four directions to signify his determination to defend the kingdom from every quarter, and once more swore to protect the country.

As the final piece of symbolism the newly crowned monarch attended a coronation banquet in the royal palace high above the Danube's waters, with only a chosen few present: the very popular Queen Elizabeth, whom the Magyars called their "beautiful providence"; dignitaries of the church; and Count Julius Andrássy, who, in his capacity as palatine, had that morning placed the crown on the king's head. Only a few years before, this spirited magnate had been condemned to death for participation in a rebellion against the very sovereign whom now he had crowned! Absent from the banquet hall was the self-effacing Magyar statesman, Francis Deák, whose sagacity and sweet reasonableness had contributed greatly to the constitutional compromise whereby Hungary's national interests were safeguarded without doing too great violence to national sentiments and traditions.

No one derived more personal satisfaction out of the coronation ceremonial than Baron Ferdinand Beust, foreign secretary of the Monarchy and Francis Joseph's principal adviser. Astride his favorite white charger, he had been fervently cheered by the crowd as he rode through Budapest; even members of parliament at a signal from Deák exclaimed in chorus, "Eljen Beust!" Francis Joseph remarked to him—so Beust records in his memoirs—that no Austrian minister had ever been so well received in Hungary. Leading up to the coronation was a chain of events which Beust had had a prominent part in forging.

II

After indecisive preliminary skirmishes, Hapsburg and Hohenzollern, long rivals for hegemony over German Europe, settled their duel in the summer of 1866 by recourse to arms. Aligned with Austria in the war were the chief states of southern Germany, while Prussia found a military companion in the rising kingdom of Italy. Prussia's soldiers pressed furiously into Bohemia, in what deserves to be regarded as the first real blitzkrieg of modern times, achieving successive victories which culminated in a decisive triumph on July 3, in the vicinity of Sadowa. Prague and much of the Bohemian province succumbed to the Prussians, and the way to Vienna lay open. Not since Napoleon's time had Hapsburg arms suffered such a crushing humiliation; Austrian victories over the Italians on land and on sea were poor compensation for the defeats by the Prussians.

Government finances, bad for years, were rendered even more precarious by the outlays that the warfare entailed. In Hungary, which was lukewarm toward the war from the outset, the veteran revolutionary general, Klapka, aided and abetted by Prussian agents and German gold, raised a legion for the purpose of staging an insurrection against Hapsburg authority as in 1848. And separatist sentiments in Bohemia, fostered by Prussian propaganda, waxed greatly.

In these melancholy circumstances, Francis Joseph, whose personal diplomacy was in no small degree responsible for the precipitation of the war, hurriedly negotiated preliminaries of peace with Prussia and on August 23, 1866 signed the painful Treaty of Prague.[1] Overriding the pressure of his king and military colleagues for Hapsburg territory, the Prussian minister-president, Otto von Bismarck, who wanted to avoid alienating Austria permanently, contented himself with the expulsion of Austria from German Europe by the dissolution of the Germanic Confederation and with a modest indemnity. Prussia's Italian ally obtained its pound of flesh in the form of the rich Austrian province of Venetia, leaving fewer than three-quarters of a million Italian-speaking people in the old Monarchy.

The future of the realm of the Hapsburgs looked dark. Could the ancient state be refashioned on more solid, more modern lines, or was it fated to stagger along to complete disruption? Could the dynasty satisfy the longings of the divergent nationalities, and so preserve the integrity of the realm? Eager for revenge on Prussia, Francis Joseph prudently resolved to go ahead with constitutional rehabilitation.

To guide the ship of state across perilous and uncharted seas, the monarch, without a native counselor on whom he could confidently rely, summoned to Vienna Baron Ferdinand Beust (1809–1886). Beust, who was a Protestant and had been foreign secretary of Saxony, was an implacable enemy of Bismarck and Bismarck's Prussia; he belonged to that band of old-school diplomatists of Germany whom the historian-publicist Treitschke crudely reviled as "diplomatic mercenaries ready to enter the service of any state which will open a field for their ambition." No more fair was Bismarck's cutting observation that if Beust's vanity were taken away, nothing would remain.

Although Beust's acquaintance with the complexities of the Hapsburg state was far from complete, he was appointed minister of foreign affairs in November 1866. He assumed office on the understanding that he would smooth the way for an international coalition against Prussia, for he, no less than Francis Joseph, was reluctant to accept the verdict of Sadowa as final. Moderately liberal in political outlook, an experienced diplomatist who was in the good graces of Napoleon III of France, Beust promised to be an ideal instrument of the crown. His task in domestic affairs he conceived in these words: "I am called in as a sort of state washerwoman to purify, if I can, the accumulation of centuries of foul linen which is tainting the atmosphere of the Austrian state."[2] Count Richard Belcredi (1823–1902), proponent of a federal solution of the Monarchy's constitutional problems, was retained as minister of the interior.

Promptly the cabinet of Vienna turned to the appeasement of the Magyars by allowing Hungary virtual autonomy so far as home affairs were concerned, but preserving unity in matters with international implications. Moderates among the Magyars were entirely prepared to resume the conversations that had been ruptured by the coming of the Prussian war. Head of the Magyar compromise party was Francis Deák, who for thirty years had been a prominent figure in Hungarian politics, and who possessed an unrivaled knowledge of his country's constitutional history. Because of his dogged insistence upon Hungary's national rights, English admirers likened Deák to their own John Hampden.

Closely associated with Deák were the liberally minded Baron Joseph Eötvös, esteemed alike as a political philosopher, an educational pioneer, and a novelist, and Count Julius Andrássy, who belonged to the most exclusive branch of the Magyar aristocracy. After formal education, which included studies of law, Andrássy had visited foreign countries, and on his return had thrown himself into the struggle for greater constitutional freedom for Hungary. In the exuberance of youth Andrássy had cast in his lot with the revolutionaries of 1848 and had been obliged to flee from his native country, a price on his head; his effigy had been put to the torch in Hapsburg market places. As an exile in western Europe for nine years, he had acquired a wide acquaintance with European politics, high and low. Amnestied in 1868, he returned to Hungary, aligned himself with Deák, and pushed into the front rank of moderate politicians, displaying talents that were to make him the most outstanding statesman to emerge in the Hapsburg Monarchy since the departure of Prince Metternich.

Early in 1866, as has been before remarked, the Hungarian diet had been called together to deliberate on an understanding to regulate relations with the crown. The moderate party of Deák commanded a decided majority, but a strong faction favored a settlement that would restrict ties with Austria to a personal union through a common monarch. There were some Kossuthists, exponents of full Hungarian independence, and a handful of conservatives, sympathetic to a centralized Hapsburg state. To prepare the terms of an agreement, a committee of sixty-seven was named by the diet and that group entrusted its responsibilities to a more intimate committee of fifteen, of which Deák was the guiding genius. This committee agreed on a program, which Deák largely devised, but on the day after it was published the Monarchy became immersed in the Prussian war and the diet was dissolved.

After the defeat at Sadowa, Empress Elizabeth was dispatched to Hungary to sound out the country's attitude toward the dynasty and reported that it was sympathetic. On July 18, 1866, Francis Joseph invited Deák to confer with him in Vienna. Asked the conditions upon which Hungary would agree to bury the hatchet, Deák made the celebrated response, "No more after Sadowa than before." Much gratified, the monarch inquired whether Deák would serve as prime minister of Hungary, but he declined, recommending

Andrássy in his stead, and promising to support him in parliament. Negoti-ations, thus initiated, proceeded until satisfactory constitutional arrangements were worked out.

Conversations had come dangerously close to a deadlock, mistrust had arisen on both sides, when Baron Beust was brought into the situation. While the Saxon's name must always be associated with the Settlement of 1867, it is improbable that his contribution was so large as he assigned to himself in his memoirs. Deák was profoundly convinced that whoever was chosen as Hapsburg foreign minister would actively promote a *rapproche-ment* with Hungary, because the Monarchy's international standing required the prompt pacification of the Magyars. However that may be, Beust was instrumental in securing the assent of the emperor to the final arrangement, and politicians and public in Budapest cordially demonstrated appreciation of his services on the day of the royal coronation.

In January of 1867, decisive discussions on the terms of the constitutional compromise or *Ausgleich* took place in Vienna. The formula that was worked out deviated only narrowly from the program drafted by the Hungarian committee of fifteen before the onset of the Prussian war; the resignation of Belcredi, in protest over the projected settlement with Hungary, helped to ensure its success. After Deák, who had not attended the January con-ference, gave his blessing to the plans and Francis Joseph acquiesced in them, the Hungarian parliamentary committee of sixty-seven was called together, and ratified the agreement on the understanding that parliament would have the right to sanction formally the necessary changes in the Hungarian constitution.

On February 17, 1867, in the great hall of the National Museum at Pest, amidst rapturous applause, parliament listened to a royal letter restoring the Hungarian constitution and authorizing the formation of a ministry respon-sible to a Hungarian parliament. The first ministry was composed exclu-sively of Deákists, Andrássy taking the post of premier, and Eötvös was the only other member of first ability. Deák held aloof, but no ministry could last, so immense was his personal prestige, without his backing.

Reconciliation between king and Hungary became an accomplished fact on May 29, 1867, when the parliament by a vote of two hundred nine to eighty-nine ratified the *Ausgleich*. Louis Kossuth from his place of exile in Italy issued an open letter to Deák condemning him for accepting a settle-ment that would be fatal to the interests of the Hungarian nation. Kossuth's gesture merely helped to swing opinion in Austria to favor the *Ausgleich,* a consequence he had not anticipated.

Francis Joseph sanctioned the law—Law XII—in 1867, and the coronation, as has been described, followed shortly afterward. The popularity of the ruler was enhanced by a declaration at the time he was crowned that he wished "a veil to be drawn over the past," and by the distribution of the customary coronation gifts among invalided Hungarians and widows and orphans of those who had participated in the insurrection of 1848-49. A general amnesty was decreed for all connected with that dismal chapter in Hungarian history.

So weak had the sentiment for revolution become that even the veteran insurgent, General Klapka, assured Andrássy that "in the resurrection of the constitution he saw the beginning of a happy period for our people and the first step toward its vital task in eastern Europe." If the *Ausgleich* of 1867 did not create a symmetrical system of government for the Hapsburg realm, it went far to conciliate the Magyar ruling class, and that was the immediate object. It is not difficult to imagine a constitutional framework superior to the one that was devised, but at the time it was probably the best that could be worked out.

III

Steps had been taken in the meantime to place constitutionalism on a solid footing in the Austrian half of the Monarchy. To ratify the *Ausgleich* with Hungary and to remodel the governmental machinery of the empire of Austria, parliament would have to be convoked.

According to the February constitution of 1861, deputies of the lower house of parliament were to be chosen by the provincial diets on the basis of socioeconomic classes or curiae. On the proposal of Count Belcredi, with Beust in support, the emperor issued a rescript, January 2, 1867, calling an "extraordinary parliament," extraordinary because it would be elected by the diets without reference to the curiae. Since this change in the electoral law promised to bring victory to the advocates of a federalized Austria, angry protests were registered by German liberals, who vainly argued that deputies should be chosen as prescribed in the February constitution.

In the election that followed, the diets of Bohemia, Moravia, Carniola, and Galicia chose friends of federalism—men who were in the main unsympathetic to the projected compromise with Hungary. From the German provinces, on the other hand, deputies were returned who were decidedly favorable to the *Ausgleich,* but they declined to take seats in the extraordinary parliament.

Beust, who had changed his mind regarding the extraordinary parliament, counseled its abandonment as federalistic and dangerous for the dualistic deal with Hungary, but Belcredi hotly dissented. Differences between the two men were ventilated before the emperor who, after his customary deliberation, sided with the Saxon. Thereupon Belcredi resigned, Beust was named minister-president of Austria, and the way was cleared for a speedy solution of constitutional questions.

On February 18, 1867, an imperial message to the Austrian diets announced that the extraordinary parliament had been given up and that a parliament elected by the several classes would be called a month later. To that body bills would be presented making such modifications in the Austrian constitution as were necessitated by the impending *Ausgleich* with Hungary, creating a responsible ministry, enlarging provincial home rule, and improving the fighting services and the judiciary. When the diets of Bohemia, Moravia, and Carniola reported that they would not send representatives to parliament, they were summarily dissolved. The Galician diet hesitated, but the others chose delegates and after the lapse of a few weeks newly chosen diets of Bohemia, Moravia, and Carniola followed suit. In the Bohemian diet a majority sympathetic to the ministry's wishes was secured by official pressure and by the personal influence of Francis Joseph among the landed nobility.

Generally pleased over the course events had taken, Francis Joseph wrote to his friend, Albert of Saxony, "Beust is already a thorough Austrian! He is developing commendable activity and energy while at the same time preserving his sense of humor; we work together excellently." The emperor openly manifested his confidence in Beust (and his approval of the *Ausgleich*) by appointing him chancellor of the empire, an honor conferred only twice before in Austrian history.

Upon the convocation of parliament, May 22, 1867, Beust announced that a responsible ministry would be chosen from the parliamentary majority, the German constitutional or liberal party. But that group refused to take over the management of the government until the settlement with Hungary had been completed. Beust was therefore obliged to organize a temporary ministry composed of men of small political influence. Polish spokesmen muddied the waters by insisting that Galicia should be given special autonomous rights, and Beust, in order to secure Polish parliamentary support, promised substantial concessions.

After receiving bills to regulate anew the relations between state and church and to establish the principle of ministerial responsibility, parliament adjourned to permit representatives of Austria and Hungary to iron out the details of joint finance. After lengthy discussions and pressure from the monarch it was decided that Hungary should bear 30 per cent of the common expenses, or approximately the proportion that had been paid annually by the Hungarian counties during the preceding decade. Without recognizing that both halves of the Monarchy were responsible for existing debts, Hungary promised to make a relatively small payment each year to meet these obligations. With the making of the financial accord, the settlement with Hungary, subject to approval by the Austrian parliament, was finished.

No sooner had the Austrian parliament reassembled than the twenty-five members of the Catholic episcopacy protested energetically against any alteration in the existing concordat with the Vatican. Beust, however, preferred to ignore the concordat as such and to concentrate on the "fundamental principles of the realm," which would eventually make possible modifications in the status of the Catholic Church and her clergy.

Parliament proceeded to revise the February constitution of 1861 to bring it into conformity with the status accorded to the Hungarian partner by the *Ausgleich*. In the debates the thorny question of the competence of the provincial diets was thoroughly aired, with the non-German deputies clamoring for wide provincial autonomy; it was agreed finally that all matters not expressly assigned to the central parliament in the fundamental laws should fall within the jurisdiction of the several diets. A motion to ratify the understanding with Hungary provoked animated debate, especially on the financial terms, but it was passed almost unanimously. In December of 1867, the fundamental laws that revised the February constitution, having received the sanction of the emperor, were published in the Official Gazette of Vienna.

Upon the adoption of the constitutional reforms Beust retired as Austrian premier and was free to concentrate on the foreign affairs of the Dual Monarchy. Praised by the emperor for his share in effecting the constitutional adjustments, he was also warmly acclaimed by the "liberal" press. Vienna's leading paper, *Neue Freie Presse*, the new mouthpiece of German liberalism, commented editorially that "the industry of the bee and the patience of the beaver" were required to carry the negotiations on the constitution to a successful conclusion. Those qualities Beust had shown and he fully deserved the almost universal respect that he had won.

IV

No state on the face of the globe had a more complicated framework of government than the Hapsburg Monarchy, the inescapable sequel to the blending of traditional constitutional rights with the requirements of practical expediency. In reality there was created in 1867 a trinitarian political complex comprising the organs of central governmental authority, of the kingdom of Hungary, and of the empire of Austria.

The settlements were made up of two parts: a permanent arrangement respecting the political institutions of Austria and of Hungary; and an impermanent section which provided for renewable agreements regarding the share that each partner was to contribute to the common expenses of the Monarchy and with respect to tariffs, the imperial bank, the currency, and those railways which served both countries. In such matters as weights, measures, coinage, the postal service, and patents, the two countries were identical. There was, however, no common monarchical citizenship; a resident of Austria had to become naturalized if he desired to become a citizen of Hungary, and vice versa.

Under the terms of the *Ausgleich,* the ruler of the dual state would be a Hapsburg so long as legitimate Catholics in the family line existed. He might not abdicate the throne of one of the countries without relinquishing his sovereign rights in the other, and before a new ruler could exercise his royal prerogatives in Hungary he would have to be formally crowned and take the traditional oaths to protect the laws and liberties of the nation. As ruler, he was commander in chief of the armed forces, and appointed and dismissed the common ministers of the realm and the ministers of Austria and of Hungary.

Three public matters of mutual concern would be managed by common or joint ministries: foreign relations, including diplomatic and consular representation abroad; the fighting services (other than "home" armies); and finances to provide for both these purposes. It was assumed that these joint instruments of government would ensure the international prestige and defense of the Monarchy entire. Since the ministers in charge were responsible to the crown, their tenure of office would not be directly affected by the ebb and flow of domestic politics.

The foreign secretary was charged with the direction of international policies and representatives, both political and commercial. As things worked out, he frequently conferred with the premiers of Austria and Hungary who, in turn, transmitted information on foreign affairs to their respective parliaments. When international trade treaties were being drafted, the foreign minister consulted with the commerce ministers in the two cabinets and such treaties had to be assented to by both parliaments. To the delegations, shortly to be explained, or to their committees on foreign relations, the foreign minister imparted such information as he deemed compatible with state interest, and occasionally volumes of diplomatic documents, illustrative of foreign policies and actions, were issued.

The common war minister was entrusted with the direction and management of the defense forces, though, ordinarily, he had no jurisdiction over the territorial levies, the Austrian *Landwehr* and the Hungarian *Honvéds,* which were controlled by ministers of defense in each country. (In practice, the Austrian *Landwehr,* except for the special militia in the Tyrol and Dalmatia, was brigaded with the common army.) German was the language of command for the joint army, though military instruction was customarily given in the several tongues of the recruits. All legislation relating to military affairs, such as the length of the term of service and the size of the annual contingent of conscripts, was reserved to the decision of the two parliaments.

Supervision over common finance, the handling of funds received from joint revenues, principally customs receipts, and from contributions to common expenditure made by the two partners, was the province of the joint finance minister. He had also to prepare annually the common budget for the approval of the delegations, and since his responsibilities were lighter than those of his two colleagues he was appointed chief administrator of Bosnia-Herzegovina after 1879.

None of the common ministers might simultaneously be a member of the cabinet of either Austria or Hungary. Without constitutional warrant, an informal crown council came into being, usually presided over by the monarch, which comprised the common ministers and the premiers of the two countries; occasionally other cabinet officers and prominent politicians and military leaders attended the council to deliberate on questions of general concern, especially foreign affairs. The crown council represented the closest approach to a common cabinet that the Dual Monarchy ever possessed.

It was stipulated in the Settlement of 1867 that every ten years the two countries should fix tariffs and related matters jointly and should decide the share or quota that each partner should pay for common expenditure. These agreements and any international accords involving financial obligations or territorial changes would have to be validated by parallel laws enacted by the two parliaments. If no understanding on "quotas" were reached, the monarch, on the advice of the cabinets of the two countries, might out of hand fix the contributions for one year. When accepting the tariff understanding in 1867, the Hungarian negotiators entered a reservation to the effect that Hungary possessed the right of customs autonomy, which it might invoke if it so desired.

Unique among political institutions was the Austro-Hungarian delegation system, devised by Count Andrássy, who regarded it as an "international" commission, symbolizing the parity between Austria and Hungary. Advocates of centralism accepted the delegation scheme in the belief that it would be the seed of a central, monarchical parliament. Each parliament would annually select from its membership a delegation of sixty members, twenty from the upper house, forty from the lower. As a sign of the absolute equality of the two countries, these bodies would meet alternately in Vienna and Budapest, and each would deliberate and vote separately unless disagreement, thrice expressed, developed; in that event—and it was in practice exceedingly rare—a plenary session would be convoked and without debate the controversial issue would be voted upon. (Should a tie result, the monarch would cast the deciding ballot.)

The delegations were assigned the task of adopting the budget for common affairs, and once they had accepted it and the monarch had given his approval the two parliaments were bound to vote the necessary appropriations. The delegations also exercised supervisory authority over the common ministers, might summon them to give an account of their stewardship, and might even impeach a joint minister, though that right was never actually invoked. The delegations, which were not really legislative organs, and which met only infrequently and then only for a brief period, and debated separately, exerted precious little weight in the shaping of public policies; on vital questions of foreign policy the desires of the delegations were seldom solicited.

Whereas the Hungarian delegation usually presented a united front, the Austrian one was often divided by nationalistic dissensions, as Andrássy had shrewdly anticipated. That difference was traceable to the different methods that were followed in selecting the delegations. In Hungary the delegation was chosen by majority vote in each branch of parliament, with the proviso that one Croat should be elected in the upper house and four Croats in the lower. Since Magyars dominated parliament, almost to the exclusion of the other nationalities, Magyars very largely made up the Hungarian delegation.

In Austria, on the other hand, the delegates from the lower house were selected by the deputies of the several provinces, thus assuring representation to the several nationalities. At the very first joint sitting of the delegations (1869), made necessary by a disagreement on the common budget, Polish and Tyrolese deputies from Austria voted with the Hungarians. Unity in the Hungarian delegation was matched by discord in the Austrian—to the obvious advantage of the former, though the practical significance of that situation may easily be exaggerated.

Changes in the political institutionalism set up in 1867 could be effected only by the concurrent action of the parliaments of the two partners, approved by the monarch. The immense difficulty involved in revising the governmental system, in view of the consistent solidarity of the Magyars and their unwavering adherence to the *status quo*, was a major flaw in the Settlement of 1867. From time to time, drastic constitutional reform was urgently advocated, particularly in the twentieth century, but changes could scarcely have been achieved without the arbitrary action of the monarch.

v

Technically, constitutionally, separate from the dualistic organs, though in practice inextricably interwoven with them, were the autonomous governments of the kingdom of Hungary and the empire of Austria. By the Settlement of 1867, Hungary's ancient constitution, which like the British constitution consisted of customs and statutes, such as the Golden Bull, rather than a single all-embracing document, was revived. Historic rights and traditional liberties that had been shelved and trampled upon after the insurrection in 1849 were now adapted to meet new conditions.

By the act of coronation Francis Joseph had been invested with the powers of a limited constitutional king in Hungary. To him belonged the right of summoning, adjourning, and dissolving the legislature; he was obligated to call that body together at least once a year and to sanction or reject all bills passed by it. Besides, he appointed the ministers of state, certain members of the upper house, the chief county officials, civil servants, and university professors. Over the Roman Catholic church the king exercised extensive authority, such as the appointment of bishops, and he was the official protector of other legally recognized religions. All royal nominations, all special ordinances and the like, had to be assented to by the appropriate minister or ministers.

The real Hungarian executive was the ministry, which was responsible to the lower branch of the parliament. It consisted of a premier, the heads of the several royal bureaus, a special minister for Croatia, and an unimportant representative attached to the imperial court. Ministers were members of parliament and were expected to explain policies or present official reports to that body when requested. By a simple majority of the deputies any minister could be impeached for acts violative of the constitution, for fraudulent use of public funds, or for neglect to enforce laws.

Legislative authority in Hungary was vested in an aristocratic table or house of magnates and a house of representatives. Not unlike the British House of Lords, the Hungarian upper chamber contained the adult males of titled families from barons to princes, the principal functionaries of the Roman Catholic and Uniate faiths, designated court officials, the lords lieutenants of the counties, and three representatives from the Croatian diet. Although constitutionally the equal of the lower house (except that they could not originate laws) and competent to defeat measures adopted by it, the magnates as a rule acquiesced in the decisions of the more popular assembly.

The house of deputies selected its own presiding officer and was allowed virtually unlimited freedom in debate, so that it was not hard to impede or block the passage of bills that were distasteful to even a few members. The right to initiate legislation, though shared with the king, was the special province of the lower house, and this body controlled the tenure of office of ministries. While the king might suspend the sessions or even dismiss parliament at any time, he was required to summon it again within three months after dissolution, and even sooner if the budget for the following year had not been passed.

In essence the Hungarian lower house was an oligarchical body, in no sense dependent on the will of the vast mass of the citizens. Of its 453 members, forty were chosen by the Croatian diet and participated in deliberations only when measures affecting the entire kingdom were under consideration. The other deputies were directly elected by adult males who met certain qualifications, qualifications which varied widely so that there were more than fifty categories of electors; candidates had in all cases to possess a knowledge of the Magyar language. Electoral districts were arranged partly in accordance with population density, partly on the basis of economic and nationality considerations. Voting for deputies was conducted orally, which opened the way for coercion and intimidation; originally, deputies were chosen for three years, but in 1886 the term was extended to five.

Hungary's county governments, which had kept alive the heritage of constitutionalism against great odds, regained something of their old prestige after 1867, though there was a marked tendency in the direction of administrative centralism. The lord lieutenant, the county's most prominent official and a nominee of the crown, had as his principal responsibility the job of securing the support of the county assembly for the policies of the Budapest government; in time of grave emergency he might temporarily suspend local laws and even dismiss the assembly. His subordinate, the vice-sheriff, who was elected by the assembly, performed most of the local administrative functions. An Act of 1870 prescribed that half of the county councilors should be chosen by the largest taxpayers, the other half by men eligible to vote for parliamentary deputies. County assemblies could pass local laws, controlled local finance, and retained their old privilege of refusing to levy taxes or raise recruits not authorized by the Hungarian parliament.

VI

Legally, that part of the Hapsburg realm known as Austria had no name, or rather was designated as "the kingdoms and countries represented in the reichsrath." On occasion Austria was referred to as Cisleithania, with Hungary as Transleithania, since the Leith, a little tributary of the Danube, separated the two parts of the Monarchy.

Austria's form of government had its direct legal warrant in the February constitution of 1861 and the fundamental laws adopted on December 21, 1867. The first statute in the "constitution" of 1867 set forth the rights of man and the citizen just like the prefaces of almost all constitutions since the famous French charter of 1791. Equality before the law and in the public service, freedom of press, speech, and assembly were formally guaranteed.

One clause made liberal provisions for the interests of the various nationalities, for it stated that "all nationalities (*Volkstämme*) in the state enjoy equal rights, and each one has an inalienable right to the preservation and cultivation of its nationality and language. The equal rights of all languages in local use (*landesüblich*) are guaranteed by the state in schools, administration, and public life. In the provinces inhabited by several nationalities public educational institutions are to be so organized that, without applying compulsion in the learning of a second language, each nationality receives the necessary means for education in its language." That article, so full of promise as written, was never faithfully enforced. Other statutes defined the organization and jurisdiction of the several political institutions of the Austrian empire.

Constitutionally, the authority of the emperor of Austria paralleled that of heads of other limited monarchies. He selected and dismissed ministers and certain other policy-making officials, created peers, and granted pardons and amnesties. He summoned, prorogued, or dissolved the legislative bodies, subject to the rule that if the lower house was dissolved a successor must be convened within six months. The signature of the emperor gave final validity to laws.

One paragraph of the constitution, the notorious article fourteen, authorized the ruler to publish decrees when parliament was not in session, which had full force of law. Imperial decrees, however, required concurrence of the ministry, and in no case might they modify the fundamental law of the empire. It was further prescribed that a decree would cease to be binding if not acceded to by parliament at its next succeeding session. Nonetheless, the dictatorship paragraph, as critics labeled it, clothed the monarch with almost unfettered authority in the event that parliament misbehaved.

The ministry, consisting of a premier and a varying number of heads of state departments, was responsible constitutionally to the lower house. Official acts of the monarch, emergency decrees included, required countersignature by the ministry. As matters turned out, ministers were less agents of the legislature than obedient servants of the emperor who appointed them. Projects for laws originated very largely in the ministry.

The constitution assigned broad powers to the parliament. To the lower house the ministry was technically responsible and deputies might freely interpellate or impeach ministers. Both houses had to approve important items of state business, including international treaties. In legislative authority the houses were coequal, although the budget and bills fixing the annual contingent of soldiers had to be considered first in the lower chamber. It was specified in the fundamental law that parliament must be convened at least once a year.

Dynastic aristocrats, heads of noble families, leading ecclesiastics, and individuals of distinguished attainments picked by the emperor had seats in the upper chamber. Originally, the deputies of the lower house were sent to Vienna by the provincial assemblies, but after 1873, as is later explained, election by districts and on a class basis was substituted.

The seventeen provinces of Austria each had an assembly (diet) of a single house ranging in size from twenty members in Vorarlberg to over two hundred in turbulent Bohemia. Instead of a ministry, assemblies chose executive committees to attend to local affairs. Legally, the assemblies possessed competence in all aspects of government not reserved to the government in Vienna. General principles on such affairs as primary education and churches were decided by the imperial parliament, and the assemblies enacted implementing legislation.

Imperial authority, moreover, imposed very real restrictions upon provincial autonomy. Legislation adopted by assemblies, for instance, required approval by the emperor, which was not at all an empty form. Besides, the crown appointed the provincial governor (*Statthalter*), an administrative overseer, and the presiding officer of the assembly who decided the order of business and could dissolve the assembly. Nevertheless, the assemblies were significant instruments of local government, growing in vigor and vitality with the passage of time.

CHAPTER THREE

GERMAN LIBERAL PREDOMINANCE
IN AUSTRIA

THAT THE POLITICAL REORGANIZATION OF THE HAPSBURG MONarchy and the introduction of formal constitutionalism in Austria presented extremely complicated problems of government was recognized at home and abroad. "Only the most perfect harmony," wrote a British agent in Vienna, "and a sincere desire on all sides to labour unremittingly for the general interests of the monarchy can afford the slightest chance of duration and success to so novel and unwieldy a system, but such complete harmony will be difficult to establish or to maintain for any lengthened period in a nation of so heterogeneous a nature as Austria."[1] Grant Duff, one of the best-informed members of the British House of Commons on European politics, remarked: "What statesman inside or outside the Empire knows anything at all of the facts of Austria? It is a science in itself. Nay, it is half a dozen sciences, and the ablest politician can only move timidly and tentatively like a mule among slippery and crumbling rocks."[2] These commentaries of the 1860's had not lost their validity half a century later.

Confronting the new regime were ever-pressing financial perplexities and readjustments in the relations of Austria with the Roman Catholic church. On the recommendation of Beust, Francis Joseph picked for the first parliamentary ministry men with a reputation for liberalism and known for their sympathy with constitutional government. At the head of the ministry was Count Charles Auersperg, called "the first cavalier of the realm," and his principal colleagues were Dr. Edward Herbst, a spirited German from Bohemia, and Count Edward Taaffe. Both federalist and centralist viewpoints were represented in the cabinet; it was a body of excellent debaters rather than of creative statesmen.

German Liberals, the largest faction in the Austrian parliament, spoke the mind of the German middle class and drew their inspiration directly from the revolutionary ideology of 1848. Stanch friends of constitutionalism and civil freedoms, the Liberals were opponents of clericalism and opponents of a federalized Austria which would spell political ruin for the Austro-Germans and might prove disastrous for the international standing of the realm.

The Auersperg ministry proceeded at once to impose limitations on clericalism, which, it was held, was blameworthy for the reversals that had recently befallen the Monarchy. In a resolution calling for the abrogation of the Concordat of 1855, the Town Council of Vienna characterized the treaty with Rome as "that baleful agreement by which the inhabitants of Austria, as regards their most sacred rights and possessions, are exposed to the arbitrary pleasure of a foreign power." Impetus had been given to anticlericalism by papal criticism of the constitutional laws of 1867 and by popular clamor against clericalism. Fifteen hundred schoolmasters, for instance, at a meeting in Vienna in September 1867, passed resolutions asking that the schools should be wholly separated from ecclesiastical control.

If the Liberals had followed their private inclinations they would have torn up the Concordat by the roots, but out of deference to the wishes of Francis Joseph they whittled away clerical prerogatives bit by bit. By one measure civil marriage was legalized and marital trials were transferred from church to secular courts. In the upper house, churchmen fought the legislation tooth and nail. Joseph Othmar von Rauscher, cardinal archbishop of Vienna, who had negotiated the Concordat, strove manfully to swing the landed aristocrats against the marriage bill, arguing that it involved a breach of faith with the Vatican and would be detrimental to the cause of religion. Count Anton Auersperg, on the other hand, a militant champion of liberalism, implored the chamber to strike "the badge of ecclesiastical slavery from Austria," and invoked stirring memories of Joseph II and his ecclesiastical innovations. Vienna's "great press" joined in the cry for secularism, and wild anticlerical demonstrations were staged on the streets of the capital.

In a dramatically tense session the upper house adopted the marriage act by a large majority, whereupon the Catholic prelates withdrew from the "infidel" chamber. Vienna celebrated the passage of the law with a grand illumination. Count Beust, who had been active behind the scenes, was popularly hailed as the real organizer of the anticlerical victory; a citizen who recognized him on the street, embraced his knees, crying, "You have liberated us from the fetters of the Concordat." "I beg you," Beust briskly responded, "to liberate my legs."

In the absence of the bishops, legislation was enacted removing the schools from church control and handing them over to the superintendence of the state; only religious instruction, noncompulsory in character, remained in the hands of the priests. Federalists and clericals, Poles and Slovenes, repudiated this measure as an infringement upon provincial rights and retired in protest from the Chamber.

Another bill was intended to put all Christian creeds on an equal plane before the law. It also prescribed that if parents of different faiths died without deciding the religion of their children, sons should follow the father's creed and daughters that of the mother. It was declared unlawful for a cleric to deny religious burial to a member of another sect, if there was only one church in the parish. And no longer might a freethinker be refused a bequest, or imprisoned for expressing his convictions. In spite of pressure exerted upon him by clericals, especially by his old tutor, Rauscher, Francis Joseph sanctioned all the church bills, and sanguine liberals even murmured that the emperor was Joseph II reborn.

Churchmen protested vehemently against the ecclesiastical legislation. In a solemn allocution by Pope Pius IX, the laws were denounced as "truly unholy," "destructive, abominable, and damnable," and "absolutely null and void." Certain Austrian spiritual dignitaries flatly defied the laws and summoned the faithful not to obey them; Bishop Riccabona of Trient, for example, declared that anyone who submitted to the laws was a despoiler of God, and Cardinal Schwarzenberg ordered his clergy to deny confession and absolution to anyone who had been married by civil authorities. So violently did Bishop Rüdiger of Linz express himself that he was haled into court on the charge of incitement to disturb the peace; condemned to prison, he was pardoned by the emperor, with whom Rauscher interceded. In the Tyrol, Vorarlberg, and other districts where clericalism was powerfully entrenched, the laity loyally backed the churchmen.

Count Beust vigorously attacked the papal allocution as unwarrantable interference in the affairs of the Austrian empire. If the Vatican thought that its action would lead to the repeal of the anticlerical legislation, as seems to have been the case, it was rudely deceived, for the spirit of the age was running heavily against ecclesiastical intervention in what were thought of as purely secular matters. Like their counterparts in Prussia, a large company of Austrian politicians, supported generally by the middle class, was intransigently opposed to anything that savored of clerical encroachment upon the sphere of the state.

Formal grounds for the abandonment of the Concordat were furnished in 1870 by the promulgation of the doctrine of the personal infallibility of the pope in matters of faith and morals at the Vatican Council. Before the Council assembled, Bavaria recommended that the interested governments should impose a veto upon the adoption of the dogma, but Beust scorned the idea, holding that religious bodies should have full liberty in their internal affairs, so long as there was no invasion of the province of the state. Almost without exception, the delegates from the Hapsburg Monarchy to the Vatican Council resisted the adoption of the infallibility principle, and acquiesced in it only with extreme reluctance.

Shortly thereafter, an imperial Austrian rescript declared that the infallibility doctrine had changed the character of the party with which the Concordat had been signed and that Austria was therefore justified in canceling the treaty. The liberal press of Vienna commented that what Austrian Liberalism had striven for years to accomplish had been quickly brought to pass by the maneuvers of the Jesuits in Rome. Beust hurriedly explained that the Austrian government in abrogating the Concordat was not hostile to religion in its appointed sphere, but that was only inadequate consolation for stanch Clericals.

The defeat at Sadowa had taught Austria many things, not least that the armed services were antiquated and no match for the modernized forces of Prussia. Therefore, a flood of reforms endeavored to raise the armies of the Hapsburgs to a footing of equality with the victorious Prussians; universal military service was voted in 1868, military tactics and equipment were radically revised, and even the traditional white coats of the Hapsburg troops were discarded. Corporal punishment was abolished, and the standard of professional competence required of officers was considerably heightened. Legislation similar in scope was enacted in Hungary, providing the Monarchy with a standing army of 255,000 and a war footing more than triple that size. "Progressing in science and in the spirit of the times," Francis Joseph promised, "the army will inspire respect in the enemy and be a stronghold of throne and realm."

Prussia was once more imitated in a school law of 1869, bold in conception and comprehensive in scope, which provided (on paper) for compulsory and free elementary education for all children. Unfortunately, administration of the law was left to the provincial diets, where religious prejudices and political passions retarded the full execution of this enlightened measure.

Other progressive laws enacted in the rosy dawn of Austrian parliamentary government established trial by jury for alleged violations of the rigorous press laws, humanization of the penal code, and the abolition of oppressive restrictions upon Jews. Viewing the reformist innovations as a whole, achieved in the face of stiff resistance from the singularly conservative aristocracy and the Catholic hierarchy, it seemed to foreign observers that Austria merited a place among the forward-moving countries. "From the defeat of Sadowa," wrote John Jay, the American minister to the Hapsburg court, "Austria has arisen to the astonishment of Europe and of herself, with modern ideas, free principles, and a new life." [3]

In the course of the negotiation of the Settlement of 1867 Beust is reported to have observed to Andrássy, "You look after your barbarians and we will look after ours." Piece by piece concessions were extended to the Polish "barbarians" which assured their loyalty to the new Austrian order, but other national groups of Austria, notably the Czechs, the Yugoslavs, and the Italians, were unappeased, and their leaders were inclined to believe that stubbornness might be rewarded with concessions as in the case of the Magyars. Guarantees of national equality that had been inscribed in the fundamental law of the state failed to satisfy, if for no other reason, because experience had shown the worthlessness of such pledges. What the minority leaders in general desired was extensive and genuine provincial autonomy. "Nowadays," a minister was heard to remark, "every nationality, even every little bit of a nationality, wants an *Ausgleich*."

It was argued by spokesmen of the Czechs that the lands of the crown of St. Wenceslaus, meaning the provinces of Bohemia, Moravia, and Silesia, possessed comparable rights with the lands of the crown of St. Stephen and should, therefore, be given a constitutional status analogous to that of Hungary. The most outspoken advocate of Czech autonomy was Dr. Francis L. Rieger, a miller's son, who had emerged as a public figure during the revolutionary storm of 1848, and who was the son-in-law of Palacký, the eloquent Czech patriotic historian.

In some respects Rieger resembled the Magyar Deák, for he was a lawyer well versed in constitutional history and tenacious of his countrymen's interests, but his case for home rule rested on less substantial ground than the Magyar's. Though Magyar rights had often been violated, they nevertheless remained in being to 1849, while Bohemian rights had not been operative since the early seventeenth century. In the diet at Prague, Rieger inveighed in shrill tones against the dualistic settlement and confidently predicted the disruption of the Monarchy unless it was remodeled. Holding that the new Austrian regime lacked constitutional validity, he and his fellows declined to attend the sessions of the reichsrat.

Aggrieved Czech patriots directed their gaze toward Russia, the big benevolent brother of Slavdom. In May of 1867, a group of Czech politicians and intellectuals made a pilgrimage to Russia, ostensibly to participate in a Slav ethnographic convention; the journey roused a storm of protest in the Austro-German press and governing circles, though Beust appears not to have been uneasy. It also caused flutterings among the Polish feudalists of Galicia, who thoroughly detested Russia.

At Moscow the Pan-Slav congress published an appeal to all Austrian Slavs to combine so as to secure a federal pattern of government. At public banquets Czech delegates declaimed against the overbearing tyranny of the Viennese administration, and Rieger tried to persuade Tsar Alexander II that Russia could furnish the moral support, if she would, that would enable Slav minorities everywhere to gain their legitimate rights. The Czechs proposed the establishment of a permanent Slav institute and biennial cultural conferences of Slavs, but without success. They left Moscow with the unforgettable words of one of the enthusiastic Russian promoters of the gathering ringing in their ears, "The Slav question has been transferred now from books and private studies to the street, to public squares, to churches, and to theaters."

Poles were conspicuously absent from the Moscow conference, and at the close of the gathering Rieger remonstrated with the Russians for the abusive treatment of the Polish minority in the tsardom. For that he was sternly rebuked, for the Russians would not countenance outside interference in domestic affairs. Pan-Slavism at the time was too closely identified with Orthodox Christianity to appeal warmly to the Roman Catholic Slavs of Austria, and linguistic disparities presented another big barrier to Slav cooperation. Some Czechs, it is true, entered the Orthodox fold in the illusory belief that Russia would act energetically on behalf of adherents of the national religion. Actually, the tsarist government was unprepared to intercede in Vienna even to secure autonomy for Bohemia.

In June 1868, when Francis Joseph appeared in Prague to dedicate a bridge, the Czech population manifested its ill-will by boycotting the city. And next month, the birth anniversary of John Huss afforded an occasion for fervent national demonstrations. Viennese ministers now entered into conversations with the Czechs for reconciliation, the first of a long series of discussions, but no common ground of accommodation could be discovered.

So that there might be no doubt of what the Czechs claimed, their deputies in the Bohemian diet published in September of 1868 a detailed Declaration of Rights and Expectations, which served until the dissolution of the Monarchy as the most authoritative exposition of the Czech position on constitutional questions. On the basis of rather flimsy historical precedents, the Czechs insisted that the organic unity of the lands of the "Bohemian Crown" should be recognized, that Francis Joseph should take the royal oath and be crowned in Prague, and that inequitable electoral laws, which discriminated against the Czechs, should be democratized. Only the diet in Prague, it was asserted, was competent to modify the historical relationship of Bohemia to the sovereign; as matters stood, no legislation enacted in the Vienna reichsrat could lawfully apply to Bohemia. Until the Czech claims were met, Czech representatives would hold aloof from the Austrian parliament; and Czech deputies in the diet of Moravia adopted a declaration of similar tenor.

Czech hostility to the dualistic regime was by no means confined to public men. Czech military conscripts, for example, in one district balked at taking the oath of allegiance to the crown, declaring, "We are ready to serve our homes, the lands of the Czechs, and for the holy crown of Wenceslaus . . . We will not, however, stir in favor of German rule in Bohemia, or for the Magyars." Anti-Hapsburg street outbursts attained such dimensions in Prague that the city was placed under a state of siege which lasted six months. Czech newspapers were confiscated and suppressed, and police were freely employed against the "Fenians of Austria," as some Austro-Germans labeled the Czech dissidents. Relying on the coöperation of the German element, the Austrian government tried to rule Bohemia by repression, as it had often done before and as it would frequently do in the future—a tyranny tempered by extremely slender concessions such as the founding of a technical high school for Czech youths.

Under the circumstances, Czech politicians looked to France for help at the very moment that the cabinet of Vienna was engaged in conversations with Napoleon III for a military alliance. Rieger on a visit to Paris conferred with Napoleon III, then esteemed as the arbiter of Europe and known to be devoted to the principle of nationality, and besought him to exert pressure in Vienna on behalf of the Czech pretensions. But Napoleon III, already sufficiently perplexed by dangerous antagonism with Prussia, was no more responsive to Czech entreaties than the Russian tsar had been.

Certain extremist Czechs thought to purchase the goodwill of Napoleon with tangible military values. "Once independent," read a secret memorandum dispatched to the French emperor, "Bohemia will keep northern and southern Germany apart so that a French army may be more rapidly thrown into Bohemia than a Prussian army could be sent to the Upper Rhine province . . . The Bohemian nation . . . can in a very short time effect a rapid diversion in favor of France . . . exasperated national sentiment if translated into action during a war could cause the [Hapsburg] monarchy to fall to pieces."

All hope of French intervention, which was never very real, disappeared with the swift defeat of the Napoleonic armies by Prussia in 1870. After that, Czech leaders looked more favorably upon the idea of a compromise with the Hapsburg crown.

III

The Austrian cabinet allowed special, though modest, linguistic and administrative privileges to the Poles, who lorded it over the province of Galicia, with its large and backward Ruthenian or Ukrainian population. In imitation of the Czechs, Polish politicians drafted in 1868 a Galician *Resolution* which called for far-reaching provincial self-government and permitted only limited participation by Galicia in imperial affairs. If Vienna had accepted the *Resolution,* the status of Galicia in the realm would have been quite similar to Hungary's and the province might well have become a rallying ground for independence-minded Poles of Prussia and Russia. As a means of showing his disapproval of the federalist ferment among the Poles, and to allay apprehensions that had been roused in Prussia and Russia, Francis Joseph ostentatiously canceled a trip that he had planned to Galicia.

Though unwilling to acquiesce in the *Resolution,* the Austrian authorities quite readily extended privileges to the Poles which gave Galicia a considerable degree of self-government and facilitated the Polonization of the Ruthenian minority. Polish was recognized as the language of public administration, the law courts included, and of secondary schools, except that religious instruction might be offered in the Ruthenian tongue. In 1871 a special Austrian ministry for Galician affairs was created and financial arrangements were adjusted along lines desired by Polish politicians. By these concessions the Vienna regime helped to cement the devotion of Polish leaders to the crown and assured the ministry of the votes of Polish deputies in the imperial parliament.

Whereas Poles in Russia and Prussia were looked upon and treated as inferiors, in Galicia they reigned supreme and they were in the main well aware of their comparatively favored status. If the Hapsburg realm should disintegrate, many Austrian Poles reasoned, Galicia would pass under the harsh scepter of the tsar or of Prussia and the last state would be infinitely less attractive than the first. Wherefore, such a respected Polish grandee as Prince Czartoryski asserted that the first duty of Galician Poles was to uphold and defend the Hapsburg Monarchy as a haven of liberty between Muscovite barbarism and Prussian militarism; and he echoed the thought of many of his countrymen.

Over the heads of the Polish landed aristocracy the Vienna government held a heavy club, the threat of social revolt, which exercised a restraining influence upon separatist activity. The precedent of 1846, when Hapsburg officials incited rural laborers against Polish landed interests, might again be invoked. As a matter of fact, that rising marked a turning point in the attitude of the Polish proprietors toward Austria, for thereafter they identified themselves with the government against the soil workers, more particularly the Ruthenians. By coöperating with the Vienna administration it was possible for the Poles to submerge the Ruthenians, though by no means wholly.

IV

As a semiïndependent province, Galicia attained a unique place in the cultural affairs of the entire Polish nation. Refugee patriots from Russian and Prussian Poland found asylum in the congenial Galician cities of Cracow and Lemberg, whose universities fostered a distinctly Polish intellectual life. Polish magnate families patronized learning and the arts, and occasionally a Polish nobleman combined an active career in politics with a lively interest in the things of the mind and spirit. Such a one was Count Leon Piniński, who, after studying in Polish and German universities, lectured on Roman law in the University of Lemberg. At his home this wealthy landowner composed music and wrote on art and on Marcus Aurelius, Dante, and Shakespeare; for a decade Piniński sat in the Vienna reichsrat and for five years he served as viceroy of Galicia.

But achievements in scholarship, in letters, and in the arts were much more largely the work of the Polish middle class than of the aristocracy. It was at Cracow, redolent of memories of medieval Poland, of which it was the capital, and the home of Poland's oldest university, that Polish national culture was most assiduously and most fruitfully cultivated. The ancient Jagellonian University, dating from 1363, to which was attached the Academy of Arts and Sciences, became the intellectual capital of the Polish nationality after the restoration of Polish as the language of instruction in 1861. It quickly enrolled more than a thousand students and by 1900 there were over a hundred professors. In the classrooms of the University men and women were trained who, upon the rebirth of Poland in 1918, organized the educational system of the country at all levels, and provided leadership in every branch of the public service. There, in the Austrian era, secret political societies were founded by students and their elders to promote the cause of Polish national resurrection.

Freedom of inquiry was permitted. Natural science flourished and Cracow University gained international renown through a school of historians who foreswore romanticized idealism, studied and published documentary materials on medieval and early modern Poland, and freshly evaluated the country's past. Where scholarship demanded it, the Cracow school, which was presided over by Michael Bobrzyński, sometime Galician governor, had no qualms about assigning the dismemberment of Poland to the grievous incompetence and blindness of the Polish nobility.

Another school of history flourished at Lemberg University, with Professor Xavier Liske, a scholar of vast erudition, in charge. In his seminar many of the leading Polish historians of the next generation received their professional training. His brilliant colleague, Szymon Askenazy, who was educated in the Russian University of Warsaw, concerned himself with polemical researches in modern history, especially the Napoleonic period and diplomacy. Historians at Lemberg extolled the constructive achievements of Poland in the past and, in contrast to their fellows at Cracow, attributed chief responsibility for Poland's downfall in the eighteenth century to the rapacity of predatory neighbors. Intellectual warfare between the Cracow "realists" and the Lemberg "romantics" enlivened Polish historical learning, infused it with a dynamic character, and brought to light a wealth of new evidence on the antecedents of Poland's spoliation. But after about 1900 the romanticizing interpreters were reluctantly obliged to acknowledge the victory of the scholars in Cracow.

Outstanding among Polish men of letters residing in Cracow was Stanislaus Przybyszewski, who was born in Russia and studied in Germany before settling down in Galicia. Around him he gathered a company of young literary rebels who lived and wrote in an unorthodox, "realistic" fashion. In his own novels and dramas, Przybyszewski treated sexual themes in unconventional ways and preached that every individual was an absolute law unto himself. His *The Children of Satan* and *Homo Sapiens* are prized as classics of modern Polish prose, but their popularity was short-lived.

Przybyszewski's foremost disciple, Stanislaus Wyspiański, has been doubly acclaimed as a prophet of Poland's political resurrection and the foremost literary genius of Polish Galicia. His fame rests chiefly on his realistic and dramatic masterpiece, *The Wedding,* which was a valuable antidote to much of the fanciful romanticism of other literary advocates of Polish resurrection.[4] *The Wedding* recounts the marriage of a Polish townsman, who was a poet, and a simple peasant maid, with guests from city and countryside in attendance at the ceremony. The dialogue deals in turn with a highly imaginative interpretation of Polish history, the present degradation of the nation, and the prospects for the future. Poles of all ranks should unite to achieve national freedom, the author pleads, but, in the pessimistic conclusion, the townsfolk, who ought to serve as leaders for the peasantry, are shown to be wanting in national ardor and conviction.

Wyspiański's *Deliverance* graphically pictured the faults and frailties of the Poles and summoned readers to assist in the rebirth of an independent Poland; more a patriotic manifesto than a piece of great literature, *Deliverance* exerted a strong influence upon a whole generation of Polish readers. In two dramatic tragedies, *The Curse* and *The Judges,* Wyspiański described the ways of the peasants and their dealings with village priest and Jewish shopkeeper; rustic ignorance and superstition and the penalties they brought were vividly depicted. Wyspiański's writings had abundant recognition while the author lived and his death was mourned by the whole Polish nation at a huge funeral in Cracow.

The most eminent poet of Galicia was John Kasprowicz. Born into a peasant household in Prussian Poland, Kasprowicz moved to Lemberg and became professor of comparative literature in the university there. In that capacity he translated Greek, English, and German poetry into Polish, but his real renown was based upon original compositions which recounted the manners and the grinding poverty of the peasantry; yet in those folk he discerned the force that would one day liberate the Poles, both socially and politically. The plain teachings of Jesus in the Gospels appealed powerfully to Kasprowicz, and in *The Christ* he drew vivid contrasts between those teachings and the practices of historical and contemporary Christianity. In the latter part of his life Kasprowicz drifted into philosophical mysticism, having grown skeptical about the peasantry, once his passion. His writings gave inspiration to the oncoming generation of Polish poets.

Adam Asnyk, who chose Cracow as his home after taking part in an insurrection against Russia in 1863, secured recognition as the outstanding Polish lyricist of his time, and was distinguished as a playwright as well. His writings were animated by profound faith in the common man and deep love of nature. *Mr. Balcer in Brazil,* a popular epic relating the harsh experiences of Polish emigrants to the New World, brought fame to Marie Konopnicka, and another of her poems, *Rota* (The Oath), in which she inveighed heatedly against German oppression of the Poles, was adopted as a national song.

Among the visual arts, Poles of Galicia excelled only in painting. The academy at Cracow was the artistic citadel and Jan Matejko, its director for many years, was the greatest creative genius.[5] His paintings, which were executed on a lavish scale, recalled romantic episodes from Poland's past and were calculated to evoke ardent national emotions. The finest of them were "The Battle of Grünwald," "Sobieski at Vienna," presented by the artist to Pope Leo XIII, and "Reytan Protesting against the First Partition of Poland." For the great hall of Cracow University Matejko painted a famous picture of the young Copernicus, greatest of the graduates of the institution. The scientist is depicted on a roof from which he studies the movements of the heavenly bodies; his face lights up with radiant joy as the faint beginnings of the great heliocentric truth associated with his name dawn upon him.

Other Galician artists employed their brushes in reviving historical memories, expressing the mute resignation of the Poles to their political fate, or hinting at happier days yet to come. Wyspiański, painter as well as man of letters, decorated stained-glass windows in Cracow's churches with dramatic representations of Polish kings, heroes, and saints.

With its splendid medieval edifices—the Gothic cathedral of St. Stanislaus, the veritable Westminster Abbey of the nation, in which reposed the mortal remains of Poland's illustrious kings, warriors, and authors; the royal castle close by, high above the Vistula, in which Polish sovereigns resided until the seventeenth century; the Gothic edifice of the old University, in whose charming Venetian courtyard was erected a graceful statue of Copernicus; the quaint, gaunt remnants of the city's medieval ramparts—with all these architectural treasures, harking back to the greater glories of Poland, Cracow eclipsed other Polish communities in interest and as a source of patriotic inspiration.

Owing to its location on the Vistula and at a commercial crossroads, Cracow prospered economically; trade and industry expanded and by 1914 the population was well beyond the 100,000 mark. The novelist Joseph Conrad, who visited Cracow in 1914 after an absence of forty years, found an alert and busy city instead of the drab provincial town he had known as a lad. Although the community was heavily Polish in composition, a large Jewish colony dwelt amidst poverty and squalor in the Casimirski district, set apart from Cracow proper.

Lemberg (Lvov), the sprawling Galician capital, at the eastern end of the province, contained a polyglot population, Polish mainly, but with a large admixture of Jews, Ruthenians, and Germans. With Ruthenian patriots Poles battled incessantly to preserve the dominantly Polish character of the city. The University in particular, in which after 1871 Polish was the language of instruction, was the scene of constant strife, not always verbal, between partisans of the rival nationalities. As the marketing point for Galician oil, wheat, timber, and sugar beets, Lemberg flourished commercially, and as a major center of communications where four railways converged, the city developed into the third largest community of the Austrian empire.

v

Like the Czechs, many Italian subjects resented the Austrian regime established in 1867, and Italian-speaking deputies elected to the Vienna parliament from Trieste refused to attend sessions until 1877. Italians in the southern part of the Tyrol agitated in the local diet, in the imperial legislature, and through petitions to Francis Joseph from scores of towns, for a separate autonomous government. Patriotic societies were organized to carry on propaganda favorable to the union of Italian-populated areas with the kingdom of Italy. The Italian national committee for Trentino thanked the city of Bassano for selecting Count Manci, a Tyrolese Italian firebrand, as its deputy in the parliament of Italy. When the government of Italy announced that in the future emigrants from "the provinces not yet annexed" would be denied Italian citizenship, a few of the *Italianissimi* moved across the border into Italy.

The reaction among Austrian Yugoslavs to the arrangements of 1867 followed no clear-cut pattern. Certain Slovenes, for instance, asked for a Slovene state in the Monarchy but their agitation was handicapped by the fact that Slovenes were dispersed in six provinces. Eventually they chose to concentrate on securing local concessions, and small grants were actually made to them, such as lecture courses in Slovene at Graz University. Among the Croats who were Austrian subjects, there was no little sentiment in favor of an autonomous Croatian state, which would include the Slovene-inhabited areas and Dalmatia, as well as Croatia proper.

The diet of Dalmatia was the theater of fierce national squabbles as the Italian Slav-hating minority struggled with Croats and Serbs. An insurrection against Hapsburg lordship broke loose in 1869 in southern Dalmatia, in the Cattaro district, being precipitated by an imperial order requiring young men to present themselves for military service from which hitherto they had been exempt. With some help from their free Montenegrin brothers, the *Bocchesi* heroically resisted imperial troops and, indeed, only laid down their arms when given assurances that conscription would not be applied and that the insurgents would be amnestied.

Dissatisfaction with the new governmental scheme inspired one clarion call from a German quarter for the reordering of the Austrian constitution along federal lines. A respected and liberal publicist, Adolph von Fischhof, who had fought in the Vienna revolution of 1848, published *Oesterreich und die Bürgschaften seines Bestandes* (1869), in which he pleaded with Austro-German Liberals to slough off their centralistic sympathies. As an empire of divergent national groups, Austria, he urged, should be remodeled on a federal basis, imitative either of Switzerland or of the United States, and allowing a large measure of home rule to the several nationalities. Federalism, Fischhof persuasively argued, was absolutely necessary to ensure the preservation of the realm. "Only centralism makes the peoples centrifugal; if Austria were decentralized they would be centripetal," he wrote. While the book created a stir in Austrian political circles and inspired other plans for the reorganization of the realm, it failed to capture the support of the predominant German Liberals; stanch Bohemian Germans blasted the author as doctrinaire and reactionary. So far as the bulk of the articulate Austro-Germans were concerned, Fischhof's was a voice crying in the wilderness, though his central idea of federalism was presently to find a place in practical politics.[6]

VI

Short-lived Austrian cabinets grappled ineffectively with the puzzling task of appeasing the dissident nationalities. No formula could be discovered that would reconcile Czech federalistic aspirations with German notions of centralism and Magyar aversion to drastic constitutional change. Debates in parliament commonly degenerated into acrid verbal warfare, more congenial to a madhouse than to a responsible branch of government. Czechs were bluntly told that they were "the barbarous vassals of Russia, the Tyrolese that they are the benighted and bigoted slaves of the pope, the Germans that they are tyrannical, bloodthirsty and irreligious."[7]

Upon the outbreak of the Franco-German war in 1870 political interest was temporarily diverted to the international scene. For Austria's internal, as well as her external, affairs the outcome of the struggle in the West had significant consequences. Austro-Germans, or at least the bourgeois element and the Alpine peasantry, rejoiced over the military success of Bismarckian Germany and lauded the proclamation of the Hohenzollern empire. Popular pro-German demonstrations in Graz grew so tumultuous that police intervened and imposed a ban on them. It was in that intoxicating hour that the Pan-German movement in Austria, which died away only with the actual union of Austria with Germany in April of 1938, had its real beginnings. Not unprophetically, Deputy Rechbauer exclaimed in the reichsrat in June of 1871, "Our fathers were Germans, and if fate should destroy Austria, we would again be Germans."

In marked contrast to the Austro-Germans, wartime sympathies among the Slavs were decidedly pro-French, and Magyars were rather French in their outlook, though the Hungarian ministry itself was stanchly Germanophile.

Along with many of his subjects, Francis Joseph wondered whether Bismarck, having acquired Alsace-Lorraine by the victory over France, would stretch out his hand to all lands where German was spoken. Pan-German effervescence cut the monarch to the quick, and that, together with dread of Bismarck's covetousness, induced the ruler to steer a new tack on the stormy Austrian domestic sea. Quietly he selected a ministry that had Slavophile leanings, detested Austro-German liberalism, and proposed to placate dissatisfied Slav nationalities by reconstructing the imperial edifice on a federal pattern.

The new premier was Count Charles Hohenwart, a cautious conservative and devout Clerical, who held that conciliation of the Slavs was indispensable for the conduct of state business and to ensure the future of the monarchy as a great power. His minister of commerce, A. E. F. Schäffle, an economist who had recently been invited to the University of Vienna from Tübingen, was the dominant personality in the cabinet. Fiercely critical of Bismarck and his ways, advocate of varied socializing reforms and universal suffrage, and a firm believer in federalism for Austria, Schäffle seemed to be the man of the hour. Two conservative Czechs and a Pole, the last as special minister for Galicia, were given places in the Hohenwart ministry.

From the outset, the German Liberals and their press, except for an unregenerate conservative bloc, savagely assailed the Hohenwart ministry, whose appointment, it was felt, indicated that Francis Joseph had taken the initiative in public business out of the hands of the parliament. Fears were openly expressed lest this Slavophile cabinet should sacrifice the Germans in Bohemia to the Czechs, even as the Ruthenians in Galicia were being handed over to the mercies of the Polish governing caste. More than one

Austro-German journalist likened Bohemia to Schleswig and visualized imperial Germany as a holy liberator. Over strong resistance, the Hohenwart-Schäffle cabinet managed to secure the passage of the budget law of 1871. Once that was done, parliament and certain provincial diets were dissolved, and a call was issued to the electorate to return deputies known to be friendly to the appeasement of the Slavs. To that appeal, with which was coupled pressure from high places, the electorate responded affirmatively.[8]

Behind the scenes, in the meantime, agents of the crown, Schäffle first and last, had been carrying on negotiations with Czech spokesmen, particularly Rieger and the leading spirit of the Bohemian landed aristocracy, Count Henry Clam-Martinič, who was wedded to the idea of federalism. Out of the parleys emerged a program for an Austrian federal union.[9]

When the Bohemian diet convened in September 1871, Czech deputies formed the majority. To that body was handed a rescript from Francis Joseph, amazing in its content. "In view of the former constitutional position of Bohemia," so the document ran, "and remembering the glory and power which her crown had given to our predecessors and full of gratitude for the loyalty with which the Bohemian nation has supported our throne, we are ready to recognize the rights of the kingdom and to confirm this assurance by taking the coronation oath." The diet was invited to specify the conditions upon which Bohemia could be reconciled; it seemed as though the constitutional aspirations of the moderate Czechs were within sight of fulfillment.

After German deputies had withdrawn in high dudgeon from the Bohemian diet, the Czechs unanimously adopted a set of fundamental articles to regulate the relation of Bohemia to the Monarchy. Thereby Bohemia would share in the deliberations on common affairs—foreign relations, the fighting services, and monarchical finance—through a delegation, similar to that of Hungary, and chosen by the Prague diet. On all other public questions the diet itself would have competence. Full linguistic and educational rights would be guaranteed to the Bohemian Germans. Seats in the diet would be redistributed so as to make sure that Czechs would always have a majority, which on the basis of history and population was legitimately theirs. As soon as Francis Joseph had sworn to observe these fundamental laws, he was to be crowned at Prague with the ancient crown of St. Wenceslaus.

Not unnaturally the Czech aspirations, which if put into operation would sound the knell of German and Magyar hegemony and might lead to further federalization, infuriated the bulk of the Austro-Germans and the Magyars. Their ire had already been roused by the privileges accorded to the Poles in Galicia. For Austro-German Liberals and for virtually all Germans dwelling in Bohemia, the Czech proposals were simply criminal; or, as one of them expressed it, "The Hohenwart ministry is pursuing a policy that will definitely oust the German element from leadership in western Austria . . . and substitute the leadership of the Slavs for that of the Germans."

In Vienna the Czech constitutional program provoked a revolutionary spirit, more threatening than had been known since the hectic days of 1848, and Hohenwart's ministers were the victims of open insults on the street. From imperial Germany, too, issued hot protests against concessions to the Czechs that would make them paramount in Bohemia. In short, by trying to appease the Czechs the Hohenwart cabinet had given mortal offense to the Germans.

Count Beust, who had originally sympathized with the idea of conciliating the Czechs, now expressed disapproval of the Czech fundamental laws in a detailed memorandum to the emperor. His aggressive rival for the favor of Francis Joseph, the Hungarian prime minister, Andrássy, also raised his voice against the Czech conditions, contending that acceptance of them would produce undesirable repercussions in the army, confuse finance, and retard industrial growth. Other Magyar politicians, fearful of the effects of concessions to the Czechs upon their own minority groups, condemned the proposals root and branch and threatened to have nothing to do with a "Slavicized Austria." Just when Francis Joseph was debating what he ought to do, an insurrection of Slavs occurred in the southern part of Austria and had to be put down with armed force.

Under these circumstances—the resistance of the German Liberals and of the Magyars and the Slav rebellion in the south—the emperor changed his mind on Czech appeasement, albeit reluctantly. The Czechs were curtly informed that they would have to seek revision in the constitutional structure by parliamentary processes. Promptly the Hohenwart ministry handed in its resignation, thus closing one of the most extraordinary episodes in the reign of Francis Joseph. Reconciliation of the Czechs was knocked into a cocked hat.

Utterly and righteously disappointed, Rieger at huge nationalistic meetings counseled his Czech countrymen to be patient and expressed the firm conviction that eventually the Czechs would be victorious. "Nedejme Se [no surrender]! We go forth," he declared, "to harder battles and in them hostitlity toward the monarchy will be intensified." The historian Palacký, who amidst the revolutionary tumult of 1848 had coined the much-quoted epigram, "If there were no Austria, it would be necessary to create one," had already modified his views and had written: "If it is decided to reverse the natural policy of Austria, if this empire, composed of a medley of different nationalities, refuses to accord equal rights to all, and organizes the supremacy of certain races over the others; if the Slavs are to be treated as an inferior people, and handed over to two dominant peoples as mere material to be governed by them; then nature will assert herself and resume her rights. An inflexible resistance will transform hope into despair, and a peaceful into a warlike spirit; and there will be a series of conflicts and struggles of which it will be impossible to foresee the end. We Slavs existed before Austria: and we shall continue to exist after Austria has disappeared."

Presently Palacký declared that "the Dual Monarchy is a despotism ruled by Germans and Magyars, who, like the Mongols, betray the spirit of the conquistadors." One day Slavdom and Germanism would clash violently, he explained, and against that time the Czechs should align themselves with their Russian relatives and make ready to march shoulder to shoulder with them to a triumphant victory.

Czech deputies in the Bohemian diet implored their fellows to defend their legitimate rights "up to the sacrifice of property and lives." Forthwith the Czechs reverted to passive resistance, withdrawing from the diet, and abstaining from attendance on the imperial reichsrat. The nationalist press conducted a campaign against Viennese authority, and antidynastic societies were founded. It was soon evident that Francis Joseph's refusal to approve the Czech fundamental laws had impaired the prestige of Czech moderates and strengthened the hands of a more radical faction.

VII

Upon the collapse of the Hohenwart federalistic project, the conduct of Austrian public business passed to the German Liberals and their allies. Simultaneously, Beust was supplanted at the Ballplatz by the stanch Germanophile, Count Julius Andrássy, who also became the chief adviser of the monarch on all manner of public questions. For a span of seven years German interests and the principles of German Liberalism were in the ascendant in Austria.

Hohenwart's successor, Prince Adolph Auersperg, younger brother of the first constitutional premier, was a military man with some training as a local administrator, and a loyal Constitutionalist. Count Lasser, the strongest figure in the new ministry, was known for his intense German sympathies; for the rest, the cabinet contained mainly Austro-Germans without much experience as public officials. Critics derided the cabinet as a "ministry of doctors," because of the predominance of political theorists; for them, liberalism was virtually synonymous with anticlericalism, administrative centralization, and, paradoxically, discrimination against national minorities.

The Auersperg ministry moved swiftly and decisively against Czech malcontents. General Koller, whose soldiers gave him an untranslatable nickname expressive of merciless severity, was reinstalled as governor of Bohemia. Czech newspapers were pitilessly persecuted and journalists were tried by hopelessly prejudiced German juries; police even confiscated copies of the imperial rescript in which Bohemia's rights had been acknowledged! The diet was dissolved; Czech boycott of the ensuing election and official pressure upon voters resulted in a victory for the Germans at the polls.

Reform of Austrian electoral institutions had meanwhile engaged the attention of the reichsrat. Instead of the existing law whereby the several diets chose the deputies, the Auersperg ministry proposed to partition the empire into single electoral districts each of which would return one deputy. In this way, it was calculated, the passive resistance of the Czechs would be partly circumvented and the forces of federalism would be weakened. The number of seats in parliament would be substantially increased, and they would be distributed in such manner as to increase the representation of the German bourgeoisie. The tradition of election by socioeconomic classes or curiae would be perpetuated, 85 deputies being chosen by the great proprietors, 116 by qualified townsmen, or double the number under the existing law, 21 by chambers of commerce, and 131 by rural electors.[10]

When the reform bill containing these provisions was offered to the reichsrat, federally minded deputies noisily protested. Poles manifested their disapproval by marching out of the chamber, spokesmen for the Czechs implored the emperor to throw his influence against the measure, and hostile mass demonstrations took place here and there in the empire. Had the Czech deputies and other foes of the law attended parliament and voted negatively, the electoral bill would probably have been defeated. But in their absence the lower house accepted the measure almost unanimously and in April 1873 it was formally sanctioned by the crown.

In the first election under the new franchise, conducted in the midst of the great financial *Krach* of 1873, Austro-German centralists and Liberals won a comfortable majority of the seats. The Czechs, faithful to tradition, refused to appear in parliament and an attempt by Auersperg to purchase their attendance by minor concessions fell flat. Parliament was called upon by the crown to enact measures fixing the position of the Catholic church in the empire and to combat the evil effects of the business depression.

The abrogation in 1871 of the Concordat with the Vatican had left a variety of church questions to be decided. A series of proposals now undertook to deal with these problems. In the future, priests would be appointed and dismissed by the government, in effect, and regulations for the education of the clergy were prescribed. Ecclesiastical property would be subject to public taxation, the proceeds being used for religious purposes. Members of monastic orders might renounce their vows simply by informing a civil magistrate of their intention to do so; building of monastic establishments would henceforth be decided by the government.

Although these acts were much less inimical to Roman Catholic interests than bills only recently enacted into law in Prussia, they evoked vehement protests from the Vatican and from Austrian Clericals. According to a papal encyclical, the laws would "subject the church to the tyranny of the state in a deplorable manner. They are subversive of Catholic discipline; they encourage disloyalty to the Church; they awaken the spirit of conspiracy and fanaticism against the true Christian faith." The Catholic faithful were summoned to battle against the obnoxious bills and the emperor was threatened with excommunication if he should support them.

Popular excitement over the church measures was reflected in angry debates in the reichsrat, where the Clericals argued that the principles of a free church in a free state and the sovereign rights of the provincial diets were being flagrantly transgressed. Proponents of the reforms, while disclaiming any intention of invading the sacred domain of religion, were firmly resolved to remove church influence from affairs not clearly religious. All the proposals except the measures on monastic societies were accepted by both houses of parliament and sanctioned by the emperor.

Devout and ardent Catholic that he was, Francis Joseph personally disapproved of the laws, but he bowed to the will of the parliament, though he decisively exerted his influence to block the passage of legislation concerning monasteries. With good grace the Austrian ecclesiastics acquiesced in the laws and Austria escaped a *Kulturkampf* such as was upsetting Prussia at the time. For that prudential policy Cardinal Rauscher was to a large degree responsible, for his sense of loyalty to the state outweighed his detestation of the anticlerical acts.[11]

VIII

If the Auersperg cabinet and the Liberal deputies could point with pride to the electoral and the ecclesiastical reforms, they could only view with distress the state of industrial and business affairs. In 1873, on the heels of a period of feverish, tinsel prosperity, Austria was gripped by the most severe economic crisis of the century.

Until the advent of the railway, industry and commerce in Austria had progressed with slow and halting steps. Though the first Austrian railroad was completed in 1832, a short road from Linz to Budweis, railway history really commenced in 1841 when the state encouraged building by private companies, guaranteeing a certain income on the capital invested, and also constructed lines with public funds.[12] The Semmering road, Europe's first mountain railway, was started in 1854. At the end of the fifties, political and financial considerations caused the government to halt construction on its own account and to sell many state-owned roads to private concerns, in which French capital participated.

Down to the War of 1859, the aims in laying down railways had been to connect the northern and the southern provinces and to link Vienna with Italy and the Adriatic with Hungary. Lines followed traditional commercial routes. In the sixties, railways were built from east to west and a rather extensive system was completed in Bohemia. By the seventies, then, a network of railways linked Vienna, Budapest, Prague, and Trieste with the outlying provinces of the realm and with the principal foreign cities. Austrian railway finance was engaged in schemes to bind central Europe to Constantinople, with spurs running off to Aegean ports.

A redundant Austrian population provided cheap and abundant labor for manufacturing, mining, and the like, fuel was plentiful and easy of access, and capital, too, was available. Since 1815, Vienna had grown into a major center of banking and finance, whose interests ranged all across the Monarchy and down into the Balkan peninsula. The famous Rothschilds established themselves in Vienna about 1820, and founded the great *Creditanstalt* bank (1855), whose fingers reached into many a financial pie. The international connections of this family attracted capital from France and Germany into Austrian banking, railway, and industrial undertakings and into government securities. British financiers, too, shared, though very modestly, in the expansion of Austrian industrialism.

The year 1866 was one of unusual material hardship in Austria. Bohemia, the richest and most industrialized province, was overrun by Prussian soldiers, severe weather ruined crops, and the repercussions of the war paralyzed commerce and manufacturing. Austria was prostrate, despondent. The state imposed additional taxes to meet the extraordinary expenses of the war, even levying a tax on the interest on state bonds, which embittered foreign bondholders; Austrian securities as a penalty were banned from the London Stock Exchange.

But late in the sixties Austrian economy recovered rapidly and business went ahead with unprecedented strides, aided by a series of excellent harvests, so that by 1871 Austria was in the midst of a veritable boom. The distinguished American statesman, William H. Seward, journeying through the country in 1872, observed, "When we look at the vigorous and varied agriculture and the stupendous works of material improvement, we might fancy ourselves at home in the United States."

For Austria, no less than for Germany, this was the *Gründerzeit* for industrial capitalism on the large scale. Banking, industry, and railways declared huge dividends; shares of new joint-stock companies were oversubscribed as much as twenty times. Coal mines were opened or enlarged, iron and steel mills and sugar factories were built. In 1869, new capital to the tune of $400,000,000 was authorized in Vienna alone, and charters were granted by the government for the organization of over a thousand companies of one variety or another. Railway construction between 1868 and

1873 far exceeded all previous records and in the same period the paid-up capital in banking institutions more than tripled. A little Austrian capital even found its way into railway undertakings in the United States.

Many of the new Austrian banks, it is true, had no more exalted mission than speculation in stocks and bonds. Prices on Vienna's Stock Exchange surged upward when companies declared huge, often fictitious, dividends, and glowing stories in the big Vienna press, which was owned by large financial and industrial interests, gaily recounted the ease with which fortunes were being accumulated. Mortgage banks and building societies sprang up like mushrooms to finance housing projects in Vienna and other cities; prices of land soared to fantastic heights and loans were floated to put up buildings whose rentals would not begin to cover the costs of construction.

In anticipation of the International Exhibition of 1873 hotels, cafés, and places of amusement were built in Vienna far in excess of what would be required in ordinary times. Temporarily, nefarious companies distributed large dividends, mostly on paper. Bribery and corruption that attended the issuance of charters for railways were matched by the inefficient and inferior manner in which the lines were laid down—if indeed they were ever constructed at all.

Visitors to Vienna were impressed with the luxury and the ostentatious display of the *nouveaux riches*. The artist Hans Canon painted the Viennese plutocracy of this feverish and furious time as noblemen and ladies of quality, like unto the newly enriched in the brilliant decades of medieval Venice. The Viennese International Exhibition of 1873 was intended primarily to advertise the material progress in the realm of the Hapsburgs, but from the first the affair was beclouded by difficulties. There was a slight epidemic of cholera, a general strike of fiacre drivers, the fair buildings were not ready; and Vienna and presently the rest of the Western world was wracked by the most acute business depression to that time.

Nevertheless, the Exhibition attracted the attention of the world. Seven hundred American firms and civic organizations, for example, were represented by exhibits; among the novelties from the New World were an Indian wigwam and a bar that dispensed mixed American drinks. Fully seven million tourists chose Vienna as their holiday resort; not since the historic peace congress of 1815 had the Hapsburg capital acted as host to so many crowned heads and other celebrities.

Speculative excitement—*Gründungs-fieber*—had run rampant through the Austrian population, infecting not alone professional stock speculators but many inexperienced amateur investors. One contemporary explained that stock gambling extended from the high aristocracy to the greengrocer, and even to the kitchen maid. Favorite "gambling securities" were bid up until they reached three or four times the amount of capital they actually represented, and the financial winnings of the few lured the many in characteristic fashion to disaster.[13] Unorthodox overexpansion of credit placed Austrian finance in a singularly vulnerable position. "Both the Vienna and Berlin markets are so overloaded and topheavy," wrote a British consul early in 1873, "that the slightest incident may produce a capsize . . . Engagements have been made out of all proportion to the annual additions to the capital of the empire . . . If any sudden political event intervenes, we may see, not an inclined plane, but a cascade like that of the English banks in 1825."

Minor financial convulsions in 1869 and 1872 preceded the disastrous crash of 1873. On May 8 of that year, it was disclosed that a hundred traders on the Vienna Bourse were insolvent. Promptly the familiar earmarks of the commercial crisis manifested themselves: panic, collapse of confidence, wild despair, suicides of ruined speculators, paralysis of credit, business chaos. Stocks were disposed of wholesale, hundreds of bubble companies collapsed, and scores of sand-built banks were obliged to close their doors; only solid investment securities, such as government bonds and gilt-edged railway debentures, managed to outride the hurricane. Confusion in the financial community was universal; unemployment and therewith popular distress in the cities were widespread.

Hesitantly and reluctantly the Austrian government moved to relieve the destitution by borrowing to complete railway projects, which had been halted by the panic. The state financed a few public works and relief projects and stimulated housing construction by granting concessions on taxes. In response to the depression, too, Austria reverted to its earlier policy of state ownership and operation of railways.

Parliamentary investigations revealed that many German Liberal deputies, spurred on by the motto "Enrich yourself," had taken bribes in exchange for votes for charters of companies whose character was extremely dubious, and prominent Viennese newspapers which supported Liberalism had also indulged in shady transactions with shameless financiers. Court trials exposed the linkage between Liberal politicians and fraudulent money racketeers, and these scandalous revelations were a factor in the ultimate downfall of the Liberal Auersperg ministry.

The melancholy events of 1873 cast a pall over Austrian economy for the rest of the decade; bankruptcies and liquidations, even among old, well-established firms, were monotonously numerous. Industrial wages dropped off and rentals and house values depreciated sharply. To combat the onslaughts of the depression, Austrian industrialists clamored for greater tariff protection, and cast about for new trade outlets in the Balkans. By the end of the seventies, the worst effects of the crisis had worn off and the return of peace in the Balkans promoted a modest revival of industry and commerce, though it was not until well along in the nineties that prosperous conditions were restored.[14]

In a manner that attained much greater popularity in a later day, enemies of Jewry assigned responsibility for the financial crash of 1873 to the Jews, whose influence in the German Liberal party was large, and many of whose deputies were mixed up in financial and commercial enterprises. Such charges were grist to the mills of Austrians who for any reason or emotion looked upon the Jews as an undesirable element. The fact that the House of Rothschild, which had refrained from participation in the giddy speculation, had emerged from the *Krach* almost unscathed made it a special target for the slings and arrows of Jew-baiters. Fanatical demagogues, grotesque generalizers, and rabid newspapers with clerical leanings whipped up anti-Jewish animosities, assailed "big business" as the cause of the economic maladies, and so prepared the way for the amazing Christian Socialist movement of the next generation.

IX

The industrial working class of Austria suffered severely by reason of the depression that accompanied the financial debacle of 1873. This social element had grown in response to the spread of machinofacture and experienced much the same hardships as its British counterpart in the first flush of machine economy: extremely low wages, long hours, paternalism on the part of management, and unsavory living quarters. So early as the revolution of 1848, leaders of propertyless urban workers had separated themselves from the bourgeoisie and started to press for social and political rights for their followers. Until 1867 strict laws forbade the organization of associations of workers, but revisions in that year permitted the formation of a workingmen's Mutual Improvement Society in Vienna and other clubs for self-help.

At about the same time, socialism in the moderate version expounded by the German, Ferdinand Lassalle, reached Vienna and attracted considerable working-class support. At the top of the agenda stood a demand for suffrage rights for workmen. A few liberally minded Austrian deputies and even some noblemen took an interest in the budding proletarian cause, but the ruling classes were bitterly hostile. Minister of State Giskra cynically remarked, "The social question is just a battle cry like freedom, which people utter without knowing what it means." Austrian spokesmen of urban wageworkers participated in 1869 in a conference of Social Democrats in Germany.

An imperial decree of 1859 defined in a formal way for the first time the rights of industrial workmen. That code indeed served, with amendments and amplifications, as the fundamental law on the subject until the breakup of Austria in 1918. Unions of workmen were declared unlawful and so were strikes, but in 1867 the ban on unions was somewhat relaxed. Even so it was permissible, for instance, for police to dissolve meetings of unions, if proceedings were considered inimical to the welfare or security of the state.

Manifestations of worker discontent in 1869, strikes, and a mass demonstration in Vienna caused the ministry of the day to allow wider freedom for workers' associations and to legalize strikes. Yet Viennese expressions of sympathy with the Communard rebels in Paris in 1871 so frightened public officials that societies suspected of socialist leanings were suppressed and the leaders sentenced to jail.

Repression, instead of stifling the workers' movement, helped to steer part of it into a more radical channel, into the Marxian ideology. Hard times in the seventies contributed to the same end. Distrust of international socialism partly inspired the Hapsburg foreign office, as is later explained, to affiliate with conservative Russia and Germany in the League of the Three Emperors. As for Austrian socialism, it was tormented for years by sharp ideological conflicts between the disciples of Lassalle and the internationally oriented Marxists.

During the depressed seventies, Austrian legislation imposed restrictions upon the employment of women and children in industry and ordered owners to install protective devices, but the laws were not effectively enforced. Representatives of workers repeatedly petitioned for the right to vote, but the Auersperg ministry would have none of it. Actually, over twenty years elapsed before Austrian wageworkers were granted suffrage.

x

Meanwhile, Prince Auersperg's liberal ministry had gone on the rocks. Weakened by factionalism, by financial jobbery involving deputies, and by the prolonged business depression, the cabinet split asunder over diplomatic policies in the Balkans. A compact minority of German Liberals, headed by the irrepressible Bohemian politician, Herbst, violently assailed the extension of Hapsburg responsibilities to the southeast. Incensed, Francis Joseph decided that the time had come for a different orientation in the politics of the Austrian empire. Government would be entrusted to the political foes of German Liberalism, to German conservatives and clericals, and to the Slavs.

After dominating the Austrian stage through most of the seventies, German Liberalism passed into eclipse, never again to attain a commanding position. And the new course on the Austrian home front was paralleled by a shift in foreign policy leading on to diplomatic alignment with imperial Germany.

‡ CHAPTER FOUR ‡

AUTONOMOUS HUNGARY
1867–1875

HUNGARY IN THE FIRST STAGE OF ITS SEMIÏNDEPENDENT EXISTENCE experienced most of the vicissitudes, economic and administrative, to which new political creations are likely to be heir. From the making of the *Ausgleich* down to World War I, domestic politics revolved round three central issues: the relations of the kingdom with the Austrian partner, the non-Magyar minorities, and the internal consolidation and material progress of the country. Numerous political parties were formed, grounded primarily on their attitude toward the settlement of 1867.[1]

Friends of the *Ausgleich,* the Right, the party of Deák and Andrássy, which organized the first ministry, regarded the great compromise as a positive advantage for Hungary, obtained without the sacrifice of any really vital national interests. Their opponents were at the outset divided into two major factions, one standing for modification of the settlement with Austria in such fashion as to enlarge Hungary's autonomous rights, while the other, a smaller and more intransigent group, which venerated Louis Kossuth as its patron saint, clung stubbornly to the revolutionary and republican ideology of 1848–49.

The first of these dissident parties, given the name of the "Tigers," after the hotel in which its members were accustomed to gather, was headed by Coloman Tisza (1830–1902) and Coloman Ghyczy (1808–1888). At a conference held in 1868, the party adopted the Bihar Agreement, calling for a free and independent Hungary and the repeal of legislation that imposed limitations on independence; Hungary ought to have its own army and diplomatic service and unfettered control over finances. The tie with Austria, it was declared, should be limited to the person of the ruler, as was the bond that existed between Sweden and Norway. This party possessed considerable influence over Magyars dwelling in the Danube valley and over Protestants everywhere in the kingdom. Kossuthist independence sentiment was strongest among small-bore local politicians and many erstwhile *émigrés* who had drifted back to their homeland imbued with Western political convictions.

Andrássy's ministry proceeded to complete the administrative unification of the kingdom by defining the status of Transylvania and Croatia-Slavonia. Transylvania, which was inhabited by Rumanians principally, many Magyars, and a substantial minority of Germans, called "Saxons," was wholly incorporated in the Hungarian state, as seemed particularly desirable in view of the recent unification of the neighboring kingdom of Rumania. For a time after the revolutionary turmoil of 1848, Transylvania had been autonomous, but home rule was thrown overboard by Vienna in order to conciliate the Magyars. In 1865, the Transylvanian diet, strongly Magyar in composition, confirmed an abortive act of union with Hungary that had been made in 1848; and over the protest of Rumanian leaders, the diet was dissolved, never again to be assembled.

Conditions of the reunion were defined in 1868 by the Hungarian parliament, after Rumanian deputies, who had been denied the right to use their native tongue in parliament, had vainly appealed for home rule. Rumanians were bluntly informed by the chauvinistic Tisza that they must amalgamate —and that speedily—with their Magyar masters. Ancient privileges of the national minorities of Transylvania were rescinded, though complete equality in rights was promised to all citizens, regardless of nationality or creed. In lieu of a diet of its own, Transylvania was permitted to send seventy-five deputies to the lower house of the Hungarian parliament, and the principal dignitaries of the region were accorded seats in the house of magnates. Autonomous privileges were conferred upon the Rumanian Orthodox Church, an institution which served in the next half century as the principal spawning bed of Rumanian nationalism.

Chief credit for the attainment of church rights belongs to the conciliatory and patriarchal Rumanian archbishop, Andrieu Şaguna, who convinced Francis Joseph of the wisdom of allowing the Rumanians religious freedom. Şaguna, whose role in the Rumanian national cause resembles that of Strossmayer among the Croatians, appreciated the value, the necessity indeed, of education for his fellows. At his metropolitan see in Hermannstadt (Sibiu), he reorganized theological learning, founded a printing establishment, and encouraged the extension of schooling facilities. On his death in 1873, the venerable prelate was extolled by friend and foe alike, even by a Rumanian faction that detested his conciliatory political tactics and favored violent action to liberate Transylvania from Magyar dominance.

In spite of the political union of Transylvania to Hungary, partly because of it, particularist sentiments, even among the Magyar-speaking population, continued to be strong. Of all the national minorities in the realm of the Hapsburgs, the Rumanians, next to the Italians, were the least devoted and least loyal to the Monarchy.

II

Croatia was assigned a unique position within the Hungarian constitutional scheme of things. Connected with the Magyar state since 1091, this kingdom, or at any rate its intellectuals and bourgeoisie, were infected in the nineteenth century with the virus of nationalism. In the 1840's an "Illyrian" movement which harked back to the era of Napoleonic control, the brightest and happiest period the Croats had ever known, was revived and encouraged by Vienna as a means of counteracting the rising tide of Magyar national sentiment. Croats in 1848 repudiated·the Magyar insurrection against the House of Hapsburg and openly aligned themselves with Vienna; and the military assistance that Croatian troops rendered the dynasty was of no mean significance in extinguishing the Magyar uprising. An equestrian statue of Jelačič, the Croat commander, stood in the Agram (Zagreb, meaning "beyond the rocks") marketplace, his naked sword pointed straight at the heart of Budapest. The great Kossuth declared that he knew of no Croatian nationality and could not find Croatia on the map.

Temporarily Croatia was converted into an Austrian crownland, but, as part and parcel of the settlement of 1867, it was remanded to Hungarian rule. Once more Croat nationalists who had dreamed of a great Croatian state, under the Hapsburg aegis, were sacrificed on the altars of Magyar arrogance. Slavonia, which before 1848 had been represented directly in the Hungarian parliament, was now wholly merged with Croatia, while Dalmatia, claimed by Croatian patriots as a legitimate part of their kingdom, remained under Austrian control.

To the moderates among the Croats, to those who favored the renewal of the ancient connection with Hungary, Deák, who during the revolutionary excitement of 1848 had stoutly condemned the racialist fanaticism of his chauvinistic Magyar compatriots, held out an olive branch, indicating that the Magyar parliament was ready to enter into negotiations with the Croats to fix the conditions of the new union. Subsequently he and his followers promised to accept any terms of settlement that did not imply the dismemberment of the kingdom of St. Stephen.

After the *Ausgleich* with Austria had been arranged, Deák remained faithful to these pledges and in collaboration with Baron Joseph Eötvös, one of the most enterprising and enlightened Magyars of the century, minister of education and religion in the Andrássy cabinet,[2] he drafted a constitutional program which was the basis of deliberations between representative Magyars and Croat delegates. These last had been chosen by the diet at Agram, after its predecessor, in which a majority belonged to the irreconcilable Croatian Liberal National party, had been dissolved, the electoral law modified, and the anti-Magyar press effectively muzzled. "Oats and the whip" were invoked to secure a majority of "unionist" deputies in the diet. The Liberal National delegation, which was reduced to fourteen, protested in the diet against the shameless electoral practices that had encompassed their defeat and then quit the chamber, against the advice of their more prominent leaders.

Most zealous and influential of the opponents of a unionist settlement with Hungary was the stalwart and fearless Joseph George Strossmayer, bishop of the Roman Catholic diocese of Diakovar, and one of the most remarkable Yugoslavs and political prelates of the century.[3] His life was guided by the motto "All for faith and fatherland." Though of German ancestry—contemporaries wrote his name Straussmeyer—he early became a stanch Yugoslav patriot, and time and experience made him more tenacious of his nationalist convictions. After passing through the normal training required of a cleric, he served for a brief time as curate and teacher in the seminary at Diakovar, and in 1849, thanks to the intervention of Croat public men, he was appointed bishop of Diakovar with jurisdiction over nearly three hundred thousand Latin Christians. In that office, with a large revenue at his command, he lived in medieval grandeur.

Strossmayer achieved wide popularity for his intellectual independence, his lavish hospitality, his patronage of culture, and his unswerving advocacy of Croatian national rights. What he wanted was an autonomous Croatian state within the Austrian framework that would embrace Croatia-Slavonia, the province of Dalmatia, and certain islands lying at the head of the Adriatic. This Croatia, Strossmayer dreamed, would be the nucleus around which all Yugoslavs—Serbs of the principality of Serbia and Bulgars too—would coalesce. Croats and Serbs, divided though they were by religion and culture, formed, in his view, but a single nationality; both groups, he pointed out, venerated Saints Cyril and Methodius, the apostles of the Orthodox version of Christianity in the western Balkans.

Politicians in Serbia at the time looked upon the prelate as a wily intriguer, though some publicists, professors, and students in the principality sympathized with his ideas and aspirations. Strossmayer's political program was of course utterly incompatible with the designs of even the most moderate Magyar leaders, and he, together with the accomplished Croat man of letters, Ivan Mažuranic (1813–1890), held aloof from the deliberations that resulted in the reaffirmation of Croatia's inclusion in Hungary.

In the course of 1868 a constitutional scheme in the nature of a compromise, the Croatian *Nagoda,* was hammered out, formally accepted by the legislatures of Croatia and Hungary, and sanctioned by the monarch. Since this agreement was given the form of a treaty, any revision would require the concurrence of all parties involved. Hot differences of opinion over the status of the seaport of Fiume almost shattered the compromise negotiations. This city, Hungary's sole window on the Adriatic, had belonged to the Hapsburg empire since about 1465, and in 1779, at the request of its residents, had been assigned to Hungary. As a reward for Croatian aid to the Hapsburgs during the rebellion of 1848–49, Fiume had been transferred to Croatian control, and the Croats desired to perpetuate that relationship, though sentiment in Fiume itself was almost unanimously in favor of direct Hungarian rule, not only on account of the recollection of former days but because material advantages were expected.

The *Nagoda* was drawn up in the Magyar and the Croat languages and the texts diverged on the subject of Fiume. In the Magyar version, Fiume was declared to be attached to Hungary and it was specified that the autonomous position of the city would be defined by agreement between Hungary, Croatia, and Fiume itself; the Croat text, on the other hand, merely stated that no understanding was reached on Fiume. When the *Nagoda* was handed to Francis Joseph for acceptance, a Croat translation of the Magyar version of the Fiume article was pasted over the Croat text. Thereafter Hungary declined to reopen the Fiume question; the Croats, however, considered it unfinished business and kept two seats in their diet vacant for deputies from the "lost city."

In the *Nagoda,* Croatia-Slavonia was defined as an integral part of the Hungarian kingdom; all decisions regarding military, commercial, and financial affairs were reserved to the government in Budapest. Matters of common concern to the entire kingdom would be regulated by the Hungarian cabinet, in which there would be a minister specially charged with safeguarding Croatian interests. When legislation touching joint affairs was under consideration in the Hungarian parliament, representatives chosen by the Croatian diet from its membership would participate in the deliberations and in the voting.[4] Whenever Croats were in attendance in parliament, the Croatian national flag would be hoisted alongside the Hungarian over the parliament building. A direct voice in the common affairs of the whole Monarchy was assured to Croatia by a clause in the *Nagoda* stipulating that the Hungarian delegation should contain one Croatian representative from the magnates and four from the deputies. Whether in the delegation sessions, or in the Hungarian parliament, or in Croatia itself, the Croats might speak their native tongue, and in like manner Croatian would be used as the language of command in the Croatian territorial army.

Under the *Nagoda,* Croatia was allowed a considerable degree of home rule, far more than was permitted, for example, in the Yugoslav kingdom constituted after World War I. Educational and religious affairs, control over the police, the administration of justice, and the determination of a large part of the civil and criminal law, were all placed within the competence of the Agram authorities. On the other hand, the local government might not raise money for any purpose whatsoever; all taxes would be voted by the Hungarian parliament and collected by agents of the royal ministry of finance. Forty-five per cent of the net receipts would be allocated to the Croatian government to be appropriated for its purposes.

The legislative organ of Croatia was a unicameral diet, or *Sabor,* made up the principal churchmen, the lords lieutenants, titled magnates who paid a specified tax, and more than seventy elected deputies, a majority of the whole, chosen under a complicated suffrage scheme based upon taxation. The chief local executive, the ban, was appointed by the crown, on the recommendation of the premier of Hungary, and he as well as any of his major subordinates might be removed if two-thirds of the diet so desired. With the approval of the cabinet at Budapest, the ban might at any time dismiss the diet.

Although the *Nagoda* involved no wide deviation from Croatia's traditional rights, it evoked indignant protests from patriotic Croatian chiefs. Bishop Strossmayer and his disciples condemned the arrangement since it thwarted their plans for a united Yugoslav state within the Hapsburg orbit, and a more doctrinaire, a more irreconcilable "Party of the Right," whose leader was Anton Starčevič, a capable lawyer and journalist, clamored for complete separation from Hungary and an independent Croatia confined to Yugoslavs who were Hapsburg subjects. Partisans of this faction would have nothing to do with Strossmayer's program of Croat-Serb union, and derided the Serbs as an inferior lot tainted with Byzantine manners and customs.

Early in the seventies, Croatian resentment against the "new deal" with Hungary expressed itself at an election for the diet, in which advocates of repeal of the *Nagoda* captured four times as many seats as the government candidates. For this victory the unpopularity of the strong-willed viceroy, Baron Rauch, the appointment of a Magyar as archbishop of Agram, and the excellent organization of the Strossmayer party, led by the clergy and schoolmasters, were collectively responsible. The *Sabor* even went so far as to declare the *Nagoda* null and void, and a minor insurrection followed which had to be put down by military force. Concessions of an administrative and fiscal character appeased the moderates, but even the appointment

of the popular poet, Mažuranič, as ban, in 1873, failed to bring about anything like real reconciliation.

III

Croat culture on the higher plane had for a long time been dominated by
foreign influences, German largely. Sons of well-to-do Croats traveled to
Vienna or to Graz to be educated and German was the language commonly
spoken by the Croat intellectuals. Croatia's national awakening was paralleled
and to a degree preceded by a literary revival which had characteristic reverberations in the political sphere. The national language was modernized and
respect for the country's past was kindled by the publication of historical
treatises and romances, by the collection and popularization of folk ballads
and songs, and by the study of Croatian national customs and traditions.

The pioneer in the cultural renaissance was Ljudevit Gaj, a poet and journalist, who in his youth succumbed to the romanticist currents prevalent
among educated Slavs of the time.[5] He initiated "Illyrismus," a literary and
political movement intended to bring together the branches of South Slavdom
and to teach them to think and act in unison. As the mouthpiece of his propaganda, Gaj founded the *Croat Newspaper* (1835), changed in the next year
to the *Illyrian Newspaper*. Articles and poetry extolled the ideal of Illyrian
unity and, while generating enthusiasm among South Slav intellectuals,
excited the susceptibilities of the Magyars, through whose influence an imperial decree was issued forbidding the use of the word "Illyrism," so the
term Yugoslav was substituted. Gaj reached the maximum of his influence
in 1848, when he was the acknowledged spokesman of South Slavdom, but
his prestige waned as more energetic leaders pressed to the fore. Stanko
Vraz, a versatile man of letters, most honored for his lyrics and popular
ballads, commenced writing in Slovene, but soon shifted to Croatian and
became an ardent propagator of Illyrism; *Djulabije* (Small Roses), which
appeared in 1840, was a typical specimen of his patriotic lyricism. For a time
Vraz edited a small literary review, *Kolo* (The Circle).

Just as Bishop Strossmayer occupied a peculiar position in the political
affairs of the Yugoslavs, so he acquired a unique place in the cultural renaissance of Croatia. He patronized and encouraged Croatian scholars, endowed Slav cultural societies in Zara, Laibach, Belgrade, and Prague, and
founded secondary schools, a seminary, and, above all, a South Slav learned
Academy. For thirteen years he and his chief adviser and closest friend,
Franco Rački, worked to obtain official sanction for the Academy in which
the arts and science would be cultivated. Magyar opposition to the project
was bitter, but appeals to Croatian patriots issued by Strossmayer procured
the necessary funds and in 1867 the Academy was opened.

No institution perhaps did more to foster Yugoslav national feeling than

Strossmayer's Academy, in which Yugoslavs from all over the Balkans regardless of creed were welcomed. Thither were atttracted the finest scholarship and scientific talent of the area: scholars who specialized in assembling and interpreting ancient historical manuscripts and works of old Slav writers; students of Yugoslav antiquities and folklore, flora and fauna. Findings were published to the world in learned periodicals such as *Rad* (Work), and in a series of volumes in Croat and Latin. Many foreign scholars collaborated in the publications of the Academy, which was affiliated with sixteen similar institutions abroad.

Strossmayer also inspired the establishment (1874) of a national university at Agram, containing faculties of philosophy, theology, and law, which furnished education on the higher level to from 300 to 350 students. Some of the original professors were brought in from Prague, but the proportion of Croat scholars and teachers steadily increased; to the energetic prelate also belongs credit for the foundation of an art gallery in Agram (1884). Even the cathedral at Diakovar, upon which Strossmayer lavished large sums, built in the Gothic style under the direction of German architects, was a monument to South Slav nationalism. Decorations in national Croat designs shared honors with symbols of the Christian religion; in the center of the apse, Yugoslav peoples were depicted being guided to the throne of Christ and his mother.

For all his patriotic zeal, Strossmayer was not unmindful that he was a Roman Catholic prelate, and in the ecclesiastical sphere he displayed the same fiery energy that distinguished his political career. For his courageous defense of Protestantism and his sturdy resistance to the adoption of papal infallibility as a sacred dogma at the Vatican Council of 1869–70, he was acclaimed as a second St. Bernard.[6] When a proposal branding Protestantism as the source of all the evils in the world and as destructive of the very foundations of organized society came before the sacred conclave, Strossmayer decried the indictment as not only uncharitable, but untrue; where the Protestants err, they err in good faith, he declared. His words provoked sensational scenes, and demands for the removal of the heretic forced him to break off his address. In a modified form the anti-Protestant proposal was accepted, with Strossmayer, alone among the delegates, absent from the balloting.

On both intellectual and practical grounds Strossmayer resisted vigorously the dogma of the personal infallibility of the pope, and more than once at the Council he was shouted down for his bold utterances. Other liberal and moderate prelates, such as Dupanloup, Bishop of French Orléans, who shared Strossmayer's convictions, submitted promptly to the Council's decision in favor of the dogma, but the tough-minded Croat held out until the pontificate of Leo XIII, when he too yielded, believing that acquiescence was necessary to advance the cause of Yugoslavdom. At Rome he had joined with a minority of bishops in asserting that the College of Cardinals and the See of St. Peter itself required reform, that the papacy to its own detriment had degenerated into an Italian institution, and that canon law was "the confusion of Babel." Nothing came of these strictures, but Strossmayer's fearlessness in making them earned him an enviable place among the exponents of a new Catholic Reformation.

Strossmayer's religious concerns were not confined strictly to his own faith, for he cherished the hope that he might be instrumental in bringing to pass the reunion of the Roman Catholic and the Eastern Orthodox Churches and that was one of his reasons for speaking out so boldly against the infallibility dogma. He conferred on the subject with other Slav intellectuals, notably the Russian philosopher and publicist, Vladimir Soloviev, who like the Latin Bishop imagined that it would be possible to bring the two faiths together. Strossmayer likewise strove to arrange a concordat between Serbia and the Vatican which he fancied would prepare the way for Serbian entrance into the Roman communion. This project failed of realization, but, by sponsoring and encouraging it, Strossmayer helped to mitigate somewhat the ancient antagonisms that embittered the relations between the Roman Catholic and the Orthodox branches of the Yugoslav nation.

On his death in 1905, at the patriarchal age of ninety, Strossmayer was universally mourned in the Slav world. And as one of the small band of men whose political and intellectual activities smoothed the way to the formation of the kingdom of the Serbs, Croats, and Slovenes, he was remembered by the celebration of his birthday in the schools of Yugoslavia after 1919.

What Gaj had meant in the renaissance of Croat culture early in the nineteenth century, that and more Franko Rački meant later on, for he is regarded as the foremost Croat intellectual of his century.[7] An ardent patriot and learned savant, Rački worked to forge intimate cultural bonds between Croats and Serbs as the prelude to religious and political unification. Of peasant stock—his father, though well-to-do, was wholly illiterate—Rački studied in Fiume and Vienna, and then entered upon a clerical career. His writings on the ecclesiastical history of the Croats brought him to the attention of Strossmayer, who sent him to Rome, where he continued his researches and made valuable contributions to the political and religious history of the South Slavs in the Middle Ages.

Rački achieved international renown as a historian and as the promoter of the scientific and cultural revival of his nation. Politically he saw eye to eye with Strossmayer, his benefactor and patron, and yet his concern for the progress and welfare of Roman Catholicism surpassed his devotion to national interests. As the real organizer and the first president of the South

Slav Academy, Rački saw to it that the interests of the whole of South Slavdom rather than narrow Croatian concerns were properly cultivated. An indefatigable student himself, Rački's learned publications, chiefly on historical subjects, numbered 287.

Croatia's cultural renewal owes something, too, to Ivan Mažuranič, one of the most brilliant representatives of Croatian literature. His poetic masterpiece, *Smrt Ismail Aga Cengića* (The Death of Ismail Čengić) vividly described the manner of life in Bosnia under Turkish rule and the endless border warfare between Christian and Moslem. This epic of hate, which was calculated to keep Yugoslav bitterness toward the Turks aflame, was extensively translated and brought its author acclaim not alone in Croatia, but among Slavs generally. Mažuranič also edited a dictionary and wrote historical and political essays, particularly on the relations between Croats and Magyars. Moderate in his political thinking, he acted as a sort of tool of Vienna in Croatia after 1848, and, following the making of the *Nagoda,* he pleaded for reconciliation of Croatian patriotism with Magyar unionism. From 1873 to 1880 he occupied the post of viceroy of Croatia.

Peter Préradovič divided his energies between a military career—he became a general in the Hapsburg army in 1866—and writing ballads and other forms of poetry. While on garrison duty in Dalmatia he abandoned the German idiom in which he had written his first poems, in favor of his national tongue, Croatian. His poetry breathed a moderate patriotism, attained considerable popularity, and was published in book form by national subscription shortly after his death. Poet and playwright too was Milan Ogrizovič, who wrote mystical and patriotic pieces, his drama showing strong evidence of Ibsen's realism.

Around these major suns circled distinguished Croatian satellites, intellectuals who devoted themselves to studies that aided in the upbuilding of a Croat or a Yugoslav conception of nationalism. Among the philologists, Franko Karelac, a pioneer, and Vastroslav Jagič stand out; as professor in the gymnasium at Agram Jagič shared in the foundation of the South Slav Academy and, when driven from the country by the Rauch administration, occupied university chairs in Berlin, St. Petersburg, and Vienna. He wrote particularly on Croat grammar and the history of Croatian literature, and published the works of early Slav missionaries.

A band of Croatian historians, mostly professors in the University of Agram, endeavored to prove by their investigations that Croatia's relation to the Magyar state was one of association, not union, and in their researches unearthed and published much valuable documentary material; Šime Ljubać, Vjekoslav Klaič, author of an elaborate history of the Croats from the earliest times to the close of the nineteenth century, and Sišic, the editor of *King Coloman and the Croats* were the most eminent. Bogoslav Šulek was the outstanding Croatian lexicographer, and A. Šenoas composed historical romances, which revived the Croatian past in an entertaining manner.

Upon Agram, the center of Croat cultural activity as well as the capital of the autonomous kingdom, was bestowed the title of the "Athens of the South Slavs." In the upper part of the town were the palace of the ban and the governmental buildings; below was the ecclesiastical quarter with a notable Gothic cathedral of St. Stephen, started in the early thirteenth century and thoroughly renovated in 1879, one of the most interesting pieces of ecclesiastical architecture in southeastern Europe. Not far away were the palace of the South Slav Academy, the university, the national theater, a museum of archaeology, rich in Roman antiquities and Slav coins, the national gallery of art, and a celebrated industrial museum. In Agram too were the headquarters of intellectual societies, of which the *Matiça Hrvatska,* founded in 1842, was the most influential; it regularly published six volumes a year, as a rule cheap editions of the writings of Croatian men of letters. By 1914 the population of Agram had reached almost 80,000.

Scattered about Croatia-Slavonia were more than fourteen hundred elementary schools in which Croatian was the language of instruction, and nineteen secondary schools. From these institutions and the university went forth intellectuals who propagated the national movement and provided leadership for it.

IV

Along the southern rim of Hungary ran a military frontier which for two centuries had been governed by the minister of war in Vienna, though allowed local autonomy, as a *cordon sanitaire* against the plague and as a permanent bulwark against the Turks. Every village had its guardhouse with a number of men on duty as police, and for generations soldiers from this district were the backbone of Hapsburg armies. This region in 1869 was handed over to Hungarian administration, as demanded by the Magyars, who based their claims on declarations of earlier Hapsburg sovereigns; in return, Hungary agreed to enlarge its contribution to the common expenses of the Monarchy.

Many of the new inhabitants in the district were Serbs (called Gränzers) who hotly resented the new dispensation. As Serbs they admired their fellows in the principality of Serbia for their heroic struggles against Turkey; the young were reared on hallowed Serb folk tales and ballads, and in this way "the history of the Serb race from the battle of the field of Kossovo in 1389 down to Karageorg" was kept fresh and green. In the homes of the dour peasantry hung pictures of the patron saint, of the emperor of Austria, of the tsar of Russia, of Karageorg, and of Garibaldi, who was esteemed as the Karageorg of Italy. But when Francis Joseph sanctioned the transfer of the military frontier to Hungary his portrait was removed.

The inhabitants of the region stoutly and fearlessly protested, "We cannot dissemble the bitterness with which we behold in the Hungarian government the arbitrary masters of our national property; but we expect nothing but evil from a nation which has so often treacherously violated its oath of fidelity to its august sovereign." One Gränzer declared to his son, "Thou shalt never be a soldier in the emperor's army. The emperor has broken his word; the emperor is a traitor in the eyes.of the military frontiersman. We despise the man who is not true to his word." That son, Michael Pupin, took ship for the United States, where he attained an international reputation as a man of science.[8]

Leadership among the Serbs of Royal Hungary was assumed by Svetozar Miletić, son of a poor cobbler, for many years a deputy in the parliament at Budapest, and honored as the uncrowned king of the Hungarian Serbs.[9] When the military frontier was abolished, he publicly berated Francis Joseph for his ingratitude in a fiery speech, to which the audience responded, "Long live the Prince of Serbia," until it was hoarse; and schoolboys boldly flaunted the Serbian national flag.

Hungary's Serb politicians cherished visions of a grand Slav confederacy in southeastern Europe which would embrace even the Bulgars. At their centers of Karlowitz and Novisad they contributed in an important way to the cultural renaissance of the Serbs. Miletić's newspaper *Zastaba* (Standard), which was read extensively among Serbs everywhere, fostered patriotism, and a semisecret political society, *Omladina,* founded by him in 1866 and financed by well-to-do Hungarian Serbs, was erroneously regarded in Budapest and Vienna as an instrument of Russian Pan-Slavism, though it did have contacts with Serbs in Serbia. A great national gathering took place at Karlowitz in 1885, in connection with the interment of an honored Serb poet, Branko Radičević, whose writings had summoned the Serbs to preserve their traditions and to prepare for political union. Representatives from all parts of the Serb world shared in the ceremony and there was "not a single dry eye." "A dismembered nation," recorded a participant, "united in tears, was a most solemn and inspiring spectacle."[10]

v

After settling the status of Transylvania and of Croatia, the Hungarian parliament, under the direction of the Andrássy ministry, proceeded to the enactment of prudential and enlightened legislation defining the rights and privileges of the national minorities. As early as 1861 a parliamentary committee had drafted a report on nationalities, based upon the principles that Hungarian citizens formed one nation politically, and that all nationalities

possessed equal rights. Specific recommendations were proposed to implement these principles, but parliament was dissolved before any decision was
reached; on the eve of the *Ausgleich,* deliberations were resumed with
spokesmen of the minorities participating. These latter argued for a federalized Hungary in which political arrangements would be fixed in accordance with nationality and each unit would have considerable home rule.

Moderate Magyars such as Deák and Eötvös, while adamantly opposed to
concessions that would impair the political integrity of Hungary, favored
equality for all citizens regardless of nationality. In support of their position
they might well have recalled the "Admonitions" of St. Stephen, the venerated first king of Hungary, which asserted that only weak and backward
countries had a single language and a uniform set of customs. Deák's thinking on the minorities question was summed up in his statement: "We shall
not forget that the non-Hungarian inhabitants of Hungary are in every respect citizens of the country and we are prepared sincerely and readily to
secure to them by law whatever their own interests or that of the country
demand." That sagacious point of view had expression in a famed Nationalities Act of 1868, which reflected the spirit of moderation and conciliation that was shown in the parliamentary committee report of 1861.

While stressing the political unity of the kingdom, the Nationalities Act
promised far-reaching rights to national minorities. Although the Magyar
language was declared to be the language of parliament, administration, the
county councils and their officials, the law courts, and the universities, in
the county assemblies members might speak in their mother tongue, and
records might be kept in a minority language as well as Magyar if a fifth
of the representatives so desired.[11] Judicial and other public officials would
be chosen, so far as possible, from candidates belonging to the several nationalities. In the local communal assemblies, every member might use his
own language; each assembly might determine its official language, and a
second language might be designated as official if a fifth of the membership
desired it. Communication between county councils and the central government might be in either Magyar or one of the official tongues. All communal officials would be obligated to speak the language of the area in
which they served and broad linguistic rights were promised in the matter
of political petitions.

In communal and district courts of justice, moreover, citizens might speak
in their mother tongue, judges would have to be acquainted with the languages of the litigants, and judicial verdicts would be translated into the
languages of all parties in a controversy. The language to be used in religious services and confessional schools would be decided by each congrega-
tion; church officials might communicate with their subordinates in any
tongue they preferred and church courts would choose their own language.

In state schools the language of instruction would be fixed by the minister of education. Individuals, communes, and churches might freely establish schools and colleges or organize societies and clubs, provided only that their objectives were lawful.

All in all, the Nationalities Act of 1868 was one of the most enlightened measures of its kind ever adopted, even more liberal than the minority safeguards incorporated in the peace settlements of 1919–20, which, indeed, were very largely modeled on the Hungarian precedent of 1868.

Many Magyars condemned the law as giving too much leeway to the minorities and inviting subversive separatist movements, but leaders of the nationalities, on the other hand, felt that not enough had been conceded. As things fell out, Magyar chauvinists had little cause for concern, since the law, except for the sections relating to ecclesiastical affairs, was permitted after a few years to become a dead letter. For non-Magyars the Nationalities Act was the law and the prophets to which they appealed—albeit in vain—whenever their rights were curtailed or infringed.

Deák sagely observed, "If we wish to win over the nationalities, we must not seek at all costs to Magyarize them; this can only happen if we create in them love and attachment for Hungarian conditions." That judicious and realistic approach to the intricate problem of minorities found no favor with the Magyar elements that were bent on thorough and rapid assimilation. Successive ministries whittled away, one by one, the guarantees given to the non-Magyar groups, and so impaired whatever prospects of reconciliation there may have been.

VI

Public schooling in Hungary was placed on a new footing by the National Schools Act of 1868. Previously, primary schools had been maintained exclusively by the churches,[12] towns, and private associations. The census of 1869 revealed that over three-fifths of Hungary's population were illiterate, another 10 per cent could read but not write, and almost sixteen hundred communes had no provision whatsoever for elementary education. Under the education bill, sponsored by the progressive and farsighted Eötvös, who was much influenced by discussions on elementary schooling then under way in Great Britain, compulsory attendance in school was required from six to twelve years of age and communes were obligated to set up schools wherever there were thirty eligible children, if no confessional or locally maintained school existed; instruction would be given in the mother tongue of the pupils. Unhappily, none of the principles in this measure was honestly executed; for instance, teachers provided by the state were insufficient in number and rarely knew any language but Magyar, and schools of all kinds were subjected to common regulations concerning buildings, training of teachers, and inspection by agents of the state. Even in the twentieth century there was only one qualified teacher for every 107 children and the disproportion was even greater in the rural areas. In a sentence, popular education in Hungary was about on a plane with that in southern Italy and Portugal.

Not a single non-Magyar secondary school was operated by the state and the Magyar secondary schools were specially designed to turn out Magyar patriots. The Serb and Rumanian minorities had a few secondary schools financed by their churches, in which their languages were spoken, but the Slovaks and Ruthenians or Ukrainians were utterly without secondary schools.

One progressive act of the Andrássy ministry relaxed the severely arbitrary censorship of the press that had prevailed for a generation, and another struck off the legal fetters that had so balefully enchained the Jews, giving them full civil equality. This reform put another feather in the cap of Eötvös, who had been employing his eloquent tongue and pen in behalf of the emancipation of the children of Israel; other progressive measures looking to religious freedom which he advocated were defeated by clerical resistance.

As a country whose population was predominantly Roman Catholic, Hungary did not escape the controversies over church and state relations then troubling central Europe. The publication of the dogma of papal infallibility, without royal permission, provoked a sharp quarrel in which so devout a Catholic as Eötvös aligned himself with the critics of ultramontanism. Certain deputies insisted that the position of Catholicism in Hungary should be regulated with greater precision, as was being done in Austria at the time.

Deák in his last major parliamentary speech set forth with studied moderation his views on the proper sphere of the church in the kingdom. Anything approaching papal interference in public affairs was wrong, state and church should be completely separated, and all law-abiding creeds should be tolerated on equal terms, as in the United States. Bishops, Deák thought, ought to be deprived of the right to sit in the house of magnates, and church property that was being used for educational purposes should be transferred to the state; civil marriage should be made compulsory. The prime minister of the day, anxious to avoid an open quarrel with Catholicism which might completely disrupt his party, contented himself with the appointment of a commission to prepare legislation in conformity with the broad objectives that Deák had enunciated.

Military bills, one establishing universal service and another creating a Hungarian national army of *honvéds,* completed the important acts of the first parliament under the *Ausgleich.* In connection with the military-service law, the old question of an independent, a purely Hungarian, army was raised anew, though authorities in Vienna imagined that the unity of the common army had been permanently settled in the *Ausgleich*. Deák and Andrássy had both opposed a separate army; now Deák spoke out against the universal-service law as an invasion of the rights of the Hungarian nation, and Prime Minister Andrássy disputed so vigorously over modifications in the law with John, the common war minister, that the latter was forced from office after only a short tenure. Magyars obtained changes in the law so that Hungarian officers as far as possible would command Hungarian regiments.

Magyar elements which were dissatisfied with the ministry's policies carried on such violent agitation through their societies and newspapers that the government felt obliged to move energetically against them; over counties in which Kossuthist sentiment was rife, royal commissioners were placed. How widespread the discontent was, was reflected in the parliamentary election of 1869, when the opposition picked up forty seats, though the Deákists retained a substantial working majority. Many peasants who had bought paper money issued by the revolutionary Kossuth government in 1849 plumped for the Kossuthist candidates in the illusory hope that, if Kossuthists won, the revolutionary currency would again be made legal tender. This election, like many another in Hungary, was attended by turbulent popular conflicts in the course of which citizens were killed or seriously wounded. "The reports from the Transleithan Electoral Districts," reported the British ambassador in Vienna, "have all the character of bulletins from the field of battle."

VII

When the ministry in 1872 proposed a revision of the electoral law and an extension of the life of a parliament to five years, Magyar separatists and conservatives alike resorted to obstruction to prevent enactment. Separatists feared that the new electoral law would reduce their representation and so militate against the attainment of their supreme objectives—the abrogation of the *Ausgleich* and the establishment of an independent Hungary. At the election of 1872 the Deákists, by applying heavy pressure on voters and by corruption, won a large majority of the seats, but it was a victory that sapped the moral prestige of the ministry. A section of the badly defeated "Tigers" now allied itself with the Deákists. Factional bickering and charges that ministers had exploited their offices to fatten their pocketbooks so weakened the ministry that an attempt was made to purchase the support of the influential Coloman Tisza, but his price was still too high.

A transitional cabinet in 1874 pushed through an undemocratic revision of the Hungarian electoral law, which remained unaltered until 1913, until the downfall of the Monarchy indeed, since the act of 1913 was never put into operation. Franchise qualifications of an educational and financial character were deliberately set relatively high so that only about 6 per cent of the population were eligible to vote, and electoral districts were gerrymandered so as to restrict the representation of Magyar separatists and to render the non-Magyar minorities politically impotent. In Transylvania, for example, in twelve constituencies where Magyars predominated, there were in all only 5,161 voters, while a single purely Rumanian district contained 5,275!

Hungary's electoral map, in short, was drawn in a manner that would ensure Magyar hegemony and the preservation of the dualistic regime. Since voting was by word of mouth, in the presence of a board composed of Magyars, free expression of an elector's convictions was prevented. Another idiosyncrasy of Hungarian electoral procedure permitted any voter to propose a candidate for the deputies, provided he did so in the first half hour after the polls opened; and if only one candidate was proposed, he was declared elected without further ceremonial. Even though two or more nominations were made, there was no balloting unless ten electors desired it. And if, while the polling was on, all nominees but one formally declined to stand for election, the remaining candidate was declared elected.

Non-Magyar deputies in the Hungarian parliament rarely exceeded 5 per cent of the whole, which meant that the peculiar interests of the minorities were neglected, except, of course, for the Croats, who participated in parliamentary transactions only when the concerns of Croatia-Slavonia were under consideration. Clauses in the electoral act of 1874 that were intended to eliminate abuses attendant upon elections were stillborn, and corruption continued to be widespread and notoriously flagrant.

VIII

In the first period of its existence as an autonomous kingdom, Hungary achieved commendable, if limited, improvement along economic lines, except in the matter of governmental finances. Overwhelmingly agrarian in character, Hungary was a country whose material welfare depended fundamentally upon the riches that the soil produced. Between 1848, the year in which the ancient seignorial rights over the peasants were abolished, and 1868, the agricultural wealth of the country nearly doubled in value. Then came a four-year period of unusually poor harvests due to unfavorable weather, wheat rust, and the inundation of sections of the kingdom by floods; the export of wheat ceased almost entirely. But more beneficent weather in the middle seventies brought splendid harvests, and exports were large, especially to Germany.

A standing handicap for agriculturalists on the Hungarian plain, the area of the finest wheat lands, was the sorry state of transportation facilities. Far too often roads were as singularly primitive as in eastern Europe, owing in part to the lack of stone or other solid road-making material throughout much of the country. These obstacles were very largely overcome by the building of railways. Construction which started in a small way as early as 1846 was greatly accelerated after 1867, with public and private capital participating. Budapest was quickly linked to all parts of the kingdom by inexpensive and rapid transportation and beginnings were made in the building of lines radiating from other natural centers. In deciding where tracks should be laid and in fixing rates, particular care was devoted to enhancing the interests of the Magyars at the expense of the lesser nationalities; lines in Transylvania, for illustration, crossed, in the main, districts that were peopled by Magyars and "Saxons," while communication with Rumania was deliberately kept inadequate.

No less than Vienna, the Hungarian government was keenly alert to the value of a railway that would reach down the Balkan peninsula to Constantinople; but Hungary adamantly insisted that the route should be so chosen as to bring the maximum advantages to the kingdom. Stubbornly and successfully the Magyars blocked railway projects to connect seaports of Croatia and Dalmatia with the hinterland. On the other side, to develop international trade independent of Austrian outlets, public funds were appropriated to run a road to Fiume and to start improving the splendid natural facilities of that port. To the same end government subsidies were given to an English shipping concern that operated commerce carriers out of Fiume for Liverpool. That Fiume, poetically "the pearl in the crown of St. Stephen," should one day outstrip its Austrian rival, Trieste, was one of the most dearly cherished ambitions of Magyar patriotism.

Hungary's industrial development was hindered by the scarcity of cheap capital, the heavy weight of taxes, the melancholy condition of the highways, and the competition of Austrian manufactures. But at the very end of the sixties, the kingdom, more especially Budapest, attracted a swarm of promoters and speculators in search of industrial El Dorados, frequently men who had fanciful notions of the swiftness with which the resources of the kingdom could be opened up. The money-making frenzy, which gripped Vienna at the time, prevailed in Budapest as well and Hungarians of all classes, strangers to the ways of business for the greater part, plunged into all manner of alluring but unsound financial transactions; public works of magnitude were initiated in imitation of the large and prosperous countries of Europe. Catastrophe was not long delayed. In the black year of 1873, honest and shameless promoters alike were overwhelmed and Hungary experienced much the same woe, though on a much smaller scale, that confounded and paralyzed the Austrian partner.

National finance was long in a parlous state, partly because of the large debt that had been incurred when emancipated serfs were given land purchased from the big owners. During the years of controversy with the crown preceding the *Ausgleich,* nonpayment of taxes was lauded as a patriotic duty, and after 1867, the practice lingered, especially among the wealthy classes. Allocation of state funds to railway construction and to armaments, together with fiscal mismanagement and slender harvests, resulted in huge national deficits, which obliged the state to borrow on a lavish scale. National credit sank so low that loans could be contracted only at very high rates in foreign money markets and an ever larger proportion of the public income had to be assigned to the service of the national debt. So grievous did the situation become that officials were paid in copper coins and daily the minister of finance sent for the fees collected for the use of the suspension bridge in Budapest—often only a few florins—in order to defray day-to-day expenses! Seeking a way out, the ministry proposed in 1875 that taxes should be strictly collected and that new levies should be voted, including a tax on incomes. These proposals stirred up bitter opposition in the deputies, enemies of dualism charging, as usual, that the ties with Austria were responsible for the desperate financial straits. Some deputies even recommended that the budget be brought into balance by scaling down the outlays for Hungary's chief hobby, the national (*honvéd*) army! In the end, the ministerial tax plans were enacted into law and soon afterward the management of the kingdom passed into the dictatorial hands of Coloman Tisza.

IX

Hungarian politics in the early seventies were in topsy-turvy condition. Leaders in the making of the *Ausgleich* disappeared one by one from the national stage. The singularly attractive Baron Joseph Eötvös passed away in 1871, and Deák, worn out by arduous labor and in failing health, gradually withdrew from active participation in public life; Andrássy, the third member of the *Ausgleich* triumvirate, was summoned to Vienna in 1871 to assume charge of the foreign relations of the Hapsburg realm. None of the other Deákists possessed either the ability or the authority of these men, and strife within the party paralyzed the ministry. Cabinets rose and fell in rapid succession, as the fiscal troubles grew increasingly more chaotic; enemies of dualism rejoiced over what they believed to be the impending collapse of the settlement of 1867.

With the domestic situation progressively more perplexing and ominous war clouds hovering low over the Balkans, which made a strong ministry even more desirable, Coloman Tisza at last consented to abandon his resistance to the *Ausgleich* and to merge his parliamentary following with the emaciated forces of Deák to form a new party. "I love my fatherland," he patriotically exclaimed, "more than my principles."

This new political creation, called the Free Principles or Liberal party, illiberal on such vital issues as agrarian and suffrage reform and the treatment of subject minorities, but unflinchingly loyal to the *Ausgleich,* dominated the public affairs of Hungary until 1914, except for a strange interlude lasting from 1905 to 1910; and its strength rested less on the appeal that it made to the distinctly Magyar areas than to its amazing success in manipulating, by one stratagem or another, the limited number of voters in the "peripheral" constituencies, whose basic national stocks were other than Magyar.

Shortly after the formation of the Liberal party, death removed Francis Deák, Hungary's wisest statesman, and the most popular. Citizens of all classes, all parties, and all nationalities paid him the tribute that was his due, and Francis Joseph testified that "the old gentleman by his fidelity to the throne and country had earned . . . the affection of his sovereign and countrymen." The experimental stage of the *Ausgleich* had now been successfully crossed; only the exponents of Kossuthism and a scattering of stiff-necked conservatives declined to accept the arrangements with Austria as something fixed and final.

‡ CHAPTER FIVE ‡

THE GREAT RENUNCIATION

FOR EVERY STATE THE PRIMARY OBJECT OF FOREIGN POLICY is self-preservation, security. To that end the modern state has sought to maintain "adequate" fighting services and, as occasion required, to search for useful allies. The quest for security by means of armaments and alliances is an old, old tale. The international policies of a state are to a very great extent determined by its geographical position and its resources, both human and material. For the Monarchy of the Hapsburgs, a crucial consideration was its location in the heart of Europe, very largely in the valley of the Danube. That, however, was only one of the broad conditions that shaped Austria's long-range tendencies in international affairs.

Great-power status had been the Austrian rank for centuries, and if that eminence were to be preserved the disparate nationalities in the realm would have to be held in line; the pull of nationalism from states encircling the Monarchy would somehow have to be overborne. The objective had not been realized in the first phase of Francis Joseph's reign; quite otherwise, for the Monarchy had lost choice territories to emergent Italy, had been ousted from her place of hegemony in German Europe, and was somewhat disturbed by the mounting swirl of nationalism among the small national groupings in the Balkans, of whom the most dangerous potentially was the Yugoslav. As for no other state in the world, the political feelings and desires of subject minorities were for the Danube Monarchy a paramount and permanent factor in international policy.

To geography and the human factor of nationalities must be added the Hapsburg historical heritage, old antipathies with other countries which were to be embittered by new rivalries and jealousies and were, as well, to be counterbalanced by new or recovered friendships. With Russia, since her emergence as a power of European stature in the mid-eighteenth century, Austria had maintained a "wavering friendship"; for the larger part of the time these two powers had lived on terms of amity, as during the common struggle against the French Revolution and Napoleon, and in the firm alignment to repress subject Poles. To the middle of the nineteenth century, a fact of cardinal importance in the high politics of Europe was a "northern alliance" comprising Austria, Russia, and Prussia. But that combination disintegrated thereafter, owing directly to clashing Austro-Russian interests in the Balkans and Russian encouragement of nationalism within the Hapsburg Monarchy. The rift was openly heralded at the time of the Crimean War and, though temporarily healed later on, was never really closed.

Austria and Russia, the astute Austrian foreign secretary, Count Julius Andrássy, once observed, "are immediate neighbors and must live with one another, either on terms of peace or of war. A war between the two Empires . . . would probably only end with the destruction or collapse of one of the belligerents. Before embarking on such a struggle there must be reasons of an absolutely binding character, reasons which make a death struggle inevitable."[1] Mutual misunderstandings, misconceptions, and suspicions plagued the relations of the two countries; thrice within the half century before 1914 —in 1878, in 1887, in 1908-09—they moved to the very brink of war; and in 1914 they went over the precipice. In each and every instance, prestige and power in the Balkans were the compelling issues.

The maintenance of the *status quo* in the Balkans, more particularly the preservation of European Turkey as long as possible, may be regarded as another lasting facet of Hapsburg foreign policy. That was in fact a corollary to the rivalry with imperial Russia, whose overarching aim was to rid Europe of Ottoman rule, to inter "the sick man" and parcel out his possessions. In keeping with that line of logic (to which the logic of facts gave confirmation) it was the Austrian intention to prevent any Balkan state, should the Ottoman empire crack up, from growing too strong, that is, strong enough in collusion with Russia—or Italy—to endanger the security of the Dual Monarchy itself. For that reason primarily, Austria occupied and subsequently annexed the provinces of Bosnia and Herzegovina.

In dealings with Italy no straight line of Austrian policy can be drawn, except the resolution to hold the territory that had been salvaged from the wreck of 1866, and to keep Italian influence in the Balkans at the minimum. Nor, on the Italian side, can a consistent tendency be discovered except as one distinguishes between the official course of the Italian government and the doings of societies and individuals that cherished ambitions of winning the last fragments of Hapsburg soil where Italians lived, or schemed to further Italian penetration in the western Balkans. Officially, the Consulta manifested in word and deed—most positively in the Triple Alliance inaugurated in 1882—the Italian wish to live on good-neighborly terms with the Hapsburgs, but the pressure of Irredentist and expansionist groups frequently disturbed relations until, in 1915, ties were completely ruptured and Italy and Austria took up arms against each other.

Reliance upon imperial Germany, once cannon had decided that Prussia, not Austria, should be the chief state of German Europe, was the cornerstone of Hapsburg foreign policy. The association was not one of abject vassal and master, as was commonly believed in influential foreign circles, but it surely was the alliance of a weaker with a far stronger power, for mutual comfort and security. For woe or weal, Germany served as the stout bulwark of the Hapsburg realm.[2]

Traditions of Austrian enmity toward France running back across the centuries of competition between Hapsburg and Bourbon—save for the alliance in the Seven Years' War—were reinforced by the struggle against the first Napoleon and the assistance which Napoleon III lent to the Italians in the War of 1859. But the alienation was not at all complete. In international politics there are neither eternal enemies nor eternal friends. Both France and Austria desired the other to be strong and respected as an asset for their own safety, as essential for the uneasy balance of power in Europe, at least until French interests were laced in with Russian ambitions in the Near East.

Harmony with Britain, intimate coöperation for mutual advantage, may be taken as another settled aim of Hapsburg diplomacy. True, these powers were on opposite sides in the Seven Years' War; true, British liberalism found much that was exasperating in Hapsburg domestic policy and warmly championed the cause of minorities; true, British traders competed with Austrian mercantile interests in the Balkans. But the two cabinets, which once worked together effectively against the Napoleonic threat to mastery over Europe, subsequently had a common bond in profound mistrust of the predatory expansionism of populous and powerful Russia. Balancing matters up, it is fair to say that London and Vienna coöperated to their common gain until the Anglo-German antagonism of the early twentieth century ushered in a new era in their relations.

II

So far as the actual direction of Hapsburg diplomacy in the dualistic period was concerned, the controlling force was Francis Joseph himself. In spite of advancing age the emperor kept his hand on the tiller to the last, albeit less firmly toward the end than in the disastrous first phase of his reign. While he invariably solicited the counsel of leading public men and in time of major crises convoked unofficial crown councils to debate foreign policies, he reserved to himself final decisions on the most momentous questions. His advisers, whether civilian or military, were, without conspicuous exceptions, men of conservative outlook with aristocratic backgrounds, who by inheritance and conviction preferred that things should be kept as they were. Although the influence of the leaders of the professional Austrian military caste on foreign affairs was large and pervasive, the civilian authorities, when their thinking diverged from that of the military chiefs, customarily, though not always, managed to secure the emperor's blessing on their views.

Of the importance of the prime ministers in the conduct of foreign relations, one Austrian foreign secretary has written: "The Prime Ministers . . . had a very considerable voice in foreign policy, for they assisted not only in determining its general lines but were also the leaders of the two parliaments or delegations and . . . provided the Minister of Foreign Affairs . . . with the necessary majority. If he could not arrive at agreement with either one of the Prime Ministers, the position of the joint minister became untenable. A good understanding with the two Prime Ministers was, therefore, of primary importance in the conduct of foreign affairs." [3]

With the advent of parliamentary institutions, political parties, pressure groups of one sort and another, and individuals made themselves heard and felt in the sphere of Hapsburg international politics, though none would be so bold as to try to estimate, except most roughly, the actual weight of such influences. Periodically, the foreign minister presented an oral account of his stewardship to the delegations, speaking, of course, only of those matters (and in a guarded manner) that appeared to him compatible with monarchical interest. In the delegations as in the two parliaments of the Dual Monarchy, deputies had an opportunity to express their opinions on international affairs—sometimes they did so in a most unsympathetic, not to say captious, fashion. A certain feeble light was shed on the transactions of the foreign office by infrequently published "Red Books," containing parcels of diplomatic correspondence, and shrewdly calculated to prove the wisdom and virtue of the course that the Ballplatz followed in any given controversy, instead of furnishing a solid documentary basis for critical discussions and independent judgments on foreign policies.

As time marched on, the press, or more exactly the "great press" of Vienna and the principal journals of Budapest, had a part—a limited part in comparison with that of the press in countries in which the democratic philosophy was in the ascendant—in shaping the trend of diplomacy. At other places in this book the general character of the Magyar press and that of the lesser Hapsburg nationalities is sketched, and just here the press of Vienna may be similarly dealt with.

III

As was uniformly true in Europe east of the Rhine, the press of Vienna was subjected to considerable government control, direct and indirect. That part of Europe still cowered under the dictum of Frederick the Great that "press freedom leads to the destruction of the foundations of the state." It was an established tradition in Austria—from which, to be sure, there were momentary deviations during the epoch of the French Revolution and Napoleon—that newspapers handling political and economic issues should at best merely discuss, not criticize. Revolutionary spokesmen in 1848 clamored for and obtained press freedom; scores of papers were started only to perish shortly. After the suppression of the revolution, shackles were once more clamped upon the press, but they were somewhat relaxed in 1863.

A quaint, flexible clause in the Austrian constitution of 1867 assured freedom of expression in print "subject to such rules and regulations as His Majesty's Government shall deem necessary in the interest of order and public welfare." Before publication of a newspaper was started, official approval had to be secured and the owner had to post a bond against which authorities could levy in case of infraction of censorship regulations, which were diverse and comprehensive; each paper had to carry a tax stamp, which, though inexpensive, tended to hold down circulation. No important modification in press laws was effected until early in the twentieth century. For the greater part, Austrian newspapers were distributed through state tobacco shops—street sale was unlawful—and it was an easy matter for public authorities to restrict the sale of an offending sheet.

In spite of handicaps, the number of Viennese papers and political reviews grew in the final decades of the nineteenth century, in keeping with the growth of literacy and wealth. Big banking interests acquired a controlling interest over the most widely circulated journals and they did not scruple to exploit the press in the hope of advancing their private interests and ambitions. Corruption of the big Vienna press in the 1870's elicited from the excited Treitschke the indictment that "the press of Vienna is the most shameless in Europe, without excepting that of France. The newspapers today are nothing but industrial enterprises and the man who would presume to speak of morality to these literary speculators would be laughed at to his face . . . in that town of easy morals, venal consciences are numerous and when a rascal's mouth must be shut money is no object." [4]

Pride of place among Vienna papers belonged of right to the *Neue Freie Presse,* founded in 1864 by a band of journalists who had seceded from the *Presse.* This latter sheet had been established as an organ of political opinion by August Zang, a man of many talents, who had grown rich as proprietor of a Vienna bakery in Paris. In the French capital he had developed an interest in journalism and shortly after the outbreak of revolution in 1848 he hurried to his native city and launched the *Presse*. Gathering round him an able group of associates, Zang attracted readers by pithy editorials and admirable articles on economic affairs. During the political reaction of the 1850's, the *Presse* was frequently in hot water with the censor; still it prospered, and was spoken of as the most influential of Austrian papers. Zang entered the ranks of the millionaires and got himself elected to public offices; eventually he sold out his interest and turned to other pursuits. *Die Presse* carried on until 1894 and then succumbed.

In the meantime the *Neue Freie Presse* had established itself as not only the foremost Austrian journal but one of the great newspapers of the world, whose editorial views were carefully scrutinized abroad and much copied in the foreign press. The accent in the *Neue Freie Presse* was on freedom; it regarded itself as the heir and the champion of the liberal principles of 1848, actively advocated constitutionalism and the integrity of the Monarchy, and took·pride in its reputation as the mouthpiece of the German "Liberals" and centralists. It came to be looked upon as a semiofficial organ, through which the ministry disseminated facts and opinions that, for one reason or another, it did not choose to circulate through the old, official sheet, the *Fremdenblatt*. This is not to say that the *Neue Freie Presse* supported every official policy, whether on foreign or domestic question, that arose. It sharply criticized, for example, the course that the foreign office pursued in the Balkans late in the 1870's and helped to undermine the prestige of Count Andrássy, the foreign secretary.

Specially devoted to German interests in the Austrian empire, though hostile to anything savoring of Pan-Germanism, the *Neue Freie Presse* freely condemned ministerial policies that tended to be Slavophile. But in the main its viewpoint on international questions was attuned to the desires of the foreign office; it was much more a mirror of Ballplatz prejudices or convictions than an independent creator of public opinion, guided by considerations of hard thinking and good conscience. So far as foreign news was concerned, it depended heavily on the English Reuter Agency and the French Agence Havas. Of the importance of the *Neue Freie Presse* an informed but shrewish British critic wrote: "The greater part of what does duty for Austrian opinion is dictated or suggested to the public by the editor-proprietor of the *Neue Freie Presse,* of whom it has jokingly but, in a sense, not untruthfully been said that next to him the Emperor is the most important man in the country." [5]

Something of the immense prestige of this paper was due to its literary quality and its finely polished articles on mercantile affairs, on the theater, and on music. For many years Edward Hanslick (1825–1904), who was professor of music in the University of Vienna, prepared distinguished and critical reviews of musical performances. Feuilletons, short popular essays on matters of gravity or bright and witty pieces on nothing in particular, composed by some of the finest penmen in the German language, occupied an important place in the paper.

The *Neue Freie Presse* profited from a long line of clever, even brilliant editors, who preferred scholarly sobriety and eschewed sensationalism, and who joined capacity as business men with talent as journalists. The original editors, Michael Etienne and Max Friedländer (brother-in-law of the Socialist theoretician, Ferdinand Lassalle), who had broken away from the staff of the old *Presse,* laid solid foundations for their famous journal. They were succeeded in time by Edward Bacher, who specialized in editorial leaders on Bohemian and foreign affairs, and Moritz Benedikt, a much-respected expert on economic questions. Financially, the paper was a huge success, deriving considerable revenue from advertisements, which were printed in almost every language of Europe. It was perhaps the wealthiest paper of continental Europe, and was accused, in its early years at least, of accepting subsidies from foreign governments.

Next in importance to the *Neue Freie Presse* was the *Neues Wiener Tagblatt,* founded in 1867, which in time attained a circulation double that of its august competitor. This paper was the child of its original editor and owner, Moritz Szeps, a talented journalist, who surrounded himself with a set of first-rate writers; occasionally Crown Prince Rudolph made anonymous contributions to the *Neues Wiener Tagblatt*. Considerable space was given over to articles on economic conditions and to sport, all written in an easy style, and intended to appeal to the lower middle class.

Szeps' intimacy with French political leaders—his daughter was married to a Clemenceau—brought him information that was unique. Editorially, the *Neues Wiener Tagblatt* advocated wider freedoms and stanchly supported Austro-German interests, but was an inveterate critic of the proponents of the union of the German areas of Austria with imperial Germany. It did not hesitate to present to its public the disadvantages of the alliance with Germany, nor the merits of a Francophile orientation in foreign policy. When financial difficulties forced Szeps out of the *Neues Wiener Tagblatt,* he set up (1886) the *Wiener Tagblatt,* perhaps with some financial aid from Crown Prince Rudolph; in it he perpetuated his earlier editorial policies. Szeps' journals, together with the *Neue Freie Presse,* earned for Vienna the title of the "newspaper capital" of Europe.

Defender of the concerns of the Austrian clerical and conservative elements was the *Vaterland* (1859), whose circulation was never large but whose influence in the circles to which it appealed was considerable. This organ of clericalism had an ally in the *Reichspost* (1894), "an independent paper for the Christian people of Austria," the spokesman of the Christian

Socialist party, and edited by embattled Catholics. In the twentieth century the *Reichspost* gave currency to the political opinions of the heir presumptive to the throne, Francis Ferdinand.

Avowedly a competitor of the *Neue Freie Presse* was the *Zeit* (1894), edited by the critically minded Heinrich Kanner. It established a reputation for independence on public questions which distinguished it among the Viennese papers catering directly to others than industrial workers.

Able organ of Austrian Social Democracy was the *Arbeiter Zeitung,* which was launched in 1889 and became a daily six years later. It replaced earlier Socialist journals and unlike them in the main it proclaimed the principles of evolutionary, rather than revolutionary, Marxism. It could be counted upon to deal with foreign policy in a moderately critical manner and its influence extended well beyond the Socialist party membership. In the early years of its existence the *Arbeiter Zeitung* was very often confiscated because of unsympathetic commentary on governmental policies.

Except for the *Arbeiter Zeitung* and the *Zeit,* the widely circulated dailies of Vienna were more or less—more rather than less—at the disposal of the ministry of the day and of the foreign office. A special press department of the foreign office, elaborately equipped, and corresponding bureaus in other state departments, supplied information to the newspapers that they wished to have spread abroad. On occasion, government officials arranged for the printing of inspired stories and subtly influenced the content of papers by awarding paid announcements on state business to sheets that were friendly. Journalists whose pens were at the service of the authorities were given access to official information that was withheld from unsympathetic critics. Besides, there were the *Fremdenblatt* (1847), founded by Gustav Heine, the younger brother of the poet Heinrich Heine, which became the official organ of the Ballplatz, and *Politische Correspondenz,* printed in French, which was called—exaggeratedly—"the most secret-revealing of all European papers"; nothing appeared in its columns without the sanction of the foreign office.[6]

The sum of the matter is that independent judgments by readers on foreign countries and their policies were only tepidly encouraged by the press of Vienna.

IV

"Wrong has triumphed over Right and Honor," Francis Joseph mourned to his one solitary friend, Crown Prince Albert of Saxony, shortly after the War of 1866. Great as was his grief over the loss of the Italian-peopled province of Venetia, the expulsion of Austria from the Germanies after centuries of intimacy was even more humiliating and distressing. Prophecies of the swift disintegration of the realm on the Danube were current, but they were soon belied, for the settlement of 1867 with Hungary ensured the preservation of the Monarchy as one of Europe's great powers, and strengthened its position in the high politics of the continent.

The idea of revenge on Prussia burned hotly within the emperor, and army circles were permeated with the resolve to regain the traditional Austrian place in German politics. "From the highest commander down to the youngest lieutenant," it has been said, "the army was filled with one idea: Revenge for Sadowa!" [7] Archduke Albrecht, wealthy cousin of the emperor and son of the Archduke Charles who had repulsed Napoleon at Aspern, headed the *revanchards* in the fighting services and coveted the honor of commanding the military forces in a victorious war against Prussia. Count Beust, who took charge of the foreign office in November of 1866, nursed hot memories of his personal vendetta with Bismarck. Among the Monarchy's leading men only Count Andrássy, the astute and resourceful premier of Hungary, favored the abandonment of ambitions to the north and concentration on the larger menace that was Russia.

Hatred of Prussia was the paramount emotion at the Ballplatz after the War of 1866, but how did Austria stand in her relations with the other continental powers of importance in her diplomatic calculations? Take France first of all, the France of Napoleon III. Austria was on reasonably good terms with France, and common distrust and common jealousy of the growing might of Prussia induced the cabinets of the two countries to forget the differences that had so long alienated them. In the humiliated and vengeful Austria the wily master of the Tuileries saw a potential ally, and a valuable one, against Prussia, and in Beust at the foreign office Napoleon had a well-known Francophile on whose effective coöperation he felt he could rely with confidence.

Italy was something else again, for Irredentist aspirations had been only partly appeased by the annexation of Venetia to the kingdom. Still under the Hapsburg flag lived Italian-feeling folk in the South Tyrol and at the head of the Adriatic. For Mazzini, for Garibaldi, and for other ardent patriots there could be no harmony with Austria until these districts were redeemed; Mazzini had eloquently outlined the objectives of Irredentism in language that ever afterward remained the law and the prophets. The Italian government, on the other side, confronted by vexing domestic puzzles and concerned with acquiring the last of the temporal holdings of the papacy, was prepared to put extreme territorial claims on Austria on the shelf—temporarily, at least.

So far as monarchical security and imperial interests were concerned, Russia was regarded in Vienna and Budapest as a far greater peril than Prussia. Both Prussia and Russia viewed with misgivings the concessions that Austria was granting to her Polish subjects, fearful that the tranquillity of their own subjects of Polish nationality would be disturbed; besides, the Russians nurtured the hope that closer alignment with Prussia, to which they were already bound by historical and dynastic ties, would make it possible to score diplomatic points, at least, against the powers that had so recently defeated the tsardom in the Crimean War.

During that war the Russians had counted on active assistance from Austria, if for no other reason because in 1849 Tsar Nicholas I, on appeal from Francis Joseph, had ordered his soldiers into Hungary to put down the Magyar insurrection. But instead of aiding Russia, Austria had pursued a course of neutrality, had striven to extend her own Balkan interests to the detriment of the tsardom, and by stationing troops close to the Russian border had forced a costly revision in Muscovite war strategy. Austria's rank ingratitude, shameless treachery in the Russian view, was never forgotten in St. Petersburg, nor would Magyar patriots forget Russia's part in crushing their struggle for independence. Seeds of hostility then sown yielded their harvest in the fullness of time.

What is more, Austria and Russia competed for top place in the economic and political affairs of Balkan Europe. In that rivalry Russia commanded unique assets, for the Balkan native populations were Slav in "race," for the greater part, and Orthodox Christian in religion. In view of her own Slavic subjects, the largest in Europe outside of Russia, and her established interests in the Balkans, Austria considered every Russian attempt to press southward as a challenge to her own security, while the Russians on their side came to look upon Austria as the principal barrier to the fulfillment of their "historic mission" in the Near East.

Deep-seated suspicions and hostility were quickened by the writings of Russian Pan-Slavs, advocating the use of force to effect the union of all Slavs regardless of creed or nationality. That messianic propaganda was systematically expounded by Nicholas J. Danilevski, in *Russia and Europe* (1871), a heavy and lengthy book, scarcely intended for popular consumption, which was hailed as the bible of Pan-Slavism, and like the Bible itself was more talked about than seriously studied.

Danilevski, who borrowed from Darwinian science the idea of a struggle for existence among nations, implored the Slavs to detach themselves culturally from Europe and "overthrow the decadent Roman-German civilization." Upon Russia, he thought, devolved the solemn and sacred obligations of delivering all Slavs from foreign domination and of organizing a vast Slav empire, from which debilitating Western influences would be excluded. As the initial step in creating this Slav state Constantinople must needs be acquired, and that would necessitate warfare with Turkey and Austria.[8]

Even more directly menacing to Austria and its interests were the outpourings of General Ratislav Fadeyev, whose *Reflections on the Eastern Question* appeared in 1869. Short, smoothly written, translated into many tongues, this work attained a unique position in the Pan-Slavist literature of the time. Fadeyev harped upon the theme that the solution of the Near Eastern question, Russia's largest problem, required the annihilation of Austria, the holder of the key to the Turkish door. Austria was a greater obstacle to the Russian mission than Britain or France, who could only bar the way to Constantinople by seapower. Therefore, Austrian Slavs and Rumanians should be incited to rebel with promises of freedom; Polish Galicia should first of all be wrested from Austria, assurances having been given the Poles that they would be allotted their rightful place in a general Slav community under the aegis of Russia. The liberation of the Hapsburg Czechs and Croats came, of course, within the purview of this Pan-Slav evangelist.[9] Sentiments of a similar order were propagated by the capable and calculating General Nicholas Ignatyev, ambassador of the tsar at Constantinople from 1864 to 1877. For him as for Fadeyev, Pan-Slavism meant an aggressively chauvinistic policy pointed against the Danube Monarchy and Turkey alike.

It seems perfectly clear that the real directors of Russian diplomacy, Alexander II and his foreign secretary, Gorchakov, were but little affected by the fervent Pan-Slav ideology, but in foreign chancelleries, particularly in Vienna, the propaganda caused considerable vexation and apprehension. Upon Serbs, including those who were Hungarian subjects, Fadeyev's teaching made a decided impression, and the political restlessness of the Czechs was traceable in some measure to Pan-Slav inspiration; among them, as in Galicia, Pan-Slav literature was distributed with a generous hand. All of this could not fail to add fuel to the fires of Austrian distrust, to conjure up fears that Russia, in the clothing of Pan-Slavism, was waiting for a favorable chance to disrupt the Monarchy of the Hapsburgs.

Moving on to the Balkans, Austrian relations with Rumania were less than happy. Vienna had steadfastly resisted the union of Moldavia and Wallachia to form the kingdom of Rumania—a goal reached in 1866— partly because it was believed that such a state would be nothing more than a Muscovite outpost in the Balkans, partly because it would encourage separatism among the large Rumanian population of Hungary. Beyond that, if Rumania were consolidated, other Balkan peoples would be inspired to strive for similar ends, which would surely cause trouble, possibly territorial losses, for the Hapsburg realm.

Only grudgingly did Vienna acquiesce in Rumanian unity, and it opposed the selection of a foreign prince to rule over the country. When the Rumanian choice fell upon Prince Charles of the Hohenzollern family, he thought it politic to travel across Austria to his new home in the guise of a commercial drummer! In collaboration with most of the other great powers, Austria put pressure on Rumania to force an amelioration in the lot of the Jewish population, which had been subjected to expulsions and other forms of abuse and persecution. That intervention, from which Russia studiously kept aloof, intensified Rumanian resentment toward its great western neighbor.

The main Rumanian grievance, however, was the Magyar treatment of the Rumanians in Transylvania. Once, when it was proposed to Prince Charles that a real reconciliation with the Hapsburgs should be negotiated, he replied, "I can work hand in hand with Hungary only when Hungary has changed her policy toward the Rumanians in Transylvania. I cannot abolish the natural sympathies which exist between Rumanians on both sides of the political boundary. I am, therefore, entitled to expect that the Hungarian government will do everything that is right and fair in dealing with the real interests of its Rumanian subjects . . . I lay stress upon this point for it is the principal condition for bringing about a good understanding between the two countries." This and similar admonitions Magyar politicians, bent upon assimilating the Rumanians, disregarded to their peril.

Serbia likewise occasioned some uneasiness at the Ballplatz because of the magnetic influence it might exert, was indeed exerting in a limited way, upon South Slavs dwelling under the Hapsburg and the Ottoman flags. Serbian patriots who dreamed of a Yugoslav state embracing all South Slavs had followed with lively interest the success of the unification movements in Italy and Rumania. Serb volunteers who had fought in Garibaldi's famous Sicilian army declared in a farewell message to their commander, "Your triumphs in Southern Italy have made every noble heart leap on the shores of the Danube and the Sava." For the purpose of wresting Yugoslav-inhabited territory from Turkey, Prince Michael of Serbia contemplated a Balkan league of nations, but an assassin's bullet removed him in 1868 and the league idea perished. Serbian foreign trade was restricted almost exclusively to Austria, which enabled Vienna to exercise a large if not a controlling influence in the foreign politics of the principality.[10]

Montenegro's ambitious prince Nicholas leaned heavily on Russia and with its blessing had tried in 1866 to obtain an Adriatic outlet from Turkey. That project was upset by the powers who suspected that the port, while nominally Montenegrin, would be in fact Muscovite. As evidence of his Russophile sentiments, Nicholas sent his daughters to Russia for an education and husbands; St. Petersburg, on its part, promoted the candidacy of the prince to the throne of Serbia, left vacant by Michael's murder.

With the Ottoman empire Austrian relations may on balance be described as cordial. True, pressure from Vienna had just obliged the sultan to evacuate his soldiers from the principality of Serbia, but during an uprising of Cretans, Austrian diplomacy worked to prevent the disturbances from spreading into the European holdings of the Turk and helped to put an end to the insurrection in a manner that was gratifying to the Turks. Francis Joseph and high dignitaries of his realm visited Constantinople in 1869 in connection with the opening of the Suez Canal and were received with marked cordiality. Undercover Austrian financial interests, effectively supported by the Ballplatz, were bargaining with the Turks for the privilege of building railways in European Turkey; competing plans, not to be reconciled with Austrian ambitions, were harbored in Russia. All in all, it was in the Austrian interest that the Ottoman empire, with its disparate nationalities, should be kept intact as long as possible.

v

Beust had been called to Vienna on the understanding that he would make diplomatic preparations to square accounts with Prussia or at least to forestall any further expansion of Prussian power, an assignment that was congenial to his convictions if not his temperament. As minister in Saxony, Beust, possibly the most talented diplomatist in a small European state of the time, who reminds one somewhat of the Czech statesman Beneš in the era between World Wars, had striven to organize a "third Germany" made up of the South German states, which would be a counterpoise to Prussia and Austria alike. But with the decisive Prussian triumph at Sadowa, Beust's grand political design crashed to the earth; and the Saxon statesman, as vain and obstinate as he was shrewd and courageous, never entirely forgave the ever-victorious Bismarck. Still, in failure there was seeming success, for Beust moved on to Vienna where he commanded larger resources and had ampler scope for his abilities. He participated effectively in the Hapsburg constitutional reconstruction of 1867 and played a major role in the liberalization of Austrian domestic institutions. But all of that was intended as the prelude to a foreign policy that would restore the international prestige of the House of Hapsburg.

Beust's appointment as foreign secretary, which was gleefully hailed in the camp of the Austrian *revanchards,* incensed Austro-German and clerical circles, which detested him as a foreigner, a warmonger, and a Protestant. And in important foreign chancelleries, that of France alone excepted, the naming of Beust was received with unconcealed mistrust and suspicion; Britain's foreign minister, Lord Stanley, for example, commented that "the Austrians have made their greatest mistake of this year (which is saying a good deal) in the choice of Beust as Minister." [11] A diplomatist in Paris was heard to remark, "Il a enterré la Saxe, il a enterré la confédération, il va enterrer l'Autriche," but the Saxon succeeded in disappointing that lugubrious prophecy. Peace, Beust knew full well, was necessary for the internal regeneration of the Hapsburg Monarchy and he informed the cabinet that "the whole efforts of the Imperial Government must now be directed to efface the consequences of a calamitous war, and it will . . . remain faithful to the policy of peace and reconciliation which it has at all times pursued."

Actions did not entirely square with the foreign minister's fair phrases. First of all, Beust contemplated the organization of a league of South German states under the aegis of Austria that would bar Bismarck's path to the fusion of South Germany with the North. Carefully he matured his plans, only to discover that the clever Prussian had once more outwitted him by arranging secret treaties with the major German states south of the river Main, making them his allies in the event of conflict with France; presently the armies of the southern German states were organized on Prussian lines. With discretion born of harsh experience, Beust refrained from public condemnation of what he considered Bismarck's trickery and duplicity.

Heartily though he despised Beust, much though he mistrusted the Austrian adventure in constitutionalism, Bismarck thought that a strong and prosperous Austria was a European necessity, and he appreciated the value of the friendship of the Hapsburg Monarchy in case the German states fought France.[12] He was therefore ready to welcome Austria with open arms, and he made somewhat vague proposals to the men on the Danube for a political agreement to which Russia should be a party. That idea of Bismarck's, more than once later presented to the Ballplatz, was to flower in time in a League of the Three Emperors.[13] Vienna spurned the overture, without, however, closing the door to some kind of bargain in the future. An official visit of the Prussian crown prince, Frederick, to Vienna tended to sweeten relations between the two countries.

Austrian diplomacy found itself in something of a quandary in 1867, when a dispute between Prussia and France over the status of the German-peopled Grand Duchy of Luxemburg, which Napoleon III was seeking to annex, threatened to precipitate an armed clash.[14] Prudence ruled out too close collaboration with France lest the large and influential Austro-German faction swing against the government. The Duc de Gramont, French ambassador in Vienna, counseled Napoleon III not to reckon on aid from Austria; it was his judgment that if France and Prussia clashed, Austria would hold aloof, ready to align herself with whichever contestant promised to be victorious. Working hand in glove with the British cabinet, Beust offered himself as the impartial mediator in the Luxemburg controversy, and a compromise was hammered out at an international conference which disappointed both disputants: Luxemburg would be retained by the King of the Netherlands, it would be demilitarized, and its neutrality would be guaranteed by the powers. After that setback, Napoleon III set about to cultivate diplomatic intimacy with Austria—and with Italy too.[15]

After the frustration of the South German design, the Ballplatz viewed sympathetically a political understanding with France to which the young Italian kingdom would be party. During the crisis preceding the outbreak of the War of 1866, Austria had angled for an agreement with France, but the latter's price was too high and the negotiations ran into sand. The Austrian defeat by Prussia was regarded in France as a defeat for France as well.

Scarcely had the cannon of 1866 been silenced when Austria and France gravitated as by natural compulsion toward one another and Napoleon III went out of his way to show his affection for Francis Joseph's representative at his court, Prince Richard Metternich, son of the famous chancellor, and for his gracious wife. For the first time, in April of 1867, the Duc de Gramont, in consequence of the growing antagonism between France and Prussia, discussed with Beust the desirability of a Franco-Austrian alliance pointed against Prussia. Beust temporized, knowing perfectly well that such an arrangement would antagonize the Austro-Germans and the Magyar chiefs to boot—those considerations were never out of Beust's calculations throughout the intermittent alliance negotiations with France which went on by word of mouth and in writing until the outbreak of the Franco-German war in July of 1870.[16]

It was planned to attest Austrian good will for France by means of a visit of Francis Joseph to Paris, but the trip was called off because of the tragic news of the execution of the emperor's audacious brother, Maximilian, Napoleon's "stooge," at the hands of a firing squad in Mexico. Instead, Napoleon III and his wife Eugénie paid a visit to Salzburg in August of 1867, ostensibly to express condolences to the emperor over the death of his brother, but really to carry forward the diplomatic conversations that had been initiated in the spring. Napoleon's presence on Austrian soil displeased Francis Joseph, who had by no means forgotten the French role in the military humiliation of 1859, and the Salzburg town council balked at presenting the French ruler an address of welcome until sternly commanded to do so. On the other side, Napoleon III, confounded by the swift upsurge of Prussian power, was exceedingly anxious to heal Austrian wounds and to establish friendly intimacy with the Hapsburg state. Very frankly he had expressed the hope that Austria would regain her traditional position in German Europe.

As Beust anticipated, the Frenchmen at Salzburg brought up the subject of an alliance, indicating that at the end of a victorious war with Prussia, Austria should have a free hand in most of southern Germany while France should take charge of the left bank of the Rhine. That alluring prospect Beust felt obliged to turn aside because of political conditions inside the Monarchy; he countered with the suggestion that the two countries should pursue a united policy against Russia or a Russo-Prussian combination, so as to pave the way for a more solid partnership. That proposal the French found unacceptable, for they felt that a Russo-Prussian coalition lay outside the range of the probable.

No basis for understanding could be discovered, and nothing concrete resulted from the Salzburg conference, though in and of itself the meeting openly advertised the emergence of Austria from diplomatic isolation and brought about greater cordiality between the two cabinets. Publicists with sharp pencils glibly wrote about the "Salzburg entente"; in November of 1867 Francis Joseph and Beust called in Paris to underscore the growing rapprochement with France.[17]

Diplomatic dickerings were renewed in 1868, the French again evading an Austrian proposal for an alignment against Russia, and once more failing to win a pledge of Austrian help should Prussia encroach upon German territory south of the Main River. Napoleon III in July of 1868 solicited Austrian acquiescence in an active alliance or in support of an international conference to guarantee the territorial *status quo* of Europe. Neither of those perspectives attract Beust, who recommended instead an international conference to deliberate on limitation of armaments. That suggestion the French agreed to take under advisement, and Napoleon urged the Austrians to accelerate the reorganization of their military services, observing that "before talking of disarmament one must be armed and you are not."[18]

Presently the French broached a proposal for a ten-year limitation on armaments which promised to benefit France to the disadvantage of Prussia, but Lord Clarendon, the prospective British foreign secretary, afraid lest the mere announcement of the project would precipitate hostilities between France and Prussia, threw cold water on the scheme and washed it away.[19]

So the French turned to the idea of a triple alliance, uniting France, Austria, and Italy. Conversations ran in the familiar vein, Beust desiring an eastern orientation for any agreement, the French seeking positive pledges of Austrian backing in case of a Franco-Prussian conflict. But Beust would not even agree to station an army corps along the Bohemian border if war broke out. Italy meantime had been drawn into the bargaining. Italian dread that Austria might interfere if an attempt were made to annex the fragment of territory still belonging to the Vatican had been diminished by the anticlerical tone that pervaded the Austrian reichsrat and by the fact that Beust was a Protestant. Francis Joseph and King Victor Emmanuel exchanged orders of knighthood and Beust wrote that his adopted country had accepted without reservation or rancor the situation which events had created in Italy. It was presently evident that the Italians were ready to come to an intimate understanding with Austria and France provided territory was ceded to them and they were given support in definitively settling the Roman question.

The upshot of intricate negotiations was a draft treaty of May 10, 1869, in which the three cabinets bound themselves to pursue a common policy in Europe, and reciprocally guaranteed the territorial integrity of each other.[20] In the event of war, the three monarchs would arrange an alliance, decide upon military operations, and settle jointly all territorial and financial problems. Under the terms of a protocol, France and Austria promised to make territorial cessions to Italy, but nothing specific was stated concerning gains for the other signatories. Throughout the exchanges, the Austrian diplomatists had stressed the applicability of the projected combination against Russia, while the French for their part conceived of it as a shield that would make intervention against Prussia feasible.

The draft treaty was never officially ratified. Insurmountable obstacles prevented that; for one thing, the Italians raised the price for their collaboration, demanding the evacuation of French troops that were garrisoning the papal possession and additional territorial pledges. Beust backed the Italians on the Roman question, "the Roman thorn," in his language. But Napoleon's authoritarian regime, beset at the moment by most serious domestic troubles, would not call the troops home, knowing full well that such a move would have completely alienated the powerful clerical party of France. That stanch ultramontane, Empress Eugénie, is credited with the aphorism: "Better the Prussians in Paris than the Italians in Rome." [21]

Instead of a formal treaty, notes were exchanged between Francis Joseph and Napoleon that amounted to a "moral" alliance. Assurances were given the Hapsburg ruler that if his country was threatened by aggression from any quarter, French forces would immediately be sent to his aid, and Napoleon indicated his readiness to put into writing the entente that existed between the two sovereigns and the king of Italy.[22] Just how Francis Joseph responded is a matter of speculation, though beyond any doubt he did not bind Austria to fight if France were attacked. In spite of the flimsy nature of the understanding, Napoleon and other French leaders regarded the commitment as morally binding and seem to have felt certain of Austrian military support should France be involved in war with Prussia.[23]

At Berlin, in the meantime, Count Bismarck, aware that serious negotiations between Austria and France were under way, had not been idly resting on his oars. In view of the possibility of joint Franco-Austrian action against Prussia, Bismarck had arranged, early in 1868, with Russia for military collaboration, and the men on the Neva had let it be known that they wanted no renewal of the Austro-Prussian feud. At the outset of 1869, Bismarck launched a furious press campaign against Beust's diplomacy, to which Viennese newspapers retorted in kind. In the midst of the newspaper war Bismarck warned foreign statesmen that Austria and France were engaged in a sinister program of *Einkreisungspolitik*.[24]

Bismarck also got into touch with Hungarian elements that were antipathetic to a Prussophobe orientation of Hapsburg diplomacy. Andrássy, the Hungarian prime minister, who kept his eyes resolutely glued on the East, on the Russian danger, made it perfectly clear that he was opposed to the resumption of the traditional Hapsburg role in German affairs. As he calculated the future, Hungary would suffer if Austria should regain her former place in Germany, and might even be reduced to a crownland once more; only if Prussia supported Russia or any other power against the interests of the Dual Monarchy would the astute Magyar look with favor upon a solid Hapsburg alignment with France. Had there been no other stumbling block to an active alliance with France, the hostility of Andrássy and his Magyar fellows would alone, no doubt, have been sufficient to prevent its consummation.

Nevertheless, communications between Vienna and Paris proceeded, and the desirability of a military convention to reinforce and implement the "moral entente" had considerable support in policy-making quarters. At the middle of February 1870, Archduke Albrecht, chief of the Austrian war hawks, appeared in the French capital with a project for joint military operations against Prussia. In essence the plan called for the invasion of southern Germany by the forces of Austria, France, and Italy, if and when hostilities commenced; the decisive battle would be fought in the vicinity of Leipzig and the victors would dictate terms of peace in Berlin. Conversations with French military specialists were initiated along these lines, but little progress had been made when Albrecht returned to Vienna, carrying with him a rather unfavorable impression of the French war machine. In the end, the French decided that Albrecht's scheme was unacceptable, because both Austria and Italy would need six weeks to mobilize their armies and their publics for war.[25]

To continue the military conversations Napoleon dispatched General Lebrun to Vienna in June of 1870 where he conferred lengthily with Albrecht and other Austrian leaders. It was made perfectly clear that Austria would not participate in a war against Prussia until French arms had scored a striking victory. Francis Joseph told Lebrun that his country needed peace and went on, "If I make war, I shall have to be forced into it . . . If Napoleon . . . occupies [steht] southern Germany with his army, not as a conqueror, but as a liberator, I shall [then] be compelled to declare that I will make his cause my own."[26]

Although the Austrian commitments were vague and "moral," Napoleon III and his Prussophobe foreign minister, Gramont, who was transferred from the Vienna embassy to Paris in May 1870, blandly counted upon some assistance from Austria in case of war with Prussia. How much that assumption affected the conduct of French diplomacy in the crisis arising from the Hohenzollern candidature to the Spanish throne it is impossible to evaluate. Certainly Austria had not given unequivocal assurances of support if France were attacked by Prussia, however much may have been hinted at or suggested; indeed, in a dispatch to Paris on the very eve of the Franco-Prussian conflict, Beust declared that Austria would not take up arms unless Russia allied herself to Prussia. In a war limited to France and Prussia, Austria would stand on the side lines unless and until it were decidedly in her interest to enter the struggle.[27] That communication was explicit enough and, if presented to the French when written, should have made Austria's intentions crystal clear; Gramont, however, claimed that the dispatch was never communicated to him.[28] Advices that Bismarck received from his envoy in Vienna assured him that Austria probably would not fight, even though the French were persistently pressing her to do so.[29] And St. Petersburg let it be known in Berlin and Vienna that if Austria went to war against Prussia, Russian troops would promptly storm against Galicia.[30]

VI

Hapsburg policy in the Franco-Prussian crisis was the subject of animated debate in a crown council, held on July 18, under the presidency of Francis Joseph. Attending were Chancellor Beust, Prime Ministers Potocki of Austria and Andrássy of Hungary, Lónyay, common minister of finance, Kuhn, minister of war, and Archduke Albrecht. Casting himself in the role of the astute Metternich, Beust argued that the diplomatic situation required a dual policy of watchful waiting and of military preparation and partial mobilization, so that Austria might be ready to take a hand in the war if such a course should seem politic. The Chancellor was restrained from advocating immediate intervention by the well-grounded suspicion that if Austria entered the war, Russia as surely would place its sword at Bismarck's disposal, and by the equally well-known sympathy for Prussia on the part of the Austro-German Liberals who were averse to another "brother's war." The Viennese press was predominantly Prussophile and in favor of strict neutrality.

No man in Austria was more eager than General Kuhn to secure revenge for the defeat of 1866, and at the crown council he recommended that Austria should immediately align herself with France and order general mobilization, even though the military reforms recently inaugurated were far from perfected, morale was still shaken from 1866, and considerable time would have to elapse before an effective army could be put into the field. Italy should be drawn into the struggle by promises of territory, Austria obtaining compensation in southern Germany and the Balkans. Kuhn contended that if Prussia triumphed over France she would turn next to the acquisition of the German provinces of Austria; if Russia entered the conflict, her war effort could be nullified by stirring up rebellion among the Polish minority, Kuhn smoothly argued. Archduke Albrecht in turn favored either general mobilization or complete neutrality; in his surprisingly optimistic opinion, French arms would penetrate to the border of Saxony by September, and there the decisive battle would be fought. Potocki's sympathies were definitely with France.

Faithful to the convictions he had previously revealed, Andrássy stoutly opposed any course that might involve the Monarchy in a war against Prussia alone. Strict neutrality, with partial preparedness, he regarded as the only sound policy. If complications arose in the East, if Russia aided Prussia, then the Monarchy would have to fight. For Hungary, his supreme concern, no positive good could result from a war, Andrássy thought, and secret advices from Bismarck confirmed him in his opinions.[31] Defeat would lay Hungary open to enemy occupation, while victory would place the kingdom at the mercy of the Austrian generals. A strong triumphant Austria would be detrimental to Hungarian interests and the dualistic arrangement might even be scrapped.

Francis Joseph, who saw in the impending Franco-Prussian contest the possibility of restoring Hapsburg prestige in German affairs, scrupulously weighed the rival contentions, and in the end adopted essentially the position advocated by Andrássy. Neutrality, accordingly, was proclaimed and only minor military measures, such as reinforcement of fortifications and buying horses, were authorized. Beust assured the British ambassador that these were merely precautionary steps and were not intended in any way to influence the military dispositions of Prussia.

Rational calculations had clearly triumphed over considerations of Hapsburg prestige and imperial honor. As is now known, if Austria had marched against Prussia, Russia would have taken the field and the struggle would have expanded into a general European conflagration. Beust evidently hoped that the French would win the initial encounters in the war, and then Andrássy and in turn Francis Joseph might be brought round to his "activist" thinking. Austrian court society, generals, and diplomatists did not conceal their Francophile leanings and the Prussian ambassador to Vienna reported that he often felt as though he were living in the enemy's country. He was instructed to get into communication with Austro-German youth and to stir them to rebellion if that were necessary to prevent Austrian armed assistance to France.[32]

Efforts which France put forth after the beginning of the war to arrange a Triple Alliance on new terms came to naught, and a similar fate befell a project sponsored by Beust for a treaty with Italy, providing for armed neutrality and concerted diplomatic action.[33] At an opportune moment that combination might have exercised effective pressure in behalf of France, but the scheme collapsed when Napoleon III stubbornly declined to recall French troops from papal territory.

Whatever plans of intervention or dreams of compensation the Austrian war party nurtured, they were utterly blasted by the rapid and smashing victories of the Prusso-German legions over France. Austrian forces could not have been put on the battle line before September, and on September 2, Napoleon III and his army surrendered at Sedan. After that, Adolphe Thiers, as the agent of the provisional French government of national defense, twice conferred in Vienna in a heroic, pitiful effort to secure foreign intervention; Beust tried his hand at arranging collective mediation, but without result. Alone of the great neutrals, Austria derived no tangible benefit from the Franco-German war. Britain profited by the sale of goods to the belligerents, Italy took over the papal remnant of Rome, and Russia cancelled the distasteful Black Sea restrictions in the Treaty of Paris of 1856.

Russia's very benevolent posture toward Prussia during the French war was a vital factor, arguably the decisive one, in keeping Austria on the side lines, and St. Petersburg insisted on a reward. Bismarck had promised to back Russia in scrapping the naval prohibitions on warships and naval stations in the Black Sea, incorporated in the Treaty of Paris in 1856, on the assumption that Russia would not bring up the matter until the war with France had closed. Prince Gorchakov, however, decided that it would be wiser to repudiate the clauses promptly and did so in October 1870.

Although Beust previously had favored the removal of the fetters on Russian naval power in the Black Sea, he now declared his opposition on the technical ground that Russia had acted arbitrarily and illegally. Britain took much the same line, but neither power was in a mood to prevent revision by force, though Andrássy boldly urged going to war,[34] and the Russians were permitted to have their way. Formal international approval of the revision was embodied in the London protocol of March 15, 1871.[35] By this change, Russia improved her strategic position in the Near East,[36] Russo-German friendship was reinforced, and the way for a political understanding with Austria opened up.

VII

After the catastrophic French defeat at Sedan, all hopes cherished in Vienna of revenge for Sadowa went aglimmering. Francis Joseph described Sedan as "terrible" and the jubilation of the Prussian king, "with his arrogance, vanity, and hypocrisy," as "shameless." Beust almost tumbled over himself in an effort to restore good feelings with his great rival, Bismarck, as a means of consolidating the peace of Europe and of preparing the way for better relations with Russia.

Bismarck, who had consistently sought Austrian friendship since 1866, eagerly seized the outstretched hand of Vienna. At a conference of the two foreign ministers, in 1871, Bismarck declared that he had no desire to take over the German-inhabited provinces of the Hapsburgs, as was widely believed in Austria and elsewhere. Treitschke, the distinguished German historian and publicist, expressed what no doubt was the prevalent Prussian opinion when he spoke out against such annexation on the ground that the Catholic element in Germany would be dangerously enlarged. "We Germans," he wrote, "have never understood the principle of nationality in the crude and overbearing sense that all German-speaking Europeans must belong to our Empire" [37]—a doctrine that might well have been applied in the Alsatian question.

In spite of Bismarck's disclaimers of annexationist designs on German Austria, Beust hesitated to accept them at face value. "It would be well for us," he remarked, "to keep our eyes open and to exercise unflagging vigilance." He believed that the Pan-German ferment among Austro-Germans was traceable in part to the line taken by the official German press; if that press urged upon the Austro-Germans the desirability, nay the necessity, of seeking harmony in an empire of many tongues the unrest would diminish, Beust thought.

Exchange of views between Beust and Bismarck tended to improve feelings between their governments and to enable them to take common precautions against revolutionary movements, dread of which had been conjured up by the bloody Communard episode of 1871 in Paris. Greater cordiality was openly manifested by meetings between the sovereigns of the two countries, which, once begun, continued almost without interruption until the death of Emperor William I in 1888.

Any lurking doubts that may have existed in Berlin as to Francis Joseph's renunciation of ambitions to recover Hapsburg influence in the affairs of Germany were removed when Beust was dismissed from the Ballplatz in November of 1871, and Andrássy, friend of Bismarck and an admirer of Germany, was appointed in his stead. The Austrian emperor had decided upon the change in ministers, which he described simply as a change of staff, without consulting anyone. Empress Elizabeth, who had been captivated by the fascinating Magyar, had urged her husband to make Andrássy foreign minister as early as 1866, and she interpreted his appointment as a personal triumph.[38]

Although it had been apparent for some time that Beust's prestige was falling and that of Andrássy on the rise, the request for his resignation smote the Saxon like a thunderbolt. His dismissal, coming as it did just after the downfall of the pro-Slav Hohenwart ministry, created considerable stir; even the abdication of the monarch was excitedly talked of by Viennese. The assigned reasons for the change at the Ballplatz were that Beust was enfeebled in health, that the title of chancellor which he bore created too many constitutional perplexities, and that his genius for intrigue together with his outlook on domestic politics had raised up a pack of enemies. But what was more weighty, the Saxon reminded his imperial master of too many unhappy memories in home and foreign affairs, and his departure would facilitate a *rapprochement* with Germany. As if to emphasize the new, Germanophile, course in diplomacy, Prince Richard Metternich, whose anti-Bismarckian and Francophile tendencies were notorious, was recalled from the Paris embassy. The Hapsburg future lay not in antagonism toward Germany but in intimate collaboration with her.

Beust finished out his checkered public career as Hapsburg envoy to London and Paris in turn, retiring in 1882, but in neither capital did he enhance his stature as a diplomatist. His conduct of affairs at the Court of St. James's earned him neither trust nor respect during the great diplomatic crisis of 1876–1878 over the Balkans; at Paris he was "the most miserable figure in the diplomatic corps," full of self-esteem, proud of his accomplishments, oblivious of his shortcomings, benevolent toward his foes.

Beust's large monument in Austria was the contribution he made in bringing to pass the *Ausgleich* with Hungary; his part in molding the Austrian constitution of 1867 was substantial, while his support of liberalizing legislation entitles him to a place among the German liberals, though contemporary politicians of that school would only grudgingly have admitted it, in consequence of his willingness to traffic with the Slav minorities. As a diplomatist, Beust shines feebly beside his dynamic and successful rival, Bismarck. The Saxon champion of lost causes stands out in marked contrast to the Prussian virtuoso of iron will, who dreamed big dreams and contrived to create a great empire.[39]

VIII

Lord Robert Lytton, the British attaché in Vienna, who was quite intimate with Andrássy, regarded the new director of Hapsburg foreign affairs favorably, in contrast with his low estimate of the character and capacity of Beust. To his home office Lytton wrote shortly after Andrássy's appointment: "[Although] he has passed many years of his life in France and England as an exile . . . all his instincts are intensely antidemocratic. He is a man of unquestionable energy and courage, who has seen much of the world. Without any great general culture, he has talents and natural political tact which are remarkable. He thoroughly understands his own countrymen and how to manage them. His administration of Hungary has been eminently successful, although by no means easy. He is a soldier, a sportsman, and something of an elegant, with a dash in his temperament of the gypsy chief . . . He is of good family, his public character is thoroughly honorable, and his manners are simple, engaging, and unmistakably sincere.

"These qualities have no doubt rendered him personally agreeable to the

Emperor, most of whose ministers on this side of the Leitha have lately been lawyers or professors and not men of the world.

"He has a sincere belief in the principles of parliamentary government, and a greater practical knowledge of their application than any minister who has yet been called to coöperate in the administration of this Empire. Having definite political ideas and convictions, he does not affect that official reserve which is so often the asylum of self-mistrust and intellectual vagueness. As a practical politician, however, he has perhaps the defect of too great an anxiety to convince; and he sometimes argues when it would suffice to affirm.

"He is fully capable of combining prudence with promptitude and forethought with firmness. If the internal conditions of this Empire were tolerably settled, I should feel no doubt of Andrássy's ability to deal most efficiently with any great crisis in its foreign relations . . . He probably lacks the *savoir faire* of his predecessor . . . who is a master in the art of political cookery." [40]

Without diplomatic experience, distrusted by German bureaucrats in the foreign office and by German Liberals, though fulsomely hailed by his own countrymen as the first Magyar ever to serve the Hapsburgs as foreign minister, Andrássy entered office with firm convictions as to the course to be steered in international affairs. Austria, he had said, "should offer her hand to Germany and show her fist to Russia," and yet he was willing to coöperate with the eastern colossus provided it did not interfere with Austrian interests or her mission in the Balkans, where Andrássy was bent upon strengthening the Hapsburg position. As a Magyar, he not only despised Russia but regarded the South Slavs as a serious enemy, and for that reason, as well as for economic advantages and out of personal gratitude to Turkey, which had given him asylum after the revolution of 1848, he desired the preservation of the Ottoman empire. Like Beust before him, Andrássy lent diplomatic support to Austrian financial interests which were engaged in providing the Ottoman empire with a railway system. The great trunk line under construction, linking Budapest and Vienna with Constantinople, with branches running off to Aegean ports, would bring obvious commercial and strategic advantages to the Dual Monarchy.

Historically, Great Britain had been friendly with Austria, the points at which their vital interests diverged were inconsequential, and with that power Andrássy was eager to negotiate an entente, mutually profitable. To his way of thinking, an Anglo-Austrian alignment might very well serve as the prelude to a diplomatic partnership embracing Germany and Italy—a combination that would have no trouble in holding Russia and France, Europe's wing powers, and the only probable challengers of the *status quo,* in leash. It was an ambitious diplomatic project, worthy of an imaginative and creative statesman.

Andrássy's first major diplomatic gesture was an attempt to secure British backing against a possible Russian thrust into the Near East. "What I have in mind," he wrote Beust, now ambassador to the Court of St. James's, "is not a military combination, not an alliance leading to war, but rather a strong understanding to preserve peace." [41] If Austria went to war to check Russia it would obviously be desirable to have solid assurances that Britain would be in the Hapsburg corner, and, as a *quid pro quo,* Andrássy was prepared to pledge support to Britain if Russia menaced India. The British ministry seems to have given serious consideration to the overture (there was considerable apprehension in London in consequence of recent Russian pressure into Bokhara and Khiva) but declined to deviate from the settled policy of splendid isolation. In the next years, though Austria drew close to Russia, the hope of making an entente with Britain was for Andrássy an *idée fixe*.

Failing to strike a bargain with Britain, Andrássy was disposed to cast about for some kind of an understanding with Russia, and it was evident that the road to St. Petersburg passed through Berlin. Quite early in 1872, Andrássy let it be known that Austria desired an alliance with Germany, preferably one pointed against Russia. However much Bismarck disliked to be too intimately bound up with the tsardom, prudence and wisdom alike counseled against an out-and-out anti-Russian policy; such a course would almost certainly drive the Russians into the wide-open arms of humiliated and vengeful France. It was in the German interest, and indeed in the interest of the peace of Europe, to have both Russia and Austria as friends if that could be contrived. Plans were matured for another meeting of Francis Joseph and William I, in Berlin this time, with their foreign secretaries in attendance; learning of that and alarmed lest something detrimental to Russian interests might be decided upon, Tsar Alexander II requested that he too be invited to the parley. To that Austria assented, albeit reluctantly.

IX

At the German capital in the autumn of 1872, the three emperors met in conference and their ministers exchanged views on diplomatic matters. Andrássy and Gorchakov talked more particularly about the Polish question, for Russian susceptibilities, as has been said, were aroused by the autonomous rights given to Galicia; they talked too about the Serb problem, and the future of the Ottoman empire. Russian suspicions that Austria coveted Bosnia-Herzegovina, Andrássy tried to brush away,[42] promising to work to maintain the *status quo* there.

With full candor the two statesmen informed each other that if either power resorted to force in the Near East, the other would go to war. In the light of his conversations with Gorchakov, Andrássy presently assured the delegations that "certain Pan-Slavist tendencies which continue to strive to bring Austria and Russia into antagonism with one another find no support in official Russian circles." Though nothing was set down on paper at the Berlin conference, the way was opening for a formal Austro-Russian *rapprochement*.

Before that came to pass, German statesmen paid a visit to St. Petersburg (May 1873) and signed a secret convention, in which Germany and Russia each promised the other military assistance in the event of an attack. Austria, when bidden to subscribe to this accord, expressed preference for something less specific; the point was that Andrássy was disinclined to bind the Dual Monarchy to aid Russia, if the latter's ambitions in the Near East brought on a clash with Turkey or Britain. And he had his way. By a special Austro-Russian understanding, the two countries agreed to consult on any issues in which their viewpoints were at variance, though apparently nothing definite concerning the Balkans figured in the pact. If a third power should endanger the peace of Europe, the two signatories would seek to find a common policy, with provision for the use of armed force should that be required. A codicil to the document united the two governments in joint resistance against the doings of revolutionary socialism. To the naked eye, this Austro-Russian understanding appeared to signify that the bitterness running back to the Crimean war had been liquidated and that the two monarchies would work together for a constructive settlement of the complex and perilous Balkan problem.

Germany promptly attached its signature to the pact and thus was brought into existence the League of the Three Emperors—first edition—which, on a longer view, revived the alignment of the conservative eastern monarchies of the first half of the nineteenth century. It was implied that if and when Austria and Russia proved unable to reconcile differences over the Balkans, Germany would act as an impartial mediator; and it was also implied that Germany would support the other powers should they agree on a common course of action.[43]

Good feelings between Austria and Russia were promoted in 1874 when Francis Joseph on a visit to St. Petersburg laid a memorial wreath at the grave of Nicholas I, his benefactor of 1849. That gracious gesture suggested to Alexander II that all parties should try to rid their memories of past grievances. Austria and Russia were in fact on better terms than at any time since the Crimean war.

Even so, Andrássy seriously doubted whether the reconciliation would long endure. He had said in November of 1873 that "although for the moment relations between the two empires are satisfactory, war might arise between them."[44] He therefore continued to solicit an entente with Britain which could be invoked in case the Russians kicked over the Balkan traces.

The Austrian clerical party would have liked the Monarchy to take steps looking to the restoration to the Vatican of its temporal possessions. But Andrássy set his face like flint against interference in Italian affairs, and in fact tried to effect a *rapprochement* with the kingdom, though he was annoyed by the ceaseless Irredentist clamor. Italy, on her side, deeply mistrustful of France so long as there was a chance that the clerical-royalist faction might take over the management of French politics, inclined toward friendship with Austria.

When Victor Emmanuel II visited Vienna in 1873, he was given assurances that Austria would not champion papal interests, either alone or in collaboration with France. Two years later Francis Joseph appeared in Venice—a call in Rome was out of the question for this devout son of the church—symbolizing thus his renunciation of territory that had been lost to Italy. Using expressions familiar to the language of diplomacy, the emperor hinted that one day the Italian-peopled Trentino area might be ceded to Italy if Austria obtained appropriate compensation elsewhere—in the Balkans, presumably. Victor Emmanuel, soon after the Venice visit, boldly declared that "behind this proof of cordial friendship between the rulers, stands the lasting sympathy of their peoples"; Italy, he went on, had given up claims to Hapsburg territory.[45] Stanch patriots, Irredentists, on the other hand, kept busily at work stirring up popular concern over the unredeemed provinces, and their agitation presently bore poisonous fruit.

For all the growing intimacy with Germany, Austria on occasion took a line at odds with German desires and policy. Toward France, for instance, the Ballplatz displayed good will in small ways, letting it be known that a strong France was necessary for European tranquillity, though it shied away from unofficial suggestions for a French alliance. On Spain, too, Vienna and Berlin did not always see eye to eye; after the proclamation of a Spanish Republic in August of 1874, Bismarck recognized the new order, but Austria, to whose ruler the republican concept was anathema, would do no more than recognize the ministry alone.

A grave war scare in 1875 involving Germany and France directly enabled Austria to improve its diplomatic position. Alarmed by the military rejuvenation of France, and the prevalence of *revanche* sentiment, the German press indulged in a campaign against the Third Republic to which French journalism retorted in kind. Responsible Germans murmured of the necessity of a preventive war. If Bismarck actually contemplated such a course (which is doubtful), he changed his mind when Russia and Great Britain rallied to the side of France. The German Chancellor's anger knew no bounds when Prince Gorchakov gave currency to the impression that Russia, by standing forth as the protector of France, had saved the peace of Europe.

Andrássy, although requested to identify himself with the Russo-British pressure on Berlin, coolly held aloof and gathered in the profits. Bismarck was gratified that Andrássy had refrained from entering the informal coalition against him, while the intensified antagonism between the Iron Chancellor and Gorchakov quickened Andrássy's hope that a diplomatic bloc might be arranged in which Russia was not a partner. He confided to Francis Joseph that "an alliance with Germany appears possible in the near future," and he renewed his efforts to secure the recall of the German ambassador, the Russophile Schweinitz, who was outspokenly unsympathetic to an alliance.[46]

During the war scare of 1875, the League of the Three Emperors had been weighed in the international balances and found wanting; Russia had substantially aligned herself with France and Britain against Bismarck's Germany. Austria, on the other side, thanks to the astuteness of Andrássy, had managed to retain the friendship of the Iron Chancellor, without at the same time rupturing the slender tie with St. Petersburg. It is not too much to say that in 1875 the diplomatic standing of the House of Hapsburg was better than at any time in a generation. But ominous storm clouds were hovering low over the Balkans.

‡ CHAPTER SIX ‡

THE NEAR EAST AND THE
GERMAN ALLIANCE

Bosnia-Herzegovina, a kind of equilateral triangle forming the northwestern section of the Balkan peninsula, with a short frontage on the Adriatic Sea, holds a distinctive place in modern European history. Conquered by the Turks in the last half of the fifteenth century, this region was the scene of almost constant insurrection, and there originated a chain of events, beginning with an uprising in 1875, that led to war between Russia and Turkey in 1877. Next year an international mandate assigned Bosnia-Herzegovina to the occupation and administration of Austria, and thirty years later the area was annexed by Austria under circumstances that came close to precipitating a general European war. It was in Bosnia's capital, Sarajevo, finally, that Francis Ferdinand, heir presumptive to the Hapsburg throne, and his wife were assassinated, the episode out of which cycled World War I. International wrangling over Bosnia, with Austria and Russia as the principals, was almost incessant.

Slightly more than 18,000 square miles in extent, this area contained in 1879 a population of about 1,158,000. Somewhat more than half a million belonged to the Orthodox Church, almost as many were Moslems, and the balance professed Roman Catholicism; there were also tiny gypsy and Jewish minorities. Not more than one resident in a hundred could read.

The rule of the Turk over Bosnia-Herzegovina caused deep discontent among the Christian peasantry. Had they been slaves they could scarcely have been more fully at the mercy of their Moslem landlords; justice simply could not be obtained and outside of a few favored places neither the person nor the property of the peasant was safe from molestation. Fanatical and arrogant Moslems solicited the coöperation of the Roman Catholic population, but quarreled constantly with adherents of the Orthodox faith. And the higher clergy of Orthodoxy, Greeks mostly, who had purchased their offices, fleeced the parish "popes," who in turn levied upon such worldly possessions of the peasantry as had escaped the rapacity of landlords.[1]

Taxation for public purposes was so devised as to extort the last coin from the unhappy countryfolk. Part of the taxes was collected by tax farmers, who assessed the value of crops before the harvest was gathered in, and if payment was not forthcoming applied force to get it. In the rocky region of Nevesinje, a dozen miles from Mostar, Herzegovina, crops failed in 1874, and when taxes were not met, brutal soldiers were set loose on the hapless peasants. That was the immediate cause of rebellion against the Turkish government in 1875.[2]

Forces from outside operating upon Bosnian clansmen fostered sentiments of revolution against Turkey. Among the Orthodox population, which honored the national heroes of Serbia, there was a growing desire for political union with the principality of Serbia, a desire that was encouraged by propaganda of Serbian origin. Roman Catholics, on the other hand, in so far as they held political convictions, were inclined to lean to the views of the Croatian Strossmayer, in whose seminary some of their clergy were trained. A suggestion of Austrian administration, which the Catholic bishop of Sarajevo broached in 1876, had precious little popular appeal.[3]

Yet Hapsburg interest in Bosnia-Herzegovina ran deep into the past. At one time the northern strip had been governed from Vienna, and Austria considered herself the protector of the Roman Catholic citizens. Besides, many a Franciscan friar who worked in the provinces had been educated in Austria, and funds for Catholic activities flowed down from Vienna; after about 1850 the proportion of Catholics in the area increased substantially. In a very real and positive sense, the Catholic Church was at once a symbol and an instrument of Hapsburg interests in Bosnia-Herzegovina.

Recurrent disorders in the nineteenth century, moreover, heightened the interest of the Yugoslav minority in Austria for their national brethren south of the border. Christian refugees who streamed into the Danube Monarchy were maintained at government expense and marauding raids of Moslem brigands onto Hapsburg territory were answered with punitive expeditions.

Aside from religious and humanitarian concerns, Austria had a strategic interest in Bosnia. Sea-borne commerce, after the loss of Venetia to Italy in 1866, passed through Trieste and Fiume and could easily be interrupted if a strong and unfriendly power were established on the eastern side of the Adriatic. Austrian possession of Dalmatia provided a measure of protection, and it was thought in some influential Hapsburg military circles that Bosnia-

Herzegovina ought to be taken over to give Dalmatia greater security. While Francis Joseph was visiting Dalmatia in the spring of 1875, the governor of that province, Baron Rodič, a Croat loyalist, urged upon the ruler the necessity of securing Bosnia-Herzegovina for the Monarchy; and representatives from Bosnia, Roman Catholics almost wholly, "begged" Francis Joseph to come and rule over their land. The Emperor returned to Vienna convinced of the wisdom of bringing the provinces into the realm of the Hapsburgs.[4]

On the other hand, Count Andrássy, the foreign secretary, disapproved the acquisition of a region that would intensify the already formidable problem of nationalities in the Monarchy. Besides, Serbia and Montenegro, which had pretensions to the provinces, would be antagonized and, what was more serious, Austria would invite fresh controversies with Russia, the patron and protector of Slav interests. Andrássy thought that the Monarchy should consider taking over Bosnia-Herzegovina only if it appeared that the Ottoman empire was about to fall apart, or if Serbia were going to pounce upon the area.

There is considerable evidence for the opinion that Austrian officials in Dalmatia, many of whom were Serbs and Croats, incited the Bosniacs to rebellion in 1875.[5] Certainly officials aided and comforted the insurgents from the very beginning of the uprising, and yet Turkish ships were permitted to enter an Austrian port to discharge military and other wares for use in subduing the rebels.

Serbian solicitude for Bosnia-Herzegovina stemmed from the twin considerations that many of the inhabitants were Serb in nationality and that an energetic party in Serbia believed that their country should be the nucleus round which all Yugoslavs should coalesce, even as Piedmont had served the Italians. Agitation issuing from Belgrade for rebellion against the sultan had a part in bringing on the Bosnian insurrection of 1875. Even more effective perhaps were urgings of a similar character that came from Montenegro; and leaders of that tiny princedom, like other politically conscious Balkan Slavs, were much influenced by Pan-Slav doctrines being preached by Russian evangelists. Although there was little Russian commerce with Yugoslav areas, the tsardom maintained consulates at key points there which served as channels for political missionary work. Consuls of the tsar boldly promised that, if the Bosnian natives rebelled against Turkey, help would be forthcoming from the big Slav brother.

II

Upon the outbreak of the insurrection, Andrássy aligned himself with the cabinets of Russia and Germany in requesting the Porte to introduce reforms in the administration of Bosnia so as to remove the internal causes of grievance. Prompting Andrássy's action was the conviction that Hapsburg interests would best be served by keeping the Ottoman empire intact, and, not less weighty, his desire to keep Serbia and Montenegro out of the fighting and to prevent any moves looking to the formation of a united Yugoslav state.

At Mostar, chief town of Herzegovina, a committee of consuls representing Europe's major powers held a meeting with rebel chieftains in September of 1875, but the insurgents declined to bargain unless the powers were ready to guarantee the execution of any reforms that might be decided upon. Long experience had taught the natives that Turkish pledges of more equitable administration had nothing more than paper value. Among the Herzegovinians in particular the untrustworthiness of Turkish promises had attained the solemnity of a proverb: "A firman is not worth the pod of a bean." So the European consular committee soon folded up.

To the delegations, Andrássy reported that he had appealed to the sultan "to put an end to the regrettable state of affairs" in Bosnia "by appropriate measures," and Austria had stationed troops along the border in sufficient numbers to fulfill the obligations of neutrality. A Russian proposal that Austria and Russia should jointly occupy the provinces and restore order was turned down in Vienna.

Andrássy next prepared a schedule of reforms for Bosnia which, after approval of the great powers, he dispatched to Turkey for acceptance. Religious freedom should be allowed to all inhabitants of the provinces, the iniquitous institution of tax farming should be abolished, and steps should be taken at once to improve the general lot of the peasants. It was recommended that a commission, part Moslem, part Christian, should be appointed to see that these reforms were carried out.

Knowing full well that the Bosnian rebels would not accept any terms without solid guarantees from the powers that they would be executed, the Turkish government blandly consented to the Andrássy program and offered to cease fighting. But Austrian efforts to persuade the rebels to lay down their arms were unavailing. So the hostilities raged on, and Russian sources now began supplying generous help to the insurgents.

In Serbia and Montenegro, meanwhile, agitation for war upon Turkey had grown ominously. Popular excitement was raised to fever pitch by nationalistic propaganda and by stories of Turkish atrocities circulated by Bosnian refugees. Seeking to prevent the Balkan conflagration from spreading, the foreign ministers of Austria, Russia, and Germany conferred at Berlin in May of 1876. But none of the proposals that were advanced suited all the delegates, and the swift course of events snatched the decision out of the hands of the "big eastern three." [6]

Among the Bulgars, a nationality so thoroughly repressed by the Turk that many otherwise well-informed Europeans possessed no knowledge of its existence, the spirit of revolt had taken hold and in May of 1876 open rebellion started. Theirs was an ill-starred piece of heroism, for the Turks quickly hurled against the Bulgars bands of their most fearless and ferocious troops, who burned and butchered without ruth. These barbarous outrages roused a wave of hot resentment against the Turk all over Europe, more so in Britain than on the continent.[7]

Serbia and Montenegro, the ruler of the first in the belief that war with Turkey was the only way to avert civil upheaval, and both egged on by Russian agents, negotiated a secret alliance and on June 30 declared war on the sultan. Bosnian insurgent leaders at once proclaimed the prince of Serbia as their sovereign, while the choice of the Herzegovinians fell on Montenegro's ruler. These developments rendered futile all outside attempts to restore peace in the Balkans by diplomatic action.

General Chernyaev, an ardent Pan-Slav, with a not undistinguished record as a soldier, though wanting in political acumen, assumed command of the principal Serb army. Volunteers from Russia, officers by the dozen, soldiers by the hundred, enlisted under the Serb flag; and funds flowed in from the tsardom for military and humanitarian ends. All of this mirrored the Pan-Slav ferment in Russia, which was nurtured by wild sagas of bestial barbarities in which Turkish troops indulged.

Much to the surprise of the outer world—and of themselves—the Serbian forces suffered defeat after defeat, so that there was real likelihood that Serbia might again fall under the full sway of Turkey. But that, Russia would not allow, would indeed fight to prevent. If Russia fought, then Austria would in all probability intervene, particularly since it was firmly believed that Pan-Slav ambitions, dangerously menacing to the very integrity of the Danube Monarchy, were in the ascendant at St. Petersburg.

Anxious to avoid an armed clash between his *Dreikaiserbund* partners, Prince Bismarck induced the rival foreign secretaries, Andrássy and Gorchakov, to talk things over again. They met in July of 1876, just after Serbia and Montenegro had gone to war with Turkey. The outcome of the parley was the vague and verbal Reichstadt Accord—or rather disaccord as it may be called because of the different versions of what was decided. Instead of drafting a joint declaration, each minister dictated his personal understanding of the agreement, and though the documents ran parallel on most items, there was wide divergence on the key question of the future status of Bosnia-Herzegovina.[8]

Andrássy and Gorchakov promised at Reichstadt that their countries would not intervene at the moment in the Balkan imbroglio. But if it looked as though Turkey was on the verge of overwhelming her enemies, then the two powers would jointly insist upon far-reaching reforms in Bosnia-

Herzegovina and the restoration of Serbia and Montenegro to their prewar boundaries. On the other hand, should the enemies of Turkey triumph, then broad alterations would be effected in the Balkan map; the Dual Monarchy, for instance, would obtain sections of Bosnia and possibly Herzegovina, and the rest of the provinces would pass to Serbia and Montenegro.

As compensation for possible extension of Hapsburg authority in the Balkans, Russia would regain Bessarabia (then belonging to Rumania) and parcels of Turkish territory on the eastern coast of the Black Sea. As Andrássy understood the Reichstadt bargain—or said he understood it—all of Bosnia and Herzegovina, save a slice of the latter, would pass under Hapsburg sovereignty, but Gorchakov understood (or said he understood) that part of Bosnia would be awarded to Serbia and Herzegovina entire to Montenegro.

Both ministers, it appears, had gaps in their geographical knowledge, and Andrássy seems to have been uncertain how much of the provinces he really desired. Against his best judgment, for he decidedly preferred reform within Turkey which would avoid dismemberment, Andrássy had bargained to take over Turkish territory; the alternative would have been to allow Russia to rearrange the Balkan map in her own sweet way. In spite of misgivings, Andrássy regarded the prospective acquisition of Bosnia-Herzegovina as "important and pleasing . . . We are following," he gleefully commented, "the great tradition of that noble knight, the Prince Eugene." [9]

Turkish military victories and the furore they engendered among Russian Pan-Slavs brought Gorchakov to the conclusion that Russia ought to take a hand in the fighting, regardless of the pledge of abstention given to Austria. That implied the open revival of Austro-Russian antagonism in the Near East and might bring on armed strife between the two eastern monarchies.

Russia therefore inquired of Germany what it would do in case of an Austro-Russian war, requesting an answer in positive language. Bismarck replied that if Russia fought Turkey he would strive to hold Austria neutral, but if Austria fought, then Germany would not intervene unless it appeared that Austria was on the verge of defeat that would endanger its position as a great power. That no doubt was the kind of answer Gorchakov had expected and he had to proceed with extreme caution.

At the end of October 1876, Russia demanded that Turkey sign a six-weeks' armistice with Serbia, and the Porte acquiesced. Andrássy, who had vainly tried to purchase Italian coöperation and to entice Bismarck into a solid commitment against Russia, welcomed a proposal for an international conference to deal with the vexing problem of European Turkey and to put an end to the fighting.

At Constantinople in December of 1876 delegates of the great powers deliberated on terms that would restore peace in the distraught Balkans. A set of territorial changes was agreed upon which would gratify, in part at least, the Christian nationalities and would cost Turkey territory and prestige. In the Christian areas remaining under Turkish sovereignty, administrative and economic reforms would be carried out by representatives of the powers.

From the first, the Turks were furious over foreign interference in their imperial affairs. Shrewdly the sultan issued a constitution for the Ottoman empire calling for a limited constitutional monarchy with an elected legislature, and promised to carry out an impressive array of improvements. That was a bombshell tossed into the lap of the foreign diplomatists and it blew the Constantinople conference to bits. Official Russia, aggrieved over the unwillingness of the powers to guarantee the execution of reforms, prepared for unilateral military action against Turkey; indeed, before the Constantinople conference convened, part of the Russian army had been mobilized and moved in the direction of the Ottoman empire.

Before invoking military force against Turkey, Russia felt it politic to assure herself of Austrian neutrality. In a pair of secret deals, military and political, whose texts were not published until after World War I, Austria promised not to intervene if Russia became involved in war with Turkey. As a reward for neutrality, Austria would obtain Bosnia-Herzegovina after the fighting ceased. Territorial understandings for the deeper Balkans were so drawn as to preclude the appearance of a large Slav state. Turkey, it is true, would lose territory by these conventions, but not so much as to be politically impotent in Europe. For Andrássy these arrangements were a gratifying diplomatic victory; merely by sitting on the sidelines, he could adequately safeguard Hapsburg interests.[10]

Unquestionably, domestic conditions influenced the Russians to agree to this unusual bit of diplomatic generosity; revolutionary unrest and financial distress were eating away the very pillars of the tsarist autocracy. Foreign adventure, on the other hand, would at once divert attention from internal troubles and appease the lively Pan-Slav sense of mission in the Balkans. Having purchased Austrian neutrality, Russia, in April of 1877, declared war on Turkey, avowing that its aim was simply to force the Moslem to improve the lot of the Balkan Christians.

Stubborn Turkish military resistance deceived the Russian expectation that the enemy would be swiftly annihilated. Rumania was then drawn into the contest and Serbia and Montenegro renewed their crusade against the Ottoman. Abroad, as the fighting proceeded, the idea gained currency that the tsar's real war aim was mastery over Constantinople and the Straits, the fulfillment of an ancient Muscovite ambition. In Austria, press and parliaments called upon Andrássy to reveal his intentions and policies; in some quarters, in fact, it was urged that Austria should take up arms against Russia and Pan-Slavism, while other voices pleaded that Austria should seize the golden opportunity to appropriate adjacent Turkish territory.

In spite of his fundamental distrust and dislike of Russia, Andrássy held his tongue and declined to become alarmed, for he believed that the tsardom would loyally abide by the secret commitments that had been negotiated. When the Turks, driven back at last by the invading Russian and Rumanian armies and scenting disaster, appealed to the powers for mediation, Austria responded negatively. But the British government, fearful lest Russia should occupy Constantinople, which would endanger the Mediterranean route to India, offered its good offices to the belligerents and warned St. Petersburg that occupation of Constantinople would mean war.

Not until the armies of the tsar were within easy range of the Ottoman capital would the men on the Neva consent to break off the fighting. The actual content of the armistice that was drawn up roused lively dreads in Vienna, matching the alarm that the Russian thrust southward had already provoked in London. But an armistice was only the prelude to a definitive peace treaty, and in the interval the Turks played upon the ambitions and cupidity of the neutral nations so as to save their country from the full consequences of military defeat.

III

Balkan events, affecting the fate of Slavs, kindled excitement among Hapsburg Slavs, the Czechs of Bohemia particularly, but also in Croatia and southern Hungary. Funds were collected, benefit concerts were given, and prayers for Slav victory were enthusiastically launched heavenward. Hungarian Serbs organized volunteer bands to fight the hated Turk; but deputy Svetozar Stratimirovič, the guiding spirit of the enterprise, was arrested and tried by Hungarian authorities on charges of high treason and condemned to prison for five years. Upon hearing of the defeat of Serb armies, Czech sympathizers bestowed a sword of honor on the vanquished commander, the Pan-Slav Chernyaev.

Russian intervention in the war against Turkey evoked warm expressions of gratitude and approval in Hapsburg Slav quarters. Czech patriotic clubs lauded the tsar for his noble decision, likened the campaign to a holy Slav crusade, and hoped for unqualified triumph; prayers for Russian success ascended in the churches. Vatican condemnation of Russian participation in the war so enraged some Czech Pan-Slavs that they publicly burned portraits of Pope Pius IX. In the name of the "Old" Czechs, Rieger wrote Aksakov, a prominent Russian Pan-Slav, "Today begins for the Russian nation and for the race in general, the period in which the task of advancing civilization has passed to the Slavs. Hitherto the youngest and largest of nations has not played a dominant role in world history . . . Today Russia battles for a grand ideal: for Christendom, for humanity, and the emancipation of our Slavic brethren. Who can doubt that the Czechs wish wholeheartedly for Russian success? The glory of Russia in so holy a struggle is the glory of the Czechs and will raise the self-respect of the Slavs universally. When mighty Russia protects the weak Slavs, it calls forth the applause of all Slavs. What great things Slavdom could achieve for mankind, if its strength were not lamed by disunion." [11] Croats in Agram passed resolutions extolling Russian valor and sympathetic to the aspirations of the Slavs of Turkey. The government banned a pro-Bulgarian rally in Slovenian Laibach.

Among Magyars, on the other hand, Russophobia touched new heights and mass meetings expressed sympathy for the Turkish "racial relatives" and even called for war upon Russia. Citizens of Budapest presented a sword of honor to Abdul Kérim, who had whipped the Serbs, and the veteran General Klapka, burning with hot memories of the tsarist invasion of Hungary in 1849, volunteered to organize an army corps to help the sultan.

When the defeat of Turkey appeared imminent, a popular mass meeting in the Hungarian capital highly resolved that the Dual Monarchy should immediately fight the Muscovites. Resolutions denouncing Russian atrocities and directing attention to the Russian peril were adopted; scores of meetings at other points in Hungary ratified these Budapest resolutions, some of them with a supplement voicing disapproval of Hapsburg expansion into the Balkans. Premier Coloman Tisza, himself a Turkish partisan, declared that his ministry shared the popular resentment over atrocities but added that the Hapsburg Monarchy alone was incapable of checkmating Russia; other powers, he hoped, would act.

IV

When the conditions of the Russo-Turkish armistice were disclosed, it was apparent that Russian war objectives, under pressure of Pan-Slavism, had risen mightily, for the armistice envisaged the almost total elimination of the Turk from the European continent. Angry and chagrined at the manner in which he had been betrayed, Andrássy declared that settlement of the war on these terms would not be acceptable, and he turned to Britain for support to thwart the perfidious Russian designs.

While the fighting was on, the British cabinet had tried several times to draw Austria into an active alliance against Russia. Without divulging his special understandings with the men on the Neva, Andrássy revealed that he would consider a Russian move upon Constantinople as grounds for war,[12] but with almost naïve confidence he relied upon Russian disclaimers of ambitions anent Constantinople and upon the fulfillment of the secret engagements that had been arranged. After the armistice terms were published, the British in turn hesitated, and only reluctantly seconded Andrássy's recommendation for an international conference to deliberate on the delicate Balkan situation.

Afraid that the Russians would occupy Constantinople (and stay there), Britain ordered a fleet into the waters adjacent to the Turkish capital and solicited Austrian coöperation in an armed demonstration should that seem necessary as a warning to the Russians. But Russophile military leaders in Vienna, ever a thorn in Andrássy's flesh, exerted pressure on Francis Joseph to avoid any measure that might involve the Monarchy in war with the eastern colossus. Wherefore, the foreign minister had to depend exclusively upon diplomacy to safeguard Austrian interests in the Near East.

Early in March of 1878 the Treaty of San Stefano, formally closing the Russian war against Turkey, was concluded. Among the provisions of peculiar interest to Austria, one article blocked out a Big Bulgarian state ranging far and wide over the Balkan peninsula; another permitted Bosnia-Herzegovina to remain under Ottoman rule, but promised improvements in administrative and agrarian conditions; and a third allocated a strip of the Sanjak of Novibazar, a wedge of territory lying between Serbia and Montenegro, to those two princedoms. Other clauses promised the fulfillment of other dreams of Pan-Slav romantic wishfulness in the Near East. All in all, the treaty virtually erased Turkey, except Constantinople and its environs, from the map of Europe.[13]

The exasperated Andrássy blasted the San Stefano document as an "Orthodox Slav sermon," which dismissed the secret prewar bargains he had struck with Russian policy makers as though they had never existed. Andrássy was sure, for instance, that Big Bulgaria, in which Russian soldiers would be stationed for two years, would be the merest puppet of Russia and an instrument of Muscovite dominance in the Near East. The Bosnian clause, moreover, tore the Reichstadt understanding to shreds, while the decision on the Sanjak of Novibazar would hamper peaceful Austrian commercial penetration of the western Balkans.

So the Hapsburg foreign secretary was full of wrath, rendered the more galling by domestic critics who derided him as a dupe, hoodwinked by the sinister, slick men on the Neva. But as Andrássy discovered, neither the Austrian military hierarchs nor the emperor were willing to fight in order to force revisions in the San Stefano program. British opinion cried aloud against items in the San Stefano treaty, particularly the Big Bulgarian creation, and even in some Russian diplomatic circles that arrangement was spoken of as grotesque, and the treaty, as a whole, as gross stupidity.

Austria and Britain now joined forces against the San Stefano treaty. If Russia insisted on carrying it out, she would no doubt have to fight, something which the shaky state of imperial finance and the dubious condition of the armies and of public morale made extremely risky. It was elementary wisdom, in other words, for the Russians to choose, not the sword, but the pen.

Andrássy invited the powers that had signed the Paris treaty of 1856 to attend an international conference at Berlin, where the San Stefano document would be laid on the diplomatic operating table. Already Bismarck had thoughtfully offered himself as the "honest broker" in this gigantic real-estate transaction. After some delay the powers, one and all, accepted the Andrássy invitation. It was not an easy decision for the Russians to take; after all, the arms of the tsar had imposed a treaty that had elicited hosannas in Pan-Slav circles, and now the conqueror was faced with the certainty that the fruits of victory—or some of them—would be snatched away. But consent the Russians did.

In the weeks between the calling of the congress and its actual convocation, European diplomatists quietly consulted on preliminary settlements. Ignatyev, Russia's shrewd ambassador to Turkey and the principal architect of the San Stefano Treaty, conferred with Andrássy on terms of peace that would be acceptable. Although the content of their discussions is still somewhat conjectural, it would seem that the Russian was agreeable to having Austria take over Bosnia-Herzegovina, but would not compromise on the questions of "Big Bulgaria" and the Sanjak of Novibazar.[14] Failure of the diplomatists to come to an understanding set off a panic on the Vienna Stock Exchange.

Ignatyev retired from Vienna without having accomplished anything in the way of blunting Andrássy's anger, and on his arrival home he found that his prestige had suffered further impairment. Rumors of Austrian troop concentrations in Galicia confirmed the suspicion that an armed struggle impended, such as Russia could hardly hope to sustain with success.

After Ignatyev's departure, Andrássy eagerly exchanged ideas with Great Britain, seeking to ascertain whether London would really fight, if necessary, to protect her interests in the Near East. Early in June, after the British and Russians had worked out an accommodation, which faced Austria with the prospect of standing up to Russia alone, Andrássy signed an accord with Britain outlining the common policies to be pursued at the Berlin parley. It was a gentlemen's agreement, in which the two governments bound themselves to insist upon a small Bulgarian state and the British pledged their support for any proposition Austria might offer concerning Bosnia. Austria and Britain, furthermore, would coöperate in the making of other settlements affecting Turkish possessions in Europe. If large-scale mobilization were needed to compel Russia to acquiesce in the Congress verdict, then Great Britain would help Austria financially. Andrássy was also assured of British backing to forestall Russian interference with Austrian shipping at the outlets of the Danube on the Black Sea.

In this manner Andrássy assured himself of British coöperation at the Congress on issues of interest to the Monarchy. Also preparatory to the conference, he agreed with Bismarck to cancel a clause in the treaty that ended the War of 1866, calling for a plebiscite in the Schleswig province. After these diplomatic preliminaries had been finished, Austria could attend the Berlin meeting confident of success.

Home-front critics of territorial expansion in the Balkans which would enlarge the Slav population of the Dual Monarchy and of the vacillating course of Austrian diplomacy embarrassed Andrássy not a little. Time and again in the Austrian parliament and in the delegations, delicate questions were raised on the intentions of the Monarchy in the Balkans, especially in Bosnia-Herzegovina. Repeatedly the foreign minister or his deputy denied that Austria contemplated extending its direct political power to the southeast. Indeed, so late as March of 1878, Andrássy told the delegations that "occupation of Bosnia-Herzegovina is not at all contemplated," adding later, "neither occupation nor annexation has been the aim of this government and will not be in the future . . . so long as our security is not endangered, such aims, I believe, are wholly impossible." [15] When the Austrian delegation was asked to authorize an extraordinary appropriation for military purposes, Herbst and other leaders of the antiexpansionist German Liberal bloc indulged in lively polemics against Andrássy's diplomacy, but the measure was adopted by a vote of thirty-nine to twenty.

In Hungary, too, vigorous objections were raised against the possible annexation of Bosnia. That attitude paralleled Andrássy's own considered judgment, but he was subjected to irresistible pressure by the emperor and military leaders, alert to the strategic importance of Dalmatia's hinterland. Andrássy, of course, was determined that Bosnia-Herzegovina should not fall to Serbia and Montenegro which, as satellites of Russia, would extend the Muscovite encirclement of the Hapsburg Monarchy, and he was intent upon consolidating Austrian influence and economic privileges in the western Balkans. Those objectives required at least the friendship of Turkey as a counterpoise to the aggressive ambitions of Russia.

Early in the Near Eastern crisis Andrássy had tried to preserve Ottoman authority over Bosnia-Herzegovina, as has been explained, by sponsoring a reform program under international auspices; that initiative failed, so he had negotiated with Russia to secure a privileged position in the provinces for Austria without depriving Turkey of sovereignty; his aim did not extend beyond obtaining the right to occupy and administer the area. Indeed, at one point in the evolution of his policy, Andrássy thought of pressing merely for a customs union between Austria and the provinces and for the privilege of sending soldiers in if and when civil disorders occurred.[16] Occupation he thought of as temporary and a necessary evil, and for that limited objective he persuaded the delegations to vote the necessary funds.

British diplomacy, in the meantime, had entered into a provisional understanding with the Russians, cutting down the size of Bulgaria, yet satisfying many of the Russian aspirations at other places in the Ottoman empire. That bargain was supplemented by an Anglo-Turkish convention, permitting British occupation of Cyprus in return for putative guarantees of British protection of Turkish territory in Asia Minor.[17]

Throughout the spring of 1878, the highly excited state of opinion in Austria, in Russia, and in Britain and the clashing national ambitions of the great powers in the Near East filled the European atmosphere with smoke and thunder and carried the Old World to the brink of armed conflict. But happily the secret diplomatic consultations relaxed the tension, and to dispel the war clouds in something like a lasting manner was the responsibility, as it was the achievement, of the Congress of Berlin.

Though diplomatic deals covering many points in dispute had already been negotiated, a wealth of intricate problems awaited final adjustment at the conference, and Russia and Turkey were bent upon battling for their particular interests at every step of the way. In spirit, and up to a point in content, the diplomatists at Berlin wrought substantial modifications in the preconference diplomatic bargains.

v

At Berlin in mid-June of 1878, there assembled one of the grandest arrays of diplomatic talent and energy that had ever been brought together in Europe. Nations, great and small, dispatched their subtlest negotiators and best-informed experts to the great conclave.

Andrássy naturally headed the Austrian delegation, the strongest, no doubt, that participated in the Berlin deliberations. Easily the most picturesque figure at the Congress, the Magyar nobleman, looking "thinner and gypsyer than ever," dazzled the peacemakers with his assortment of brilliant uniforms. One of the Russians pictured Andrássy as "evil and lean with shaggy hair and hideous hands always clasped in front of him." At the outset grave doubts, encouraged by his devious diplomacy during the Balkan crisis, were murmured as to his reliability. Andrássy's intimacy with Bismarck stood him in good stead, and he worked wholeheartedly with the British delegation. When dealing with the smaller diplomatic fry he did not scruple to employ domineering tactics.

Andrássy carried back to Vienna almost everything he had hoped for. At his right hand was Count Alois Károlyi, for many years Hapsburg ambassador in Berlin, and peculiarly gifted for the discharge of the social obligations of diplomacy. Baron Henry Haymerle, a career diplomatist, who was thoroughly versed in the intricacies of the Balkans, and a smart negotiator, completed the Austrian official delegation. Flanking these leaders was a bevy of excellently equipped and hard-working specialists, full of facts and advice.

Russia sent the aged, decrepit, and senile Prince Alexander Gorchakov as titular head of her diplomatists. By this point in his career, his glory had departed, and his technical knowledge of Balkan problems was limited in quantity and fuzzy in quality. Disliked by Bismarck, Gorchakov was distrusted by his first lieutenant, Count Peter Shuvalov, careful, indefatigable, a model diplomatist, with an established reputation for moderation and reliability. Their associates and assistants made up a formidable team, but friction within somewhat enfeebled the Russian delegation.

The defense of British interests was entrusted to Disraeli, prime minister, irritable, arrogant, and pugnacious, and to Lord Salisbury, who had to look after the details which his chief contrived to avoid. Salisbury's conciliatory tactics on secondary issues and his ability to work out compromises with Shuvalov helped substantially in the success of the Berlin meeting.

Great as was the reputation of the other peacemakers, Prince Otto von Bismarck, the presiding officer, towered head and shoulders over the lot. Ill at the time, he brusquely pressed for speedy action and, off stage, in private bargaining, urged accommodations that more than once probably saved the conference from disruption. On controversial points, especially those involving Russia and Austria, the Iron Chancellor endeavored to be judicially impartial, with the result that both disputants accused him of favoritism.

The other delegates at Berlin had little to do with the final decisions. The Turkish spokesmen were taught to be seen rather than heard, and the French and Italian diplomatists were sweetly reasonable; representatives of the Balkan powerlets and of special-interest groups hovered round the edges of the parley without much influencing its course.

Of paramount concern to the Dual Monarchy was, of course, the settlement on Bosnia-Herzegovina, the region that had broken open Pandora's box. Taking into account the repugnance at home to fresh commitments in the Balkans, Andrássy desired to have it appear that the Congress had obliged Austria to occupy the region and that he had acquiesced with sad reluctance. "I do not request that Bosnia-Herzegovina be annexed by Austria-Hungary," he said in a document reciting how the affairs of the Monarchy had been adversely affected by the Bosnian insurrection. "I only urge the congress to reach some decision. Should it appear at all practicable, Austria-Hungary will endorse it." [18] The Russians consented to Austrian occupation provided that the harbor of Antivari was assigned to Montenegro.

It was a surprise to Bismarck, who before the Congress convened had recommended that Austria dispatch troops into Bosnia, to learn that mere occupation, not annexation, was preferred by Andrássy. After Lord Salisbury endorsed the Austrian pretensions and formally proposed an Austrian mandate to occupy and administer the provinces—"left-handed annexation," the Britisher thought it—only the voice of Turkey was raised in opposition and that was quickly smothered. Precise conditions of occupancy, it was announced, would be hammered out by Austrian and Turkish negotiators.

For his monarch Andrássy also secured special privileges in the Sanjak of Novibazar, described as the area "between Serbia and Montenegro stretching in a southeasterly direction to the other side of Mitrovitza." To protect the line of communication to the Aegean, Andrássy insisted that Austria must have the right to garrison the Sanjak and to maintain military and commercial roads there; Turkish sovereignty over and administrative jurisdiction in the area would not be impaired. After a little hesitation, the Russians acquiesced and Austrian wishes were incorporated in the Berlin treaty.[19] High Austrian military officials recommended that Austrian administrative authority should be established as far south as Salonika, but Andrássy was satisfied with the prospect of constructing a railway that would terminate in the "pearl of the Aegean," and he persuaded Francis Joseph of the wisdom of that point of view.

Serbia, which had been alienated from Russia by the latter's sponsorship of Big Bulgaria, turned to Austria for help in its claims to independence from Turkey and territorial aggrandizement. Andrássy drove a hard bargain with Ristić, the Serbian minister for foreign affairs, whom he mistrusted because of his well-known Pan-Serb convictions. For support of Serbian aspirations, Andrássy extorted promises of commercial and railway treaties that would place the little kingdom in economic bondage to its great northern neighbor. At Berlin, Serbia was granted full independence and a modest extension of its territory to the south.

Montenegro, too, was wholly freed from Ottoman lordship and awarded a slice of Turkey. After heated debates with the Austrian delegates, the Russians managed to obtain international sanction for the inclusion of Antivari in Montenegro, though Russia was forbidden to keep warships there. Besides, Montenegro could not undertake the construction of new roads or railways without the approval of Vienna; up to a point, Montenegro, not unlike Serbia, was put in economic servitude to Austria.

Like ancient Gaul, the Big Bulgaria of the San Stefano Treaty was divided into three parts. In making this settlement Andrássy faithfully and vigorously backed the British, for whom the definitive destruction of Big Bulgaria was the supreme issue at the Congress, and it kicked up the most serious controversies. Though extremely reluctant to do so, the Russians were compelled to give ground on almost every point of material importance, but it was conceded that tsarist soldiers might linger in "Bulgaria" for nine months. That part of Bulgaria lying to the north of the Balkan mountains was erected as an autonomous principality, tributary to Turkey; immediately to the south a semiautonomous area, baptized as Eastern Rumelia, was carved out, in which the sultan would exercise direct military and political authority; and what remained of "Big Bulgaria" was retained by Turkey without reservations.

Without much trouble, except in the matter of shipping rights on the Danube, Rumania's case was disposed of. For coöperation with Russia in the war, the Rumanians hoped to keep Bessarabia and to secure a financial indemnity from Turkey, but the Congress would not have it thus. Rather, Bessarabia was transferred to Russia and Rumania was "rewarded" with the sterile Dobrudja district and nearby islands. The loss of Bessarabia cut Rumanian national pride to the quick and presently induced the kingdom to move into the diplomatic orbit of Vienna, which was quite in keeping with the desires of Andrássy. Particularly to protect the rights of the Jewish community, Rumania, whose full liberation from Turkey was recognized, was obliged to guarantee religious freedom to all citizens.

So far as the Danube was concerned, Austria sought the neutralization of the river by international guarantee from the Iron Gates to the Black Sea, which would have kept Russian warships away. That proposal was, however, vetoed, yet the existing Danube commission, which had authority over navigation and kindred matters, was set up as a permanent body. And it was arranged that the Dual Monarchy should undertake the removal of the hazards to shipping at the Iron Gates.

Though Greece had not been at war, it was decided at Berlin that her northern frontier should be rectified at the expense of Turkey.

Questions relating to Asia Minor consumed the energies of the delegates in the final week of the Congress. The future of the port of Batum caused a sharp dispute, second in gravity only to that over the frontiers of Bulgaria; but in the end, Russia secured the city, with the limitation that it should not be fortified. Two other parcels of Turkey-in-Asia were also allotted to Russia, which, *ipso facto,* brought into force the preconference convention between Turkey and Britain, respecting the island of Cyprus and British guarantees to preserve the territorial integrity of the section of the Ottoman empire lying in Asia Minor.

VI

Shortly after the adjournment of the Berlin Congress, Austria, armed with a European mandate, prepared to assume its responsibilities in Bosnia-Herzegovina. Andrássy, lightheartedly, calculated that military occupation would be little more than a formality—a march in of a regiment of Hussars accompanied by a band of musicians! An imperial Austrian proclamation announced to the Bosniacs that the sultan had entrusted Francis Joseph with the protection of the province, and promised that peace and prosperity would reign and that cherished local customs would be scrupulously respected. Into the promised land moved a small army of occupation, whose commander, Baron Philippovič, adjured his men, "It is not to victory that I lead you, but to hard work, to be done in the service of Humanity and Civilization."

Instead of welcoming the Hapsburg troops as liberators, Moslems and Orthodox Bosniacs, many of whom had defied the Turk in 1875, took up arms. They lived very close to the earth, these Bosniacs, and though that earth was penurious and unrewarding they loved and coveted it and saw no reason for exchanging Ottoman domination for Hapsburg. What the Orthodox leaders desired was political union either with Serbia or with Montenegro; only the more affluent citizens and the articulate Roman Catholics rejoiced over the verdict delivered at Berlin. Albanian mountaineers and some Turkish officers and regular soldiers rallied around the Bosnian rebels, though the Turkish government held studiously aloof from the insurrection. The natives put up a fierce resistance, resorting to guerrilla tactics for which the configuration of the region was so admirably adapted.

Additional Austrian soldiers had to be shipped in, and with the capitulation of Sarajevo, the headquarters of the insurgency, the back of the rising was broken, although sporadic fighting continued for several weeks. To effect the conquest of the provinces almost 150,000 Hapsburg troops in all were employed—more Hungarians than Austrians, the Magyars characteristically complained—and casualties passed the 5,000 mark. Insurgent troops exceeded 90,000, not a sixth of whom had formal military training; gruesome outrages committed by the Hapsburg armies lengthened the casualty lists of the Bosniac rebels.

The rebellion was crushed, but at the cost of undying hatred among the natives and with a loss of military prestige such as a giant sustains when he unsheathes the sword against a pigmy. Memories of the "holy and heroic rising" against Turkish tyranny in 1875 and of the sturdy resistance against the Austrian occupation in 1878 were enshrined in popular Serb ballads and folk legends and handed on to later generations. Revolt was no longer feasible, but conspiracy and assassination, using dagger and bomb, might yet be the path to freedom. "History" made an imperishable impression upon the minds of the fanatical and the irresponsible among the Bosnian Serbs.[20]

While the subjugation of Bosnia was in train, the Ballplatz entered into negotiations with Turkey to define the Austrian position in the provinces and in the Sanjak. Parliamentary controversies, rising bitterness in Constantinople over Austrian military methods, Russian intrigue, and suspicions that Andrássy coveted more territory than was assigned at Berlin hampered the deliberations. But at length in April of 1879, a detailed convention was concluded, acknowledging the sultan's sovereignty over Bosnia-Herzegovina and his peculiar rights there as head of the Moslem community. Austria, moreover, promised to engage Turks as officials until natives were adequately trained, to ensure religious liberty, to devote all revenues collected to provincial needs, and to allow Turkish currency to circulate. These reservations and pledges apart, Hapsburg authority in the provinces was thorough.

Bosnia's status in the constitutional complex of the Dual Monarchy was worked out in an ingenious way. Instead of adding the area to either Austria or Hungary, or making it a *Reichsland*, after the manner of Alsace-Lorraine, or putting it on a plane with Austria or Hungary—alternatives which the Magyars in particular rejected—the provinces were placed under the supreme jurisdiction of the common Hapsburg ministry of finance. That branch of the joint administration was selected because it had fewer burdens than the other two departments. The finance minister was charged with supervision over local administration and finance, and made responsible to the delegations for the manner in which he performed his duties.

Legislative power for Bosnia-Herzegovina was vested in the monarch, who would issue ordinances having the force of law. Local administrative authority was entrusted to a governor, *Landeschef*, in command of the armed forces, and a civilian associate, *Ziviladlatus*, assisted by a council composed of the heads of the political, financial, judicial, and public-works bureaus. That division of responsibility, between an army man and a civilian, turned out to be productive of much dissension and strife.

Local expenses would be defrayed as far as possible out of local revenues and deficits would be covered by appropriations authorized by the delegations. Public-works projects, including the construction of railways, and undertakings that affected the affairs of the rest of the Monarchy, required the approval of the Austrian and Hungarian parliaments, and no modification in the Bosnian governmental structure could be carried out without the concurrence of the two parliaments.

Within a very short time Hapsburg officials, mainly Croats, who were detested by the native Orthodox population as minions of a foreign ruler, had supplanted the Turks. Ottoman currency was banned, the Austrian system of weights and measures was introduced, the provinces were embraced in the Hapsburg postal and customs system, and young men were made liable to military conscription. For most practical purposes, in other words, Bosnia-Herzegovina became an integral part of the realm of the Hapsburgs; Turkish sovereignty extended little beyond the rights that Moslems possessed of murmuring the sultan's name in prayers and of flying the Ottoman flag over mosques during prayer time.

Under the convention of 1879 with Turkey, Austria was also permitted to station garrisons for an indeterminate span of time in three key towns of the Sanjak of Novibazar, though it was given no part in administrative, judicial, or financial affairs. Accordingly, in the autumn of 1879 a small detachment of Hapsburg soldiers moved in, without exciting any popular resistance or friction with Turkish officials. These troops were an insurance that Austrian commercial interests in the district would be safeguarded and they blocked the possibility of a merger between Serbia and Montenegro. Britain's Lord Salisbury, in a public address, rejoiced over the "Austrian sentinel" who barred a Russian advance into the lower Balkans, and Andrássy shared that feeling of satisfaction, but he would have preferred that the Britisher think his thoughts and not speak them, for they tended to enflame public sentiment in Russia and to aggravate Muscovite antagonism toward the Dual Monarchy.

As it was, Austria had trouble enough with Russia in the execution of the articles of the Berlin treaty touching the eastern Balkans, especially the Bulgarian settlement. Throughout critical months of dispute and grave tensions, Austria and Britain loyally coöperated, and the isolated Russians were forced to give way at almost every turn. By August of 1879 boundary lines had been drawn, a native government had been set up in autonomous Bulgaria, with Alexander of Battenberg as prince, a working administrative regime had been established in Eastern Rumelia, and the last soldier of the tsar had been withdrawn from the Balkans.

VII

Andrássy returned from the Berlin conference, bringing peace with honor and striking diplomatic successes: the occupation of Bosnia-Herzegovina; rights in the Sanjak of Novibazar; guarantees for Austrian trade routes overland and on the Danube; safeguards for economic interests in the deeper Balkans—and, not least, confirmed friendship with the Iron Chancellor of Germany. It has been said on high authority that "Russia acquired Bosnia-Herzegovina for us! Russia made the sacrifices but the advantages . . . accrued to us." [21] Yet Andrássy's Balkan policies had definitely antagonized two factions in the Dual Monarchy: Francis Joseph and many diplomatic and military leaders, proponents of expansion who thought the Magyar had not obtained enough, and civilian political groups, which felt he had got too much.

Backed by the columns of the *Neue Freie Presse,* opponents of a forward course in the Balkans complained sharply over Andrássy's diplomacy, and protestations mounted with the actual military occupation of Bosnia-Herzegovina. The foreign minister in fact became the most unpopular figure in the Monarchy. One hundred sixty Austrian deputies protested to the emperor that "irreparable sacrifices in blood and money have been made before the representative assemblies have been permitted [even] to discuss the Treaty of Berlin according to their constitutional right." [22]

The presentation of the Berlin Treaty to the Austrian reichsrat unloosed acrid criticism of monarchical diplomacy, condemnation of the dispatch of troops into Bosnia without parliamentary approval and of the inadequacy of the military preparations that had resulted in unnecessary shedding of blood. Premier Auersperg and his colleagues handed in their resignations but continued to carry on their official functions. Defending his course of action, Andrássy asserted that the occupation of Bosnia would come to an end once the objects for which it was undertaken were achieved and Turkey had reimbursed the Monarchy for the expenditures that had been made and had given solid guarantees that order and prosperity would prevail in the future. Gladstone, it is worth recalling, made analogous professions with regard to Egypt, under not dissimilar circumstances.

Actually, Andrássy's parliamentary adversaries—they belonged principally to the Herbst wing of the German Liberals—could do nothing to stay the march of events. But by their criticisms they might (and indeed did) undermine Andrássy's public prestige and speed along his retirement. By a majority of forty-two the Austrian reichsrat ratified the Treaty of Berlin.

Similar denunciations of Andrássy's policies and their cost resounded in the Hungarian parliament and press, most stridently in the "Independence" and extreme conservative sections. Premier Coloman Tisza retorted that occupation of Bosnia-Herzegovina was imperative in order to counteract Russian-sponsored Pan-Slavism. Unfriendly critics turned on the prime minister, precipitated a ministerial crisis, and forced drastic reconstruction of the cabinet. But, in the end, the Hungarian legislature, like the Austrian, confirmed the Berlin Treaty by a decisive margin. Andrássy had expected hostility from Herbst and his followers, but the vigor of the assault on the part of some of his Hungarian countrymen surprised and wounded him grievously, and helped to form his decision to retire from the Ballplatz.

In both Hapsburg legislatures factionalism and divergencies over foreign policy had run high, yet devotion to the dynasty and unwillingness to thwart the known minimum wishes of the emperor in the Balkans had triumphed. Francis Joseph was thought of as above the battle; and, in April of 1879, the silver wedding anniversary of the imperial and royal couple was celebrated with enthusiastic and spontaneous rejoicing all over the realm.

VIII

By extending her authority into Bosnia-Herzegovina, Austria invited fresh trouble with the Kingdom of Italy.[23] In the early phases of the Balkan troubles advocates of Irredentism in Italy intensified their agitations, hoping that Austria would become so enmeshed in the imbroglio with Russia that it would be willing to purchase Italian good will by ceding the areas containing Italian populations. It was an encouragement to Italian extremism that a "Liberal" ministry was at the helm in Italy, with the stanch Irredentist, Crispi, in its personnel. At the death of Victor Emmanuel II, king-liberator, early in 1878, the popular Garibaldi asserted that "the call of the patriots of Trieste and Trent must find an echo in the hearts of all Italians, and the yoke of Austria, no better than that of the Turk, must once for all be broken from the necks of our brethren." [24]

After it was learned that Austria might establish herself in Bosnia, demands for compensation to Italy rose prodigiously. Sections of the Italian press took up the hue and cry and a new and militant Irredentist society enlisted something like a hundred thousand members. No ministry could remain utterly indifferent to this ferment; yet it was well known that Austria was of no mind to cede territory, if for no other reason, because that would tend to intensify separatist tendencies among Slav and Rumanian minorities. The "great press" of Vienna charged the Italian ministry with trafficking with the Irredentists and forced the recall of certain Italian officials stationed in Vienna, who were accused of espionage. Andrássy was much annoyed by a fruitless Italian effort to further the interests of Montenegro—the first overt gesture of united Italy in the western Balkans.[25]

During a tour round the major European capitals in 1877, Crispi had unsuccessfully solicited support for compensation to Italy in the event that Austria gained Bosnia. All that he got for his trouble was pointed suggestions that Italy might pick up land in northern Africa at Turkey's expense; even Andrássy thought that was a legitimate sphere for Italian expansionist appetite.

Although in his youth Count Luigi Corti had engaged in anti-Austrian intrigues and as Italian ambassador in Constantinople had sided with Russia against Austria, he accepted the office of foreign minister in March of 1878 on the understanding that a *rapprochement* with the northern neighbor would be sought and that the occupation of Bosnia-Herzegovina would be approved. In the instructions that he carried to the Berlin Congress, Corti was told not to put in a claim for compensation unless Austrian occupation of Bosnia should be unqualified and permanent. At the meeting, accordingly, the Italian acquiesced in all the Hapsburg claims with scarcely a murmur of dissent.

When Austrian troops began to move into Bosnia, confirming popular Italian suspicions, and Corti returned from Berlin with clean but empty hands, Irredentists organized public meetings and indulged in violent demonstrations against Austria, "the crime of Berlin," and the "incompetent and pusillanimous" Italian government. "At Berlin we were treated as the least important nation of Europe. We were insulted and disgraced," cried Crispi, and what he said Italy quite generally felt.[26] Violent outbursts occurred throughout the length and breadth of the peninsula, the most serious taking place in Venice and Rome; in the "Queen of the Adriatic," an inflamed mob stormed the Austrian consulate and committed acts of vandalism, while in Rome the Austrian embassy itself was assaulted and insulted.

The Austrian ambassador, Baron Henry Haymerle, was keenly disliked in Italy because he was held responsible for a pamphlet, actually written by his brother, sometime Hapsburg military attaché in Rome, that was sharply critical of Italian politics and military forces. The closing observation of the pamphlet that "Austria can perhaps lose a province in an unfortunate war . . . never however will it voluntarily give up a region that has belonged to it for a thousand years," aptly condensed the Austrian official opinion on the matter.[27] So great did the Irredentist furore grow that doubts were expressed in foreign circles whether the Italian government was strong enough to curb it. Foreign Secretary Corti, who was popularly branded as a traitor, and the Italian ministers of war and marine were obliged to resign their offices.

In September of 1878 a plot was organized, with the knowledge of some Italian government officials, for an armed invasion of Austria. Local rioting among Austrian Italians reinforced the belief that a general insurrection could easily be fomented. In readiness for any challenge, Austria increased the defense forces in the vicinity of the Italian border, and, before the year was out, the veteran soldier, Archduke Albrecht, was placed in command. But the Italian government let it be known that it would apply force, were that necessary, to prevent the extremists from moving into Austria, and that declaration, combined with the reluctance or the inability of the *Italianissimi* in Austria to rebel, caused the conspiracy to evaporate. In spite of the prudent policy that the Italian government followed during the crisis, the suspicion somehow got abroad that it had identified itself with radical, violent Irredentism. As for the Irredentist movement itself, it never, thereafter, wholly lost the bellicose and militant character it took on in the summer of 1878.

Irredentist excitement, it is true, receded from the heights of 1878, but it flared up anew the following year and with Garibaldi as titular leader another project for a violent assault upon Austria was prepared. The murder of the Italian consul in Sarajevo and the death of the Irredentist chief,

General Giuseppe Avezzana, a disciple of Mazzini, furnished texts for extremist homilies and demonstrations condemnatory of Austria. The general's funeral was a state affair; Crispi participated in it, and the obituary address delivered by Matteo Renato Imbriani, "a fanatic from a family of fanatics," provoked a stir in Vienna; more soldiers were ordered into the Tyrol.

Rome took the hint, announcing once more that it would prevent activities that compromised good relations with Austria. Italy's real task, explained a government spokesman, the real *Italia Irredenta,* was the improvement of economic conditions within the kingdom; that job would require all the energies the country could muster and victory on that front would not fall like manna from heaven. Not very long after the most rabid manifestations of anti-Austrian feeling United Italy had ever known, the Roman government entered into an alliance with the hated Hapsburgs—the famous Triple Alliance of 1882.

IX

Andrássy crowned and closed his career as foreign secretary by arranging an alliance with Germany that was destined to endure until both the Hapsburg and Hohenzollern dynasties crumpled in the autumnal fury of 1918. Personal friendship between the Magyar and Bismarck, dating from Andrássy's Germanophilism before and during the War of 1870, had deepened in the stormy seventies. Step by step Andrássy moved toward closer intimacy with Germany, much against the will and the wish of an influential party at the Viennese court.

At the Berlin Congress, Bismarck's backing had stood Andrássy in good stead, and the decisions made there infuriated the Russians, wrecking the League of the Three Emperors. Andrássy strongly desired a solid alliance with Germany pointed against Russia, which Britain and Italy might subsequently enter. With Germany as an ally, Andrássy reasoned that Russian ambitions could be held in check and the freshly acquired Austrian position in the western Balkans could be consolidated.

Bismarck, on his side, was well aware that his diplomacy had produced grave deterioration in German relations with Russia. He who had benevolently offered himself as an honest broker at the Berlin conference was charged with partiality which had brought about a grievous diplomatic humiliation for Russia. Russian friendship had been invaluable for the Iron Chancellor in the epoch of empire building and he had now rewarded her with shocking ingratitude; or so, at least, it was thought by the men on the Neva.

The evidence, however, points to the conclusion that Bismarck's course at the Berlin Congress had in reality benefited Russia. His underlying purpose had been to assist both Austria and Russia in bettering their positions in what he considered their rightful spheres in the Balkans, the first in the western area, the other in the eastern. Russian gains at Berlin were in fact considerable, although not so large as the doctrinal nonsense of Pan-Slavism had bemused the gullible into expecting. Furious Russian press criticisms, ominous military maneuvers near the German border, and suspicion that official Russia was courting the friendship of vengeful France, seem to have persuaded the Iron Chancellor that an attack was being matured, an interpretation by no means wholly shared by other influential Germans, the Emperor William included.

Could Bismarck have suited his own inclination, he would gladly and immediately have resurrected the League of the Three Emperors, but that being out of the question, Germany had either to tie up with Russia or Austria or be left in diplomatic isolation. The last alternative might have had as its sequel a reconciliation between the two eastern monarchies, as was being urged in fact by a powerful Austrian military clique, or more likely by the growth of Anglo-Austrian collaboration, exhibited at the Berlin Congress and before, into an entente, to which France might conceivably attach herself. For Germany to ally with Russia, were that at all possible, would have antagonized Austria and Britain at a moment when acute domestic troubles in the tsardom raised doubts of her value as an ally. All things considered, Bismarck reasoned that Germany's safety would be best secured by close alignment with Austria against Russia.

It was a difficult task for Bismarck to convince his master, William I, of the necessity and the wisdom of an alliance with Austria. The ruler, indeed, assented only after signs suggested that Russian policy makers were coquetting with France and after other German leaders lined up with Bismarck in advocacy of tight bonds with Austria.

Bismarck, in the meantime, had been communing fruitfully with Andrássy. At Gastein in August of 1879 the Magyar seems to have convinced him that the Dual Monarchy had no intention of arranging a deal with Russia; rather it desired an alliance with Germany, and to effect that objective Andrássy, who had decided to quit the Ballplatz, would stay on until negotiations were finished. Much as Bismarck tried, he could not persuade Andrássy to undertake a commitment against France; any treaty would have to be designed to protect both signatories against Russia directly.

Draft treaties prepared by both foreign offices served as the basis for further discussions when Bismarck appeared in Vienna in September of 1879. The hearty ovation given the chancellor on that occasion by the Viennese populace attested that the memories of the "brothers' war" of 1866 had grown dim. Again Andrássy insisted that Austria could not assume a commitment that might obligate her to fight France, and Bismarck had grudgingly to acquiesce.

By the terms of the famous alliance of 1879, if either Austria or Germany was attacked by Russia, the other signatory would rally to its support with all its military forces. Should either be attacked by a country other than Russia, its ally would pursue a policy of benevolent neutrality. If, however, Russia should aid a country with which either signatory was at war, its ally would fight shoulder to shoulder. Made for a term of five years, and renewable, the treaty would be kept strictly secret, although the contents might be divulged to Russia, in the event that Muscovite war preparations seemed to be menacing.[28] This treaty created an alliance essentially defensive in character, a mutual safeguard against Russia. There was no provision for military agreements by the general staffs of the two countries, for Bismarck feared that arrangements of that order might unwisely bind the hands of diplomacy in an hour of international crisis. Not until 1909 were there even regular conferences between German and Austrian military staffs for the consideration of plans of campaign, distribution of troops, and the like.[29]

It was no small matter to persuade William I to approve the alliance, for he had consented only to a general treaty, not one pointed against Russia alone. Only after Bismarck and other prominent German statesmen made acceptance the price of their continuance in office would the emperor agree to sign, and on October 17, 1879, ratifications were formally exchanged. On that very day, Lord Salisbury, the British foreign minister, declared that all those who valued the peace of Europe and the independence of nations might regard the reported defensive alliance between Germany and Austria as "good tidings of great joy." Disraeli, however, felt less confident, and his reservations were shared by many another foreign statesman.

Andrássy evidently hoped that the alliance with Germany would divorce that country from Russia and would be the first link in a grandiose chain of partnership that would embrace Britain and Italy. In that, however, he was deceived, for in 1881 something like reconciliation between Germany and Russia was achieved and these countries revived, with Austria, the League of the Three Emperors.

Austro-Germans, especially those with Pan-German leanings, and the Magyar ruling caste looked upon the diplomatic bond with Germany as something natural and altogether desirable. The dominant Polish aristocracy, whose hatred for Russia matched that of the Magyars, applauded the German alignment. Only rigidly conservative Austrian diplomatists and military chiefs clung to the belief that an alliance with Russia would have been more judicious, more in conformity with monarchical interest. From the beginning, Austrian Slav leaders in general, except the Poles, disapproved of the

German orientation, and in time they manifested active hostility toward the alliance.

x

Scarcely was the ink dry on the German treaty when Andrássy handed in his resignation as foreign minister, something he had decided upon more than a year before. Physical illness, the loss of personal prestige which his Russian and Balkan policies had produced, and dislike of the Slav twist that Francis Joseph was giving to the internal affairs of the Austrian half of the Monarchy, prompted his decision. He felt that having completed the alliance with Germany he had achieved the maximum of success and anything that might follow would be in the nature of anticlimax.

It is fair to say that during Andrássy's tenure at the Ballplatz the prestige and influence of the Hapsburg Monarchy were elevated to a height unknown since the great Prince Metternich had been swept off the scene. Proudly the haughty Magyar remarked, "I had rather leave the stage a favorite opera singer than go on till I am broken down and have to sing at cafés." That was a pretty figure of speech, though hardly an accurate one.

Francis Joseph, who during the peak of the tension with Russia had debated dismissing Andrássy but had decided against it as unwise until the Russian controversy had been ironed out and ties with Germany had been solidified, allowed him to nominate his successor. Andrássy's first choice, Count Alois Károlyi, the distinguished ambassador in Berlin, declined because of his inexperience in parliamentary affairs and his disinclination to shoulder the worries of the foreign office; so Andrássy turned to his other principal colleague at the Berlin Congress, Baron Henry Haymerle, who accepted.

After his retirement Andrássy was occasionally called upon to advise the emperor on foreign affairs, but his expectation that he, whose policies had done so much to rehabilitate the Monarchy's diplomatic standing, would again be put in charge of the Ballplatz, once he had recovered his health, was never realized. He engaged actively in Hungarian politics as a member of the house of magnates, and at meetings of the delegations he freely expressed his convictions on foreign problems, not least his suspicions and mistrust of Russia.

Always the grand seigneur, dwelling in the sumptuous surroundings of his country estate, Andrássy lived on until 1890, honored by his Magyar fellows as an architect of the Settlement of 1867 and as the ablest diplomatist his nation had produced. At his death he was given an earned place in the Hungarian national pantheon.

CHAPTER SEVEN

THE HAPSBURGS AND THE
AUSTRIAN ARISTOCRACY

VIENNA SHELTERED THE MOST VENERABLE REIGNING FAMILY OF Europe, and the proudest. For centuries the House of Hapsburg had furnished dukes, archdukes, kings, and emperors to preside over the political destinies of a continent. Rival dynasties rose, some of them fell, but the Hapsburgs seemed immune to the common fate of political families. To be sure, the house experienced eras of impotence as well as of grandeur and, with the exception of Charles V, it gave Europe no royal statesman worthy to be classed in the very top rank. Maria Theresa, however, vies with Elizabeth of England and Catherine II of Russia for the title of the most distinguished of women monarchs. Her son, Joseph II of the "Enlightenment," was full of grandiose ideas for the rejuvenation and modernization of his state, but at his death the realm was in a condition of extreme turbulence. Francis I had contrived somehow to outride the storms of the French Revolution and Napoleon, carrying on in a truly authoritarian manner, which his grandson, Francis Joseph I, the penultimate Hapsburg sovereign, found wholly admirable.

Toward the end of the 1870's, Francis Joseph reached the golden epoch of his career. The constitutional quarrel with the Magyars which he had inherited had been settled for the nonce at least; the Slavic orientation that had been given Austrian domestic politics promised to placate the dissident northern Slavs; and the fierce social discord unloosed by the *Krach* of 1873 had largely spent itself. The ruler's fond dream of rewinning at least something of his family's traditional influence in the politics of German Europe had been frustrated, so he had aligned himself diplomatically with the successful Hohenzollern rival, and in the rising economic and political might of the German empire he saw the strong right arm of his own realm. That, however, did not mean that his fundamental opinion of the Hohenzollerns had changed; parvenus they were and parvenus they remained.

All men are enigmas to everyone, including themselves, and Francis Joseph was no exception, for he was not one but several personalities. An English journalist, who was anxious to obtain opinions on the ruler and his traits, addressed inquiries to an array of Austrian public men about the man, and learned nothing substantial. Finally he approached the Magyar, Khuen-Héderváry, who was for years close to the monarch, his personal confidante indeed. "You ask me," he replied, "to tell what I do not know. If anybody knows the emperor I suppose I know him; but the truth is that I do not know him and never shall . . . The monarch takes counsel of none save the Deity to whom alone he feels responsible." [1]

In his personal life Francis Joseph displayed many of the qualities of the stoical Spartan, without warmth and devoid of sentimentality. Tragic domestic experiences, which earned him the sobriquet of "the most sorely tried character in modern history," had remarkably little lasting effect upon him. From boyhood he was accustomed to the stiff formalism of the military barracks and the stern etiquette of Europe's most punctilious court, and those traditions he dogmatically preserved and enforced as essential for imperial prestige. He avoided literature dealing with modern and contemporary trends of thought and had a positive aversion for theoretical study; newspapers he scarcely bothered about, except in the form of terse summaries placed on his work desk each morning.

Simplicity in personal living was certainly one of the earmarks of Francis Joseph. Luxury made almost no appeal to him; his plain tastes in clothing and food lasted as long as his life, and Viennese may still point with pride to the iron bedstead in the imperial summer palace of Schönbrunn on which the frugal monarch once slept. In the Hofburg in Vienna, the favorite Hapsburg residence for six hundred years, he frowned upon up-to-date improvements that would make living easier and more comfortable. Illumination was provided by horrible kerosene lamps that smoked constantly; if the chimneys broke, as sometimes they did, the company sat in darkness until repairs were made or replacements brought in. The primitive toilet facilities in the palace so irritated Stephanie, Francis Joseph's daughter-in-law, that she had two bathrooms installed at her own expense. Even in his conversation, the monarch was simple and changeless; his talk was sober, monotonous, soporific.

On each day that was spent in the capital, Francis Joseph followed an unvarying routine. Usually he rose at five, much to the annoyance of some of his ministers; it is said that when the emperor and King Edward VII visited one of their favorite spas they frequently met at five in the morning, the emperor just beginning his day's work, Victoria's pleasure-loving son en route to bed. After a meager breakfast, he set about dispatching regular business and writing brief, conventional congratulations and formal condolences. Then he devoted himself to interviews with ministers, generals, and other prominent personages, always austerely and ceremonially.

The spheres of activity of state servants were defined with something like mathematical precision. Austrian ministers complained that they could not make even passing reference to Hungarian affairs; to which Francis Joseph replied that for Hungarian business he had Hungarian ministers—and experience had taught him that they were a tougher lot to deal with, exceedingly jealous of their kingdom's rights, than the Austrians. For high offices this "civil-servant" emperor preferred men like himself: masters of routine, skeptical of novelties, meticulous, persevering, reticent; he insisted that ministers should refrain from public discussion of public affairs as far as possible.

Almost all transactions had to be executed for Francis Joseph in writing. Such newfangled contrivances as the typewriter and telephone he shunned, but of the telegraph, which had been invented while he was very young, he had no dread. Only with extreme reluctance would he enter a motorcar in his latter days.

So much of the monarch's time and energy were consumed with the details of public and household affairs that he was unable to deal effectively with the broader and deeper problems in his monarchy of many tongues, though he was by no means unversed in them.[2]

Another legitimate criticism of Francis Joseph as ruler was that he was brutally callous in the way in which he dismissed officials, even the highest, not excluding members of the judiciary, however faithfully they may have served. If a public man seemed to have outlived his usefulness to the dynasty, if the sacrifice of an official seemed necessary to expiate a political blunder, he was unceremoniously, though with utter politeness, cast into the discard and forgotten.

Throughout his long reign Francis Joseph was guided by strong convictions of personal dignity and of high, even sacred responsibility, half by heritage, half in emulation of the "Iron Tsar," Nicholas I, who had helped to save his realm in 1849. He conceived of his authority in terms of the divine right to rule and the grace of God. To Theodore Roosevelt he described himself as the last European monarch of the old school. Down to his dying day he referred to "my house" and "my people" with greater assurance than any other Western ruler of the age. For popular participation in government this archconservative had positive detestation; only grudgingly and with much misgiving had he accepted the principle of constitutionalism, and when, late in life, he spoke out in advocacy of manhood suffrage, it was not because of reasoned belief in the principle but rather as a matter of political expediency. His philosophy of government was definitely authoritarian, cloaked in the institutions of parliamentarianism. Sense of public duty was strong within him; forced into bed on the very eve of his death, he is said to have protested, "I still have much to do . . . I must get on with my work." [3]

Always Francis Joseph was faced with the thorny problem of nationalities, but long experience made him a master in the difficult and devious art of alleviating that peril by granting concessions. He contrived to stand above all nationalities, all social classes, all political parties; the large and permanent bureaucracy was his effective tool, the army his loyal instrument, and everything touching his military prerogatives he guarded intransigently. While not unready to make concessions to Magyar nationalism, for example, in other spheres of government, he was absolutely inflexible on the unity of the monarchical army.

Foreign policy Francis Joseph regarded as the peculiar province of the monarch, and that he shaped, at least in the first decades of his reign, more fully than he did internal affairs. Diplomatic dispatches he scrutinized carefully, and he knew the language of the diplomatic profession to a nicety; in the use of delicate shades of expression he was the peer of a foreign-office specialist. In his last years, as his physical and mental powers declined and he isolated himself more and more, he was obliged, perforce, to follow closely the advice of diplomatic and military specialists.

His puritanical personal traits, which contrasted vividly with the habits of some of the members of the imperial Hapsburg household, were matched by extraordinary religious piety. To the end he cherished clerical teachings that had been inculcated in his youth by Jesuit fathers. A loyal and devout son of the Church, he found in the absolutes of Catholicism the satisfactions and the consolations required to buoy up his spirit in a life that was replete with bewildering dynastic vicissitudes and harsh domestic tragedies. And he was alert to the value of Catholicism as one of the very pillars, one of the strong unifying forces, of his realm.

Quite openly, even ostentatiously, he performed his penitential obligations. Regularly on Maundy Thursday (Gründonnerstag) the emperor washed the feet of a dozen or more old men brought to the Hofburg from an almshouse. Notables of the realm and curious foreigners were permitted to witness the elaborate pageant. Behind the chairs on which the humble pensioners were seated, guardsmen stood in resplendent dress uniforms and helmets with flowing plumes. The monarch entered, flanked by religious and secular dignitaries and followed by archdukes; solemnly he walked up to the awed old men, who had removed their right boots and socks and had a linen cloth across their knees. While a high churchman read from the Scriptures, Francis Joseph, half kneeling, washed and dried the foot of each man with fine linen. That done, the honored guests were given new socks and boots, ate a meal, with the monarch as waiter, received purses of cash, and then were driven back to the poor house.[4]

Annually on Corpus Christi day Francis Joseph and his ministers paraded through Vienna in a hallowed religious procession, and, before an altar erected in the middle of a street, the sovereign knelt on a cushion and devoutly told his beads. At a Eucharistic congress in Vienna in 1912, he obediently opened and closed the door of the carriage in which the papal legate rode, and then, with head uncovered, knelt piously in a public square. Upon the church and her clergy he showered gifts with the utmost liberality. Francis Joseph stubbornly declined to pay his respects to the king of Italy in Rome, though his political advisers repeatedly urged him to do so, because of the quarrel the latter had with the Vatican over the temporal possessions of the papacy, and in the knowledge that the papacy would regard a call upon the "robber king" as a grievous offence.

For all his devotion to Catholicism, Francis Joseph did not hesitate to disagree with the church authorities or to interfere in ecclesiastical affairs if he thought higher interests of state required it. The belief that he was subservient to the higher clergy is as legendary as the parallel tales of the dominance of the Freemasons and the Jews over him.[5] Even his favorite tutor, Cardinal Rauscher of Vienna, could not persuade him to veto the Austrian ecclesiastical reforms of the seventies, and, in the late eighties, when Pope Leo XIII contemplated withdrawing from Italy because of friction with the Quirinal, Francis Joseph strongly advised him against it and flatly disapproved of a papal plan to solicit international guarantees for the safety of the Pope's person and palace. In 1903 he successfully blocked the elevation of Cardinal Rampolla, Leo XIII's first lieutenant, to the papal chair, apparently because of the cardinal's imagined hostility to the diplomatic coalition to which the Danube Monarchy belonged and because of the emperor's personal dislike of him, due to his attitude at the time of the death of Crown Prince Rudolph and to controversies over the selection of bishops.[6]

During World War I Cardinal Piffl of Vienna, on instructions from the Vatican, conveyed to the emperor the Pope's hope that hostilities might swiftly be terminated or, failing that, that the area of strife might not be extended. Crimson with rage, the old ruler pushed the Cardinal from the reception room, for he was interfering in Caesar's business. "For three new regiments of cavalry," dryly remarked Count Paar, one of Francis Joseph's personal adjutants, "the emperor would give all his bishops."[7]

Unlike the up-and-coming William II of Germany, Francis Joseph restricted his social relations to the conservative nobility and the most exalted bureaucrats, as seemed proper to an earthly divinity, and that strengthened his ingrained aversion to innovation, to new ideas. In his closest male friend,

Albert, crown prince of Saxony and subsequently king, he had boundless confidence, and they had many pleasures and dislikes in common.

After the death of his wife in 1898, Francis Joseph absented himself more and more from court society, finding innocent companionship and intellectual friendship in Katharina Schratt, a sprightly, amiable, close-lipped, and gracious bourgeois actress of Vienna whom Empress Elizabeth had also admired. "Katha," who had a cottage on the edge of the Schönbrunn gardens, he saw or wrote to daily, and the Viennese affectionately labeled him "Herr Schratt." She seems studiously to have avoided intrigue and exerted little if any influence on public affairs. Intimate though their friendship was, Francis Joseph never unbent sufficiently to use the familiar *du* in addressing her; that was reserved for his nearest relatives.[8]

For hunting, his only absorbing diversion, Francis Joseph had a genuine passion, as aristocrats had from time immemorial. In the saddle even in old age he sat as straight as a ramrod and took every ditch. Each autumn with a few companions he withdrew to his favorite hunting preserve at pleasant Ischl, near Salzburg; there in leather breeches, bare-kneed, with a green hunter's jacket, a Tyrolese hat with a quaint "Gamsbart," and hobnailed shoes, the ruler of all the Austrias thoroughly enjoyed living. There he entertained the notables of this world, such as the German kaiser, William II, and Edward, Prince of Wales, later Edward VII, neither of whom Francis Joseph really liked. After one of Edward's visits he commented, "Wales was so delighted that there seems to be some danger of his wishing to repeat his experiences." [9]

Francis Joseph's personal characteristics, his tireless devotion to public duty decade after decade, made him an object of general, if not universal, veneration. Britain had its Victoria, the Danube Monarchy had its Francis Joseph, and just as the queen-empress' long, dignified reign endeared her to her many and motley peoples, so the emperor-king was revered by his subjects, only more so, for respect for royalty was more deeply entrenched in conservative Austria-Hungary than in democratic, industrialized Britain.

His role as the linchpin of the realm, the human cement, was generally recognized and it was openly predicted that his departure would be the signal for the downfall of the Monarchy. As things turned out, the bells that tolled the passing of Francis Joseph also sounded the death knell of his realm.

To the public popularity of Francis Joseph, instruction in the schools of the realm made an unmistakable contribution. Historical lore and patriotic exercises glorified the accomplishments of the Hapsburg House and extolled the majesty, the achievements, and the exemplary virtues of the wearer of the crown. The monarch's portrait adorned the walls of every classroom and children were taught dynastic loyalty by the Hapsburg anthem, set to the moving music of Joseph Haydn.

> God save, God guard
> Our emperor, our country!
> Powerful with the Faith's protection
> Shall he lead us with wise hand!
> The crown of his fathers
> Shall defend us from all enemies;
> Closely with the throne of the Hapsburgs
> Austria's fate remains united.[10]

Not unnaturally, in minority areas of the realm where consciousness of nationality was on the march, enthusiasm for the ruler and the dynasty lacked something of the ardor displayed in solidly German-speaking districts.

This sketch of Francis Joseph may well be concluded with the impression that he—and Viennese society—made upon Theodore Roosevelt,[11] who was his guest in 1910.

"The Emperor was an interesting man . . . He did not strike me as a very able man, but he was a gentleman, he had good instincts, and in his sixty years' reign he had witnessed the most extraordinary changes and vicissitudes. He talked very freely and pleasantly, sometimes about politics, sometimes about hunting; and after my first interview, when he got up to tell me 'good bye,' he said that he had been particularly interested in seeing me because he was the last representative of the old system, whereas I embodied the new movement, the movement of the present and future, and that he had wished to see me so as to know for himself how the prominent exponent of that movement felt and thought . . .

"The dinner at Schönbrunn was interesting, of course, and not so dull, as those functions are apt to be. The Emperor and all the Austrian guests had one horrid habit. The fingerbowls were brought on, each with a small tumbler of water in the middle; and the Emperor and all the others proceeded to rinse their mouths and then empty them into the finger bowls . . . However all the guests were delightful; both the men and the women who came in after dinner were on the whole charming. I was told that Viennese society was frivolous, but it happened I suppose naturally that those men whom I saw were most of them interested in real problems of statecraft and warcraft."[12]

II

We have it on high authority that Francis Joseph committed one irrational act: he became enamored of and married his cousin, Elizabeth, of the Bavarian dynasty of Wittelsbach. This princess, a veritable child of nature, almost a shepherdess, had lived in the mountains with her sisters and her jolly old father, who dressed himself in coarse cloth and his children in wool. At their first meeting Francis Joseph called her "the fairy of the forest." From youth onward, Elizabeth had a deep and abiding longing for the open sky, for the wilderness and the wanderer's staff.

All witnesses testify to Elizabeth's incredible beauty. Her classic loveliness has been frozen into a marble statue which adorns Vienna's Volksgarten. An American who met the empress in 1863 sketched this portrait: "She is a magnificent creature, moves with grace and dignity and carries off her great height with perfect ease. Indeed, instead of appearing tall herself, she has the effect of making others look small. She is far handsomer than her photographs, which, of course, cannot convey the impression of youth and bloom, which is one of the effects she produces. Her figure is beautiful, her complexion that sort of *mot* white which is so brilliant in the evening. Her eyes are dark and her whole expression singularly gentle with even a shade of timidity. She spoke English to us, which she knows very well, in a very low voice." [13]

Elizabeth found the stiff conventionality of imperial Vienna an unpalatable contrast to the freedom and independence of her native Bavarian countryside. By disposition and training she was ill-suited for the role of Hapsburg empress-queen. Francis Joseph's autocratic and domineering mother, Archduchess Sophia, and the archduchesses disapproved of her, for her elder sister had been picked by them as the proper wife for the young monarch and there was endless bickering and intrigue over precedence at state ceremonies. Against the strict rigidity of Spanish court etiquette the "maid of the mountains" openly rebelled, and she found Francis Joseph's reticence and pedantry insufferable.

In interests and convictions the imperial pair differed vastly. She much preferred fine literature to inane court ceremonials; she much preferred riding and walking to prosaic receptions; she much preferred men of wit and learning to stuffy old dukes and dowagers. She bitterly resented the hard necessities of imperial living which kept her like a prisoner enchained. Politics concerned her little, unless she felt called upon to upbraid a minister because of real or fancied anti-Magyar leanings, for the Magyars were her pets. Nothing akin to intellectual companionship developed between emperor-king and empress-queen. Coolness rather, and that gradually gave way to estrangement; and Elizabeth commenced the practice of seeking greener and unfenced pastures abroad for several months each year.

Of all the peoples of the Hapsburg realm, Elizabeth found the Magyars most charming and lovable, or at least those aristocrats among them who shared her notions of freedom—mad gallops, hunting, adventure, escapades —and she was happiest when at her Hungarian shooting château at Gödöllö, not far from Budapest; away, she suffered a "terrible Hungarian homesickness." She learned the complicated Magyar tongue, admired Hungarian men of letters, wept compassionate tears over the tragic pages of Hungarian history, and by little gestures captivated the Magyar population. As her *dame de confiance* she selected a Magyar countess, Marie Festetics, of whom it has been said that she knew more important and more interesting things about the Hapsburg history of her time than the imperial Viennese Academy of Sciences entire! Elizabeth exerted her influence to bring about the reconciliation of the moderate Magyars with the crown in 1867, but thereafter she eschewed politics, though unfriendly critics in Vienna accused her of being a sinister Magyarophile. For the Magyars, the gracious and charming queen became a kind of legendary figure, the *Patrona Hungariae*. A statue to the memory of "the divine Elizabeth," encircled by a small temple, was dedicated in Budapest so late as 1932.

Elizabeth never recovered from the tragic fate that befell her only son, the Crown Prince Rudolph, in 1889. After that disaster she became more than ever a wanderer on the face of Europe and more than once she intimated that she was contemplating a journey to the New World. Melancholia steadily gained upon her. On the island of Corfu she had built a spacious Greek palace and in it she raised a monument to her favorite poet, Heinrich Heine, another impassioned and freedom-loving rebel; Lord Byron held second place in her literary affections. "Heinrich Heine," the empress confided to her diary, "it is for you that my soul sobs and my spirit longs . . . Since I wedded myself to you spiritually, I think and feel as you thought and felt . . . Verily you sang as the nightingale sings." [14] Her passion for freedom led her to choose the eminent Hungarian Jewish journalist, Max Falk, to give her instruction on political and economic matters, and she counted among her friends Baroness Julie Rothschild, a Jewess of rare charm and distinction.

In spite of her eccentricities and her ceaseless roaming, Elizabeth never lost the favor of Francis Joseph. Their relationship was likened to that which might exist between a wayward, alluring kitten and a big Newfoundland dog. Parsimonious though he was, Francis Joseph set no bounds upon her lavish expenditures; yet his notes to her rarely went beyond perfunctory inquiries on the state of her health or comments on the state of the weather. On one occasion he warned her of the danger of traveling without protection, but she nonchalantly went her way.

At Geneva in 1898 Elizabeth was stabbed to death by an Italian anarchist, Luigi Lucheni, like herself a rebel against things as they were. He selected her as his victim in the belief that the deed would be a blow struck at the ruling class everywhere and that his name would be heralded round the globe. On learning what had happened Francis Joseph remarked with uncommon stoicism, "I must not lament the empress. She found the death which she had always desired—sudden and painless." [15]

The monarchy was plunged into indignation and grief by the crime at Geneva; Magyars grieved over the empress-queen's death almost as much as they had mourned the departure of the heroic Kossuth a few years before. Protestations from Hungary obliged court officials to have the inscription on her coffin read: "Elizabeth empress of Austria *and* queen of Hungary." Upon Elizabeth's sarcophagus in the imperial vaults of the Capuchin Church in Vienna was placed—appropriately—a crown of thorns.

To the imperial couple three daughters and one son were born. Sophie, the first child, died in infancy; Gisela married Prince Leopold of Bavaria; and Marie Valerie wedded the Archduke Francis Salvator of the Tuscan wing of the Hapsburg House. Francis Joseph's attitude toward his daughters was patriarchal without any real paternal affection; nor did he exhibit any special fondness for his grandchildren, though all were welcome at Ischl or at Wallsee on the Danube.

III

Rudolph, the only son of Francis Joseph and Elizabeth, was, like his mother, a rebellious spirit. Born in 1858, he was given a formal education in keeping with orthodox Hapsburg traditions as befitted the heir to the throne. Among his teachers, and there were more than two score of them, Joseph von Latour exerted the most profound influence and earned the lifelong confidence and esteem of his pupil; his instructor in economics was a leader of the "Austrian school" of economics, Carl Menger; Rudolph's innate bent for the sciences of nature was quickened by the stimulating companionship of Alfred E. Brehm, perhaps the most distinguished ornithologist of the time.

For languages the crown prince displayed unusual aptitude, speaking and writing several tongues fluently. Conventional studies were supplemented by travel to England, to Spain, and to the Near East, and from these experiences Rudolph learned and remembered much. His last travel journey he described in *Travels in the East*,[16] which was translated into several languages and inspired the authorities of the University of Vienna to confer the doctorate upon him, an honor which the recipient believed would not have been granted to an ordinary person for a comparable contribution to knowledge. Though unlike his father in many ways, Rudolph shared the paternal passion for hunting, and much of his time was consumed in the chase.

Rudolph's thinking and personal convictions strayed widely from the stereotyped and conservative patterns of his father and rather closely resembled those of Empress-Queen Elizabeth. His religious outlook was that of a free thinker at least, traceable half to the influence of some of his tutors and half to his studies in natural science. Under his direction, in part, a magnificent, though uncritical, work on the ethnography and history of the diverse peoples in the Hapsburg realm was prepared. Entitled *The Austro-Hunga-rian Monarchy in Story and Picture,* this monumental synthesis ran into twenty-four stately volumes and is a permanently useful repository of in-formation.[17]

Rudolph shared the aversion of his mother for his imperial relatives and the Austrian aristocracy and for the rigors of court routine, much preferring the companionship of men of demonstrated ability and intellectual talent. Among them a peculiar place was reserved for Moritz Szeps, a left-wing journalist of international repute, who had intimate ties with French poli-ticians, and whose political outlook was that of a typical Viennese intellec-tual. Association with Szeps was a kind of liberal education on an advanced plane for the inquisitive and impetuous scion of the House of Hapsburg, and to the columns of Szeps' *Neues Wiener Tagblatt* the crown prince made anonymous contributions, based occasionally on information originating in the foreign office. And with Baron Moritz Hirsch, a prominent Jewish finan-cier and the principal promoter of railway projects in the Balkans, Rudolph did not hesitate to fraternize in a perfectly open and frank fashion.

Rudolph was different from his father in many ways, but in none was the divergence more striking than in the sphere of politics. In Rudolph, writes his most reliable biographer, "Fate seemed for once to want to place a philosopher on the Hapsburg throne." [18] As a lover of freedom by convic-tion, not unlike Joseph II, he railed against the conservative tendencies of the Austrian government and what he regarded as the unholy alliance with clericalism and the forces of obscurantism. Menger's teachings convinced him of the necessity of heavier taxation on the great landed estates and of the parceling among the peasants of the properties belonging to the aristoc-racy and the church.

Rudolph's affection for the Slavic minorities, notably the Czechs and Croats, appears to have been real and abiding, and yet he, like Elizabeth, was singularly fond of the lighthearted and politically stiff-necked Magyars, however much he disapproved of their treatment of minority groups and the clamor for Hungarian independence. As Rudolph saw it, "Our Hapsburg state has actually put into practice, in a miniature form, Victor Hugo's dream of a United States of Europe." [19]

Rudolph's views on foreign policy conformed fairly closely to the gener-ally liberal pattern of his thought. On the virtue of the alliance with Ger-many he had grave misgivings, yet he favored its continuance as protection against Russia. Deep-seated dread of Russia, as a menace to freedom in Eu-rope, was matched by his conviction that Austria-Hungary must outwit the tsardom in the competition for hegemony in the Balkans—an area in which he felt the Hapsburgs had a high and holy mission to impart the blessings and institutions of German civilization. Toward the end of his life, Rudolph came to mistrust Italy and to believe that in a crisis Italy would, at the very least, leave her ally in the lurch. Before engaging in any forward enterprise in the East, the monarchy, he thought, ought to square accounts with the fickle and treacherous southern neighbor—an attitude that earned him the reputation of a warmonger.

It can hardly be doubted that Rudolph favored diplomatic intimacy with the French Republic, for whose culture he had warm admiration. To ensure the security of the realm, and as an instrument to advance Austrian concerns in the Near East, the prince pleaded for the upbuilding of the army, in whose ranks he had served and to which he freely proffered advice on methods of improvement.

Whatever his desires in the conduct of public affairs, however much he longed to alter the prevailing governmental policies, Rudolph had almost no opportunity to have his convictions put to the test because Francis Joseph treated him as a negligible quantity, too immature to concern himself with intricate problems of state.

In very modern history two outstanding instances of the grand passion in royal palaces belong to the House of Hapsburg: Crown Prince Rudolph and Crown Prince Francis Ferdinand. The former in 1881 contracted a *mariage de convenance* to a stiff stick of a girl, Stephanie, daughter of the artful Leopold II of Belgium. Neither of them found the marriage productive of much happiness; in interests and in intellect they were ill-mated, and the prince mourned the fact that no son was born to the union. After a few years Rudolph sought romance beyond the bounds of the princely bed-chamber and of accepted convention. The final object of his affections was an attractive young baroness of Greek extraction, Marie Vetsera. Her corpse was found alongside of his own in the fateful hunting lodge at Mayerling on January 30, 1889.

Presumably the mysterious Mayerling tragedy will long furnish a subject for debate in both popular and academic circles, but it is the most reliable opinion at present that Rudolph killed himself and his mistress as well. His most authoritative biographer, Oscar von Mitis, after a rigorous and careful scrutiny of the admissible testimony, confesses to being puzzled as to the motives that inspired the hideous crime.[20] Certain it is that the mind of Rudolph had for some time been less than balanced, and he may have been affected by the fact that his uncle, King Louis of Bavaria, had recently drowned himself and a companion in a fit of insanity. Certain it is, too, that the autocratic, patriarchal stiffness of Francis Joseph caused the heir apparent deep anguish of mind and spirit. Yet it is by no means clear that Rudolph committed suicide because he would not give up Vetsera under pressure from his father; nor is it clear that he acted as he did under the impression that a treasonable intrigue in which he was interested, to separate

Hungary from Austria, was about to be disclosed, as some critics have asserted. Anything like a complete exposition of Rudolph's behavior must await the appearance of documentary evidence at present under lock and key. Certain of the relevant papers have been destroyed, so that Mayerling may always remain a mystery and a topic for subjective speculation.

Francis Joseph, who was crushed by the Mayerling blow, practiced deception concerning what had happened in order to assure an ecclesiastical burial for his son. Had it not been for the sturdiness of soul of Elizabeth, the emperor might have cracked under the terrible strain. With exemplary nobility of character, she sustained her husband in an hour which for both must have been the most painful of their whole checkered careers.

Upon Hapsburg citizens of a freedom-loving cast of mind, the violent death of a prince who was known as a friend of freedom and individuality left a profound impression. Even a shopworker with revolutionary inclinations was heard to refer to the crown prince as a saint. For weeks after the tragedy, Vienna was strangely silent and reserved and the very name Mayerling was murmured with bated breath.

IV

Together with the political absolutism of the crown and the secular authority of the clergy, the Great Revolution in France swept away the feudal privileges of the nobility. But east of the Rhine innovations inspired by the French example proceeded at a leisurely pace and reached flood tide only after World War I—a point sometimes missed by students who approach the European scene from the vantage ground of France.

In Austria the institutions of the *ancien régime,* the pattern of conservatism, possessed remarkable tenacity. The noble caste, proudly jealous of its historic rights, learned nothing and forgot everything. Here indeed was the international aristocracy of birth par excellence, partly recruited from and intermarried with foreign nobility, disdainful of everyone who lacked sixteen noble quarterings. Sharp social distinctions separated the older and upper nobility, those clans which boasted an ancestry that had performed meritorious political or social services in a bygone century, from the *Briefadel,* a growing class of newly created barons, mostly wealthy financiers. All alike looked down their noses at lesser and inferior breeds of humanity who had not shown sufficient wisdom to be born with a title or sufficient energy and shrewdness to acquire one.[21]

At the top of Austrian aristocratic society, the elite of the elite, stood the archducal families, which were closely related to the imperial family. Time had written or given sanction to a host of rules of etiquette which members of the archducal clan were expected to obey. But much to the annoyance of Francis Joseph some of the archdukes rebelled against these conventions and provoked endless bickering and trouble; it must be said that their levity and transgression of accepted moralities would have ruined the patience of a modern Job. Certain of the archdukes, however, in keeping with family tradition, concerned themselves with the fighting services of the Monarchy or served as patrons of art and science.

One of the archdukes, Francis Ferdinand, who became heir presumptive after the death of Rudolph, and who with his wife was slain at Sarajevo in 1914, deserves passing comment. Emperor Francis Joseph found his nephew scarcely more congenial than Rudolph, though not for precisely the same reasons. The two men fell out when Francis Ferdinand asked approval to marry Countess Sophie Chotek, a Czech woman of minor noble stock, whom he met while courting a daughter of the fabulously wealthy Archduke Frederick.[22] Since the lady was not of the blood imperial, the emperor refused the request, but the crown prince persisted and in the end Francis Joseph grudgingly acquiesced, though he never forgot nor forgave. In fact he insisted that any children born to the union should not be eligible to the throne and formal renunciation took place fourteen years to a day before the unfortunate couple rode to their death at Sarajevo. That marital episode suggests much about the character of Francis Ferdinand: his independence of spirit, his resolute will, his dogged stubbornness.

After a conventional education on the traditional Hapsburg pattern, which included service as a cavalry officer with Bohemian and Hungarian regiments, Francis Ferdinand toured the globe, half to enlarge his knowledge of the world and its affairs, half for reasons of health. An extensive diary of his experiences and observations reveals a personality of ordinary quality without much social sympathy or understanding of the trends of the age. Except for the grandeur of Niagara Falls, he discovered little in the United States that appealed to his tastes, and a great deal that was irritating.[23] For the things of the mind, apart from politics, he had small concern, but he greatly relished hunting for game and collecting curiosities, especially statues of St. George, patron saint of huntsmen, of which he accumulated hundreds. Seemingly he was a sincere believer in the Roman Catholic creed; certainly he was a stanch supporter of the interests of mother church, and highly respected in clerical circles. After listening to a fervent sermon by a Jesuit father on the blessings that flowed from the harsh Counter Reformation in Austria, the archduke, deeply moved, thanked the preacher for one of the finest addresses he had ever heard.[24]

While not the chauvinist many of his contemporaries imagined him to be, Francis Ferdinand believed confidently in the future of the Monarchy and was alert to the perils that threatened it. He pressed energetically for greater efficiency in and the expansion of the fighting services—the navy was his special pet—and he advocated diplomatic policies that did not always conform to the views of the monarch or the foreign office. Italy and Italians he detested as traitors masquerading as friends of Austria, and as the despoilers of papal and his family's landed properties. He shared the official distrust of Greater Serbia propaganda and desired that the kingdom of Serbia should somehow be inveigled into the Hapsburg realm. For imperial Russia, as for Germany, he had real affection and he worked intelligently to improve relations with St. Petersburg. In the final years of his life, the archduke thought that a coalition embracing Austria, Russia, and Germany was the quintessence of diplomatic wisdom and to bring such a league into being he was ready to go far in an effort to satisfy Russian ambitions in the Balkan area.

Like Rudolph before him, Francis Ferdinand chafed under the limitations imposed by the emperor and greatly feared that a "do-nothing" policy on constitutional questions would bring ruin to the venerable Monarchy. At the Belvedere palace, crowning one of Vienna's splendid hills, the crown prince collected a kind of "brain trust," a band of followers, mostly experts on some phase of public business, upon whom he relied for information and advice, and he contrived to place some of his henchmen in key governmental posts.

Just how the archduke thought the constitutional framework of the Monarchy should be reformed is not entirely clear, for at different times he was interested in alternative programs, all of them grounded, however, on principles of federalism. Any such reformation would have curtailed the weight of the Magyars in the Dual Monarchy and for that reason, as well as because he captiously criticized Magyar treatment of minorities, the archduke was disliked and detested in the governing circles at Budapest. That attitude he cordially reciprocated; "It was an act of bad taste on the part of these gentlemen ever to have come to Europe," he caustically remarked.[25] Explosive in temperament, ambitious, iron-willed, suspicious, Francis Ferdinand has been called the strongest personality that the House of Hapsburg produced in more than a century.

Outside his immediate circle of friends and sycophants the crown prince was more hated than loved. His home life was, however, singularly idyllic; husband and wife were drawn close together by the social discriminations against the countess and by the rigid punctilio of the Vienna court. News of their foul assassination in 1914 evoked few tears at court or among Magyar politicians—and even they were of the crocodile variety.

v

By grants from the crown or as the result of conquests and rebellions, the higher Austrian patrician stocks had come into possession of wide and scattered estates. Kinsky, Starhemberg, Schönborn, Liechtenstein, Schwarzenber symbolized authority and power from the twilight of medievalism onward; Harrach, Auersperg, Windischgrätz and Lobkowitz attained prominence in early modern times, while branches of Polish noble families, such as Goluchowski and Potocki, and others of Italian antecedents, Belcredi, Odescalchi, and Montecuccoli, entered the Austrian elite even later.

The prestige of the aristocracy rested on the wealth of their rural properties, over which they ruled rather like petty kings, with small armies of retainers at their beck and call. The Starhembergs, for example, had over a dozen castles and palaces which they called home. The Liechtensteins owned more than a score of castles and surrounding soil in Austria proper, in Bohemia, and even in imperial Germany, quite apart from the principality of Liechtenstein, sandwiched between Austria and Switzerland, which the family ruled uninterruptedly from 1608 onward; in Bohemia thirty-three magnates owned 238 castles and 137 palaces. By custom the eldest son in the greater families inherited the bulk of the property; land, houses, plate, and jewels were entailed. Nearly all the nobles had fat incomes, which enabled them to live in a semiregal fashion; the poorer ones, however, kept to the seclusion of their rural châteaux.

With the coming of industrialism some Austrian nobles dabbled in finance, a few even sharing in the directorates of banks and insurance companies. Many an aristocrat played the stock market, less in hope of gain, it would seem, than as a sport, just as he bet on the turf. Some were quite crippled if not entirely ruined in the financial crash of 1873, while others won large sums. The lordly Schwarzenbergs and their imitators built sugar refineries and distilleries on their properties for the conversion of primary products of the soil; near Bohemian Krumau, the site of the most palatial Schwarzenberg castle, was erected the largest paper factory in the Danube Monarchy.

For the greater part, however, the landed aristocracy shunned industrial enterprises, either because of a certain intellectual indolence or as incompatible with caste code. As the pushing, self-reliant bourgeoisie crowded upward, the economic importance of the aristocracy declined and some of the princely estates passed into the ownership of members of the energetic middle class. Material changes disturbed the nobility but little, for as Peacham wrote in *The Compleat Gentleman,* "riches are an ornament, not the cause of nobility."

From early youth Austrian nobles were trained in the belief that they were the chosen of the Almighty and of destiny in the best of all possible worlds. Private tutors, Jesuit fathers commonly, and special schools for nobles steeped them in aristocratic conventions and taught them standards of personal conduct. Seldom did Austrian aristocrats pursue studies on the university level, and if they did they attended institutions in Germany by preference.

They cared little about "liberal" education, and actively disliked learned men who were not afraid to think, men whose heads were supposed to be full of unorthodox ideas, dangerous for the noble scheme of things. The opinion was generally prevalent in aristocratic circles that serious study made people stupid; "a nice, superficial" education was quite enough.

In maturity, Austrian nobles displayed singularly little interest in the affairs of the great world beyond their enchanted circle, and of the forces and secular currents of their time they were abysmally ignorant. Rather exceptional was Count Ferdinand Harrach, who attained a certain distinction as a painter of historical and religious subjects. Complacency, it is fair to say, characterized the attitude of the nobility toward religion, with the ladies distinctly more pious and more strict in the observance of the rites of the church. Catholic dignitaries rarely appeared in high society, except for an occasional cardinal at a dinner party.

Austrian nobles were taught and believed profoundly that they were born to rule and that their set alone, as for centuries past, was fit to monopolize politics. It was impossible for them to reconcile their inherited convictions with the growth of popular participation in public affairs. As a class, the nobility venerated the existing social order, espoused conservative causes and reactionary policies, and aligned themselves with the clerical forces, to which some of them were allied by family connections. The princes Liechtenstein, Alfred and Alois, Jesuit-educated and clerical to the core, participated actively in the doings of the Christian Socialist party, the Austrian version of political Catholicism.

The Austrian suffrage laws were so drawn that great landlords, either directly or through their influence over peasant voters, were able to play a role in parliamentary transactions out of all proportion to their numbers. Members of Austrian princely families occupied seats in the upper house by hereditary right and some nobles were elected to the lower house or to one or another of the provincial assemblies; with a single exception, every premier of Austria in the constitutional era belonged to the nobility. And the nobility furnished a good deal of the leadership in the minority nationalist movements of Austria, invariably in the conservative wing. Polish aristocrats of Galicia were conspicuously loyal to the Hapsburg crown and carried with them the clergy and the majority of the peasantry.

For the specialized and tedious tasks of bureaucratic administration, counts and barons had small taste, gladly welcoming middle-class men to these responsibilities. What they doted on were the higher posts in the diplomatic and fighting services, and most of these offices were filled by them.[26] A thousand Austrian nobles are reported to have perished on the battlefield in World War I. Not a few blue bloods took employment at the imperial court, busying themselves with the intricate Spanish etiquette of the hidebound household. Conspicuous here was Prince Albert Montenuovo, grand master of the imperial court, the grandson of Marie Louise, Napoleon's second wife, and Count Neipperg; no servant of the crown was a greater stickler for ceremonial than this guardian of the elaborate rules of Hapsburg ceremonial.

Whether in castles on their ancestral acres or in town residences in Vienna or Salzburg, in Prague or Cracow, the Austrian nobility lived a social existence of peculiar charm. Pride and clannishness made high Vienna society more exclusive than any other in Europe; its members were on terms of easy familiarity, having known each other from childhood, sharing the same patterns of interest, tastes, and ideas. Aristocratic matrons presided over regal salons, which were meeting places for the exchange of frivolous wit and worldly chatter. Late in the nineteenth century the most popular figure in Viennese high society was Princess Pauline Metternich, an intimate of Empress Eugénie when her husband was ambassador to the court of Napoleon III. She was a woman of intellectual and artistic gifts, full of ideas, friendly with the wealthy Rothschilds, and eager to make the acquaintance of the self-made American, Charles M. Schwab. Cheers of an infatuated public followed the princess when she drove through the streets of the capital, for Vienna admired her no less than she adored Vienna. Princess Pauline's leading competitor, the old Princess Croy, presided over a rival salon, and baited shafts were bandied back and forth.[27]

High society in Vienna vied with that in Paris in setting the fashion in dress, furniture, and carriages for the European continent. Daughters of famous aristocratic houses, however unattractive or poor they might be, rarely thought of marrying outside their circle for money; wealth gave no title of admission to the most exclusive Austrian patricianate.

Careless of the future, the aristocracy loved sport, dancing, dinner parties, and competed in banquets, hunts, and entertainment that swallowed up a large share of the income from their estates. In the 1880's old families indulged in table rapping, crystal gazing, and planchette writing in the expectation that they would be able to recall the spirits of their departed ancestors.

Family residences in Vienna were concentrated in the Inner Town, the medieval walled city, where space was at a premium. Usually designed in the Italian Baroque style, which became popular in the seventeenth and eighteenth centuries, the palaces were ideal for entertaining, but cheerless, unsanitary, and dark. The palace of the Lobkowitz clan, for instance, in which Beethoven, while librarian to the family, had composed some of his immortal works, had to be artificially lighted at all hours. The huge Liechtenstein palace contained one of the world's finest private art collections.

One Austrian prince, on the occasion of large balls—and dancing was the supreme passion of this set—imported scores of peasant lads from his estates, arrayed them in the eighteenth-century livery, swords girt at their sides, and used them for decorative purposes or to serve the supper. At every ball, a special room was reserved for young unmarried ladies—the *Comtessen Zimmer*—whither they withdrew at the end of each dance, emerging only when the orchestra struck up the music for the next whirl. Young ladies were hedged round by iron-clad social conventions; custom permitted them neither to walk alone nor to drive in carriages unaccompanied. Society maidens customarily married early or withdrew from social activity, prefer-ably to a nunnery. Aristocratic ladies presided over benevolent societies and busied themselves in charity balls of which there were a great many; at such affairs they and their families deigned to fraternize with Vienna's wealthy and very fashionable upper bourgeoisie.

Of all social functions, the most exclusive were the balls at the court (*Ball bei Hof*), which were limited to the very highest circle of the aris-tocracy. Not even a Vanderbilt wedded to a lordly Széchényi of Hungary or the beautiful Countess Károlyi, whose husband long served as Hapsburg ambassador to Berlin, were welcome at these affairs, for they lacked the indispensable sixteen noble quarterings. Questions of social precedence were burning issues and distinctions in rank were strictly observed.

Male members of the elite gathered in their clubs, where conversation revolved round racing, shooting, and dicing. Facility in speaking English slang was looked upon as the certain sign of an authentic gentleman. Nobles talked of horses and stables, of the curious horseman, Count Zderko Kinsky, who broke every bone in his body, except his neck and spine, or of his even more eccentric uncle, who once drove a four-in-hand up a staircase into the large banqueting hall of a mansion. For a time the quaint pastime of snail racing was extremely popular, and one of the most fashionable clubs in Vienna was given over to the craze.

Vienna's horse-racing season from April to June brought the social year to a giddy climax; the army steeplechase, the *Preisreiten* and *Preisspringen,* which Francis Joseph usually attended, closed the social season in a blaze of glamour and colorful military uniforms. Gambling ranked high among the favorite indoor diversions; scarcely a young noble escaped being hard hit at one time or another, and then his friends and relatives were expected to rush to the rescue. Plutocratic "social climbers" of the middle class knew well that the surest way to win recognition from the upper stratum was to dis-play an ardent interest in gaming.

Taken as a whole, Austrian upper society, while charming and pleasant, was gripped by moral indolence and without much initiative or sense of public responsibility. It was, in fact, an anachronism, out of place in an age of capitalistic industry and bustling commerce. The class was astonishingly ignorant and narrow-minded; shallow, pompous, futile; there was much marital infidelity and unconventional licentiousness. Bourgeois morality represented a code of personal conduct beneath the notice of the aristocracy. One writer characterized the patrician order in general as "irresponsibly frivolous, irresistibly gay, fundamentally ignorant, devotees of sport and fashion, hopelessly gregarious, and class conscious."

Courageous critics of the ways and works of the Austrian aristocracy were not wanting, and a most vigorous one was the ill-starred Crown Prince Rudolph, who collaborated with the distinguished economist, Carl Menger, in composing a brochure entitled "The Austrian Nobility and its Constitutional Profession; A Warning to Aristocratic Youth by an Austrian." [28] For its special privileges, the nobility owed special services to the state, the treatise argued, but in actuality the aristocrats were incompetent, falsely and inadequately educated, and unwilling to fulfill their high obligations. Rudolph, no Puritan himself, upbraided the young bloods for engaging in frivolous prodigality and for squandering their time and energies in hunting and dancing. Preachers sometimes preach what they themselves find difficulty in practicing.

Rudolph's shrill castigation of the nobility recalls the no less unfriendly indictment of the liberally minded Emperor Joseph II, who, toward the end of the eighteenth century, exclaimed: "The good gentlemen believe they have achieved everything when they have produced a statesman, when their son officiates at the mass, when he fingers his beads, confesses every fortnight, and knows nothing more than what the limited intelligence of his father confessor tells him." [29]

Another and smoother critic of the parasitic nobility, of the easygoing habits of the higher aristocrats, their glacial aloofness from the rest of mankind, and the artificial character of their existence, was the poet and novelist, Marie von Ebner-Eschenbach.[30] She showed, however, that among the insipid and dissolute many, there were some enlightened, sober, and principled patricians. A noblewoman herself, she defied the code of her caste by turning authoress. At the height of her career she was regarded as the foremost woman of letters writing in the German language and she was the first of her sex to be awarded an honorary doctorate by the University of Vienna. Her writings are of inestimable value, for they faithfully and boldly portray slices of Austrian life now vanished beyond recall. Nowhere else were the interests, the prepossessions, the frailties, the outlook of the Austrian nobility more competently related.

In the pages of her novels Ebner described the way of life of her noble friends, telling more of their behavior than their feelings, and she also depicted the customs and manners of the estate peasantry, the rough conditions of living among the villagers. Her writings eschewed sensationalism, but were full of bright wit and sharp satire. *Countess Muchi,* a typical specimen of Ebner's work, was a series of letters in which a young countess quite naïvely unveiled herself without restraint as an archfoe of learning and culture in any sense. Her range of interest stopped with the animals that were used for sporting purposes. Woven into the letters was much enlightening information on the matrimonial vicissitudes of the Austrian patricians. Another piece, *After Death,* was a revealing tale of a noble landlord who had real affection for the good earth and for those who toiled upon it.

Interspersed in Ebner's pitiless criticism of the aristocracy were appeals to the nobility to alter their ways and to devote themselves to the progressive reformation and regeneration of the Monarchy. But her pleas, like those of Rudolph, irritated rather than inspired the heirs of great traditions and great wealth. Like their counterparts in eighteenth-century France, they shunned anything savoring of reform, chose ease instead of action, and paid the penalty in the revolutionary tumult that attended the downfall of the venerable Monarchy in 1918.

Members of archducal families who then agreed to renounce all special privileges were permitted to live on in Austria, eking out a livelihood in agriculture or in some form of business. The others took refuge abroad, in Switzerland, or Hungary, or Poland, and eventually not a few of them emigrated to the United States; more than once personal possessions of archdukes and archduchesses were sold under the auctioneer's hammer in New York City. Shortly after Hitlerian Germany annexed the Austrian republic in 1938, the crowning blow was delivered to the Hapsburgs: the family was dropped from the *Almanach de Gotha.*

‡ CHAPTER EIGHT ‡

THE AUSTRIAN "OTHER HALF"

WELL OVER HALF OF THE AUSTRIAN POPULATION AT THE outset of the twentieth century earned a living from soil and forests, a somewhat smaller proportion than in 1870. Conditions of rural life and labor varied considerably across the empire, for climate was not the same everywhere, terrain was diversified in character, great disparities in land tenure prevailed, and social habits and customs diverged widely. During the revolutionary storm of 1848, encumbrances upon the peasantry, lingering on from medieval times, were removed and many rustics acquired full proprietary rights over pieces of ground while retaining traditional privileges of pasturage in common meadows and of gathering firewood in the common forests. It was unlawful to divide a peasant holding under sixty acres; when a proprietor died, his land normally passed to the eldest son, who was obligated to compensate other children appropriately. That custom often put the inheritor of a property hopelessly and permanently in debt.[1]

At first the abolition of serfdom brought agricultural and social gains. The material lot of the rustic population showed some improvement, and great proprietors, who had been compensated by the state for the property rights of which they had been deprived, tended to have their estates cultivated more carefully, so that many doubled and even trebled their incomes in the space of a single generation. Land values shot up over a hundred per cent, even more in some districts.

In sections of the Austrian empire, peasant holdings adequate to provide sustenance for a family, though rarely producing an appreciable surplus for the market, predominated. This was the case in the provinces of Upper Austria, Styria, and Carniola, and in the Alpine areas. In Lower Austria there was a marked tendency toward independent proprietorships on which gardens and vineyards were cultivated to satisfy the requirements of Vienna and other populous centers. Ownership of landed property in Carniola was especially widespread, a heritage of the land redistribution effected while the province belonged to the Napoleonic kingdom of Illyria. As of 1870, small Austrian farms were not, as a rule, heavily mortgaged; it was exceptional to find a little holding mortgaged to as much as half its value, and on the independent farmsteads there was considerable material comfort and contentment.

In certain areas of the empire peasants supplemented their incomes in special ways. Tourist traffic, for example, in the Austrian Alps, in the health spas of Bohemia, and on the Dalmatian coast created seasonal employment; in one Styrian district, peasants turned amateur veterinarians and traveled far and wide over eastern Europe doctoring animals by rule-of-thumb techniques; many a Bucovinian rustic was hired as a "beater" on a large game preserve. Work in forests and in timber industries was an important source of revenue for some poor peasants; and almost everywhere household handicrafts were carried on in cottages when the weather was inclement and in the winter months when the ground could not be worked. Womenfolk spun and wove, made lace and embroidery, or plaited straw articles, while the men turned out baskets and pots or worked up articles of wood and leather; wages for this toil were invariably small, miserably small.

The growth of factory production, which had ruinous consequences for cottage industries, and competition from mechanized agriculture both at home and abroad seriously affected the economy of the small proprietor of Austria. Service of mortgages reduced some peasants in time to the living standards their fathers had known in the serf period, when they were obligated to turn over part of their harvests to noble lords. Many a small owner sought escape from his economic plight by moving into factory centers or to a new home beyond the Atlantic. Increasing pressure of population in the countryside likewise swelled the exodus to cities and overseas.

In some mountainous districts of Austria wealthy townsmen bought up peasant holdings, planted them with trees, and used them as hunting preserves. What happened was poetically depicted by the novelist Peter Rosegger in *Jacob the Last,* a tale of rural Styria. In the novel many peasants sell their properties to a rich city chap, who allows trees to grow up on land that once had been tilled. Ravenous deer ruin the crops of those peasants who linger on in the community. So the peasants, with one solitary exception, part with their holdings and move off to cities, where they find living drab and unsatisfying. But the obdurate Jacob clings tenaciously to his good earth, though conditions of existence grow progressively more harsh. He is caught killing a deer for food; imprisoned, and in terrible misery of mind and spirit, he takes his own life. To his memory an old friend raised a rude tombstone, into which was cut: "Jacob Steinruther, the last peasant of Altenmoss."

Except in the Adriatic region, there was not much farm tenantry in the Austrian empire and where it existed the landowner commonly supplied seeds and fertilizers. The tenant's share of the produce was as little as a third, though in the least fertile districts his portion might reach as much as four-fifths. So long as a tenant cultivated the land properly he could not lawfully be evicted, and if he desired he might purchase the property. There was a distinct trend toward the conversion of tenant farmers into independent proprietors.

The conspicuous features of rural economy in the provinces of Bohemia, Moravia, and Silesia were the large estates of the aristocracy and the dwarf properties of the peasantry. Census reports of 1896 disclosed that more than a quarter of the land of Bohemia belonged to fewer than 2 per cent of the landowners, while in Moravia a third was owned by fewer than 1 per cent. Huge properties in Bohemia, extending over more than five thousand areas, covered more than a quarter of the province; the largest of the holdings, belonging to the powerful Schwarzenberg clan, reached almost five hundred thousand acres, a veritable kingdom. In Moravia and Silesia the proportion of big estates was almost as great, and properties of thirty thousand acres were not unusual. A considerable part of these latifundia was forested and much of the arable soil was leased to peasants. On the big estates agricultural machinery was increasingly the vogue and there was a tendency to grow crops that required a minimum of labor.

In the northern provinces peasant holdings capable of supporting a family were relatively rare, by no means typical. As of 1896, 45 per cent of the farms were under an acre and a quarter and 58 per cent were smaller than two and one-half acres; owners of these dwarf properties often rented additional land from the great estates. Similar conditions of land tenure existed in Galicia, where three-fifths of the productive soil belonged to big estates and many peasants owned only an acre or two. In the Cracow district, for each big property there were thirty to forty dwarf farms, and a like situation prevailed in the heavily wooded province of Bucovina.

The insufficiently landed rural class, wherever found, depended heavily for livelihood upon employment on the large estates, while the wholly landless class, an enlarging company, lived entirely on their pay as farm laborers. Treated with scant consideration, illiterate and inefficient, paid poorly and worked long hours in the busy seasons, the Austrian rural proletariat resembled that of Hungary, Russia, and sections of Italy. On the wide Schwarzenberg domains, the workers, some Germans, some Czechs, lived in a feudal environment, subject to eviction from their rented huts if, for instance, they married without the sanction of their lord.

II

Human conditions among rural workers were perhaps worst in Polish Galicia, where a huge surplus of labor normally existed and the nobility had almost unlimited authority over the poverty-stricken field hands. Not infrequently half the wages was liquidated in spirits which the proprietors alone had the legal right to distill and distribute. In the 1870's a Galician rustic toiled from daylight to dusk for the sum of twelve cents a day in winter, eighteen cents in summer, and as much as twenty-nine cents during the arduous harvest season. Women in Silesia cultivated potatoes for ten cents a day and a spot of corn brandy; male workers, hired by the year, were given maintenance and twenty dollars. And yet in these northern provinces wages had advanced anywhere from 50 to 150 per cent since forced labor had ceased a generation earlier. Many Galician field workers owned a plot of ground, or rather several small, scattered strips, and a dwelling, as a rule a miserable and flimsy structure of wood and clay covered with thatch. On the larger Silesian estates workers were furnished cottages and garden patches by employers.

Housing at best left much to be desired; at worst, the situation horrified foreign travelers. An English agricultural specialist reported these findings in the late 1860's: "At one village . . . I had an opportunity of seeing how they [the laborers] were lodged: one large barnlike building, with only a ground floor, was divided into two rooms. In one, forty feet long, twenty feet wide, and ten feet high, were six beds and four families; in the other, somewhat smaller, were five beds, and three families. Smallpox having broken out a fortnight before, I was told some tenants of this wretched abode had been removed in order to thin it. There was one common cooking stove to the whole, and to add to the wretchedness of the place, it was infested with rats. A more deplorable scene it had never been my lot to witness."[2]

Pauper standards of living inspired strikes, rioting, and home burnings in Galicia, which were particularly serious at the end of the nineteenth century, and landowners were forced to raise wages. Workers in Bucovina had a habit of falling into debt to local usurers and spent much of their lives trying to liberate themselves.

Low living standards among the rural poor and land hunger were incentives to seek economic improvement in the industrial communities of Austria or seasonal work on the great estates of eastern Germany and Russia, and for the bolder, the more venturesome, to emigrate across the sea. It was about 1880, after oceanic transportation rates had fallen and when industry and agriculture were expanding rapidly in the United States, that the migration from Austria took on impressive dimensions, reaching its peak early in the twentieth century.

Legislation dating from the era of Metternich and even earlier attempted to prevent emigration entirely, but later the government tried to regulate and restrict it. It was stipulated in the constitutional laws of 1867 that "freedom of emigration is limited only by liability to perform military service"; but a good many emigrants departed secretly and so escaped duty as conscripts. Statistics on the number of departures vary greatly in completeness and accuracy and can be regarded merely as suggestive. Something like four out of five of all emigrants in the period from 1876 to 1910 sailed for the United States and most of the rest found new homes in Canada.

Methods of cultivation, like systems of landowning, showed considerable differences in various sections of the Austrian empire. Modern improvements in farm technique were confined pretty largely to areas in which extensive estates were located; on these big properties, annual rotation of crops, the use of artificial manure, periodic change of seeds, deep plowing with machinery came into use, the Galician landlords being less progressive in these respects than the others. Peasant producers generally preserved the wasteful, uneconomic scattered-plot system and the old custom of allowing one-third of the arable soil to lie fallow each year in order to recuperate its fertility. Since Galician peasants were able to obtain animal fertilizers only in insufficient quantities, night soil in powder form was applied extensively, as in China and Japan. Tools of peasant cultivators were frequently no newer than the Old Testament; grain was threshed, for example, chiefly by women with flails after the outdoor work was finished in the autumn.

III

Blessed with varied climatic conditions, ranging from rather dry Bohemia to the well-watered and semitropical Adriatic districts, Austria yielded a wide variety of soil products. Everywhere rye, the largest single crop, and wheat were grown, and oats and barley in many regions. Bohemia, which was the most productive province agriculturally, raised large crops of potatoes and clover, and made a specialty of sugar beets; the output of sugar beets per acre even surpassed that in Germany, and, apart from furnishing sugar, they yielded molasses, fodder, and fertilizer. Turnips were widely cultivated in the northern areas, and small quantities of tobacco were grown in Galicia and Bucovina. In Dalmatia and the region around Vienna, vineyards were of considerable significance.

Stock raising was an important source of income and provided substantial surpluses for export. In the Alpine highlands much care was devoted to the breeding of horned cattle; peasants had pasturage privileges on the hillsides as well as in the meadows of the lowland. Toward the end of May, cattle and sheep were driven to the lower part of the highland and gradually ate their way upward as the summer progressed. Feed for winter consumption was scarce; it was mostly hay, with turnips occasionally, but clover was reserved for horses. In the Vienna area, milch cows and sheep were raised in large numbers, but few cattle were bred in the southern provinces, for there land was minutely divided and the soil was stony. Dalmatia, however, was famed for goats and sheep and Istria for sheep.

On the large estates of the north, livestock thrived on the abundant natural pasturage and the waste from breweries and sugar refineries. Galicia exported cattle, especially oxen; it was a common practice for the large estate owners to buy animals in Russia, fatten them during the winter months, and ship them to the market in the spring. The more enterprising Polish landlords went in for superior breeds of sheep and of horses. Bohemia and Moravia raised pigs on a large scale.

Before 1914, the Danube Monarchy was the largest wood-exporting country in the world. About a third of the Austrian empire was covered with woodlands, the proportion being highest in the Alpine areas and Bucovina, and smallest in Galicia. Spruce, beech, and oak had the largest commercial importance and much spruce was shipped to Germany, Italy, and other Mediterranean countries. Forests furnished part-time employment for peasants in the making of furniture and charcoal, and in pulp and cellulose mills. Rigid laws regulated the care and cutting of woodlands; yet before World War I Austrian timber was being felled faster than it grew. Excellent schools for the training of expert foresters were maintained.

For the agriculturist the world around, the problem of credit to meet emergency expenses or to tide him over until crops were harvested and sold presented perennial difficulties. Scarcity of credit was a constant source of distress among landowners, small and large, and village usurers fleeced without ruth the simple rustics who needed cash. Old-line Austrian savings banks extended loans on landed property, but the newer commercial banks restricted rural lending almost entirely to the large estates, which offered better security than the peasant farmsteads. In the 1880's peasant borrowers had to pay as much as 12 per cent a year in interest; large proprietors, only half that figure. A few special mortgage institutions in the Austrian provinces made loans to agrarian interests at relatively low rates.

Of special importance for peasant welfare was the development of cooperative banking on principles that had been devised by a Rhineland mayor, Raffeisen, and that had worked successfully in Germany. The first Raffeisen society of Austria appears to have been organized by Germans in Bohemia in 1888; the value of the institution was quickly appreciated, so that by 1912 over eighty thousand banks were in operation. Some artisans and factory workers joined the societies but most members were soil workers;

peasant banks in Galicia served as depositories for emigrants who had gone to the New World.

Each society restricted its sphere of activities to a limited area, ordinarily to a single village. From deposits made by peasants and others loans were extended to needy members. When a peasant required funds he applied to the bank's committee of management, indicating the purpose to which the loan was to be put. Proof of financial solvency and of the good character of the borrower were prerequisites to lending and management was obligated to see that the funds were expended for the specified purpose. Loans were extended for as long as four years at a general interest rate of 4¾ per cent, or about a third of the charge for loans from other sources. Eventually, both Czechs and Germans in Bohemia set up central Raffeisen banks to reinforce the local societies.

Out of the coöperative banks developed other coöperative societies to benefit the Austrian peasantry. They spread most rapidly in the 1880's and 1890's, when the twin peril of American and Russian agricultural competition was most serious. Dairying societies were pioneers in producers' coöperatives and their success in obtaining higher prices inspired imitation by winegrowers, by olive raisers in Dalmatia, and by flax producers in the northern provinces. Peasants also formed societies to purchase farm machinery, to operate distilleries, to store grain, and so on; in parts of the empire the practice of buying goods in bulk and coöperation in the sale of products were remarkably well developed by the twentieth century. Almost without exception these organizations netted economic gains for their members and they probably did more to improve or at least to hold steady the living standards of the landed peasantry than all the government legislation, tariff protection included, put together.

IV

It is a truism that none but a peasant can really penetrate the peculiar psychology, the distinctive mentality, of the European countryfolk.[3] Ignorance, stupidity, and habit combined to make them, particularly if they were owners of property, incredibly patient and industrious, extremely conservative, cautious and mistrustful. The range of peasant interests was confined to the necessary and the traditional: the exacting routine of land labor, the satisfactions and consolations afforded by mother church, the simple diversions of the countryside, and reluctantly, under duress, a term of service in the conscript army, and the payment of taxes.

A peasant's overarching pride was his land; his loftiest ambition, if he was landless, was to obtain land. Both the soil and the tools that turned the soil were sacred, the very stuff and staff of life. However few his acres might be, the peasant clung to them tenaciously and cultivated them in keeping with the time-tested customs and methods that his forefathers had followed century upon century. Normally not much affected by the economic ebb and flow of the wider world, the tiller of the soil was content to remain brother to the ox, to walk where his fathers had trod, willing to labor from dawn to dark for a bare subsistence, happy if his money income sufficed to procure homely necessities such as matches, oil, and salt, and to meet dues to state and church. Farming for the authentic peasant meant the raising of enough food to supply the wants of his family, and his wealth was reckoned, not in terms of money, but in foodstuffs to feed so many mouths from grandparents on down. Without the spur of capital accumulation, the peasant had little conception of labor value and small regard for efficiency in work. If his land was decently productive, if he was diligent and frugal, if the exactions of government and clergy did not weigh too burdensomely upon him, he and his family somehow managed. Let the big estates produce the surpluses required to feed the teeming populations of the industrial towns and cities.

Apart from the good earth, mother church bulked largest in the concerns of the peasant as she had done in bygone centuries. With the church and her divine services he associated the interpretation of the mysteries of existence, if any was required, and the explanation of the good and ill in the daily and seasonal round, as he engaged in the everlasting struggle with the elemental forces of nature. In the peasant beliefs, there was a large admixture of superstition, of notions and customs handed on by his pagan ancestors; woven into the rustic creed were strands of old, old earth worship. Belief in spirits, ghosts, fairies, and the like were prevalent, and soothsayers were often called upon for advice. The peasant felt that he, his family, his cattle, and his crops were somehow kindred phenomena. The good earth bore them, the good earth would reclaim them, when their life's task was done. Wayside shrines scattered generously about the countryside, and crowds of peasants marching in procession to hallowed pilgrimage places, such as Maria Zell in Styria, testified to the active interest of the Austrian villagers in the world beyond this world.

For the typical peasant, the voice of the priest was the voice of the Almighty. If the priest condemned "progress," it stood condemned; if the priest inveighed against city-bred innovations, they were anathema; if the priest said think this way and vote that way, thus the peasant thought and, if an elector, voted. Priest and great landed proprietor, exalted personages indeed, knew about these matters and deserved to be respected and obeyed, as they had been for century after century.

The Austrian rural masses were taught, and few doubted, that Francis Joseph was their divinely appointed guardian and peasant affection and loyalty for the ruler were impressively vast. It was almost pathetic to observe the enthusiasm with which the villagers celebrated the name day, the birth-day, and other days associated in any fashion with events in the career of their sovereign.

Marriage for the peasant was a transaction of the utmost importance, for a wife meant another pair of hands, a new piece of farming equipment, possibly an acre or two of land as dowry. Bachelor peasants were rarities. No doubt the round of the rural woman was even more prosaic and exacting than that of the man. By old established custom she started the fire and fetched the water, cooked the meals, made the clothes with primitive spindle or loom out of flax or wool, washed garments at the water's edge, mended, endlessly mended, and cared for cow or goat. She and her children performed such field tasks as their strength permitted; in the winter months many worked away at cottage handicrafts. Often the peasant woman gave birth to as many as ten children, usually without benefit of professional medical care, and a couple of days after childbirth she was back at her accustomed household tasks; quite likely half the children would die in infancy. Inability to bear children was the supreme disgrace for a country woman and sterility was legitimate ground for separation.

As a rule the woman was treated coarsely by her husband, considered inferior in value to a cow, for a cow after all cost money. Now and then the drab routine of drudgery was interrupted by folk festivals with colorful costumes, songs and dances; wild, boisterous affairs those peasant dances, requiring great physical endurance and expressing all facets of feeling and passion. The peasant woman, wrinkled and unattractive before she reached middle life, was "aged before she was old." But the really old woman—the chronologically old—was very often an austere matriarch, occupying a place of dignity and respect in her family and community.

Apart from the occasional folk festival and parties in the winter, from low-thatched cottage to low-thatched cottage, such social life as the peasantry knew centered on the village tavern. There dances were held on Sundays and holidays; there was staged part of wedding pageantry. Weddings were no doubt the most thrilling rustic social functions, accompanied by an elaborate peasant etiquette, with guests attired in their peculiar national costumes. After the church ceremony, guests assembled in the tavern and spent days drinking, roystering, dancing, and singing, to the neglect of their homework. One chronicler comments ruefully that as the nineteenth century moved along only the customs of drinking and boisterousness at weddings were honored. Christenings and funerals were also occasions for drinking and hilarity.

Illicit love was rife in Austrian countryside and there was much illegitimacy, more in some districts than in others, to be sure. Children born out of wedlock ranged (1910) from under ten in a hundred in Dalmatia to more than thirty-seven in a hundred in Carinthia; but the peasant attitude toward unblessed unions diverged from that of the American farmer, with his heritage of Puritanism and his generally higher standard of living and education.

Peasant codes concerning crime such as robbery and murder varied a great deal, but it may safely be asserted that the peasants distinguished between misdeeds committed against the government and the well-to-do and similar wrongs against their own fellows. A peasant who outwitted the tax-gatherer or the shopkeeper was likely to be thought of as clever, while he who fleeced one of "God's poor" merited and received the condemnation of the rural community; thievery seems to have been the largest source of trouble in the villages. Changes were introduced in traditional morals as schools brought some enlightenment and therewith a deeper sense of social responsibility and greater opportunity for personal improvement.

This or something like this was the way of life of the Austrian peasants, sowing and reaping, toiling and spinning, with little thought of gain or plan for profit, but rather so that they and their households might dwell in peace, close to the level of subsistence, and be allowed to worship in freedom.

v

For centuries Austrian society was composed essentially of nobility, clergy, and land workers, but in the very modern age a new element intruded, or rather a small older category was greatly enlarged: the town-dwelling burghers and wage earners. This social grouping expanded in proportion as trade and banking, transportation and industry progressed. Accumulation of wealth afforded greater leisure in Austria as elsewhere; the arts of civilized living could be and were more thoroughly cultivated, and the more widely culture was diffused, the larger the educational opportunities, the weaker became the fixity of classes. The Austrian bourgeoisie, thrusting forward in economic affairs, disputed the monopoly in politics and learning which the aristocracy and the clergy had so long held. The city of Vienna was the home of one of the most cultivated and subtly civilized middle classes to be found anywhere in the world.

Like their counterparts in other countries, the bourgeoisie of Austria prized diligence, creative work, and self-reliance as virtues. They heartily believed in the religion of progress, in the optimistic faith that there was an iron law of inevitable human improvement. They cherished the belief that, with the help of applied science and the growing prestige of reason, humanity was proceeding to a social paradise on this earth. They tended to substitute happiness in the here and now for eternal bliss or everlasting torment beyond the grave. Many Austrian middle-class spokesmen rallied round the banner of anticlericalism, when indeed they were not unsympathetic to organized religion in any form.

As possessors of wealth or culture or both, the Austrian bourgeoisie disputed the monopolistic pretensions of the aristocracy to political power. Yet underneath, middle-class folk—or some of them—secretly envied the "bluebloods" and in their social attitudes and appetites paid them the most flattering variety of flattery—imitation. Plutocratic bourgeois families built splendid residences in the hope of forming social friendships with patricians and they allied with them against the haunting specter of socialism.

In actuality, the bourgeoisie of Austria was a heterogeneous grouping with very real gradations, just as was the case with the aristocracy and the rural population. The wealthiest bankers and manufacturers ranked above the owners of small shops and independent mechanics, who endeavored to safeguard their interests by supporting the Christian Socialist party, as did well-to-do peasants.

Also in the petite bourgeoisie were the salaried public servants and "blackcoated" private employees; both of them had advanced educational training, often of university grade. There were, too, the members of the "free professions," physicians, lawyers, university professors, and others. Practitioners of the liberal professions spent long years in study and training and earned next to nothing before they were thirty years of age. The Austrian lawyer, for instance, after completing his university studies at about twenty-three, served seven years as a sort of apprentice before he was fully qualified to engage in practice. The economically more successful professional men enjoyed incomes and had living standards comparable to the plutocratic among the banking and industrial gentry.

There was a growing class of citizens, beneficiaries of higher education, who, on completion of their studies, found only inadequate opportunities to apply their talents—which were not always equal to their ambitions. Among this element there was a feeling of frustration and therewith, not infrequently, the conviction that the prevailing social and economic order required far-reaching transformation. From their ranks issued some of the leaders of the vigorous Austrian Socialist movement. Part of the middle class, too, was the "labor aristocracy," that is, well-paid skilled artisans, and some officials of trade unions and coöperative societies.

VI

In the bourgeois society of Austria, Jews occupied a peculiar, and as time went on, a powerful position. According to the census of 1910, the empire contained 1,314,000 professing Jews, or just under 5 per cent of the whole population. Apostasy, intermarriage with Christians, and Christian baptism, growing in volume among the educated Jews in the western cities of Austria, made heavy inroads into Jewish ranks. It is probable that Jews and "non-Aryan" Christians formed, as of 1914, the greater part of the cultivated and well-to-do classes of Vienna.[4]

Children of Israel actually resided in the realm of the Hapsburgs before the arrival of the Hapsburgs themselves, and it may be that Jews were dwelling in Vienna when the community was still a military outpost of the Roman empire. But most Austrian Jews lived in the province of Galicia, which was finally incorporated in the Hapsburg Monarchy in 1815. After about 1870, when legal limitations upon Jewry were removed, many migrated from Galicia to the west, and their numbers were swollen by impoverished newcomers who streamed in from Hungary, Russia, and Rumania to find better economic and cultural opportunities or to escape discrimination, abuse, and persecution. The wandering Jewish peddler was a familiar figure in all sections of the Austrian empire. By 1914 there was scarcely a village without its Jewish shopkeeper or tavern proprietor, many of whom combined moneylending with their other business, and many great landed estates employed Jewish stewards. Thousands upon thousands of Jews crowded into Vienna, Prague, and other cities. To the Jews, Austria was indebted for many pioneer industrial undertakings, such as leather and silk manufacturing, the processing of tobacco, and the large-scale distillation of spirituous beverages.

Vienna was the focal point of Jewish migration and concentration. One district of the capital, the *Leopoldstadt,* an island between the Danube canal and the river, was formally assigned to the Jews as a place of residence in 1622. At the middle of the nineteenth century only a few thousand Jews actually resided in Vienna, and there were only sixty-three officially authorized Jewish traders; yet many shops and stores were operated by Jews and they were supreme in the wholesale textile trade. In the years after 1870, Viennese Jewry increased rapidly, and by 1900, 146,926 residents were classified as Jews.

Down through the Christian centuries, Vienna's Jewry experienced the typical and familiar cycle of favoritism, discrimination, persecution, and then toleration again. Welcomed at times as valuable for the economic welfare of the community in general, or as financiers and counselors of rulers and princes, on other occasions Jews were the victims of destructive pogroms, wholesale pillage of property, and banishment.

During the reign of Emperor Joseph II, many traditional limitations upon the Jewish population were revoked or relaxed; Jews were allowed, for example, to engage in almost any trade, and to make loans on real property, though they might not buy it. Ancient regulations obliging Jews to wear distinctive costumes and debarring them from public places of entertainment were abolished. Those who lacked hereditary names were required to adopt them, so no longer were they designated simply as Jew Isaac, Jew Sara, and so forth. And Jews were made liable for military service on the same conditions as Christians. On the other side, special taxes upon Jews went untouched, and until 1823 the privilege of building a synagogue in Vienna was withheld. Down to 1848 Jewish residents were obliged to report to a Jewish Bureau every three days and to pay a tax every fortnight; they were not allowed to acquire land, nor to enter the civil service or the legal profession. As a result, they concentrated mainly in finance or handicraft industry, or became tutors or physicians.

Certain energetic and thrifty Jews pressed into prominent positions in the financial and banking affairs of the country. All other Jewish banking houses were eclipsed or crowded aside by the Vienna branch of the ramified and powerful financial dynasty of the Rothschilds. Solomon Rothschild, who arrived in the Hapsburg capital about 1820, quickly forged to the front in the banking world and, aided by his international connections, remained until his death in 1855 the most influential figure in the financial affairs of the empire. Befriended by Prince Metternich, he was particularly active in the flotation of government bonds, in the building of the early railways, and in lending to impecunious nobles.

Solomon's son, Anselm, a shrewd and cautious banker, launched the famous Viennese *Creditanstalt* on its fabulous career, and his heir, Albert, carried the fortunes of the Viennese House of Rothschild to dizzy heights. Albert and his brother, Nathaniel, whose preferences followed artistic rather than business lines, built palatial mansions in Vienna, frequented exclusive social circles, and even gained admission to court society; they were the admiration of their coreligionists and the envy of many a Gentile. The Rothschilds were merely the most conspicuous representatives of the culturally refined Jewish moneyed aristocracy of Vienna.

Equality of rights was formally extended to Austrian Jewry in 1867, but deviations from the law were frequent in places. Allowed greater freedom of movement and in choice of vocations, Jews after about 1870 penetrated the learned or "free professions" and went into journalism in large numbers. In time a large percentage of the physicians and lawyers of Vienna and a predominant portion of the newsmen, even on papers notorious for their anti-Jewish proclivities, were Jews. They forged to the front rank in literature, in the theater, and in intellectual affairs, broadly, and pressed into lower positions in the civil service. And Jewish participation in the commercial and financial affairs of the empire increased prodigiously, with by far the greater proporton of Jews in the category of the small operator in wholesale or retail trading. Though no statistics on which reliance may be placed are available, it is safe to say that by 1914 the industry and trade of Vienna were to an overwhelming extent in Jewish hands. Not uncommonly Gentiles filled conspicuous offices in business concerns, where they were known to the general public, while Jews, who were the real directors, kept behind the scenes.

After restrictions on Jewish landownership were fully removed in 1867, some prosperous Jews commenced to purchase real property and by 1902 they owned something like 7 per cent of the cultivable area of Galicia. A few wealthy Jews managed to secure titles of nobility, and some who accepted Christian baptism were able to marry into the bottom levels of the Austrian aristocracy. Among the Jews dwelling in the western cities, Vienna and Prague particularly, there was a distinct tendency to abjure the faith of their fathers, to accept Christian baptism, and to merge pretty thoroughly with the rest of the population. Assimilated Jews frequently discovered that they were regarded by conforming orthodox Jews as traitors and renegades, and that they were looked upon by the enemies of Jewry as undesirable and unwelcome intruders.

Deeply ingrained social prejudices persisted against all but the most polished and most affluent children of Israel. Old, insurmountable barriers kept Jews out of the Hapsburg diplomatic service, out of responsible positions in the army and in the bureaucracy (with rare exceptions), and denied them top rank in the universities of Austria. Dr. Sigmund Freud, the world-famed pioneer in psychoanalysis, was only the best-known Viennese scholar whose Jewish antecedents debarred him from a full professorship.

Very modern anti-Judaism in Austria, serious, open, organized agitation against Jewry, first assumed importance after the financial crash of 1873. The prosperity of a handful of Jews in a time of general hardship was strummed upon by adroit demagogues in whipping up popular passions and latent emotional prejudices, and Jewry entire was condemned as the author and the beneficiary of the economic distress. Thereafter suspicion, distrust, and hatred of the Jew were constant forces in the public and private life of the empire.

Competition of small Jewish tradesmen, competition of Jewish artisans, the displacement of handworkers by machine industry in which Jewish business men played a part—all furnished fuel for anti-Judaism. Not untypical of the antipathy toward Jewry on economic grounds was the comment of the clerical *Reichspost* on the death of Albert von Rothschild: "The state has long been the productive milch cow of a syndicate at whose head stands the firm of Rothschild, and some of the most recent profits pocketed by it might be considered anything but justified."

The fires of anti-Judaism were fed by the steady migration of *Ost Juden* from Galicia and other East European sources into the Austrian cities, especially Vienna. Small islands in the broad Christian-Slavic sea, the *Ost Juden* had largely preserved their medieval outlook on man and the world and cherished the belief that they were, peculiarly, the chosen of God. By choice as well as by social pressure they insisted on exclusiveness in marriage and in other ways, to a degree unmatched by Gentiles. Consciously and deliberately they were a folk apart and that was conducive to unpopularity.

Down to the minutest details of everyday living, the way of life of the eastern Jew was regulated by religious dogma and moral rule. Attempts to acquaint the Galician Jewry with modern ideas by innovations in education and in synagogue service met with small success, and efforts at cultural and intellectual reformation fell pretty flat; eastern Jewry, for the greater part, preferred to walk in the conservative paths which the fathers had followed.

Poverty-stricken ghetto dwellers for the most part, victims of hazardous living and inequalities and misunderstanding across the centuries, restricted and exploited by officialdom, subjected to recurrent physical attacks, despised and mistrusted by their Gentile neighbors generally, the Galician Jews were, by and large, unappealing specimens of humanity, uncouth, tricky, penny-grubbing, cringing. These tendencies, as well as their exotic costumes and their outlandish speech, wandering Jews carried to new homes in Vienna's *Leopoldstadt* and other centers of settlement.

Given time in their new and freer environments, the *Ost Juden* abandoned something at least of their medieval heritage, just as they shed their traditional garments, but in the interval they encouraged dislikes and suspicions among Gentiles that affected the whole Jewish community. Critics echoed the shrill warning of the German savant, Treitschke, that "year after year there pours in from the inexhaustible Polish reservoir a host of ambitious pants-selling youngsters, whose children and children's children will some day control . . . the stock exchanges and the newspapers." Westernized, assimilated Jews in Austria, or some of them, greatly resented the steady influx of *Ost Juden* and, out of fear for their own position, tried to prevent immigrants from settling in and about Vienna and Prague.

In Austrian clerical circles, antipathy toward the Jew was relentless, for he belonged to an alien, accursed folk, the denier of the Christian Saviour, the veritable offspring of the devil. Besides, Jewish purchasers of landed estates became patrons of the churches on their properties, and that the clergy resented; and the activity of Jews in both press and parliament in connection with anticlerical legislation accentuated the ill-will of churchmen. The growth of secularism and irreligion was ascribed to malevolent influences fostered by Jewish-controlled newspapers and by the allies of the Jews in the liberal wing of the Austrian parliament. Father Sebastian Brunner, a versatile, voluminous, and polemical writer, has been called the father of modern anti-Judaism in Austria. In his savage diatribes against the children of Israel, Brunner did not scruple to resurrect the monstrous medieval calumny of ritual murder, devoting an elaborate brochure to allegedly authenticated specimens of that superstition. It was among the lower clergy that anti-Judaism appealed with especial force; bishops as a rule held aloof from the agitation when they did not flatly condemn it.

Clerically minded laymen played leading roles in Austria's most potent political expression of anti-Judaism, the Christian Socialist party. From 1897 to World War I that party dominated the municipal government of Vienna, and was a powerful force in Austrian parliamentary affairs.[5]

Political considerations, too, occasioned dislike and dread of the Jew in Austria. If Jewish children in Bohemia attended a German school, Czech patriots were angry; if they went to a Czech school, they antagonized the Germans. Polish patriots in Galicia often denounced Jews as Pan-Germans, while Pan-Germans reviled them as internationalists. Because Jewry furnished a large share of the leadership in socialist and radical movements, believers in the *status quo* were prone to indict the whole Jewish population as subversive and dangerous.

Anti-Jewish feeling seems to have penetrated pretty deeply into the Gentile population of Austria. *Kikeriki,* a sheet of political doggerel, carried on a running attack against Jewry and indulged in coarse, vulgar propaganda. At least one Jew-baiting Austrian politician posted over the gate of his country place: "Hunden und Juden ist der Eintritt nicht gestattet" (Dogs and Jews must not enter). In the Austrian parliament it was actually proposed, in 1900, that sexual relations between Gentiles and Jews should be punished under a law prohibiting intercourse between humans and brutes, and that at the Easter season Jews should be scrupulously watched by officers of the law, to prevent them from perpetrating ritual murders.

Not unnaturally, Jews resented the constant vituperation of which they were victims. The naturalness of that reaction was appreciated in some Gentile quarters, as the testimony of Count Wilczek, a prominent member of the Austrian Catholic nobility, illustrates. "The Jews are not exactly congenial to me," he wrote in his memoirs, "especially when I come into contact with their less agreeable qualities, but I can well understand their hostility to us when I reflect that from morning to night they are always hearing the word 'Saujud'—Jewish swine—hurled at them. If they have any sense of honor or of self-respect, how can they help being hostile to us?" Wilczek accepted Nathaniel Rothschild as an equal, found him an "unusually charming man and a really noble character," and addressed him with the familiar "du," an example which was later imitated by some other aristocrats.[6]

The hope cherished by many well-to-do Austrian Jews, that Jewry would eventually blend with the Gentile population, was challenged by the continuing discriminations, social and civil, and by the rising surge of anti-Judaism. Certain Jews became convinced that salvation must be sought in a new Zion, in a Jewish national state, to which the discontented and the abused might emigrate. The Zionist idea had considerable popularity among eastern Orthodox Jews, who thought of it not only as a means of checking the assimilationist drift but as a way of ensuring the political and cultural prestige of the Jews as a nationality.

In Vienna, messianic Zionism found an eloquent champion and able organizer in Dr. Theodor Herzl, who nowadays is honored as the father of political Zionism in its most modern and positive form. Into the Zionist movement, which had a considerable history but at the time little vitality, Herzl infused new vigor and energy, which was to carry the cause to eventual, if incomplete, success. Budapest-born, Herzl drifted to Vienna, where, as literary editor of the *Neue Freie Presse,* he preached the virtues of assimilation to his coreligionists. In a moment of exaltation he even recommended that leading Vienna Jews should set an example to their fellows by receiving Christian baptism en masse. At one point he thought that Socialism would be the cure for discrimination against Jews. But denunciations of the Jews, personal insults, and the notorious Dreyfus affair in France eventually persuaded Herzl of the futility of the assimilationist philosophy. So he avowed himself a political Zionist, explaining his beliefs and his dreams in *Der Judenstaat* (The Jewish State; 1896).

Under the influence of a Russian Zionist society and of friends in Vienna, Herzl concluded that a Jewish homeland ought to be obtained in Turkey's Palestine, the ancient dwelling place of Jewry. Accordingly, negotiations with the sultan were initiated and, when Emperor William II of Germany rode into Jerusalem on his famous Holy Land tour of 1898, Herzl and a Zionist delegation solicited his weighty support for their enterprise. The kaiser, while at first sympathetic to the plan, shied away after learning that the sultan was opposed. Herzl, in the meantime, organized societies to promote the Zionist cause and to purchase land for settlements in Palestine; annually Zionist congresses resolved in favor of "a home in Palestine secured by natural law." A tireless worker, Herzl arranged great Zionist gatherings, wrote extensively on his project, and sought the personal endorsement of European sovereigns for his plan.

After the sultan declined to approve a Palestinian colonization scheme, Herzl took up a proposal of the British government to create a free Jewish Commonwealth in African Uganda. But strait-laced orthodox Zionists would be satisfied only with the realization of the messianic dream in the old homeland of Palestine. They hotly condemned Herzl's acquiescence in the Uganda alternative as a betrayal of a sacred cause, and divisive controversy broke out within Zionist ranks. When Herzl died in 1904, the prospect of founding a Jewish state seemed remote indeed; nevertheless, the dynamic impetus he had given Zionism encouraged feelings of self-respect among many Jews, quickened hopes, and stimulated lively interest in the historical traditions and distinctive culture of Jewry. Galician Jews elected four Zionists to the

Austrian parliament of 1907, the first to be chosen by equal and manhood suffrage.

Far more than Hungary, where large and earnest Protestant and Orthodox Catholic minorities flourished, Austria was a Roman Catholic country, qualified to supersede anticlerical France as the most reliable, though scarcely the most devout, daughter of the papacy. Latin rite and Uniat Catholic believers together accounted for over 90 per cent of the Austrian population, if official figures may be accepted as satisfactory evidence of religious affiliation.[7]

Austrian Catholicism profited from a large and active hierarchy, whose close-knit organization reached into every urban district and almost every hamlet. For thirty-five years, Prince Frederick Schwarzenberg, brother of the statesman, Felix, who battered down revolution in 1849 and proceeded to restore absolutism, presided over the Austrian episcopacy and jealously guarded the interests of mother church. His successor, Count Francis Schönborn, who also belonged to the highest aristocracy, perpetuated the tradition, and both were ably supported by Vienna's great cardinals, Rauscher, Gruscha, and Piffl, and a line of energetic bishops. Many of the higher clergy came from the lower classes, especially from the peasantry, rather than from the nobility.[8]

Catholic prelates had the title and dignity of princes with all the rights and privileges pertaining thereto. They comprised a substantial bloc in the upper house of the Austrian legislature and maintained their own ecclesiastical courts; clergymen were subject to state courts only when church tribunals consented. And a prince bishop could punish laymen for offenses that the civil law did not recognize as unlawful; individuals sometimes were condemned to the greater excommunication, involving not merely exclusion from the religious fellowship but often an economic boycott as well.

Stubbornly the Austrian episcopate fought to preserve the historic privileges of Catholicism, but in the years just after the *Ausgleich,* as has been explained, it was obliged to bow to laws that modified the position and prerogatives of the church. On historical grounds and for reasons of expediency, leading Austrian churchmen were unsympathetic to the doctrine of papal infallibility; both Schwarzenberg and Rauscher composed pamphlets criticizing the dogma and at the Vatican Council of 1869 voted against its promulgation. But when the majority at the conclave accepted the dogma, the Austrian bishops, except for Strossmayer, promptly fell into step, though they well knew that the decision would destroy the Austrian Concordat.[9]

Although the state took away some of the special rights of the church, it did not disturb her administrative freedom or touch her landed property; but churchmen were obligated to present annually an abstract of their accounts to the secular government. To supplement the revenues from landed estates and the gifts of the faithful, the state furnished subventions for the maintenance of Catholic worship. Through ecclesiastical pressure in the seventies, larger appropriations were secured from the public treasury, so as to assure curates a minimum income of about two hundred dollars a year and full-fledged priests somewhat more than double that amount; at the same time, pension provisions for the clergy were brought more into conformity with newer economic conditions. Parish priests as a rule pieced out their incomes by teaching the catechism in state-operated schools.

Drawn from the common people, the Austrian lower clergy, or many of them, performed their duties without notable devotion and displayed little interest in doctrinal or philosophical questions. Moral laxity was rather prevalent among rural churchmen—the priest's cook was the subject of many a robust, earthy tale. Clerical deviation from the loftiest standards of personal behavior caused no consternation among the faithful, for priests were to be respected as spiritual guides, and not to be judged by ordinary human codes. Many clergymen, of course, discharged their responsibilities conscientiously and lived in a manner that was beyond reproach.

Something of the prestige of Catholicism in Austria stemmed from the wealth that it possessed, represented by land and securities, and not improbably this was the richest branch of the church in Europe. Individual prelates boasted princely incomes; the archbishop of Prague, for example, had revenues in 1868 valued at $62,000, while the Cardinal Archbishop of Olmütz was able to donate $20,000 to the Vatican annually, and at his death left a fortune reputed to be $10,000,000. In every province of the empire there were properties belonging to the church, the most extensive being in Bohemia, Moravia, and Styria. And monasteries often owned and operated inns, wine cellars, dairies, sawmills, small factories, and banks. Although legally required to pay taxes to defray the costs of the ecclesiastical establishment of the empire, church authorities often managed to evade their obligations.

Austrian monasteries preserved much of their medieval flavor and performed in the nineteenth century the peculiar services they had rendered an earlier, less complex, and more otherworldly society. As of 1868, more than three hundred monasteries and over five hundred convents were flourishing in the empire. Commonly monks conducted schools for the training of children of well-to-do families and some of them carried on scientific researches. The ancient school of the Scottish Benedictines in Vienna catered originally only to the nobility, but in the nineteenth century youths of all classes were admitted; Charles I, the last Hapsburg monarch, the Social Democratic leader, Victor Adler, and Arthur Seyss-Inquart, the first Nazi governor of Austria, all attended this famous school. And it was in the monastery of Brünn that Abbot Gregor Mendel, a peasant by birth, working among his peas and beehives, made discoveries on the physiological process of heredity that earned him a place just below Darwin in the gallery of modern biologists. His studies, which were published in an obscure journal, remained unknown to the world of science until a generation after his death. They opened up the wide field of research and speculation in heredity associated with the name Mendelism or Mendelianism.

As centers of learning below the universities, and in spirit remote from them, monastic schools accumulated large book collections, carefully preserved and diligently studied. Members of older religious brotherhoods exerted little effort to keep abreast of contemporary currents in thought, and their theology was untainted by traces of modern heterodoxy. Monks were often well versed in science—not always up-to-date, to be sure—and in the politics of their time; and many among them were keen sportsmen. As progressive farmers, monks wielded a beneficent influence upon the peasantry in the neighborhood of their cloisters.

Along the Danube valley stood (and stand) some of the most historic monasteries of Christendom, the property of easygoing Benedictines, Cistercians, and Augustinians. These orders regarded themselves as the superiors of the newer and poorer Jesuits, whose actual impact upon the life of the times was far more extensive.

The noble Benedictine abbey at Melk, on the edge of the Wachau, dates from the eleventh century. It was really a single building, magnificent and palatial, mostly erected in the early eighteenth century, on a hilltop commanding marvelous vistas in every direction. The library, which was inlaid with costly woods, contained over eighty thousand volumes of rare incunabula, including a copy of the first Bible in German. Apartments in the monastic quarters were reserved for the use of the emperor and his retinue whenever he visited in the region. Tastefully laid out grounds surrounded the monastery and the fat acres that it owned yielded lucrative returns. Part of the landed estates was tilled by hired workers, under the supervision of the monks; the balance was leased to the peasants. To the Melk monastery belonged twenty-seven nonresident livings, and about a hundred monks devoted themselves to educational and religious ministrations. The great abbot of Melk of the nineteenth century, Alexander Karl, who was a peasant in origin and a skillful manager, impressed travelers as a territorial magnate not less than as a spiritual leader.

Scarcely less affluent than Melk were the Augustinian monastery at St. Florian, famed for its organ, which the composer Anton Bruckner once played and beneath which he is buried, and the Benedictine chapter at Krems. Each owned some of the most fertile fields along the Danube; and

at Salzburg the venerable Benedictine abbey of St. Peter preserved fragments of early Christian art and owned large zoölogical and mineralogical
collections, which had given the monastery distinction as a scientific center
in the eighteenth century.

Members of the Jesuit and Redemptorist societies took their religious responsibilities more seriously than other monastic orders in the Austria of
Francis Joseph. Colleges conducted by Jesuits sent forth many graduates
who entered the public service, and through that channel their ultramontane teachers were able to exert a not inconsiderable influence on state business. Learned Jesuit fathers also filled many chairs in the universities of the
empire.

VIII

For Austrian churchmen, the two major forms of mass education, the
state schools and the press, were an unending source of perplexity. Taking
as its slogan "Catholic schools for Catholic children," the church persistently
pressed for confessional schools and struggled to have religious instruction
the central feature of the training of children. Proposals of laymen to lengthen
the time devoted to schooling or to teach agricultural methods in rural
schools had always to contend with the resourceful resistance of bishop and
priest. Prelates never ceased to complain about the materialistic and anticlerical temper of the universities and discrimination against Catholic student societies; indeed, church authorities battled for a purely clerical university at Salzburg from which lectures at variance with Catholic belief and
practice would be rigidly excluded.

As an instrument to combat the secular press and to strengthen Catholic
journalism, the *Puisverein* was established in 1906. Over a hundred thousand
members were quickly enrolled and contribution boxes for the purposes of
the society were installed in many churches. Funds were allotted to such
stanch organs of clericalism as the *Reichspost* and the *Vaterland,* but the success of the churchmen in the battle against the secular press was distinctly
limited. It is very probable that the influence of the Catholic press was much
smaller in 1910, say, than in the seventies when the percentage of literates was
far smaller.

In Austria, as elsewhere in Western Christendom, allegiance to conventional religion tended to diminish under the impact of secularizing forces
such as scientific progress and expanding industrialism. Nationalisms, too,
invaded the traditional sphere of Christianity. Yet as late as the sixties the
wealthier Austrian nobles and the peasantry were still obedient to the
clergy even though rationalism had penetrated the leading town classes and
in professional circles the clergy were the object of scorn and derision. Among
German shopkeepers and the more comfortably situated peasants, as well as

among liberal intellectuals, it was widely felt that churchmen should confine themselves to the appointed task of caring for souls, and that they should eschew participation in secular affairs. Anticlericalism was likewise fostered by the latitudinarian outlook of emigrants to America who, by their letters or their conversation upon returning to the homeland, affected the outlook of relatives and neighbors. Along with this, Jewish ill will toward Catholicism, as the abettor of discrimination, augmented the forces of anticlericalism.

With the passing of the decades, secularizing currents gained speed, so that Austrian cityfolk grew increasingly this-worldly and that part of the wagearners which accepted the Socialist gospel became almost wholly so. Among the males in the aristocracy, interest in Christianity was in many cases merely formal and perfunctory. Only the mass of the countryfolk, as is elsewhere remarked upon, held tenaciously to the historic faith, and for them Catholicism was likely to be "a leisurely religion without fervor."

Take it all in all, the Catholic Church formed one of the more solid pillars of the Hapsburg state, a strong unifying institution in this realm of many tongues. Intimacy between Catholic altar and Hapsburg crown had its roots deep in the past; they had coöperated to mutual advantage during the campaigns against Protestantism in early modern times and more recently their common interests had found expression in the famous Concordat of 1855. Historically, movements against the crown had been organized and promoted by non-Catholics for the most part, while Catholics, in the main, had been conspicuously loyal to the dynasty. Quite apart from its services as a spiritual institution, Catholicism was a valuable political asset for the Hapsburgs, bringing together rich and poor, townsmen and rustic, German and Czech, Pole and Ruthenian, Italian and Slovene.

Committed as it was to upholding Catholic principles, the Austrian state adopted positive measures against critics and enemies of the national creed. Freemasonry, for example, was not allowed to take root, and swift and certain punishment was meted out to mockers of religion; a citizen who made light of a Corpus Christi procession, for instance, was sentenced to hard labor, rendered the harder by fasting. Under imperial law, Catholics were denied the right of seeking a divorce whatever the circumstances, even if they changed their religious affiliation. An Italian Socialist agitator who delivered unbridled attacks upon the church and her clergy was repeatedly imprisoned and in the end (1909) unceremoniously hustled across the frontier by the public authorities. He was Benito Mussolini, known at the time as Professor Mussolini.[10]

Austrian clericals on their part lauded prevailing political institutions as possessing the sanction of divinity and as such to be cherished, respected, and obeyed. Cardinal Rauscher proclaimed that true patriotism was identical with devotion to the ruling dynasty and love for the divinely chosen Francis Joseph. "Next to God," in Rauscher's words, "we place our hope in His Majesty, the Emperor." With tongue and pen this spirited patriot kept hope and courage alive after the military reverses of 1859 and 1866 and exhorted the bishops to promote the purchase of state bonds. At election times some clerics circulated pamphlets instructing parishioners how to vote and disseminated political propaganda from their pulpits. That activity was quite in harmony with an imperial decree issued by Joseph II: "Although a priest's province is the cure of souls, he must also be considered as a citizen and as a state official engaged in religious work, for he can directly and indirectly exercise the greatest political influence over the people by working on their feelings."

The role of Catholicism in imperial Austria was summed up by a sober French scholar in this way: "The Catholic Church of Austria is less a state church than an ecclesiastical state bureau, working like the army, the bureaucracy, and the police in the interests of the government." [11]

Churchmen who in the first stage of the Austrian constitutional period identified themselves with the officially styled Clerical party later rallied to Christian Socialism when that movement emerged as an important force in the public affairs of the empire. Aristocrats with clerical convictions helped to give leadership to the party, and individual priests aided it as a bulwark against the rising tide of materialistic Socialism. The enthusiastic Jesuit Father Abel of Vienna compounded masculine Christianity with Christian Socialism as a medicine for keeping wageearners from aligning with Social Democracy. Some clerics branded Socialism as the foul brew of Satan and did not scruple to threaten hell-fire punishment to workers who embraced the Marxian faith. Socialist journalists and orators in turn excoriated churchmen in vituperative language and taught their followers that clericalism was the supreme enemy of the working class.

Officially, Austrian Catholicism was *Hapsburgtreue* in outlook and resisted political movements that were inimical in their implications to monarchical unity and solidarity. Just where the hierarchy stood on questions of nationality was cogently expressed by Cardinal Schwarzenberg during a controversy over a proposal to divide the theological faculty of Prague University into a German and a Czech section: "The Church does not wish the separation of nations, but their union in one body . . . She recognizes the right of every people to independence, she respects and supports the demand of a people for its own language and own form of instruction. But the Church cannot give to the claims of nationality the first place; they must always be for her a secondary interest . . . In this country [Bohemia] it is a special duty of the priesthood to seek to soothe and unify." Catholicism dared not forget that Hussite secessionism was woven into the Czech national pattern nor could it be unmindful of the possibility that Yugoslav and Ruthenian Catholics might, under the spur of nationalism, pass over to the schismatic Orthodox wing of Christianity.

Yet among Catholic Slavs in the empire some prelates and priests openly identified themselves with national strivings, as was conspicuously the case with the great Yugoslav bishop, Strossmayer, and with Cardinal Friedrick Fürstenberg, who was an ardent advocate of Czech national interests. Among the Polish clergy there were lively national sentiments, but as a body Polish churchmen were largely Austrophile, and the same generalization held for the clergy in the Italian-peopled districts, who fought Irredentism and secessionist agitation. Roman Catholics among the Yugoslav minority were notably faithful to the Hapsburg crown, while Orthodox Yugoslavs inclined toward the Greater Serb idea and some of their priests were outspoken apostles of the Pan-Slav gospel. As has earlier been mentioned, the presence of Roman Catholics in Bosnia and Albania furnished the Vienna government with a ready pretext for political intervention in those areas.

At the end of the nineteenth century Austrian Catholicism was confronted by a new foe in German ranks: the "Los von Rom" agitation conducted by advocates of the union of the German areas of Austria with imperial Germany. Pan-German hot-gospelers contended that the Catholic character of the Austro-Germans was a big barrier to *Anschluss,* an obstacle that would be swept away should they enter the evangelical fold. In literature and in speeches Pan-German zealots tried to rob Catholics of confidence in priests, in the sacraments that they performed, and in the church herself. Schönerer, the leading spirit of "Away from Rome," turned Protestant himself and exhorted his followers: "Let us break the chains which tie us to a church hostile to Germanism."

Catholic clergymen energetically combatted the movement, charging that "Los von Rom" involved "Los von Hapsburg" as well, which was quite correct. Emperor Francis Joseph roundly condemned the agitation and Archduke Francis Ferdinand assumed the patronage of a Catholic school league whose objective was to battle against "Away from Rome" and other tendencies hurtful to Catholicism. The society of St. Boniface, which was originally founded to care for the spiritual needs of German Catholic emigrants, likewise directed its energies against "Los von Rom."

Financial and other help was rendered the secessionist cause by Protestant organizations in Austria and in Germany. Evangelical propaganda societies of Germany generously contributed; the Odin Society of Munich, for instance, obtained funds for the Pan-Germans by selling post cards on which the crest of the House of Hapsburg was shown crushed in the claws of the Prussian eagle. Without aid from across the frontier it is doubtful whether "Los von Rom" would have amounted to much. As it was, outside of Austrian student circles defections from Catholicism were extremely small, probably not more than sixty thousand altogether. What the agitation really accomplished was to advertise the Pan-German party, to embitter the already tense relations between German and Czech in Bohemia, and to galvanize Austrian clericalism into greater political activity. In a longer view, certain of the converts to Protestantism, as mature men, promoted the Austrian *Anschluss* movement in the years after World War I, which culminated in 1938 in the forced union of Austria with the Third Reich of Adolf Hitler.

Protestantism in Austria, which was a mighty force in the age of the Reformation, was almost wholly extinguished by the agents and agencies of the Counter Reformation. It revived somewhat after Joseph II published an edict of toleration (1781), though Protestants obtained religious freedom only in 1861. Under that grant—which was not fully applied until 1875—Protestant churches were allowed to manage their internal affairs and were given subsidies from the state treasury; and a faculty of evangelical theology was established in the University of Vienna. Protestantism had its largest following in scattered communities of Upper Austria and Styria; as of 1910, 589,000 Austrians were recorded as evangelical.[12]

Followers of Orthodox Christianity in Austria, only slightly more numerous than Protestants, lived almost entirely in Dalmatia and in Bucovina. They were organized into a single fellowship in 1873, under a metropolitan see at Czernowitz; the real purpose of the merger was to keep the Orthodox worshipers in Austria organically separate from their coreligionists in Serbia and Rumania and so avoid possible political complications.

IX

The concern of Austrian churchmen over state schools and the endless wranglings among the nationalities over schools were indicative of the rising importance of popular education in the life of the country. Under imperial law the whole educational system was subject to supervision and inspection by the ministry of education, though actual control of elementary schools (*Volksschulen*) was vested in the provincial governments. On several occasions the imperial minister of education belonged to a Slav nationality and was not at all sympathetic to the diffusion of the traditional German culture, but his real power was limited.

In each province there was a school council presided over by the local governor and containing representatives of the provincial diet, churchmen, and professional specialists. This body regulated the conditions of education and subjects of study, and decided what language or languages should be used in instruction. Elementary schooling was financed almost entirely by provincial and other units of local government; provincial autonomy in educational matters made it possible for the Czechs, for instance, to have by 1914 a well-developed elementary-school system in which the mother tongue was spoken.

Under Austrian legislation enacted in 1869, attendance on common elementary schools was compulsory for eight years, though in practice there was considerable variation from province to province in the length of the school day and of the school year. Differences in the financial resources of the provinces meant differences in the quality of the instruction and the school facilities. Instruction in many rural communities seldom passed beyond the very rudiments of formal learning; inadequate though that was, it represented sheer gain over the schoolless tradition of the past. For all its faults by any ideal standards, the Austrian school system served as the ground plan for elementary education in the nations that issued from the empire after the smash-up in 1918.

The quantitative benefits of the spread of popular education were clearly revealed in the sharp decline in Austrian illiteracy. Before 1860, ability to read and write was general only in the provinces of Lower Austria (Vienna) and Upper Austria; in Dalmatia at that time only one youth out of a hundred called up for military service was literate. But by 1914 probably fewer than 10 per cent of the children of the empire of school age were not receiving instruction. Popular education was most fully developed in the German-language areas, and there the proportion of illiterates was lowest; the Czech districts stood next, with Galicia, Bucovina, and Dalmatia at the foot of the scale. A Dalmatian spokesman indeed was heard to protest: "Over three hundred Dalmatian villages have no schools at all; in half the country the number of illiterates is not 50 or 60 but 99 and 100 per cent."

On the qualitative side, the object of Austrian elementary education, above all other objects, was to contribute to the preservation of the state and the prevailing order of society. Schools were designed to send forth obedient subjects, not critically minded citizens. Religion, which was taught in conformity with the faiths represented in a given province, was a compulsory subject of study; a prescription in the constitutional laws of 1867 that other subjects were to be "independent of the influence of any church or religious grouping" was not strictly carried out. Debatable issues, such as obligatory participation of pupils in religious exercises, were decided from time to time in the light of the relative influence of clerical and anticlerical forces. In the seventies the opponents of clericalism very largely had their way, but after that, decisions on schools tended to conform to the desires and convictions of churchmen. So heavy was the emphasis on inculcation of loyalty to the monarchical order, so considerable was the influence of the clergy in educational affairs, that when experiments in more democratic forms and freer ways were introduced after 1918 in the new states formed out of the Austrian empire, the populations were lacking in proper preparation.

For apprentices who had completed their elementary schooling, continuation schools were created in the empire. Instruction was concentrated on industrial and commercial subjects, which were intended to supplement the training that the youth received in his place of employment, but some attention was devoted to the civic and general education of the pupil. Attendance on the continuation school was compulsory for apprentices for two or three years and classes were held in the evening or on Sunday. In the larger Austrian communities, there were special schools for the principal crafts and a limited number of continuation schools offered instruction in agricultural subjects.

Secondary schools (*Mittelschulen*), in which advanced general education was offered, were maintained either by provincial governments or privately, and the private schools were required to conform to the standards of the publicly supported institutions. As of 1914, there were 518 schools of this character for boys, attended by only 160,753 learners, while similar schools for girls enrolled less than a tenth of that number. Attendance at these schools was entirely optional and rather expensive. Broadly speaking, a pupil matriculated in a secondary school after having spent four or five years in a common elementary school and pursued studies for eight years.

For the greater part these institutions, which were in fact preparatory schools for the university or a technical high school, were organized like their counterparts in imperial Germany. The leading type, the gymnasia, provided training in the traditional humanistic culture, but *Realschulen,* in which modern and technical subjects were taught, became increasingly popular; after 1908, secondary schools of all types were put on a plane of equality. Certificates of proficiency in a secondary school, tested by examination, entitled holders to enroll in an institution of the highest learning. Some secondary schools furnished technical training at various levels.

From a Czech pen we have an enlightening portrait of a secondary school of the nineties in a Prague suburb: "Facing us was the teacher's desk and platform next to a sliding blackboard, a crucifix, and a framed photograph of the old emperor Francis Joseph—hated by us as a symbol of the Austrian yoke. The instruction was in Czech but the textbooks and oral explanations were devised to imbue us with devotion to the Hapsburg dynasty and to expel any thoughts of an independent national destiny . . . The secondary schools were considered principally as mills for turning out obedient civil servants of the Hapsburgs . . . The teachers belonged to two distinct types; one very officious, leathern and dry, the other trying to engage our interest and sympathizing more or less openly with our chronic state of youthful revolt . . . The Austrian school authorities severely punished any participation in debating circles or political organization . . . Passionately we took part in frequent mass demonstrations in the streets. These were followed by police reprisals. Any boy caught was liable to be expelled from school, and this added spice to the adventure." [13]

CHAPTER NINE

TAAFFE'S IRON RING
1879-1893

By ENTERING UPON THE ALLIANCE OF 1879, FRANCIS JOSEPH gave foreign policy a German orientation, yet at the same time he turned against German ascendancy in Austrian domestic politics. Criticism of the occupation of Bosnia by German Liberals pained the monarch deeply. He appreciated, however, that in the event of warlike complications with Russia his German subjects could be relied upon, but disaffection might cause trouble among the Slav minorities, apart from the Poles. It was, therefore, elementary and prudential statecraft to try to appease the Slavs, above all, the militant Czechs. With that objective in mind Francis Joseph chose as prime minister Count Edward Taaffe, a chum of his youth.

Taaffe was descended from an Irish family, one of whose members had drifted to central Europe to fight under Wallenstein; the Taaffe name in fact was not dropped from the Irish peerage until World War I. Entering the Hapsburg civil service in 1852, Taaffe, by reason of his industry and organizing talents, had advanced to the governorships of Salzburg and Upper Austria. At the outset of the constitutional regime he had functioned, successively, as minister of national defense, premier, and minister of the interior. Subsequently appointed governor of the Tyrol, he there notably improved conditions of life and labor and enhanced his reputation as a statesman of talent.

A typical old-school Hapsburger, this accomplished bureaucrat was an ideal collaborator for Francis Joseph, with whose conceptions of government he had much in common. Chary of abstract principles or far-reaching programs, distrustful of independent thinkers, Taaffe much preferred clever little expedients whereby dissident national interests could be conciliated and the country could somehow muddle along. His public record had endeared him to many political factions without seriously alienating any. As a fervent Catholic, the Clericals looked upon him with sympathy; by speaking out against the Concordat with the Vatican, he had earned the sympathetic regard of the German Liberals; Czechs and Poles liked his federalistic leanings, and even the anti-Jewish fringe fancied Taaffe on their side, even though his chief counselor was a Jew named Blumenstock.

At parliamentary legerdemain and political bargaining Taaffe was a past master, and long experience had taught him how to handle politicians and their foibles. Whether dealing with friends or foes, he assumed an air of flippancy and cynicism, and apparently was incapable of treating issues with sobriety and seriousness. In reality, however, these were only surface phenomena, for he was a deadly earnest man, cunningly concealing his deeper designs. As Austrian premier Taaffe bent his energies toward enhancing the sphere of the bureaucracy, seeking to lessen the real authority of the legislative organs of government. As the faithful servant of his imperial master, he guided Austrian destiny for fourteen years, longer indeed than any other premier of the constitutional era.

For his first assignment Taaffe was charged with conducting an election —parliament had been dissolved in May 1879—and laying the groundwork for a durable ministry. He arranged a heterogeneous political coalition, composed of Clericals, German aristocrats, and Slavs, Poles and Czechs principally, which came to be spoken of as the "Iron Ring." With that alignment of parties and a bit of pressure and manipulation at the polls, Taaffe secured a comfortable parliamentary majority. Pitted against the ministry were the German bourgeois deputies, the Liberals and their allies, who had dominated the political scene in the seventies, and even now the Liberals formed the largest single bloc in the reichsrat. Promptly the Taaffe cabinet embarked upon a course intended to ensure the allegiance of the Slav minorities to the Monarchy—a policy that could scarcely fail to antagonize the German centralists in proportion as it gratified the Slavs.

The novel feature of the Austrian parliament that assembled in the autumn of 1879—and a bitter pill for the German Liberals—was the presence of Czech deputies from Bohemia, who for a dozen years had boycotted the reichsrat. During the seventies, a fissure had opened in Czech political ranks; one faction, the "Old Czechs," while devoted to the principle of Bohemian autonomy, preferred to seek that goal by moderate measures in league with conservatism and clericalism. In this camp were about half of the most influential Bohemian landed aristocrats, members of families that historically had filled prominent positions under the Hapsburgs. The fidelity of these nobles to the crown was beyond question; they lent prestige to the

Czech national cause and brought to it the backing of feudal and clerical elements. Younger Czech hotspurs, led by the journalist Edward Grégr, advocated more radical action and cherished democratic and liberal principles of government.

These differences were, however, sufficiently smoothed over to allow the Czechs to present a united front in the reichsrat of 1879. Taaffe bought their appearance with promises of concessions to Czech nationalism without committing himself on the long-standing Czech demand for an autonomous Bohemian kingdom clothed with the same rights as Hungary.

It was, however, understood that the Czechs had not renounced their pretensions regarding states' rights. Deputy F. L. Rieger at the very first parliamentary session read a statement of his nationality's claims, and that practice was repeated by other Czechs at each meeting of parliament down to the collapse of the Monarchy. Praźak, a leading Czech, was given a place in the Taaffe cabinet, and two other Slavs, both Poles, were allotted portfolios. The Pole, Julian Dunajewski, professor of economics in the University of Cracow, who was put in charge of imperial finance, became the most powerful personality in the ministry next to Taaffe himself; during his tenure of office posts in the ministry of finance were gradually filled with Poles.

For their support of a military appropriations bill the Czechs extracted from the ministry a special language ordinance obliging all judicial and administrative officials in Bohemia and Moravia to render their decisions in the language of the petitioner and to conduct trials in the language of the accused. For Czech patriots this was a meaningful advantage, for they regarded their language not merely as a means of communication but as a symbol of political equality with their German neighbors. Of necessity the new ordinance would require civil servants to speak both German and Czech, a handicap for Germans since as a rule they neglected to learn Czech, while Czech officials were bilingual and so qualified for offices that Germans were incompetent to hold.

As predicted by German deputies, who protested hotly against the ordinance, the number of Czechs in the lower branches of the state service increased. Also beneficial to the Czechs was the tendency of sons of well-to-do German Bohemians to shun the civil service for more remunerative employment in private business. Officials of Czech antecedents secured appointments to inferior posts in heavily German districts, and the Hapsburg bureaucracy, once solidly German in composition, became increasingly a training school for civil officials of Slav origins. Thus a body of experienced Slav public servants was built up, which was to prove a valuable asset in the Czechoslovak and Polish Republics created at the close of World War I.

As another concession to the Czechs, the Taaffe ministry sponsored a measure to split the venerable University of Prague into a Czech and a German section. In the sixties, professors at Prague had been authorized to lecture in the language of their choice and students had been allowed to take examinations in Czech. Chairs from which the Czech tongue was spoken increased from two in 1864 to twenty in 1880, and repeated proposals to divide the University had been approved by the Prague city council, by groups of Czech scientists, and by other bodies. To many Austro-Germans the plan seemed to be nothing short of a wanton and intolerable desecration of the most ancient of German seats of higher learning, and German deputies fought partition tooth and nail. Czech intellectuals not only disputed the German origin of the University, but pointed out that for years Czech students had exceeded German; in 1882 the faculties of philosophy and law were separated and the process of divorce was completed a decade later. Czechs angrily complained that in dividing the physical assets of the institution the Germans were given preferential treatment.

At its opening the Czech university enrolled a thousand learners and by 1914 the attendance had quadrupled, while less than half as many were studying in the German university. Even so, state appropriations for the German institution were disproportionately large, as Czech spokesmen never ceased to point out. To the Czech university young Slovaks and Yugoslavs were attracted by talented and inspiring professors; and university-trained Czechs in excess of the needs of their homeland took employment in Russia and Bulgaria. Efforts of the Czechs to secure a second university at Brünn, the capital town of Moravia, were successfully blocked by the Germans.

State and private initiative provided the Czechs with other institutions of learning, including two technical colleges, many secondary schools—the source of students for the national university—and a large number of elementary schools. It became in time an official policy to establish an elementary school in any area where forty Czech children of school age lived within a radius of half a mile. Once a school had been set up, aggressively Czech teachers, sometimes abetted by priests, pressed forward the work of Slavicization; classes for Czech pupils were also formed in predominantly German schools. As an instrument to fight German influences and to foster Czech consciousness the *Matice Skolská* (mother of schools) was founded in 1880; it established private schools in districts of mixed language. Funds for this cause were raised by the sale of picture post cards and commemorative stamps, and by popular subscription; and in many a Czech restaurant it was customary for the head waiter to pass a collection box for the "mother of schools."

Revisions in the suffrage laws favorable to the Slav groups were carried through by the Iron Ring. Over the fierce opposition of German Liberals, the privilege of voting in the town and rural curiae was extended in 1882 to all males who paid five florins direct tax, instead of ten as formerly; and the landlord curia of Bohemia was enlarged so as to benefit the Czechs, and the growth of the Czech bourgeoisie enabled them to capture several of the seats assigned to chambers of commerce.

Taaffe had not only to retain the goodwill of Slavs, he had also to keep conservative Clericals in line. To that end, and over the strenuous protests of German Liberals, schools were placed under the direct control of the Catholic clergy and compulsory school attendance in rural Austria was reduced from eight to six years.

On the rising wings of material prosperity the Czech middle class grew more aggressive politically and converted Bohemia into a battleground on which they intended to vanquish the Germans. National controversies in Bohemia became so vehement indeed that the consul general of the United States in Vienna reported (1886): "The irrepressible parliamentary conflict between the slavery and antislavery parties [in the United States] was not waged with more acrimony and determination than the political strife now in full progress between the German and the Bohemian [Czech] subjects of the Austrian empire. There is not a political move on the European chessboard which to the participants in this internal warfare seems of any importance whatever in comparison with the great and overwhelming question whether the German-Austrians or the Czech-Austrians shall obtain predominance in the Empire." [1]

The Slav orientation of the Taaffe ministry heightened confidence among the Czechs and encouraged a mood of belligerence. At elections to the Bohemian diet in 1883 Czechs scored heavily, taking one hundred sixty-seven seats, with only seventy-five going to Germans. A well-intentioned gesture by Rieger to smooth out national antagonisms with Schmeykal, a prominent German leader, foundered, for the latter held that only the imperial parliament, not the provincial assembly, had authority in these matters. On the other side, German proposals to partition Bohemia into Czech and German administrative and judicial zones fell flat, because Czechs tenaciously insisted that Bohemia must be kept intact and the two languages treated as equals. In 1886, German deputies started a boycott of the Bohemian assembly that lasted four years.

Provincial elections in 1889 resulted in remarkable gains for the militantly nationalistic "Young Czechs," at the expense of the "Old Czechs"; the veteran Rieger himself escaped defeat by an exceedingly narrow margin. The Young Czechs appealed chiefly to the rising bourgeoisie, many of them newly enfranchised "five-florin" taxpayers. Adroit campaigners, such as the journalists Grégr and the physician Engels, painted glowing visions of the transformation that would come over Bohemia once the young Czechs were in command and home rule had been secured.

On foreign policy, the Young Czechs espoused a course diametrically opposed to that being pursued in Vienna, for they desired friendship with France and Russia and the abandonment of the alliance with Germany. During the War of 1870 a prominent Czech newspaper had declared: "From the beginning of the war we have been friendly to France and in the future we will align ourselves with any state or people which makes war on the Germans. The enemies of our enemies are our friends." For the Young Czechs that confession of faith remained the law and the prophets.

Infuriated by the astonishing success of the Young Czechs at the polls and by the nomination of the Czechophile Count Francis Thun as governor, German Bohemians feared that autonomous status might in fact be conferred on their province. Taaffe, however, quieted German apprehension— and punctured Young Czech dreams—by announcing that "the government has no intention of advising His Majesty to sanction any change in the constitution or to consent to his coronation as king of Bohemia."

Shortly (1890) the Taaffe ministry convoked a conference of Bohemian moderates of both nationalities to canvass the possibility of an amicable settlement of Bohemian language questions. The Young Czechs, whom Francis Joseph considered "queer customers," were not invited to share in the deliberations. Out of this parley—the most important that was held before 1914—emerged a promising set of accords, which seemed calculated to satisfy all factions except extremists. The Germans acknowledged the justice of having a Czech school in any district in which lived forty Czech children, provided their families had resided there for five years; Czech negotiators on their part agreed to the division of Bohemia into two ethnic areas for administrative and judicial purposes, and promised to be contented if a majority of the judges in the supreme court of the province were bilingual, the others to be German in language.

Crown and ministry endorsed these understandings and the semiofficial press showered praise upon Taaffe for his share in making reconciliation possible. In May 1890, a series of bills to execute the accords was presented to the Prague diet, which German deputies attended after an absence of four years.

But the Young Czechs, who saw the unity of the Bohemian kingdom imperiled by the compromise proposals, resorted to filibustering in a determined effort to prevent their adoption. Some of the Old Czechs lined up with them, so that the reconciliation scheme was nullified. Electoral opinion seemingly endorsed the intransigent stand taken by the Young Czechs, for in the reichsrat voting of 1891 they were hugely victorious; even the venerable Rieger, taunted by critics with cries of *Haimba* (Shame) and charged with clericalism, went down to defeat. After a melancholy farewell to his people, the "Grand Old Man" of Czech politics, who had done more for the advancement of Czech nationalism than any other living person, retired from the public scene. Not only was the projected Bohemian settlement pigeonholed, but Taaffe's parliamentary majority was weakened and political disorders in Bohemia increased.

Bohemia, indeed, was swept by a fresh and fervent wave of Czech nationalism, which had a strongly antidynastic tinge. When the imperial Hapsburg anthem was played at the Prague Exhibition of 1891, the audience studiously refrained from applause. And a bomb, set by Czech zealots, damaged a railway bridge on the line from Prague to Reichenberg over which Francis Joseph was to travel after visiting the Exhibition. As part of a Slav festival at Prague in the summer of 1891, the coronation of Leopold II as Bohemian king a century before was commemorated and evoked an outburst of Czech national enthusiasm. Extremist political sentiments were floridly voiced by Edward Grégr, the recognized mouthpiece of the Young Czechs, in a speech to the reichsrat. "Bohemia," he declared, "is being sucked dry by Austria, which resembles a vampire. The majority of the Czech population is utterly wretched in the midst of this alien empire . . . Their nationality is oppressed and persecuted in this Austrian state, which is a state of violence and tyranny toward all Slav races. The Bohemian people are made to hate this state—I repeat—hate this state, and mark my words, the day of reckoning will come."

To this intemperate utterance, Prince Charles Schwarzenberg, an "Old Czech" moderate, responded: "If you and yours hate this state—and it is unfortunately a fact that hatred of Austria is spreading in Bohemia through your teachings—what will you do with your country, which is too small to stand alone? Will you give it to Germany or to Russia, for you have no other choice if you abandon the Austrian union."

Despite the stubborn resistance of the Young Czechs, the Taaffe ministry resolved to proceed with the partition of Bohemia into two judicial zones. Thereupon, the Young Czechs, in an address to the crown, rehearsed their stock claims and grievances and intimated that if Austria became involved in war Bohemian loyalty could not be depended upon;[2] in their view there could be no settlement of the nationality controversy unless autonomy were bestowed upon an integral Bohemia.

The presentation of the Bohemian partition bill to the diet was the signal for the most disgraceful outburst that that turbulent body had yet known. Young Czech deputies snatched addresses from the hands of German deputies and tore them to ribbons; books and inkstands were hurled promiscuously about the chamber, and a free-for-all fight, knock-down-and-drag-out, broke loose. There was no alternative but to prorogue the diet; demonstrations were continued on the street, attacks were made upon the persons and property of Germans; antidynastic Czechs desecrated imperial eagles on public buildings and postboxes and a noose was looped round the neck of a statue of Francis Joseph. To put an end to the disorders, Prague and a large part of Bohemia were placed in a state of minor siege; in reply, Young Czechs at an immense banquet defiantly sang the *Marseillaise* alternately with the Russian national anthem, and resounding cheers were given for the tsar and the recently completed Franco-Russian entente.

On the assumption that Czech extremists were plotting a revolutionary conspiracy, the police made many arrests. Investigations revealed the existence of an antidynastic and republican society, the *Omladina,* composed of Czech university professors, students, young bourgeoisie, peasants, and wage-workers. After trial, thirteen of the arrested men were sentenced to years of hard labor and over two score were given lighter penalties.

Taaffe's appeasement policy had patently failed to win the Czechs over to the existing Austrian system. Rather it had fostered Czech "radicalism" and had likewise intensified national feelings among the Germans. But Bohemia, meantime, was making economic progress and Czech culture was advancing famously, all of which redounded to the profit of the Czech national cause.

II

During the Taaffe era the region that once had formed the Bohemian kingdom became not only the most highly industrialized section of the Hapsburg Monarchy but one of the major manufacturing areas of Europe. Traditions of fine craftsmanship, which had been created late in the Middle Ages but had declined in consequence of the seventeenth-century wars, were revived, and Bohemian districts once noted for the manufacture of high-grade linens flourished anew as centers of textile manufacturing.   In the refining of sugar and the making of fabrics, woolens, cottons, linens, and silks, Bohemia attained first place in the Hapsburg Monarchy. Northern Bohemia indeed boasted more textile establishments than any comparable district in Europe. Cheap goods were disposed of among the peasants of eastern Europe and the Orient, while finer cloths met the demand of the Old World aristocracy and plutocracy. Bohemian cotton-spinning mills compared favorably with the most up-to-date English factories, though costs of production were somewhat higher owing to more expensive plants, greater provision for the welfare of the workers, and the comparative inefficiency of labor and fuel.

Illustrative of the advance of the Bohemian textile industry was the record of the Liebig family. Johann Liebig, a journeyman weaver, set up a tiny plant at Reichenberg in 1826; the business prospered, and products were diversified, so that in 1886, 7,200 employees were at work, and the company had become one of the very largest in the Monarchy. Johann died an Austrian baron and a multimillionaire. For the welfare of the workers and their families, the Liebig firm established a sickness and old-age pension club, stores that sold food and other necessities at low prices, kindergartens, trade schools, and a colony of workers' dwellings, each with eight apartments; these social-welfare institutions compensated somewhat for the meager wages that were paid.

At Pilsen, Emil Škoda took over in 1868 a concern to manufacture machines, and later turned to the production of steel goods and of armaments. By 1900 the Škoda company was operating coal mines as well as steel plants employing 3,300 workers, and had emerged as the rival and competitor of the great German Krupp firm. Škoda had created, in fact, the greatest of all Bohemian industrial establishments and had become the most successful of all Austrian manufacturers. Though born·a Czech, Škoda abandoned the Czech nationality after he became wealthy and he had his children brought up as Germans.

Over in Moravia, at Zlin, the foundations of Europe's largest shoe and leather company were laid before 1914 by Thomas Bata, the son of an obscure village cobbler. Ambition drove Bata to quit his father's shop and, after misadventures in Prague and Vienna, he started manufacturing cheap shoes on his own account. Part of the capital was supplied by a Czech coöperative bank, but the enterprise, though it employed fifty workers, was never a financial success. Bata decided in 1904 to go to the United States, to Lynn, Massachusetts, to learn advanced processes of shoemaking, and took with him a few shopworkers. Each of them secured employment in a different factory and after a year's experience in the United States returned home, spending a short time in English and German plants on the way. Applying methods of standardization and mass production that he had picked up abroad, Bata created a boot and shoe industry which in 1914 had almost 2,000 names on the payroll. Profit sharing with workpeople and paternalism were conspicuous features of Bata management. During World War I the operations of the company expanded fabulously and by 1918 Bata was coming to be called "The uncrowned king of Moravia," or, alternately, the "Henry Ford of Europe."

Porcelain, china, and articles of glass, called "gablonz" wares, mock jewelry, beads, and buttons were specialties of Bohemia. These goods were largely made by peasants for miserable pittances and sales depended upon the whims of fashion; changes in the ornamentation of feminine apparel, for instance, spelled hard times or good for multitudes of Bohemian cottagers. In winter months whole peasant families engaged in making lace, baskets and barrels, shoes and gloves, cheap oil paintings and artificial flowers; around Karlsbad, workers toiled in factories by day and in cottages at night. Beers brewed in Pilsen and Budweis set standards for the world, owing to the high quality of hops and to skillful brewing. Special institutes carried on researches to improve methods of beer production.

Austria was generously endowed with medicinal springs of varying chemical combinations that alleviated or cured certain diseases. Each major spring was the site of a flourishing health resort, with a *Kurhaus* containing reading and music rooms, halls for band concerts, and living quarters. Spas in Styria, Carinthia, the Tyrol, and Upper Austria attracted crowds of patrons, but the baths of Bohemia, Karlsbad, Marienbad, Franzensbad, and a multitude of smaller ones were world-renowned for the curative qualities of their mineral waters. Sufferers from nervous ailments, gout, stomach and kidney disorders, rheumatism, and throat afflictions by the tens of thousands visited the Bohemian health resorts annually, and the export of mineral waters was a not unimportant source of income. Besides furnishing employment for hotel attendants, visitors purchased the productions of provincial cottage industries and stimulated export trade in these commodities.

Czech industrial progress was displayed to the world in an exhibition held at Prague in 1891, precisely a century after Europe's first affair of this kind, which had also been held in Prague. Ignored by the German-language press and with only a few Bohemian Germans exhibiting, the Prague fair had a distinctly Czech character. A wide variety of machinery, utensils, and textiles demonstrated Czech achievements and was highly gratifying to national pride.

Before the end of the nineteenth century Bohemia supplied a quarter of Austrian revenues, produced more textiles and sugar than the rest of the Monarchy combined, brewed over half the beer, manufactured a third of the paper, and had two-fifths of the railways of the empire. Bohemia and Moravia together turned out the greater part of Austrian machinery and railway equipment, and mined upwards of half of the coal and graphite, four-fifths of the lignite, and all of the small output of tin and precious metals. No other part of the Hapsburg realm, in short, approached Bohemia in mining or manufacturing.

Standards of life among industrial workers in Bohemia left much to be desired. Employment of children was unusual, it is true, but the normal workday was eleven or twelve hours. Wages were low, among male cotton spinners in the late eighties ranging from $1.90 to $3.80 a week. Primitive cottages contained a single room, a kitchen, and a woodshed. Breakfast and a forenoon lunch consisted of black bread, butter, and coffee; for a few cents the worker bought a midday meal of soup or a chunk of bread and a vegetable; fried sausage, potatoes, and bread were the normal supper; a piece of pork or beef brightened the Sunday table.

Lowly conditions invited organized activity to better the lot of wage earners. Spurred on by Socialists of Vienna, a Social Democratic party was founded which, in 1892, split into two factions, the Czech group, which repudiated ties with Austrian Social Democracy as "Jewish, international, and German," taking the name of the National Socialists. Trade unions were organized and strikes conducted, but seldom did the workers win their objectives.

Economic discontent in Bohemia, as in other provinces of the Dual Monarchy, stimulated emigration to Vienna or across the broad Atlantic. Bohemia in the eighties probably sent more emigrants to the United States than any other part of the realm, some Germans, but mostly Czechs. Before that Bohemia had contributed to the peopling of the New World, Protestants who settled in Quaker Pennsylvania, for instance, and revolutionaries who fled after 1848. Newspapers in the Czech language were appearing in the United States by the sixties, and a Czech gymnastic society founded in 1878 established branches in centers where immigrants congregated. At Prague University, Professor Thomas Masaryk, who had married an American, delivered lectures on the United States.

For the most part Czechs took up farms in the Mississippi valley and in Texas, baptizing their communities with Old World names and even teaching Negroes to speak Czech. Other Czechs, preferring an urban existence, planted themselves in Midwestern cities and towns. The Czech colony in Chicago, for instance, constituted a city within the city, with its own language, schools, and churches; by 1930, citizens of Czech origin or descent in Chicago exceeded 160,000. A Czech, Cermak, was chosen mayor of the Midwestern metropolis and on a visit to Prague in 1932 greatly pleased an audience with the remark that he presided over the second most populous Czech community in the world.[3]

Machinofacture in Bohemia was attended by the growth of the Czech bourgeoisie and of the wage-earning class. German managers in the sixties started to attract Czechs into textile mills and lignite mines and craftworkers in leather and cloth drifted from the countryside into German towns. Coöperative credit societies and a strong banking institution, *Zivno,* organized in 1868, assisted enterprising Czechs in advancing into the capitalist class.

Town-dwelling Czechs, to the consternation of their German neighbors, showed small inclination to merge with the older German element. Indeed, Germans in predominantly Czech areas tended to assimilate with the newcomers, owing to German practices of employing Czech house servants and nurses for children, and entrusting German foundlings to Czech baby farms. Czechs, moreover, had a higher birth rate than Germans and intermarriage was not uncommon. In consequence, Czechs bore obviously German names like Jungmann, Rieger, and Sontag, while Germans were known as Kallina,

Schmeykal, and Schuselka. At a meeting of Socialists in 1913 a leading Czech had the name of Nemeth, the Czech term for German, while a Dr. Czech was prominent on the German side of the aisle!

Wherever Czechs moved they held tenaciously to their national peculiarities and customs. Czechs who took up residence in Vienna—and by 1900 nearly 200,000 had done so—preserved their language, and maintained schools, churches, welfare societies, and militantly patriotic clubs; some Czechs edged into the municipal government.

Communities in Bohemia that once were regarded as German were year by year converted into dominantly Czech towns and cities. Conspicuous was the transformation that took place in Prague, which for centuries had been overwhelmingly a German city; in 1856 Prague's population was made up of 73,000 Germans and 60,000 Czechs; thirty years later there were 30,000 Germans and 150,000 Czechs, and not a single German had a seat in the city council. In the earlier year both languages had been used impartially in public documents and street inscriptions, but by the end of the eighties only Czech street names were to be seen and German firms had largely removed their names from shops and stores. By 1910 Prague had become more thoroughly a Czech metropolis than ever before in its history, the German-speaking element having dwindled to under 19,000 while the Czechs exceeded 200,000. Pilsen, the Škoda works center, which was a German town at the middle of the nineteenth century, had by 1890 been converted into a Czech city, with only a fifth of the inhabitants reported as German, and the same trend characterized other cities in the province of Bohemia, except in the west and northwest; certain rural villages shed their traditional German character in as short a time as a decade.

Despite the onward march of the Czech population, Germans continued in the ascendant in sections of the former Bohemian kingdom. In the province of Bohemia, at Aussig on the Elbe, the Monarchy's busiest internal port, at Reichenberg, a textile center, in the "Egerland," whose chief city was Eger, a lovely old German community, at the Karlsbad health resort, and in southern Bohemia, where they were mainly poor soil workers and handicraftsmen, Germans still outnumbered Czechs. The Moravian capital of Brünn (Brno) contained a German majority, but if suburbs were reckoned in the Czechs stood first. Taking the province as a whole, Czechs were ahead, though Germans, by reason of tradition and wealth, dominated the local assembly until 1905.

Population was extremely mixed in Silesia, the third fragment of the medieval Bohemian kingdom. In 1880, Germans totaled almost half, Poles rather more than a quarter, and Czechs somewhat less; by 1910, the German element had fallen off fractionally. Silesia, because of the heavy German population, considered itself separate from Bohemia and Moravia, and was so regarded by the Austrian government; as a rule, linguistic concessions given to the Czechs did not apply in Silesia.

Sharpening national animosities reflected themselves in the daily life of Bohemia. Boycotting societies fostered discrimination in business, and the circumstance that Germans owned factories in which Czech workpeople were employed embittered the social scene. Workmen founded competitive trade unions and university students of the rival nationalities engaged in street brawls or joyously consigned one another to inferno. Czech zealots heard themselves called "reptiles" and in turn labeled Germans "bugs," to recall merely the more polite zoölogical epithets that were in vogue.

III

Czech national consciousness, which had been steadily unfolding in the preceding century, grew apace as the Czech population expanded in wealth, numbers, and culture. The focus and symbol of the emergent Czech patriotism was the historic Bohemian capital and ancient commercial metropolis, Prague, set upon seven hills and served by the Moldau (Vlata). So long ago as the tenth century, an informed Jewish trader and traveler, Ibrahim ibn Jacob, described Prague as the richest of cities by reason of its trade. "Russians and Slavs come to it from Cracow with their wares," he chronicled, "and Moslems, Jews and Turks come . . . with goods and money and they take away slaves, lead, and various furs." Prague in the nineteenth century seemed to be fulfilling the destiny predicted for it by Libuše, the mythical first queen of the Czechs, who, according to legend, envisaged "a city whose glory shall reach the stars."

After 1867, when the medieval walls were demolished and surrounding suburbs were absorbed, Prague's growth was rapid. The building of railways and the coming of modern factories transformed the city into an industrialized community, but the diversified architecture was a silent reminder of medieval and early modern splendor. Old "imperial" Prague with its cathedral, castle, and aristocratic palaces was outclassed by the modern quarters of thriving commerce and industry. In the new day, Czech speakers came greatly to exceed the German, and Czechs took control of the municipality, without, however, distinguishing themselves in administration; for years, in fact, the finances of Prague were deplorably mismanaged, corruption was not unknown, and funds were appropriated for luxuries while sanitation was neglected.

In propagating national consciousness Czech patriots paid especial attention to schools. Czech nationalism was inculcated by appeal to heroic chapters in the national past; instruction, not accident, made John Huss the national saint and the warfare of his era the most glorious memory of the Czech people. The work of the school was reinforced by newspapers, scores of which circulated after the relaxation of the censorship. Most widely read was *Národní Listy* (National Journal), founded (1861) by Julius Grégr, which disseminated the opinions of the Young Czechs; fearlessly it encouraged and fostered Czech national interests, and where it led lesser sheets followed.

Active in the national revival, too, was the *Matice Česká* (1830), an association of intellectuals concerned with the regeneration of Czech literature and scholarship generally. Patriotic clubs and choral and gymnastic societies cultivated national faith and hope. Especially effective were the *Sokols* or athletic organizations which combined physical training with the promotion of patriotic and cultural interests.[4] Although the dream of the founder of the Sokols, Miroslav Tyrš, to enlist all Czechs fell short of the goal, nevertheless by 1914 upwards of 130,000 belonged to this important agency. The *Sokol* idea, incidentally, was adopted by other Slav nationalities and promoted some sense of solidarity within the broad Slav family.

While these bodies were at work spreading patriotic sentiments among the masses, Czech scholars, mostly attached to Prague University, achieved for their nation a distinguished place in the republic of letters and provided inspiration and leadership for the national cause. The greatest of them was Thomas Masaryk, properly honored as the father of the Czechoslovak Republic and its first president. Of humble origin, once a locksmith's apprentice, Masaryk contrived to work his way through the University of Vienna, and was appointed a *privatdozent* there. Without by any means giving up his youthful ambition to become a public man, Masaryk dedicated himself to an academic career. In 1882 he was nominated professor of philosophy in the Czech university at Prague, a post which he accepted with considerable reluctance, since he was not a thorough Czech either in language or spirit at the time, but he soon attained a unique position in the faculty.

Whereas his colleagues tended to be narrow and pettily nationalistic in their outlook, Masaryk extolled cosmopolitan ideas and sought to weave the Western cultural heritage into the Czech pattern. His conception of intellectual honesty impelled him to repudiate as crude forgeries the celebrated Königinhof Manuscripts, which allegedly showed that Czech literary culture was older than German and which had for years been the subject of violent controversy among Czech and German pundits. Masaryk's scholarly verdict brought down on his sturdy head the wrath of Czech chauvinism, which accused him of being bribed by Germans to betray by belittlement the glorious heritage of the Czechs. For Masaryk, the issue at stake possessed high moral implications; "Our pride, our culture," as he put it, "must not be based on a lie." In the end, truth scored a notable victory over sentimental romanticism.

Nor did Masaryk hesitate to intervene (1899) in a notorious ritual-murder case. A Jew, Hilsner, was accused of murdering a Czech peasant girl to obtain blood for ritualistic services. By the great mass of the people, even in learned circles, it was superstitiously believed that ritual murder was in fact a part of normal Jewish procedure, so that there were few doubts of the guilt of the accused, and popular passions provoked attacks upon Jewry. When appealed to, Masaryk scrupulously examined the evidence in the case and proved that the charge was utterly false. Nonetheless, Hilsner was committed to prison for life and Masaryk was hounded as a philosemite, who had been suborned by Jewish gold to exculpate the Israelite. When the feeling against Masaryk was at its peak, it was impossible for him to deliver his university lectures, streets leading to his residence were closed by the police, and two officers of the law accompanied his son on the way to school. Heedless of the unpopularity his battle against discrimination and injustice caused, Masaryk pursued truth wherever it led, and his reward was an enviable reputation for sound judgment, candor, and intellectual integrity.

From his university chair in philosophy, Masaryk lectured on the philosophical systems of Western thinkers such as Locke, Hume, Pascal, and Comte, seeking, among other things, to impress upon his students that others than Germans had speculated profoundly on the great and central problems of life and the universe. He was more a sociologist than a metaphysician, and an ardent democrat, and his teaching was permeated with moderate patriotism and with appeals to translate ideals, taught in university cloisters, into realities in the great world of practical affairs. "If you love your country," he implored, "don't talk about it, but *do* something worth while; that is what matters." Adding to precept example, Masaryk contributed to the columns of *Národní Listy,* later published a daily of his own, and vigorously engaged in political discussion. Elected to the Vienna parliament in 1891, as an ally of the Young Czechs, Masaryk retired after a brief and disenchanting experience. But subsequently he founded a "realist" party, returned to parliament, and defended the interests of Hapsburg Slavs with skill and eloquence.

Czech history, which had been given a patent of respectability by the romantically minded Palacký, was cultivated by a notable company of scholars. Wenceslas Tomek, for instance, composed a monumental history of Prague to 1608, illuminating many dark corners in the era of Huss; only gradually was this humanistic cosmopolitan "converted" to Czech nationalism. Scientific history, perhaps better called "university history," had its best treatment at the hands of Professor Jaroslav Goll, who insisted that the Czech past should be studied from a broadly European approach rather than in the narrowly patriotic framework that Palacký had chosen. Disciples who went forth from Goll's seminar on Czech history in the Reformation period were imbued with the objective qualities of their master, and themselves earned distinction as historical craftsmen.

Cast more in the Palacký mold was Joseph Kalousek, a thorough Czech partisan, who selected subjects for study that would reveal the Czechs in a favorable light in their century-long struggle with *Deutschtum*. With Bohemian German scholars, Czech historians waged fierce literary polemics that brought to light much new knowledge on medieval Bohemia and quickened national fervor in both camps.[5]

Without allotting a disproportionate amount of space to the subject, it is impossible to convey more than a sketchy impression of the wealth and variety of the Czech literary output in the half century under review. Only with the relaxation of the stern censorship in the sixties were Czech men of letters able to resuscitate the long-neglected literary language and traditions. In the vanguard was the lyrical poet Jan Neruda, whose compositions showed warm social sympathy and discontent with the prevailing order; a nationalist, but no chauvinist, Neruda taught democratic and liberal ideas in matters of politics and religion. His charming short stories described realistically the manner of living of the Prague petite bourgeoisie.

More attractive to the patriotic were the writings of Svatopluk Czech, whose epic poems glorified the Czechs in the spacious epoch of Huss. Of all the Czech litterateurs the palm for versatility and erudition must be awarded to Jaroslav Vrchlický, the pseudonym of Emil Frída. In one of his best-loved sonnets, addressed to the bejeweled royal crown of Bohemia, he voiced the political longings of his countrymen:

> How long wilt thou languish in thy retreat,
> O splendid jewel, sacred symbol of our nation?
> How long wilt thou slumber in thy cell?
> It is not in vain that upon thy circlet
> Gleams the brilliance of our precious stones.
> Our love is the ruby; our faith is the sapphire,
> The emerald our hope, and the pearl our silent abdication.[6]

Whereas authors of erudite Czech historical treatises counted their readers by tens, popular historical novels, imaginative, rich in detail, and vivid in coloring, had a far wider appeal. Most successful of the writers of this literary genre was Alois Jirásek, who turned out tales dealing chiefly with the Hussite wars and the Counter Reformation, though some of them recounted the nineteenth-century Czech renaissance. *Against All, Brotherhood, Darkness* were clarion calls from a romanticized past to a realistic present, acquainting Czech readers with the heroic qualities of their forebears and summoning the patriotic to emulate their courage and resolution. Similar traits characterized Jirásek's dramas glorifying the famed heroes of the Czech nationality. What Jirásek preached he did not disdain to practice, and during World War I he helped to force the idea of political separation from Austria upon Czech politicians who were hesitant and vacillating. Carolina Svetlá, the most popular Czech woman novelist, fostered national sentiments in her later productions, and became an ardent nationalist.

From a world viewpoint the eminence of Czechs in music in the age of national reawakening eclipsed the achievement in literature. Bedřich Smetana laid the groundwork for a distinctly Czech pattern of music; he belongs to that small group of artists who demonstrated that the little Czech nationality possessed elements of authentic genius. Involvement in the convulsions of 1848 left impressions on his mind that were never erased; love of country as the prelude to affection for a broader humanity inspired much of his creative activity. "My Country," a cycle of symphonic poems composed in the seventies, glorified the Hussite heritage and heralded a brighter future for Bohemia; one of the pieces, "Moldau," a paean to the noblest of Czech rivers, has been a favorite of music lovers the world over.

For the gala opening of the National Theater (1881), Smetana prepared a warmly patriotic opera, *Libuše*. The theater itself manifested the progress of Czech culture; over the stage in gilt letters were the words *Národ Sobe* (The Nation for Itself). Funds for the building, as well as for a successor when fire destroyed the original, were raised by patriotic subscription.

National extremists on occasion accused Smetana of not being sufficiently Czech and of wilfully neglecting the folk songs of his own people, while German critics, on the other hand, derided him because of the decidedly Czech flavor of his productions. The international renown of Smetana rested chiefly on his comic operas, of which *The Bartered Bride* (1866), full of rich scenes drawn from peasant life, achieved and retained immense popularity. His successor in the writing of opera, Zdeněk Fibrich, recalled episodes from the romantic past of the Czechs in *Šarka*.

Better known in the United States, no doubt, than Smetana is Anton Dvořák, who composed for a time in the New World. Son of a village butcher living near Prague, Dvořák came into prominence with a patriotic hymn, "The Heirs of the White Mountain." While his music had a nationalistic flair, it was less nationalistic than Smetana's, and much of it showed Pan-Slav inclinations. Folk tunes, Czech ones particularly, Dvořák exploited in "Slav Dances" and "Slav Rhapsodies," which established his reputation on a solid basis; in the final phase of his career he undertook to preserve bits of Czech mythology in symphonic poems. For his artistic accomplishments Dvořák was appointed to the upper house of the Austrian parliament, the only Czech musician so honored, and his funeral occasioned national mourning.[7]

Music apart, Czech contributions to the fine arts deserve only brief mention, for there were no painters or sculptors of European stature. The brothers Mánes, Joseph and Guido, drew their inspiration from historical and religious themes; Joseph, the more distinguished, has indeed been cited as the emancipator of Czech painting from German influences. Like them, the foremost Czech sculptor, Joseph V. Myslbeck, drew his materials from the legends and history of his countryfolk; the noble equestrian statue of St. Wenceslas in Prague is the finest expression of Myslbeck's talent.

All things considered, the advance of the Czechs, both materially and in the things of the mind and spirit, progress accomplished in the face of heavy odds, stands out as a shining example of what a small nationality, imbued with a growing consciousness of national individuality, can accomplish in a relatively brief span of time.

IV

The sympathetic treatment accorded by Taaffe's Iron Ring to Slav and Clerical interests, and the upward thrust of Slav minorities, in particular the Czechs, irritated and worried the politically articulate among the Austro-Germans. German Liberal deputies seized upon almost any pretext to deliver passionate philippics in the reichsrat against the ministry and to engage in wild demonstrations punctuated by cheering, hissing, groaning, whistling, and raucous hand clapping—practices which deputies of other factions later imitated and perfected. A manifesto published by the German Liberals concluded: "We protest against all attempts to convert Austria into a Slav state. We shall continue to agitate for the maintenance of German as the official language and to oppose the extension of federalism." But, however critical these Germans were of domestic policies, "we are steadfast partisans of the alliance with Germany and the foreign policy now being followed by the Empire."

Outside of parliament, Germans raged and ranted against the submergence of their nationality and language by the Slavs. Politicians and university men drafted in 1882 a celebrated program at Linz, which contemplated the restoration of German dominance in Austrian affairs. It proposed that Galicia, Bucovina, and Dalmatia, non-German provinces, should be detached from Austria and handed over to Hungary or given full autonomy; then the territory that remained to Austria should establish close economic bonds, a customs union indeed, with the German empire, and should recognize German as the official tongue. And the Austrian political tie with Hungary should be whittled down to mere union through the person of the monarch. This essentially defensive program, which diverged sharply from the traditional centralist doctrines of the Germans, was thereafter regarded as authoritative in moderate German circles.

A more radical and noisier wing of German opinion, antidynastic and anticlerical, advocated the political union of the German-inhabited provinces to Germany, and reviled the Slavophile tendencies of the Taaffe cabinet. General Horst, sometime a colleague of Taaffe's, remarked in 1881, "What a thousand Prussian agents could not have done has been accomplished by Taaffe's policies. A Pan-German party hitherto nonexistent has come into being." This Austrian version of Pan-Germanism has significance not alone for its role in Austria, but because of its affinity with the National Socialism of Germany, personified by Adolf Hitler. Wherever Austro-Germans were actively in competition with Slavs, especially in Bohemia and Styria, this movement struck root; fervor was greatest among the young, university students in particular.

The moving spirit in the Austrian version of Pan-Germanism was the fiery-tempered, demagogic, almost pathologically chauvinistic George von Schönerer. Educated in Germany, he inherited considerable wealth from his father, an enterprising Viennese railway magnate, who had been rewarded with knighthood. Schönerer devoted himself to Pan-German propaganda and was the first exponent of those doctrines to be elected to the reichsrat (1873), where he represented the very district in which Hitler was later born.

Proud of imperial Germany's achievements in war and diplomacy, in industry and commerce, the Pan-Germans venerated Prince Bismarck, who only a few brief years before had entangled Austria in a humiliating war, as their patron saint, and to his memory they raised monuments and dedicated streets and squares. With affection for imperial Germany was associated a kind of Wotan cult, calculated to appeal to youthful enthusiasms and sentimentalities; in lieu of the conventional calendar, Pan-Germans adopted one that commenced with the Teutonic triumph over Varus's Roman legions. Ancient Teutonic religious rites, customs, and costumes were resurrected and dramatized in ceremony and pageant.

Schönerer and his mesmerized followers did not disguise their convictions of German racial superiority and of the inferiority of the Slavs. "I hold," he once remarked, "reconciliation with the Slavs to be a useless effort . . . One hears talk of equality between Germans and Slavs. It is as if one compared a lion to a louse because both are animals." And the Pan-German gospel contained a large admixture of rabid "racial antisemitism." To the reichsrat, Schönerer presented a bill in 1882 that would have prohibited Russian Israelites from entering Austria; it attracted twenty-three votes. When, in March 1888, the *Neues Wiener Tagblatt,* the most widely circulated Austrian newspaper, prematurely announced the death of Emperor William I of Germany, a Schönerer mob raided the offices of this "Jewish sheet" and thrashed the staff for deliberately spreading false news about "their emperor." Whereupon the paper entered suit against Schönerer; he was convicted, imprisoned, and stripped of his title of nobility and of his seat in parliament. However, instead of lowering his prestige, the newspaper episode converted Schönerer into something of a popular martyr.[8]

Apart from political agitation, the Austro-Germans sought to safeguard their nationality by the establishment of patriotic societies of one variety or another, covering a wide range of interests. Notable was the *Deutscher Schulverein,* founded in 1880 with the assistance of university student fraternities, which in a decade boasted more than a thousand branches and 100,000 members; its principal objective was to subsidize schools and libraries in areas where the German minority had to fight to preserve its identity. Under its auspices German Catholic priests were sent around to teach the catechism, books were circulated that extolled *Deutschtum,* and the society made itself generally useful in promoting the German national cause. A parallel society, the *Allgemeine deutscher Schulverein,* was set up in Berlin to lend comfort and help to the brethren in Austria. Local German societies in Bohemia dedicated to the struggle with the advancing Czechs included the energetic *Böhmerwaldbund* (1884), and the *Bund der Deutschen,* whose special activity was to keep farm land from passing out of German hands.

Austrian Pan-Germanism attracted little sympathetic response in the highest quarters of Berlin. Bismarck's interest in Austrian affairs was restricted to the effect which domestic policies had upon the Hapsburg Monarchy as a factor in high politics. Yet his detestation of Taaffe and the Slav reconciliation course was complete, and he saw to it that the coveted German order of the Black Eagle, which was conferred upon the Hungarian premier, Coloman Tisza, was denied the Austrian prime minister. Bismarck positively despised the doctrinaire German Liberals and frowned on the Linz program; for one reason he feared that if the German areas of Austria were separated from the Slav the latter would gravitate toward Russia, and an enlarged Slavdom might join in an unholy coalition with France.

It was Bismarck's opinion that the Austro-Germans should subordinate their *Deutschtum* to the larger concerns of Austria-Hungary as a great power; and at no time during the Taaffe era did he intercede directly on behalf of the Austro-Germans. Had he tried to exercise any influence in domestic affairs, the strong anti-German passions of the Czechs and Poles might have imperiled the Austro-German alliance. The Iron Chancellor also reproached journalists in imperial Germany who inveighed against Magyar efforts to denationalize the German minority in Hungary; he himself was engaged in a similar process among the Prussian Poles, and he believed that the retention of the friendship of the Magyar ruling caste was indispensable for the preservation of the alliance with the Dual Monarchy.

Among dynastically loyal Germans, for whom the Pan-German doctrines were anathema, there appeared in the Taaffe period a new and vigorous current in Austrian public life, which was destined to exert a large and at times a controlling influence in the affairs of the country until the merger of Austria with the Third Reich in 1938; it bore the intriguing name of Christian Socialism. Christianity this party identified with Roman Catholicism and the concerns of the clerical traditionalists, while its socialism consisted of repudiation of laissez-faire economic principles, interest in the well-being of the small enterpriser and the peasant, unflagging enmity to "big business," which Christian Socialists held to be equivalent to Jewish capital, so that Judeophobia figured conspicuously in its propaganda, and interest in legislation that would improve the social and material lot of the common mass.

Whatever was liberal in the historical sense of the term was hateful in the sight of Christian Socialism. Old-fashioned liberalism it regarded as responsible for the anticlerical legislation, for the "dechristianization" of the schools, for the economic depression of the seventies, and for the financial power of Jewry. From these evils, Social Catholicism would first emancipate and then protect Austria. In foreign affairs the party was a stanch supporter of the alliance with Germany.

The original leadership of Christian Socialism came from aristocratic, journalistic, and religious circles, and the intellectual and spiritual father of the movement was Baron Karl von Vogelsang.[9] A Protestant nobleman, born in Germany, Vogelsang embraced Catholicism, quarreled with his family, and rather late in life drifted to Vienna, where as an editor of the clerical *Vaterland,* previously an obscure journal, he thundered against political and economic liberalism. In pamphlets and in a learned journal dedicated to social reform on "Christian principles" he elucidated his views on the proper means for combatting industrial injustices and ushering in a better and brighter era for humanity. Individualism he repudiated as socially and personally harmful; rather, the state should intervene in social and economic affairs and legislation should be shaped in the light of the Christian teachings of fairness, love, and mutual welfare. A study that Vogelsang published on the condition of the Austrian working class hastened the adoption of labor-welfare legislation in the eighties; other reforms for which he and his disciples campaigned were the preservation of handicraft industry, the elimination of monopolistic capitalism, the establishment of coöperative credit societies, and other aids to peasant agriculture.

At the outset the Austrian Catholic hierarchy, conservative by instinct, opposed Christian Socialism, fearful lest it should divide the forces of clericalism, and repelled by demagogic attacks upon wealth. But slowly attitudes shifted and clericalism eventually allied itself with Christian Socialism; in rural Alpine areas the backing of the clergy was of the utmost importance in capturing the broad mass of the peasantry for the party. That rustic element, together with small tradesmen and other petits bourgeois in the cities, all or most of whom were admitted to the suffrage by the enfranchisement of "five-gulden men" in 1882, furnished the voting strength of Christian Socialism.

It was not in the countryside, however, but in imperial Vienna that Christian Socialism scored its initial and most astounding successes. There its outstanding leader was one of the most remarkable figures of modern Austrian politics, Doctor Karl Lueger.[10] Son of an ordinary Viennese concierge, Lueger attended the University of Vienna and entered the legal profession. As a German Liberal he was elected in 1875 to the Vienna municipal council and he attracted attention by his eloquent and unrestrained indictments of corruption and mismanagement in the conduct of municipal business; he exposed profiteering in the administration of municipal cemeteries and flagrant dishonesty in the building of street railways. In courts of law this man of the people stood forth as the advocate and protector of the underprivileged and the "little man." An individual of robust dislikes, Lueger delivered fervent diatribes against Jewry as the source of the corrupting forces in public and private affairs and leveled his guns at the Magyars, or the Judaeo-Magyars, as he was wont to call them. Magyars he despised because they had assimilated many Jews, allowed Protestants a prominent place in politics, discriminated against Germans, and exerted a decisive voice in the foreign policies of the Dual Monarchy.

To genuine devotion to the interests of the Hapsburgs, Lueger joined consuming love for his native Vienna and high moral courage. Endowed with amazing physical vitality and a resonant voice, he shone as an orator; he had perfect command of the Viennese vernacular and mixed much homely wit into his popular addresses. With the backing of anti-Jewish journals and societies, he was elected to the Austrian parliament in 1885 on the platform of "a united Austria, German in fabric, Slav in sympathy, Hapsburg in dynasty." He was well on the way to a career that was to make him the darling of Vienna and one of the very strongest personalities in Hapsburg public affairs.

The brothers Liechtenstein rallied the clerically minded among the aristocrats to the banner of Christian Socialism. Tall, elegant Prince Alois made public appearances for the party on festival occasions, delivered highly chiseled academic discourses, replete with epigrams, which the crowd greeted with frenzied applause. Then after shaking hands with a few favored ones he withdrew to the solitude and quiet of his palace and library, leaving the lesser fry to carry on the popular propaganda. At the reichsrat balloting of 1891, Lueger and thirteen others were elected as Christian Socialists, and by that time the movement had become a potent factor in the municipal affairs of the imperial capital. Before long, as will later be explained, the Christian

Socialists captured Vienna, though outside of the capital and the Alpine provinces the party attracted little support.

v

The Poles of Galicia preserved their reputation as the favored children of the Austrian empire and were granted additional privileges from time to time, such as the right to use the Polish language on the railways of the province. Francis Joseph won the hearty applause of Poles everywhere when in 1889 he elevated the archbishop of Cracow, universally esteemed as the primate of Polish Catholicism, to the dignity of a prince. "Every writer," exulted an Austrophile Pole, "blesses the sovereign who has fostered the national resurrection of the Poles under the aegis of Austria." Thus the Poles had their rewards for the steady support that the deputies gave the government in Vienna on both domestic and foreign policies.

The Polish Club in fact formed the most thoroughly disciplined, most politically astute and relatively the most influential bloc in the Austrian parliament, and invariably voted as a unit. German Liberals openly displayed their aversion for the Poles. When Vienna, at the time a stronghold of German Liberalism, celebrated (1883) the bicentenary of the deliverance of the capital from the Turks, the vital role of the Polish hero Sobieski was deliberately depreciated by the German managers of the affair. Outside of Vienna, the Christian world, on the other hand, hailed the festival as a "Sobieski celebration."

Hatred of Austrian Poles for Russia, oppressor of their kinsmen, showed no abatement, and lively interest was displayed in fellow nationals in the Prussian kingdom. Land-expropriation schemes sponsored by Bismarck evoked angry protests, and press criticisms grew so acrimonious that the Austrian ministry, sensitive to the feeling of the German ally, applied repressive censorship. Although consistently loyal to Austria, Poles did not neglect to keep alive their national heritage; the centennial of the heroic rising of Kosciusko, for example, was commemorated (1894) at Cracow, with representatives of the Russian and Prussian Poles in attendance. Similar all-Polish gatherings marked the burial of the national poet Mickiewicz in Cracow (1895) and the anniversary of the ancient university there.

It was during the Taaffe epoch that industrialism entered Galicia in a significant way. New railways were laid down, small factories built, and the output of petroleum increased. Though wells had been dug as early as 1853, half a dozen years before petroleum was discovered in Pennsylvania, scarcity of capital and crude techniques retarded production, until Stanislas Szczepanowski became interested. He had studied abroad and on his return invited Canadian technicians and foreign capital to participate in the production and refining of oil; before his death in 1900 Galicia was not only supplying the petroleum requirements of the Monarchy but was marketing a small surplus in Germany. A man of many talents, Szczepanowski was an active figure in politics, in coöperative societies, and in popular education, and his leadership gave a lasting impetus to the economic development of backward Galicia. In all of this he was abetted by a line of skillful governors, such as Count Casimir Badeni, who held office from 1888 to 1895.

Polish politicians worked tirelessly to strengthen Polish lordship over the Ruthenian or Ukrainian minority, which predominated in eastern Galicia and was almost as numerous as the Poles in the province as a whole; Ruthenians were spoken of as the sworn foes and worst enemies of the Polish nationality. Ruthenian deputies in the Galician diet, who in 1861 formed a quarter of the entire body, were gradually eliminated; Ruthenian representation in the imperial reichsrat, too, suffered a sharp diminution, and treason trials of Ruthenians in Galicia, priests and journalists, believed to be intriguing with Russia, were familiar occurrences. Poles habitually spoke of educated Ruthenians as mere tools of Russia, which was true only of one faction, the Old Ruthenians, who held that the salvation of their countrymen lay in political union with the tsardom. Dominated by the clergy—their headquarters was the Uniat Cathedral in Lemberg—the conservative Old Ruthenians encouraged the use of the Muscovite language and poked fun at the idea that there was a definite Ukrainian language and literature.

At odds with these elders were the Young Ukrainians, Ukrainian nationalists, who considered themselves members of a distinct nationality and gloried in the Ukrainian dialect. They dreamed of building an independent Ukrainian state, and on the way to that goal they desired an autonomous Ukrainian unit inside the Dual Monarchy, embracing areas in Hungary in which Ruthenians predominated as well as similar districts in Austria. Ardently interested in the peasant masses, who lived in a semiservile relation to Polish landlords, the Ukrainophiles were responsive to democratic political principles and were inclined to be anticlerical in outlook. These ideas they circulated in several patriotic publications.

Ukrainophilism in Austria was fostered by the repression of the Ukrainian population in Russia. Tsar Alexander II, rendered uneasy by the growth of Ukrainian sentiments, ordered (1876) the suppression of Ukrainian learned societies, forbade the publication or circulation of books in Ukrainian, and imposed other restrictions upon the use of the Ukrainian tongue. Thereupon Russian Ukrainophile intellectuals took up residence abroad, some in Swiss Geneva, others in Austrian Galicia, which, it was hoped, would serve as the nucleus round which all areas inhabited by Ukrainians might coalesce—another Piedmont. Unhappily, the Ukrainians of Galicia could not agree upon a common front and competed against each other at the polls, which redounded to the benefit of their Polish adversaries. As time moved on it was apparent that the Ukrainian nationalist faction was making headway at the expense of the Muscovite Old Ruthenians.[11]

The Viennese government was alert to the value of Ukrainophilism in the event of war with Russia, and not unmindful of the fact that if necessary the Ruthenians might be serviceable in restraining the Poles in Galicia. It was gratifying to Vienna to hear a Ruthenian spokesman, Polenowski, declare at a time when relations with Russia were acutely strained that his countrymen were ready "at any moment to sacrifice their lives for their country and their emperor, under whose scepter they had experienced so many blessings."

Ukrainian nationalists pressed for the conversion of the University of Lemberg, which had a mixed German and Ruthenian character until the seventies when Polish was made the language of instruction, into a Ruthenian institution, or failing that the establishment of a new Ruthenian university. Eight hundred Ukrainians, it was urged, were in attendance at institutions of higher learning, and enough Ruthenian professors were at work in various institutions, it was claimed, to staff an independent university. Polish politicians, however, vetoed that demand, though they authorized a professorship of Ukrainian history in the University of Lemberg. In 1894, the foremost Ukrainian historian, M. D. Hrushevsky, was invited from Kiev to occupy the new chair; in collaboration with other intellectuals, he founded a journal, *Literaturno-Naukovy Vistruk* (Messenger of Literature and Science), which was a serviceable instrument in propagating an anti-Russian version of Ukrainian nationalism. The review was published under the auspices of the Shevchenko Scientific Society, founded at Lemberg in 1873 to promote scholarly study of Ukrainian history, philology, and natural science.

A rallying ground for Ukrainian scholars of both Russian and Austrian citizenship, the Schevchenko Society attained international repute for its learned publications. Writers of fiction, drama, and poetry enriched the slender stock of Ukrainian literature, and the centenary of Kotlyarevsky's *Aeneid* (1898), perhaps the most prized piece of literature in the Ukrainian language, occasioned effusive patriotic demonstrations. Libraries, privately financed schools, gymnastic and coöperative societies, each contributed distinctively to the slowly emerging Ukrainian national consciousness. The battle with the Poles went merrily on, and little enough had the Ukrainians to show for their zeal—aside from the chair of history at Lemberg, only a single Ukrainian gymnasium, the publication of notices in official places in the Ukrainian language, and the use of the mother tongue in courts of law.[12] But as the ensuing years disclosed, it was perilous for Polish politicians in Galicia to ignore Ukrainian sentiments and aspirations.

VI

The Slovenes, who were distributed among several of the southern provinces of Austria and were almost the sole nationality in Carniola, achieved linguistic and cultural gains in the Taaffe era at the expense of their German neighbors. The Slovene language, which a German minister had once derisively labeled "baby talk," was ordered to be spoken in the schools of Laibach, the chief Slovenian center, and in a short time Slovenian politicians had supplanted Germans as the controlling faction in the administration of the city and in the diet of Carniola (1883) as well. The Taaffe ministry frankly befriended the Slovenes. By ministerial decree of 1892, for example, the town of Klagenfurt in Carinthia, in which Germans outnumbered Slovenes by more than eighteen to one, was declared to be a "mixed" community so as to justify the use of the two languages in official transactions.

Such Slavophile gestures infuriated the German population, which with official help had been combatting the upthrust of the Slovenian nationality for almost a century. Angry clashes between representatives of the competing nationalities tormented the diets of Styria and Carinthia, until the Slovenes picked up their belongings and marched home. During one outburst of Slovenian patriotism a statue erected in Laibach to the memory of the liberal Austro-German man of letters, Anastasius Grün, whose pen had familiarized cultured Europe with the simple lyricism of the Slovenes, was foully desecrated.

Constant struggles with the Slovenes deepened the sense of *Deutschtum* among Styrian Germans, many of whom matched extremists of the Sudetenland in their Pan-German fervor. The mental outlook of that element was admirably sketched in a popular novel on provincial ways and manners by Rudolph Hans Bartsch, himself a Styrian. From a ridge on the southern Alps, the hero of the tale gazed toward the blue Adriatic, but between his home and the sea dwelt the alien and despised Slav; in disgust he turned northward and fastened his eyes on imperial Germany, the certain and, as he thought, predestined savior of the Austro-Germans from Slavic engulfment. Standing alone, the Austro-Germans, Bartsch was sure, were helpless, nothing more than a withered branch cut from the flourishing parent oak.

The success of the Czechs in winning concessions from the Taaffe ministry emboldened Slovene leaders to press similar demands with turbulent vehemence. Their battle to secure a national university was barren of result, though they did force the division of the gymnasium in Laibach into a Slovenian and a German section. As an instrument of war upon Germanization, the Society of Saints Cyril and Methodius was established in 1884, and by it schools for Slovene children were built, adult cultural societies were organized even in the most remote villages, and coöperative economic societies were formed. These last proved hugely successful; the Slovenian districts in fact became a classic area in which to study the virtues and defects of coöperative societies.

For both the national political and economic movements, Slovene priests, under the twin impulse of patriotic conviction and social Catholic teachings, furnished effective leadership. Since Slovene lay intellectuals largely succumbed to the lure of Germanization, political guidance passed to the clergy; ecclesiastical sowers planted the seed of Slovene unity with neighboring Croat and Serb populations and in due season the harvest was reaped.

Laibach, the "capital of the Slovenes," with large stone houses and baroque churches, has been called a "Salzburg inhabited by Slavs." There were built a Slovenian national theater, a national opera house, a national museum, and a national art gallery; and organizations were founded to encourage scientific investigations and Slovenian literature. Several poets, novelists, and philological scholars, some of them priests who carried on in the tradition of their fellows of an earlier day, such as Bishop Anton Slomšek, a sturdy fighter for the interests and intellectual advancement of the Slovenes, wrote in the Slovenian tongue.

The pioneer Slovene novelist and dramatist, Joseph Jurčič, quickened interest in the medieval history of his folk and in the way of life of the humble peasantry. Ivan Tavčar, a lawyer and public servant in Laibach, won something more than local acclaim for the realistic and satirical talents he exhibited in historical novels. The dramatist Ivan Cankar shied away from romantic themes, choosing rather to expose the actualities of social living and to cudgel his countrymen for acquiescence in alien political overlordship. *For the Nation's Good* (1901), by Cankar, in which politics and politicians are surgically examined and caustically chastised, is esteemed as the finest political comedy from a Yugoslav pen.[13] At a Slovene Congress held in Laibach in 1897 a stillborn plan was formulated for an autonomous state of Slovenes, to include Slovenes under the Hungarian flag as well as those in Austria.

Slovenes likewise fought the Italians in the Küstenland area, which included Trieste. Slovenes formed a majority in the suburbs of Trieste, though they were heavily outnumbered in the city itself. The Italian majority prohibited the use of the Slovene language in the proceedings of the diet of Trieste and tried to remove Slav names from the voting rolls. Under the watchword "Trieste must be Slav," the Slovenes in turn clamored for educational and political equality, and physical clashes between members of the two nationalities were almost daily episodes. As a rule, the small German minority in Trieste lined up with the Italians.

Agitation among the *Italianissimi* for union with the kingdom of Italy was ceaseless. Societies were founded to preserve and promote Italian culture throughout Italia Irredenta; municipal councils in Trieste, Trent, and other communities raised monuments to the memory of Dante, Petrarch, and other famed Italians. Irredentist newspapers were tolerated so long as they kept within reasonable bounds, and Austrian officials raised no objections to the public solicitation of funds in Trieste for the Dante monument. When, however, the educational society *Pro Patria* of Trieste adopted resolutions that were interpreted as traitorous, it was summarily broken up. That act caused Irredentist societies in Italy to revive anew the old cry against the "Austrian monster," until the Italian government felt obliged to intervene and disband the groups responsible for the agitation. Prime Minister Crispi charged Irredentist firebrands with playing the game of the papacy and lacking proper patriotism; when his finance minister, Doda, failed to protest at Austrophobe speeches delivered at a banquet, which he attended, Crispi promptly invited him to resign. These signs of Italian official good will elicited praise from the Austrian press. The school society of Trieste was permitted to carry on its work under the name of the *Lega Nazionale*.

On their side, Germans tried to spread their language and culture among the Italian minority. The German-Austrian Alpine Club, the *Deutscher Schulverein*, the most active protagonist of Germanization, and local societies such as the *Tiroler Volksbund*, aided in the erection of schools, libraries, and orphan asylums. Economic advantages and favors were bestowed upon the Italian peasantry of Austria in the hope of winning them to *Deutschtum*.

It is impossible to determine accurately whether the use of the German language was gaining over the Italian or vice versa—the claims of controversialists are the claims of controversialists. That the fanatical among the *Italianissimi* were ready to go to any lengths to manifest their dissatisfaction with Austrian rule was shown in the Oberdank affair. With a view to counteracting Irredentism in Trieste and to participating in a celebration of the five hundredth anniversary of the attachment of the city to Austria, Francis Joseph, Elizabeth, and other members of the imperial family planned to visit Trieste in 1882. Learning of the projected visit, one William Oberdank, a Triestiner who had fled to Italy to escape Austrian military service, plotted to assassinate the monarch. Whether his conspiracy was part of a plan for a general rising against Austrian authority is a matter of conjecture; at any rate, during a parade of veterans in Trieste a bomb was thrown by an Irredentist that killed two spectators and wounded fifteen. Oberdank's movements had been carefully watched by Austrian police, and when he crossed the border into Austria he was arrested and the bombs

he carried were taken away. At his trial he confessed that he had intended
to kill the monarch, and he was executed.

The episode created great excitement and caused anti-Austrian demonstrations among Italians everywhere, but the behavior of the Italian government—the treaty of the Triple Alliance had just been signed—was perfectly
proper and beyond reproach. In Irredentist circles, Oberdank was hailed
as a glorious martyr to the cause of Greater Italy; an Oberdank cult grew
up, with adherents in Italy as well as on Austrian soil, including some civil
servants. Italian youths in Trieste sang an Oberdank anthem and a monument was erected to his memory; even in Rome a street was given the name
of the conspirator.

Certainly the intensity of anti-Hapsburg feeling in the Italian districts
fluctuated. In 1885, for example, Crown Princess Stephanie was sent to
Trieste on a mission of good will. Upon arrival she was greeted with anti-
Austrian songs and cries of "down with Austria," but in a short time she
had so captivated the populace that the crowds broke out in patriotic imperial anthems. And a few years later Francis Joseph was greeted by the
Italian population in the Trentino with effusive demonstrations of loyalty.

VII

Throughout much of the eighties Austrian industry, along with that of
the rest of Europe, was in a generally depressed state, owing partly to recurrent crises in international politics and partly to circumstances peculiar to
Austria. Compared with the great industrial countries, manufacturing techniques in Austria were generally unprogressive, productivity of labor inefficient, and the tax burdens heavy. Outlays for the fighting services, for the
construction of railways, and for service on the public debt necessitated steady
increases in taxation.

No country, it may be, surpassed Austria in the complexity of its tax
structure, for the laws filled three volumes, each of six hundred closely
printed pages! Indirect taxes on consumers' goods, and on documents, newspapers, and the like, made up the principal sources of state revenue; taxes
on property and income were steadily raised, and small sums for state purposes were even secured through lotteries, which gave the poor man who
bought a ticket for two cents the thrills that the wealthy obtained by playing
the stock market. That part of public expenditures not covered by revenues
was met by borrowing from Viennese banking houses or from foreign
capitalists.

As a capital-poor country, the Hapsburg Monarchy was largely dependent upon foreign finance for funds to balance governmental budgets as
well as for commercial and industrial enterprises. French capital, much of it
channeled into the Monarchy through the medium of the Rothschild family,

participated in Austrian railway, banking, and manufacturing undertakings; and Frenchmen purchased large blocks of Austrian and Hungarian government securities, so that the total stake of citizens of the Third Republic in the Danube Monarchy was of the order of two billion francs by 1890. Thereafter, considerations of diplomacy, especially Russian pressure upon Parisian finance after the making of the Franco-Russian alliance in 1893, checked French lending, and Hapsburg financial needs were met to a large extent by German bankers. Two of the great German financial institutions, the Darmstädter Bank, which was closely associated with the House of Rothschild, and the Deutsche Bank, virtually monopolized German lending to the Dual Monarchy. Funds were invested in the bonds of public bodies and in a wide variety of financial and industrial projects. About 1890 the German investment in Austria-Hungary passed the French, and by 1914 it was at least 50 per cent greater; by then the Monarchy had started borrowing in the expensive Wall Street market.

For the first time in years the imperial Austrian budget was balanced in 1886, and four years later the gold standard for the national currency was adopted, though a considerable time elapsed before the change-over from silver was completed. For the purposes of protecting home producers and of swelling the revenues of the common Austro-Hungarian treasury, upward revisions in the tariff were effected, as is elsewhere explained. Dalmatia and Istria were brought into the imperial customs system in 1880 and Trieste, previously a free port, in 1891.

Austrian industry and trade were promoted by the extension of transportation facilities. In the eighties the government bought several railways that had been privately constructed and additional trackage was laid down, so that by 1893 the length of the state system reached nearly 5,000 miles apart from lines owned jointly by the Austrian and Hungarian governments. Communications with France were improved by the opening of the Arlberg road to Switzerland, and through connections with Constantinople were at long last completed in 1888.

This latter enterprise attested the keen interest of Austrians in the commercial possibilities of the Balkans—might not Vienna grow wealthy from eastern trade as once Venice had done?—and, of course, the strategic value of the road to Constantinople was not missed. Austrian capital, aided and spurred on by the foreign office, shared heavily in the building of railways in Turkey and elsewhere in the Near East, and Austrian shipping companies operating on the Danube and the high seas were beneficiaries of government subsidies. At Vienna the Oriental Academy offered special training for consuls in the languages and customs of Near Eastern peoples, and an Oriental museum there kept on display samples of the wares that were marketable in the Balkans.

At the time of the commercial panic of 1873, Austrian financiers had pioneered in the creation of cartels, leagues of industrialists to fix prices and to regulate output. First organized among producers of steel rails, the cartel idea spread to textile, glass, sugar, brewing, and chemical industries, and eventually these trade rings very largely dominated the manufactures of the empire. Among Austrian economists it was widely believed that cartelization was not only desirable but necessary in a country that was industrially backward. Since "big finance" of Vienna controlled the combines, they were subjected to endless criticism by spokesmen of the "little men" and champions of national minorities.

That machinofacture progressed notably in the eighties was revealed in one way by the heavier concentration of the Austrian population in cities. While the total population increased by less than 8 per cent, the population in cities of more than 10,000 grew by about a third. Vienna and the region round about it specialized in the manufacture of cotton and silk fabrics, chemicals and carpets, machinery and armaments, beer and paper, leather, furniture, and musical instruments, while towns in Styria developed the production of iron and steel wares and textiles; elsewhere small industries flourished in the making of goods from locally produced raw materials.

Unwholesome living and factory conditions, low wages, excessively long hours of toil—tempered, to be sure, by an unusual number of holidays—and recurrent waves of unemployment caused unrest and disorders among the industrial working class.[14] In 1883–84 a series of fires, murders, and the discovery of a "Poison League" in Vienna, whose members were suspected of plotting to overthrow the existing social order, occasioned alarm in governing circles. Emulating Bismarck in Germany, the Taaffe cabinet placed Vienna and other industrial centers under a stage of siege and issued decrees that resulted in the expulsion of scores of radicals from the capital and the suppression of working-class societies and newspapers.

But simultaneously the Austrian administration busied itself with legislation of a social-reform character. Laws were enacted or made more stringent regulating conditions of employment in factories and mines and establishing compulsory insurance against accident and sickness, more or less in imitation of the pioneer workers' welfare legislation enacted in Germany at the same time. Acts of 1884–85 fixed the maximum working day in factories at eleven hours and in mines at ten, required the Sunday rest day, prohibited the employment of children under twelve, and strictly regulated the employment of older children and women. Employers were ordered to install equipment to guard workers against accidents and to keep workrooms clean and adequately lighted. The first real factory inspectorate system in Austria dated from 1883 but the number of inspectors was ridiculously insufficient;

so late as 1908 only eighty-five inspectors were at work. Public employment bureaus were set up in Vienna and Prague and a valuable bureau of labor statistics was established.

It was during the Taaffe period, too, that the workers' political movement, the Social Democratic party, emerged as a considerable force in the public affairs of Austria. For years the Socialist cause had been lamed by fierce doctrinal controversies, but a campaign for unity was successfully conducted by Viktor Adler, the son of wealthy Jewish parents, who learned of the harsh lot of the Vienna poor from those whom he treated as a physician. While on a study tour of England and Germany, Adler definitely adopted Marxian Socialist principles and resolved to devote his life to the welfare of workpeople; he was a persuasive speaker and writer, and admirer and critic alike paid tribute to his honesty, his earnestness, and his tenacity of purpose.

At the end of 1888, in the village of Hainfeld, Adler shared in the formal organization of the Austrian Social Democratic party and in drafting a famous manifesto of party doctrines and objectives. The Hainfeld program boldly condemned private ownership of productive property, class privileges, and the standing army; and at a time when Austrian public affairs were wracked by the sharpening conflict of nationalities, the Social Democrats flatly asserted the international solidarity of the working class and appealed for a united front of all wageworkers in the Monarchy regardless of their national attachments. Set as immediate goals of Social Democracy were universal suffrage, the complete secularization of public education, the extension of workers' welfare legislation, and an eight-hour working day.

Within a few years over fifty Socialist newspapers were in circulation, of which Vienna's *Arbeiter Zeitung,* with Adler as the leading editorial writer, carried the greatest weight. Ably edited and more solid was a monthly publication, *Der Kampf,* started in 1907 by prominent Marxist intellectuals. It laid particular emphasis on nationality tensions and problems in the Danube Monarchy and in eastern Europe. Socialist workers of Vienna and other cities staged their first May Day demonstrations in 1890, which, much to the surprise of outsiders, was a very orderly affair. Elaborate police precautions, such as the removal of railings around the Prater, where the marchers were to converge, so as to facilitate cavalry charges, proved to be quite unnecessary. The party concentrated its main energies on building up trade-unions and in agitating for the democratization of the suffrage; in the campaign for electoral reform the Social Democrats made lavish use of pamphlets, mass meetings, and a suffrage anthem set to the tune of the "Marseillaise."

Gradually the party attracted to itself a large part of the urban working class. An earnest band of reforming intellectuals, many of them Jews, supplied the leadership, organized demonstrations and political mass strikes, and waged incessant war on Roman Catholicism, the strongest and most tenacious foe of Austrian Socialism.

VIII

An Austrian parliamentary sitting of the early nineties presented a scene without equal in Christendom. In the course of a few hours impassioned speeches were delivered in half a dozen languages, some of them not understood by a majority of the deputies, often on matters of no more profound public moment than the respective merits of German and Czech men of letters.

German Liberal deputies and their allies, the largest single bloc, stood stanchly for constitutionalism and the interests of their nationality, complained against Slavophilism, and hated the Clericals. Schönerer's noisy Pan-Germans proclaimed their boundless admiration for imperial Germany; Christian Socialists envisaged the regeneration of the empire by the elimination of many accepted political and economic policies and joined with their officially anti-Jewish colleagues in reviling Jewry. German Clericals, Catholics first and Austrians later, pressed for the complete restoration of church authority and for Austrian coöperation to revive the temporal power of the papacy.

The "Old Czechs," their prestige on the decline, cherished the ideal of an autonomous Bohemian kingdom and hoped to realize the goal piecemeal by bargaining with the ministry, while the Young Czechs clamored for immediate autonomy, the coronation of Francis Joseph in Prague, and the adoption of a Russophile foreign policy. Only the solidly disciplined Polish phalanx held to a really imperial course, yet ever seeking to increase Polish mastery over Galicia; the slim Ruthenian delegation, on the other hand, struggled for the liberation of their fellows from Polish lordship and for home rule. Slovene deputies railed against Germans and Italians and solicited special concessions for their nationality, while Italian representatives were a hopeless jumble of clericalism and Irredentism. Strangely enough, a handful of Austrian deputies chose to regard themselves as independents!

From the vocational standpoint the representation in parliament was quite diversified, though the urban working class was as yet unrepresented. In the reichsrat chosen in 1891 sat fifty lawyers, forty professors, twelve physicians, nine writers and journalists, eight architects and engineers, twenty-nine civil servants, thirty merchants and manufacturers, twenty priests, one hundred forty-six landowners, and six gentlemen of leisure.

Linguistic confusion corresponding to the babel in the reichsrat prevailed in all branches of the Austrian government. Thousands of lawsuits had to be tried in two or more idioms; briefs, pleading, sentences, had to be translated and retranslated; time and money were consumed by interpreters, and the jury system was reduced to a farce by nationalistic prejudices and the inability of many jurors to understand any language other than their own. Postal and telegraph services, the collection of taxes, the conduct of business and industry, the exchange of ideas and education suffered seriously from the absence of a common language.

Taaffe's ministry rested squarely upon a coalition of conservative German, Polish, and moderate Slav deputies; and that bloc seemed impervious to the unrelenting and at times venomous assaults of the German Liberal opposition. The election of 1885, in which the newly enfranchised "five-gulden men" voted for the first time, actually reinforced the Iron Ring, but the Ring suffered a setback at the polls in 1891 due to gains by the antiministerial Young Czechs. Only with difficulty and with some help from German Liberals was legislation on currency reform enacted; and on the solid rock of suffrage reform, the Iron Ring broke down.

Growing demands for remodeling of the electoral laws came from political groupings which calculated that their fortunes would be improved by the broadening of the suffrage base and a more equitable distribution of seats: the Christian Socialists, the Pan-Germans, the Social Democrats, and the Young Czechs.[15] Doctor Emil Steinbach, an extremely competent and far-sighted public servant, who was Taaffe's last finance minister, strongly favored the extension of the franchise as a possible means of allaying nationalistic antagonisms and of placating the urban working class. He succeeded in converting Taaffe and even Francis Joseph to his views.

Under Steinbach's guidance a suffrage bill was prepared in 1893 that would allow virtually every literate adult male to vote, though the old institution of classes or curiae would be perpetuated. That proposal brought together in opposition to Taaffe the German Liberals, the conservatives, and the Poles, each of whom scented a loss of parliamentary strength and all of whom were apprehensive of the specter of Socialism. Shrill Magyar blasts condemned democratization of the Austrian suffrage as an incitement to clamor for comparable changes in Hungary. Certain that the Steinbach proposals would be defeated in parliament, Taaffe chose to retire from official activity. Francis Joseph reluctantly accepted his resignation and named a ministry mostly of German Liberals, the implacable enemies of Taaffe and his Slavophile policies.

As for Taaffe, his public career came abruptly to an end and never again did the emperor even solicit the counsel of this long-trusted and faithful servant. Instead of mitigating national discontents, as had fondly been hoped, the Iron Ring had in fact accentuated them. Yet the Slavophile course could not be utterly abandoned, nor could the issue of a democratic franchise be indefinitely pigeonholed.

CHAPTER TEN

THE SOCIAL AND ECONOMIC STRUCTURE
OF ROYAL HUNGARY

THEODORE ROOSEVELT, DURING HIS PEREGRINATIONS AROUND Europe in 1910, stopped in Hungary, made the acquaintance of many prominent men, and departed with a distinctly favorable impression of the land and its inhabitants. On them he wrote these flattering comments:

"I was struck in Hungary . . . by the fact that I was really more in sympathy with the people whom I met than with the corresponding people of the larger continental nations. Their ways of looking at life were more like mine, and their attitude toward the great social and economic questions more like those of my friends in America. The Hungarian women, for instance, were almost the only women of Continental Europe with whom I could talk in the same intimate way that I could with various American and English women whom I have known . . . The Hungarian women are charming. They seemed to have the solid qualities of the North Germans, and yet to have the French charm, which the Germans so totally lacked . . . I greatly liked the Hungarian men . . . I met an unusual number who were both interesting, and interested in things that were worth while; and who were keenly alert about political and economic matters, and yet were enthusiastic sportsmen or were well read or had other interests that were not merely stodgy . . .

"Altogether I could not overstate how thoroughly at home I felt in Hungary . . ."[1]

At the top of the Hungarian social pyramid were the great landed magnates, some of whom owned estates covering tens of thousands of acres, petty kingdoms.[2] Almost a third of the arable soil of the kingdom, and that the most productive, was possessed by 1,945 large landlords; in the main these were properties that their ancestors had acquired as the Turkish flood receded. In northern Hungary the concentration of landholding in the hands of the aristocracy was greater than in the kingdom as a whole. For the greater part the gigantic latifundia were located in the central area, in the Slovak districts, and in Ruthenia; there were relatively few large properties in Transylvania. On some of the estates small industrial establishments were operated, though this type of development failed to progress to the extent that it did in Austria. Although the peculiar rights of the hereditary nobility had been officially canceled in 1848, the law was never fully effective and this caste continued to give tone to Hungarian society. Conservative, faithful to the Hapsburg dynasty, yet genuinely Hungarian in spirit, the Magyar feudalists exercised considerable influence on the course and conduct of the public affairs of the kingdom.

Wealthiest and most glamorous of all Magyar magnate families was the Esterházy, which claimed an ancestry reaching back to Attila, king of the Huns, but which had pushed into prominence so recently as the late sixteenth century. Nicholas I, son of an ordinary country gentleman, managed to marry two widows with landed property and in that way became the owner of an extensive acreage. For political and military services rendered the Hapsburgs, he was made a baron, then a count, and for a generation he acted as viceroy over that section of Hungary which escaped Turkish domination. His third son, Paul, wedded a countess and increased the family territorial holdings to 860,553 acres. Viceroy of Hungary, chief of the Hapsburg loyalists, sturdy warrior against the Turks, he was named a prince of the empire and given the privileges of coining money, conferring patents of nobility, and governing his subjects in an absolute manner.

Nicholas Joseph, grandson of Paul, sustained the family tradition as a distinguished commander and as a lover of the arts. At his command a colossal palace in the Renaissance style was built at Esterház in a region of swamp and thicket, which eclipsed even Versailles in magnificence and dimensions. But after his death the château and grounds were neglected and the property slowly decayed. Surnamed "the Brilliant" for his love of pomp and luxury, Nicholas Joseph was the proud owner of warrior's equipment for man and horse made wholly of pearls, and valued at four million gulden; each time the outfit was worn repairs costing a small fortune were necessary. So vast in fact was the family wealth that it was said that a Prince Esterházy on gala occasions covered his Magyar national costume with such an array of diamonds and jewels that he looked as though he had been caught in a rain of precious stones. A patron of music, Nicholas Joseph engaged Joseph Haydn as musical director and for the entertainment of the family the famous composer wrote many of his most prized works.

Napoleon thought of making Nicholas III the king of Hungary, but the prince would have none of it and, faithful to his Hapsburg liege, raised a private army to break the hold of the Corsican on the Austrian state. Inordinately fond of the ladies, a lavish spender on art and architecture, this prince dug deeply into the family fortunes, and his son, Paul Anthony (1786–1866), was in many ways a chip off the old block. Though his gigantic estates were broader than the kingdom of Württemberg and his income reached a million gulden a year, he contracted enormous debts, which necessitated borrowings from foreign and domestic bankers. Many properties had in time to be disposed of to pay off mortgages, but vast acreages were entailed, so that even after World War I the Esterházys still owned a small empire, containing scores of villages in Hungary alone, while other estates were located in the countries carved out of the Hapsburg Monarchy in the peace settlements of 1919–20.

In many respects the fabulous Esterházys exhibited the typical traits of the great Magyar magnates: devoted loyalty to the Hapsburgs, readiness to serve as soldiers, diplomatists, or administrators, joviality, lavish hospitality, and gross extravagance. And their anachronistic feudal outlook, their patriarchal attitude toward social inferiors, their scorn and detestation of lesser breeds without the law, were characteristic of the hereditary aristocracy of eastern Europe generally. "Beneath the rank of a baron," a Prince Esterházy scornfully remarked, "no one exists."

Magyar noblemen thought nothing of flogging a villager caught wandering in their parks or of setting mantraps to ensnare poachers. Costly living and the inveterate habit of gambling ate heavily into noble resources and many were obliged to place mortgages on their estates, sometimes losing them. As a class, the large landlords looked after their properties inefficiently, gloried in their ignorance of economics, and displayed gross incompetence when confronted with tough workaday problems. Some of them leased portions of their estates to the peasantry, while others fleeced the peasant by the process of commassation, or the concentration of strips of soil, broadly similar to the English enclosures; in exchange for land of inferior quality, the politically influential magnates often acquired fertile plots from the peasantry. To a very modest extent the nobility shared in the industrial growth of the kingdom; Countess Ladislas Károlyi was the first woman to sit on the directorate of a Hungarian joint-stock company.

Magyar aristocrats, as a rule, were charming, chivalrous, and discriminating patrons of the arts. Some of them were intelligent and refined, and a few contrived to combine a carefree manner of living when on their estates with notable careers as statesmen. Count Alois Károlyi, of whom it was said that he kept as many shepherds as other folk had sheep, laconically described his existence in this way: "In the mornings I go for a ride, in the afternoons I pay visits and play whist . . . in the evenings I go to parties or give parties myself"; yet as Hapsburg ambassador to Berlin in the stormy seventies, Károlyi distinguished himself.[3]

But far the larger proportion of the Hungarian aristocrats were noted for loose living, luxurious Bohemianism, passion for the chase, horse racing, dandyism, and intellectual emptiness. Much of their time was frittered away at spas such as Karlsbad, battling liver complaints and combatting corpulency. That astute Englishman, Arthur Nicolson, thoroughly disgusted with what he saw of the indolence and arrogance of the Magyar aristocracy, lamented the fact that "the young magnate in general is not to be compared with his father. The latter with all his eccentricities and peculiarities was a fine specimen of manhood. The youth of the present day in many instances are poor pallid representatives of the race. The energy and activity for which the fathers were distinguished are not cultivated by the sons, who spend their nights card playing and listening to gypsy music, pasting five-pound and ten-pound notes on the foreheads of their favorite musicians. The vigor of the race will be preserved chiefly in what are called the gentry here —or what we should call the squirearchy; and though these are mostly ruined, they have the grit and determination so characteristic of the Magyar and which have pulled the country through so many difficulties."[4]

Parasitic beneficiaries of the prevailing social order, the Hungarian aristocrats, like their French counterparts of the eighteenth century, believed theirs to be the best of all possible worlds.[5] As privileged folk they paid only modest taxes, a hangover from the long generations when the nobility was exempt from taxation; in the country of Bekes, for instance, a large owner paid only a fifth of the taxes exacted from a peasant for soil of like quantity and quality. The Magyar aristocrats consistently supported the dualistic arrangement, of which in fact they were a principal prop.

II

The strong stable foundation of Hungarian society, as Arthur Nicolson perceived, was the country gentry. Together with the upper aristocracy, this element constituted the "Hungarian nation" in the precise, historical sense. These folk, very like English squires, lived close to their estates and the peasants who worked them. Masters on their own properties, which they managed with the assistance of stewards, they acknowledged no overlord save the king, in whose service they were everlastingly prepared to fight and bleed and die, provided only that the monarch did not transgress the bounds of his constitutional authority.

On their self-sustaining properties, the Magyar gentry lived in comfortable villas, modest enough when compared with palaces of the aristocracy but sumptuous alongside peasant dwellings. The household economy was supervised by the housewife, rather a slave of the home, unlike the slothful spouses of the grand nobility; tutors imparted the rudiments of education to the oncoming generation. Love of the soil and love of country, concern for the common weal, simplicity in thinking and living, stern discipline, stubbornness—these were the earmarks of the Hungarian lower nobility. From the magnates, who were tainted by association with the court at Vienna, the patriotic gentry tended to hold aloof.

During the long centuries of Turkish and Hapsburg rule this self-sufficient Magyar squirearchy had managed to preserve the tradition of self-government, as old as that of England. In the ancient county organizations which the gentry dominated, they kept green the memory of Hungary's rights. After fear of the Turk had receded, dislike of and contempt for the German intruders who streamed in as Hapsburg officials took its place. The gentry fought to regain control over domestic affairs, many of them rallied round the banner of Kossuth, and insisted upon full autonomy as a minimum; and that they gained by the settlement of 1867. "The magnates led the nation into the promised land," writes Macartney, "but it was the gentry who made the journey possible." [6]

After 1867, squires formed the principal element in the Hungarian parliament, and as such they denied to non-Magyars the elementary political rights, which the Magyars had struggled so valiantly to wrest from Vienna for themselves. Intelligent, nationalistic to the point of chauvinism, tenacious of Hungarian rights, the country gentry looked upon others than Magyars as social inferiors and treated them as such.

Economic changes, the emancipation of the serfs in 1848, burdensome taxation, and depressed agricultural conditions impaired the material position of the Magyar gentry and drove many of its impoverished members to seek new occupations. Many small bankers, teachers in universities, men of letters, and army officers emerged from this class, but the preferred vocation was the civil service, into which the gentry crowded in large numbers. Premier Coloman Tisza, himself a man of the gentry, was accused of trying to save his class by creating state positions to absorb the sons of the squires as rapidly as they quit the countryside.

III

For centuries the peasantry of Hungary—Magyars, Slovaks, Rumanians, Ruthenians, Yugoslavs—had been regarded by their social superiors as chattels to be exploited and to be fobbed off with the barest necessities of existence. True, in 1848 the institution of serfage had been officially abolished, as the culmination of emancipating statutes begun a decade earlier. Many of the peasants became landowners, and the nobles were compensated by the government; but the long-established conventions between master and man, the haughtiness of the noble, the servility and docility of the soil worker, could not be extinguished by any legislative enactment. General statements concerning the character of the Hungarian peasants on the basis of nationality possess at once all the virtue and the vice of rough generalizations. As a member of the dominant nationality, the Magyar peasant was likely to be prouder, less docile, and more thrifty than the Slav or Rumanian; and yet the Magyar peasant was conspicuously less chauvinistic than the upper and ruling classes.

Fathers ruled in their households as autocrats, and for old folk great respect was shown. In dealing wtih superiors, Magyars were reverential, and a distinct vein of politeness, the usual accompaniment of a society with a powerful hereditary aristocracy, ran through their social customs. Peasants delighted in colorful costumes, decorated the walls of their cottages, carved their own furniture; cleanliness in the home rather distinguished the Magyar household from that of lesser nationalities, except the German. A wooden floor in a cottage was looked upon as the mark of prosperity.

Of the 19,000,000 inhabitants in the Hungarian kingdom of the twentieth century, 14,000,000 lived by agriculture, and 10,000,000 of these belonged to families that were insufficiently landed or landless. Reference has already been made to the vastness of the large Hungarian estates; in twenty counties from 40 to 60 per cent of the agricultural land was in the hands of the big owners; in 1913 middle and small farmers owned 44.2 per cent of all the land and 55.5 per cent of the arable, and in addition, many peasants rented land from the great proprietors, paying in labor. Collectivism persisted in the rural economy in places.[7]

After emancipation of the serfs a relatively small group of energetic peasants added to their own holdings the land of their weaker fellows, and largely usurped the place in the national economy that had been occupied by the incompetent among the lower gentry. The rest of the villagers, owning dwarf farms or, in a much greater number of instances, no land whatsoever, were no better off after 1848 than they had been before. Peasants sometimes sold their land for trifling considerations; it was not uncommon for the holder of five or six acres to barter them away for as many gallons of wine.[8]

The ranks of the Hungarian rustics dependent upon wages increased constantly, while their living standards after the nineties were steadily depressed. Sharp social cleavages separated the independent small proprietor from his less fortunate landless fellows; a "horse peasant," for instance, stood much higher in the social hierarchy than a "cow peasant," and ownership of a couple of horses was for the peasant a socially gratifying end in itself. Seldom did a peasant proprietor give his daughter in marriage to a day laborer, and at village festivals his children were likely to avoid those of the landless.

Wage-earning peasants were divided into three categories according to the terms of employment: the permanent employee, who was hired for a quarter of a year or longer, the worker engaged by the month, and the day worker. Day laborers found employment less than half the year, as a rule, and the rest of the time this huge class lived on the verge of starvation, consuming their savings, borrowing from the local usurer, subject to epidemics of typhus and pellagra. Rural destitution prevailed on a large scale.

Women were engaged at the same work though for lower wages than men. "Here the women seem to take an equal amount of the hardest labor with the men," commented an American observer in 1877. They were frequently seen "traveling the road bearing on their backs large baskets or wooden tubs filled with various commodities or dragging by hand small wagons which seemed heavy enough for horses . . . I have often watched them laboring in harvest fields as long as there was sufficient light." A day's wages, he continued, were for a man twenty to twenty-three cents, for a woman five cents less. "They eat but little or no meat, and work on food which our people would regard as starvation." The main items on the diet, he reported, "were brown or rye bread, a little milk and such vegetables as onions and potatoes." [9]

"Nevertheless," the American went on, "they are strong and robust, amiable and kindhearted. In the matter of education they rank relatively with us as their farming, that is, they are neither so well educated as our northern farmhands, nor so ignorant as those of the South." Rural children were obliged to attend school in the evenings and on Sunday. [10]

From the pen of an American consul in Budapest, we have an illuminating description of the peasant way of life in the northern counties of Hungary:

"There the peasantry, Slovaks almost all, occupied primitive, straw-thatched cottages, containing a single small room and a kitchen. A kind of fireplace whose chimney was rudely constructed out of tree limbs and mud and homemade furniture which had been handed down for generations were typical features of households; in the more remote districts the smoke of fires escaped along the length of the roof, since there were no chimneys, and at nightfall it looked as though clusters of dwellings were on fire.

"Except for immoderate indulgence in ardent spirits the northern peasant lived in frugal existence; coarse black bread made of middlings mixed with rye flour, beans, potatoes, corn-meal mush and dishes of rye meal formed his unvarying diet. Garments for summer wear consisted of a rough linen shirt reaching to the waist and wide-flowing linen trousers; in the winter, pants made of felt and a sheepskin coat. The more fortunate had roomy, long sleeveless mantles fashioned out of half a dozen tanned sheepskins, often decorated and serviceable as a bed away from home. A coarse, wide-brimmed felt hat, a broad leather belt with pockets, and sandals or boots completed the peasant's wardrobe.

"Feminine vanity expressed itself in gaily colored handkerchiefs and ribbons for head and shoulders, varying from village to village, and in boots with distinctive red or yellow tops. Workers who were employed on the larger estates were paid from eight to sixteen cents a day for light field operations and as much as forty cents for the arduous toil of harvesting." [11]

By 1914, crude wooden huts had in many places replaced the chimneyless "smoke-houses" of the previous century. Yet in some sections of northern Hungary, Slovak rustics were unable to earn enough to build houses and lived in caves in dire degradation.

The Ruthenian peasantry existed on even lower and more sordid levels than their Slovak neighbors. Many of them supplemented their meager earnings from toil on the soil by working in forests, saw mills, or small woodworking establishments, or as beaters on big deer preserves. To a degree the acute destitution of the Ruthenians was due to their aversion to sustained effort of any kind and to their habit of celebrating the many saints' days as holidays.

Real wages in the Hungarian countryside increased between 1865 and the nineties, but after that they declined, with wide fluctuations in keeping with the season of the year. Quite commonly remuneration was paid in kind, an important item being slivovitz, a fiery brand of brandy made from prunes or potatoes, and often the employer furnished cottages for his field workers.

Social habits reflected the poverty that held the Hungarian rural millions in thrall. Illegitimacy was high because of "wild marriages" or concubinage, a widespread evil, and because young men were almost barred from matrimony until after military service had been performed; it was a common custom for a conscript to marry the mother of his child after returning from service with the colors. Crude care of babies, ignorance of hygiene, and superstitious medical practices caused a high child-mortality rate, especially among the Slovaks. Nonetheless there was a steady increase in the population that was dependent upon the land for its livelihood.

For all its reputation for forbearance, and mute acceptance of things as they were, the rural proletariat, in the purely Magyar districts especially, occasionally rebelled against its intolerable lot. [12] Symptomatic of rural poverty was the seasonal migration of landless peasants to other parts of the kingdom or emigration to foreign countries. From the districts along the rim of Hungary laborers by the thousands shifted to the fertile Alföld every year to work in the fields, particularly in the harvest period; in the twentieth century this seasonal movement involved in excess of 200,000 workers annually. Government agencies were established to find jobs, to furnish transportation gratis or at low rates, and to see that the workers obtained something like decent terms of employment and living conditions. In this way proprietors secured cheap and docile workers to beat down local wages or for use as strikebreakers; the wageworkers in turn obtained food—remuneration was largely in kind—to tide them over the idleness of the winter months; some Transylvanian peasants found seasonal employment in Rumania.

IV

Emigration from Hungary, which drew off the more resolute among the discontented, first assumed significant proportions in the eighties and reached flood tide in the early years of the new century. Small groups moved to Austria, to Germany, and to the Balkan countries, but the vast bulk of the wanderers crossed the Atlantic to the modern El Dorados in the New World. Between 1890 and 1910, approximately 1,500,000 Hungarians landed in the United States alone; in the single year 1907 Hungary and its Austrian partner sent 338,452 people to the United States, the largest voluntary movement of humans from one country to another in a single year that very modern history records. Of these "Hunjaks, Hunkees, Slabs, Polacks, and Bohunks," as they were crudely labeled, 203,332 were born under the Hungarian flag.

By far the greater part of the Hungarian emigrants were males ranging in age from fifteen to forty and they were almost wholly land laborers without financial resources and dependent upon their brawn for their daily bread; only after about 1905 were skilled artisans drawn into the emigration current. Something like two-thirds of the emigrants settled abroad permanently, and most of those who returned to their native villages had accumulated sufficient funds to satisfy their land hunger. Some Hungarian families sanctioned their daughter's marriage on the understanding that the husband after a reasonably long honeymoon would set off for America, make his fortune, and come back and purchase a farm.

Economic and social hardships, though fundamental, were not the exclusive cause of the overseas exodus. As in Austria, emigration was encouraged by aversion to military service, by political discontents, and by the activities of representatives of American state governments and steamship companies, who scattered leaflets telling of the matchless opportunities in the New World and exhibiting, among other things, a solid gold Statue of Liberty and skyscrapers edged with two-carat diamonds! From their pulpits clergymen in northern Hungary read circulars promising a settler in Canada a farmstead of one hundred sixty acres gratis.[13] American agents signed contracts with Hungarian emigrants and managed their business "a good deal in the manner of the coolie trade . . . emigrants are shipped to the United States about like so many slaves," reported the American consul at Budapest in 1880. An act of Congress of 1882 which debarred Chinese "contract-labor" immigrants was applied to Hungarians as well.

From the beginning the Slovaks, who were noted for their roaming propensities, supplied the largest contingent of Hungarian emigrants to the New World. Wages offered in Yankee mines, rolling mills, stockyards, and railway-construction enterprises were five times or more those at home and appealed powerfully to the hard-pressed Slovak farm laborer. Between 1899 and 1914 over 300,000 Slovaks settled in the United States, and the total Slovak population in the latter year exceeded 400,000; Cleveland and Pittsburgh were the principal centers of settlement. In their new homes, Slovaks preserved something of their Old World culture and their "racial" hatreds; they organized societies to promote Slovak national interests, and sent funds back to their homeland to establish small banks and a few factories. Newspapers that Slovak emigrants in America published were barred from the Hungarian mails because of their anti-Magyar temper. Returned Slovaks bought up farmsteads and imparted to their fellows something of the political practices and social ideals and customs with which they had become familiar abroad.

The Ruthenian movement overseas never reached the dimensions of the Slovak emigration. In the twentieth century about 50,000 Ruthenians from Hungary left home, and concentrated in the bituminous and anthracite coal mining districts of Pennsylvania, though several hundred wandered afield to the sugar plantations of Hawaii. The Ruthenians preserved their folk manners and customs, founded cultural and benevolent societies, and had a press of their own. By 1914 the Ruthenian colony in the United States, only partly of Hungarian origin, of course, approached 300,000, and remittances that emigrants mailed home formed an important item in the budget of many poverty-stricken families.

Croats, too, drifted from their native communities to foreign parts, seeking employment or wider freedoms. Many of them turned to the sea; they were especially fond of service under the British flag. In some Croatian villages English was the language generally spoken, the residents having come back from the United States or a British Dominion where their children had attended school. A few Hungarian Serbs and an appreciable company of Hungarian Jews, too, took up homes in the New World.

Emigrants who returned to their native villages acquainted their fellows with life and labor beyond the seas in a way that stimulated further emigration and disturbed local officials. One of them, a Hungarian Serb, Michael Pupin, who rose to a professorship in Columbia University, relates how villagers gathered round him to learn of the marvelous American agricultural machinery or to listen to political sermons on American freedom. Pupin's discourses caused such a stir that the local functionary, a young Hungarian nobleman, ordered him to desist.[14]

Frequently the departure of the men from a village was followed by a good deal of family disorganization. Emigrants sometimes forgot their marital vows and in some cases contracted a second marriage, and husbands after sojourning in America often found their Old World wives uncongenial. American experiences wrought profoundly upon the outlook of the simple rustic, as a cloud of witnesses have testified. One American investigator of these matters has written:

"He leaves his village, a simple peasant in peasant dress, usually not only unable to read and write, but even not desiring to. Ingrained in him are the traditions of his obligations to the church and to his superiors. Unresisting he had toiled from early morning until late at night for a wage insufficient for even his meager wants. Without money and totally unprepared for the complicated industrial life he comes to the New World. His new environment soon brings about changes in this respect, and when he goes back to his old home he is a different man. He is more aggressive and self-assertive. His unaccustomed money gives him confidence and he is no longer willing to pay deference to his former superiors. Frequently, too, the church has lost the influence it had had with him. Moreover, if he has not learned to read and write himself, he has at least seen the value of that ability and is more anxious than before to send his children to school." [15]

The *Budapesti Hirlap* lamented the loss of Hungarian character that occurred in the United States. "The new generation inevitably becomes entirely American . . . The mighty ocean of American cultural and economic life swallows up the Hungarian drops of rain. But these drops are very dear to us."

In several directions emigration reacted upon Hungarian rural economy. From a Hungarian viewpoint it was advantageous to have repatriated workers explain to their fellows that only by hard work could one get on in America and that if men worked as strenuously at home they would be able to raise their living standards. On the other side, in parts of northern Hungary the movement overseas reached such dimensions as to create grave danger of depopulation, and landed proprietors were obliged to import Polish harvest workers and even considered bringing in Chinese coolies. Rural wages increased in consequence of the shortage of field hands and land values shot up as returning emigrants bid for property; at places in Croatia the price of land advanced more than fivefold.

Alarmed by the virtual depopulation of entire villages, "the irreparable loss of national lifeblood," in the language of one Hungarian official, and by the critical when not downright rebellious spirit of returned emigrants, the national and local governments endeavored to discourage emigration by legislation.[16]

So early as 1881 a Hungarian law imposed limitations upon the operations of steamship agents and laid down strict rules for the purchase and payment of tickets. Emigration solicitors were kept under close police surveillance, hundreds were arrested, and publicity was given to unfavorable news about the United States, such as catastrophic cyclones, atrocious murders, attacks by Apaches, and labor troubles. At the turn of the century, in response to pressure for a total ban on emigration, laws were enacted prohibiting advertisements and public exhortations designed to promote emigration, and rigidly regulating emigration agents, who had to be Hungarian subjects. Parents who could not provide for those who would be left behind, individuals without sufficient funds, young men who lacked parental consent, and young women without responsible companions were forbidden to leave the country; and a special frontier police force was created to enforce the law. A supplementary act of 1908 prohibited men from emigrating who had children under fifteen or parents incapable of supporting themselves. While these measures may have restrained emigration, and certainly eliminated abuses of foreign emigration solicitors and domestic go-betweens, they by no means stopped the trend overseas, as the statistics eloquently testify. After emigrants had settled in America, Hungarian agencies tried to get them to move back to "the sweet Hungarian Fatherland" or at least to keep them from becoming "Americanized."[17]

v

Agriculturally, Hungary was divided into four main sections: the Alföld plain, which has extremely fertile soil and is largely arable, lying north of the Danube and drained by the Tisza River; the little Alföld to the south, stretching from the Danube westward into Croatia and Austria, the most highly cultivated and prosperous area of the kingdom, whose rich black soil produced the finest wheat and heaviest corn for the Vienna and Budapest markets; the northern zone, mountainous and wooded, in which less than a fifth of the land was productive, much of it in fact suitable only for stock raising or for game preserves (Ruthenia, in particular, depended upon the rest of the kingdom for all kinds of foodstuffs except potatoes); and Transylvania, half of it too rough for farming, but containing large and fertile valleys, capable of supporting good-sized towns. Transylvania was long a self-contained economic unit, which had made possible political independence in the past; in the modern age, a good deal of trade was carried on with Rumania, for commerce with Hungary proper involved costly transportation.

The section of Croatia adjacent to Hungary proper was an extension of the fertile lowland, broken only by forests of beech and oak, where swine picked up abundant food. On the coast, vegetation grew in abundance; and between these two districts lay the Karst, a rough, inhospitable, mountain area, part of it inhabited by the Pandurs, a brave and revengeful stock, with an established reputation for ferocity. Peasant mothers of southern Germany were wont to frighten their children into obedience with the threat, "Hush! If you are not good, the Pandurs will come and eat you!"

Hungary was one of Europe's major granaries. Its chief productions were wheat, by far the largest crop, barley, rye, oats, corn (maize), and potatoes. Output increased prodigiously after 1870, the wheat yield, for example, rising threefold between 1870 and the end of the century, and much of the wheat was exported in bulk or as flour. Uniformity of quality and reliability of grades accounted more than anything else for the popularity of Hungarian flour in foreign markets, and it was claimed, too, that it had a peculiar buoyant quality lacked by competing grain. England was the principal customer for the finer grades of wheat, followed by France, Germany, and Switzerland; flour of commoner grades was disposed of in the manufacturing communities of Austria. Hungarian competition drove many Bohemian millers to the wall; it was charged that Hungarian millers illicitly imported inferior wheat from the East and converted it into flour to be sold at a price that Bohemian producers could not meet. In the raising of tobacco Hungary ranked just below Turkey among European countries.

Methods of cultivation in the kingdom varied greatly; some of the large proprietors used most up-to-date techniques, while peasants preferred to work very much as their ancestors had done for centuries. The triennial rotation system was generally followed, more than a fifth of the land on the average lying fallow each year, but the proportion was steadily reduced as green fodder was planted and artificial fertilizer applied. Small farms, on which shallow plowing was the vogue and methods were skill-less, were less productive per acre than large properties. In spite of the superior quality of the soil, in general, Hungarian crop yields were only about half as large per acre in the twentieth century as in Germany; in Transylvania the anachronistic, if picturesque, water buffalo served as the chief work animal.

As early as the sixties enterprising large owners started importing agricultural machinery and the steam threshing machine slowly eliminated the primitive custom of treading out wheat on archaic threshing floors. In 1870 antiquated wooden plows were still being used on half the Hungarian farms, but gradually steel plows superseded them, and in the nineties steam-driven plows came into favor on the big estates. Storage buildings were notoriously scarce; hay and straw were kept in stacks, grain in dried pits; well-built granaries were found only on the larger holdings.

In the late seventies Hungarian agriculturalists, like their Austrian fellows who produced for the foreign market, began to feel the effects of the opening up of virgin plowlands in the United States and of the cheapened cost of oceanic transportation. The United States became the national bugbear and the phrase "America is smothering us" was frequently heard; the nub of the matter was that Hungarian methods of production and distribution were no match for those of the enterprising and energetic Yankees. The absence of labor-saving grain elevators, for example, made the handling of wheat in Hungary unduly expensive. Accumulated grain was stored in ancient cisterns or vaulted cellars and loading and unloading were done by man power; Budapest's first grain warehouse was not built until 1880.

Horse breeding was the chief glory of Hungarian agriculture. The foundation stock was the small Asiatic horse with which the conquering Magyars had ridden into Central Europe. During the Napoleonic war, stallions were imported from France, and subsequently from England, and the result of the interbreeding was a large, bony creature, light but tough. Thousands of horses were annually exported from Hungary to the Balkans and Russia. For breeding purposes the government maintained stud farms, and distributed cattle of a superior quality. Hungarians were proud too of their swine, the *mangalica,* a type peculiar to the country, yielding generous quantities of lard, fat bacon, and woollike bristles. As the cost of oceanic shipping dropped and Australian competition increased, sheep breeding in Hungary declined. Cattle raising was the most profitable branch of Croatian agriculture, and swine were the major form of peasant wealth there.

Forests of hardwoods, beech and oak mainly, abounded in the northern regions of Hungary and in Transylvania, but large-scale exploitation of the timber wealth of the north had barely begun by 1914; much of what was cut was marketed in Austria or Italy. The state carefully regulated the exploitation of woodlands and encouraged reforestation. Culture of the grape and wine making had commercial significance in some sections of the kingdom; vineyards were terribly scourged by the dread phylloxera in the eighties, but recovered rapidly with government assistance.

VI

State aid to agriculture assumed a variety of forms, ramifying to meet changing conditions, to mitigate rural destitution, or to combat foreign competition. Tariff measures to safeguard agrarian interests are elsewhere explained. A ministry of agriculture was set up (1889) to promote agriculture in general and to foster coöperative societies in the countryside. Under government auspices seeds, saplings, and stock for breeding were furnished on easy terms, and to a very limited extent farm implements were made available; farmers were compelled to organize societies to prevent floods by regulating rivers and streams.

Agricultural schools offered elementary technical instruction, and courses were arranged for peasants, but the response was disappointing, for they preferred time-tested methods. A dozen academies and specialized institutes supplied advanced training in agriculture; Hungarian agricultural technology dates in fact from 1797, when an academy was founded at Keszthély on Lake Balaton. Veterinary education started toward the end of the eighteenth century in the University of Budapest, and in 1899 a separate veterinary college of the highest grade was organized; the principal forestry school dated from 1808.

Agricultural credit, in a country where interest rates on loans stood as high as 18 to 20 per cent in the 1850's, presented a troublesome and constant problem for the public authorities of Hungary. Private joint-stock banks existed only in the large cities, and they were reluctant to grant rural credit, even though mortgage loans to small holders were acknowledged to be the safest possible investments. Under governmental guidance the Hungarian Land Mortgage Institute, which had the character of a coöperative society, was founded in 1863 to supply loans (on mortgages) to the larger estates and to make advances for the regulation of waterways or to improve land. Similar was the National Small Holdings Land Mortgage Institution (1879) to furnish credit for well-to-do proprietors. To assist the poorest ruralites, the National Federation of Land Mortgages Institutes was set up in 1911; it granted cheap loans, aided poor parishes in purchasing common pastures, building dwellings, or buying seeds and equipment, and it also leased land from aristocrat and church. An Esterházy property of over thirty thousand acres, for instance, was rented and over eight thousand farmers were settled on it.

Local credit societies, mostly on Raffeisen principles, were organized by wealthy Hungarian landowners and in 1898 they were amalgamated in the Hungarian Central Coöperative Credit Society. Business was confined to members only and each local society was limited as a rule to a parish. Loans were extended mostly for agricultural purposes, but sometimes to buy furniture or build a house, or for a daughter's dowry. Interest rates in 1900 ranged from 5 to 8 per cent. In some places credit societies erected small granaries, leased land for cultivation, or purchased artificial fertilizers and farm machinery, and they were increasingly active in supplying agricultural training to members. Managers were the natural local leaders: priests, teachers, in a few instances, large landlords; a central board had jurisdiction over the local units, and furnished them with capital. By 1912, branches of credit coöperatives had been established in half the counties of the kingdom and there were nearly 700,000 members.

Credit coöperatives in Hungary were a definite success. Where they operated, usury was practically unknown and managers kept a watchful eye on the farming methods and the moral conduct of the borrowers. Some non-Magyar groups organized Raffeisen credit coöperatives of their own; the largest was a Croatian society, the most prosperous a Saxon society, a model institution. And there were also several mutual insurance societies.

Producers' coöperative societies had only a limited development in Hungary, though there were some dairy unions and grain coöperatives, which received state aid to build granaries and benefited from the government policy of buying from them for the armed forces. To relieve distress in the Ruthenian area a coöperative movement under government auspices was launched (1898); considerable sums were appropriated to buy land for distribution among the peasants, and to supply better seeds, livestock, and implements, but improvements failed to keep pace with the "incredibly prolific" Ruthenians. A consumers' coöperative league, *Hangya* (1898), established over 1,200 branches in smaller communities mainly, selling food for man and beast, artificial manure, and machinery. At the society headquarters in Budapest there were facilities for processing salt, sugar, coffee, and other commodities. Linked up with *Hangya* was a credit-store chain in Ruthenia with a hundred outlets, and there was also a small Christian coöperative league.

What thoroughgoing economic coöperation could really accomplish was demonstrated in the village of Totmegyer, lying midway between Budapest and Vienna. Most of the property belonged to Count Alexander Károlyi, the leading promoter of coöperation in Hungary, a man who was animated by a deep sense of moral responsibility and a personal version of applied Christianity. The remainder of the land in the community was cut up in small holdings; sugar beets, corn, and barley were the chief products. Between 1896 and 1902 a producers', a consumers', and a credit coöperative were organized, and, owing largely to the guidance of the village priest and the estate physician, all were successful. This model coöperative community maintained two elementary schools, two kindergartens, a small library, a hospital, bowling alleys, and tennis courts; in the winter, lectures and entertainments were provided. Totmegyer proudly exhibited the advantages of coöperation in rural Hungary, and Károlyi fondly hoped that the whole kingdom would find example and inspiration in his pattern village.

VII

The true Magyar was a lover of the land, a kind of Bedouin, in Treitschke's phrase, with a congenital aversion to town life. Trade and commerce he regarded as beneath his dignity; a son of the aristocracy disgraced his family if he turned merchant. Wherefore, historically, the Hungarian town populations had been made up of foreigners, Germans in majority and Jews next. But well along in the nineteenth century, as business expanded, Magyars of the middle and lesser nobility drifted to the towns to swell the middle class; they became small businessmen, bankers, manufacturers, government officials, professional folk. Members of national minorities who took up residence in towns and cities commonly forswore their original nationality under the pressure of official and private Magyarizing influences. So late as the nineties the German idiom was still generally spoken in the Hungarian world of business and commerce, but by 1900 something like two-thirds of the burghers were recorded as Magyar in nationality. In Budapest slightly more than half of the inhabitants spoke German in 1850, but in 1910 the reported ratio had fallen below a tenth.

No Hungarian bourgeois was more Magyar in his outlook and feeling than the assimilated, Magyarized Jew; and nothing gratified such an individual so much as to be able to pass for an authentic Magyar. Before 1800, except in the northern counties, Jews formed a very small fraction of the Hungarian population; some were innkeepers, small-scale moneylenders and tradesmen, more served as stewards and business agents on the estates of the nobility, invaluable assets for the happy-go-lucky aristocrats. So numerous were Jews in the north that the region was referred to colloquially as the Magyar Israel. A prominent personality in every Transylvanian village was the Jewish tavern keeper, who lived in a stone house and whose wife wore a hat — both marks of affluence. He was also likely to be grocer, clothier, hardware merchant, selling everything the peasant bought and buying everything the peasant sold.

With the coming of industrialism and the relaxation of old and oppressive disabilities against Jewry, the Jewish population multiplied. Migration took place from the towns and villages of the north into Budapest and other cities, and Jews wandered in from Galicia, Rumania, Russia, precisely as was the case in Austria, though in somewhat smaller numbers. Yet the Jewish element in Budapest became proportionately more than twice as large as in Vienna. Whereas Hungary's recorded Jewish population was 270,000 in 1840, it had reached almost 1,000,000 by 1914.

Thrifty, hard-working, ambitious Jews pushed to the front in the commercial and professional life of the kingdom and became in time, next to the Magyars themselves, the most powerful group in Hungary. It has been said that the transformation of Budapest from a quaint, charming hill town into one of Europe's loveliest capitals was largely a Jewish achievement. Magyarized Jews crowded into the professions of medicine and law and obtained a controlling influence in industry, banking, commerce, and the press—so much so that it was said, exaggeratedly, that "the entire wealth of the nation runs through Jewish channels." Jews turned to the purchase and leasing of land, and entered the class of big owners; many a property passed to them upon the failure of a borrower to meet his obligations on a mortgage. Certain Jewish families amassed great wealth, gained admission to the baronial class, became in title as in feeling aristocrats, as was true of the Herzogs, the Kornfelds, the Hatványs; some Jewish landed proprietors indeed were permitted to adopt the name of their estates just like the traditional Magyar nobleman. How the Jew advanced in worldly goods and the social graces out of rural obscurity has been entertainingly recounted by Baron Hatvány in a novel known in its English dress as *Bondy Jr.*[18]

Below the very top group of Jews were well-to-do bourgeois, untitled, but financially quite comfortable, the owners of successful factories and stores, journalistic and professional folk, often men and women of rare cultural refinement. At the bottom of the Jewish scale were the shopkeeper, the village moneylender, the huckster, the peddler, and the handworkers, miserably poor, receptive to ideas of radical innovations in state and economy. From Jewry's ranks issued the greater part of the leaders of Hungarian Social Democracy and a substantial share of the members, so that Magyar critics nicknamed the Socialist movement *Jock,* an epithet for Jews.

Social assimilation of Hungarian Jews was closely related to their economic status. The affluent readily responded to the pervasive Magyar pressure to become Magyars in name and feeling; Weiss was transformed into Fehér, Block into Ballagi, Schwarz became Fekete, and some Jews wholly forsook the faith of their fathers and accepted Christian baptism. Another large group (Neologs) were assimilated to the Magyar cultural pattern in everything but religion. Their interpretation of the Hebrew creed deviated from orthodoxy, for they abandoned every vestige of tribalism and the messianic faith, rejected the verbal inspiration of the Hebrew Scriptures and the authority of the Talmud, and adopted the Magyar language for much of the synagogue service. Budapest was indeed one of the more important centers of "Reformed" Jewry in Europe. Orthodox Jews, however, among them the zealous Chassidim Jews of the north, held tenaciously to the traditional beliefs and customs of their people and lived in cultural and social isolation, little affected by Gentile society. They disputed angrily with their coreligionists who had accepted radical revisions in the theory and practice of the ancestral Hebrew creed.

In the main, Hungary's Jews were ardent patriots, advancing the material and intellectual life of the country, sturdy defenders of the rights of Hungary in its dealings with Austria, fervent apostles of Magyarization.[19] In season and out the Jewish-owned press, the largest part of the Hungarian journalistic world, vigorously supported the campaign to denationalize non-Magyars and eloquently proclaimed the convictions of Magyar chauvinism.

The attitude of the Hungarian government toward Jewry was consistently liberal, an encouragement to immigration and assimilation. Medieval restrictions upon Jews were gradually removed, and in 1867 full rights of citizenship were conferred upon them; they were allowed to occupy university chairs and to serve as officers in the national army. After 1885 a Jewish rabbi was given a seat in the house of magnates, legal barriers to marriage between Jews and Christians were overthrown, and in 1896 the Hebrew faith was put on a plane of official equality with other religions.

For reasons and prejudices akin to those which operated in Austria, anti-Jewish feelings were evident in Hungary from the eighties onward, without, however, attaining anything like the intensity that prevailed across the Leitha. Literature condemnatory of Jewry, such as translations of crude "racialist" writings, coming in from Austria and Germany, stirred up latent antipathy toward Jewry. A hitherto obscure member of parliament, Victor Istóczy, attracted attention (and ridicule) when he proposed that the sultan of Turkey be compelled to hand Palestine over to the Jews and that all Israelites be deported thither. Round his anti-Jewish banner Istóczy rallied a handful of fellow deputies who joined him in clamoring for the repeal of the law giving equality to the Jews; scores of anti-Jewish clubs were organized that engineered raids upon Jewish moneylenders and participated in an international conference on the Jewish question at Dresden. A rising against Jews in Poszony (Bratislava) in 1882 was put down by the military, only to break out in neighboring villages, but fears that the scandalous outrages then raging in southern Russia would be repeated in Hungary proved groundless.

In the same year a typical charge of ritual murder was raised in the town of Tisza-Eszlár. At the trial of the accused man it was conclusively shown that his idiot son had been suborned to bear false witness against him. He was released, but an infuriated mob, angered by the outcome of the trial, set upon his lawyer and demolished his residence. That incident set off outbursts against Jewry in which personal and property damage was done; excesses subsided only after police intervened and Premier Coloman Tisza declared unequivocally that the government intended to protect the rights of all citizens. Seventeen deputies were elected to parliament in 1884 as anti-Semites. They demanded drastic limitations on the economic liberty of Jewry, and thereafter animosity toward Jews continued to be a constant though definitely a secondary phenomenon in Hungarian affairs.

Owing to the remarkable growth of the Jewish population, an aphorism of Count Stephen Széchényi, "the greatest Hungarian," was often on the lips of Jewry's foes: "The Jew in England is as a bottle of ink thrown into the ocean; the Jew in Hungary is as a similar bottle of ink thrown into a glass of water." By the old aristocracy ennobled Jews were regarded with varying degrees of reserve; concerning the converted Jew, a Hungarian proverb taught: "A dog will never become bacon"; Jews were commonly referred to as dogs, which recalls another Magyar adage: "Whenever a Slav speaks a dog yelps."

While Jews made up a part of the Hungarian industrial working class, that social element was recruited principally from landless villagers and in large measure from the national minorities. As peasants they had the rural lust for landownership and looked forward to the day when they might abandon the factory for the farm, for the millworker was thought of as socially beneath the tiller of the soil. Given that outlook, it was not easy to build up a sense of class consciousness or to develop class solidarity among industrial workers.

Industrialism in Hungary was restricted pretty largely to small establishments and never affected as much as a fifth of the kingdom's population. Only Budapest was an industrial city by Western standards; Pozsony and Pécs (Fünfkirchen) were other centers of large-scale production, and Szegedin, Debreczen, Kassa, Arad, Temesvár, and Kolosvár had importance in milling and manufacturing. Hungary's oldest industry was mining, carried on principally in the Slovak counties and Transylvania; iron ore of fine quality was mined in the Slovak area and about half the output was shipped to Austria for fabrication. Scattered about the peripheral districts of the kingdom were minor deposits of coal, copper, zinc, manganese, salt, and the precious metals.

Textile manufacturing employed the largest number of industrial workers, and the milling of flour made Budapest famous; among flour cities it stood next to Minneapolis, though the gap between them was wide. Small numbers of workers were engaged in the processing of tobacco, the manufacture of chemicals, and the making of products of wood. Heavy industry grew rapidly after 1900, principally in the Slovak area, where governmental aid was generously given; the large Reşiţa iron and steel works of southern Hungary belonged to Viennese financial interests.

Without political rights and quite at the mercy of employers, Hungarian industrial workers lived under conditions more suggestive of imperial Russia than of western Europe. Long working days—in 1900 the normal stint for miners was twelve hours—were rewarded with extremely low wages. On a visit to Budapest in 1909 the American labor leader, Samuel Gompers, discovered skilled millers receiving less than eighty cents a day, women cigar makers under half that, and miners in northern Hungary a daily wage of sixty cents; yet wages were appreciably higher than a generation earlier.[20] Housing congestion was probably worse in the Hungarian capital than in any large European city west of Russia, and police often raided and closed up disease-breeding pest holes.

Organizations of Hungarian workers to improve conditions of employment were strictly banned until 1872. An act of that year, following demonstrations of factory workers in Budapest, legalized the formation of labor unions provided they had no political purposes, and recognized the right to strike, though with reservations. But linguistic differences among the workers, the prevalent peasant mentality, and the unsympathetic attitude of government militated against the growth of vigorous trade-unionism. Nevertheless, twoscore unions were formed and congresses were held in which demands were made for Sunday as a rest day, better wages, and shorter hours. However, when local general strikes achieved partial successes, the government imposed fresh restrictions on the right to strike, labor's most potent weapon. By 1914, slightly more than 100,000 workers were enrolled in unions, and intimately, though illegally, allied with trade-unionism was the Hungarian Socialist movement.

Grudgingly the state intervened to protect or improve the lot of the industrial wageworkers. The first factory law of 1872 prescribed the manner in which wages should be paid, fixed the maximum work day at sixteen hours, and placed certain restrictions upon the employment of children. Another act of 1884 provided protection for employed women and ordered management to install safety devices in factory and mine; a system of state inspectors for factories was authorized but was not faithfully carried out, and in fact did little to remedy abuses or safeguard workers' interests. A compulsory insurance measure was passed into law in 1891 and two years later Sunday was prescribed as a rest day, though numerous exceptions were permitted. Efforts of Hungarian workers later on to secure the right to vote were barren of result. To relieve the housing congestion in Budapest the government appropriated funds in 1908 to build dwellings for six thousand families, principally for workers on the state railways, and tax exemption was granted to inexpensive apartment blocks.

IX

Hungarians prided themselves on the fact that in the past, as in the present, they were "the shield of Christendom" against the infidel Turk. As in Austria, the Roman Catholic church was a mighty bulwark of the Hapsburg regime and the *status quo*. High dignitaries of the church rivaled the great secular grandees in their landholdings; three of them possessed estates in excess of 100,000 acres—the bishop of Nagy-Varád had 266,000 acres—and most bishops owned more than 35,000 acres. Monasteries, too, were richly endowed with land. Just like the entailed estates of the aristocracy, the landed property belonging to the Catholic church doubled after 1867, and in 1914 ecclesiastical holdings covered fully 2,250,000 acres, some of them the fattest in the kingdom.

The primate of Hungary, who filled the archbishopric of Esztergom (Gran), four other archbishops, and twenty-three Catholic bishops were entitled to sit in the house of magnates. All priests and some of the monks enjoyed the social standing of nobles, and a few churchmen occupied local public offices, lord lieutenancies of counties, for example. In the age of the Reformation Hungary had turned almost wholly to Protestantism and only three of the powerful aristocratic families held faithfully to Rome, but by the nineteenth century the vast majority of the wealthy grandees had returned to the Catholic fold, carrying their peasants along with them. As of 1910 over three out of five of the Hungarian population were communicants of the Roman Catholic or Uniat Church.

The "apostolic" king possessed considerable authority in the selection of Hungarian prelates, though the concurrence of the pope was nominally required. Governmental pressure in 1891 obliged the Vatican to confer a cardinal's hat on Louis Haynald, archbishop of Kalocsa, which Pius IX had refused because the cleric had fraternized with the Italian "robber king," Victor Emmanuel II. As a rule, Hungarian churchmen were not less loyal to the dynasty than the Austrian, but they allied themselves with Magyar nationalism and so escaped charges of lack of patriotism, which would have driven high-spirited Magyars into the Protestant camp; seldom was the august voice of Catholicism raised on behalf of non-Magyar peoples. Nobles, younger sons, and poor squires filled the chief places in the church hierarchy, forming an intimate link with the lay aristocracy. Yet the Catholic Church was no doubt the most democratic institution in the kingdom, since it supplied a ready way for gifted peasants to lift themselves out of their original social class. Religious liberty was placed on a solid basis late in the eighteenth century and complete religious equality for all Christian creeds was established in 1848, while Judaism was recognized as the equal of the other faiths in 1896.

Orthodox or Eastern Catholicism accounted for one out of seven of Hungary's inhabitants. The head of the Serb branch of Orthodoxy was the patriarch of Karlowicz, and of the Rumanian, the archbishop of Hermannstadt (Sibiu); and each group had autonomous privileges. Confessing Jews comprised a twentieth of the population and Protestant sects accounted for the balance, almost 20 per cent of all, a fractional falling off since the mid-nineteenth century. Followers of Calvin in the Reformed Church were the largest and by far the most influential of Protestant groups, the Lutherans came next, and there were tiny islands of Unitarians in Transylvania. Full equality among faiths was recognized and each was free to administer its own internal affairs.

While Lutheranism's strength lay in the Slovak districts and among the "Saxons" of Transylvania, Calvinism was emphatically a Magyar faith, enrolling a few grandees and many gentry. By its adherents Calvinism was thought of as the "Magyar religion" par excellence. At Debreczen, the

"Rome" of Hungarian Calvinism, an excellent denominational "college" was maintained which educated children at college levels and offered professional training in law and theology. It was in the massive Calvinist church of Debreczen that, on Louis Kossuth's motion, the resolution was adopted in 1849 declaring that the Hapsburgs had forfeited the crown of St. Stephen, and there the insurgent government had its headquarters until the legions of Russia captured the city. Because of these historical associations Debreczen occupied a unique place in the affections of Magyar patriots regardless of their creed.

Throughout the prolonged struggle to prevent the Hapsburgs from completely wiping out Hungarian political rights, Protestantism was one of the deepest sources of national moral energy, and from its ranks came a surprisingly high proportion of the anti-Hapsburg chiefs; Kossuth, for example, the doughty and irreconcilable antagonist of Francis Joseph, belonged to the Lutheran church. And after the *Ausgleich* Calvinism gave the kingdom a long line of prominent public men, among whom the two Tiszas, father Coloman and son Stephen, stood out most conspicuously.

x

Before 1867 popular education in Hungary was provided only to a very limited extent and was controlled exclusively by the several religious confessions. That tradition of ecclesiastical influence was perpetuated in the new era; the great majority of the schools were operated by churches, though state schools were of increasing importance.[21] The ideal of universal education had a vigorous champion in Baron Joseph Eötvös, minister of education and worship in the Andrássy cabinet of 1867. Much influenced by the currents of educational thought in England at the time, Eötvös asserted jurisdiction of his ministry over state schools and sponsored an act of 1868, making school attendance compulsory from the age of six to twelve. Wherever parishes were unable to maintain schools, they would be built and financed by the royal government. Elementary schools of all kinds were subjected to uniform regulations by the state regarding buildings, teachers, and the like, and their internal organization was minutely prescribed.

But enforcement of the obligatory attendance law was imperfect, so that in many sections instruction started when the snow fell and ceased when it melted and teachers were simply intelligent farmers or tradesmen. Even so, by the twentieth century more than 80 per cent of the children of school age were receiving some sort of formal education, and Hungary seems to have made relatively greater progress in the war on illiteracy than her Austrian partner. Ability to read and write was most widely diffused in the predominantly German and Magyar areas and in the city of Fiume. Taking the kingdom as a whole, the proportion of illiterates dropped from almost sixty in a hundred in 1880 to under forty-eight in 1900, but in the northern and eastern sections the illiterates formed anywhere from 60 to 80 per cent of all.

Primary schooling was regarded by the Magyar governing class as an indispensable instrument to ensure national solidarity and to impart a sense of national consciousness. Among the whole population knowledge of the Magyar language, literature, and history was inculcated through the schools; legislation to that end, to be described later, was enacted from time to time. While the customary three R's, religion, and ethics had places in the curriculum, the rights and duties of citizens comprised the very core of instruction and in the twentieth century Magyar was used as the exclusive language of instruction in seven out of ten elementary schools, as compared with about five out of ten in 1880. Glorious epochs in Hungary's past were exalted and the incessant struggle against Hapsburg tyranny was subjectively treated; much praise was showered upon Deák for the negotiation of the *Ausgleich* of 1867, and the idea was fostered that that arrangement had given Hungary carte blanche to pursue her own ends without restraint from the ruling dynasty. Minority peoples were treated with disdain in instruction in the schools and their languages and literatures cavalierly minimized or avoided. Subjects that were loaded with political dynamite, such as the cultural rights of minorities and the basic economic tensions of the kingdom, were adroitly sidestepped. Into the minds of the rising generation was insinuated the conservative maxim that "whatever is, is right, and whatever is right, is." [22]

Above the elementary level there were secondary schools, some with religious foundations running back to the sixteenth century but many established under state auspices after 1867. Graduation from a secondary school—and those in which classical literatures were emphasized attracted vastly more learners than the "modern" schools—was a prerequisite to admission into a university or entry upon a professional or official career. As of 1911, over 57,000 youths were studying at secondary schools, and over three-quarters of them were of Magyar (including Jewish) antecedents and a majority of the rest were Germans; the language of instruction, except in Fiume, was Magyar and the spirit of the institutions was uncritically and proudly Magyar. Hungary was also rather well supplied with specialized industrial, commercial, and art schools, and institutions for technical training in agriculture, forestry, mining, and education; all were financed by public authorities. Religious groups offered theological training of a mature character.

Education at the highest level was available at the University of Budapest, founded in 1635. This institution gained greatly in quality and reputation in the late nineteenth century, so that it was no longer thought necessary for an educated person to pursue advanced studies in Vienna. By 1910, almost 7,000 students, fully a third of them Jews, were in attendance, or almost four times as many as in 1880; women were admitted with reservations, though few actually enrolled. Magyar scholarship on the highest plane centered in the University of Budapest, which was organized on the German pattern.

Smaller institutions of the highest learning were located at Kolozsvár (Klausenberg) (1872), the Transylvanian capital, and at Agram (Zagreb) (1874), attended by Croats and other Yugoslavs. The college at Debreczen, which was founded in 1538, was raised to university rank in 1914, and given the name of Stephen Tisza, in honor of the institution's most distinguished graduate; and in 1912 an embryonic university was organized at Pozsony (Bratislava). The Polytechnic School of Budapest (1844) furnished training of the highest grade in engineering, architecture, and related vocations.

Apart from the Croatian institution at Agram, the Hungarian universities were permeated with the Magyar spirit, and it has been estimated that fully nine out of ten of the students with non-Magyar backgrounds who attended became Magyarone, many of them positively scornful of their own national folks. Stanchly Rumanian-feeling or Slovak-feeling youths preferred in general to matriculate at a university outside the boundaries of the kingdom and only a ninth of the more than 10,000 university students in 1911 professed to belong to non-Magyar minorities.

CHAPTER ELEVEN

THE REIGN OF COLOMAN TISZA

FROM 1875 TO 1890, HUNGARY'S POLITICAL AFFAIRS WERE DI-
rected by the dictatorial and domineering Coloman Tisza (1830–1902) to such
a degree that this epoch may well bear his name. With him at the helm
Hungary attained unprecedented influence in the affairs of the Danube Monarchy, and one overly enthusiastic admirer wrote at his death, "Hungary of
today is his work and his monument." That Tisza was a remarkable personality admits of no doubt. Small and thin, with long flowing hair, sparse
beard, large blue spectacles, dressed in ill-fitting clothes, he resembled Shy-
lock as represented in old prints. Eagerness for parliamentary combat, ruth-
lessness in debate, persuasiveness in oratory, an unbending iron will, intense
devotion to Magyar interests were the personal qualities that enabled him to
stand out from the crowd, to dwarf his ministerial colleagues, so that it appeared that Tisza was in fact the cabinet. Admired and respected by many,
he was loved by none.

Tisza belonged to a Magyar gentry family, which had long been active in
public affairs and in furthering the interests of their Reformed or Calvinist
faith. In a small country seat at Geszt, the Tiszas lived in austere simplicity,
ruled their peasants as patriarchs, and hewed close to the Puritan way of life,
in marked contrast to the ostentation and pomp of the wealthy Magyar
aristocracy. Of the Tiszas it was said they had three overmastering concerns:
"horses, politics, and the Bible." No family better typified the Hungarian
gentry class, none exceeded it in passionate loyalty to the Magyar fatherland.
"I am as wholly and solely Hungarian," Coloman remarked, "as the river
whose name I bear."

After the revolutionary rising in 1848–49, in which because of physical frailty he had no part, Tisza went abroad to complete his education, and on his return he followed the normal and prosaic round of a country squire. By marriage he was brought into association with the Károlyi and other grandee families.

Debreczen, the Calvinist stronghold, sent Tisza to parliament in 1861, and he attained immediate prominence in the party that advocated the restriction of the Hungarian bond with Austria to the person of the ruler, far less than the Deákists agreed to in the settlement of 1867. For a time he wrote editorials for a free-trade journal, conducted by his admiring follower, Maurus Jókai.

After the making of the *Ausgleich*, Tisza stood forth as an opponent of dualism, though gradually his enmity cooled as he came to appreciate the economic advantages of the new regime and discovered that the monarch was sympathetic to Hungarian viewpoints in foreign relations, as was attested in one way by the selection of Andrássy as foreign secretary. Forsaking his earlier political principles, Tisza merged his parliamentary following with the Deákists, to form the new Hungarian champion of dualism, the Liberal party. In the fall of 1875, Francis Joseph named Tisza prime minister, though he regarded him with suspicion as a renegade who had deserted the anti-*Ausgleich* camp. But reservations swiftly vanished, for as prime minister Tisza, who had been an outspoken foe of centralization, worked for more complete centralization and was undeviatingly faithful to the settlement of 1867.

Twice during Tisza's tenure of power, in 1878 and in 1887, the decennial commercial and financial pacts with Austria were renewed, each time over the obstinate resistance of the Kossuthists in Hungary and the protests of bureaucrats in both Austria and Hungary who felt obligated to raise objections. Each time business interests were uneasy lest the economic *Ausgleich* should be jettisoned and each partner be permitted to pursue independent commercial policies. Three items came up for deliberation and settlement: the proportion of the common expenses to be paid by each partner, the future of the monarchical bank, and tariffs, with the last the most fertile source of discussion and dissension.

Hungary, whose economy was predominantly agricultural, leaned in the direction of free trade except with respect of farm products, while Austria, whose industrialists had to face stiff competition from Western and German manufacturers, favored tariff protectionism. Neo-mercantilism, then rising to popularity on the Continent generally, had considerable support in the Austrian empire, especially after the commercial crisis of 1873 and the attendant fall in prices. International treaties fixing tariffs which had been arranged with foreign countries continued in force until 1875, when Hungary served notice of its intention to insist upon a revision in tariff schedules.

Negotiations on all the joint economic issues started in 1875, but were not completed until June 1878, when the two parliaments ratified agreements that had been reached after prolonged deliberation, angry polemics, and ministerial crises which irritated feelings in both sections of the realm.

In the making of these economic arrangements an extremely complicated procedure had to be gone through. First of all, representatives of Austria and Hungary prepared tentative accords on the matters at hand, which were transmitted to the two ministries for acceptance. They in turn presented the proposed bills to the two parliaments, and committees of each parliament examined them and made modifications after consultation with one another; that done, the bills were finally communicated to each parliament for adoption. In 1877 the Austrian reichsrat balked at increased tariffs on coffee and petroleum and created a ministerial crisis. Thereupon a crown council, presided over by the monarch, was summoned, and an acceptable compromise, mainly in accordance with Hungarian wishes, was hammered out.

Under the tariff act of 1878 raw materials entered the Monarchy free of duty, and relatively low tariffs were set on some manufactured articles, and on coffee, petroleum, sugar, and brandy. Provision was made for raising duties on imports from countries that did not grant most-favored-nation treatment to Austro-Hungarian wares. Since all duties had to be paid in gold coin rather than in silver as previously, the new tariff law involved an advance of about 15 per cent in rates.

Thoroughgoing revisions in the tariff, with a view to protecting agriculture and manufacturing and the enlargement of monarchical income, were effected in 1882 and 1887.[1] How the tariff provided protection was illustrated by the case of hogs, which in 1874 brought twelve cents a pound; foreign competition depressed the price to 7.3 cents. But behind the tariff act the price rose to 11.1 cents, which encouraged the breeding of hogs and again the price fell. Partly to reduce competition, partly for hygienic reasons, Hungarian frontier authorities strictly inspected every hog imported from Balkan countries and if the slightest trace of epidemic disease was discovered a whole drove was denied admission. Hungary, which was intent on building up native industry, combatting transatlantic agricultural competition (great alarm was caused among agricultural producers by a report that the United States intended to establish six offices in the Monarchy to sell wheat), and retaliating against Germany, whose tariff policy hindered the sale of Hungarian grains and cattle,[2] gradually passed over to the protectionist position.

Virtually all articles produced in the Monarchy were accorded protection in 1882, as Austria-Hungary joined the triumphant procession of continental lands which saw and sought salvation in state intervention on behalf of commerce and agriculture. Competition of American pork products led to complete prohibition of the importation of American pork, the official reason being the prevalence of disease among American hogs. In the same neo-mercantilist vein, subsidies were given to shipping concerns and reductions in duties were permitted on articles imported through Trieste and Fiume. Monarchical customs receipts almost doubled in the eight years that followed the raising of tariffs, but the new commercial policy caused such severe strains in dealings with Germany that, in spite of the diplomatic alliance between the two countries, they came repeatedly to the verge of an economic war, and with Balkan countries the Monarchy actually fought severe customs wars.

Large agrarian interests, of Hungary in particular, supported by individual economists of repute, argued for a customs union with Germany, the market for fully half of the Monarchy's exports. They wanted an agreement that would give preference to grain and meat, or better still a tight *Zollverein* which would eventually embrace all of central Europe. Such a league would have been pointed against the foreign trade of Russia and the commercial invasion of Europe by the energetic New World. "Against imports from Russia and America," Tisza, once a partisan of free trade, observed, "we may all feel bound to protect ourselves."

As time moved on, the apprehension of agrarians because of American intrusion into European markets was increasingly shared by Austrian manufacturing interests. Declared the president of the Vienna Chamber of Commerce, a semiofficial institution, in 1902: "America is destined to be a most powerful country. We regard it as the most dangerous competitor in all our markets. The marrow and bone of her prosperity we believe to be her protective tariff . . . Whenever we discover that American competition is hurting any of our industries, we shall certainly shut out America if we can."

But the Hapsburg-sponsored idea of a grand customs league against the United States failed of realization, if for no other reason because of the divergent interests of the several countries. Yet the Danube Monarchy joined with Germany and Italy in forming a very loose central European tariff union (1891), which, among other things, tended to supplement the political Triple Alliance, and excited groundless dreads lest it might be the prelude to a solid commercial union.

The economic union of Austria and Hungary enabled the former to capture the lion's share of Hungarian trade. In the eighties almost three-quarters of Hungarian exports passed to Austria, and in Austria, Hungary made about four-fifths of its foreign purchases. The relationship was, to be sure, mutually advantageous, since Hungarian cattle raisers secured a virtual monopoly over the sale of meat to Vienna, where consumers complained that the Magyar partner forced prices to inordinate heights. To bring prices down, special railway rates were extended to cattle transported from Galicia, and shipments from Hungary were somewhat obstructed by strict sanitary inspection.

It was anticipated in Austria that, in the economic negotiations of 1877, Hungary could be induced to shoulder a larger share of the common expenditures of the Monarchy, for, as matters stood, Austria paid the bulk of these charges and also carried almost all of the pre-1867 imperial debt. But Hungary adamantly refused to increase its contribution to the common expenses, and nothing could be done about it. Upon Hungary's insistence, a reorganization was effected in the Austrian national bank, which served the financial requirements of the whole monarchy. During the deliberations of 1867, Magyar negotiators had thought of holding out for an independent bank but had abandoned the plan because their country was without adequate capital resources. The existing Austrian bank, which had many offices in Hungary and carried on a thriving business in mortgage loans, was therefore allowed to continue its operations unaltered. For some Magyars national honor, no less than national interests, required an independent bank; businessmen and landholders, in debt to the Austrian bank, favored a separate institution that would issue cheap paper with which their obligations could be liquidated, while Austrian financial interests, which would be injured by the division of the banking system, tenaciously resisted any change.

Yet in the economic settlements of 1878, Magyar pride was appeased by refashioning the imperial bank along dualistic lines so that the Hungarian government had comparable influence with the Austrian in bank affairs, and by changing the title to the Austro-Hungarian bank. From a financial angle that arrangement unquestionably benefited the weaker Hungary, which could secure credit cheaper than would have been possible from an independent institution lacking the financial resources of Vienna. At the same time it was agreed that bank notes in the future should have an Austrian side and a Hungarian; not insignificantly, the inscriptions on the Austrian half were done in all the major languages of the empire, while on the reverse side only the Magyar language was printed. At the renewal of the economic arrangements in 1887 no changes were introduced in the banking establishment nor in the quotas for the common expenses of the Monarchy.

II

From the moment he came into power Tisza posed as the deliverer of Hungary from its financial difficulties; it was indeed the critical fiscal situation that had induced him to enter the ministry in the first place. In line with pledges of strict economy, reductions were effected in the number of judicial and administrative officials and the collection of taxes was slightly better enforced. But the crucial problem was the national debt, which had doubled between 1867 and 1875 owing to financial mismanagement and huge outlays for railways and military purposes; over a third of the state income was absorbed by service of the public debt. A succession of able finance ministers, Széll, Szapáry, and Tisza himself, guided the country out of the financial doldrums. By refunding the national debt at much lower interest rates annual expenditures were substantially cut down, and a state loan of 1881 was oversubscribed twenty-five times by domestic and foreign investors, in itself a vote of confidence in the new Hungary tendered by financial interests.

Economies in other directions, the virtual completion of railway lines, which had been a prime source of state deficits, more orderly administration and collection of taxes, and remarkably good crop yields in the eighties (the harvest was the axle on which all else revolved) made possible a balanced budget in 1889, for the first time since the establishment of the autonomous kingdom. Judging by quotations for government securities, the credit of Hungary showed greater relative improvement in the eighties than that of the other principal European countries. Tisza was hailed as "the best statesman Hungary ever boasted," and "the regenerator of national finance."

As has been mentioned, a network of railways was built in Hungary in the seventies, following in the main the natural routes that transportation had taken since the dawn of the modern era, and in the eighties and nineties large additions were made to the trackage tapping agricultural areas previously out of the reach of markets. Ten trunk lines departed from Budapest alone, and railways crossed the national frontiers at nineteen points. Spokesmen of minorities charged that lines were laid out and rates manipulated so as to benefit Magyar interests rather than those of the nationalities, and there was some substance to the contention. But in the case of communications with the Balkans, the deliberately restrictive policy of the government met with general approval, since the commodities that Serbia was accustomed to export competed directly with products of southern Hungary, where costs were higher because of a different and more expensive living standard.[3]

By 1890 the railways of the kingdom were almost wholly under state control, either owned by the state or privately owned and worked by the state, and even stanch critics of public ownership of railways acknowledged in time that state operation was more satisfactory in Hungary than anywhere else in Europe. Rates were adjusted for the purpose of promoting national economic interests as a whole.

Seeking to enlarge railway revenues, Hungary pioneered in the application of the principle of uniform charges for passengers regardless of the distance traveled, the "postalization system," as it was called. Responsible for this innovation in rates was the energetic and iron-handed minister of communications and commerce, Gabriel Baross. Under his direction the entire kingdom was divided into fourteen railway zones, with Budapest as the center, and enormous reductions were made on long-distance journeys; farm laborers in gangs were carried at half the regular fares.

Baross was typical of the Magyar statesmen who believed in fostering national prosperity and in making the kingdom industrially self-sufficient by mercantilist legerdemain. Ardently devoted to national welfare, he wanted Hungary to have industries that would render it independent of Austria and would offer greater opportunities for employment. Industrialism had developed tardily in Hungary, for before the *Ausgleich* Austria had deliberately prevented the growth of manufacturing, intending to keep Hungary as a market for Austrian manufacturers. Capital and industrial raw materials were scarce, means of transportation primitive; as late as 1873 only four small textile factories were operating in the kingdom and their output went largely into uniforms for the Hungarian army. Clothing for the masses was prepared in the home, garments and patterns varying from district to district, nationality to nationality. Articles requiring skilled labor came largely from Austria, or in the case of finer qualities from Britain or France.

After a web of railways had been completed, the building of a native Hungarian industry became practicable. Beginning in 1881, capital was attracted from Austria and Germany by granting tax exemption to factories for a period of years; over 400 firms were thus benefited in the eighties. On occasion the state furnished direct subsidies to "baby industries," and railway rates were manipulated to promote industrial growth. Youths were dispatched abroad to study manufacturing processes, and engineers and skilled artisans were invited to Hungary to operate plants. Legislation prescribing that public contracts should be awarded to Hungarian companies stimulated the growth of textile and metal industries.[4]

Natural economic advantages dictated primarily the location of manufacturing establishments, although it was alleged that official pressure was exerted to keep plants out of areas inhabited by minorities. In reality, industrial development was encouraged in the more backward, non-Magyar districts with the twin objective of bettering living standards and of checking the tide of emigration. One third of all the financial assistance appropriated by the state for industry went to Slovak areas and the proportion allotted to textile manufacturing was even greater in the Slovak counties. And subsidies were also granted for schools to give training for cottage industry.

Measured by the number of workers engaged, Hungarian industrialism went forward with giant strides during the Tisza period, far exceeding the progress achieved in the Dual Monarchy as a whole. Milling made the most striking advance, and sales of flour to Austria tripled between 1882 and 1893. The passage of Hungary from a purely agrarian economy was demonstrated at a national industrial exhibition at Budapest in 1885. The fair was opened with great pomp, such as the city had not seen since the coronation of Francis Joseph; court and high society were present in their ceremonial regalia, and Crown Prince Rudolph asserted that "the great and surprising progress in the work of civilization in Hungary is manifested in this gorgeous display. The exhibition gives evidence of development as wide as it is sound." An English visitor called the Hungarians "the Yankees of the empire," praise that might more deservedly have been bestowed upon the Bohemians.

As a rival to Trieste, the Hungarian government lavished great care on Fiume, the country's sole seaport, whose approaches were safe and protected, and the waters were deep. With the completion in 1875 of a railway running down from Budapest and Agram, the commercial history of Fiume really commenced. Large sums were invested in breakwaters, loading facilities, piers and warehouses, and subsidies were given to native and foreign shipping companies; whereas in 1867 the trade of Fiume was valued at less than $3,000,000, it exceeded $36,000,000 in 1882. Lesser economic improvements of the time were the regulation of the Danube and its tributaries, progress in widening the Danube's perilous Iron Gates, and currency reform, whereby fiat money was redeemed and the gold standard introduced.

III

In the first parliamentary election under the Tisza ministry, held in 1878 while troops were engaged in the unpopular task of subduing Bosnia-Herzegovina, the government party lost almost fifty seats.[5] In the Debreczen area, the three victorious deputies belonged to the extremist 1848 or Independence party; Tisza was himself defeated there, but was elected in another district. In spite of this setback at the polls the ministerial Liberal party still commanded a large majority in the lower chamber. That was due partly to the application of favoritism, bribery, and terrorism in districts with a limited number of electors, over two hundred of which were thus controlled by the government and handed out to Tisza's trusties, the "Mamelukes," as they were appropriately called. The united opposition of seventy represented a faction sympathetic to the existing bond with Austria, but intensely hostile to Tisza's dictatorial rule; the extreme left won sixty-six seats and there were fifteen independents. Shrewd statecraft and the immense personal influence of Count Andrássy were required to secure parliamentary approval of the occupation of Bosnia-Herzegovina.

Subsequent elections—1881, 1884, 1887—the second marred by scandalous and bloody outrages, strengthened the position of Tisza. The opposition, consisting of archconservatives, of an extremely tiny representation of minority peoples, and of the Kossuthist independence faction, was almost reduced to impotence. Only the last group caused any noteworthy concern, for it utilized every opportunity to manifest hostility to the union with Austria and, by the same token, to the Tisza ministry. A curious manifesto issued by Louis Kossuth from his exile in Italy, affirming that "the present situation in Hungary is in accordance with the real wishes of the nation" and that "loyalty to the dynasty was unshakeable," made little impression upon his more radical followers.

Kossuthist deputies in 1881 denounced an extradition treaty arranged with Serbia which provided for the return of any fugitive who had made an attempt upon the life of the ruler or any member of the Hapsburg family; regicide under certain circumstances, the Kossuthists felt, might be justified. When Tisza heatedly berated the opposition, he was charged with being a liar and cheat; a "court of honor" that the prime minister appointed to decide whether as a gentleman he was bound to seek personal retaliation for these insults decided in the negative. Tisza indeed found the Kossuthists a handy bugbear to be invoked when necessary to extract concessions from Vienna.

The outstanding constitutional change of Tisza's reign was the reorganization of the unwieldy house of magnates so as to eliminate deadwood from that aristocratic body. It had experienced little alteration since its establishment in medieval times. Proposals for reform had been in the air for some time, and the action of the magnates in twice rejecting a law legalizing marriages between Jews and Christians finally induced the Tisza ministry to bring in a reform measure. Catholic clergy voted against the marriage bill, as did sixty other members who had not appeared in the house before and whose right to vote had to be proved, eleven of them Austrian noblemen, and the marriage measure was defeated by nine votes.

Under the reform act of 1885, Hungarian magnates who had a hereditary right to a seat in the chamber were deprived of the privilege unless they paid land taxes of 3,000 gulden ($1,200) annually. The king, moreover, might assign hereditary seats to new peers and grant membership to the chief dignitaries of the several religious creeds. He might create nonhereditary peers for services to public welfare, though their number might not exceed a third of the total. The reformed chamber contained 376 members, as compared with over 1,200 before. At about the same time the term of office of deputies was raised from three to five years, and minor changes were effected in the civil service and in local government.

Tisza's steady support of the foreign office in the Bosnian occupation and general coöperation with the crown on military and diplomatic issues brought their reward, for he was conceded a free hand in domestic matters and was able to proceed with a program of systematic Magyarization in defiance of the Nationalities Act of 1868. If the original aim of Magyarization was to strengthen resistance against any Hapsburg effort to recover its old authority, the long-range objective was nothing less than to press the diverse national minorities of the kingdom into the Magyar cultural and linguistic mold.

It was in the field of education that Magyar chauvinism exhibited itself in the most pronounced and consistent form, on the obvious principle that as the twig is bent so will the tree incline. An act of 1879, for example, made instruction in the Magyar language obligatory in all state-supported primary schools and a knowledge of Magyar was made prerequisite for a teacher's diploma; schools that failed to conform to regulations on the teaching of Magyar as issued by the ministry of education might be closed. Schools operated by religious denominations—and they formed the largest part of the elementary educational facilities—remained beyond the scope of this law, but if any of them accepted state financial aid, as some were obliged to do, they were subjected to state supervision. If confessional schools failed to maintain educational standards acceptable to the ministry of education they might be replaced by a state school.

Particular attention was paid to the building of state schools in non-Magyar districts. Over 100,000 non-Magyars attended state schools in the twentieth century, and in all but one of them—there were more than 2,000 —the instruction was exclusively in the Magyar tongue. Consequently the proportion of citizens able to speak Magyar but claiming to belong to a minor nationality increased prodigiously.

A parallel measure of 1883 placed the secondary schools frequented by non-Magyars, Germans and Rumanians, under rigid state supervision,[6] and the Magyar language and literature were made compulsory studies. Thenceforth the language of instruction in state secondary schools was Magyar and the schools were thoroughly Magyarized; in all the highest institutions of learning under state control, Magyarization was already complete. Even in the nursery schools efforts were made to spread the Magyarization ideal; by the kindergarten law of 1891, which professedly aimed to provide children of employed mothers a place where they would be properly cared for, it was permissible to teach tiny tots Magyar history, music, and language. The act had small practical significance since few children attended, but the law was symptomatic of Magyar intentions and hopes.

Magyarization was promoted in yet other ways. With the sanction of the crown, Slovak intellectuals had established in 1863 the *Matice Slovenská,* an educational, literary, and scientific society, similar to associations that furnished the dynamic for the cultural renaissance of other Slav nationalities. It published collections of peasant melodies, proverbs, poems, and fictional and learned works in the Slovak idiom. But in 1875 this promising society and all other Slovak societies were suppressed, the property of the *Matice* was confiscated, and for a quarter of a century no similar Slovak cultural organization was allowed. Slovaks were even denied the right to have a chair in the University of Budapest for the scholarly study of their language; Slovak cultural progress was stifled, and educated leaders were kept few in number.

Magyar was the only language used in the state postal and telegraph services and had to be spoken by railway workers in the kingdom proper. This order was directed particularly against German-speaking railway officials, and severe criticism of it in the "great press" of Vienna led Magyar chauvinists to demand restrictions on the circulation of Vienna newspapers in Hungary. For workers, as for schoolchildren for whom Magyar was an alien tongue, to learn the language was no light task. And Magyar was, of course, useless outside of the kingdom, since it was an Asiatic tongue, allied to Finnish and Turkish, and without any similarity whatsoever to the Aryan languages of the rest of Europe.

Magyar had words an ell long, stuffed full of consonants; real linguistic genius was required to master *legmegvesztegethetetlenebbeknek*, meaning "the most incorruptible of men," and not extensively used in even the purest Magyar circles. R. Nisbet Bain, a savant attached to the British Museum, who was extraordinarily proficient in languages, Magyar among them, once described a Magyar sentence as "a miracle of agglutinative ingenuity." There was no term in the language to express the distinction between a citizen who was a Magyar and one who professed allegiance to another nationality; in the Magyar tongue the word for Hungary was Magyarland.

Against the Rumanian minority special measures with Magyarizing implications were applied. Methodically the public authorities hampered the Rumanian-language press by petty annoyances, confiscations, imprisonment, and heavy fines. Journalists accused of offenses against the press law were tried in special courts in which the juries were composed almost invariably of non-Rumanians, since the property qualifications for jurymen were so high. Because juries made up of "Saxons" often freed Rumanian journalists, such cases were transferred to the strongly Magyar community of Klausenberg and then acquittals were rarities.

Of the same order were the practices of posting public notices, even warnings of danger, in the Magyar language only and of expelling children from school who uttered Rumanian words. Matriculation of Rumanians at the University of Koloszvár, founded in 1876, was made difficult, the organization of Rumanian student fraternities was prohibited, and the display of the Rumanian national flag was declared a crime. An effort was made to force Transylvanian civil servants who were not Magyars to do their names over into the Magyar. Few did so; indeed some parents deliberately gave children names that could not be translated into the tongue of the ruling nationality. To promote Magyarization, the Transylvanian Magyar Cultural League, *Emke,* was organized and it soon had 20,000 members and commanded a substantial revenue, part of which came from the public treasury in Budapest.

Magyarization evoked angry if futile protests from all sides. Germans who resented assimilation positively manifested their determination to preserve their national identity by founding a national newspaper in their language, but their contention that school legislation violated the legal rights of the "Saxons" went unheeded and accusations of tyranny hurled against the Magyars were answered with scorn. Certain newspapers in imperial Germany zealously championed the interests of the Germans in Hungary, condemning Magyar efforts to denationalize young Germans, and a school union was formed in Germany to support German institutions in Hungary. At the request of the Hungarian government, responsible German citizens of Hungary (and the *Pester Lloyd,* the great German-language newspaper of Hungary) emphatically repudiated foreign interference in Hungarian affairs.

A Kossuthist deputy, Louis Mocsáry, in a speech to the chamber, ridiculed the Magyarization program as utopian, erroneous, and provocative of trouble in the future. For his courageous audacity he lost his seat in parliament and was expelled from the Independence party. A Rumanian who was a retired general of the Hapsburg army was heavily fined and imprisoned for two years as a penalty for raising his voice against the Magyarization policies of the government.

Among the Rumanians political leadership, after the death of the saintly Şaguna, passed to an activist group, headed by Vincent Babes, sometime professor at Bucharest, and Georges Baritsiu. These intellectuals inveighed incessantly against the oppression of their countrymen, but the clergy adopted a passive attitude and the peasants remained largely immune to Rumanian national propaganda. The influential archbishop, Miron Roman, in a circular letter to his priests urged full loyalty to the Hungarian government.

In 1881 Baritsiu founded the Rumanian National party and at a conference of Hungarian Rumanians the objectives and demands of this minority were specifically formulated.[7] Transylvania should again become autonomous and the Nationalities Act of 1868 should be enforced. More exactly, the Rumanian language should be used by administrative officials and in law courts wherever Rumanians lived; the Rumanian Orthodox Church should be allowed the same rights as the Catholic Church. and its schools should be financially aided by the state. Suffrage laws should be reformed so that at least every adult male who paid direct taxes might vote.

Unrelenting Magyarization induced Rumanian politicians to seek redress through the intervention of the crown, before 1867 the traditional defender of minority interests. At this period the national revival in Transylvania had scarcely passed beyond the embryonic stage and the Rumanian political leaders still looked to Vienna rather than to Bucharest for succor and comfort. Early in 1892, representatives of the National party compiled a dossier of injustices and demands for presentation to Francis Joseph. Arguing that the Budapest government was Magyarizing public life in its entirety and seeking to convert the polyglot kingdom into a purely Magyar land, the petitioners begged for reforms in the electoral, educational, and press laws, for the elimination of corruption and bribery at election times, and for the admittance of qualified Rumanians to the civil service. They deplored the denial of autonomous political privileges in Transylvania.

"The Rumanians dwelling in Hungary," the memorandum protested, "are not treated as considerately as are the people of a conquered country." The document affirmed the desire of the Rumanians to live on friendly terms with the Magyars and to work for the progress of the common realm, but the conclusion warned that "a national policy which is mistaken in its foundations and its final purpose can only lead to serious consequences for those who continue that policy, for the country and for the throne." When Francis Joseph declined to receive this memorandum, it was transmitted to the Austrian ministry, which forwarded it to the authorities in Budapest, and they in turn sent the document back to the petitioners, unopened!

To place their case before the bar of European opinion, the sponsors of the memorandum had the document translated into several foreign languages and distributed in hundreds of thousands of copies. It was freely alleged in Magyar quarters that the Rumanian politicians responsible for the *cahier* of grievances were exponents of secession, in the pay of the kingdom of Rumania if not indeed of Russia. On charges of "incitement against the Magyar nationality," twenty-eight of the protestants were arrested and held for trial at Kolozsvár, the Transylvanian capital. The trial itself attracted the attention of Europe. Rumanian peasants flocked to the city to demonstrate against the jurymen, Magyars all; anti-Magyar mass meetings were organized at which the black and yellow flag of imperial Austria was much in evidence and the Hungarian tricolor conspicuously missing. Armed forces were held in readiness to intervene if tempers should boil over. Counsel for the defendants was browbeaten and fined by the presiding judge—all of which was vividly reported in the foreign press. In the end, the chief defendants were adjudged guilty and given jail sentences; and the Rumanian National party was dissolved by ministerial decree.

This much, however, the Rumanian dissenters had accomplished: their grievances had been called to the attention of opinion outside of the Hapsburg Monarchy. It was already appreciated in Germany that the Magyar treatment of the Rumanian minority was alienating the kingdom of Rumania from the Triple Alliance. While the trial at Kolozsvár was being conducted, Irredentists gatherings were assembled in Rumania, orators in the Bucharest parliament loosed their sharpest shafts against the Magyars, and a military detachment had to be stationed round the Hapsburg embassy in Bucharest to protect it against mob attack. In consequence of the oppression of Rumanians beyond the Carpathians, and as an agency to foster Irredentism, a "League for the Cultural Unity of All Rumanians" was founded at Bucharest in 1891, which undertook to combat Magyar denationalizing influences; money, for example, was collected to finance Rumanian confessional schools in Hungary. Inevitably the society was charged with being responsible for stirring up political disaffection and Irredentism among Hungary's Rumanians, as indeed it was.

Tacit encouragement to Irredentist sentiments among Rumanians in Hungary was given by officials in Bucharest, and in the schools of the Regat children were inoculated with the virus of "Greater Rumania." Lessons in geography, for instance, distinguished two types of country: areas where Rumanians lived and areas in which there were no Magyars! Lessons in history taught that the Rumanian-inhabited districts of Hungary were once part of the Rumanian state and should be reclaimed. Nevertheless, officially, the Rumanian government avoided any act that might compromise relations with the Hapsburg ally, and Foreign Minister Kálnoky more than once remarked upon the friendly attitude of Rumania to the Dual Monarchy.

IV

Down in Croatia political conditions in the middle seventies were unusually tranquil, marred only by Serb outbursts in protest over the exclusion of Orthodox clergy from the management of schools. But when the Dual Monarchy occupied Bosnia, Croat nationalists raised the familiar cry for a Great Croatia which should embrace Bosnia. In reply the Hungarian government dismissed Mazuranič, popular national poet, from the office of Croatian ban, though he had taken no part in the political clamor. Croat animosity toward the Magyar overlord flared up in a serious manner in 1883, when Agram (Zagreb) was convulsed politically as it had recently been upset physically by a series of earthquakes, the worst Europe had experienced since the destructive Lisbon quake of 1755. Mass disorders, organized by moderate nationalists, broke out after the head of the tax department did violence to custom by placing the Hungarian national escutcheon beside the Croat on his office and ordering that both the Magyar and the Croat languages should be used in public notices in the future.

Smoldering Croatian grievances, resentment over the inequitable franchise and tax laws and muzzling of the press, burst into destructive flame. Partisans of an independent Croatia fed the fire. Mobs in Agram and other towns went on the rampage, wrecking property and resisting officers of the law. The government in Budapest replied by suppressing the Croatian assembly and the constitution and instructing a military man to quell the popular disorders. Those decisions prompted renewed rioting; to outward appearance it seemed as though Croatian nationalism as in 1848 had thrown down the gauntlet to Hungarian rule. Slav spokesmen across the Hapsburg Monarchy applauded the courage and the spirit of the Croatian rebels. By free application of the bayonet and promises of appeasing concessions, which were only partly fulfilled, the Hungarian authorities contrived to restore peace and security.

As the new ban, Tisza named his own relative, Count Charles Khuen-Hédérváry, a magnate owning lands in Croatia. This pleasant-mannered "strong man," a personal favorite of Francis Joseph, governed Croatia until 1903. At the outset the viceroy curried favor with moderate Croats, paying a courtesy visit to the venerable Strossmayer and delivering speeches that flattered native pride; his son paraded on the streets with a peasant who was giving him lessons in the Croatian language. But Khuen-Hédérváry soon abandoned finesse for force. Skillfully he exploited the latent antagonism between Croats and Serbs, who comprised more than a quarter of the population; Serb schools were opened, Serbs were appointed to public offices—one was made president of the diet—Serb material interests were catered to, and their Orthodox religion was given special concessions.

Still Croatia could not be ruled simply by enflaming one section of the population against another. The native press was severely restricted; gross corruption and inequitable electoral laws held the antiadministration factions in the diet at a minimum, and even they were effectively stifled by closure or expulsion. Behind the fair façade of constitutionalism Khuen-Hédérváry exercised the power of an Oriental despot. On the other side of the shield, the ban encouraged economic progress; agriculture was improved, schooling facilities were enlarged, highways and railways were bettered and extended. Revision of the financial arrangements with Hungary (1889), modestly raising the charges upon Croatia, caused renewed popular protest.

In his camp Khuen-Hédérváry counted the Magyarone Croats or Unionists, almost all landowners and officials, and the reconciled portion of the Serbs, who together controlled the diet. Antagonistic to his rule and to the prevailing constitutional system were those Serb politicians who were coquetting with their kinsmen in the kingdom of Serbia,[8] the followers of Strossmayer, and the extreme Croats, the party of the National Right, which stiffly declined to recognize Francis Joseph as lawful sovereign. Pure, uncompromising Croat nationalists, only a genuinely autonomous state, covering not alone Croatia proper, but Fiume, Dalmatia and Bosnia-Herzegovina as well, would pacify them. It was openly declared that if the court at

Vienna would not meet their wishes the Croat extremists would appeal to Russia for assistance in the struggle for liberation. How confident this Croatian element was of the ability of the Croats to manage their own affairs is reflected in the battle cry coined by their leader, Ante Starčević: "To exist, Croatia needs only God and the Croats."

So serious was the rumpus raised in the diet by the Croat extremists that police ejected them, and Starčević was imprisoned in 1888 on charges of embezzlement. His friends insisted that the accusation was trumped up and that he had really been put in "quarantine" for his political convictions and the violence with which he attacked the arbitrary administration of Khuen-Héderváry. Aside from these extremists and the Pan-Serbs, the politically articulate among the Croats were not less devoted to the Haps- burg crown than they had been in the past. That loyalty was demonstrated in one way by the warmth of the welcome given to Crown Prince Rudolph, who was keenly concerned about Croatian affairs, when he visited Agram and lavished praise upon Croats who in times past had sacrificed their lives in Hapsburg armies.[9]

v

In the spring of 1890, Coloman Tisza resigned the Hungarian premier- ship, directly as the result of a clash with incorrigible Kossuthists, partly because of the antagonism of the clerical and old aristocratic groups who were alienated by the reformation of the house of magnates and by a project for mixed marriages which Tisza was sponsoring.

Military questions involving the Austrian partner furnished Tisza's foes, especially the Kossuthists, with a wealth of ammunition. Gratifying to Hungarian national pride was the decision taken in 1882 to reorganize the common army along "nationality" lines. Whereas previously each brigade and division was composed of a mixture of national groups, in the future they would be made up entirely, or almost entirely, of Slavs, Hun- garians, and so on. That arrangement tended to keep the troops raised in Hungary distinct from those recruited in Austria. But popular resentment against Austria flared up in connection with the notorious Jansky affair.

On the anniversary of the capture of Buda by the Hungarian rebels in 1849, it was customary to deck the common burial ground of fallen heroes with decorations. In 1886 General Jansky, commander of the Budapest garrison, annoyed by the neglect of the graves of imperial officers who had been killed in the fighting, persuaded a group of subordinates to join him in honoring the loyalist martyrs and in placing a wreath on the statue of the Austrian General Hentzi, who had been mortally wounded defending Buda against the insurgents. By the native populace, especially by lusty adherents of the Independence party, this gesture was resented as a wanton insult to revolutionary worthies and to the Hungarian nation.

Riotous demonstrations took place on the streets of the capital, Hentzi's statue was desecrated, and the windows of Jansky's residence were bashed in. Police and troops with sword and bayonet dispersed the rioters, wounding many and killing one; hundreds were arrested. Parliament and press rang with denunciations of General Jansky, Austria, and the monarchical army. Tisza in alluding in parliament to the desecration of the Hentzi statue branded the act as unwise and tactless, defended the guardians of the law, and hinted that the highest Austrian army authorities disapproved of what Jansky had done. But Archduke Albrecht, commander in chief of the common army, on his return from an inspection tour praised Jansky. Whereupon *Pester Lloyd* took the Archduke to task in phrases that the Viennese press dared not reproduce; the editor eventually was obliged to apologize to the Archduke. Fresh street disturbances occurred, the Archduke was burned in effigy, and troops again had to intervene to repress disorders.

The Jansky affair lent momentum to the agitation for separation of the Hungarian armed forces from the Austrian. As a step in that direction Kossuthist deputies, supported by members of the clerical Peoples party, demanded that Hungarian troops should be given commands in the Magyar language.[10] Tisza set his face like flint against this demand, holding that a single language for the army of the entire Monarchy was indispensable for military efficiency, and he cavalierly brushed aside the argument that the disciplined and effective armies of Prince Eugene of Savoy and of Napoleon had spoken a variety of tongues.

To parliament Tisza presented a bill on national defense which fixed the number of recruits and stipulated, among other things, that officers of the common army should possess a thorough knowledge of German. This proposal provoked noisy disturbances, and demonstrators roamed the streets of Budapest yelling "Down with Tisza." Enraged opposition deputies threatened to set off a revolution, and the premier had to be given a protective guard. The veteran Count Julius Andrássy, as faithful to the Hapsburg crown as ever, raised his voice against the "separatists" and warned of the dangers implicit in arrogant national chauvinism. Sops were thrown the dissenters by changing the title of the joint army from imperial-royal to imperial and royal and by inserting a ten-year clause in the army bill; otherwise the law was enacted as presented.

Chauvinistic hysteria touched a new high in 1890 when a bill was offered in parliament to grant full citizenship to the exiled Louis Kossuth, aged eighty-eight, the incomparable idol of the Independence party. After Tisza had expressed himself strongly against the proposal, arguing that the bill was superfluous since many communities had already conferred honorary citizenship on the revolutionary chieftain, Kossuth's admirers in the chamber indulged in scandalous scenes. Tisza then seized the opportunity to retire from the premiership, leaving his satellites in control of the government.

Looked at in the large, Tisza's reign had notable results for his country. Economic and financial conditions had improved; the house of magnates had been modernized and the policy of crude Magyarization had been given an impetus that was to endure almost until the dismemberment of the kingdom. Off stage, until his death in 1902, Tisza exerted an active influence upon Hapsburg and Hungarian politics and without flinching he defended the dualistic arrangement with Austria, as his son, Stephen, would do later.

‡ CHAPTER TWELVE ‡

THE TRIPLE ALLIANCE
1880–1897

Baron henry haymerle, who succeeded andrássy at the Ballplatz, belonged to a German family which for generations had resided in Bohemia. During the revolution of 1848 he had been arrested as a republican, but he was quickly released. Entering the Austrian diplomatic service, he had risen steadily through the ranks, and acquired a wide knowledge of affairs and peoples in the Near East. Unusually well-versed in languages, though he spoke no Slavic tongue, he made a hobby of archaeological research, and earned the favorable regard of the permanent officials in the foreign office by perspicacious reports on the countries where he was stationed.[1]

After the war of 1864, Haymerle was dispatched to Copenhagen to restore normal diplomatic relations with Denmark, and in 1877 he was sent as ambassador to Italy, a post on which he had long set his affections. At the Berlin conference, where he was one of the Austrian delegates, his exact knowledge of the Near East was employed to good advantage. Much against his personal wishes he was transferred from the Rome embassy to the foreign office on Andrássy's nomination, remaining as director of the Ballplatz until his sudden death in October of 1881.

Not an adroit statesman like Beust, nor a brilliant diplomatist like Andrássy, Haymerle was cautiously conservative, an indefatigable worker, and a capable organizer. Bismarck, with his customary flair for the pithy phrase, once likened him to "a schoolboy eager to get out of school," and, on another occasion, spoke of him as "the colorless, lusterless, wooden, Viennese bureaucrat."[2] Haymerle resolved to conduct foreign policies along the lines and in the spirit of his predecessor: the alliance with Germany would be consolidated, the decisions of the Berlin Congress executed, and caution would characterize dealings with St. Petersburg, where Haymerle was considered a cunning and dangerous troublemaker. He studiously avoided any act that might be interpreted as interference in the domestic affairs of either Austria or Hungary. To the delegations he announced, soon after becoming foreign minister, that he would strive to win the friendship of all countries and to preserve the balance of power in the Balkans and in Europe more generally. That Russia was the major concern was revealed in one way by the request of the minister of war for large appropriations to reinforce the defences of Galicia.

Austrian relations with Britain were somewhat disturbed because Gladstone, the tireless champion of Balkan Christians, more than once assailed Hapsburg diplomatic tactics in the course of his impassioned Midlothian electoral campaign of 1880. "Austria," he imprudently observed, "has been the unflinching foe of freedom in every country of Europe . . . There is not a spot upon the whole map where you can lay your finger and say, 'There Austria did good.'" The Ballplatz naturally entered a stern protest against that sweeping indictment; Gladstone acknowledged that he had been indiscreet, and after he became prime minister he apologized handsomely, saying that he had been incorrectly informed and that he had used the language he did on the basis of "secondary evidence."[3] Francis Joseph was satisfied, but the memory of Gladstone's utterance lingered on in Vienna. Presently Austria and Britain were working hand in glove to execute the territorial pledges given to Montenegro and Greece in the Treaty of Berlin.

II

Ottoman territory that the treaty had awarded to Montenegro contained Albanian tribesmen, Moslem in religion, who rebelled rather than accept Montenegrin authority. An Austro-British proposal that Montenegro should have the seaport of Dulcigno and a strip of the Adriatic littoral in lieu of the area originally assigned was approved by the other great powers, though rejected by Turkey until a naval demonstration brought her to terms. So Montenegro obtained (1880) Dulcigno and its environs, which gave her modest frontage on the Adriatic; and Prince Nicholas, concealing his deep affection for Russia, expressed gratitude to the Vienna government for the benevolent assistance it had rendered.

While other foreign offices recommended further pressure on Turkey to wrest away more territory, Austria, which desired a strong Turkey, dissented. Said Haymerle, "It is not yet clear to the European areopagus what would take the place of Turkey . . . [probably] a war between the Balkan nationalities would ensue." In keeping with the terms of the Berlin Treaty

Austria collaborated with Britain to secure parcels of Turkish land for Greece; small areas in Thessaly and Epirus were transferred, less than the Greeks had expected, and they did not conceal their disappointment.

On two occasions (1880, 1883) Greece made overtures to Austria for an alliance, without accomplishing anything. Relations were, however, quite cordial and intimate and the Greeks looked upon the Danube Monarchy as their "most sincere and natural ally." Sultan Abdul Hamid of Turkey, too, endeavored to align himself (1882) with Austria and Germany, but Austria, unwilling to pose as the ally of the sultan in his endless friction with Russia, rebuffed the overture, and the most Bismarck would do was to allow Prussian military experts to assist in the rehabilitation of the Turkish army.

Greece lay rather outside the orbit of Austrian vital interests, but it was quite otherwise with Serbia, Bosnia's neighbor and a country of Yugoslavs. Belgrade was aggrieved because of the position that Austria had recently acquired in Bosnia and in the Sanjak of Novibazar, but even more indignant because Russian diplomacy had left Serbia in the lurch at the Congress of Berlin; with the support of the Austrians, Serbia had contrived to obtain from Turkey the Pirot and Nish districts, both of which Bulgaria coveted. Austrian help to Serbia was a reward for an agreement negotiated by Ristič, the Serbian foreign minister, providing for a railway convention and closer commercial ties. In keeping with that understanding a railway contract was drawn up in 1880 and much enlarged three years later, with other interested powers participating. These arrangements called for the building of railways across Serbia and Bulgaria to link up with the existing road to Constantinople; but the execution of the plans progressed at a snail's pace, so that it was not until August of 1888 that the first through train passed from Vienna to Constantinople.

Commercial transactions between Serbia and Austria caused sharp controversies. Austria insisted that her manufactures should be admitted by Serbia on the same terms as comparable goods of British origin. After several angry exchanges Haymerle peremptorily demanded that Serbia should apply the most-favored-nation principle to Austrian wares and threatened to invoke whatever measures of coercion seemed necessary if the Serbs balked. Holding that acquiescence would be an invitation to Austria to exercise intolerable influence upon Serbia, Ristič resigned in favor of a more conciliatory man, and it was only by inches that a diplomatic rupture was avoided. In conformity with a trade treaty of May 1881, Serbia lowered duties on Austrian articles and was allowed to ship livestock, prunes, and the like to the Monarchy. That settlement, which was to run for ten years, infuriated Austrophobic elements in Serbia, who thought of it as a phase of the Austrian "softening" process preliminary to the absorption of their land.

With Ristič out of office, the Serbian King Milan, who was Austrophile to the core, proceeded in 1881 to conclude a very secret political convention with Vienna. For practical purposes that document converted the little Slav kingdom into an Austrian vassal, and yet it was not without putative benefits for Serbia. If satisfactory assurances were given that Serbia would not become a mere Muscovite outpost in the western Balkans, then Austria was prepared to see Serbian territory extended farther to the south.

During the discussions on the treaty, Haymerle reputedly remarked to the Serb negotiator, "We are ready to bind ourselves by a formal convention to recognize the Serb pretensions to the vilayet of Kossovo and in Macedonia—up to a certain point—and to use all our influence in the next European Congress to bring the great powers to recognize the annexation of these territories to Serbia." And an ambiguously phrased article embodying that pledge appeared in the Austro-Serb treaty. Serbia, on its part, promised not to negotiate with another country for a political accord without the sanction of Vienna; Russia, of course, was the power that Austria had principally in mind. It was explicitly understood, however, that Serbia might freely arrange nonpolitical treaties with other powers.

By this bargain of 1881, which was paralleled by the railway and commercial conventions with Serbia, Austrian preponderance in the western Balkans was guaranteed. It was easy to believe that Vienna lusted for political mastery right down to Salonica, "the pearl of the Aegean," but that hypothesis rested on a dubious factual foundation. Certainly the desire for territorial expansion southward, once Bosnia had been occupied, was extremely small; neither Germans nor Magyars in the Dual Monarchy wanted the Slav population of the realm enlarged, as had been so unmistakably revealed in connection with proposals to annex Bosnia outright.

Late in 1881, the Monarchy was confronted by an insurrection in Bosnia which spread over into southern Dalmatia. By that time Austria had reorganized the civil administration and the police service of Bosnia, had introduced medical services, and had started to improve highways. The Austrian administration entailed tax increases, and natives complained that officials flagrantly robbed them. Besides, Bosnians resented the intrusion of merchants from the Monarchy, and the Orthodox Christians, who had been hostile to Austrian rule from the beginning, grew more resentful because of the refusal of the authorities to dispossess the Moslem landowners. Discontent reflected itself in increasing brigandage, and when, in November 1881, military conscription was applied in the province, the population, egged on by Russian agents, rose in rebellion.

In Vienna, fears were expressed lest the rising should repeat the sequence of 1875 and involve Serbia, Montenegro, and even Russia. Actually the enemies of King Milan were itching for a favorable opportunity to expel the ruler, and Montenegro's prince found it difficult to hold his chiefs in leash.

Taught by the military occupation of 1878, Austria treated the Bosnian insurrection as though it were an authentic war; troops in excess of 60,000 were ordered into the occupied province, and even the fleet was mobilized. The rebellion was suppressed rather quickly in southern Dalmatia and with more difficulty in Bosnia, for the insurgents retreated to the roughest part of the province and resorted to guerilla methods of fighting. At home the foreign office experienced real difficulty in securing the sanction of the delegations for the funds that were needed to crush the rebellion.

While the insurrection was being put down, Benjamin von Kállay, a Magyar, was appointed common minister of finance, a position he filled until his death in 1903. By reason of that office he was chief secretary for Bosnia. Kállay had a merited reputation for administrative skill and was recognized as an authority on Balkan affairs. He had written a useful history of Serbia and a volume on Russia's Near Eastern policies, and had translated John Stuart Mill's *On Liberty* into the Magyar language. As consul general in Belgrade from 1869 to 1875 he had studied Serb conditions sympathetically and had learned the Serb language; no man, perhaps, was better qualified to undertake the proconsulship of Bosnia.

Kállay accepted the office of finance minister on the understanding that he would be allowed considerable latitude in administering Bosnian affairs. It was proved beyond question that several Austrian officials had fleeced the natives and the guilty ones were immediately dismissed; old-fashioned Hapsburg bureaucrats were sent in to govern the territory, and agriculturists and artisans were imported to teach their techniques. And there were other improvements; the Narenta, for example, was dredged so as to make it accessible to the larger boats plying the Adriatic, and aqueducts were constructed from the mountains to furnish Sarajevo with a public water supply. Kállay advertised the provinces by sumptuously entertaining prominent foreigners and members of learned societies. By 1890, Bosnia had fully three hundred miles of railways and would have shown a surplus in the public treasury had it not been for the cost of maintaining the large garrison; probably no part of the Balkans made as great material progress as did Bosnia under the able direction of Kállay.[4]

III

At the Congress of Berlin the slender diplomatic threads that knit Austria, Germany, and Russia together had been violently rent asunder, and Russia's undisguised hostility to Germany had smoothed the way to the Austro-German alliance, as has been explained. Yet before that treaty was signed Bismarck was engaged in conversations with St. Petersburg for a revised version of the triple partnership of the seventies; his underlying aim was the preservation of tranquillity in eastern Europe, where the supreme enemy to peace was the rivalry between Austria and Russia for hegemony in the Balkans. It was Austria's settled objective to be politically preponderant in the western half of the peninsula and to reap the economic advantages that would follow therefrom. Repeatedly, responsible Hapsburg officials disclaimed any territorial ambitions in the Balkans, but peaceful economic penetration was quite another matter, and to that end the Monarchy had bent its efforts to improve the railway and other transportation facilities.

Russia, on the other hand, was obsessed with the strategic and commercial advantages that would accrue from control of Constantinople and the Straits, and Russian public men were not unmindful of an obligation to the Orthodox Christians who lived under the thrall of the sultan. Tsar Alexander III in 1885 tersely and secretly outlined Russian ambitions in the Near East in this manner: "We ought to have one principal aim: the occupation of Constantinople so that we may once for all maintain ourselves at the Straits and know that they will remain in our hands . . . everything else that takes place in the Balkan peninsula is secondary to us . . . The Slavs [in the Balkans] must now serve Russia and not we them." Austria had only a relatively slight interest in the fate of Constantinople, but the future of the Christian nationalities of Turkey, above all of the Serbs and the wider Yugoslav family, was for her a crucial monarchical interest.

What Bismarck contemplated was a triangular pact that would assure Austria paramount influence in the western Balkans, and would recognize Russian preëminence in the eastern side and at the Straits. Germany then would act as mediator in any specific dispute that might embroil the other two countries. It was reasoned, too, by Bismarck that by drawing Russia to his side he would be better able to forestall a Russo-French diplomatic alignment.

Diplomatically isolated, militarily prostrate, and navally defenseless, Russia at the end of the seventies was haunted by the possibility of a clash with Britain, aided perhaps by Austria. Wherefore the men on the Neva were exceedingly anxious to restore normal, preferably close, relations with the ever-victorious Iron Chancellor. Peter Saburov, the tsar's ambassador in Berlin, disclosed to Bismarck that Russia desired solid assurances of help in case Britain threatened to advance into Constantinople and a pledge that no territorial revision would be effected in the Balkans without Russian consent. Bismarck was entirely ready to strike a bargain on these terms, but insisted that his ally, Austria, should be brought into the combination, something the Russians disliked.

For Austria a triple accord that would create formal friendship with Russia would tend to stabilize her position in the Balkans. But Haymerle hesitated to accept Bismarck's proposal, for he was toying with the idea of an entente with Britain which would checkmate Russia and might be useful if

Irredentist stirrings in Italy caused serious trouble with the southern neighbor. Besides, the Ballplatz had no desire to share the friendship of Germany with Russia, and it had small confidence in Russian loyalty to any pledges that it might take concerning the Balkans.

While the Austrians debated, Bismarck plunged ahead with negotiations with Russia and brought them to a mutually satisfactory conclusion. Francis Joseph was then won over to Bismarck's tripartite enterprise, and to his friend, Albert of Saxony, the monarch confided, "I lay the highest value on a closer union between the three powers and to this end I have welcomed Prince Bismarck's initiative . . . and given it my support . . . I wish for nothing better than . . . good and confidential relations between Russia and ourselves." [5] Haymerle grudgingly agreed to the project when assured by Bismarck that the Alliance of 1879 would in no wise be affected by an entente of the two allies with Russia.

By the *Dreikaiserbund* of 1881 documentary endorsement was given to Bismarck's pet doctrine of a Balkan peninsula divided into Austrian and Russian spheres; yet the treaty, which was to run for three years, authorized territorial changes in the Balkans under certain circumstances. Specifically, the treaty pledged the signatories to benevolent neutrality, should one of them become engaged in war with a fourth power, but that clause would be operative in the event of a Russian war with Turkey only if a previous understanding had been reached by the three powers regarding the peace settlement. Furthermore, without the approval of the three signatories no change in European Turkey would be allowed, and all would coöperate to keep the warships of a fourth country from moving upon Constantinople. Austrian rights in Bosnia were reaffirmed and it was agreed that Austria might annex the region "at whatever moment she shall deem opportune." [6] Finally, the three empires bound themselves to sanction the union of eastern Roumelia with Bulgaria, if and whenever force of circumstances brought such a merger to pass.

The advantages that accrued to Austria by the new League of Three Emperors were more apparent than real. True, Russia had indicated that Austria might annex Bosnia, but there was no intention in Vienna at the time of changing the technical status of that region; Austria's it was and Austria's it would remain. Germany, by reason of the *Dreikaiserbund,* might be able to influence Russian Balkan policies, but the basic Russian political competition with Austria, the deep-seated mutual suspicions, had in no wise been altered. If the Russians would keep their hands off the western Balkans all might yet be well; and for Austria that was a gamble worth taking.

In signing the *Dreikaiserbund* treaty Russia had gained much and conceded little. It had wormed into the charmed Bismarckian orbit and had secured a pledge which would be serviceable in holding British seapower south of the Straits. And Bismarck likewise had occasion for gratitude, for the wire to Russia on which he set such great store, had been rebuilt, and the chances of preserving peace in the Balkans and of keeping the tsardom out of the loving embrace of France had both been bettered. Until the end of World War I the text of this treaty remained a secret closely guarded in the three chancelleries, but an exchange of cordial messages between Francis Joseph and Alexander III of Russia apprised the world that some sort of *rapprochement* between Europe's great eastern empires had been completed.

IV

The Hapsburg sovereign testified again to his desire for good relations with Russia by appointing Count Gustav von Kálnoky as foreign minister, upon the death of Haymerle.[7] As ambassador to St. Petersburg, Kálnoky had collaborated with the Russians in carrying out the Treaty of Berlin and he had shared actively in the negotiation of the *Dreikaiserbund;* he was admired by the men on the Neva and respected by Bismarck. Kálnoky hesitated to take charge of the Ballplatz for, though experience had schooled him thoroughly in Austrian foreign policy, he was only superficially acquainted with the internal affairs of the realm, a common deficiency in Austrian diplomatists who served abroad. But Francis Joseph smoothed away his anxieties.

A member of the hereditary Magyar aristocracy, calm, austere, passionless, Kálnoky favored a prudential and unadventuresome foreign policy. On his family coat of arms was inscribed the motto: "Nec timide, nec tumide." An extreme conservative and a confirmed clerical, he refrained as a rule from meddling in domestic affairs; and he confined his social contacts to the aristocracy, boasting that he never deigned to read a newspaper. Here was a man, in fine, after Francis Joseph's own conservative heart. Count von Monts, the German ambassador, described Kálnoky as "of medium stature, rather fat, and with a pudgy face. His outward appearance was not attractive, nor could his manner be called engaging . . . [His] rudeness to diplomats was notorious." He treated the French ambassador, M. Decrais, who had once been a schoolmaster, as he treated a bootblack; so incensed was the Danish minister by Kálnoky's brusque manners that he communicated with him only in writing.

As foreign minister, Kálnoky personally wrote many of the diplomatic dispatches and held a tight rein on subordinates. From them he expected unquestioning obedience, not initiative, and he frowned upon expression of opinions at variance with his own. He deliberatedly kept himself out of the public eye and, except for reports on foreign affairs which he delivered to the delegations, little was known about him and his doings beyond court circles. With Francis Joseph he agreed that the alliance with Germany should be consolidated and that serious controversy with Russia must be avoided, if at all possible; yet, not less than Andrássy, Kálnoky was prepared to unsheathe the sword should diplomacy prove unable to forestall Muscovite pretensions to dominance in the Balkans.

Although the League of the Three Emperors was not scheduled to expire until June 1884, Russia, rendered uneasy by Austrian diplomatic maneuvers and smalltime intrigues in the Balkans, raised the question of renewal several months in advance of its expiration. Bismarck gave the men on the Neva unequivocal promises that Germany would go the limit to keep her partners at peace. The chancellor's distrust of Francophile tendencies in Russia had lessened after the death of General Skobelev, an impassioned preacher of an alliance with France and hero of the recent war with Turkey, and the withdrawal of Bismarck's archfoe Gorchakov from the foreign office in favor of the pacifically inclined Giers (1882). Bismarck was himself convinced that Russia sincerely desired the preservation of peace and so persuaded the Austrians. Without significant revision, then, the League of Three Emperors was renewed in March of 1884 for another term of three years.

v

Safeguarded by the solid bond with Germany, the semiprotectorate over Serbia, and the friendly tie with Russia, the security of the Monarchy was rendered even stronger by an alliance with Italy, the historic Triple Alliance signed in May 1882. Much patient, canny diplomacy was required to bring the Austrian and Italian rivals to an understanding; without the master hand of Bismarck and the colonial aggressiveness of France, an alliance could hardly have been arranged.

Italian memories of the long dominance of Austria over the peninsula and of the arduous struggle to strike the Hapsburg chains from Lombardy and Venetia were still green. And nationalistically minded Italians kept their eyes glued on Austrian areas peopled by Italian-speaking folk. Irredentist outbursts in Italy, as has been explained, were constant and frequently matched by unrest in Italia Irredenta; Irredentist passions were more pronounced, it is true, in Italian popular circles than official, but they were not unknown there. On the Austrian side, resentment was fanned by recurrent Irredentist spasms, and the unwillingness or inability of the Italian government to appease the Vatican antagonized powerful clerical forces in the Dual Monarchy. Given these obstacles, it was no light matter to effect an Austro-Italian reconciliation, even on paper.

The idea of an Italian alliance with her northern neighbors dated from 1877, when Premier Crispi undertook a secret diplomatic mission to Bismarck. He solicited German support for Italian territorial claims upon

Austria, in the event that the latter should occupy Bosnia. With his usual candor the old Junker bluntly informed the Italian emissary that the road to Berlin lay through Vienna, but it was common knowledge that Austria had no intention of relinquishing Italia Irredenta. Wherefore, it behooved Italy to divert its expansionist appetite toward the Balkans and northern Africa, as had been recommended by influential foreign diplomatists.

Northern Africa might serve as the beginning of a very modern version of the old Roman Empire; covetous Italian eyes were fastened upon Tunisia and less avidly upon Tripoli. But France, too, saw in Tunisia a field for aggrandizement and for acquiring prestige. French pressure upon the region in 1880 induced Italian diplomacy to turn anew to Berlin for an alliance which would be helpful against France and would enhance the international standing of Italy. Bismarck, who was much annoyed by the provocative doings of the Italian Irredentists—and who could see little virtue in an Italian alliance, except as it would keep Italy away from France—once more directed the Italians to Vienna.

Italy discovered that Haymerle was sympathetic to the idea of reciprocal pledges of neutrality in case either Italy or Austria was attacked by another country. As the Austrian foreign minister diagnosed the international situation, a deal with Italy would have more real value for the Danube Monarchy than the league with Russia that Bismarck at the moment was warmly recommending; and it was only with great reservation that the Russophobe Haymerle consented to the *Dreikaiserbund*.

The actual occupation of Tunisia by French arms in 1881 completed the estrangement between the Latin sisters, and rocked the ambitious young Italian kingdom to its very foundations. Fierce resentment against France tempered the traditional animosity toward Austria and made the Italians more than eager for an accommodation with the detested Hapsburg, which would enable them to escape from uncomfortable isolation. "Friendship with Austria is for us," declared the rising young politician Sonnino, "an indispensable condition for a conclusive and effective policy"—a doctrine that was heartily applauded, except in the most intransigent Irredentist circles. Even some Italians who had spent time in Hapsburg prisons openly advocated a treaty of alliance with Austria.[8]

At just this time the Italian government learned that Pope Leo XIII was sounding out foreign offices on intervention to restore the temporal dominions of the papacy. Austrian good will would be an invaluable asset for Italy in frustrating European action on behalf of the papacy. In the autumn of 1881, King Humbert and his queen were dispatched to Vienna on an errand of good will, and for five days the royal pair were feted amidst much popular enthusiasm. The contemporary observer might warrantably conclude that the royal mission signified Italian desire to establish amicable relations with the hereditary Austrian enemy and an inclination to forego the well-known pretensions to the unredeemed areas.

Undercover, dickering for a triangular alliance proceeded quite leisurely. The Italians suggested that each ally should guarantee the other's territory, but Kálnoky, who had now succeeded Haymerle, rejected that idea, for he did not think that the territorial integrity of Italy was in any real danger, nor did he want to confirm Italy in the possession of the Vatican lands. He had small confidence in Italian capacity to fight alongside of Austria should the latter's territory be placed in jeopardy. From the point of view of Kálnoky, an Italian promise to remain neutral in case of an Austro-Russian war was much to be preferred to elaborate territorial guarantees. Robilant, the Italian envoy in Vienna, proposed as the price of a neutrality pledge that the central powers should promise to veto any attempt to restore the papal possessions, to support Italy's colonial aspirations in northern Africa, and to allow Britain to enter the diplomatic combination. Austria and Germany rejected these terms, though they were ready to declare that the projected alliance would not be directed against Great Britain.

On May 20, 1882, diplomatists of the three countries put their names to a secret, strictly defensive treaty, which was to endure for five years.[9] Each power promised not to enter into diplomatic arrangements pointed against the others. Austria and Germany would go to Italy's assistance in case France attacked her "without direct provocation." And if France attacked Germany, Italy was to fight, though Austria assumed no obligation to do so. If, however, one or two of the allies were attacked by two or more great powers, the other signatory, or signatories, would then fight alongside its allies. Moreover, if one ally should make war on a fourth power that menaced its security, the other two would preserve benevolent neutrality. Provision was made for consultation on the military measures necessary to implement the alliance, and a codicil excluded Britain from the list of possible enemies.

For Austria, as well as for Germany, the Triple Alliance implied that Italy would not align itself with either Russia or France. If Austria fought with Russia, Italy was pledged not to fall upon the Monarchy in the rear; while if Austria and Russia clashed and France entered on the Russian side, Italy then was committed to help Austria. It was also assumed in the Ballplatz that the alliance would lessen Irredentist ardor and lead the Italian government to disavow anti-Austrian agitation, though no concrete pledge of that sort had been given. Actually, however, the government roundly condemned the Irredentist effervescence that boiled up in connection with the Oberdank affair. "Why," inquired Foreign Minister Pasquale Mancini, "because some Austrian districts are Italian should we demand them? We should have to make similar claims on France and England which own

Nice, Corsica, and Malta." [10] For a time it was the official policy of the Italian government to restrain the more extravagant varieties of Irredentist zeal.

Italy, the originator of the Triple Alliance project, profited less by the treaty than had been hoped for, but secured all that should have been reasonably expected. If Italy were the victim of an unprovoked French attack, she would then have the assistance of central Europe. And whatever likelihood there may have been of Austrian or German intervention to restore the papal lands was removed, an advantage which Italian statesmen prized highly. From the standpoint of international prestige, too, the alliance meant much to the young Latin kingdom; she could now swim with the big boys with greater confidence. Once made, the Triple Alliance—in the geography involved, the Holy Roman Empire reborn—was periodically renewed, with important textual revisions, to be sure, and was in force when World War I broke over Europe.

VI

After Germany, after Serbia, after Russia, after Italy, Austria entered into a useful and enduring diplomatic understanding with Rumania. It was intense resentment against Russia for the shabby treatment meted out in 1878, the loss of Bessarabia, and the decisions of boundary commissions set up by the Berlin Treaty, that impelled Rumania into the Hapsburg diplomatic orbit. Italy had officially submerged its territorial claims upon Austria chiefly because of distrust of France; dread and detestation of Russia dictated a similar course in Rumania.

And yet the path to the Austro-Rumanian marriage of reason was not strewn with roses; big obstacles stood in the way. First of all, Rumanian patrioteers longed for the inclusion in the Regat of their linguistic brethren dwelling in the Hapsburg Monarchy. Only a few months before the treaty with Austria was sealed, a prominent Rumanian politician, in a speech delivered in the presence of the king, bewailed the fact that the crown was incomplete since it was not adorned "with the pearls of the Bucovina, Transylvania, and southern Hungary"; the Bucharest government apologized to Vienna for this indiscreet and provocative utterance. In the second place, commercial relations were disturbed by quarreling over a trade treaty of 1875 which enabled Austrian manufactures to compete most effectively with Rumanian industry; antigovernment newspapers in Bucharest had in fact gone into mourning when the trade pact was published. And Austria (as well as Germany) was at odds with Rumania over railway concessions and discriminations against the Jewish minority.

Navigation on the Danube was another perennial source of friction between the two countries. Improvements in the riverway facilitated a large increase in traffic in the sixties and seventies, with Austrian shipping second to British, Russian a poor third, and Rumanian nonexistent; except for the transportation of Rumanian wheat, the Danube was little more than an artery of local traffic in freight and passengers. Austrian commerce had been injured by the closure of the Danube during the War of 1877 and Vienna was resolved that neither Russia nor one of her satellites should have any large measure of control over the river.

As prescribed in the Treaty of Berlin of 1878, an international commission drafted a program for the navigation, policing, and regulation of the Danube from the famous Iron Gates to Galatz. The plan provided, among other things, for a permanent board of supervision containing representatives of Rumania, Serbia, and Bulgaria, and presided over by an Austrian nominee. But, in the belief that Austria would exploit her position to obtain monopolistic control on Danube shipping, Rumania scorned the project and relations between the two countries almost reached the point of rupture. King Charles publicly demanded exclusive Rumanian jurisdiction over the section of the Danube passing through the kingdom; Austria retorted by ordering the minister in Bucharest to suspend personal contacts with the Rumanian foreign office. That brought the king to book, he apologized, and the incident was declared closed, though Rumania adamantly refused to share in the mixed Danube commission, and it never came into existence.[11]

Yet however diverse and contentious the disputes with Austria, Rumanian hostility toward Russia at the moment was greater. Whatever the restraints Magyars were imposing upon the Rumanian minority, Rumanians in Russian Bessarabia were treated even more evilly; they were being "annihilated," it was said. Besides, who could tell when Russia would again seek to use Rumania as a land bridge into the lower Balkans, as had been done in 1877–78? For the official class of Rumania, the Russian peril outweighed the grievances that the country held against Austria. As early as February 1880, Premier Jon Bratianu had applied to Bismarck for admission into his diplomatic confederacy, but for three years the Iron Chancellor took little interest in the overture until it seemed that Russia contemplated interfering with armed force in Bulgaria. Then Bismarck recommended that Rumania should arrange a purely defensive treaty with Austria, to which Germany would append its signature. Kálnoky in Vienna readily fell in with the idea, and negotiations with Bucharest quickly produced an understanding in October of 1883.

Only King Charles and a few of the more prominent Rumanian politicians were familiar with the content of the Austrian treaty, and it was never presented to the Rumanian parliament for ratification. Even the king had misgivings about the alliance—we are "leaving ideals aside," he murmured —and upon him really depended the validity of the alliance. Germany at once adhered to the treaty and Italy signed in 1889. Originally made for five years, the alliance was regularly extended, for the last time in 1913.

By the treaty of 1883, Austria was promised Rumanian support if she were attacked by Russia (or Serbia) while Rumania was assured of Austrian assistance if she were the victim of an attack from any quarter. It was implied that if Russia attempted to move into Bulgaria overland, Austria would immediately take up arms. By the treaty Rumania was tied diplomatically to the central powers and they secured in consequence a virtual monopoly on Rumanian foreign trade. But the alliance was sown in thin soil, and though there was a meeting of minds on some matters, a wide and potentially dangerous area of divergence remained and mutual suspicions and ill will between the peoples of the two countries were not diminished.

The limited character of the Austro-Rumanian *rapprochement* was shown in commercial strife which started when the Danube Monarchy banned the importation of Rumanian livestock, allegedly for hygienic reasons. Presently commercial war to the knife was declared on behalf of Magyar landed proprietors and Rumanian manufacturers, respectively, and waged vigorously to the end of 1891. Rumanian merchants diverted orders for finished goods, which they had been accustomed to purchase in the Dual Monarchy, to Germany and Britain, and Austrian sales dropped to less than a third of what they had been; Transylvanian Saxons, who bore the full weight of the conflict, protested. On the other side, Rumanian cattle exports to the Monarchy were cut to a tenth and grain shipments fell off precipitately. Rumanian grain growers were incapable of competing effectively in the markets of western Europe with American and Russian producers, nor could cattle raisers discover a satisfactory substitute for the former Hapsburg market.

Economic distress among the Rumanian peasantry, due alike to the reduction of trade with Austria and to poor harvests, provoked revolutionary disturbances in 1888 when taxgatherers sought to collect normal payments. But a new commercial treaty arranged in 1891 brought the ruinous tariff war to a close; free trade on grain and livestock was revived and Austrian reprisals against Rumanian commodities were discontinued. Austria quickly regained first place in the sale of goods to Rumania, but the latter's exports to the Low Countries and Italy far exceeded those to Austria.[12] Without much success, the Rumanian government tried to foster home industry by subsidies; new textile mills that were built depended almost entirely upon army contracts for survival.

VII

Outward appearances notwithstanding, relations between Austria and Russia were marked by the utmost vigilance, not to say mistrust, on both sides. As always, discord issued directly from conflicting interests and ambitions in the Balkans. The truce that had taken form in the *Dreikaiserbund* crashed to earth in 1887 because of strife involving Bulgaria. As arranged at Berlin in 1878, Russia had withdrawn her troops from Eastern Roumelia and an autonomous government had there been established. But Russian maneuverings certified the intention to bring about the union of this district with the principality of Bulgaria, a consummation devoutly wished for in patriotic Bulgarian circles.

To the principality itself Russia generously shipped military supplies and military men to train the conscript army, and a favorite nephew of Tsar Alexander II, Alexander of Battenberg, had been chosen prince of the autonomous state. Although extremely charming, the prince was not qualified either by talent or by experience to rule over this turbulent country. Equipped with the essential institutions of a parliamentary regime, Bulgaria to outward seeming was well launched on a course of enlightened progress.[13] Russian agents prepared a program of railway construction, which Austria successfully countered, securing instead Bulgarian assent for lines that would link the principality to central Europe.

The obvious design of Russia to convert Bulgaria into a Muscovite satrapy, presently symbolized by the naming of Russian military men as premier and minister of war of Bulgaria, could not fail to antagonize Austria and Britain as well. If Russia lorded it over Bulgaria there would no doubt be undesirable repercussions among Austrian Slavs and the Serbs which might prove damaging to Austrian commercial and railway ambitions in the lower Balkans. Ardently patriotic Bulgarian politicians likewise resented Russian intrusion into their affairs, and Prince Alexander marched with them. The Bulgarian government dismissed the Russian army officers in 1883, which provoked a loud outcry in Russian Pan-Slav circles, but the tsarist government showed little open concern over the decline of Russian influence.

Secretly, however, it was decided in St. Petersburg that the union of the two Bulgarias would not be sanctioned, unless Prince Alexander first retired. In Berlin it was suspected that Austria might be intriguing to establish a position in Bulgaria similar to that which it had gained in Serbia. Such a design, if realized, would cut athwart Bismarck's cherished policy of reserving the eastern Balkans for Russia, and would almost certainly precipitate war between Russia and Austria. The theory that Austria was entirely, some observers said slavishly, under the dominance of Berlin cannot be squared with Austria's independent policy toward Bulgaria at this time.

In the autumn of 1884, not long after the renewal of the *Dreikaiserbund,* the sovereigns of Austria, Germany, and Russia and their foreign secretaries conferred on matters of common interest, Balkan affairs almost wholly. In itself the meeting was a visible sign that the governments preferred that pending issues should be adjusted pacifically. Kálnoky seems to have informed the Russians that the anti-Russian temper in Bulgaria was not of Austria's making, but he would not grant Russia a free hand in the principality. On the flimsiest evidence, it was suspected by some Magyar politicians that Kálnoky had actually made some concessions to Russia, and they put some embarrassing questions to him in the delegation meeting, which the foreign minister allowed to go unanswered. Premier Tisza undertook to allay the suspicions of his countrymen by announcing that the sole purpose of the meeting of the emperors had been to consolidate peace; in ignorance, apparently, he added that the Monarchy had no written understanding with Russia.[14]

Alexander of Battenberg, aware that Russian antipathy was jeopardizing his crown, steered on a new tack and tried to effect a reconciliation with the men on the Neva. Shortly, in September of 1885, a miniature, almost bloodless revolution occurred in Eastern Roumelia and the leaders at once proclaimed the union of the province with Bulgaria. Although Prince Alexander had been officially informed that Russia was now opposed to the merger, he eagerly accepted the invitation of the rebel chiefs to become ruler of Roumelia.

What happened in Roumelia caused anxious flutterings in all of Europe's major chancelleries. Might not the Bulgar-inhabited sections of Macedonia now rebel and demand incorporation in the Bulgar state? And might not other Balkan peoples find encouragement for similar moves in the doings of the Bulgarians? Kálnoky condemned the apostles of a big Bulgaria as agitators, whose rash deeds would promote anarchy in the Balkans. Turkey warned that she would fight if necessary to prevent the union of the two Bulgarias. And Serbia let it be known that if Bulgaria were enlarged, she should be awarded territorial compensation. The Serb ministry showed that it meant business by mobilizing troops along the Bulgarian frontier and beseeching her patron and benefactor, Austria, for support.

Since the making of the convention of 1881, Serbia had been for Austria the veriest problem child. Milan, become king in 1882, was tame enough, as befitted a puppet, but his Austrophile predilections made him increasingly unpopular with the politically articulate in the kingdom. Ristič, leader of the pro-Russian faction, who had been ousted from the premiership in 1880, intrigued against the crown, and a new political party, the Radical, was a thorn in the king's flesh. This party, founded in 1881, adopted as its program a weird amalgam of Pan-Slavism, Yugoslav nationalism, and Western liberalism. It was antidynastic and republican, and eager for an alliance with Bulgaria, economic emancipation from Austria, and the deliverance of Yugoslavs under the Turkish and Hapsburg flags. At the polls, in 1883, the Radicals triumphed and their chief, Nikola Pasič, was designated as premier, but

King Milan arbitrarily passed him over. An armed rising that followed was suppressed with much difficulty, and Pasič and others escaped abroad, a price on their heads.[15]

More than once it appeared as though Austria might intervene with an army to crush the enemies of King Milan. So unsure in fact was the king of his throne that in 1885 he even offered to place Serbia wholly under Austrian authority, a proposal that the men in Vienna turned down for both domestic and international reasons. After the union of the two Bulgarias had been proclaimed, popular agitations and a desire to rehabilitate his personal prestige impelled Milan to seek territorial compensation for Serbia.

Milan's appeal to Austria for assistance against Bulgaria placed the Ballplatz in a perplexing position. If it backed Serbia, a war between that country and Bulgaria might break out; this in itself would have only local significance, but if Russia should help Bulgaria, the situation would become extremely dangerous. Possibly, however, Russia might prove indifferent; in any case, unless Austria backed Milan, he would almost certainly be deposed by his restive subjects, and the anti-Austrian element in Serbia would take charge; a Serbia governed by that group would exert an undesirable attraction upon the Hapsburg Yugoslavs.[16]

Reluctantly the Austrian foreign office assured Milan that he could rely on the Monarchy for assistance and a Serbian loan was floated in the Vienna money market. All of this thoroughly alarmed Bismarck, who feared the outcome would be war between Austria and Russia.

When Bulgaria declined to make territorial cessions to Serbia, the latter, in November 1885, charged Bulgaria with "unprovoked aggression" and declared war. But to the amazement of Europe and the consternation of Austria, the Bulgarians whipped the Serbs and advanced irresistibly onto enemy territory; if the fighting had gone on much longer Serbia would have been totally humiliated. Anguished appeals from Milan caused Austria to threaten military intervention against Bulgaria unless the warfare was promptly broken off. Reluctantly Bulgaria bowed to Austria, promising to withdraw her troops from Serbian soil and to sign an armistice. A peace settlement based upon the *status quo ante bellum* was completed in March of 1886.

Austrian intervention on behalf of Serbia infuriated St. Petersburg and enraged Bismarck, ever fearful of war between his imperial partners. If the Serbo-Bulgar war had been permitted to run its course, both belligerents would have been weakened, Bismarck observed, and Serbia at the end would have been more than ever dependent upon Austrian favor and friendship. Besides, Russia would have had no legitimate grounds for fresh bitterness toward Austria. In a manner not always imitated by his successors in the

German foreign office, Bismarck warned Vienna that he could not and would not back her in the Balkan course that she was pursuing.

Russophile critics of King Milan charged that Austria was really responsible for Serbia's military defeat, since Vienna had induced the ruler to hold off military operations until Bulgaria was fully prepared for war. Imprudently they urged that national pride should be assuaged by a renewal of hostilities, a proposal which Milan brushed aside, and which indeed the condition of the Serb fighting forces made fantastic. The Austrian minister, Count Khevenhüller, reported that Milan's reputation had been so grievously impaired that Austrian pressure ought to be exerted to force him to abdicate; the alternative, he thought, would be a successful revolution by the pro-Russian party. But the Ballplatz declined to act upon Khevenhüller's advice, much to Milan's gratification.

To strengthen his position, Milan authorized political concessions, including a liberalized constitution, the release of his political enemies from jail, and amnesty for "guilty rebels" in exile. In 1889 the new constitution was formally promulgated and then Milan renounced the throne in favor of his son, Alexander. Since he was a minor, a regency was created and that body was compelled by Milan to extend the term of the secret political convention with Austria to 1895. Francis Joseph reported to the delegations in June 1889 that the Serbian regency "has given me the assurance that it will preserve and foster the friendly relations hitherto existing between us." Kálnoky added that unless Serbia ventured upon an Austrophobe course Austria would not interfere in Serbian affairs.

Nevertheless Ristič, the arch-Russophile, was appointed president of the Serbian regency, the anti-Austrian Pasič returned from exile, and his Radical party dominated the politics of the land. Kálnoky concluded in 1890 that the anti-Austrian faction in Serbia was stronger than the government itself, and he condemned as "morally deficient and politically immature" certain Serbian journalists who preached hatred of the Hapsburgs. He warned Serbian firebrands that in a struggle with a great power there could be but one outcome.

Commercial controversies envenomed feelings in both countries. Veterinary regulations hindered the sale of Serbian pork products in the Monarchy and Serbia retaliated by refusing to prolong the existing trade treaty unless economic concessions were granted. A bitter tariff war ensued, with melancholy consequences for the foreign trade of Serbia. No satisfactory alternative market to replace traditional outlets in the northern monarchy could be found and the Serbs grudgingly signed (1892) a commercial treaty advantageous to Austria though not without benefits for their own economy.

Young King Alexander, on coming of age in 1893, abolished the regency and presently suspended the constitution. Pro-Russian Radical politicians were unhorsed, and friends of Austria, directed by ex-King Milan, who had returned from his foreign wanderings, hopped into the saddle.

VIII

After the union of the two Bulgarias was proclaimed in 1885, Russia officially declined to consent, and Austria and Germany sided with her. The three powers in fact ordered that Eastern Roumelia should be restored to the sovereignty of Turkey, as prescribed in the Treaty of Berlin. Britain, on the other hand, supported the union, for it had reversed its policy on the Bulgarian question as radically as had Russia, and had become convinced that Bulgarian nationalism not only would prevent the country from passing under Russian domination, but would serve as a bulwark against Russian pressure upon Constantinople. Britain's stand compelled Russia to modify its tune, and, making a virtue of necessity, Russia agreed to sanction the union. The central powers at once wheeled alongside of their Muscovite partner.

Then in August of 1886 there occurred one of those merry episodes that supplied stuff for the composers of light opera with a Balkan setting. Bulgarian plotters, abetted by Russian agents, forced Prince Alexander to vacate his throne and a pro-Russian ministry took charge of Bulgarian affairs; kidnapers placed the prince on the princely yacht and steamed off to Russia with him, but he managed to sneak back to Bulgaria, only to have a Russian representative tell him bluntly to go away and stay away. Afraid of an assassin's bullet if he remained, Alexander formally abdicated and left his adopted country, never to return. His abdication and the selection of a successor produced fresh international tensions.

Machinations of Russians in Bulgaria gave credence to the well-grounded belief that Russia was seeking to dominate the country, something that Austria would not tamely permit. "St. Petersburg," wrote Francis Joseph, "is utterly undependable . . . There is a limit to all things and the patriotic feelings of our people must not be trampled upon.[17] At a Hapsburg crown council it was decided that if Russian troops moved upon Bulgaria, Austria would have to act; and Premier Tisza declared in the Hungarian parliament that "no power is entitled to undertake any singlehanded armed intervention or to set up a protectorate in the Balkan peninsula."

To the delegations Kálnoky announced in November 1886 that any act which impaired the freedom of Bulgaria would be regarded as unfriendly and he hoped for British coöperation to preserve Bulgaria's integrity, if that should be necessary. Andrássy ascribed the trouble over Bulgaria to the "unnatural alliance" of the three emperors; Germany, he averred, anxious to retain Russian friendship, was sacrificing Austrian interests to sinister Muscovite ambitions. Other Magyars in the delegation argued that if Russia marched into Bulgaria, Austria must declare war at once; but Austro-German spokesmen wanted to know first what Germany would do in case of an Austro-Russian conflict, and Slav delegates, other than Polish loyalists, were opposed to war under any circumstances.

Divided counsels in the Hapsburg Monarchy encouraged Russian Pan-Slavs to believe that the tsardom could fulfill its historic mission in the Balkans without fear of effective resistance from Austria; and so they whispered in the receptive ear of Alexander III. Austria, however, warned Russia that if her soldiers moved into Bulgaria that would be legitimate cause for Austria to interfere. It is difficult to see how the frequently predicted Austro-Russian war could have been avoided had the army of the tsar entered Bulgaria.

Austrian aversion to Russian lordship over Bulgaria was shared by Britain and Italy, but Bismarck, who considered Bulgaria as Russia's legitimate sphere, almost ostentatiously aligned himself with the tsar. "To us," he thundered in the reichstag, "it is of no importance who rules in Bulgaria, or even what becomes of Bulgaria," but secretly he counseled Russia against military occupation. Bismarck well knew that an influential faction in Austria preferred a diplomatic alignment with France against Germany, for memories of 1866 had not altogether vanished. Should that opinion become policy, Germany might find herself isolated or too heavily dependent upon Russia.

At the moment that the Bulgarian crisis darkened the diplomatic sky in the east there was ominous thunder in the west. The Boulangist excitement in France and the enlargement of the French fighting services signified the growing French desire for *revanche* for 1871. If Russia was blocked in her Bulgarian designs she might ally herself in fact with France and seek to gain her ends by war. Very naturally, then, Bismarck, for whom a Franco-Russian alliance was a haunting nightmare, worked for an accommodation in Bulgaria that would keep his Austrian and Russian friends from flying at one another.

IX

At the outset of 1887—a year of extraordinary diplomatic complexity— it seemed to many observers as though Europe was on the verge of a general conflagration. French and German journalists were engaged in a fearsome newspaper war; in view of the dangerous international situation Bismarck sought and secured greater military appropriations, and thereby aggravated the international tension. It was widely believed in the Hapsburg Monarchy that Germany and France would go to war and that Russia would seize the opportunity to fight Austria for mastery in the Balkans. Support for that hypothesis was given by the concentration of Russian troops along the

Galician frontier, and the Austrian High Command countered by increasing the military forces in Galicia, laying an embargo on the exportation of horses, calling conscripts to the colors months in advance of the scheduled time, and ordering new repeating rifles. The gravity of the crisis arising out of the Bulgarian imbroglio necessitated these warlike measures, Kálnoky explained to the delegations. Upon the Viennese Stock Exchange and on Austrian business generally, war alarums had a very depressing effect.

On the diplomatic front three major events of 1887 reacted upon the Austrian international position: the renewal of the Triple Alliance, an entente with Britain to which Italy was party, and the replacement of the League of the Three Emperors by Bismarck's famous Reinsurance Treaty with Russia. This last agreement was, however, unknown in Vienna.

The stormy international scene of 1887 played squarely into the hands of the Italians, who felt that the Triple Alliance had done little to further their national interests. In 1885, when Italy laid hands upon Massawa on the Red Sea, she was told by Austria that she would be expected to withdraw as soon as Britain retired from Egypt, which seemed like an ungenerous stand for an ally to take. Actually Italy expected and wanted diplomatic support from her Triplice allies to enable her to carve out a really impressive African empire. And Italy envisaged the western Balkans as a convenient field for expansionist energy; in any case Austrian power in the Balkans ought not to be increased unless Italy secured appropriate compensation.

As early as November 1885, Italy had informed her allies that she would renew the Triple Alliance only if given assurances of backing for her colonial aspirations and promises that her interests in the Balkans would be protected. Count Robilant, the new Italian foreign minister, felt strongly that the original Triplice treaty was insufficiently profitable to Italy and was determined that the alliance, if renewed, should yield larger dividends for his country. But Kálnoky declined to meet the Italian wishes and Bismarck was of like mind for a time, though eventually he shifted his ground. He approved a draft treaty that Italy produced in November of 1886, and he pressed Austria to concur. But Kálnoky still hung back, for he feared embroilment with France as a result of Italian colonial aspirations and he was unwilling to concede to the Italians a foothold on the Balkan side of the Adriatic. Austria, he said, would consent only to the renewal of the treaty of 1882 without alteration.

Afraid lest Italy might gravitate toward France or Russia, Bismarck then made the ingenious proposal that the original treaty should be perpetuated but should be supplemented by bilateral pacts, which would satisfy Italian desires. There would be a pact between Germany and Italy in which the former would commit itself to back the Italian colonial aims, and also an Austro-Italian convention in which Vienna would promise compensation to Italy should the Austrian position in the Balkans be bettered. To that plan Kálnoky assented, with the reservation that Austrian annexation of Bosnia would not entitle Italy to a reward. Italy eagerly accepted these terms, and in February of 1887 appropriate diplomatic instruments were signed.

Under the terms of the Austro-Italian convention, the two allies would coöperate to preserve the territorial *status quo* in the Near East, but if changes should become necessary, then the two powers would decide in advance on the division of the spoils. By the special treaty with Germany, that power was pledged to fight at Italy's side to prevent France from appropriating Tripoli or Morocco, even though Italy should start the war; in this wise, an unmistakably aggressive character was imparted to the Triple Alliance.

Austrian and British diplomacy had, in the main, followed parallel lines with reference to Russian activities in the Near East. Both were bent upon holding Russian influence in Bulgaria at the minimum; yet each cabinet was suspicious of the other's diplomacy and hesitant about promising positive support. In the autumn of 1886 Anglo-Austrian discussions were held on a formal understanding which would be pointed against Russia, but Britain would do nothing more than assure Austria of her good will.

Behind the scenes, in connection with the conversations on the renewal of the Triple Alliance, Bismarck urged Italy to strike a bargain on the Mediterranean with Britain. At odds with France over Egypt and distrustful of Russian pretensions in the Balkans, Britain responded cordially to Italian overtures. Notes were exchanged in February 1887 between the two governments binding them to act together to maintain peace and the *status quo* along the Mediterranean and adjoining seas.

Meantime, Austro-British *pourparlers* had been revived and after the Anglo-Italian entente was negotiated, Austria immediately signed the document. This tripartite Mediterranean league, designed to preserve things as they were, could be turned effectively against France or Russia or both. Later on in 1887, the Mediterranean understanding was made much more specific, for all three signatories promised, among other things, to uphold Turkish rights in Bulgaria, in the Straits, and in Asia Minor. Plainly this was an entente directed against Russian expansion in the Near East— Austria's central concern—and it might also be applied to restrain French imperialism in north Africa.

Austro-Russian antagonism over Bulgaria fatally destroyed the League of the Three Emperors. Russia would not renew it. Yet the men on the Neva, afraid of being isolated, addressed overtures to Bismarck for a treaty committing Russia and Germany to neutrality in case of war. Because of the Austrian alliance, which Bismarck was determined to preserve, he could not sign a general neutrality pact; he indicated, however, his readiness to enter into an understanding of limited scope.

On the principle that half a loaf was better than none, the Russians acquiesced and in June of 1887 arranged a very secret bargain with Germany, which is often referred to as Bismarck's Reinsurance Treaty. Each signatory was committed to benevolent neutrality should the other go to war, with the exceptions that Germany would not be bound to neutrality if Russia attacked Austria, and that Russia would become a free agent in case of a German attack on France. Germany, moreover, promised to support Russia diplomatically in the Near East; more exactly, Russia could rely on help from Berlin in regaining a dominant place in the affairs of Bulgaria.

The wisdom and the morality of Bismarck's deal of 1887 with Russia have been the subjects of lengthy and acrimonious debate in the world of scholarship. Germany had promised in 1879 to stand on the side lines if Austria should attack Russia. Was that pledge incompatible with Germany's obligation to fight alongside of Austria in case she were the victim of a Russian attack? It is not difficult to believe that the arrangement with Russia was diplomatic behavior on the grand design, for so long as Bismarck kept in friendly contact with Russia he was in a stronger position to smooth out Russo-Austrian quarrels to the advantage of peace. Unless it be assumed that Austria had a reasonable right to ascendancy in Bulgaria, one must accept the verdict of Langer that "It is hard to see how he [Bismarck] can be accused of having betrayed Austrian interests." [18]

x

Austria had renewed the treaty of the Triple Alliance, arranged an entente with Britain, and broken off the diplomatic tie with Russia, but the future of Bulgaria still hung in the balances. Russia seemingly held a trump card in Bismarck's pledge of support in Bulgaria; how useful that was the event would presently show.

In July of 1887, the Bulgarian assembly chose as ruler Prince Ferdinand of Saxe-Coburg, another young, inexperienced, and headstrong individual, to whom time was to assign the epithet of "The Fox." He was the owner of a large estate in Hungary and held a lieutenancy in an Austrian regiment, which he was obliged to resign before accepting the Bulgarian princedom; Austrian agents probably had a good deal to do with his selection as prince. In any case it was not unnatural, despite Kálnoky's disclaimers, for Russia to look upon Ferdinand as Austria's man, and Russia complained vehemently against his election. But a Russian appeal to Bismarck to have Austria oppose Prince Ferdinand fell on stony ground. Wherefore, Russia took steps looking to the expulsion of the Hapsburg puppet from Sofia by force; general preparations for war were speeded up, and more soldiers were posted along the Galician border.

In high Vienna quarters it appeared as though an armed clash was now unavoidable, and Austria sought definite assurances of German help. Bismarck, however, held back until rumors reached Berlin that tsarist troops were being mobilized in the vicinity of Prussian Poland; then he applied the financial brake to the Muscovite war chariot by making it impossible for Russia to borrow funds in the Berlin money market. That revelation of Germany's attitude had a dampening effect upon Russian military ardor. Nevertheless, prominent Russians delivered bellicose speeches, and army concentrations close to Galicia went on apace; certain German officials conjectured that Russia would pounce upon Austria in the spring of 1888. Bismarck admonished Austria to prepare for an attack, while avoiding any move that might legitimately cause provocation in St. Petersburg.

On the assumption that war was in the offing, Austria tried to arrange with Germany on the way in which the troops of the two countries should be employed. The patriarchal war hawk, Archduke Albrecht, approved a plan for a joint Austro-German preventive war on Russia, but the Hapsburg political authorities scorned it, for Bismarck kept dinning in their ears that Germany would fight only if Russia was the attacker. Military chiefs of Austria and Germany conferred, it is true, on plans of campaign, without, however, reaching positive conclusions. Nothing was clearer than that Germany was unwilling to pull Austrian chestnuts out of the Balkan fire.[19]

In spite of military preparations the Vienna cabinet seems to have been averse to taking the initiative for war. Prime Minister Tisza declared to the Hungarian parliament that although the Monarchy was in shape to deal with any emergency, it desired neither extension of influence "nor increase of territory, as had been falsely ascribed to us . . . We desire foremost of all the preservation of peace." At the end of the year Russia, too, displayed a less bellicose tone, her ambassador in Vienna asserting that his country had no intention of warring upon Austria nor even of resorting to force in order to establish its ascendancy in Bulgaria. War fever was further reduced in February of 1888 when Bismarck caused the terms of the Austro-German alliance to be published. All the world then knew that Germany was bound to fight Russia, if that power should attack Austria. The disclosure had a sobering effect upon warmongers in both St. Petersburg and Vienna.

By April 1888, the clouds of war which had hung so low over Europe had largely been dispelled. The Vienna stock market, invariably a reliable barometer on the state of the international weather, boomed in a way reminiscent of the early seventies, and the press began to speak of Francis Joseph as the "peace emperor."

Once more, as in 1878, the "old diplomacy" had succeeded in keeping the swords of Europe in their scabbards, and much the largest part of the credit for that achievement belonged to Prince Bismarck. Austro-Russian rivalry, concentrated this time on Bulgaria, might well have resulted in war; nations had taken up arms for slighter reasons before. But Bismarck, in the name of German vital interests, had toiled effectively to preserve peace between the eastern empires; had a conflict occurred in the east, a Franco-German war might well have been unloosed simultaneously.[20]

It is noteworthy that a school of opinion in Austria felt that Germany had not backed her ally adequately during the Bulgarian crisis. Some Austrian Clericals and the Czechs, of course, had at no time been in sympathy with the German alliance, much preferring an alignment with Russia. Late in the summer of 1888, the great Viennese press subjected the German alliance to much adverse criticism, and when William II visited Vienna that autumn, the crowds that lined the streets exhibited no particular enthusiasm for the new monarch of Germany.

Bismarck, on his side, was worried lest the Slavophilic domestic policies of Count Taaffe might impair the fighting ardor of the Hapsburg army and be reflected in Austrian foreign policies. He could, however, count confidently upon the Magyars, whose Slav antipathies, distrust of Russia particularly, were notorious. Pointing to a map the Iron Chancellor remarked in 1884: "There between the Danube and the Carpathians live the Hungarians. For us it is just as though the Germans were there, for their destiny is tied to ours—they stand or fall with us. That is the fundamental difference between them and the Slavs and the Rumanians. The Hungarian factor is the most important for us in the whole Balkan region." [21] As a mark of his friendship for the Magyars, Bismarck decorated Tisza with the Order of the Black Eagle and conferred slighter honors upon lesser Hungarian officials and Austrians, too, though Taaffe, the Slavophile, was conspicuously passed over.

XI

Hapsburg foreign policy was thoroughly ventilated at the end of 1888 in the Vienna reichsrat during debate on a bill to raise the size of the standing army. For the Austro-German Liberals, Plener rang the changes on the inconsistency of an alliance with Germany and the anti-German, pro-Slav course that the Taaffe ministry was pursuing in internal affairs. Czech spokesmen, on the other hand, warned against allowing the Dual Monarchy to degenerate into the merest tool of crafty designers in Berlin. "We must remain Austrian," remarked Rieger, the "Old Czech" war horse. "We have no future outside this empire. That is why we shall vote for this bill. But the Austrian emperor must not sink to the rank of a noble governor of a German province. There is no place for us outside of Austria, but there is at the same time no future for the dynasty without us."

Speaking for the "Young Czechs," Edward Grégr supported army expansion in order to keep the Monarchy from falling under Germany's thrall. "We want Austria to be strong, ten times stronger than now. Austria's minorities live on no bed of roses but may the Lord and all his saints preserve us from Prussian rule. We want Austria to have an imposing army, in order that the German alliance shall not crush her . . . An alliance of the weak with the strong is slavery." Few voices were raised in parliament against military expansion and the measure was passed into law by an overwhelming majority (182 to 23).

Societies and private individuals in Germany and in the Dual Monarchy, too, carried on active propaganda for tighter trade bonds between the two countries which would reinforce the diplomatic partnership and relax tensions that had arisen. A customs union, certain partisans of the idea reasoned, would surely yield mutual benefits and, if extended to neighboring countries, would be an instrument for the preservation of European peace. Though discussion never got beyond the stage of projects, the essential principle was applied in the Caprivi commercial treaties of 1891, in which duties were reciprocally scaled down, so that Austro-Hungarian agricultural products and cattle were, in general, admitted to Germany at lower rates, while German manufactured goods entered the Monarchy more cheaply than before. Railway rates were adjusted so as to facilitate rather than hinder exchange of goods.

For over a decade trade between Austria and Germany increased, as did discussions on a *Zollverein*. But as the century turned, the recurrence of business depression brought other viewpoints into the foreground. German agrarians, for example, protested energetically against competition from the plains of Hungary. When commercial treaties expired in 1904, Germany raised duties on farm products and the new Austrian tariff of 1906 dealt damaging blows to the importation of German manufactured goods.

Nevertheless, the desirability of a mid-European customs union continued to be preached in Austria and Germany. The opinion of the learned and respected economist, Gustav Schmoller, served as the theme for innumerable academic treatises. In 1900 Schmoller wrote: "The states of central Europe must put into the background the political and economic factors which divide them, and concentrate on what unites them. Far off as a mid-European *Zollverein* may be, the tasks of the new century lie in the direction of a combination between the medium and smaller Central European states." [22] On the eve of World War I, projects for an economic union were again under serious consideration.

The Triple Alliance, first renewed in 1887, was extended again in 1891.

In the interval Bismarck had departed from the Wilhelmstrasse and his supreme nightmare, the alignment of Russia and France, had taken concrete form. Austro-Italian relations, however, had taken a turn for the better, half because the Italian government imposed restraints upon extreme Irredentism, half because of Italian squabbling with France over colonies and commerce. Just as Italy's value to Austria depended upon the state of Austrian relations with Russia, so the Italians prized the bond with Austria in proportion as tension with France was acute or modest. The Italian premier, Crispi, in the spring of 1889 begged Austria to coöperate navally with Italy in case of a French attack.

But the Ballplatz was averse to committing itself in any way that might be regarded as encouraging Italian colonial pretensions in northern Africa. If Italy robbed Turkey of its African holdings, that volcano which was Turkey-in-Europe might erupt and that could not fail to endanger Austrian interests. Bismarck, when appealed to by Italy to exert pressure on Austria for a naval pact, evaded the issue, recommending instead that Italy should consolidate its Mediterranean bond with Britain.

Crispi, while he pleaded for considerate treatment of the Austrian Italians, struck decisively against radical apostles of Irredentism in Italian public life and without. Certain Austrophobe clubs were broken up, collection of funds in Italy for a memorial to Dante in Trieste was prohibited, and the finance minister, Seismit Doda, Dalmatian-born, was dismissed because he failed to protest at a meeting in which an anti-Austrian address was delivered. On the other hand, Crispi's foes in parliament fulminated against the Triple Alliance, and reviled "a hateful treaty which binds us to our enemy." Although Crispi was driven from power in 1891 and a cabinet with rather pro-French inclinations acceded to office, it was nonetheless felt that the Triplice was, on balance, a national asset, and in May of that year the treaty was renewed.

In the course of the negotiations leading up to the renewal it was arranged that the three documents of 1887 should be merged in a single instrument. The Austrian pledge of reciprocal compensation to Italy, should the Hapsburg position in the Near East be improved, formed Article VII of the new treaty; and Germany gave greater precision to her commitment to back Italy with regard to African empire, notably with reference to the Turkish colony of Tripoli. For the Italians, the Triple Alliance became in a very real sense the Tripoli alliance.

After Bismarck's withdrawal from the Wilhelmstrasse in March 1890, his successors declined to continue the secret neutrality treaty of 1887 with Russia, chiefly because that accord was thought to be incompatible with German commitments to Austria. So strong in fact was Austrophile feeling in the German foreign office that assurances were given in Vienna that no change in the Balkan situation would be permitted if Austria dissented—a striking, though momentary, deviation from the Bismarckian doctrine of a strict division of interests in the Balkans between Austria and Russia.

After the Germans had refused to renew the neutrality treaty, Russia was inclined to be more cordial toward Austria. An exchange of princely visits between the two eastern empires betokened better feelings, and the Russians intimated that any ruler for Bulgaria other than Ferdinand of Coburg, who still lacked international sanction, would be acceptable. Publicly Kálnoky described relations with Russia as very friendly, adding that "the Triple Alliance . . . is purely defensive and peaceful and no attack upon other countries will come from Austria." [23]

Nevertheless, Hapsburg mistrust of Russian designs would not down, and temporary fortifications and barracks which had been hastily constructed in Galicia during the war scare of 1886-87 were replaced by permanent structures. Bulgaria continued to be the direct obstacle to amicable relations between the cabinets of the two countries. When in 1890 Bulgaria applied in Constantinople for independent status, Austrian diplomacy seconded the request, but Russia successfully blocked it; and when Prince Ferdinand sought to revise the Bulgarian constitution so that his children might be baptized in the Roman Catholic faith, Austria approved, while Russia roughly dissented. As for forcing Ferdinand from the throne, as Russia desired, that was remote indeed from the thinking of the Ballplatz.

On a visit to Vienna in 1893, Prince Ferdinand was given a hearty reception, though politely admonished to restrain Bulgarian ambitions in Macedonia, for Austria was wholly opposed to any political change in that troubled province. Kálnoky reiterated in 1894 the Monarchy's settled policy in the Balkans. "I have to declare in the most positive terms," he said, "that the principle of nonintervention in the domestic policy of the Balkan states, adopted by Austria as part of her foreign policy, several years ago, still exists in force, and that it has been the steadfast desire of this country to see the Balkan states develop independently on the basis of the Berlin Treaty, and that there ought to be no intervention by any foreign power in their internal affairs."

Prince Ferdinand endeavored to purchase the friendship of Russia by ousting the notoriously Russophobe premier, M. Stambuloff. Frequently Prince and Premier had quarreled acrimoniously over the management of public affairs, and in 1894 Stambuloff handed in his resignation. Before long he was slashed to death by "wretched Russophile" killers, and two years later Russia at last recognized Ferdinand as the legitimate ruler; Austria promptly followed suit. Austria had won a point in that its candidate for the Bulgarian throne had obtained recognition, but in reality he was ruler by the grace of Russia; for neither contestant, in other words, was the Bulgarian

settlement a clear-cut victory. Yet the Bulgarian problem which had perplexed eastern Europe for more than a decade had been settled, and the way
was opened for a new epoch in Austro-Russian relations, looking to cooperation to preserve a semblance of order in European Turkey.

Before the Bulgarian question had been fully resolved, the Ballplatz
was disturbed by the implications of the recently sealed Franco-Russian
alliance, which might encourage the eastern colossus to resume the tradi-
tional pressure in the Balkans in a manner inimical to the Dual Monarchy.
Inquiries in Berlin disclosed that Germany was of no mind to invoke force
to keep Russia out of Constantinople; rather if Russia moved upon the
Ottoman capital, Austria should occupy Salonica by way of compensation.
Plainly in its Balkan policy the Wilhelmstrasse had now reverted to the
Bismarckian formula of having the peninsula divided into spheres, and
Vienna had to steer her course by the light of the great northern star.

Austria turned to London to ascertain what British policy would be in
case Russian pressure upon the Ottoman empire should be resumed. The
British let it be known that they would hold fast to the tradition of blocking
Russia, but that the British fleet could not keep both Russia and France in
check. In the event of an Anglo-Russian clash the Triple Alliance, so London
contended, would have to compel France to remain neutral. But Germany
shied away from any commitment of that nature, arguing that Britain should
safeguard her interests by hooking up definitely with the Triplice, something
the island kingdom, still devoted to the principle of diplomatic isolation,
would not do.[24]

Much to the astonishment of the European chancelleries, the British
foreign office in 1895 issued a kind of diplomatic feeler, which contemplated
the disruption of the Ottoman empire and the distribution of the territories
among the powers. Russia would control Constantinople and the Straits;
Albania would pass to Italy, unless Austria strenuously objected, in which
case Tripoli or Morocco would be substituted; Austria itself would be assigned a free hand in the western Balkans, while France and Britain would
make colonial gains; how Germany would profit by the division of the
Turkish estate was not divulged.

Austria, like the other continental powers, rejected the British overture
(if it could be so dignified), scenting danger over the actual partition. Austria expressed a preference for the maintenance of the uneasy *status quo*
in the Ottoman realm. Thereupon, Britain declined to renew the Mediterranean Pact with Austria, dating from 1887, which had nourished the belief
that in the event of an Austrian war with Russia Britain would fight shoulder to shoulder with the Dual Monarchy.

XII

For some time signs had been multiplying that the Ottoman empire was growing steadily weaker and that the oppressed nationalities, in Armenia, in Crete, in Macedonia, were bent upon striking off the Turkish yoke. Those longings could not fail to have reverberations upon the high politics of Europe.

Toward the end of 1895 Christendom was horrified by a fresh wave of brutal Turkish atrocities against the Armenians in reprisal for seditious activities of reckless, patriotically intoxicated Armenian enthusiasts. European humanitarianism reacted violently against this barbarism, and realistic diplomatists dreaded the repercussions of these disturbances on the Christian minorities in Macedonia.

At the Ballplatz, Kálnoky, who had fallen afoul of the Hungarian government, had by now been supplanted by Count Agenor Goluchowski. Goluchowski recommended an international naval demonstration against Turkey to impel the sultan along the road of reform, but the proposal fell on deaf ears.

Presently, in the summer of 1896, hundreds of Armenians in Constantinople were foully butchered in retaliation for deeds of fanatical Armenians in the capital and for new stirrings of their brethren in Armenia. That bloody outrage profoundly shocked Europe, and if any country had intervened at once and deposed the sultan, probably no nation would have protested. But as matters stood, no power was willing to apply force, though had Britain decided to do so, and Russia had objected, Austria would almost certainly have ranged herself alongside Britain. Except for interminable haggling among diplomatists and various paper schemes for remedying evils in Armenia, nothing was done. The Armenian problem remained as vexed as ever.

Attention was soon diverted from Armenia by events in Crete, culminating in a brief and inglorious Greco-Turkish war and followed by the establishment of Cretan autonomy under the ægis of the great powers. For much of the nineteenth century Crete had been the scene of ceaseless agitation on the part of the Christian and Greek-feeling majority for liberation from Turkey and union with the kingdom of Greece. Revolutionary outbreaks were invariably aided and abetted by Pan-Hellenists in the Greek kingdom. During a Cretan insurrection in 1896, the sultan, under international pressure, promised administrative reforms, and Austria thereupon requested Greece to persuade the Cretan rebels to lay down their arms. Austrian initiative was not dictated by any love for the Cretans, but rather by the dread that the revolutionary flame would excite disturbances in Macedonia, and hence have undesirable repercussions upon the Balkan interests of the

Dual Monarchy. But the Athens government scorned the counsels of Vienna and, owing to popular pressure, eventually dispatched military assistance to the insurgents in Crete. It was made clear that Greek national sentiment could be appeased only if Crete were actually annexed to the kingdom; in fact, the commander of the Greek expeditionary force proclaimed Crete a possession of Greece. The powers declared the annexation invalid and ordered the withdrawal of the Greek forces, but the Greeks refused to comply.

War with Turkey broke out in April of 1897, and occasioned modest fear in Austria lest the fighting incite the population of Macedonia to arms to end Turkish rule. Instead, the swift Turkish defeat of the overambitious Greeks exerted a pacifying, or at least a restraining, influence upon restless Macedonia. Greece was spared the full penalties of her audacious bellicosity by the intervention of the powers, Austria among them, and Crete was recognized as autonomous, with Prince George of Greece as governor general. Austria and Germany, who were currying the favor of the sultan, opposed the prince's candidacy, but the other great powers, including Italy, backed him and secured his acceptance by Turkey.

While the agitation in Greece for the annexation of Crete was at its peak, Hellenic expansionism spread into the Turkish district of Macedonia—a geographical term embracing the vilayets of Salonika, Kosovo, and Monastir. With the reawakening of Balkan nationalisms this region had become an angry battleground of competing Christian powerlets. "Into that dark and turbid lake," it has been poetically said, "flow many waters—Serb, Bulgar, Albanian and Greek—coloured with the soils of the land from which they come." [25] The writer might as well have remembered the Turkish element there and the splinter minority of Vlachs claimed by the Rumanians as blood brothers. Not only were national groups mixed in Macedonia, they were intermixed, religious differences aggravated the confusion, and the residents were cursed with an unruly and anarchic disposition. Historians, geographers, and ethnographers with sharp pencils could (and did) fashion a persuasive claim to all or part of Macedonia for each of the rival national claimants.

Until after the middle of the nineteenth century Greek influence, by reason of Greek control of the churches, predominated in Macedonia. But in 1870 Bulgarian clergy were assigned a special position by Turkey, which they exploited, by means of schools and political societies, to convert Macedonians to Bulgarian sympathies. And in this they were surprisingly successful. After several false starts Serbian propaganda in Macedonia gained vigor in the eighties, being aided by Serb-operated schools, and Greek patriotism likewise bestirred itself. Abetting the rival agencies of cultural penetration were guerilla bands, subsidized by the several pretenders, to promote their particular version of nationalism. The sequel was raids, brigandage, and devastation.

Europe's great powers could not remain indifferent to the vexed Macedonian convulsion in the Turkish empire. For while Armenia and Crete were rather remote geographically, Macedonia lay in the very heart of the Balkan peninsula. Austria had railway and commercial interests at stake, nor could Vienna view with equanimity too large an accession of territory by Serbia if Macedonia should be partitioned. Not less than Austria, Russia, with her long-standing concern for the Balkans, preferred at the time the preservation of the *status quo*. In the Treaty of Berlin (1878) Turkey had bound herself to grant home rule to Macedonia and her neglect to do so furnished grounds for appeals to the powers to intervene and compel fulfillment.

Through diplomatic channels, Serbia in 1892 tried to arrange with Greece for the division of Macedonia into spheres of interest, but the Greeks scorned the proposal. In the autumn of 1896, when Bulgar terrorism was working havoc in sections of Macedonia, rumors spread abroad that the claimants to the region were drawing up a bargain to parcel out the province. In fact a Serbo-Bulgarian understanding was reached in March of 1897, the signers promising to adjust conflicting claims amicably and to coöperate for mutual benefits. But Austria and Russia immediately reiterated their opposition to any change in the Balkan *status quo*. That declaration in itself signified that Austrian relations with Russia had improved. And presently the Austro-Russian entente, which had been dissolved by the collapse of the League of the Three Emperors in 1887, was resurrected.

XIII

The way toward Austrian reconciliation with Russia had been smoothed by the formal recognition of Prince Ferdinand of Saxe-Coburg as ruler of the Bulgarian principality. And while the war between Greece and Turkey was being fought Francis Joseph and Foreign Minister Goluchowski visited St. Petersburg, ostensibly to repay a call of the tsar, though really so that diplomatists might discuss an understanding on the mutual concerns of the two monarchies in the Balkans. Russian expansionist energies had now shifted heavily to the Orient and for that reason the foreign office was minded to strike a bargain with Austria in the Near East.

Austria, on its part, wanting the *status quo* maintained in the Balkans, and riven by fierce domestic strife, was ready to talk of an entente; her German ally urged the merits of such a deal as a guaranty against a conflict with Russia. Personally Foreign Minister Goluchowski, a Pole who shared the common detestation of his countrymen for Russia, would have liked a merger of the Triplice and Britain, if that could have been arranged,

to checkmate Russia in the Balkans, or failing that, an Austro-German alignment with France, but neither of those alternatives fell within the range
of practical politics.[26]

Conversations in St. Petersburg brought into being an Austro-Russian
gentleman's agreement in 1897, an armistice, which relaxed the old tension
and put the Balkan question "on ice" for ten years. It was agreed that so
long as it was practicable the two cabinets would work together to preserve
the Balkan *status quo;* they would not themselves seek Balkan territory
nor permit another power to do so. Austria, however, reserved the right
of annexing Bosnia and the Sanjak of Novibazar at her discretion, or thus
at least Goluchowski summed up this portion of the conversations.

If and when territorial revision should become unavoidable in the Balkans, a new state, Albania, would be carved out along the Adriatic, and
the rest of European Turkey, except for Constantinople and the Straits zone,
would be equitably distributed among the Balkan Christian states. But no
Balkan country would be permitted to become so strong as to be able to
dictate the politics of the peninsula. Austria and Russia, finally, would work
in "perfect harmony" on specific Balkan questions and would avoid any act
that might create "elements of conflict or of mistrust" between them.

On two major points the men on the Neva demurred on the foregoing
summation which Goluchowski drafted upon his return from St. Petersburg.
Austrian annexation of Bosnia, they said, "would require special scrutiny at
the proper time," and the boundaries of the Sanjak would need definition.
The Russians expressed reserve, too, concerning the eventual partition of the
Turkish lands in Europe.

This Austrian understanding with Russia, incomplete and imprecise
though it was, precluded a forward Russian program in the Near East. The
"Eastern Question," that Banquo's ghost of European high politics, had been
temporarily, at least, laid to rest, and the way was opened for the resurrection of the *Dreikaiserbund,* which, like the new Austro-Russian arrangement, had been designed to keep things as they were in the Balkans. If peace
in the Balkans could be preserved, then the chances of maintaining general
European tranquillity would be vastly improved.

In the address of the crown to the delegations of November 1897, Francis
Joseph expressed gratification over the *rapprochement* with the eastern
colossus. "Upon [this accord] has been founded," the message declared, "a
relation of mutual confidence between our countries, the consolidation of
which cannot but promise well for the future." Both powers, Goluchowski
publicly explained, rejected any notion of conquest in the Balkans and were
resolved "to respect the independence of the individual Balkan states and
their right themselves to mold their destinies" without interference from
outside.

The understanding with Russia was, in the main, welcomed enthusiastically in the Hapsburg Monarchy. Slav elements rejoiced with especial fervor, for they descried the possibility that Austria might withdraw from the Triplice and give a Slav orientation to foreign policy. In other quarters it was imagined that the Austro-Russian entente might lead on to a union of the Triplice and the Franco-Russian alliance in a grand continental league. Yet when that possibility was suggested to Goluchowski, he responded, "I would never consent to it, for Austria's *one* foe is Russia." [27]

By 1897, Italy's devotion to the Triplice had weakened, as her failure to march with her allies in the Cretan affair certified. Anti-Austrian agitation was less restrained than hitherto and the efforts of Irredentists to cause bad blood with Austria were unrelenting. The antagonism between Britain and Germany as it developed in the late nineties reacted importantly upon Italian diplomacy, as indeed upon that of Austria and the other European powers.[28] Crispi, the champion of the Triplice, was hurled from power for the last time in 1896, following the defeat of Italian arms in a war with Abyssinia. Then Francophile politicians took command of Italian public affairs and smoothed out the long quarrel with the Third Republic. After the setback in Abyssinia, Italy displayed greater interest in the Balkan peninsula, as the marriage of the Italian crown prince, Victor Emmanuel, to a Montenegrin princess bore witness. Perhaps the chief reason for Italy's growing activity in the Balkans was to exert pressure on Austria with regard to Italia Irredenta.

Austria, on her side, valued the alliance with Italy, as has been suggested, in proportion to the danger of a clash with Russia. The Austro-Russian gentleman's agreement, therefore, lessened Italy's worth to Vienna, yet Goluchowski arranged with Italy in 1897 that, if European Turkey should disintegrate, an autonomous state of Albania would be set up. The strong anti-Italian party in Vienna, to which the heir presumptive, Francis Ferdinand, belonged, considered the Italian alliance a millstone, more a liability than an asset. Italy could not be trusted, this group thought; if Austria became involved in war, Italy would at once claim the "unredeemed areas" as the price of neutrality and if Austria were defeated in war Italy would surely pounce upon the coveted districts.

XIV

Count Kálnoky yielded up the direction of Hapsburg diplomacy in May of 1895. His health was poor but the immediate cause of his resignation was a quarrel with the Hungarian government. Kálnoky holds an honorable place on the roll of Austrian foreign ministers; for fourteen years he had presided at the Ballplatz, longer than any of his successors or any of his predecessors, in fact, since Prince Metternich. In an era of stress and storm, when relations with Russia were recurrently critical, he managed to hold the Hapsburg ship of state off the rocks of war; if relations with Rumania, and less so with Serbia, had deteriorated, that should be charged up primarily to the growing nationalism in those two powerlets and Austrian resistance to it. Bulgaria and Greece, on the other hand, had been drawn closer to Vienna, and, except for minor disputes, relations with Turkey were reasonably tranquil; the unhappy memory of the occupation of Bosnia had dimmed somewhat.

The bonds of common interest with Germany had been tightened, and Austrian diplomatic calculations almost always revolved round the alliance with Germany. But the alliance with Italy, never really popular in either country, was exhibiting marked evidence of decay. Moreover, Austria's traditional reliance upon Britain in the Near East was slackening visibly, the inescapable sequel to the growing British antagonism with Germany. Britain's coolness was not due to the fact that London loved Austria less, but because it feared Germany more.

As the new chief of the foreign office Francis Joseph appointed the Pole, Count Agenor Goluchowski, a choice that occasioned considerable surprise. Yet his family was reputed to be one of the most faithful to the Hapsburgs in the Polish aristocracy and his father had been a respected figure in Galician and imperial politics. A protégé of Kálnoky's, who recommended him as foreign secretary, Goluchowski had been in the Hapsburg diplomatic service for years without attracting particular attention; his most responsible post had been that of minister to Rumania. Jovial, easy-going, Goluchowski scarcely qualified as a first-class diplomatist; but he was a master in the art of making awkward situations look pleasant, however much his facile optimism was belied by cold facts.

The change in the Austrian foreign office represented a shift merely in personalities, not of policies. Owing to the critical domestic situation in the two halves of the Monarchy, if not for other reasons, the paramount objective of Hapsburg diplomacy was to work for the maintenance of European peace. Caution, passivity, conservatism, safety first, last, and always were the guiding rules of the Ballplatz during the Goluchowski period: eschew all thought of expansion, hold fast to the Triplice, improve relations with Russia, if that were possible without sacrifice of Balkan interests, keep the Ottoman empire intact as long as possible. Those were the specifics of Viennese international policy until the autumn of 1906, when Count Alois Aehrenthal became foreign secretary and admitted fresh, intoxicating currents into the musty chambers of the Ballplatz.

CHAPTER THIRTEEN

AUSTRIA: *KULTUR UND STURM*
1893-1899

IN THE HAPSBURG REALM OF PEOPLES, MANY NOTABLE CITIES abounded, the chief of them the focal points of the political and cultural affairs of a nationality: Budapest for the Magyars, Prague for the Czechs, Cracow and Lemberg for the Poles and Ruthenians, Laibach for the Slovenes, Agram for the Croats. But supreme above them all, German in tradition, extremely cosmopolitan in population, unique among the major metropolises of the world, was the ancient seat of the Hapsburg dynasty, the *Kaiserstadt,* Vienna. Nature herself intended that a great city should arise at precisely the place where Vienna stands, at the point where trade routes from the north crossed the Danube on their leisurely way to the Adriatic; Vienna's basin, in fact, is the only break in a continuous mountain chain extending from the Gulf of Liguria to the Black Sea. Here was a veritable meeting place of peoples, the crossroads of European humanity. For south central Europe and the East as far as Asia Minor, Vienna was the capital of Western civilization; for the Westerner it was the gateway to the East.

Haughtily, though not untruthfully, Prince Metternich once remarked: "Asia begins on the Rennweg," the thoroughfare leading from Vienna toward Hungary. To that relatively backward East, Vienna imparted in the latest age, as it had done historically, some part of the civilization of the West, and Vienna's own character responded to influences coming in from the East and the South. Vienna was the capital of finance and banking, of commerce and insurance, of fashions and gaiety, and of culture, not alone for the Danube Monarchy but for southeastern Europe as well. It served as the exchange mart between the industrialized area of central Europe and the agrarian regions of the lower Danube; Vienna's own inexpensive manu-factures found markets among the Balkan peasantry; her families supplied organizers and managers for finance and trade, and her university and spe-cialized technical institutes sent forth men trained in all lines of human ac-tivity. And as the political capital of the polyglot Hapsburg Monarchy, Vienna was the headquarters of the court and the aristocracy, of the vast bureaucracy, of the police, of the fighting services, and of diplomacy.

Marching with the times, Vienna had expanded beyond the limits with which the European peacemakers of 1815 had been familiar. Medieval ram-parts that encircled the Altstadt, or inner city, were razed (1858–1860), making possible the magnificent Ringstrasse, one hundred fifty feet broad, two miles in length, with fine trees and monumental edifices along its course, one of the noblest boulevards known to man and the distinctive glory of Vienna. The Danube was spanned in the seventies by new bridges and regulated so as to remove the peril of floods and to improve the value of the river commercially; hundreds of acres of ground were reclaimed for building purposes by this engineering feat.[1]

A generation later, the demolition of the outer girdle of fortifications brought suburban districts, some residential, some industrial, into the mu-nicipality. Parks, woods, and farmland covered about three-quarters of the Vienna area; no other city of comparable size boasted such varied environs, such extensive tracts of forests and lofty mountains at its very gates. In 1869 the population of the city and suburbs stood at 842,951; by 1890 it had risen to 1,341,900, and by 1910 to 2,031,498.

Vienna teemed with magnificent secular structures and shrines of divine worship. Grandest of all was the Gothic Cathedral of St. Stephen, which was started in the twelfth century and completed in the Renaissance period. The soaring spire, the lofty choir of purest Gothic, the fretted network of the vaulted roof, the splendid stained glass in its traceried windows, the sculp-tured pillars, marble altars, and a profusion of statuary—all these made St. Stephen's the architectural masterpiece of Austrian Catholicism, the wonder and amazement of worshipers and of the casual visitor. Not far away was the dull and cumbrous pile of the Hofburg, the city residence of the Hapsburg family, an array of buildings, diverse in age and design, several of them in the favorite style of medieval urban architecture, and enclosing spacious courtyards.

Vienna's baroque churches, monasteries, and sumptuous palaces of the aristocracy harked back to the early eighteenth century in the main. The newer city, the Vienna of the second half of the nineteenth century, con-tained a noble line of structures, varied in architecture and purpose, front-ing upon the Ring. There were the massive Opera House of the sixties, with tasteless interior ornamentation, the imperial museums of fine arts and natural history, in Renaissance style, twenty years in the building, and the law courts, which like Paris' Tuileries before it, were destroyed by mob violence, in 1927.

Farther along were the chaste parliament house, a fine replica of Greek architecture, the somber and huge Rathaus in Gothic, built on the very site where Turkish marauders two centuries before had raised redoubts and forts; and across the boulevard the Renaissance Burgtheater, once the leader in the dramatic art of German-speaking Europe. Toward the end of the Ring were the main building of the university, another Renaissance conception, and, finally the Votivkirche, erected on the spot where an assassin had tried to murder Emperor Francis Joseph and commemorating the monarch's escape.

Business establishments were largely concentrated in the inner city, world-famous for fashionable shops, and in the Leopoldstadt, the Jewish quarter; manufacturing was carried on in the districts lying round the core of the old city. Well-to-do families lived mainly in the suburbs, a few of them in individual dwellings; but the bulk of the Viennese population was crowded into the metropolis proper. Congestion and associated evils were the perpetual bane of Vienna and a perpetual challenge to the municipal administration.

Houses for the mass of the Viennese were generally large structures, four to six stories in height, built almost entirely of stone or brick, and furnishing quarters for a dozen families or more. It was officially reported in 1872 that in one sordid tenement sixty-three persons were crowded into three rooms, while 104 lived in six rooms; an investigator discovered thirteen workers of both sexes "in the garret of a small house, twelve paces long and eight paces wide; an old man had his quarters in a remote corner, among the rubbish, for which he paid 1.20 florins [about 48 cents] a week." To relieve the fearful overcrowding, the construction of residential structures was promoted by tax exemption for as long as thirty years and by other concessions; yet building failed to keep pace with the enlarging population.

Housing deficiencies profoundly molded the social habits of the Viennese. For the poor and the *petite bourgeoisie* the coffeehouse, the inexpensive restaurant, the public gardens, the spacious Prater, and the woodlands encircling the city were substitutes for the home as places of relaxation and diversion; cheap streetcar fares, which came into vogue in the nineties, enabled families "to get into the country" with comparative ease.

Costs of living in Vienna generally exceeded those anywhere else on the continent; indeed, except for clothing, the necessities of life were probably as expensive as in the United States, where wages, of course, were much higher. For the working classes a typical breakfast consisted of a bowl of gruel, a roll or dry bread, and a substitute for coffee; for dinner, soup and vegetables, rye bread, pork two or three times a week, on holidays beef boiled in the soup; and for supper, bread, a piece of sausage, and beer. A report of 1891 revealed that even skilled artisans earned less than was necessary to maintain ordinary standards of decency for a family; household budgets were normally balanced by the earnings of the wife and children. The rate of illegitimacy was comparatively high.

Despite the harsh conditions of existence, the workers of Vienna displayed an interest in culture, not always discernible in their counterparts elsewhere. "I have conversed with many Viennese workingmen," reported the secretary of the British legation in 1869, "who appeared to be thoroughly acquainted with all the classics of German literature and had highly intelligent judgments of their respective merits. I fancy that on political and economic subjects the Viennese is more poorly informed than the British. His daily life is influenced by refining drama and music." Drunkenness, the Briton commented, was rare, habitual intoxication rarer still.[2]

Natural increase in population by no means accounted for the congestion in Vienna. Much more important was the magnetic attraction which the capital had for inhabitants of all the provinces of the realm and peoples in countries to the east. Only a trifle more than half the population in the twentieth century was Viennese by birth. It has been fairly remarked that only on Constantinople's Pera bridge could one observe such an intermingling of nationalities or hear such a babel of tongues as at the favorite rendezvous spot of Vienna, in front of the Opera House. With a bit of exaggeration a reporter once described the diversified character of the population of Vienna in these words: "Swamped for long centuries by the Slavs, the Magyars, and the Italians, this town, they say, has no longer a drop of pure German blood. You find at Vienna a Bohemian theatre as at Prague, an Italian opera, French and Hungarian singers, Polish clubs; in the omnibus it is sometimes impossible to exchange a word, since nobody understands German; in some of the cafés there are Hungarian, Czech, Slav, Polish, Italian journals and not a single German newspaper. If you have not lived long in Vienna, you may still be a German of pure breed, but your wife will be a Galician or a Pole, your cook a Bohemian, your nursemaid an Istriote or a Dalmatian, your valet a Serb, your coachman a Slav, your barber a Magyar, and your tutor a Frenchman . . . No, Vienna is not a German town."[3]

Cosmopolitanism and a climate conducive to languor contributed to Vienna's peculiar social and cultural atmosphere, much dwelt upon by writers who delight in the romantic and the sentimental, and for whom the darker side of mass living had small appeal. The joviality, the amiability, the politeness, the gay good humor, the easy-going tempo, the willingness "to drift lazily down the stream of life with as much enjoyment and as little trouble as possible," the fatalistic nonchalance, the lack of energy of the

Viennese, always dreaming and seldom achieving, these traits possess the prestige of proverbs and therewith all the virtue and vice of proverbs.[4]

Withal the Viennese exhibited fond affection for and deep pride in their city. Berlin, which replaced Vienna as the largest German-speaking city, was looked upon as a parvenu, pushing and crude. The popular estimate of the Prussian capital was frozen into a merry jingle:

> Es gibt nur eine Kaiserstadt,
> Es gibt nur ein Wien;
> Es gibt nur ein Räubernest,
> Und das heisst Berlin.

Dislike of Berlin extended even to the culinary art as there practiced. Viennese skill in pastry cooking inspired the contemptuous description of a Prussian blancmange as "something that they call a sweet in Berlin, but that we use for paperhanging in Vienna."

Like many another metropolis, more so perhaps than most, Vienna cherished quaint customs of its own. After ten in the evening, for instance, dwellings were bolted and barred, and the porter exacted a small gratuity from every person entering or leaving; in restaurants, servants were tipped in precise proportions: the food waiter, the wine waiter, and the bill bearer. Patrons of coffeehouses (and each Viennese had his favorite coffeehouse), lingered for hours, reading newspapers, sipping coffee or water—the waiter kept two glasses of water always before a guest; orchestras entertained with popular melodies and light tunes. Singing clubs and bands in public gardens brought merriment to living; all that was part of the Austrian tradition of music everywhere, the peasant's yodel in the Styrian Alps, the zither in the wayside inns; and well-presented anthems in churches were often rewarded with cries of "Bravo" and handclapping.

II

After the revolution of 1848, a city council and the mayor selected by it were given extensive authority over the business of the Vienna municipality. Most of the councilmen were elected on a three-class system, arranged in keeping with taxes paid, and nontaxpayers shared with the rest in choosing a fourth section of the lawmakers. Before assuming the office the mayor had to have the formal approval of the emperor.

Up to the nineties, German Liberals dominated Vienna politics, but in that decade they were crowded aside by the militant and exuberant Christian Socialists, marshaled by Karl Lueger. At the municipal balloting in April of 1895, the Christian Socialists and a small Pan-German party captured more seats than the Liberals for the first time. Christian Socialist battle cries of religious intolerance, destruction to Jewry, and war to the knife on "big business" netted astonishing results; party chiefs in the campaigning promised that if they were victorious at the polls many types of business enterprise would be taken over by the municipality and that middlemen would be squeezed out of commerce. By a political stratagem the Liberals put Lueger in the office of mayor in 1895, in the belief apparently that his party if given enough rope would hang itself. On the assumption that another election would bring his party a clear majority, Lueger dissolved the council and ordered a second balloting.

In the electioneering, street demonstrations and mass meetings against Jewry whipped up great popular ferment; but for the excellent discipline of the police, backed by garrisons of army troops, grave disorders might have resulted. The outcome of the voting confirmed the Christian Socialist prognostications and Lueger was chosen mayor by his own followers. It was feared in some quarters that foreign capital would take wings, for every capitalist was regarded by Lueger's party with unfriendly, suspicious eyes, as a thief who would despoil Vienna and the Viennese and make off with his ill-gotten gains.

Furious attacks during the campaigning had been delivered against foreign-owned concerns in Vienna, public utilities especially; foreign wheat merchants who frequented the international grain market in Vienna were subjected to public and private insult, so that attendance fell off sharply, and in 1896 the market was actually transferred to Budapest. Recurrent panics on the stock market—one in November 1895 was the worst since the dark year of 1873—had damaging effects upon the financial and commercial health of the community. Besides, wealthy Jews threatened to move to Hungary, and the Jewish element, dreading violence after the Christian Socialist victory at the polls, lived in a state of panic, until assured by Francis Joseph that he would protect all his subjects, regardless of creed or tradition.

In view of all this, influential German Liberals besought the Austrian premier, Badeni, to advise the emperor not to confirm Lueger as mayor. Spokesmen for Hungary, incensed by Christian Socialist criticism, likewise urged Francis Joseph to veto Lueger's election. Anxious to conciliate the Magyars on the eve of the renewal of the Austro-Hungarian economic accords—the negotiation of which promised to be sufficiently difficult as matters stood—Francis Joseph denied Lueger the mayoralty and approved the nomination of an imperial commissioner in his stead. Whereupon fanatical anti-Semites nicknamed the ruler the *Judenkaiser*.

Another municipal election produced another Christian Socialist triumph and the reëlection of "Handsome Karl" as mayor, but once more he was refused imperial confirmation. Again in February 1896, the popular electoral verdict went to the Christian Socialists and for the fourth time Lueger was selected to preside over Vienna. Lueger's personal appeal had much to do with the repeated victories of his party, but even stronger, no doubt, were fervent, demagogic outcries against Jewry and big business, and appeals to the "little man" and to Catholic workers. Intellectuals by and large were hostile to Christian Socialism and so were the socialistically inclined wage-workers, but because of the inequitable electoral law their influence bore no exact relation to their numbers. At the personal request of Francis Joseph, Lueger, after his fourth election, accepted the post of vice-mayor.

For a fifth time, in April 1897, Lueger was elected Bürgermeister and at last the emperor reluctantly consented to confirm him. Promptly the Council revised the municipal franchise laws, so as to enlarge the voting strength of the poorer classes and to diminish the relative power of the well-to-do German Liberals. Reëlected in 1903 and again in 1909, Lueger was also active in the provincial diet and in the Austrian parliament, and more than once he was seriously considered for the premiership. In season and out Lueger fought for the interests of the "little man" and of the church, battled against the Social Democrats and Magyar influence in the common affairs of the Monarchy, and wholeheartedly supported the closest diplomatic intimacy with imperial Germany.

Lueger's popularity attained such proportions that he was called "the uncrowned king of Vienna." Incorruptibly honest, though frequently less than wise or tactful in his remarks, effervescently cheerful, physically attractive, Lueger displayed traits as a politician that would have served him in good stead in any democratic country. He was a past master at handshaking, acted as godfather whenever invited, attended golden-wedding anniversaries (much-feted affairs in Austria), visited the sick, and courted the friendship of children.

For Magyars and Social Democrats, Lueger's aversion showed no lessening with the passing of time. When Nicholas II of Russia stopped at Vienna in 1903 (and bestowed a decoration on the mayor), Lueger railed against the Socialists for protesting the visit and tactlessly reminded an audience that imperial Russia had crushed the rebellious Magyars in 1849. But his detestation for Jewry declined and since he counted several Jews among his friends—"I myself decide who is a Jew," he is said to have remarked—it was rumored that he had never entertained very deep anti-Jewish convictions. He was the idol and hero of a large share of the population of Vienna; his death in 1910 evoked almost universal mourning and his funeral was the most remarkable the old city had ever witnessed. Watching the procession was a young Austrian provincial, Adolf Hitler, who had recently drifted to Vienna. In his autobiography, Hitler lauded Lueger as "the greatest German mayor of all times," and "the last great German whom the ranks of the colonizing people of the 'Ostmark' brought forth . . . a statesman greater than all the so-called 'diplomats' of that period put together."[5]

With Lueger at the helm, Vienna embarked upon a program of municipal socialization and civic betterment intended to benefit the common man and to free him from the clutches of monopolistic capitalism. "Everything that we do, we do for the people, with the people, and through the people," the mayor was wont to say. Municipal ownership of public utilities appealed strongly to the Christian Socialists. For half a century gas had been supplied to Vienna by an English firm, the Continental Gas Company; to crowd the company to the wall, a municipal gas plant was built, and eventually the city purchased the facilities of the foreign concern. Transportation lines in Vienna, electric-power plants, and the water system were gradually bought up by the municipality and rates were lowered.

Among other noteworthy accomplishments of the Christian Socialist administration were improvement or extension of bridges and canals, enlargement of schools and playgrounds, public gardens and parks, orphanages and hospitals; school children of poor families were furnished milk and food. Under municipal auspices a wide variety of welfare services were provided: public markets, a slaughter house, an unemployment bureau, an insurance company, savings banks, and homes for municipal servants. The cost of funerals was cut to a minimum figure by means of municipal funeral homes and city-owned burial grounds. In the large central cemetery, the most conspicuous monument was Lueger's mausoleum, a symbol perhaps of the "welfare city" he had so energetically sponsored.

Christian Socialism understood the publicity value of circuses as well as bread. National festivals were celebrated with lavish splendor and the cellars of the city hall were converted into an attractive rathskeller, where only Austrian (not Hungarian) wines were dispensed. All in all, Lueger's administration considerably altered the physical appearance of Vienna and put into operation social-welfare reforms unsurpassed in any other city. Necessarily, "municipal socialism" involved large financial outlays, unbalancing the budget for a time, but in the long run the public services seem to have netted profits and taxation was not increased.

III

In imperial Vienna, the arts of culture and the pleasures of the mind and the finer emotions were assiduously cultivated. Talent in literature, in music, in painting, and in scholarship was diversified, abundant, and steadily replenished by newcomers attracted to the capital as by a magnet. Here we can comment on only a few of the artists and men and women of learning who reinforced the reputation of Vienna as a capital of civilized living. Some Austro-Germans not Viennese also merit mention in this connection.

Austro-German literature diverged from that of Germany proper owing to environmental differences and to the peculiarly cosmopolitan complexion of Vienna. For a generation or so Austro-German letters were dominated by a literary circle called "Young Vienna" which was much influenced by Western literary tendencies; its principal personalities were Hermann Bahr, Hugo von Hofmannsthal, and Arthur Schnitzler.

Bahr had one of the most versatile and kaleidoscopic careers in modern literature. A moderate Socialist in his youth, he became successively an atheist, a Pan-German, a realist, a symbolist, a Liberal, and a Clerical, dying a convinced monarchist and Catholic, all of which was reflected in his voluminous writings. In the prime of life Bahr was respected as the foremost literary critic writing in the German language, being specially liked for smart epigrams and wide knowledge, but he soon fell out of public esteem and was almost forgotten. *The Renaissance* (1897) is a typical specimen of Bahr's writing, and *The Apostle* is his most popular drama.

Distinguished as a writer of lyric verse and as a playwright, Hofmannsthal personified rather well the closing chapter in the history of Hapsburg culture. A member of a well-to-do Jewish family, he earned the doctorate in Romance philology at the University of Vienna. He learned much from Hugo, Swinburne, and D'Annunzio and was tremendously interested in pathological phenomena, which imparted to much of his writing a repulsively morbid quality. He succeeded remarkably well in capturing and distilling the peculiar qualities of Vienna and his compositions were notable for vivid and subtle beauty, for richness and melody in vocabulary. A writer of neorealistic drama—*Death and the Fool*—Hofmannsthal also collaborated with his friend Richard Strauss, supplying the libretto for *Elektra* and *The Rose Cavalier,* and in the last phase of his career he composed society comedy and mystery plays. He had a swarm of imitators in Vienna.

For his starkly realistic short stories Schnitzler has been called the Maupassant of German letters; his novels and plays savor of Ibsen and earned him a place alongside of Sudermann. A brilliant analyst of character and of mental and emotional aberrations, he wrote charmingly and sardonically on the master themes of life and death. Skepticism, nihilism, aesthetic epicureanism, unconventionality, lust for the pleasurable, pervaded Schnitzler's thinking and writing. His personality and his productions rather faithfully reflected the mental outlook, the *Weltanschauung,* of cultivated society in the Vienna of the early twentieth century. "Schnitzler sang the swan song of old Vienna," one of his biographers has said. "He caught in his gentle hand the last golden glow of its setting glory and converted it into art." [6] Schnitzler's imitators, like Hofmannsthal's, were legion and unimportant.

Nothing more exalted than the quest for purely personal happiness, untrammeled by inherited conventions, was the aim in life of many of the characters that Schnitzler created. Squeeze the best out of living while you may, abjure ambitious struggling for power and pelf, leave the future to whatever gods there be, were recurrent themes in his writing. Dithering dilettantism mixed with unorthodox romance make existence tolerable and satisfying, he taught. Viennese society, as Schnitzler knew and understood it, he depicted in the semiautobiographical *The Road to Freedom;* therein were described members of the lower aristocracy and the upper *bourgeoisie,* "lounge lizards" who knew no material cares, and carefree pretty girls concerned only with gratifying their inborn passions.

Subjected himself as a Jew to the slings and arrows of Jew-baiters, Schnitzler handled the Jewish problem with penetration and calmness in *Professor Bernhardi.* As an alien minority with ineradicable peculiarities, Jewry, he thought, could not escape the vicissitudes common to minorities: suspicion, ill will, hatred. Philosophical idealism could not smooth out the tensions, and the individual Jew should manage as best he could in an insoluble situation. Although he was the friend of Theodor Herzl, the Zionist apostle, and paid warm tribute to his memory, Schnitzler balked at committing himself to the Zionist formula for the salvation of Jewry.

Fine insight into men and manners distinguished the writing of Ferdinand von Saar, who composed short stories, poetic tragedies, and lyrical verse.[7] Sometime an army officer, Saar was especially interested in the Austrian military caste and its ideals, but he also dealt with aristocrats who mourned the passing of the good old days and of craftsmen and merchants whose conventional way of life had been disrupted by the intrusion of machine industry. Teachings of defeatism and of mute resignation to the inescapable permeated productions of Saar, of which *Tales of Austria* and *Vienna Elegies* were most popular. The environment and traditions of Vienna were sketched by Edward Pötzl in *feuilletons* for the press, which were subsequently collected in a row of volumes.

Provincial Austria, as well as Vienna, attracted the attention of German men of letters, who depicted the joys and cares of rural existence and the sharpening strife between contending nationalities. Peasant living had an especially entertaining and brilliant expositor in Ludwig Anzengruber, son of a minor Viennese official and perhaps the most accomplished playwright of very modern Austria. His own career was far from happy, for it was marred by cruel disappointments as he struggled for fame as an artist, an actor, and a dramatist. For years Anzengruber led a tantalizing hand-to-mouth existence, not all dross, however, for he picked up ideas and information which, when woven into literature, earned him an honored niche in the republic of Austrian letters.

Acrid criticism of petty human prejudices, ardent anticlericalism, and keen-eyed rustic realism were conspicuous in the thinking and writings of Anzengruber. His *The Priest of Kirchfeld* (1870) owed something of its immense popularity to the contemporary interest in religious questions, excited by the anticlerical ferment of the hour; therein he realistically described the mind and customs of Austrian villagers. Central in the drama was an unconventional Tyrolese priest, who preached compassion for all men, without reference to religious or class distinctions. His intolerance of intolerance, his struggle to surmount his own inner frailties, his approval of the liberalization of the church laws earned him the affection of his parishioners. Not so, however, the local nobleman, for whom any change spelled disaster, and a villager who hated church and priest for refusing to solemnize his marriage to a Protestant; poisonous rumors of the cleric's illicit love spread by the vindictive peasant (to his remorse later) caused the church authorities to unfrock the good priest. Anzengruber's clerical hero made a triumphant appeal to Austrian "liberalism."

The Star Stone Court (1884) was, no doubt, the most popular of Anzengruber's many novels and tales. Here was depicted a village maid, extremely poor, extremely glamorous, extremely unscrupulous. Her consuming ambition was to become the mistress of the rich "court" or farm, a goal she attained by marrying the heir to the estate, a weak and simple-minded fellow. Death in war removed the husband and the erstwhile beggar watched her inherited property flourish abundantly. Gross vice and earthy passion were pictured alongside of rare human self-denial; lesser characters were charmingly portrayed and the story abounded with rich and faithful descriptions of rustic Austrian folkways.

Written with much bucolic humor and moving pathos, Anzengruber's works were intended to enlighten and uplift the peasantry, to lead them into ways of broad-mindedness and humanity. Gifted with rare insight into the peasant mentality, Anzengruber succeeded admirably in imparting his understanding to readers.

A disciple of Anzengruber, Peter K. Rosegger, interpreted the humble folk and the countryside of his native Styria in short tales and novels. Rosegger, who as a youth had been a shepherd, deplored the progress of industrialism and of the moneyed bourgeoisie, which was having ruinous consequences for the sturdy yeomanry. *Papers of a Schoolmaster* (1875) presented a somewhat sentimentalized picture of the rustic way of life and exhibited the personal emotions of the author better than the social realities. Rosegger's views as a freethinker were reflected in *The God-Seeker,* the story of a gross religious crime on the eve of the Reformation, in which the ancient pagan heritage of the Styrian Alps was sympathetically and beautifully portrayed.

Not less successful in the depiction of simple Styrian ways was Rudolph Hans Bartsch, who, disgusted with metropolitan Vienna, extolled the humble peasant, the Austro-German peasant. *Twelve from Styria,* a characteristic piece, was written with fervor and in a highly florid fashion. Otto Hauser in his *1848* depicted the German-speaking populace locked in mortal combat with their South Slav fellows.

The provincial tale in the Tyrol had its most perfect expression in the work of Adolf Pichler, a geologist by profession, the author of *Tales of the Tyrol,* and of Karl Schönherr, who mingled quaint sentimentality with ruthless realism after the manner of Anzengruber. One of his comedies, *The Earth,* was focused upon a peasant custom that regarded the father as master of the household until the eldest son married and took over authority. *Belief and Home,* which was almost a tract for religious tolerance, was set in the era of the Reformation when Tyrolese Protestants were commanded to abjure the new religious teaching or be expelled from their homes. But many peasants chose to perish rather than give up Luther's Bible.

For the soil and towns of Galicia there were the warm and moving *Galician Tales* and *Jewish Tales* of Count Leopold von Sacher-Masoch, who was spoken of as the Galician Turgenev. The leading poet of the ghetto was K. E. Franzos, a Jew with a Western outlook, who extolled the superiority of German culture over Polish.

Folkways among the Germans of Bohemia were gracefully presented in the novels of Adalbert Stifter. His *Indian Summer* was judged by some critics to be one of the most beautiful pieces of prose in the German language, and *Witiko,* a leisurely historical romance, was much prized. The work of a native of the Bohemian forest and a devout Catholic, Stifter's fiction reflected the sobriety and simplicity of his environment and the certitudes of his religion; trivial, everyday commonplaces were etched into a background of highland forest and lowland heath. As documents of social history the writings of Stifter have unique value.

Out of Bohemia, too, came one of the most powerful pacifist tracts of the century, Baroness Bertha Suttner's *Lay Down Your Arms* (1889), which was in the form of a German nobleman's journal and recounted in vivid and realistic language the personal experiences and tragic sufferings of one who lived through the wars of German unification. It is indeed a long sermon on the kind of pacifism that rested its case on ethical and humanitarian considerations. Suttner, whose father was a field marshal, was the first president of the Austrian peace society, editor of a pacifist magazine, and Nobel prize winner. Among others whom she befriended was Alfred H. Fried, a tireless and persuasive preacher of international peace in German Europe.[8]

IV

Austro-German contributions to exact scholarship may first of all be illustrated by the historians of distinction. A landmark in Austrian scientific historiography was the founding of the Historical Institute at the

University of Vienna in 1855 by the Tyrolese scholar, A. Jager. Theodor Sickl, who followed him as director in 1869, devoted himself to discovering and editing medieval documents from Austrian and Italian sources. From his seminar and that of Fickler at Innsbruck, a specialist in medieval law and institutions, emerged a set of top-rank historical investigators, some of whom moved on to Germany.

At the time that the Historical Institute was starting its memorable career, the Austrian government relaxed the censorship and adopted a more generous policy with regard to the study of the rich manuscript resources concentrated in Vienna. A pioneer in applying the scientific approach to the study of the past was Alfred Arneth,[9] who as custodian of the imperial archives after 1868 had a unique opportunity to exploit original state documents. Already he had eulogized the House of Hapsburg in an elaborate biography of Prince Eugene of Savoy (3 vols., 1858), the dashing cavalier of the eighteenth century who had done so much to revive the drooping prestige of the imperial dynasty. In ten weighty volumes, the *History of Maria Theresa* (1863–1879), Arneth presented a vast array of original materials loosely strung together; much less a biography of the energetic empress than an encyclopedia of her times, this monumental work is indispensable for an understanding of the politics of Europe in the eighteenth century. Into it was woven an illuminating portrait of Emperor Joseph II, a man whose broad outlook was congenial to Arneth's own moderately liberal convictions. As an archivist, Arneth introduced methods that were copied in other historical treasure houses, and his innovations were perpetuated in Vienna by a line of admirable successors in the office of director of the state records.

Overshadowed though they were by historians in Germany, Austro-German scholars added not insignificantly to the stock of historical learning. A *History of Italy in the Middle Ages,* by Ludo M. Hartmann, dealt in an enlightening manner with economic and social affairs, and skillfully revealed the important impact of medieval Italy upon German life. In dramatic prose, Heinrich Kretschmayer composed a *History of Venice,* which adequately emphasized the economic and cultural evolution of the "Queen of the Adriatic." Ludwig von Pastor's massive *History of the Popes* cast fresh light on the Reformation era from the inexhaustible resources of the Vatican library; though sympathetic to the papacy, it was a singularly balanced study, and an invaluable one. Onno Klopp in studies on the seventeenth century vigorously defended the politics of the Hapsburgs in the early phases of the Thirty Years' War; his *History of the Fall of the House of Stuart* displayed greater erudition on continental affairs than on England. Francis Krones, in a *Handbook of Austrian History,* broke new ground by showing the influence of geography and ethnic factors upon political development, and August Fournier's elaborate and stylistically appealing study of Napoleon promises to be permanently useful. Czech-born Joseph K. Jireček studied the medieval history of the Bulgars and Serbs, preparing volumes which have not yet been superseded in their entirety. For the nineteenth century there was a solid and brilliant analysis of the duel for mastery in German Europe, *The Struggle for Supremacy in Germany, 1859–1866,* by Heinrich Friedjung, half historian, half publicist, who patriotically, if indiscreetly, lent his name and fame to the secular intrigues of the Austrian foreign office.

In no sphere of thought were Austrians more conspicuous than in economics. A group of theoreticians gave the name of their country to a body of doctrine, which enlisted exponents elsewhere, most prominently perhaps in the United States. Emerging in the seventies, the Austrian school of economics represented at once an attempt to reconstruct "Manchester" economics and a revolt against the "historical" school, then in the ascendant in German universities. In their thinking, Austrian economists took the principle of value as basic and reasoned that the explanation of the problem of value was to be found in the idea of final utility; as that concept was explained by Eugene Böhm-Bawerk, best-known member of the group, "the enjoyment derived from the least enjoyable unit is what we understand by final utility."

The actual founder of the school was Carl Menger, a graduate of Cracow University, who moved to Vienna as a civil servant. His book, *Foundations of Economic Doctrine* (1871), was the original treatise of the Austrian school, and he followed it up with other works defending his conclusions against critics. Besides holding a chair in economics at Vienna University, Menger was private tutor and traveling companion to Crown Prince Rudolph and in 1900 he was named a life member of the Austrian upper house. Böhm-Bawerk and Friedrich von Weiser combined theoretical studies on economics in the university with fruitful careers as public servants; on several occasions Böhm-Bawerk was head of the Austrian finance ministry.

The last of the band, Eugene von Philippovitch, who concerned himself principally with urgent problems of social reform, believed strongly in a state-regulated economic regime and was adamantly opposed to unrestrained capitalism. For almost half a century the ideas of the Austrian economists exerted wide influence on economic thought, but by 1914 the group had practically ceased to exist as an independent school.[10]

Alongside of the Austrian school of economics an effort was made to establish an Austrian school of sociology under the leadership of the tough-minded and pugnacious Ludwig Gumplowicz. Born a Polish Jew, Gumplowicz drifted to the University of Graz, where he expounded a personalized version of social Darwinianism, finding the key to the development of society in the ceaseless struggle between social groups. In that strife, he held, a dominant minority, the fittest to survive, had invariably gained the ascendancy, and no political changes whatsoever could alter this iron law of sociology. The idea of international coöperation Gumplowicz brushed aside as the wishful imagining of the ignorant. His studies on the origins of "race" and the family yielded doctrines that were eagerly taken up by admirers in Austria and beyond, but their influence was ephemeral.

Among other Austrian savants of European stature were Francis Brentano, who endeavored to reconcile the philosophy of Aristotle with the "positivism" of August Comte; Sigmund Freud, pathfinder in psychoanalysis; Constant Wurzbach, editor of a learned biographical dictionary of Austria, running into sixty volumes; and Richard Heinzel, distinguished student of German philology. In legal studies the most productive Austrian scholars were Rudolph von Ihering and Joseph Unger, who, like the eminent Austrian authority on international law, Heinrich Lammasch, combined a teaching career with active participation in public affairs.

The University of Vienna was not only the intellectual stronghold of the Hapsburg Monarchy but one of the most renowned institutions of the higher learning in the world.[11] Founded in 1365, on the model of the University of Paris, the Vienna institution was originally assigned quarters near the ducal castle. Foreign scholars and students flocked to the university from all over Europe and within a century after its establishment between five and seven thousand learners were listening to lecturers. War and political confusion long retarded growth, but a genuine revival set in at the middle of the nineteenth century. A new building for the university was erected in the eighties on the Ring. This structure in the form of a square was built round a spacious court, whose colonnaded corridors were adorned with busts and tablets commemorative of the university's ablest men of learning; scientific collections and laboratories were concentrated nearby. At the end of the century fully six thousand students, half of them in the faculty of law, were in attendance; except in the medical school, students from foreign countries were not numerous, partly because of the relatively high cost of living in Vienna.

It was in the realm of medicine and in the seventies and eighties that Vienna stood supreme among universities. That reputation resulted from the talented men of science, teachers and explorers in the wilderness of the unknown, the variety of the courses that they offered, and the unusually excellent clinical facilities that Vienna afforded. Most distinguished, perhaps, was Theodor Billroth, who performed a famous operation on the stomach for cancer and generally advanced antiseptic surgery. As the foremost surgeon of his time, Billroth was much in demand as a consultant, was the recipient of many official decorations, and was honored with a seat in the Austrian upper house.

Among the other world-famed members of the Vienna medical faculty were the anatomists, Joseph Hyrtl, the teacher of almost all the other comparative anatomists of Austria, Carl Rokitansky, one of the founders of modern pathological anatomy, Emil Zuckerkandl, and Theodore Meynert, possibly the foremost brain anatomist; Joseph Škoda, great diagnostician; Carl Gussenbauer, Billroth's most accomplished pupil; Ferdinand Hebra and Isidor Neumann, pioneers in modern dermatology; Ernst Brücke, who was in charge of the famous Vienna institute of physiology; John Oppolzer and Hermann Nothnagel in internal medicine; Moritz Benedikt, neuropathologist and a founder of criminal anthropology; Julius Wagner-Jauregg, psychiatrist, who discovered that imbecility was sometimes caused by the abnormal functioning of the thyroid gland which could be cured by iodine salts, a discovery that brought him the Nobel prize. These were only the outstanding individuals in a large company of Viennese investigators, whose researches added richly to the stock of medical learning and practice.

Vienna had eminent representatives in other branches of science: in physics and mathematics, Ludwig Boltzmann and Ernst Mach, the latter noted for his contributions to philosophical materialism; Theodor Oppolzer in astronomy; Michael Haberlandt, botanist; Edward Suess, geologist and geographer; and Rudolph Pöch, who distinguished himself as a bacteriologist and then turned to anthropology. Only Berlin, among universities, surpassed Vienna in the quality of its faculties; and the institution heightened the fair fame of the imperial capital.

v

A distinguished line of composers and conductors upheld the reputation of Vienna in the world of music. Classical compositions reluctantly yielded pride of place to romanticism, so luxuriantly cultivated by Richard Wagner. As a disciple of Wagner, Anton Bruckner composed spacious, deeply romantic works, tinged with Catholic mysticism; no symphonist since Beethoven had been so lavishly acclaimed as Bruckner. His pupil, Gustav Mahler, carried the romantic tradition forward and for a decade was conductor of the Vienna Opera, no doubt the highest honor open to a musician; Mahler trained eminent conductors, Bruno Frank and William Mengelberg among them, and eventually took charge of the Metropolitan Opera House in New York.

Called Schubert reborn and a warm admirer of Wagner, Hugo Wolf excelled in songs for voice and piano, while Johannes Brahms stood in apostolic succession to the celebrated Austrian masters of a century earlier. Though born in Hamburg, his productive years were spent largely in Vienna, where he enriched every musical form except opera. The classical purity of his symphonies repelled critics at first, but gradually he won favor and a secure place among the Viennese immortals. Richard Strauss, another émigré from Germany, consolidated his reputation with operas making extensive use of the Viennese waltz, as was vividly shown in *The Rose Cavalier* (1911).

Vienna reigned supreme in dance music and light opera, with Johann Strauss the younger, well-known composer of the "Beautiful Blue Danube" (1867), as the uncrowned king of the waltz. His *Die Fledermaus,* doubtless the most popular of all Viennese light operas, full of lilting dance melodies, expressed the charm and traits that are labeled "Viennese." Of the same order were the productions of Franz von Suppé, *Boccaccio* and *The Gascon;* of Karl Millöcker, *The Student Beggar;* and of Franz Lehár, a Hungarian émigré to Vienna, and composer of *The Merry Widow,* no doubt the most popular light opera ever written.

The other fine arts suffered in Austria from the competition of music, which absorbed so much of the available aesthetic talent. The leading painter was Hans Makart, who had no peer in Germany. A rebel against classical art, Makart tried to emulate Rubens by painting huge canvases, lavish in color and glowing with sensuous emotion. His drawing was defective, his execution careless, his materials of inferior quality, and he was guilty of glaring anachronisms. For his subjects Makart chose historical and mythological episodes—"The Plague in Florence," "The Chase of the Amazons"—and he also painted landscapes and genre pieces.

Extremely popular, Makart reached the peak of his fame when he was authorized to arrange a grand pageant in 1879 to celebrate the silver-wedding anniversary of Francis Joseph and Elizabeth. For once he was able to give free rein to his florid imagination; fully fifteen thousand people participated in the pageant, wearing costumes of the Rubens and Rembrandt period which Makart had designed; the artist himself, a little man with dark beard and penetrating glance, was decked out in Velasquez finery, astride an enormous white horse. All Vienna mourned his death and soon forgot him, and his paintings faded almost as rapidly as his reputation.

Before Makart, Joseph von Führich, who specialized in religious painting for churches, had been the unquestioned artistic leader. Hans Canon, a pugnacious soul, a revolutionary fighter, and student of galleries from Madrid to St. Petersburg, established his reputation by painting scenes of the *nouveaux riches.* E. J. Schindler's charming portraits of Viennese landscapes imported French impressionistic ideas into central Europe. Distinguished for military scenes was August von Pettenkofen, himself a cavalry officer; he also reproduced on canvas the prosaic round of the yeoman of the Hungarian plain, and painted portraits of easygoing folk who took life pretty much as they found it. Rudolf von Alt was the chronicler with the brush of old Vienna, a landscape artist and a refined water colorist; the pride of his career was a decoration in St. Stephen's Cathedral.

At the end of the nineteenth century a set of young Viennese artists broke away from the Old Society of Artists and organized the Secessionist School, which gloried in freedom of expression, unrestrained individualism, and rebellion against tradition. The principal figure of the group was Gustav Klimt, who painted refined portraits, pleasing landscapes, and decorative pieces; of the last, the most admired were the ceiling paintings in the University of Vienna representing philosophy, medicine, and law. His portraits of women, "Nuda Veritas," for example, provoked sharp criticism from orthodox circles; nonetheless, Klimt was hailed as the leading Austrian painter of the time. Tyrolese yeomanry had faithful reproduction in the works of Albin Egger-Lienz, whose compositions, such as "Anno Neun," resemble those of the Frenchman Millet.

Sculptors raised monuments in Vienna to illustrious characters in the political and cultural history of the community. Anton Fernkorn, for instance, molded vigorous equestrian statues of Prince Eugene of Savoy and Archduke Charles, commander in a victory over Napoleon, for a courtyard of the Hofburg; Kaspar Zumbusch made statues of three Viennese favorites, Maria Theresa, Beethoven, and Field Marshal Radetzky; Victor Tilgner and Edmund von Hellmar carved chaste memorials to Mozart and to Goethe, respectively. Vienna's splendid new buildings of the late nineteenth century were the conceptions of a company of gifted architects: Fredrick Schmidt designed the Rathaus; Edward van der Null and August von Siccardsburg created the Opera House; Theophil Hansen, of Danish birth, who attained popularity first for buildings in the Byzantine style, turned to the classical model in designing the Austrian parliament building; Heinrich Ferstel was the architect of the University and the Votivkirche, and Karl Hasenauer designed the museums of art and natural history and the Burgtheater. These talented workmen made Vienna the city beautiful.

Vienna of the late nineteenth century, in sum, stood out as one of the noblest cities on the face of the globe. No matter what one's interest, whether business or finance, whether scholarship or music, whether the arts or the sciences, the old Hapsburg capital had accomplished representatives in that field, and the peculiarly cosmopolitan character of the Viennese population gave the city singular distinction and rare charm. Men of a later age looked back to the "old Vienna" with a deep feeling of nostalgia.

VI

From 1893 to 1896 Austrian domestic politics were dominated by the problem of franchise reform, which even submerged nationality squabblings momentarily. To replace the discredited Taaffe ministry, Francis Joseph selected a cabinet headed by Prince Alfred Windischgrätz, a wealthy high Tory and grandson of the field marshal who had helped to save the dynasty in 1848. He had the backing of the German Liberals, the Clerical Conservatives, and the Polish deputies; the strongest personality in the cabinet was the respected leader of the German Liberals, Dr. Ernst Plener, who managed the country's finances remarkably well.

In keeping with promises that had been given, the Windischgrätz ministry proposed to extend the suffrage privilege by allowing essentially all male workers to elect deputies to a new curia or "sphere," to be added to the four existing curiae, which would contain forty-five representatives. That project was indignantly rejected by advocates of thoroughgoing revision of the franchise laws, who wanted voting to be equal, direct, and universal. Spokesmen of the social Democratic party, with Viktor Adler in the lead, threatened to call a general strike of organized workmen to force real democratization of the suffrage. In October 1894, a gigantic workers' demonstration, perfectly orderly and unprecedented in size, was staged in Vienna; crowds paraded the streets with banners demanding equal voting rights and similar demonstrations took place under Socialist auspices in other populous centers. Christian Socialists, too, whipped up interest in electoral reform.

Replying to the popular agitation, Windischgrätz blandly declared that he would not be moved by "the arguments of the streets." Nonetheless, his ministry presented to the reichsrat a measure setting up a fifth curia, thirteen of whose deputies would be elected by insured wageworkers, the rest by all other citizens who paid a small tax.[12] Except for some support from German Liberals no party responded sympathetically to the proposal; Poles and Clericals disliked the measure because it was too radical, while the proponents of a truly democratic franchise condemned it because it did not go far enough. But before debate on the bill could be begun in parliament, the funeral bell was tolling for the Windischgrätz ministry.

It was a very insignificant school question, involving national interests, as usual, that wrecked the Windischgrätz coalition. For years Slovene intellectuals, backed by Clericals, had been demanding a Slovene gymnasium in the Styrian town of Cilli, but German Liberals contended that the German gymnasium there was perfectly adequate to meet all requirements. When the ministry authorized a Slovene gymnasium in the budget of 1895 as a concession to Slovene sentiments, the Liberal deputies withdrew their support from the cabinet, obliging Windischgrätz to resign. Much annoyed, Francis Joseph protested that the German Liberals by ruining their own ministry had reduced parliamentary government to an absurdity; he would select a cabinet that would be independent of fickle legislators.

Windischgrätz's ministry enacted laws that humanized the criminal code, restricting capital punishment, for example, to premeditated murder and attempts at regicide; it also took steps preparatory to the purchase by the state of the remaining private railways, extended the term of service in the *Landwehr,* and continued the state of siege in Prague, to which the Young Czech deputies responded with violent outbursts in parliament.

At the time that the Windischgrätz cabinet retired, imperial Austria was confronted by three delicate problems: reform of the suffrage, appeasement of the belligerent Young Czechs, and renewal of the decennial economic pact with Hungary. As he had warned, Francis Joseph picked a cabinet of officials, removed from the strife of party politics, and headed by Count Casimir Badeni, lately governor of Galicia; in that capacity Badeni by his vigorous and effective administration had won the sobriquet of "a strong man." Admirers touted him as a Hapsburg Bismarck, a title somewhat warranted by his aristocratic manners and physical resemblance to the Iron Chancellor. Badeni's fidelity during the Russian war scare of 1887–88 had endeared him to the Austrian High Command, which recommended his appointment as first minister against the advice of higher civil bureaucrats.

Of the affairs of Austria as a whole the new premier had small knowledge, and the empire had little knowledge of him. He seemed constitutionally averse to consulting public men who could have counseled him wisely on matters of which he was ignorant. Techniques of government that this self-confident Polish grandee had pursued successfully in Galicia simply would not work in Vienna, as Badeni quickly discovered. Since the new minister of finance was a Polish railway expert, Leon Bilinski, and the Ballplatz was presided over by Count Goluchowski, another Pole, Polish politicians held a commanding position in the affairs of the realm. Badeni's ill-starred policies soon made the name Pole more odious to German ears than ever it had been, though for a time German Liberals applauded the prime minister for declining to approve Lueger as mayor of Vienna.

The Badeni cabinet offered to parliament a new measure for the extension of the franchise right. In that bill the principle of manhood suffrage was engrafted on the old electoral scheme without in any way impairing the institution of class voting. A fifth curia or sphere would contain seventy-two deputies to be chosen by every male over twenty-four who had a fixed residence for at least six months. In other words, about 5,250,000 voters would participate in the election of these seventy-two deputies, while 1,750,000 eligible to vote in the four traditional and favored curiae would return 353 representatives.

Badeni's bill was full of intricate absurdities, from a democratic point of view, and full of complicated discriminations. The gross inequities were fully revealed in the way in which the law would operate in the provinces of Bohemia and Moravia; whereas between 40,000 and 50,000 electors there would choose a deputy in the new fifth curia, nineteen landed aristocrats,

3,000 bourgeoisie, and about 9,000 peasants would each elect a representative in their respective spheres. This measure failed utterly to meet the expectations of the advocates of equal and direct suffrage—the Social Democrats and the Christian Socialists—nor did it satisfy the desires of the German Liberals who stood to lose in relative importance, or the rabid Jew-haters, who would deny every Israelite the franchise. Nevertheless, the proposal attracted the support of a majority of the deputies, was passed, and was sanctioned by the emperor.

As soon as the bill became law the reichsrat was dissolved, and elections under the new franchise were ordered. Francis Joseph expressed his satisfaction that the issue of franchise reform had been happily settled, an opinion not at all shared by exponents of political democracy, who considered the battle only just begun.

The outcome of the balloting in March of 1897 might very well have been expected; representatives of no fewer than twenty-five parties were elected. The Young Czechs annihilated their Old Czech competitors; Social Democracy captured fourteen seats, though none in the Vienna area, for there the Christian Socialists repeated their recent triumphs in municipal elections. German deputies won 202 of the 425 places but they were split into nine disparate, warring factions. Friendly toward the Badeni ministry were the Poles, the Yugoslavs, the Clericals, the Conservatives, and the Czechs, a safe majority if the Czechs could be kept in line. Taaffe's "Iron Ring" had seemingly been remolded.

To secure the coöperation of the Czechs for the impending economic agreements with Hungary, Badeni treated their special interests generously. The state of siege that had hung over Prague and its environs for many months was lifted, the Draconian press censorship was mitigated, imprisoned members of the *Omladina* were pardoned, certain political prisoners were given their freedom, and the Bohemian governor, Count Thun, who had incurred the disfavor of the Young Czechs, was dismissed. These gestures formed the prelude to two famous language ordinances published in April of 1897, broadening the linguistic concessions that had been granted the Czechs in the eighties. After July 1901, civil servants in Bohemia and Moravia would have to be able to speak and write in Czech as well as German. Every public official, imperial as well as provincial, from top-rank bureaucrats down to letter carriers and street cleaners, would have to possess a knowledge of both languages. And in a lawsuit involving members of the two nationalities the language of the plaintiff would have to be used by the local magistrate and on up to the highest court of appeal.[13]

The Badeni language decrees loosed upon Austria the most fearful nationalist struggle known since the inception of the constitutional regime. It affected every phase of life and for a time even called into question the very continuance of the state. Throughout the empire nationality leaders were ever on the alert to extend the use of their particular language and to oust every other tongue wherever possible. The fierce controversy that developed over the Badeni ordinances dramatized the deep underlying jealousies and antagonisms of the competitive nationalisms. Smoldering flames blazed into a roaring fire.

Germans without regard to province or party, except for the stanchest of Conservatives and Clericals, reviled the language ordinances as an insult, a wanton challenge to their nationality, another stride in the direction of autonomy for the Czechs. It was utterly unjust and downright provocative, in their opinion, to require German officials to know Czech, a "mere dialect," difficult to master, and useless internationally. And the ordinances should not have been arbitrarily ordained, the Germans argued, but should have been presented to parliament for debate and decision. Germans denied that the ordinances had legal standing, because Francis Joseph had not signed them. Czech spokesmen hastened to point out that the laws would require no more linguistic equipment of civil servants than Bohemian landlords expected of stewards and gamekeepers. Badeni insisted that considerations of imperial welfare dictated the course he had taken.

Austro-Germans, high and low, joined in demanding the revocation of the language decrees. Hotheads arranged mass demonstrations in German centers of Bohemia against Badeni, to which Czechs retorted with pro-Badeni meetings. Tension between the two nationalities rose to such a pitch that even waiters in German restaurants refused to serve Czech patrons and vice versa. Partisans of the unification of the German districts of Bohemia with imperial Germany redoubled their activity, launching the "Los von Rom" agitation already described; they wore blue sunflowers, emblem of Emperor William I, flaunted the flag of Germany, and decorated homes with likenesses of Bismarck and William II. Not to be outdone, Czech zealots brought forth banners emblazoned with portraits of Huss, Napoleon III, and a reproduction of the imperial rescript of 1871 promising home rule for Bohemia. In view of the fierce excitement, it is surprising that destructive civil fighting did not break loose.

The major Austro-German newspapers savagely assailed the language ordinances, and deputies resorted to obstruction in parliament. A small but noisy Pan-German delegation, headed by Karl H. Wolf, an uninhibited journalist, indulged in irrelevant speeches or drowned out friends of the prime minister by rowdyism; pugilistic bouts upset legislative procedure.

Filibustering so completely interrupted the parliamentary deliberations that Badeni sent the deputies home. Infuriated Germans blocked activity in provincial assemblies; taxes could not be collected. Appeals of the prime minister to German moderates to recommend a compromise elicited no effective response. When parliament was recalled, the Germans resumed obstruction, establishing new records for loud and long speeches, one of which dragged on for almost thirteen hours. Badeni suffered a slight wound in a duel with Wolf, who had grossly insulted him.

Unprecedented excesses broke over the chamber when the presiding officer attempted to curb speech-making German obstructionists; "a day of shame for everyone," mourned the *Neue Freie Presse*. In a notable cartoon, *Der Wahre Jakob* of Stuttgart portrayed a perspiring Badeni dragging the Austrian chariot of state, belabored by a priest, a financier, a landlord, and wild-eyed Young Czechs, while urchins, Deputy Wolf among them, pelted the miserable prime minister with stones.

To restore tranquillity in the chamber Badeni resorted to arbitrary action such as he had applied in dealing with Ruthenian malcontents when governor of Galicia. His henchman, Count Falkenhayn, proposed that "any deputy who continued to disturb a session after twice being called to order could be suspended." Amidst immense hubbub the presiding officer declared the adoption of the proposal, which struck at unfettered freedom of expression.

Democratic Socialist deputies lined up with Pan-Germans in denouncing the *Lex Falkenhayn,* and both groups were ejected from the chamber by gendarmes. Bedlam then broke loose. Young deputies engaged in fist fights, while their elders hurled inkstands at one another or blew whistles; the dignified professor of Roman law in the German university at Prague sounded off on a fire-brigade trumpet!

On the streets of Vienna, popular turbulence recalled the revolutionary episodes of 1848. Police scattered a throng of protestants before the parliament building, while at the nearby city hall Mayor Lueger shouted: "Badeni must go!" German communities of Bohemia witnessed huge mass meetings, and soldiers charged into an anti-Badeni demonstration at Graz, killing one participant. The dead man was given the funeral of a martyr.

It was plain that unless Badeni withdrew from the public stage, order could be preserved only by military force. Francis Joseph, though he felt that only a "turbulent minority" was responsible for the convulsions, forced the prime minister to resign. German enemies of reconciliation in Bohemia had scored handsomely, but in so doing they had impaired the prestige of parliament and encouraged similar tactics on the part of Czechs and other dissenters.

In the fervent struggle against the Bohemian ordinances, Austro-Germans had the support of Reich-Germans, public men, university professors, students, and journalists. The learned historian Theodor Mommsen, reputedly a liberal, published a letter in the *Neue Freie Presse* in which he excitedly exhorted the Austro-Germans not to waver in their resistance nor even to accept a compromise; Czech skulls, said he, ought to be cracked.[14] Representatives of all classes in the great cities of Germany dispatched pledges of assistance or letters of sympathy to the Bohemian Germans, and in places sympathetic mass meetings were organized. Reichstag deputies in a debate on the Austrian imbroglio warned that if the Badeni ordinances went into operation the Czechs would predominate in Bohemia and the alliance with Germany would be imperiled. There was, however, little sentiment in favor of official German intervention in a purely domestic Austrian quarrel; Berlin police refused to permit a Pan-German meeting which Wolf and other Bohemian Germans were scheduled to address. Badeni's resignation, on the other hand, was greeted in Germany with transports of joy.[15]

VII

Baron Gautsch, sometime minister of education and an obedient servant of the crown, assembled a ministry of Germans, and cast about for a solution of the impasse over Bohemia. German agitators who had been imprisoned during the campaign against Badeni were set free, which only intensified bitterness in Czech hearts. Rioters in Prague stormed homes, shops, and even a German hospital. German students in Prague countered with a public celebration, which led to street fighting. Authorities forbade German students to appear in public wearing university insignia; out of sympathy for their Bohemian fellows, students at Vienna, Graz, and Innsbruck went on the rampage, until lecture halls were closed.

Prague and its suburbs, in the meantime, had once more been placed under martial law, rigidly enforced. Angry quarreling marred the proceedings of the Bohemian diet until the German deputies, thoroughly exasperated by the content of a Czech-sponsored petition to the throne, vacated their seats. As a sequel to the political turmoil, trade languished, business was depressed, and some Czech soldiers manifested their patriotism by responding to the roll call with *"Zde"* instead of the customary German *"Hier."* Francis Joseph, ever hypersensitive to anything that hinted at disloyalty in the armed forces, ordered severe discipline for the Czech dissenters. Czech officers clashed with Germans and grave doubts were raised regarding the loyalty of Czech troops in case of war.

Speculations of that sort were encouraged by frank and open expressions of Czech devotion to Russia and Pan-Slavism. In June of 1898, Slavs from all over Europe foregathered in Prague to celebrate the birthday of the most venerated of Czech patrioteers, Palacký, who had taken a prominent part in the Pan-Slav congress held in Prague just half a century earlier. The Russian general and publicist, Komarov, wearing the uniform of a Serbian officer, delivered an impassioned Pan-Slav sermon, which was received with thunderous applause; after recalling that a coalition of Poles, Russians, and Czechs had vanquished the Teutonic Knights at Tannenberg in 1410, the Russian pleaded for a united Slav front to combat the common peril of Germandom. Once such a union was effected, the differences that separated the Slavs could readily be disposed of, he said. In German circles the Russian's exhortation was interpreted as wanton incitement to the Slavs of Austria to war upon their German fellow citizens. And General Rittich, professor in the military academy at St. Petersburg, in a communication to the editors of *Národni Listy,* assured the Czechs that they could rely with confidence upon the might of Russia. "Until you have learned to know Russia," he wrote, "you will not realize the source of Slavonic strength. 'In this sign thou shalt conquer.'"

Young Czech politicians, on their side, expressed extreme repugnance to the alliance with Germany and once more demanded diplomatic alignment with Russia and France. An article by a Young Czech preaching these diplomatic doctrines which appeared in December of 1898, in the *Revue de Paris,* created an immense sensation in Vienna, and the Austrian authorities banned the circulation of the journal. The blatant Russophilism of the Czech extremists raised fresh doubts in Germany concerning the future of the Triple Alliance; many German officials in fact looked upon Prague as a Muscovite outpost in central Europe and even alluded to it as the "western Moscow."

No public figure among the Czechs more abundantly embodied the militant chauvinism of his countrymen than the author of the *Revue de Paris* article, Dr. Karel Kramář, who was to serve as the first premier of the Czechoslovak republic. Elected to the Austrian parliament in 1891, Kramář became the acknowledged and unchallenged leader of the Young Czechs and retained that distinction down to World War I. A man of personal charm and great forensic skill, with a flair for picturesque invective, Kramář was "as courageous as an eagle and as obstinate as a mule." The son of a wealthy, self-made industrialist, internationally educated, and wedded to the daughter of a prominent Moscow manufacturer, the "Austrian Parnell" blended ardent Slavophile leanings with ardent Czech nationalism.

Kramář condemned the Austrian alliance with Germany as "a piano out of tune." In parliament and in fiery pamphlets, he reviled Germany as the supreme enemy of Slavdom and extolled his countrymen as the bulwark that would prevent Prussia from overwhelming Europe; one day, he felt sure, tsarist Russia would be the agent of Czech liberation. Although Kramář pleaded in public for Bohemian autonomy within the Hapsburg framework, he privately preferred an independent Czech state in a Slav federation under the aegis of Russia.

The Gautsch cabinet, meanwhile, had turned its attention to the thorny Bohemian language laws. After consultation with moderate Czechs and Bohemians, a compromise formula was hammered out. Bohemia and Moravia would be partitioned into three types of administrative areas; where Czechs predominated, civil servants would have to know Czech, in German districts, German, and both languages in very mixed districts. Czech criticism of the plan caused Gautsch to resign without even a parliamentary debate and the flaming ministerial torch was passed to Count Leo Thun, a Bohemian aristocrat.

As governor of Bohemia for seven years Thun had served with distinction, but he was *persona non grata* to Young Czech firebrands. Moderate Germans and Czechs were drawn into the ministry and an appeal for discipline was addressed to parliament so that "social reforms, educational progress, and the advancement of the material and moral conditions of the people, especially labor" might be enacted. Austria, Thun reminded the deputies, had been brought to a standstill by nationalistic tempests, while other countries were going forward. Essential governmental business, incidentally, was transacted under article fourteen of the constitution, the "dictatorship paragraph," which authorized the crown to issue decrees having the full force of law.[16]

Foes of the Bohemian language ordinances presently resumed obstruction, and Thun antagonized Germany by championing the interests of Austrian Poles. He threatened reprisals because Poles who were Austrian citizens had been expelled from Prussia. Government and press in Berlin retorted sharply to these protests and William II alluded to the "serious consequences" which the attitude of the premier must have for the Austro-German alliance. Without ceremony Francis Joseph tossed (1899) Thun into the discard.

The hateful Badeni language laws were formally revoked by a ministry presided over by Count Manfred Clary, but the promise to offer a substitute measure was not fulfilled. Czech extremists stultified parliamentary activity by filibustering, without descending, however, to the low level of the Pan-Germans. Clary quit after a hectic month and parliament was prorogued.

VIII

The figures poised for flight on the four corners of the Austrian parliament building neatly symbolized the national antagonisms inside the empire. As someone remarked, it was a case of "bellum omnium contra omnes." Imperial concerns were swamped beneath the high waves of national passions; every schoolhouse, every railway station, every public office excited intrigue and scheming. Bohemia and Styria were violently churned up and a peasant rising swept Galicia. Armed rustics there rebelled against harsh living conditions, pillaged property, and caused some deaths; martial law had to be proclaimed before peace was restored.

Dissenting passions were somewhat stilled in 1898, it is true, because of the assassination of the beloved Empress Elizabeth and the celebration of the fiftieth anniversary of the accession of Francis Joseph to the throne. Political factions, except for the Pan-Germans, united in honoring the monarch, and popular celebrations testified that the turbulence in politics had not reached the throne. "No one nationality is inferior to another," wrote the Czech publicist, Count Lützow, "in its veneration for a sovereign whose sagacity and kindness are acknowledged by all." [17]

Nonetheless, as the century drew to its close, the smashup of the Monarchy was freely predicted, at home and abroad. [18] After Bismarck's death in 1898, his confidential and pessimistic judgments on the Hapsburg future were disclosed to the public. Austria, he thought, would soon disintegrate, since the Germans who had long held it together were in eclipse; Clericals and Poles had manipulated affairs so as to extend the sway of Catholicism and to conciliate the Slavs, whose coöperation would be essential in the event of war with Russia. But, said Bismarck, concessions would never appease the Slavs, the Czechs above all, and Austria's days therefore were numbered; the time would soon come when Germany would be obliged to say that "it is vain to ally onself with a corpse."

Western publicists and politicians, too, were alert to the possibility that Austria might collapse and speculated on the consequences thereof. The learned Frenchman, Pierre Paul Leroy-Beaulieu, in *La France, La Russie et L'Europe* (1898), portrayed the Danube Monarchy as the very cornerstone of European peace and dreaded its disintegration, which would redound to the benefit of Germany and be detrimental to French security. And the most influential writer on the Pan-German danger, André Chéradame, in *L'Europe et la question d'Autriche* (1901), expatiated upon the theme that the preservation of the Monarchy, an essential for European tranquillity, depended upon its transformation into a federal union. He urged that France and Russia exert pressure in Vienna on behalf of federalization. In a similar vein René Henry, who like Chéradame was in intimate touch with Kramář, contended in *Questions d'Autriche-Hongrie* (second ed., 1903) that the preservation of the Monarchy was at once a necessity for Europe and for the divergent nationalities in the realm.

French scholarship, parenthetically, contributed its mite to the unfolding of Czech national consciousness and to the political stirrings of the Czech nation. Pioneer work undertaken by such intellectuals as Saint René Taillandier and Henri Martin was carried forward by Louis Leger, historian at the Collège de France, who devoted a long and fruitful career to study and writing about European Slavs; *La Renaissance Tchèque* was one of his most competent publications. In *La Bohême depuis la montagne blanche* (1903), Ernest Denis interpreted Czech political history in the light of the current strife with the Germans, and admonished the Czechs that they must be a living bulwark against the sweep of barbarism southward. Out of gratitude a monument to Denis' memory was erected in Prague after World War I by the Czechoslovak republic.

CHAPTER FOURTEEN

A LEAP IN THE DARK

Francis joseph in 1900, for the first and last time, se-lected a commoner as prime minister, Dr. Ernest Koerber, with a cabinet of prominent public officials. "The right man at the right place," as the friendly press called him, had worked his way up through the bureaucracy and twice had held ministerial portfolios. Well acquainted with the Austrian economy, Koerber was expected to sponsor legislation for economic improvement—an assumption justified by the event.

Under his direction press laws that had gone untouched since the sixties were liberalized; taxes, for instance, on newspapers were canceled. Equally, restrictions on speech and assembly were relaxed and democratic Socialists were given the same rights as other political groupings.

Koerber, of course, had to deal with and try to remedy the running sore, the German-Czech feud centering on Bohemia. His ministry revived indeed the old plan for dividing Bohemia and Moravia into three types of admin-istrative districts, one German, another Czech, and mixed areas—regions in which the minority equaled 20 per cent or more—where familiarity with both tongues would be required of public servants. But these reasonable and practicable proposals, like earlier ones, were defeated by the invincible resist-ance of Czechs and Germans; while Czechs harped upon the administrative unity of Bohemia and Moravia, Germans refused to admit that mixed dis-tricts were actually mixed.

To forestall debate on the ministerial project, Czech deputies in the reichsrat presented fully two thousand petitions and asked that a roll call be taken on each one. When the ministry attempted to stop this obstructionism, the Czechs replied with an arsenal of instruments for emitting noise, and hurled inkstands and rulers at their parliamentary foes—instead of the daggers and lances of medievalism. Whereupon parliament was dissolved and new elections ordered; the ministry at the same time published a long list of economic reforms that would be undertaken if parliament concurred. Francis Joseph intimated that the forthcoming election might be the final effort to end the parliamentary deadlock and obstruction; inferentially, the monarch threatened to suspend the constitution and govern arbitrarily.

Election results in 1901 reflected the universal excitement that had been aroused by the Badeni language ordinances and the attendant struggle in parliament and public. From Bohemia extremist partisans, Pan-Germans and Young Czechs, were returned in larger proportions than ever before; the Pan-German strength in fact jumped from eight deputies to twenty-one.[1] More stridently than ever the Pan-Germans clamored for the union of German Austria with imperial Germany. Schönerer climaxed a speech in parliament with: "Hurrah for and God save the Hohenzollerns," and his followers screamed out a German national anthem. Shortly after, however, quarreling inside the movement seriously weakened Pan-Germanism as a political force.

The Social Democrats, meanwhile, had tailored their creed to meet the peculiar problems of nationality in Austria. They took the position that the maintenance of the Monarchy was desirable from the standpoint of Socialist interests, but proposed that the state should be reconstructed on federal principles so as to ensure wide latitude to the cultural concerns of the divergent national groupings. Reformation along federal lines, Socialist spokesmen reasoned, would counteract disruptive national agitations and open the way for a frontal assault on economic and social ills.[2] On narrowly social issues, the Czech National Socialist party saw eye to eye with the Social Democrats, though it was stanchly nationalist on political questions; this party returned almost as many deputies in the election of 1901 as the Social Democrats.

Political emotions ran high upon the convocation of parliament. Czech hotspurs and German extremists tried to outdo one another in filibustering techniques. While various plans to put an end to the parliamentary comedy were canvassed, state affairs were carried on by imperial decree.

II

It was the assumption of the Koerber ministry that a progressive economic program would mitigate the acrid strife among the nationalities. Plans were announced for a second railway to Trieste, larger shipping facilities there, and the extension of canals on a grand scale; and parliament readily adopted the necessary legislation. For two years in a row the atmosphere of the chamber was so tranquil that imperial budgets were enacted as prescribed by the constitution.

The new railway to Trieste, the Tauern line, tapping the trade of southern Germany, was opened to traffic in 1909. In the interval the established policy of state acquisition of private railways was carried forward, so that the only important road outside of government ownership was the southern line from Vienna to Trieste. Austrian state railways operated at a deficit, but it was argued that the benefits resulting from low rates on merchandise for foreign markets and on products, such as sugar, that the government desired to foster, more than compensated for state losses.

Trieste prospered by reason of the enlargement of harbor facilities. Wharfage was increased by half and warehouse capacity doubled; "the heiress of Venice" competed effectively with Genoa, Hamburg, and Fiume. By 1913, tonnage at the port had doubled over 1900 with sugar, timber, cotton yarns, iron products, and paper as the principal exports, and coal, cotton, and coffee at the top of the imports. Shipbuilding concerns and shipping companies expanded their operations; the Austrian Lloyd, which the government generously subsidized, handled traffic to Adriatic ports and to the Near East and Asia. Smaller companies carried on business with the Latin countries and the Americas; permission was granted to the Cunard line in 1903 to pick up emigrants at Trieste for the New World and an Austro-American Company was organized to share in the profitable emigrant traffic.

The Dalmatian coast contained excellent harbors, but none attained much commercial significance, owing to the competition of Trieste and Fiume and to the unproductive hinterland. Ports concentrated on local traffic, except for Gravosa, terminus of a narrow-gauge railway running into Bosnia. Pola, at the tip of the Istrian peninsula, was the principal naval station of the Monarchy, with the spacious bay of Cattaro second in importance. Sailors for the Hapsburg fleet and the merchant marine were recruited largely in Dalmatia.

The Koerber canal plans called for the building of more than a thousand miles of waterways. Commerce within the empire would be facilitated and cheaper transportation to and from Germany and Russia would be made available. Critics contended that certain of the projected canals would never be economically practicable, and in fact only one project, linking the Danube to the Moldau, had by 1914 passed out of the blueprint stage.

Austrian industry at the opening of the century experienced acute depression, partly as a reflection of conditions in Germany, but aggravated by nationalistic strife, labor troubles, and tariff policies of foreign countries. The cartel system was extended, government subsidies were authorized for certain industries, and tariff rates were jacked up. Only Russia, after the tariff act of 1906, had a higher tariff wall than the Hapsburg Monarchy. Given protection, Austrian manufactures prospered without precedent, industrial output in 1912 being reported about 50 per cent ahead of a decade earlier; factories in Bohemia increased faster than the supply of skilled workmen.

III

Order prevailed in parliament until irrepressible Czech deputies sounded the national trumpet anew. Pan-Germans answered in kind, again legislative activity stopped, and the conduct of government by imperial decree was revived.[3] The price of peace which the Czechs enumerated in 1903 included a federal regime for the empire, equality of the Czech and German languages in central administrative bureaus and in state offices in Bohemia and Moravia, democratization of the franchise, and a Czech university in Moravia. That set of demands merely brought the thinking of Czech autonomists up to date.

Many of the provincial diets, too, were paralyzed by nationalistic squabbles. Germans filibustered in Bohemia, Slovenes in Styria, Italians in the Tyrol, Italians and Slovenes vied with one another in obstructing the diet of Istria, and Ruthenians withdrew in hot anger from the Galician assembly. Eastern Galicia in 1902, as four years earlier, was harassed by bloody clashes between soil people and magnates or workers imported as strikebreakers. Battles of students at Lemberg mirrored the high tension that prevailed in the province. The Polish ruling class would not hear of a separate Ruthenian university, though appropriations were voted for a Ruthenian theater and an additional secondary school.

The desire for a national university stood high on the demands of Ruthenian, Italian, and Slovene minorities. Only in such an institution could national cultures be properly cultivated and men obtain in their mother tongue the education that was prerequisite for important government posts. Austrian subjects of Italian speech had attended the University of Padua until 1866, when Venetia was ceded to Italy; then some courses for Italians were offered at Innsbruck, but friction between students and German-speaking townsmen was unending. Spokesmen of Italians asked for an independent university at Trieste, but that request was vetoed in Vienna, on the score that it would surely degenerate into a hotbed of Irredentism and would intensify the clamor of other minorities for separate universities. Instead, the ministry of Koerber proposed that a distinctly Italian faculty of law should be established at Innsbruck.

That plan was actually carried out but when the institution opened (1904) Germans and Italian students clashed and a German was killed. The excitement raced into sections of the Tyrol where Italians lived, and some property was destroyed before troops restored order. Italians everywhere interpreted the episode as fresh evidence that Austro-Germans regarded them s undesirable intruders; the Irredentist cause was quickened and Italian deputies in the diet of the Tyrol invoked the weapon of obstruction.

German spokesmen in the Austrian parliament charged the Koerber ministry with responsibility for the melancholy events in Innsbruck and demanded its resignation. Physically worn down by his unenviable responsibilities and defeated on a minor fiscal measure, Koerber retired at the end of 1904.

IV

Prolonged political turmoil strengthened the conviction that domestic tranquillity could be achieved, if indeed it could be achieved at all, only by a genuinely democratic franchise. Social Democrats, for example, incessantly declaimed against the mere sop thrown to democracy by the creation of a fifth electoral curia in 1897. Direct and equal manhood suffrage, the able socialist thinker Karl Renner urged, would prove a powerful counterweight to national antagonisms for in that way the political power of the poorer classes would be greatly increased, and these elements were favorably disposed to the preservation of the empire and interested in social-welfare legislation, while the *bourgeoisie* were immersed in the special interests of their particular nationalities.[4]

Renner's conception of a parliament divided along horizontal and class lines instead of vertical national groupings won considerable acceptance outside of Socialist ranks. Cheek to jowl with the Social Democrats on the franchise issue were the Christian Socialists and the Czechs. The threat to introduce democratic suffrage in Hungary in order to break a deadlock there between crown and parliament, the revolutionary upheaval of 1905 in Russia, and the news that a Russian parliament (*duma*) would be elected on a broad franchise aided the cause of political democracy in Austria. Victory was virtually assured when, in November of 1905, Francis Joseph, profoundly moved by the implications of the Russian revolution, and in the belief that the alchemy of political democracy would somehow soften the nationality conflicts, expressed his approval of franchise reform.

The task of formulating an equal-suffrage bill fell to the cabinet of Baron von Gautsch, the emperor's "public utility" man, who had repeatedly bobbed up in the ministerial kaleidoscope. Favorably regarded by Czech politicians, who quit their obstructionist tactics on his nomination, Gautsch contrived to secure parliamentary ratification of a new military recruitment law, an economic arrangement with Hungary, and foreign-trade and tariff treaties. While the premier personally shared the conservative apprehension that democratic suffrage would inevitably bring on the ruin of the realm, he bowed to the wishes of the sovereign in the matter.

On the day that parliament convened to consider the franchise question, the Social Democrats organized mass suffrage rallies in the leading cities of the empire. They were aware that pressure of that sort by Belgian workers had brought about franchise reform, and even more vivid was the recent success of the political strike in forcing liberalizing changes in Russia. In Vienna a monster procession, participated in by a quarter of a million workmen, who had laid down their tools for the day, was managed by three thousand marshals without any assistance from the police. For four hours the human tide flowed before the parliament building; banners calling for franchise reform in the diverse languages of the empire jostled with the red flag of Socialism. In full view of Francis Joseph a Socialist deputation handed a suffrage petition to the prime minister.[5]

That same day, Gautsch presented a bill to parliament enfranchising all males over twenty-four, distributing seats on the basis of nationality, and dropping the curiae system. Social Democrats, Christian Socialists, and Czechs applauded the proposals, but other elements, the Poles notably, complained that they had not been assigned a fair proportion of the deputies. Rather than acquiesce in Polish demands, Gautsch handed over the seals of office.

But Francis Joseph, intent upon broadening the franchise, summoned as prime minister Prince Conrad Hohenlohe, who as governor of Trieste had established a reputation as a liberal. Negotiations with political leaders on the distribution of seats had scarcely started, however, when Hohenlohe resigned in protest over the consent of the emperor to a separate tariff regime for Hungary.

The unwillingness of Hohenlohe to endorse this concession to Magyar independence sentiments precipitated a lively constitutional discussion in the Austrian parliament. Spokesmen indignantly decried the frequent appeal to article fourteen. "We have lived," one deputy blurted out, "for a decade under a regime of pure absolutism, decorated with a formal parliamentary life." Deputies warned the ministry that vital public issues should be debated and decided by the lawmakers.

Franchise reform was finally achieved under Baron von Beck, in many ways the ablest and most enlightened of the Austrian prime ministers. The Gautsch proposals were overhauled so as to enlarge the number of seats and redistribute them among the nationalities. The revised measure passed the lower house by a handsome majority and was approved almost unanimously in the upper body, though not without deep misgivings on the part of apprehensive conservatives. Francis Joseph, in January of 1907, put his signature on the law. Men everywhere quoted the phrase about "a leap in the dark" uttered forty years earlier when the right to vote was extended to the industrial workmen of Great Britain.

By the act of 1907 practically all male citizens became eligible to vote for deputies of their own nationality. German voters would elect 233 of the 516 deputies; Czechs, 107; Poles, 82; Ruthenians, 33; Slovenes, 24; Italians, 19; Serbo-Croats, 13; and Rumanians, 5. In distributing seats, taxpaying capacity and cultural considerations as well as numbers were taken into account; otherwise Germans and Poles would have had considerably fewer deputies than they were in fact allotted.[6]

The first elections under the democratic franchise, conducted in May of 1907, drastically altered the composition of the legislature. Broadly speaking, national extremists suffered sharp losses, while advocates of social innovations gained substantially. The Young Czechs, for example, were reduced to a mere shadow and the Pan-Germans were relegated to obscurity, even Schönerer, prince of the apostles, failing at the polls. German Liberals, neither well led nor well organized, dropped behind in the race, carrying only three of the seats in Vienna, once the Liberal bastion.

Christian Socialists, on the other hand, and democratic Socialists, both of whom had fought for manhood suffrage and were close to the urban masses, gained many seats. Christian Socialism profited from the indefatigable activities of Dr. Albert Gessmann, who ranged from the Bodensee to the Bucovina, propagandizing for the cause; the illness of the persuasive Lueger while the electioneering was under way probably cost his party some seats. Nonetheless, the Christian Socialists, together with their intimate allies, the German Clericals, constituted the largest faction in the new parliament.

Social Democracy won eighty-seven seats as compared with eleven in the balloting of 1901. It captured many districts in Vienna, all the deputies of Linz and Trieste and twenty-four Czech constituencies. The Socialist delegation in the Austrian parliament was larger than in any other country; deputies were mainly intellectuals and journalists, few of them manual workers. Excellently organized and supported by the trade-unions, the Socialists advocated a moderate program of social change to be achieved by parliamentary processes and the preservation of the supranationality realm refashioned on federal principles. Unlike their fellows in Germany, the Austrian Socialists seldom indulged in criticism of the armed services or of the monarch, and that was a source of strength of the movement.

All told, over thirty parties, mostly splinter groups, returned deputies in 1907. Czech deputies, to illustrate, were divided into six fragments, based upon economic or political interests, the peasant Agrarian group being the largest. Poles likewise were represented by several factions, though an inner cohesion ensured a common response whenever Polish special interests were at stake; the Polish delegation remained, no doubt, the most effective force in the parliament.

v

In the speech from the throne welcoming the new parliament, it was explained that the crown expected orderly transaction of business and the passage of much-needed social and economic legislation, now that the suffrage had been democratized. A reconstructed Beck ministry secured approval of the purchase of the Bohemian Northern railway and of a measure ratifying a new economic arrangement with Hungary, which raised the Hungarian contribution to the joint expenditures of the Monarchy and defined the customs agreement between the two partners as a treaty.

Parliamentary waters were churned up by the Wahrmund affair which brought the issues of clericalism and academic liberty to the fore. Clerically minded men had long inveighed against the prevalence of unorthodox tendencies in the universities of the empire. Lueger, for instance, in an address of November 1907, denounced the universities as "hotbeds of subversive ideas, revolution, godlessness, and antipatriotism." Presently Wahrmund, professor at Innsbruck, who had for years battled against the clerical spirit, published a pamphlet, *The Catholic Attitude and Free Learning,* arguing that an unbridgeable chasm separated Catholic orthodoxy from contemporary scholarship.

Infuriated Catholics demanded the dismissal of Wahrmund, and the papal nuncio joined in the cry, for which he was sternly reprimanded by the Austrian foreign office. The offending professor, nonetheless, was forced from his chair and the offensive brochure was confiscated. Thereupon student friends and foes of Wahrmund clashed violently at Innsbruck, causing the suspension of lectures; students at other institutions who admired Wahrmund laid aside their books. Deputies in parliament took sides on the case, the Czech scholar Masaryk delivering a memorable plea for academic freedom. State authorities poured oil on the troubled waters with assurances that freedom of inquiry would not be further infringed, and Wahrmund was assigned a post in the German university of Prague, which he filled to his death in 1932.

In Moravia, meanwhile, real progress had been achieved in mitigating German-Czech animosities. By action of the diet in 1905, seats in the provincial legislature were distributed closely in keeping with the comparative numbers of each national group; and for certain kinds of legislation the concurrence of two-thirds of the representatives was prescribed. Local civil servants would be chosen from the two nationalities in the same proportions as assemblymen, and local areas would themselves determine the language to be spoken by civil servants. That accommodation generated a better temper in Moravia and demonstrated that the highly combustible national issue would yield to treatment if an attitude of moderation and compromise prevailed in both camps.[7]

It was hoped in Viennese ministerial circles that a comparable formula might be discovered for Bohemia, where, of course, national antagonisms were much more bitter than in Moravia. Moderate Czechs and Germans seemed not far apart, were separated merely by "a wall as thin as paper," as an optimistic current phrase ran. But to rupture the paper proved impossible; the ancient feud proceeded briskly. Again the Bohemian diet was dissolved, again Prague witnessed disorders and street battles and Czech deputies in Vienna withdrew their support from the Beck ministry, which soon folded up.

Relations between Poles and Ruthenian intellectuals in Galicia, meanwhile, showed no sign of betterment, rather grew more embittered as the Ruthenian educated class clamored for equality of rights for their countrymen. High hopes that Ruthenian leaders cherished while the universal-suffrage law was under debate were dashed to the earth when the final act discriminated against them and in favor of their Polish adversaries. Despite official pressure in the election of 1907, twenty-two Ukrainophiles and five Russophiles were returned to the reichsrat.

These deputies declaimed in Vienna against Polish oppression and upbraided the ministry for refusal to authorize a separate Ruthenian university in Lemberg or to organize an autonomous Ukrainian province. And to emphasize their discontent they had no hesitancy in indulging in obstruction, wildly singing a national anthem: "The time has gone for serving Muscovite or Pole." One deputy who tried to deliver a speech in Russian was silenced by the reichsrat's president; another wrenched the top off his desk, intending to hurl it at the executive, but his aim was bad and he struck and seriously injured a Slovene deputy.

Within Galicia itself, Ruthenian malignity was concentrated on Count Andrew Potocki, who had assumed the governorship in 1903. A genial Polish nobleman, Potocki was firmly convinced that the Ruthenians must be kept in leash. As governor, he vetoed an application for a Ruthenian savings bank, ordered the dissolution of Ruthenian clubs, restricted the migration of seasonal farm workers to Germany, and winked at terrorism in elections. Ruthenian deputies in Vienna clamored in vain for the dismissal of Potocki.

Matters took a turn for the worse early in 1908, when Polish police by their brutality caused the death of a Ruthenian peasant, Kahanets. Thereupon a Ukrainophile student at Lemberg, Miroslav Sichinsky, assassinated Potocki, shouting as he did so, "For the wrongs done to the Ukrainian people, for the elections, for the death of Kahanets." At his trial Sichinsky expressed regret for the murder but insisted that a deed of violence was necessary to call universal attention to the malevolence of the Polish administration and the terrible plight of the downtrodden Ruthenians. His attorney pleaded that the culprit should be judged in the light of the fierce national antagonisms in Galicia. Sentenced to prison, Sichinsky escaped and contrived to reach the United States, where he became an active leader among Ukrainians, who hailed him as a selfless patriotic hero, worthy of high praise.[8]

International complications soon diverted attention from the domestic politics of Austria. The annexation of Bosnia, proclaimed in October of 1908, provoked sharp differences of opinion, recalling the cleavage in 1878 when Hapsburg armies had marched into and occupied Bosnia. Premier Beck thought annexation imprudent, which infuriated the heir presumptive, Francis Ferdinand, previously a devoted admirer of Beck, who was once his tutor. Many Czech and Christian Socialist deputies had fallen out with the prime minister, which gravely undermined his parliamentary position. When the dangerous crisis over Bosnia was nearing a climax, Beck resigned, having learned in the rough school of experience, as had his predecessors, that the job of managing heterogeneous Austria demanded almost superhuman faculties.

CHAPTER FIFTEEN

DUALISM IN CRISIS: HUNGARY
1890–1910

THE RELATIVELY LONG PERIOD OF HUNGARIAN MINISTERIAL stability associated with the name of Coloman Tisza was succeeded by an era of short-lived cabinets. Upon Tisza's withdrawal, his finance minister, Julius Szapáry, became prime minister, promising to carry forward the "General's" policies. Hungary soon found itself in the throes of a *Kulturkampf* arising directly from marital questions, but involving the wider issues of religious freedom and the authority of Catholicism in the secular sphere.

Controversy over mixed marriages, that is, of unions between persons of different Christian faiths, had its roots deep in Hungary's past. Until 1791 such marriages had been unlawful, but an act of that year declared them valid. Priests of the Roman Catholic faith, however, refused to solemnize mixed marriages unless the parties promised to raise their children in the Catholic faith. Louis Kossuth, for example, a Lutheran engaged to a Catholic, was married by the Lutheran ritual after a priest declined to perform the ceremony without a formal pledge respecting the religion of the children. Under pressure, the Hungarian parliament enacted a law (1868) requiring the offspring of mixed marriages to follow the faith of the parent whose sex was inherited. But Catholic clergy willfully evaded the law, appealing alike to the dictates of their conscience and the holy ordinances of their church. Wherever possible they baptized all children of mixed unions, entering their names on Catholic registries; the imposition of heavy fines was no deterrent to clerical zeal.

That bit of history formed the background (or part of it) for demands that all births should be recorded by state authorities and that civil officials should be authorized to perform the ceremony of marriage. Linked up with this was agitation for uniformity in the matter of divorce. Considerable and bewildering diversity prevailed among the several religious confessions on divorce. Roman Catholicism, for example, strictly denied the right of divorce, and yet a Catholic who changed his religion after marriage was subject to the divorce regulations of the adopted church. Uniat Catholicism recognized almost a hundred legitimate reasons for divorce, "invincible repulsion" among them.

A divorce could be easily obtained in the Orthodox church, which had other marital practices peculiar to itself. For instance, both parents of an Orthodox youth had to consent to a marriage, and marriage to a close relative was banned; a widow with children might not remarry, while a childless widow might marry as many as four times, if she had not passed her fortieth year. And Transylvanian Protestantism, to add to the confusion, prohibited a man from marrying a woman thirty years younger or twenty years older than himself. Owing to the frequency of marriages between Hungarian citizens of different confessions, the extremely complicated marriage customs produced endless difficulties and plenty of lawsuits. A marriage considered indissoluble by the church usages of one party might be declared null and void by another; in one notorious divorce trial, the parties to the suit changed their religion five times in order to annul their marriage!

To regularize marital customs and eliminate causes of misunderstandings, the lower house of the Hungarian parliament passed bills in 1890 requiring civil registration of births and civil marriage. It was indicated that legislation was being prepared to remove marital trials from ecclesiastical courts and to ensure untrammeled freedom of conscience for all citizens. Catholic spokesmen expressed uncompromising hostility to these secularizing innovations.

Before the House of Magnates could act on these bills, the ministry dissolved parliament as a lesson to Kossuthists, who, by filibustering, had blocked the carrying on of debate. In the electioneering that ensued, Catholic clergy participated actively, catechizing candidates on their viewpoint concerning secularizing acts and instructing parishioners on the way to vote. As usual, the election itself was attended by riots and the shedding of blood. The followers of the Szapáry ministry captured 230 seats, "Independence" deputies won 110, and the National Party, 65. This last group espoused clerical interests and Magyar nationalism; at its head was Count Albert Apponyi, who belonged to one of Hungary's most respected patrician families. A member of the Hungarian legislature from 1872 onward, Apponyi, who has been likened to a Whig duke of eighteenth-century England, acquired a considerable reputation as a politician, thanks in part to his moving eloquence. He had a hand in organizing the National party, but as nationalism gained upon him he wandered into the separatist fold and eventually became a leader of the Independence party.

Promptly the new legislature turned to the secularization legislation, which had the powerful, undercover support of ex-premier Tisza. Without opposition a flabby resolution affirming freedom and equality for all creeds was adopted, but bills designed to make civil marriage compulsory and to give Judaism formal equality with Christian faiths met with intransigent resistance. The ministry in fact was driven from office, and one headed by a Protestant bureaucrat, Alexander Wekerle, esteemed as the savior of national finance, replaced it. Wekerle's cabinet presented bills requiring civil marriage before religious ceremonies, permitting divorce to all citizens, and depriving church courts of jurisdiction in divorce cases. A companion measure prescribed that in mixed marriages participants should agree in a prenuptial pact regarding the religion of their children. If none was made, all children would belong to their father's confession; children born out of wedlock would be registered in the religion of the mother.

Stigmatizing civil marriages as pure concubinage, the Catholic hierarchy declared war to the knife on the church bills, while Louis Kossuth from his Italian exile summoned his followers to vote for them. By a large majority the lower house accepted the civil-marriage act, but the conservative magnates defeated the measure and repeated their negative after the lower chamber had repassed it. When Francis Joseph, to whom the secularization legislation was highly distasteful, hesitated to appoint a sufficient number of new peers to ensure the passage of the bill the Wekerle ministry resigned in May 1894. But it was quickly reinstated.

Grudgingly Francis Joseph appealed to a group of magnates to vote for the measures making civil marriage obligatory and fixing the faith of children of mixed marriages, and with that august pressure the bills were enacted into law. As a by-product of the ferment occasioned by the secularization legislation, a new political party, the Catholic Peoples' party, was founded by Counts Julius Szapáry and Aladár Zichy. While the central objective of this party was to bring about revision of the marriage laws in keeping with Catholic principles, it was also sympathetic toward minority groups and the underprivileged. It attracted the favorable regard of the heir presumptive, Francis Ferdinand.

Wekerle's cabinet, which had incurred royal displeasure by its attitude at the time of national mourning for the sainted Kossuth, presently handed over the seals of office. A new ministry was organized by Baron Desider Bánffy, a prominent Liberal and Calvinist, a man of Coloman Tisza's stamp, under whose guidance the ecclesiastical laws were put into execution. At a moment when religious passions were burning at white heat, Monsignor Agliardi, papal nuncio in Vienna, toured Hungary, abjuring Catholics "to continue their noble struggle" against the secularizing reforms. Resentful of that interference in the domestic concerns of the kingdom, Bánffy roundly censured the nuncio and besought the foreign office to demand his recall.

Foreign Minister Kálnoky temporized; he personally disliked the secularization legislation and besides he was regarded as generally unsympathetic to Hungarian interests. He had tried, for instance, to prevent Francis Kossuth from returning to his homeland after the death of his father, fearing that he would encourage antidynastic sentiments, and his unwillingness to employ stern language in communications with Rumania about Irredentist activities had infuriated Magyar patriots. Before Kálnoky had complained to the Vatican about Agliardi's conduct, Bánffy prematurely announced that he had done so, a declaration which put the foreign minister in an extremely embarrassing position. Recriminations between the two statesmen created a tense situation in which the delicate question of personal honor was raised; Kálnoky concluded that it would be politic for him to end his long tenure at the Ballplatz, and resigned.[1]

II

The tide of Hungarian separatist sentiment, of Kossuthism, had, meantime, been steadily rising. A veritable Kossuth cult had emerged and was fed by tales of the heroic achievements and the lofty character of the legendary revolutionary chieftain. Popular patriotic songs were replete with uncritical adulation for "our father, Kossuth," and young Hungarian pilgrims paid their respects to him at his refuge place in Italy.[2]

Tisza's downfall in 1890 was directly the result of a quarrel involving the famous exile, and two years later, on the ninetieth anniversary of his birth, Budapest conferred on him the freedom of the city, staged a grand commemorative parade in his honor, and listened to orators and poets extol the rebel and recount the epic exploits of the revolutionary days—much to the annoyance of the ministry.

At long last, in 1894, Kossuth died at the patriarchal age of ninety-two, the last of the mid-century revolutionary leaders to pass away. For two generations from his haven near Turin, where he had supported himself by his pen and by giving language lessons, he had exercised a limited influence upon the course of Hungary's politics. From time to time he published manifestos in which he disclosed his convictions and wishes to his followers, though in extreme old age he did little more than brood sorrowfully over the past and write part of his recollections. Never would Kossuth recognize the legitimacy of Francis Joseph's rule; never did he renounce the hope of seeing Hungary separated from Austria and independent. Uncompromising to the end, he declined in his last days to allow either of his sons to return to Hungary to share in the consecration of a church in which he had been baptized and which had been restored by his worshipful admirers.

Just before he died, Kossuth reiterated the dire warning that he had never tired of sounding: the Hapsburg Monarchy was doomed to destruction and Hungary would perish in the conflagration, unless it broke away. At his death, national mourning was proclaimed in Hungary for the illustrious foe of Francis Joseph; and half a million citizens, reportedly, marched in his funeral procession—among them veterans of the War of Independence, flaunting bullet-riddled battleflags. The pomp and circumstance surrounding the burial of the "Liberator" have been likened to the ceremonial when the bones of Bonaparte were finally laid to rest in Paris. The funeral inspired "radical" demonstrations and riotings, which troops suppressed. In parliament, Julius Justh, a Kossuthist hotspur, eulogized the patriotic hero in glowing phrases: "In Louis Kossuth," said he, "we mourn one of the greatest, most honorable, and most selfless figures of history. He is not only our dead, but the dead of humanity . . . for the services of Kossuth were large, world-wide in significance, immortal."

Such evidences of the popularity of Kossuth and of the independence cause that he symbolized seriously disturbed the emperor-king—and with reason, for the impetus that Kossuth's death and funeral gave to separatism endured. His son, Francis, took up residence in Hungary, mumbled the formal oath of allegiance to the crown, and assumed formal leadership of the Independence party. Seditious antidynastic opinions which he uttered at patriotic banquets caused disquietude among the adherents of the dualistic regime. But his speeches, commented the American minister in Vienna, "seem rather the indiscreet utterances of a young man vain of his birth and origin rather than the words of a prospective statesman"—an estimate which later events proved to be extremely shrewd. As his father's son, the younger Kossuth attained a position of high prominence in Hungarian affairs; intensely patriotic and a secessionist, he was stubborn and wanting in the foresight and breadth of vision which are the prerequisites of the statesman.

III

Amidst great pomp and ceremony, Hungary celebrated in 1896 the thousandth anniversary of the Magyar invasion and conquest of the Danube valley, and during the festivities an unwonted calm ruled in the sphere of politics. In preparation for the decennial tussle with Austria over economic agreements, the Bánffy cabinet dismissed parliament in October 1896 and conducted new elections; by curbing freedom of assembly and of speech and employing terrorism and unparalleled pressure upon voters, the "Liberal" ministry achieved an overwhelming success at the polls. Antiministerial candidates were arbitrarily thrown into jail and disorders on election day cost the lives of over thirty citizens. The Clerical party dropped many seats and the outcome of the balloting was hailed by the victors as the triumph of "liberalism" over clericalism.

Backed by a solid phalanx in parliament, Bánffy's ministry entered upon discussions with representatives of Austria on the quotas for common expenses, the joint bank, and the customs and commercial treaties. Since Hungary's wealth had increased and the Hungarian population had grown more rapidly than the Austrian, the Austrians proposed a substantial enlargement in the Hungarian contribution to the monarchical exchequer, 42 per cent of all expenses instead of $31\frac{1}{2}$. But the Magyars would not consent; true, the kingdom had made great economic progress—that had just been trumpeted abroad by the Millennial Exposition—but Hungary, the Magyars contended, was still backward compared with Austria, and anyway the ratio fixed in 1867 had been too heavy for Hungary. Mayor Lueger and his Christian Socialists worsened matters by incessant attacks upon "greedy and grasping Magyar politicians," who were "the tools of Jews and capitalists," and who had adopted anticlerical legislation. Before any agreements could be worked out, Austrian parliamentary affairs were utterly disrupted by the Badeni language ordinances. Hungary's Independence party seized the chance to proclaim that the time had come to break off all economic connections with Austria and, by recourse to filibustering, Kossuthist deputies blocked the prolongation of the prevailing economic accords with Austria for one year. Officials were permitted, however, to collect customs duties pending the retroactive approval of parliament, and in Austria the economic arrangements were extended for a year by imperial decree.

Throughout 1898 parliamentary confusion in both Hungary and Austria stalled deliberations on the economic pacts, though delegates continued to haggle and bargain on financial quotas. Over the protests of the Hungarian separatists, the Bánffy ministry extended the accords with Austria without parliamentary consent. The ministry drew up a separate tariff schedule, to be invoked in the event that no agreement on tariffs could be reached with the Austrians, that called for the exclusion of all articles customarily bought in Austria which Hungary might be able to produce at home.

From Austria issued threats of reprisals on Hungarian agriculture, if high duties were imposed upon manufactures. The danger of a tariff war between the two Hapsburg partners loomed large. Austrian business interests charged Hungarian policy with responsibility for the deterioration of the Monarchy's political and economic relations with Balkan countries. "If," an Austrian remarked, "the past ten years had not been spent in bitter customs warfare to please Hungary, Austrian exports to the Balkans would certainly have increased."

Separatist feeling in Hungary was quickened by the commemorative celebration of episodes in the revolution of 1848. On the fiftieth anniversary of the beginning of the uprising, Budapest gave itself over to holiday making; shops and stores were closed, buildings were decorated with patriotic bunting, fulsome speeches honored the revolutionary saints and heroes. On order of the prime minister, the anniversary of the day on which Austria had recognized Hungarian autonomy became a national holiday.

Patriots themselves, the Magyars intransigently declined to acknowledge the legitimacy of kindred emotions in the breasts of minority stocks. Bánffy indeed intensified the Magyarization policies which as a provincial bureaucrat had earned him the epithet of "Iron Baron." At his official headquarters he set up a special agency to keep watch and ward on the doings of minority leaders and to scan the contents of the minority press; civil servants were urgently advised to provide themselves with Magyar names, and names of minority towns were casually assigned Magyar equivalents.

On the other hand, minority politicians, Rumanians, Slovaks, and Serbs, were allowed to hold a conference in 1898 that marked the beginning of a united front to preserve and protect their common interests. Vigorous protests were delivered against Magyar racialism, and the delegates drafted a set of demands that included honest execution of the Nationalities Act, ordinary civil liberties, universal and secret suffrage, and special ministries for each of the minority groups.

Magyar enemies of the ministry carried on obstructionist tactics in parliament and clamored for the head of the gruff and tactless Bánffy as the price of peace. And they obtained it. Széll, foster son and disciple of Deák, and an accomplished financier, superseded Bánffy and resumed negotiations on economic questions with Austria. After long discussion an agreement was finally hammered out which raised Hungary's proportion of the common expenses to 33 3/49 per cent of the total—a much smaller amount than Austrians had hoped for. The *Neue Freie Presse* termed the compromise the tribute that Austria was required to pay in order to ensure the continuance of dualism. To Hungary was given a larger part in the management of the monarchical bank, whose charter was extended to 1910, and the customs union was temporarily prolonged. It was understood that conversations for the renewal of the customs union should go on and if no understanding were come to, each partner after 1907 might adopt independent tariff schedules. These several economic settlements were formally accepted by the Hungarian parliament and made operative in Austria by imperial decree.

Lengthy deliberations on tariffs which followed aggravated the mutual jealousies and antipathies of the two countries. The chief obstacles to concord were Hungarian insistence on higher duties to protect agriculture while Austria sought guarantees against the competition of the growing and mercantilist-fostered industry of Hungary. Besides, the Independence faction in

Hungary pushed for the complete abandonment of the customs union so that tariff legislation could be adopted which would accelerate the conquest of the home market by Hungarian industry and smooth the way to political independence.

Imitating the action of the municipality of Budapest, many local governments called for an independent Hungarian tariff. Societies for the encouragement of national industry, whose immediate objective was to get purchasers to buy Hungarian goods instead of Austrian, cropped up; financial sacrifices due to buying homemade goods were hailed as marks of high patriotism. Former premier Bánffy serenely recommended that the economic bonds with Austria should be dissolved and declared that "individuals hurt [thereby] must be likened to those slain or wounded in military battles." Magyar coal-mining interests implored the government to declare it illegal for any citizen to burn anything but Hungarian coal, and a ministerial order instructed schoolmasters to require pupils to write only on paper made in Hungary and to learn only from books printed in the kingdom!

Patriots who boycotted Austrian goods proudly wore porcelain tulips in their buttonholes or on their dresses. For Kossuthists, the boycott was a holy tradition, for in the 1840's Kossuth himself had organized a league against the purchase of foreign-made articles. Ironically enough, the tulip was not a flower native to Hungary but had been brought in by Turkish conquerors, and the symbolic tulips that were worn were, alas, manufactured in foreign factories! Foreign manufacturers were forbidden to use the tulip as a trademark or to ship goods into the country packed in the Hungarian national colors. Such ludicrous regulations, inspired by nationalism, it would have been hard to match anywhere else in the world.

Sober, farsighted Hungarian leadership appreciated to the full the ruinous consequences that the ending of the customs union would have for the economy of each partner. Austria at the time was shipping a third of its exports to Hungary, while almost three-quarters of Hungarian surpluses were disposed of in the Austrian market. Therefore, over the protestations of the Independence deputies, the Széll ministry pressed on with tariff conversations and contrived to reach an agreement. A hard battle had been fought with Austria, Széll informed his countrymen, without either contestant emerging victorious. The fact of the matter was that the new tariff accord benefited Hungary, on balance, more than Austria, something which Magyar separatists refused to concede. So great indeed was the commotion that they kicked up in parliament that the customs treaty could not be ratified and had to be put into force by executive order.

Toward minority groups Széll's administration adopted a saner and more conciliatory policy than its predecessor. Prosecution of the Rumanian- and Slovak-language press, which was little other than thinly veiled persecution, was considerably diminished, and Bánffy's hateful nationalities bureau was discarded. To eliminate gross irregularities and abuses in elections, such as had disgraced the voting in 1896, parliament in 1899 enacted a model electoral-practices act. Among other things, many public servants, government contractors, and persons connected with concerns that were recipients of state subsidies were debarred by the law from standing for election as deputies. Deputies were expressly forbidden to seek positions or favors for their friends or constituents.

This bill was ornamental rather than efficacious, as was disclosed in the general elections of 1901. By the familiar devices of official pressure and private bribery the ministerial (Liberal) party increased its following in the lower chamber.[3]

The Kossuthists and their allies missed no opportunity, even in connection with exceedingly trivial matters, to insist upon Hungarian equality with Austria and to raise the cry for independence. At the time of the morganatic marriage of Francis Ferdinand in 1900, for example, it was declared that the Hapsburg family law, which excluded the heir presumptive's children from the throne, was inapplicable in the Magyar kingdom; and when a son was born the infant was acclaimed as the legitimate heir to the crown of St. Stephen. Any slights, real or fancied, to Hungarian rights were seized upon as pretexts for chauvinistic diatribes against the dualistic regime, as, for example, when Francis Ferdinand selected only one Hungarian but three Austrians for his entourage to the coronation of King Edward VII of Britain. At the formal opening of Budapest's magnificent parliament building a Kossuthist deputy, Barrabac, upbraided the king for abstention from the ceremonies and denounced the Széll ministry for failure to take part in the centennial of Louis Kossuth's birth, which had recently evoked great popular demonstrations.

IV

In 1902 the wildest and most protracted political storm which Hungary had experienced since the making of the *Ausgleich* was unloosed. The military bill of that year proposed that the Hungarian contingent in the common army should be increased in keeping with the growth of the population, precisely as was being done in Austria. The troubled situation of the moment, in Macedonia specifically, furnished the High Command with justification for a larger army. Just when tempers were worn thin because of sharp controversies over tariffs, the new army bill was offered to parliament.

Backed by Apponyi's National Party and a scattering of Liberals, the Kossuthist deputies announced that they would resist increases in the army unless concessions of a military character were first granted to Hungary. Positively, they demanded that the Magyar language should be used in commanding Hungarian regiments, that Hungarian officers should be placed in charge of Hungarian soldiers, and that the Hungarian flag should be carried by Hungarian forces. If granted, these concessions would facilitate the creation of an independent Hungarian army and would convert the military services into a more effective instrument of Magyarization. And there were other considerations and complications; Czechs and Poles would surely seek comparable military rights, and the Croats plainly indicated that they would rebel if Magyar were used in commanding Croatian soldiers.

After the Széll ministry refused to accept the Kossuthist demands, the opposition paralyzed parliament by systematic filibustering which the standing orders of the chamber were incapable of overcoming. Full freedom of speech prevailed, so that it was possible for a single deputy by talking interminably to prevent debate on any measure; the presiding officer might call a speaker to order and request him to sit down, but the utmost penalty at his disposal was to enter the name of the offender upon the official proceedings.

Since no business could be transacted, the ministry ordered that conscripts who were already with the colors should remain in service even though their terms had expired. But that decree provoked such violent explosions that it was quickly replaced by another inviting youths liable for training to appear voluntarily.

For six dreary months, the obstructionists carried on their battle, and then Francis Joseph ousted Széll in favor of Khuen-Héderváry, who as viceroy in Croatia had gained a reputation for accomplishing things by iron-handed tactics. In this way the king served notice that he was unalterably opposed to any concessions which might impair the integrity or the fighting power of the common army. Although the ill-starred army bill was withdrawn, the opposition minority persisted in clamoring for the Magyar language of command in Hungarian regiments and in preventing the conduct of parliamentary business. Demonstrations on the street, crowds chanting the refrain of a national air, "The Magyar shall be free and shall rule the world," and ardently patriotic articles in the press attested the popularity of the course which the opposition deputies were pursuing. Hungarian obstinacy in the period after 1849 had been rewarded with the *Ausgleich* of 1867, and Magyar zealots harbored the belief that a fresh show of stubbornness would produce another victory.

It was, however, a vain hope, for where military issues were at stake Francis Joseph was unyielding. Egged on by the military chiefs, the king delivered in 1903 a famous address at Chlopy, hitherto an obscure Galician hamlet, in which he asserted that "he must and would hold fast" to "the existing organization of the army . . . Common and unified as it now is shall my army remain, the sure shield of defense of the Austro-Hungarian

Monarchy against every foe." Never before had the ruler spoken on a controversial topic when addressing troops, and the unequivocal character of the utterance was a warning to all and sundry. Generally applauded in Austrian political circles, the Chlopy statement simply aggravated chauvinistic excitement in Hungary. Filibustering continued to paralyze parliament; no taxes were authorized, no appropriations approved, there was no provision for recruiting soldiers; defiantly the Magyar separatists agitated for "military independence." The issue between the crown and Kossuthism was sharply and squarely drawn. "The clouds of evil times, a heavy, dense, and death-dealing fog," mourned the moderate Széll, "have descended upon our nation. Since Mohács no situation has been fraught with greater difficulty."

In the face of the grave situation which the parliamentary deadlock had created, Liberal party leaders cast about for a compromise on army questions that would be acceptable to moderate Magyars without jeopardizing the unity of the monarchical military forces. Such a formula was worked out, and, after some revisions by the king, Stephen Tisza, Coloman's eldest son, a son in the spirit as well as in the flesh, was called upon in November 1903 to drive the act through parliament.

v

Tisza the younger was firmly convinced that Hungarian interests would best be served by the maintenance of the dualistic regime in its entirety. An independent Hungary, he thought, would be incapable of resisting the magnetic attraction of Rumania and Serbia upon their respective minorities in the kingdom, not to mention the larger if more distant menace of Russia. In the thinking of this ardent patriot, unless the controversy with the crown were quickly settled, the subject minorities would be encouraged to demand a "new deal," and the international prestige of the Monarchy would be gravely impaired. Because he was persuaded that a general European war was inevitable, Tisza favored the preservation of the unified army. So long ago as 1889 he had remarked fatalistically and prophetically, "For this war we must prepare in time of peace . . . This war will be no child's play. It may well be that it will determine the life or death of the Hungarian nation." For Tisza, the Magyar independence ideals of 1848 were a grand dream but the settlement of 1867 was the great reality.

As a youth Tisza had studied in Germany where he learned to admire Bismarck and the political discipline and military power of the German nation. After serving in the Hungarian army and for a short time in the ministry of the interior, he was elected a deputy and immediately plunged into the parliamentary turmoil, as befitted his father's son. Reared in the Calvinist faith, Tisza cherished high ideals of duty, uprightness, and loyalty, and belonged to that galaxy of statesmen with a Calvinistic outlook which counted Coligny, Cromwell, and Guizot in their company.

Congenitally conservative, Tisza preferred slow orderly progress to sweeping changes in policy and practice. His enemies derided him on occasion as the "man of the Bible"; at times he was the best-hated man in the kingdom, hated by the Catholics for his Calvinism and by extreme chauvinists for his unswerving fidelity to the partnership with Austria. It has been well said that "the homeric abuse rained upon him" by critics was a kind of recognition of his power. Followers knew him as a trustworthy friend to whom the very word compromise was anathema. Autocratic, arrogant, fearless, Tisza was at his best in handling public problems that seemed to require a frontal assault rather than diplomatic finesse.

An old and intimate friend of Tisza's, Baron Stephen Burián, summed up the nature of the man in these words: "Whether one agreed with him or not, any subject that one discussed with him gained in clarity and precision. He was definite in his views and expressed them forcibly . . . When he was right—and sometimes when he was wrong—he could be most convincing, carrying one away with his genuine personal conviction and the powerful logic of his own conclusions . . . Tisza's dialectics proved an admirable touchstone for the value of one's own opinions . . . In his will he was obstinate. When he had made up his mind on a thing, it was exceedingly difficult to move him . . . He was the best-loved and the best-hated statesman in Hungary."[4]

Francis Joseph was strongly attracted to this hardworking and transparently honest man and thrice named him prime minister. Even Wickham Steed, for many years the London *Times* correspondent in Vienna and a notorious critic of Hapsburg public men and their policies, credited this Hungarian, who was "a cross between a gamekeeper in his Sunday best and a fanatical monk," with the quality of a statesman.[5]

In 1903 Tisza became premier of Hungary for the first time, with the understanding that he would secure the enactment of an army expansion bill. In return the king promised to allow the Magyars the right of flying their national colors alongside of imperial emblems on military buildings in Hungary, to permit Hungarian military officials to correspond among themselves and conduct military trials in the Magyar language, and that Hungarians would be appointed as officers in proportion to the Hungarian soldiers in the common army. But on the question of the language to be used in commanding troops Francis Joseph would not budge an inch.

Upon that demand opposition deputies harped when Tisza presented the new army measure, and debate soon degenerated into factious wrangling between the prime minister and the irreconcilable Kossuthists and their allies. Tisza taunted his critics with being unable to create as much noise as "fifty hired fishwives," to which an opponent retorted that "the Tiszas are like chimney sweeps; the higher they climb, the blacker they get." By threatening to revise the rules of procedure in parliament so as to obstruct the obstructionists, the prime minister managed to secure passage of the military law and other imperative measures.

While Tisza battled to preserve dualism, he no less manfully fought for the constitutional rights of Hungary. To a Liberal party conference he asserted in 1903 that the *Ausgleich* of 1867 rested only on an understanding between the crown and the Hungarian parliament and like any other Hungarian law could be changed without the consent of Austria, an interpretation which provoked a sharp verbal duel with Koerber, the Austrian premier. Koerber declared that Austrian assent would be needed to alter the *Ausgleich;* Tisza tartly retorted that the view of Koerber was merely the dilettante opinion of "a distinguished foreigner," which was devoid of significance. The Hungarian parliament enthusiastically applauded and all Europe pricked up its ears over this strange exchange between the two premiers.

When parliament convened in 1904 the ministry was subjected again to venomous criticism, partly because Tisza had broken a railway strike by arbitrarily calling the workers to the colors and ordering them to operate trains. Once more parliament was unable to get on with its work. So the ministry resolved upon a "surgical operation" to put an end to obstruction; the standing rules of the chamber were revised so as to permit the shutting off of debaters and a corps of chamber police was created to enforce the rules. This infringement of hallowed parliamentary freedom caused deputies who considered the remedy worse than the disease to secede from the Liberal party and precipitated furious excesses in the legislative hall. As the climax of the disorders, the enemies of Tisza wrecked the furniture in the chamber, ripped woodwork from the walls, and had themselves photographed in the midst of the ruin they had wrought. Prominently featured in the picture was Baron Bánffy, sometime premier of the kingdom!

VI

On the assumption that the electorate would repudiate the aims and the doings of the opposition and would ratify the policy of reconciliation with the crown which he espoused, Tisza dissolved parliament and ordered a national election. For purposes of the campaign, the Magyar antiministerial parties, five in all, combined in a loosely knit coalition commanded by Count Julius Andrássy the younger, who had seceded from the Liberal party, and Francis Kossuth. The sons of the three men, Tisza, Andrássy, and Kossuth, who had confronted one another in the sixties now competed in different groupings from their fathers. Another notable preliminary of the election of 1905 was the resurrection of the Rumanian national party, which published a manifesto reaffirming the old claims to Transylvanian autonomy, universal and equal suffrage, and the cessation of Magyarization.

In spite of the lavish expenditure of money and the extensive use of troops brought into Hungary from all parts of the Monarchy, Tisza's Liberal party, after thirty years of political dominance, went down to defeat before the opposing coalition. Victors and vanquished alike were greatly surprised by the outcome of the balloting. Kossuth's Independence party was far and away the largest bloc in the coalition camp. Eight condidates of the Rumanian national party won seats and several other non-Magyars were chosen under the Liberal party label. All told there were twenty-six non-Magyar deputies as compared with a mere ten in the preceding chamber, apart, of course, from the customary forty representatives of Croatia.

Without indulging in abuse of either voters or victors, Tisza calmly resigned his office, the first Hungarian premier to retire after an adverse decision at the polls. On the king's request, the ministry continued to carry on administrative functions, since no other acceptable politician would undertake the arduous and thankless task of the prime minister. Promptly the coalition majority repealed the limitations that had been imposed upon freedom of parliamentary debate.

Agitation for Hungarian independence and antidynastic feelings which had a considerable place in the electioneering of 1905 were further stimulated by the formal separation in that year of Norway from Sweden. Praise for Norway resounded in the parliament at Budapest. A cartoon in a Budapest paper pictured King Oscar of Sweden thrown from the Norwegian horse, sprawling abjectly on the ground. Francis Joseph, who sat unsteadily in the Hungarian saddle, chided the Swede because he was not a better rider; to that King Oscar retorted: "Look out for yourself; your horse Hungary is getting balky." At a banquet of Budapest University students the atmosphere was rent with cries of "Down with the dynasty" and "Long live the Republic." A statue of George Washington presented to Budapest by Magyar emigrants to America was unveiled in a public park amid speeches appealing for freedom from Austria.

Once the coalition had established itself as the dominant group in the Hungarian parliament, the question arose whether it could strike a bargain with the king and undertake the management of the government. The factions that composed the coalition diverged greatly, ranging from liberals, in the Western sense of the term, to ultramontanes; they were united only by their common detestation of Tisza's tactics and the resolve to uphold what they conceived to be Hungary's legitimate constitutional rights. Key man was Francis Kossuth, chief of the large Independence party, but scarcely a statesman; his first lieutenant was Apponyi, no friend of the Hapsburgs. Andrássy led the Liberal secessionists and vied with Kossuth for headship of the coalition. Count Aladár Zichy was leader of the Clerical Peoples party, and Bánffy, a soured and not overscrupulous politician, controlled a party of his own making.[6]

In a formal address to the king the coalition leaders listed the conditions under which they would organize a cabinet. They asked for modest extension of the franchise, arrangement of electoral districts in conformity with the interests of the historic nation (i.e., in such fashion as to keep non-Magyar representation at a minimum), readjustment of tax legislation, tariff independence for Hungary, and the use of the Magyar language in commanding soldiers recruited in Hungary.

That program was, of course, wholly unacceptable to Francis Joseph. He manifested his disapproval by appointing as prime minister Baron Géza Féjerváry, a faithful and popular old Magyar general, who recruited a cabinet of little-known civil servants. In coalition quarters the appointment of Féjerváry was interpreted as the initial step toward military dictatorship, a hypothesis not incompatible with the new premier's own philosophy of government, picturesquely defined by him in these words: "Hungary can only be governed with a cudgel; but the cudgel must be painted red, white and green"—the national colors.[7]

Parliament greeted the Féjerváry ministry with stormy outcries, shouts of "Norway forever," and by a large majority passed a motion of lack of confidence offered by Kossuth. The lower chamber condemned the ministry as an unconstitutional body, because it was nonparliamentary, and called upon patriots to quit paying taxes and to refuse to appear for army service if conscripted; and similar resolutions were carried in the upper house. Thereupon parliament was prorogued and arbitrary government was ordained; restrictions were imposed upon the press and public assembly, refractory civil servants were discharged, and local governments were coerced.

Throughout the rest of 1905 and into the spring of 1906, passive resistance against the crown was widespread. Towns and counties declined to pay taxes to the royal government or to furnish recruits for the army; Austrophile aristocrats who replaced local officials had to be protected by gendarmes and some of them were roughly treated in the localities to which they were assigned. If the ministry had resorted to more drastic measures, an uprising of serious proportions might have resulted; 1848 might even have come again.

Almost entirely the conflict with the crown was Magyar, not Hungarian, and only of a section of the Magyars at that. The mass of the kingdom's population was lukewarm if not completely indifferent to the controversy. It has been truly said that "the constitutional and political struggle between the adherents of dualism and the adherents of independence existed only within the ruling caste and signified little more than a comedy to delude people about the real conditions and essential needs of the country and its peoples." [8]

Yet the Hungarian crisis could easily be exploited by the crown. The king could bend the coalition recalcitrants to his will by ordaining, or threatening to ordain, universal suffrage and the secret ballot. The devil, in other words, could be overcome by Beelzebub. The introduction of political democracy would at a single stroke put an end to the dominance of the Magyar governing classes and indeed to the supremacy of the Magyar nationality itself.[9] Joseph Kristóffy, minister of the interior, caused a sensation by expressing strong sympathy for radical franchise reform as the means of stopping parliamentary turbulence and of allaying social and minority discontents. Democratization of the suffrage, moreover, had the secret backing of Francis Ferdinand, who firmly believed that Magyar separatism and Magyarization were fatally undermining the very pillars of the Monarchy over which one day he would be called to rule. In line with the views of Rumanian and Slovak politicians, with whom he had established direct liaison, the heir presumptive believed that universal suffrage, far removed though that was from his personal political philosophy, would make Hungary safe for the Hapsburgs.

Austrian Socialist spokesmen, Karl Renner among them, contended that Magyar separatism was merely a smoke screen, designed to divert the growing industrial and agrarian unrest into hatred of dualism and to stave off much-needed social and economic reforms. Socialists of Budapest, sheep without a very good shepherd, imitating Renner and inspired by the revolutionary upheaval of 1905 in Russia, organized a great mass demonstration on behalf of suffrage reform. They threatened to call a strike of press workers unless the newspapers adopted a more sympathetic tone with regard to political democracy; a mob actually invaded the offices of the *Budapesti Hirlap* but was repulsed by editors and printers.

More important than all this, Francis Joseph took up the idea of coercing the recalcitrant coalition by the suffrage weapon.[10] Before announcing his decision the monarch invited the coalition chiefs to Vienna and in a five-minute interview brusquely told them the terms on which peace might be restored: no changes in army matters and no revision of existing agreements with Austria, except by decision of both parliaments and concurrence by the crown. Peace at that price, the coalition indignantly spurned. Not improbably, this stubborn attitude was related to Russia's recent military humiliation by Japan and to the Russian revolution of 1905, which made the tsardom less dangerous for Hungarian security.

After the Vienna interview Féjerváry bluntly told parliament that the franchise ought to be extended to all literate males over twenty-four, that balloting should be conducted in secret, that the tariff treaty with Austria should be prolonged to 1917, and that far-reaching social and economic legislation should be enacted. Coalition deputies jeered at the ministerial pronouncement and would not even allow debate on it.

As the crown had correctly calculated, the mere threat of manhood suffrage struck alarm and terror into the hearts of the Magyar ruling classes. Kossuth assailed the proposal as "an unholy alliance," between the ministry and the Socialists, to disrupt the coalition, for while the Independence party looked with favor on general suffrage "with proper educational restrictions," the other parties in the coalition were absolutely opposed to it.

Whatever happened, suffrage reform, said Kossuth, must not be brought about by unconstitutional action; if it came at all it must only come by parliamentary decision. The contention of the non-Magyars that political democracy would enable them to obtain their just rights and end oppression, Kossuth ridiculed as without substance, weak, and unconvincing. "It is only of late years," he wrote, "under the influence of the restless literary proletariat composed of Rumanians and Slovaks . . . that we hear of the 'oppression' of these nationalities, though as a matter of fact they enjoy precisely the same political and civil rights as Magyars, while the State endows their several religions and separate schools." Whether the Independence chief was really ignorant of the status of the non-Magyars or deliberately falsified it would not be hard to determine.

Aristocratic Count Andrássy scented even greater peril in political democracy than the bourgeois Kossuth. He, who had a reputation for calm and measured statement, denounced radical suffrage reform root and branch, and called attention to the fact that in England the franchise base had been broadened by an evolutionary process extending over decades and even yet had not become general. True, manhood suffrage prevailed in Germany but there it was counterbalanced by the strength of the army, the bureaucracy, and a powerful dynasty. To admit a vast body of inexperienced and politically ignorant citizens to the franchise would spell the certain ruin of Hungary in Andrássy's view. And coalition spokesmen were not alone in protesting against a democratic suffrage. Tisza, who after his withdrawal from the premiership had retired like Cincinnatus of old to the seclusion of his country estate, flooded the press with articles inveighing against the grant of equal voting privileges to the backward non-Magyar nationalities.

However much the Magyar politicians might expostulate, it was apparent that suffrage reform would be royally ordained if the coalition did not come to terms. As an earnest of his intentions, the king decided to dissolve parliament. In February of 1906, a cordon of troops was thrown round the parliament building, and a colonel marched Rumanian troops into the chamber and read a royal rescript to the deputies: "Whereas the majority constituted by the allied parties of the chamber have . . . refused to take over the government on an acceptable basis . . . we . . . are not able to expect from this body activity conducive to the interests of the country," and for that reason parliament was ordered to go home. The violence which it was imagined in Vienna the act of dissolution would provoke failed to materialize; the coalition deputies contented themselves with verbal protests alone.

But outside of parliament resentment took more concrete forms. The *Budapesti Hirlap* declared that "dissolution is a positively unjustifiable act of despotism." Patriots were reminded of the heroic sacrifices of their ancestors for the Magyar fatherland and were summoned neither to make nor drink beer, not to travel on the railways except in cases of extreme necessity, not even to mail letters—all for the purpose of curtailing the income of the government, which already had fallen sharply because of refusal to pay taxes.

VIII

Behind the scenes, however, coalition chiefs, deeply impressed by the royal dissolution of parliament and the evil consequences that the constitutional struggle was having upon business, entered into fresh negotiations with the king. The upshot was a secret understanding whereby ex-premier Wekerle would serve as nominal head of a coalition ministry, the coalition deputies would vote essential fiscal and military legislation, and the existing franchise laws would be drastically revised along democratic lines. Formal consideration of Magyar pretensions relating to the army would await the enactment of a new suffrage law. Accordingly, a cabinet of all the dissident political talents was constructed and elections for parliament were ordered. No one could doubt that the constitutional battle had resulted in a victory for the crown and a setback for the separatists, yet the defeat was in no sense a rout. To the coalition parties had been entrusted the work of revising the suffrage laws, which was virtually equivalent to saying, as the sequel amply demonstrated, that no really important change would be undertaken.

The coalition won another resounding success in the national election of 1906, the Independence party alone capturing more than half the seats. Twenty-six deputies of minorities were returned, sixteen of them Rumanians; Magyar politicians seriously considered debarring the Rumanians from the chamber and three Slovak deputies were actually imprisoned.

Right away parliament passed laws on military recruits and credits, approved negotiations with Austria on the common economic agreements, and authorized the collection of taxes which had not been paid during the years of resistance to the crown. Fortunately, Hungary had a bumper harvest in 1906 so that overdue taxes could be met.

As results of negotiations on economic pacts with Austria, the Hungarian quota on common expenses was upped to 36.4 per cent and the Hungarian tariff, while identical with the Austrian, would be technically independent. That concession to Magyar pride produced an explosion in Austria and the resignation of the ministry, as has been earlier explained. Magyar separatists waxed jubilant over the tariff arrangement as a milestone on the road to full independence. Inasmuch as the charter of the joint bank ran to 1910, the bank question had no place in the discussions at this time.

The Wekerle ministry had been installed in office on the explicit understanding that the right to vote would be broadened, but it showed small enthusiasm for fulfilling the pledge. Popular demonstrations in Budapest, orderly and disorderly, clamored for a democratic franchise. At last, in November of 1908, in the midst of the excitement generated by the annexation of Bosnia, the ministry brought forward suffrage proposals which were no more democratic than the electoral laws of Mississippi, for example. To make certain that "the Magyar state idea would . . . suffer no diminution," as Andrássy quaintly phrased the matter, plural and oral voting would be perpetuated; and nothing actually came of the proposals, for they were eclipsed by the Bosnian business.

From its inception the coalition ministry contained factions that were too discordant for real coöperation, and time widened the gap between those who were friendly to the dualistic regime and the partisans of independence. The Independence party demanded in 1908 that when the charter of the joint Austro-Hungarian bank expired in 1910 a separate bank for Hungary should be set up; that demand, with a plan to carry it out, was referred to Francis Joseph and the Austrian ministry, but the king declined to consider it, particularly since the Wekerle ministry had not implemented the promise of franchise reform. Rebuffed by the crown, Wekerle resigned.

Francis Kossuth intimated that he would enter a new ministry friendly to the preservation of the joint bank, if Hungary were given small concessions on army organization. His conciliatory attitude produced a decided rift in the Independence party; militant extremists headed by Julius Justh, a wealthy man of the gentry and a stanch separatist, would be satisfied only with a Hungarian national bank, and he and his followers repudiated the leadership of Kossuth.

Since it was impossible to assemble a ministry that had the backing of a parliamentary majority, Hungary experienced another season of "unconstitutional" government with the hardened veteran, Khuen-Héderváry, in charge. Dualism was still in crisis.

‡ CHAPTER SIXTEEN ‡

MAGYAR CULTURE AND THE MINORITIES

THE PRIDE AND THE GLORY OF MAGYAR PATRIOTISM WAS THE capital city, Budapest on the Danube. Venerable tradition has it that Buda derives its name from the brother of the dreaded Hun, Attila, who made the town his residence. In the year of the *Ausgleich* Budapest presented a primitive, antiquated appearance; though the population had grown from 38,000 in 1780 to almost 200,000, the community still resembled a provincial hill town, with winding streets, flanked by yellow cottages of one story. The Danube was unregulated and heaps of gravel, garbage, and discarded utensils littered the river's bank, along which later was laid one of Europe's most splendid promenades.

Budapest betrayed the proverbial aversion of the genuine Magyar to town life, for the inhabitants were preponderantly German and Jewish. Magyar patriotism had started to dislodge the German language, to be sure, but German persisted as the principal tongue in business and financial transactions. For all its primitiveness Budapest profoundly impressed the Hungarian peasant who chanced to visit it; one who made its acquaintance in 1872 recorded: "The sight of Buda Pest . . . nearly took my breath away. Many legends were told in my native village concerning the wonderful things there. But what I saw with my own eyes . . . surpassed all my expectations. I was overawed."

In the closing decades of the nineteenth century, Budapest grew as rapidly as Berlin and Munich, the expansion dating from the union in 1873 of Buda with its neighbor Pest on the left bank of the Danube. The building of railways, the growth of industry and commerce, which were focused on the capital to a degree unapproached in other countries, the increase in numbers of public officials, and an almost incredible rise in the birth rate, caused the population to grow almost fourfold in thirty years. Moderate enthusiasts likened the growth of Budapest to that of San Francisco or Johannesburg, while the more exuberant drew an analogy with Chicago, a page in fact from the Arabian Nights! So much of the progress was due to the energy and initiative of the Jewish population that the new Budapest was not uncommonly referred to as a "Jewish creation."

Had a Magyar Rip van Winkle fallen asleep in the city in the sixties he would scarcely have recognized it had he been roused from his slumbers at the time of the Millennial Exhibition of 1896. In the interval the broad Andrássy boulevard, two miles in length, had been laid out; it was lined at one end with splendid mansions and at the other with attractive little villas. An Opera House, an Academy of Music, an Academy of Sciences, magnificent university buildings and technical institutes attested the Magyar interest in the life of the mind and spirit. A massive parliament building, late Gothic in architectural design, was dedicated in connection with the Exhibition (though not finished until 1902); the imposing royal palace on Buda's hilltop, built while Maria Theresa reigned, was much enlarged and modernized, a symbol in a sense of the past glories of Hungary. On the terrace Prince Eugene of Savoy proudly rode his warhorse and in the great Hapsburg Hall Maria Theresa kept undisturbed her watch in marble. Near by, the church of St. Matthias, one of Budapest's few medieval structures and the scene of royal coronations, was restored. The Danube, flowing through the center, was spanned by fine bridges and on its banks sumptuous hotels and clubhouses were beginning to rise. The queen city of the Magyars was being transformed in truth into the dream city of Europe. Railways and street-car lines, office buildings, mills, factories, the squalid tenements of the working class mutely testified, moreover, that Budapest had responded to the impact of industrialism.

II

Like trade and finance, Magyar intellectual and cultural affairs were largely concentrated in the capital city. Hungary's foremost man of letters, a storyteller of international renown, and an editor and politician as well, was Maurus Jókai. The term prolific only faintly describes his literary output; he produced more than a hundred novels, thirty plays, and scores of short stories and poems. His fertile imagination gave birth to no fewer than ten thousand characters! Jókai's novels fall into two broad classes: those in which he undertook to portray and assess the traits of his countrymen, albeit none too critically, and essentially historical romances. For the latter, in which established fact was generously interspersed with patriotic fiction, he has been called the Magyar Walter Scott.[1]

From the past, especially from the failure of the Turks to crush Hungary in the seventeenth century, Jókai borrowed the inspiriting lesson that Austria would similarly fail in the present. He wrote in full confidence that the pen in politics would prove a mightier weapon than the sword. Many of his outpourings were nationalistic clarion calls to his countrymen and his time; patriotism and warm sympathy for freedom for the Magyar oppressed are the golden keys to an understanding of the man and his works.

For editing a rebel newspaper during the revolution of 1848, Jókai was outlawed by the Austrian authorities, and during the rigorous Bach era he lived in seclusion, writing patriotic volume upon patriotic volume and publishing a patriotic newspaper to keep hope and courage alive among the Magyars. After the settlement of 1867, he sat in parliament, a steadfast follower of Coloman Tisza, and in 1897 he was given a life peerage in the upper house; to his political speeches Jókai contrived to impart the suavity and resplendent color of his literary productions.

Of Jókai's artistic talent there can be no dispute, but whether he will be much read a century hence may be doubted. His narratives were too long, and there was too much of the Oriental in them to make them popular in the colder, less vivid Western world; his thrills were too sinister and too abundant for any but the most hardened devotees of the more lurid Hollywood productions, however faithfully they might reflect the actualities of real existence in Europe's semi-Oriental East.

The Hungarian Nabob, Black Diamonds, and *The Strange Story of Rab Ráby* are characteristic and popular specimens of Jókai's genius as a novelist. *The Hungarian Nabob* portrayed the ways and manners of the Magyar squirearchy, their earthy diversions, their robust good humor, their hospitality; rustic festivals and fairs, horse races, and the like were described with a wealth of imagery and great literary power. Brilliant sketches of minor figures crowded the canvas. The rich nabob made merry with women and gypsies, gamblers and fools; at seventy he married a poor girl who presented him with a son, who turned out to be a ne'er-do-well. After the baron's death, his relatives brought suit against the widow, charging that the old aristocrat could not possibly have been the father of the dissolute youth. Into the narrative the novelist wove a prayer for Hungarian political and intellectual revival, a plea for constancy and courage, and confidence in better days to come.

Black Diamonds dealt with coal mines and the life of the upthrusting Hungarian *bourgeoisie,* the aristocracy, and the toiling miners. The hero, young as usual with Jókai, was an energetic and competent owner of a mine. A powerful combination of capitalists tried to strangle him by competition, but the resourcefulness and transparent honesty of the young man thwarted the evil ones. A beautiful village lass whom the hero loved moved off to the city, married a wealthy financier, grew weary of the vicissitudes of fashionable society, and returned to the colliery owner. *Black Diamonds,* like many another of Jókai's novels, was a valuable document for the student of Magyar society.

The troubled era of Emperer Joseph II, the "Enlightened One," and a public-spirited young nobleman's effort at reform in Hungary were the time and the theme of *The Strange Story of Rab Ráby.* To the "revolutionary emperor" the youth recommended innovations that would liberate the commoners from the incompetence and corruption of the bureaucracy. Acting on his suggestions, the emperor ordered reforms, but officials appealed to the ancient constitution of the Hungarian kingdom and stirred up the country against the changes. Only by the repeal of the edicts in the nick of time was the hero saved from destruction at the hands of the very people he had hoped to uplift.

Jókai summed up his own career, the politics and social manners of his time, in *Eyes Like the Sea.* The "eyes" belong to the heroine, a girl of good family with adventuresome inclinations which led her five times into matrimony. Each husband was of a different social rank, from nobleman to peasant, and each was described in lavish detail. Among the grooms was Jókai himself, and neither he nor the heroine could forget one another after their separation. Jókai tried to drown his sorrow by seeking fame as a writer, fighting in the revolution of 1848, and marrying an actress, who was devoted to him. Still the "eyes like the sea" haunted him, glared remorselessly at him.

Jókai had many imitators, of whom Coloman Mikszáth, called the Magyar Bret Harte, was probably the most successful. His particular concern was the lower strata of rural society and his *The Good Paloczok* is a convincing portrait of the drab round of the Magyar villagers.

Hungarian critics regarded John Arany as the most illustrious poet of the nation in the second half of the nineteenth century. Unsurpassed for perfection of form and depth of patriotic feeling, Arany was at his best in the composition of ballads depicting the ways and interests of country dwellers, whether proprietor or peasant (*Toldi; The Love of Toldi*). Through translations of Aristophanes and Shakespeare, Arany, like other litterateurs of small European national groups, opened up new vistas of thought and style to Magyar intellectuals. Also active in translating works of Western poets was Charles Szász, and in his epic *Salamon* he vividly recounted intoxicating legends of medieval Magyar chivalry.

Foremost among Hungarian playwrights was Gregory Csiky, who responded to the new currents of industrialism as is shown in the vigorous *The Proletariat* and *The Irresistible.* Csiky, who had been trained for the priesthood, adopted Protestantism and dabbled a bit in ecclesiastical history.

Rural folkways had dramatic exposition in the works of Edward Tóth, notably *The Ousted Pauper*.

Toward the end of the century conventional types of Magyar literature competed with literary forms and ideas that came in from France and Germany and had no roots in the national heritage.[2] Magyar men of letters in fact separated into two schools, each scornful of and hostile to the other. One faction preferred the subjects and modes of inherited literary tradition, while the other drew inspiration from western Europe and reflected the social changes which industrialism was bringing in its train. This latter group published a review, *Nyugat* (The West), founded in 1908 by a refined Jewish patrician, Baron Louis Hatvany, himself an author of European stature; around him there gathered a cosmopolitan set of unconventional sons of the gentry and critically minded Jewish intellectuals. These writers hailed the progress of machinofacture, shot arrows at anachronistic agrarian feudalism, and taught an essentially materialistic outlook on life. By the Hungarian reading public the "Westernizers" found only a limited reception, but criticism from conservative, chauvinistic sources only hardened the hearts of the exponents of realism and naturalism.

The *New Verse* by Andrew Ady is considered the pioneer expression of "Westernism" in Hungarian literature. His lyrics castigated in shrill tones the faults and flaws in the Hungarian nation, which laid Ady open to the charge that he was wanting in patriotism, and his vivid portrayal of the emotion of love deviated widely from standard conventions. Michael Babits, novelist, erudite poet, and philosopher, has been acclaimed as the most gifted Magyar writer since Jókai. A son of the gentry, like Ady, he minutely analyzed his own social class in a novel, *Sons of Death,* in which he attributed the woes of Hungary to the disintegration of the solid and virtuous squirearchy.

Close to these authors in restlessness of spirit was the best novelist of the generation, Sigismund Móricz, who exalted naturalism, excelling in expositions of the life of the peasantry. *Earthen Gold,* a representative specimen of Móricz's writing, was focused upon a villager of immense physical strength and presented a full panorama of rural existence. Louis Kassak, who was to be commissar of literature during the Communist interlude of 1919, sketched his struggle to achieve literary distinction in a *A Man's Life*.[3]

Over against the rationalistic and unorthodox Westernizers was a school of national writers. They found rich inspiration in the Asiatic origins of the Magyars, extolled the ethnological and historical bonds with the Turks, and espoused Pan-Turanianism. Francis Herczeg (*Susanna Simon*) was the outstanding novelist of the "Easterners," while Alexander Endrödi and Joseph Lévay upheld traditional themes and techniques in poetry.

Hungary's only painter to attract international attention was Michael

Munkácsy, who studied in German art centers and finally settled down in Paris. Though he painted some pastoral scenes and portraits, Munkácsy attained distinction by dramatically spectacular and colorful episodes from the life of Christ, "Christ Before Pilate" and "Christ at Calvary," both of which adorn the great Wanamaker store in Philadelphia. "Milton Dictating Paradise Lost" to his daughters is generally appraised as Munkácsy's most distinguished canvas. Just when Munkácsy was at the height of his powers, his mind became unbalanced and he remained hopelessly insane to his death.

Michale Zichy, an aristocrat, became the court painter of Russia, specializing in historical and sporting subjects. Of purely national interest were the paintings of Julius Benczur and Karl Lotz, who, responding to rising national sentiments, produced works suggested by Magyar saga and history; the latter decorated the walls of public buildings in Budapest with large historical pictures. History also inspired Hungary's most eminent sculptors. George Zala carved monuments in neobaroque style for Budapest to commemorate the millenium of Hungary and to honor Queen Elizabeth and Count Julius Andrássy the elder. Another sculptor, John Fadrusz, is best known for memorials of Maria Theresa in his native Pozsony (Bratislava) and of King Matthias Corvinus in Kolozsvár (Cluj), which won him a grand prize in Paris.

In the musical realm the supreme Hungarian was Francis Liszt, who is also claimed as a German and is perhaps most accurately described as a cosmopolitan. Liszt pioneered in composing symphonic poems and utilized primitive folk tunes extensively, fancying them to be Magyar though in fact they were of gypsy origin; he imagined that national uniqueness was most faithfully revealed in simple and soulful peasant melodies. For the crowning of Francis Joseph as Hungarian king, Liszt prepared a coronation mass, and he composed two national anthems, *Szozat* and *Hymnus*.

More genuinely Magyar than Liszt were the composers Béla Bartók and Zoltán Kodály. Together, though working independently, they collected thousands of Magyar, Slovak, and Rumanian peasant tunes and proved that Hungarian gypsy rhythms, which had been popularized across Europe, were not in fact authentic folk melodies of their homeland.[4] In their own compositions, they patriotically exploited original songs, some of them picked up in the most remote villages, which recalled the heroic spirit of the ancestral conquering Magyars. Except for their intensity, the compositions of Kodály resemble Schubert's. Bartók, who attained international prominence as a pianist, was the Magyar nationalistic composer without peer. He wrote an ultrapatriotic *Kossuth* symphony, a variation on the Austrian national anthem; at its first performance the artist appeared in the national costume of the Magyars. Bartók was horrified to learn as the result of later investigations that he had confused Magyar and Slovak folk tunes in his early productions. Bartók's "Allegro Barbaro" evoked glowing memories of the fearless Magyar horsemen as they set out from their Asiatic haunts on forays into Europe.[5]

III

The character of Magyar scholarship is well exemplified in its contributions to historiography. As a rule, Hungarian historians dipped their pens deeply in nationalistic ink, indulged in fulsome panegyrics of national heroes of other centuries, or strove to justify by an appeal to the past the attitudes of the governing class toward the Austrian partner and the submerged minorities. There was a pronounced emphasis on broad historical surveys instead of microscopic research, and, as was so true in other countries, considerable industry was devoted to the collection and publication of documentary materials of Magyar history.

Several of the more productive Magyar historians merit individual comment. Bishop Michael Horváth, for example, minister of education in Kossuth's revolutionary cabinet, wrote extensively on the early nineteenth century, preaching pure nationalism and the enlightened political principles of Francis Deák. Another Deákist in outlook, Francis Salomon, taught "scientific" techniques of historical investigation in his university seminar; an excellent study of the Turkish epoch in Hungary, which he prepared, concerned itself with commoners as well as with the aristocracy. With great erudition the director of the national archives, Julius Pauler, recreated the life of the Magyars after their original settlement in the Danube Valley and in the seventeenth century, while the researches of Bishop William Fráknoi clarified phases of the most glamorous age in Magyar annals, the late fifteenth and early sixteenth centuries.

Objective historical writing had its foremost practitioner, no doubt, in Henry Marczali. Professor in the University of Budapest from 1895 to 1924, Marczali was especially interested in the eighteenth century and the constitutional evolution of Hungary; less detached, more patriotic was a brilliantly written survey of the country which Marczali prepared for popular consumption. Oriental history, or more exactly the traditions and pre-Moslem paganism of the Arabs, was illuminated by Ignatius Goldscher, the first Jew, incidentally, to be advanced to professorial rank in the University of Budapest.

In anticipation of the millennial celebration of 1896 a monumental history of Hungary was written by a team of specialists. Running into ten stately volumes, lavishly illustrated, and emphatically nationalist in tone, this famous work exhibited at once the merits and the shortcomings of Magyar historical scholarship. New viewpoints on Hungarian constitutional and agrarian history in the Middle Ages were brought forward by Karoly Tagányi, who, though he held no university chair, exerted considerable influence upon younger scholars who were attracted by economic interpretations of the past; and only inferior to Tagányi in influence was Ignatius Acsady, a specialist on financial and economic class history.

The multiplication of magazines and the growth of the press reflected the growing Magyar intellectual activity and the greater literacy of the kingdom. In the age of Metternich only ten periodicals were printed in the Magyar tongue (Latin was still the language of the learned), but by 1890 there were almost six hundred, the number having doubled in the eighties, a decade of intensified Magyarization. These publications were diverse in content, some scholarly journals, others literary, professional, or trade organs.

Budapest's press was much more animated, less restrained in expression than that of Vienna. It represented and propagated Magyar national interests to the detriment of the minorities and was less concerned with considerations of monarchical solidarity. In the twentieth century the leading newspaper was the *Budapesti Hirlap* (Budapest News), which professed to stand above political partisanship but in reality was the mouthpiece of moderate chauvinism, the spokesman of Magyar nationalism in time of controversy with the crown, and a tireless propagandist of national efficiency and industry; it maintained correspondents in foreign countries, even having one in the United States. One of the owners and editors of *Budapesti Hirlap,* Eugene Rákosi, gained a European reputation as a literary critic and playwright.

Pesti Napló, which was founded in 1850 and contrived against immense odds to weather the fury of the Bach reaction, disseminated the views of Francis Deák and his disciples. But after the *Ausgleich* the importance of this journal dwindled, for it spent itself in unbridled criticism of the Liberal party, its personalities rather than its policies. Toward the end of the century, Ambrose Neményi, an astute, broad-gauged pressman, took over the editorship of *Pesti Napló,* and as the voice of the Liberal party it recovered much of its former prestige.

Kossuthist doctrines of separation from Austria, of Hungarian independence, were circulated in several papers, of which *Magyarorszóg* (Hungary) attracted the largest following. Often this paper carried articles from the pen of Francis Kossuth. Narrowly Magyar in emphasis, and flippant and sneering in tone, was *Pesti Hirlap* (Pest News), which inherited its name from a short-lived sheet published by Louis Kossuth in the forties. The leading exponent of immediate secession from Austria was *Egyétertés,* whose editor, Martin Dienes, was repeatedly haled into court for breaches of journalistic etiquette, but invariably he was judged "not guilty."

Sympathetic to the preservation of the partnership with Austria were *As Ujság* (The News), the personal organ of Stephen Tisza, and *Pester*

Lloyd, printed in German, and the only Hungarian paper in a non-Magyar tongue of more than local importance. Thanks to excellent coverage of foreign news and the considerable space allotted to cultural affairs, *Pester Lloyd* ranked with the distinguished newspapers of Europe; Max Falk, editor from 1868 to 1906, belonged in the very front rank of European journalists. These journalistic supporters of the dualistic regime argued that economic advantage and considerations of national safety demanded that Hungary live amicably with Austria, even though the partnership involved the sacrifice of some cherished idealisms. Spokesman for financial and business interests, *Pester Lloyd* roused the ire of extreme chauvinists because of its relative indifference to Hungarian national rights.

Freedom of the press was narrowly circumscribed in Hungary—university professors had much more latitude in expression—and special courts existed to try those charged with infractions of the stern press law. Jurors in these cases were required to be men with a substantial income and to understand the Magyar language, which excluded large sections of the population. Owners of newspapers were obliged to post "caution money," from which fines were deducted for violation of the press code. Laws concerning the press could be and were manipulated so as to hobble publications in non-Magyar languages, and only financial help from emigrants in the United States enabled the Slovak- and Rumanian-language press to keep going at all.

IV

The prolonged constitutional controversy with the crown, attended as it was by clamor for the abandonment of the customs union with Austria, had unhappy repercussions upon Hungarian commerce and finance, but that was counterbalanced by steady promotion of Hungarian business by the government. "Hungary," commented Fiorello La Guardia, the American consul at Fiume in 1904, "is the land of subventions and subsidies." Periodically, new legislation was enacted to foster the manufacture of wares which Hungary produced only in insufficient quantities to meet national requirements or did not produce at all; and when subsidies were awarded it was invariably prescribed that the beneficiary should employ only Hungarian workers and use only Hungarian materials. Partly because of these official policies, Hungary's industrial facilities steadily expanded.[6]

With state aid an independent Hungarian navigation company was launched to compete with an Austrian firm for traffic on the Danube. It has been well said that the history of trade is the history of transportation, and the Danube with its tributaries and connecting canals was Hungary's cheapest means of communication. Shipping on the Danube was long retarded by two obstacles which seemed insuperable: the lower end of the river was icebound several months of the year, and at Orsova, between Serbia and Rumania, formidable rocks, rapids, and cliffs, which the Turks called the Iron Gates, rendered navigation extremely hazardous. At the Congress of Berlin, Austria-Hungary was authorized to widen the channel at the Gates and the task, done largely under the auspices of the Hungarian government, was finished in 1896. A canal five miles long and thirty feet below the level of the Danube was blasted out of the rocky bed of the river. From the technical standpoint this canal was not entirely satisfactory for navigation, and the tolls charged for its use were steep and discriminatory; Rumanian oil companies, for instance, found it cheaper to ship to Germany by the Mediterranean Sea than along the Danube. Rate discriminations and the regulation that only the Magyar language should be spoken by the canal administration were much resented by the Rumanian and Serbian governments. Though the improvements at the Iron Gates failed to make the Danube as important commercially as the Rhine, they nonetheless assisted in the growth of Hungarian shipping.

Fiume, the Hungarian national seaport, continued to profit from the fostering care of the government. Exporters of wheat were granted special rates on the state railways if they shipped through Fiume and on vessels of Hungarian ownership. To divert emigrant traffic to Fiume and away from German ports, the government arranged with the Cunard company for direct steamship service to New York, and even guaranteed 30,000 fares per year. Fiume developed into a flourishing community with fine public buildings and squares and a considerable industry: oil refineries, naval yards, and a world-famous torpedo works, the property of the English inventor, Robert Whitehead.[7] Shipping traffic at Fiume increased by half between 1900 and 1912, a much slower rate than at Trieste, but impressive nevertheless.

Hungarian industrial progress was accompanied by the rise of Socialism. In many particulars the history of the movement in Hungary paralleled that of Austria, proper allowance being made for the much smaller size of the industrial working class in the land of the Magyar. Hungarian Socialism had its beginnings late in the sixties, but was repressed after the Paris Communard of 1871, and more thoroughly restricted in the eighties by legislation similar to that enacted at the time in Austria and Germany. Formal organization of Hungarian Socialism took place in 1890 and the Hainfeld program, which had been adopted by the Austrian Socialists in the preceding year, was taken over by the Hungarian Social Democracy as its very own; intellectuals, Jews very largely, furnished the leadership.

As in Austria, so in Hungary, the Socialist party was tormented by factionalism over doctrines. Secessions and purges were recurrent and in 1903 the party underwent thorough overhauling. Leader of the strait-laced Marxist wing was Ervin Szabó, who translated Marx's *Das Kapital* and other pieces of "scientific" Socialist literature into Magyar. Szabó emphasized the importance of winning not alone the Hungarian industrial workers but likewise the underprivileged rural masses to the Socialist cause; his disciples were the leaders of the brief Hungarian Communist republic of 1919. An ably edited Socialist press championed the interests of the working class, pleaded for suffrage reform and social-welfare legislation, criticized sharply official minorities policies, condemned capitalistic economy as well as the top-heavy bureaucracy and the Church—all, to be sure, within the narrow limits permitted by the stringent laws on the press. The principal Socialist daily, *Népszava* (The Peoples' Voice), was repeatedly confiscated for violation of press regulations and its editors fined.

At the general election of 1905, Socialist candidates were presented in fully a hundred constituencies, and during the ensuing constitutional conflict the anticoalition ministry permitted Socialist propaganda greater freedom than ever before. But after the crown and the coalition struck a bargain, the laws on the press and public assembly were rigorously enforced against the Socialists.

As a counterweight to Socialism, university students banded together in the national Széchényi association, which propagated patriotic and conservative principles among workers. And a small Christian Socialist party, managed by churchmen, aspired to emulate its namesake in Austria. The founder of the party, the prelate Sándor Giesswein, also organized Christian trade-unions, and preached supranational emphases in education, prohibition of intoxicating beverages, and full emancipation of women. And a government newspaper, printed in six languages, waged incessant war upon Socialist principles and their exponents.[8]

v

Agriculture, the economic mainstay of Hungary, experienced severe hardships in the nineties. Swine were ravaged by epidemics, harvests were particularly poor in 1894 and 1898, and for the decade as a whole the yield of wheat and rye touched a record low level. Discontent with prevailing conditions increased in the rural laboring class, and it was at this time that emigration overseas attained mass dimensions. Some rustics embraced and acted upon radical economic doctrines. Socialist evangelists and literature summoned the landless to overturn the existing order and to distribute the soil equitably among all families; one proclamation declared: "The people shall divide the land. Each shall have an equal part. If the owners resist, kill them." Secret societies of radical peasants held meetings in which members solemnly swore that there should be neither masters nor servants in the new Hungary that was to be.

Anarchic disturbances, rioting and bloodshed, upset the fertile Alföld time and again, reaching a peak in 1897. In that year Social Democrats organized an agricultural labor congress, which demanded shorter hours and higher wages for seasonal workers; and not long afterward laborers joined in a general strike and some landlords expressed fears that a general peasant rebellion was in the making. Strikers in some places succeeded in obtaining their demands, and widespread rural strikes also occurred in 1905, 1906, and 1907.

Lasting improvement in the status of rural labor was adversely affected by combinations of landlords, by quarreling among peasant leaders, and by the hostile policies of the government. Stephen Várkonyi, most resolute of the leaders, born a peasant but become wealthy as a horse trader, broke away from the official Socialist party and founded the "Independent Socialist party," which contemplated organizing the poor peasants in every village. Such success as the movement had, and it was never large, was confined to Magyar-inhabited districts.

Public authorities sternly repressed agrarian disaffection with whip and gun. Wherever a strike broke out, strikebreakers were thrown "like bales of goods" into the disaffected areas. Several laws, half palliative, half coercive in character, were enacted to deal with rural labor problems. An important act of 1898, "to secure the undisturbed execution of agricultural labor contracts" by casual workers, set up state labor bureaus to bring employers and workers together and to register contracts; workers were obliged to sign contracts with managers in the presence of a government agent. To each laborer was handed a "work book" in which his terms of employment were entered and officially approved; if the worker violated the contract he could be imprisoned or compelled to fulfill his agreement by the police. If the worker had a grievance he might not quit, but had to apply to a local public authority for redress. Unions of agricultural workers were banned and it was declared a punishable offense "to address, attend, or hire a hall for meetings with a view to organizing a union"; landowners, on the other hand, were not allowed to discharge a laborer without reasonable cause and were obliged to carry out contractual obligations under pain of fines. Nicknamed the "slave law," the act of 1898 was still in force at the beginning of World War II.

Small sums were appropriated by the Hungarian government to assist rural workers to buy land or build houses, and prizes were awarded to the most efficient laborers and dwarf-holders. A rudimentary scheme of accident and sickness insurance for landless workers was introduced. The Farm Laborers' Act of 1907, which avowedly was intended "to prevent abuses to the laborer and to improve his social and economic condition," was properly criticized as a law to hinder emigration and to curb agrarian unrest by shackling a laborer to his employer. Workers might not leave a landlord's estate on which they had contracted to toil, nor receive visitors from outside without permission; workers under eighteen might even be disciplined with corporal punishment, and heavy penalties were provided for incitement to strike and for participants in strikes. Proprietors, on their part, were expected to furnish decent living quarters, medical care for women and children, and schools; workers had a theoretical right to appeal to local authorities if they felt the employer was dealing unfairly.

VI

Not long after Wekerle's coalition ministry took charge of Hungarian destinies, Count Andrássy the younger, as minister of the interior, expressly renounced forcible Magyarization measures. He promised that in the future civil servants would be required to know the language of the national group among whom they worked; only the seditious among the minorities would feel the heavy hand of public authority. But deeds soon belied these enlightened professions, for the systematic process of Magyarizing the oncoming generation was pushed with redoubled intensity through the schools of the kingdom. Alarmist reports purported to show that the minorities were increasing faster than Magyars, and manifestations of national feeling among non-Magyars were somewhat disquieting to the ruling nationality. Had they not returned twenty-six deputies to the parliament chosen in 1906, aside from the forty Croatians? Were not their deputies speaking up for universal suffrage and "racial" equality and a "united army"? Had they not established a personal liaison with the heir presumptive, Francis Ferdinand, no friend of Magyar separatists?

Early in the twentieth century, the time devoted in the primary denominational schools to instruction in Magyar was considerably increased. It was seriously proposed that for three years schools attended by non-Magyars should confine themselves exclusively to speaking and singing in the language of the dominant nationality. Two laws of 1907, known as the Apponyi acts from the name of their ministerial sponsor, were designed to convert the schools into even more effective agencies of Magyarization than they had been. One measure, for example, ordered teachers to emphasize Magyar instruction and restricted membership on local school boards to persons acquainted with the Magyar tongue; the other converted teachers in confessional schools into state officials under the supervision of public functionaries. Teachers' salaries were set at such a level that confessional authorities would have to apply for state aid in order to meet them, and salary subventions were conditional upon the ability of the instructor in question to teach the Magyar language; as a result, in many instances the ministry of education virtually appointed teachers in church schools.

Instruction in Magyar and in history, civics, and geography—studies so vital in creating national attitudes—had to conform to official syllabi, and textbooks, not excluding church catechisms, had to bear the imprimatur of the state minister of education. Teachers in confessional schools would cultivate Magyar patriotism by displaying the national flag and placarding schoolrooms with pictures of inspiriting episodes from Hungarian history; they would take an oath of fidelity to the state in the Magyar language and in the presence of a government official; refusal to take the prescribed oath would be punished as "a tendency hostile to the state." These acts, which unmistakably contravened the principle of church autonomy prescribed in the famous Nationalities Act, were not fully executed when World War I broke out. They reveal, however, with crystal-clear clarity, the intention of the Magyar ruling caste to harness the schools wholly to the national purposes of the Magyars.[9]

The rising tempo of Magyarization was exhibited in other spheres than schooling. Standing regulations governing the organization of clubs and societies were stringently enforced and fresh curbs were imposed upon public assembly. To erect a public sign in a non-Magyar tongue required considerable personal hardihood; it was even ordered that tombstones in Budapest should carry inscriptions in Magyar and that names in public records should be entered in Magyar or their Magyar equivalent.[10] Schoolchildren who spoke their mother's tongue at play were sometimes punished by teachers, and attractive inducements were held out to non-Magyars, officials especially, to change their names.

VII

While the intensification of the Magyarization process was directed against all minority groups, it was given special point by political stirrings among the Slovaks, the sequel to a modest cultural renaissance. Unhappily, the Slovak movement was gravely handicapped by Magyar educational policies which tended to convert educated Slovaks into Magyarones and by wide political differences among the handful of patriotic Slovak intellectuals. An older group preferred to write in the Slovak language, a regional variant of Czech, cherished strong Russophile sympathies, and in politics desired merely the autonomy of the Slovak counties within the Hungarian framework. But in the nineties a new literary faction emerged which acknowledged the community of interest and tradition with the Czechs, wrote in the Czech language, and advocated political unity with the Czechs.

In the final quarter of the nineteenth century, when hope for the Slovak nation still seemed a fantastic dream, the patriotic flame was kept alight by two men of letters who had been trained as lawyers: Svetozár Hurban Vajanský and Paul Országh. The former looked to great Russia as the champion and the eventual liberator of the Slovaks; yet so late as the eighties he had little faith in national deliverance, for he prefaced a book of his verse with the words: "I send forth a new song into a deaf world. Silence prevails on all sides, as in a graveyard." Creator of the Slovak novel, Vajanský painted illuminating portraits of the social customs and manners of his countrymen in *The Withered Branch* and *Roots and Offshoots*.[11]

Orszách, who published under the pen name of Hviezdoslav (meaning "star-glory") won acclaim as the leading Slovak playwright and poet. Educated in Magyar schools, his first verses were written in Magyar, later in Slovak. A deep religious sense, romantically patriotic idealism, and sentimental affection for Slavdom pervaded his lyric and epic poetry. In *Psalms and Hymns* Orszách voiced bitter anguish over the oppression of the Slovaks and the ardent hope that the day of emancipation would presently dawn. "Truth has been crucified," he mourned, "but the time will come when it will rise from the dead, and, holy as the reverent Sun, it will sit on the throne, seizing the reins of government, of might and right in its just hands." A familiar Biblical story, *Herod and Herodias,* supplied Orszách with the theme for the most-prized drama in the Slovak language.

It was only toward the end of the century that Czechophile currents appeared significantly in the Slovak literary stream. A set of patriotic authors, with Jaroslav Vlček, historian of Slovak literature, in the van, joined with journalists and politicians in diffusing the notion of Czechoslovak solidarity and Western economic and political principles. Outstanding among them was Dr. Milan Hodža, son of a Lutheran clergyman, who studied law at Budapest, took a degree in philosophy at Vienna, and later practiced journalism in Hungary. Elected to the Hungarian parliament in 1905, Hodža missed no opportunity to expound his federalistic and democratic convictions to whomsoever would hear, high or low; he was to become premier of Czechoslovakia in the terrible years just preceding the destruction of the republic in 1939.[12]

For this small but earnest company of Slovak nationalists the intellectual and spiritual lodestar was the distinguished and enterprising Prague savant, Professor Thomas Masaryk, himself part Slovak in ancestry and a confirmed believer in the fundamental community of Czechs and Slovaks. In his university lecture hall, Masaryk convinced Slovak students of the validity of his views, if indeed persuasion were needed, for often the youths had been excluded from Hungarian institutions because of their Slovak outlook. Masaryk fraternized with Slovak intellectuals in their home communities and helped to found a Slovak summer school as an agency to tighten Czechoslovak bonds. Thanks to Masaryk's intervention, a section of the Prague journal *Cas* (Time) was given over to the interests of Slovaks and under his guidance Slovaks founded a monthly review, *The Voice,* which circulated Czechophile doctrines and contributed signally to the Slovak awakening.

At about the same time a Czechoslovak society in Prague began to furnish educational opportunities at Czech institutions for Slovak youths and to arrange for others to serve as apprentices to Czech craftsmen. In addition, this society distributed Czechophile literature and puzzled out methods of combatting Magyarization. So it came to pass that the idea of Czechoslovak solidarity, after lying dormant for a long time, experienced a revival, which was heavy with consequences for the future of central Europe.

The Czechophile trend, extremely modest though it was, stirred up a hornet's nest in Magyarland. Magyarone Slovaks repudiated the idea of alignment with the Czechs, contending among other things that the Slovak language had closer affinity with Yugoslav dialects than with Czech. And Czechophiles, largely Protestants or freethinkers, fell out with clerically minded countrymen, whose leader was Father Andreas Hlinka. Hlinka admitted the essential unity of Slovaks and Czechs, but on the political plane his aspirations were centered on obtaining autonomy for the Slovak area alone.[13] Conservatives and progressives among the Slovaks, Russophiles and Czechophiles, clericals and anticlericals, clashed heatedly and thereby lamed the Slovak national cause.

The Slovak cultural renaissance extended beyond literary boundaries. Folk tunes, some Christian in content, others pagan, harking back to ancient heathen divinities and to preliterary customs, were collected by the thousand, published, and utilized by native and foreign musicians; the most popular of the folk ballads recounted the exciting exploits of the Slovak robber-hero, Janošik, Robin Hood's counterpart. At Bratislava a Slovak national theater was erected, but the Slovaks lacked an opera company of their own. Bratislava, a city of strange architectural contrasts and rich in Hapsburg history, was the "capital" of the Protestant Slovaks as Trnava was of the Catholic element. For the greater part the Slovak Protestants, Lutherans, turned Czechophile and used the Czech language in their services, and their clergy had an active part in creating a literature for their countrymen.

Slovak nationalists did not neglect to emphasize the value of preserving the distinctive heritage of the land in costume and customs. Someone has said that if John Ruskin wanted to find a region in which art was woven into the very fabric of a people he should have visited the picturesque Slovak districts. Despite the extreme poverty of the masses, here was a region of gorgeous festival dress, distinctive pottery, and interesting hand-painted furniture.[14]

At the century's end, the Slovak revival had open political expression in the formation of a National party. It professed social and educational objectives and claimed equal rights for the Slovak language with the Magyar. This party in 1906 elected six deputies to the royal Hungarian parliament, a success disturbing to fervent and fearful Magyar patriots.

The attention of Europe was drawn to the Slovaks in 1907 by the notorious Csernova affair. Customarily Magyarones were appointed to Roman Catholic bishoprics in the Slovak area, but among the lower clergy an occasional Slovak nationalist was found. Such an one was Father Andreas Hlinka, for forty years a sturdy apostle of Slovak rights and interests. Born of simple Slovak peasant stock, Hlinka was ordained a priest in 1889 and quickly achieved local renown as a fighter for the economic and cultural liberties of his countrymen. He helped to organize a coöperative society and bank and edited a newspaper, *Slovak*. Settled as priest in the village of Csernova, he harangued his parishioners against Magyar rule, discriminations against the Slovak language, and related matters.

On charges of seditious agitation, Hlinka was arrested, convicted, and sentenced to jail, and the Magyarone hierarchy suspended him from his priestly office. His parishioners, however, secured the consent of the bishop for the consecration of a newly built church, though they failed to obtain permission for Hlinka to participate in the ceremonies. Rather, another priest was instructed to repair to Csernova for the dedication; on the way he was warned by partisans of Hlinka that if he set foot in the village he would place his life in jeopardy. Discreetly he turned back and other clerics, escorted by an armed guard, were sent to inform the inflamed villagers that the rites of dedication had been postponed. As the cavalcade approached Csernova a mob pelted it with a barrage of stones, injuring a priest and several gendarmes. When the crowd refused to disperse guardsmen opened fire, killing sixteen and wounding four times as many. Almost half a hundred villagers were arrested and, after a perfunctory trial, were severely punished; Hlinka's sister, the alleged ringleader of the "insurrection," was sentenced to three years in prison.[15]

The sanguinary Csernova affray not only quickened the Slovak national consciousness but excited general indignation among Hapsburg Slavs and called forth sharp denunciations of Magyars in the press of Europe. To all critics the Hungarian government and its unapologetic apologists retorted that the inhabitants of Csernova had been peaceful and contented until fanatical Slovak agitators egged them on to challenge established authority.

Slovaks were victims of petty, though vexatious, irritations, which aggravated popular hostility to Magyar rule. Numerous illustrations of the policy of "pin pricks" might be cited. For example, Slovak emigrants to the United States presented a Slovak author with an American flag, to which were attached streamers in Slav colors; the recipient intended to place the banner in a local museum but was dissuaded from doing so by Magyar officials, who warned that it would be confiscated. Again, a Lutheran clergyman asked in his Slovak mother tongue for a ticket at a railway station. The clerk, who happened to be a Slovak Magyarone, complained angrily because an educated man had dared to address him in Slovak, accused him of being a suspicious character, a Pan-Slav indeed, and would not sell him a ticket. Complaint to the stationmaster brought a repetition of the first experience; a policeman arrested the pastor as a spy, but he was released when he fully established his identity. The train meanwhile had gone its way and the clergyman's parishioners were that day deprived of his services.

Authors of international standing took up the cause of the Slovaks and acquainted the outer world with the nature of Magyar administration. Count Leo Tolstoy, for instance, raised his patriarchal voice against the ill-treatment of his fellow Slavs, and the Norse author, Björnson, having helped with pen, speech, and deed to obtain Norwegian freedom from Sweden, engaged in a lively private crusade against the Magyar governing class. In a passionate, Luther-like protest of conscience Björnson charged Count Albert Apponyi, minister of public education, with responsibility for the oppression of the Slovaks; it was gross hypocrisy, Björnson protested, for Apponyi to pose as a stanch friend of international peace at the very time that he was conniving at shameless persecution at home.

British and French writers, too, excoriated Magyar racialism. The most compelling and effective of them was R. W. Seton-Watson, a Scotch intellectual, who spread before the Western world almost incredible evidence of political and social injustices inside Hungary.[16] Magyar publicists attempted to brush aside these searing indictments by saying that foreign critics were extremely biased, or lopsided liberals, ignorant of Hungarian realities, or Pan-Slav hirelings, or freemasons leagued together to defame the Magyar character.[17]

As for the Hungarian government, it was totally unaffected by criticisms of liberally minded foreigners. The program of Magyarization was driven forward without reserve and with undoubted success. The consequence was that despite the emerging Slovak national movement, the stronger trend early in the twentieth century was not in the direction of the liberation of the Slovaks from Hungary but rather toward the eventual absorption of the Slovaks in the Magyar national community.

VIII

Magyar assimilationist measures produced resentment among some of the Hungarian German-speaking citizens, who were assisted in their struggle to preserve the German language and culture by Pan-German agencies abroad. In Transylvania, for example, "Saxons" fought their fight with newspapers and pamphlets and strove to keep their schools free from denationalizing Magyarisms; part of the literature that was circulated originated in Dresden and Munich. On one occasion the German chancellor von Bülow protested publicly that Magyarization was causing unpleasant sensations in Berlin.[18]

Magyar officials struck hard at exponents of Germanism. Arthur Korn, a "Saxon" journalist, was arrested four times for criticism of the government and was finally expelled, while the politician Korodi found it desirable to emigrate to Germany. Premier Széll in 1903 characterized the Pan-German ferment as "an absurd, inexcusable, and dangerous movement, which I will oppose with all my power"; personally he felt that no responsible statesman of imperial Germany was lending aid and comfort to the German malcontents. Like Bismarck before him, William II valued the friendship of the Magyars, took little notice of German protestations, and sedulously cultivated the good will of the Hungarian ruling classes.

The German population of Hungary outside of the larger Transylvanian communities responded only feebly to the call of *Volkstum*. The well-to-do, in fact, readily succumbed to the pervasive Magyar influences and the peasantry went their accustomed way, little concerned about politics. Once a German family had emerged in fortune or outlook from the general mass, the chances were that they would feel themselves Magyars in spirit. That, however, was less true of the town-dwelling "Saxons" of Transylvania, who preserved their German ways and their Lutheran creed, sent their sons to Germany to be educated, and would not bow down before the Magyar golden calf.

IX

In the kingdom of Croatia, as time passed, events betokened an alliance of the Croat and Serb politicians in a common front against the lordship of the Magyar. Yet until 1903 Croat patriots time and again fought with the Serbs, who were the recipients of favors from the strong-willed viceroy, Khuen-Héderváry. In 1895, for instance, when Agram acted as host to Francis Joseph, the Serbs flew their national flag from a church, as they had a lawful right to do; infuriated Croats, students mostly, stormed the church, cut down the flag, and proceeded to pillage Serb property. Not content with these displays of vandalism, Croats ripped down a Hungarian flag and burnt it in the street. Police intervention to quell the disorders cost several lives. Again in 1902 the old feud between Croat and Serb provoked serious riots, resulting in physical injury to Serbs and damage to their property. In view of the constant squabbling an acute French observer who toured Croatia early in the twentieth century concluded that the idea of uniting Croats and Serbs was nothing other than wishbone politics.[19]

The Croatian extremist party, meantime, had split into two factions after the death of its leader Starčević in 1896. The larger wing, known later as the Party of Pure Right, agitated for complete repudiation of all special links with Hungary and the formation of a Yugoslav state which would form the third member of the Hapsburg Monarchy. The chief spokesmen of these "trialists" was Dr. Joseph Frank, a journalist and lawyer with clerical leanings. From Bishop Strossmayer's conception of trialism Frank's version differed in that the "third state" would embrace only Yugoslavs who were Hapsburg subjects, while the Bishop contemplated the inclusion of Serbia and Bulgaria as well. This party recruited its following mostly from the Catholic clergy and students; it flayed the existing regime ceaselessly, condemning the undemocratic suffrage laws, the restrictions on fundamental civil liberties, and excessive taxation.

Into Croatian politics a new political grouping entered at the turn of the century. This was the Peasant party, whose leading spirit, Stephen Radič was, next to Strossmayer, the most remarkable figure of very modern Croatia. The emancipation of the Croatian peasantry and the liberation of Croatia from foreign authority were the twin objectives of his long, busy, and stormy career. The son of poverty-stricken peasants, Radič attended the gymnasium in Agram, and later visited Russia, returning with ideas for radical reform in landownership. He studied in Prague and Paris, after being expelled from Agram for taking part in the riot of 1895.

Radič founded the Croatian Peasant party and was elected to the Croatian assembly, where vitriolic attacks on Magyars, Magyarones, and landlordism made him a celebrity. In 1902 he brought forth a grandiose plan for the transformation of the Hapsburg Monarchy into a federation of five states, three of them essentially Slav, with one embracing all the Yugoslavs of the Monarchy plus Fiume; rights of minorities in the quintuple monarchy would be adequately safeguarded. But outside of Radič's immediate circle this federalistic blueprint met with small favor.

By 1903, when Khuen Héderváry withdrew from Croatia to become Hungarian prime minister, the tide had started to swing toward *rapprochement* between Croats and Serbs. Representatives of both groups took part in disorders in 1903 expressive of discontent with Magyar rule, and in the countryside peasants rose against landed proprietors. In fact a state of siege had to be proclaimed in three districts, hundreds were arrested, and ten were reported to have been slain by the military.

From Croatia the ferment leaped into Yugoslav districts of Austria. Deputies from Istria and Dalmatia requested an audience with the emperor to present the grievances of their fellow nationalists in Croatia, but the cabinet of Budapest intervened and an interview was denied. Francis Joseph's refusal to listen to complaints cost him the good will of many Croats, a people whose reputation for loyalty to the Hapsburg crown had been proverbial. Informed and farsighted Magyars acknowledged the validity of Croatian complaints, at least in part. The great proconsul of Bosnia, Baron

Benjamin Kállay, exclaimed: "My countrymen have treated Croatia badly, hindered its development, and profited financially from it. Someday the Hungarians will have to pay for this."

To the movement for a united front of Croats and Serbs Professor Masaryk made a real contribution. Students of both groups listened to his lectures in Prague, read his books, and returned home with their hearts strongly warmed. One of them, Mile Pavlović, later a professor in Belgrade, has written: "I remember how the young Serbs and Croats listened to his lectures and absorbed his ideas when . . . I studied in Golden Prague . . . Masaryk contrived to kindle a flame of enthusiasm in our hearts. From Prague our young men returned home as thorough revolutionaries." [20] Masaryk's ideas exerted an incalculable effect upon the rising generation of intellectuals and helped prepare the way for the political activities of the Serbo-Croatian coalition, soon to be described.

The trend toward Serbo-Croat unity was furthered by the constitutional struggle between the Hungarian anti-Tisza coalition and the crown. While the controversy was raging, Francis Supilo,[21] a leading Croat politician and editor in Fiume, who had been arguing for Serbo-Croat unity, arranged a conference of Croat politicians from Croatia, Dalmatia, and Istria, which adopted (1905) the historic Fiume Resolutions. Asserting the right of every people "to decide its own life and destinies freely and independently," the Resolutions called for franchise reform, free elections, civil liberties, and the faithful execution of the *Nagoda* of 1868 in Croatia; it was also proposed that Croatia should be politically united (or reunited) with Dalmatia. If the anti-Tisza coalition would accept this program, then the Hungarian South Slavs would side with it in the dispute with the crown.

At Zara, subsequently, a delegation of Serb deputies from Croatia endorsed the Fiume Resolutions and appealed for political coöperation of Serbs and Croats throughout the Dual Monarchy. Finally, representatives of both "races" put their names to an agreement declaring themselves parts of a single nation and beseeching Francis Joseph to incorporate Dalmatia in Croatia. These several accords, hinting at the organization of a Yugoslav state within the realm of the Hapsburgs, actually proved to be landmarks in the formation of the kingdom of Yugoslavia. Not all Croats by any means favored coöperation with the Serbs; the trialistic scheme was frowned upon by partisans of an independent Croatian state and, as well, by those who desired the merger of Croatia with the kingdom of Serbia.

In the Agram diet and in the parliament at Budapest the Serbo-Croat deputies worked together, backing the anti-Tisza coalition and expecting substantial concessions should the coalition form a ministry. That hope proved vain. Instead of allowing greater freedom, the coalition, soon after it came into office, brought forward a Railway Servants Act which required all railway workers in Croatia to speak Magyar, a direct violation of the *Nagoda;* though Magyar had been extensively used in the railway service of Croatia, it had not hitherto been obligatory. Magyars contended that military and commercial considerations alike made it imperative that a single language should be spoken on all railways of the state. But Croat spokesmen considered the Act simply a device for extending the use of Magyar in Croatia and feared that it would be the forerunner of other measures that would infringe upon Croatia's local institutions.[22] That prospect united all Croatian factions, except the Magyarones, in resistance to the Hungarian ministry, and they had the hearty support of the handful of non-Magyars in the royal Hungarian parliament. By executive order, the Railway Servants Act was declared law; in that way Croat deputies were stopped from delaying enactment by obstruction and, by the same token, Croatian resentment was accentuated.

Croatia's ban, Baron Pejačević, resigned in protest over the railway act. Patriots asserted their intention of boycotting everything made in Hungary, and, in imitation of the Magyars themselves, wore lime leaves as badges of their patriotism. To tame Croatia and its diet, in which anti-Hungarian sentiments had grown almost universal, the Wekerle ministry in 1908 appointed as viceroy Baron Paul Rauch, son of the man who two generations earlier had brought about the acceptance of the *Nagoda.* Upon his arrival in Agram, Rauch was greeted with hoots and catcalls and some zealots chose to express their animosity with small stones. Promptly the diet was dissolved and new elections were ordered.

Although the Croatian franchise laws were even less democratic than those of Hungary proper, not a single candidate who could be relied upon to coöperate with Rauch was elected; in other words, the disgust of the electorate with Magyar rule was virtually unanimous. The Croat-Serb league won a clear majority of the seats, fifty-seven in all; Frank's Party of Pure Right had twenty-four, and Radič's Peasant faction, seven. When the diet was convoked the president eulogized Garibaldi and the Italian *risorgimento,* citing them as models for Croatia, and deputies lustily applauded the address. By royal decree the diet was again dissolved, an act which the Croat-Serb league denounced in a flaming manifesto. For two years Rauch governed in arbitrary fashion, censoring the press, severely curbing the right of assembly, and so forth. A grand design that he had prepared for the betterment of Croatian agriculture was ruined by the uncompromising hostility of his political opponents.

Rauch's authoritarian rule reached an unsavory culmination in notorious treason trials at Agram in 1909. In the hope of destroying the spirit of co-operation between Croats and Serbs, of discrediting the agitation for Pan-Serbia, and of proving that the kingdom of Serbia was fomenting revolutionary disaffection among Yugoslavs in Austria-Hungary, Rauch arrested more than fifty Croats and Serbs, "little men" all, on vague charges that they were conspiring to unite Croatia and Bosnia with Serbia. The accused were tried in Agram before a court that was obviously prejudiced. As star witness the prosecution offered one George Nastič, who, after plotting with Serbian fanatics at Belgrade to assassinate the prince of Montenegro, had fallen out with his confederates. In July of 1908, Nastič published at Budapest an astonishing brochure entitled *Finale* in which he offered "detailed evidence" on Pan-Serb revolutionary intrigue in the Hapsburg Monarchy; among the guilty ones were the Croats and Serbs whom Rauch had imprisoned. According to Nastič, the anti-Hapsburg cause was fostered by a terroristic political society with headquarters at Belgrade, called *Slovenski Jug* (The South Slav). The prosecuting attorney accused the defendants of high treason because they had written in Cyrillic characters and had said that the Serbian franchise law was more democratic than Croatia's!

Although no persuasive proof of treasonable activities was adduced in court, more than thirty of the Serbo-Croat culprits were convicted and sentenced to prison at hard labor; the others were set free. And the climax? The condemned men appealed their case to a higher tribunal which annulled the sentences on the ground that the court at Agram had not really tried to ascertain the trustworthiness of the evidence, and the accused Serbs and Croats were released.

Practically the entire Slav press of the Dual Monarchy denounced the Agram trial as a monstrous judicial scandal, and Masaryk in parliament tried to pin responsibility upon the Austrian foreign office. International journalism reiterated the Slav charges and a group of distinguished Europeans collaborated in a pamphlet condemning the Agram proceedings and blackening the reputation of the Hapsburg Monarchy in foreign countries.

Before the Agram trial had closed, another *cause célèbre,* the Friedjung affair, had crowded to the fore. Heinrich Friedjung was an eminent Austrian publicist and historian, a patriotic Hapsburger, and an intimate of the foreign secretary, Count Aehrenthal. He was allowed to use documents in the possession of the Ballplatz in preparing an article in which he categorically asserted that Croat and Serb politicians were trafficking with the Serbian government with the ultimate object of creating a Greater Serbian state. Friedjung published the article in the liberal *Neue Freie Presse* toward the end of March 1909, at the very moment indeed when Serbia was about to acquiesce in the Austrian annexation of Bosnia and ordinary diplomatic relations were about to be resumed. Precisely why the article appeared at the time it did is even now uncertain; perhaps it was intended to fire the mind of the Monarchy for an armed conflict with Serbia, which seemed imminent. Friedjung asserted that the article was based upon unimpeachable evidence and that in composing it he had exercised the same caution as when writing authoritative historical works.

Prominent Hapsburg Serbs and Croats whom Friedjung had implicated brought libel suits against him (and against the editor of the clerical *Reichspost*, who had published similar accusations). After considerable delay the trial was conducted before a Vienna jury and attracted even greater international attention than the Agram case. The plaintiffs protested that the documents which Friedjung had drawn upon were blatant forgeries. Friedjung at first boldly defended what he had written, insisting that his evidence was trustworthy, and expatiated eloquently on the diabolical nature of the Pan-Serbian conspiracy against the Dual Monarchy. But as the suit progressed Friedjung was forced to acknowledge the fraudulent character of certain of the "incriminating documents" he had drawn upon, and in the end he admitted the innocence of the accused men. Friedjung declined to reveal in court the actual source of the documents he had used, but that the foreign office had furnished them few doubted, and it was this aspect of the affair that gave it European notoriety. After Friedjung conceded that the Serbs and Croat politicians were guiltless of the accusations, they agreed to settle the case out of court (and similarly with the editor of the *Reichspost*).

The Austrian foreign office never admitted that it had anything to do with Friedjung's article. It seems not improbable that Foreign Minister Aehrenthal thought the documents that were turned over to Friedjung authentic and that he was as badly deceived by them as the historian. In the light of revelations from Hapsburg diplomatic archives it appears that the authorities in the Ballplatz were ignorant of the fact that the documents were fabrications when Friedjung was given access to them. However that may be, the ill-starred Friedjung trial seriously damaged the reputation of the Ballplatz for reliability and simple honesty in foreign countries; many an informed foreigner believed that Aehrenthal had deliberately winked at the manufacture of documents and had cynically exploited Friedjung as his cat's-paw in an endeavor to fan ill will and hatred of Serbia and to justify his aggressive Balkan diplomacy.[23] As for the politically articulate among Hapsburg Serbs and Croats, the Friedjung suit, coming as it did on the heels of the Agram trial, intensified discontent with the existing scheme of things.

CHAPTER SEVENTEEN

THE HAPSBURG MONARCHY AND EUROPE
1897–1908

FOR ALMOST A DECADE AFTER 1897, THE FOREIGN POLICY OF THE
Hapsburg Monarchy ran a singularly passive and pacific course. The Italian
ambassador in Vienna, Nigra, remarked in 1899: "Austria pursues a policy
of complete effacement . . . and has no inclination to make conquests or
extend its sphere of influence." Nationalistic convulsions within the borders
of the "ramshackle realm" consumed Hapsburg energies and enchained
diplomacy. The alliance with Germany was conceived of as the very mainstay of Austrian integrity and existence, and a favorable turn in the wheel
of diplomatic fortune presently enabled the Monarchy to strengthen its position in the partnership. The diplomatic bond with Italy was preserved
though its value had largely ebbed away. The Austrian *rapprochement* with
Russia and Russian absorption in a predatory Asiatic adventure facilitated
the collaboration of the eastern monarchies in the Balkans in an unexampled
way that augured well for the future.

Externally the major direct challenge to the security and integrity of the
Hapsburg Monarchy lay in the Yugoslav peril, or more precisely in the intensification of the "great idea" of a Greater Serbia in the kingdom of Serbia.
In and of itself Pan-Serbism carried little menace but imperial Russia stood
in the background, and, after the defeat by Japan in 1905, the weight of
tsarist diplomacy shifted from the Far East to the Near East. More than that,
France was allied to Russia and Britain ranged herself alongside of this bloc
in the first years of the new century.

In both Germany and Austria there were misgivings about the alliance.
Growing national passions among the Czechs, and in a less formidable way

among the Poles, encouraged doubts in Germany as to the value of the league with Austria; yet the foreign office had no intention of giving up the alliance. William II indeed profusely expressed friendship for the Monarchy; in a speech delivered in Francis Joseph's presence in September 1897, at the close of a tour round Hungary, the Kaiser exclaimed: "What has most profoundly impressed me during my sojourn in Hungary . . . is the sentiment of enthusiastic devotion to Your Majesty . . . I, too, cherish this enthusiasm and . . . with the feelings of a son, I regard Your Majesty as my paternal friend." Though it was evident that separatist convictions were rising in the Hungarian ruling class, the emperor felt confident that "the descendants of Arpád would in the future, as in the past, be undeviatingly loyal to the Hapsburg dynasty." (Could the Kaiser have been ignorant of 1848–49?) Such glowing phrases from the lips of the German monarch tickled Magyar pride and fostered Magyar admiration and affection for things German.

Relations between the Dual Monarchy and the German partner were on occasion disturbed by outspoken criticism of Germany by Young Czech or Polish leaders. Studied attempts on the part of Prussian officials to force Polish schoolchildren to speak the German language provoked angry anti-German demostrations in Galicia and inspired a Polish campaign to boycott goods made in Germany. A few prominent Poles advocated in fact that the Monarchy should break off the alliance with Germany but their more realistic fellows preferred to march along with the Ballplatz.

Germany's unwillingness to restrain Austro-Germans who were preaching *Anschluss,* together with German tariff policies at the turn of the century, which were injurious to Austrian commerce, evoked not a little adverse comment in the "great press" of the Hapsburg Monarchy. The populace of Vienna greeted von Bülow with much less warmth when he appeared in 1902 to arrange for the renewal of the Triplice treaty than had been shown Bismarck on his mission to conclude the original alliance in 1879.

II

It was widely believed that domestic discords would surely tear the old Monarchy apart after the death of Francis Joseph, if not indeed before. So late as 1905 the German foreign office talked of coming to an understanding with Russia on the distribution of the territory of Europe's "second sick man" in advance of his death.[1] And responsible Germans were not alone in such conjecturings. More than one British statesman intimated that Germany might annex the Austro-German provinces if the Dual Monarchy cracked up. The shrewd French foreign minister, Théophile Delcassé, awaited the impending dissolution of the Monarchy and therewith the ending of the Triple Alliance. Such a sequence would end the French treaty with Russia, since it was prescribed that the Dual Alliance should last only so long as the Triplice. After the breakup of the Monarchy, Delcassé supposed, Russia and Germany would quarrel over the liquidation of Hapsburg lands and out of the dispute would evolve a general European war.

Thinking similar in content and conclusion prevailed in St. Petersburg. It behooved the allies, therefore, to be prepared against the day of possible Austrian disintegration. Delcassé journeyed to the Russian capital in August of 1899 and arranged for the perpetuation of the Dual Alliance even though the Triplice should dissolve. If Austria broke up and if Russia and Germany went to war over the territories at stake, the Third Republic was committed to back the eastern colossus to the limit. On the same mission, Delcassé specifically pledged French support of Russian interests in the Balkans.[2]

There were public men in Germany who firmly believed that the strong right arm of their country would be capable of averting the downfall of the venerable ally, and to that view Chancellor von Bülow came around. His considered reflections on the matter he summed up in this wise: "The imminence of the dissolution of the Hapsburg state is being freely canvassed abroad. But Germany and Austria standing together like a solid bloc may be able to withstand all storms, whether of internal or external origin . . . Loyal coöperation with Austria-Hungary will and must remain in the future the fundamental basis of German foreign policy."[3]

Yet when the first Moroccan crisis broke over Europe in 1905–06 and the menace of a general war was very real, Austria proved less than wholehearted in support of Germany. As Premier Gautsch explained, Austria's direct interests in Morocco were exclusively economic in character. "Austria-Hungary holds strongly," he declared, "to the principle of equality of rights and of the open door . . . to keep our export interests, which are increasing yearly, from damage," and Goluchowski, the foreign minister, made it perfectly clear that "Morocco was not worth a war." At the conference of Algeciras (1906), in which Morocco's destiny was decided, the Austrian delegate (Count Welsersheimb) posed as a kind of honest broker, offering compromise proposals for the police services of Morocco which were eventually adopted, though they by no means corresponded with the desires of the Wilhelmstrasse.[4]

Italy flatly identified itself at the Algeciras Conference with the Franco-British diplomatic bloc, and the lukewarm attitude of Austria underlined the uncomfortable isolation in which Germany found herself. Nevertheless, German diplomatists tried to give the world the impression that Austria had faithfully coöperated with her ally; in one of his more spectacular telegrams, William II lavished praise upon Austria as Germany's "brilliant second" in the Moroccan diplomatic encounter. Abroad, the term "brilliant second" was accepted as an accurate description of Austrian subordination to her German ally, but in Austria itself the characterization was repudiated as humiliating and indiscreet—and it was not exactly true. *Die Zeit,* a Viennese paper noted for comparative independence, bluntly remarked: "This sensational telegram does not please us." But a visit of William II to Vienna in May 1906 helped a little to soften the resentment his melodramatic telegram had caused.

The fact of the matter was that Austria had failed to measure up to the expectations of the Germans. Von Bülow therefore resolved to knit the bonds between Germany and Austria more tightly, in the hope that in the next diplomatic engagement Austria would coöperate more fully. "Instead of Berlin's boldly dominating Vienna," it has been well said, [Bülow] now slavishly decided to become the tool of the outworn, antiquated" Austria, "if in return Austria would give Germany the feeling of having at least one friend in the world." No matter how adroitly Germany might seek to conceal the fact, her international position had become exceedingly unenviable; it was even felt in Vienna that it was Austria's duty "to mediate between Germany and Europe." [5] To avoid total isolation and to merit Austrian gratitude, the Wilhelmstrasse resolutely backed her ally during Balkan railway disputes and the grave crisis over Bosnia in 1908–09.

III

At the very moment that Germany was drawing closer to Austria, Italy, the third member of the Triplice, never happy in the partnership, was edging farther away. Italy's open defection from the Triplice at the Algeciras Conference caused no surprise in official Austrian or German quarters; that was the anticipated sequel to the Francophile orientation given Italian diplomacy at the end of the nineties, to the increased Italian interest in the unredeemed lands under the Hapsburg flag, and to rising concern over the political future of the Balkan peninsula, including the Italian desire for mastery of the Adriatic. Tension with Austria inescapably followed, and that was damaging for the stability of the Triplice.[6]

Political tumult inside the Dual Monarchy and the assumption that its disintegration impended stimulated the faith and hope of Italian Irredentists. Public schoolbooks asserted that the southern Tyrol and Istria were "beautiful provinces wrongfully possessed by Austria." On one occasion, while the king was reviewing troops in northern Italy, Triestiners flaunted banners of mourning and presented petitions of grievances from Austro-Italians. Friction touched a high point at the turn of the century when M. Zanardelli, a veteran Irredentist and a native of the Trentino, was serving as Italy's first minister. Previously he had been obliged to decline the foreign secretaryship because of veiled protests from Vienna. He and his foreign minister, M. Prinetti, no friend of the Triplice, arranged a very secret entente with France, which gave Italy a foot in each European diplomatic camp. Incidents along the Austrian border inspired predictions that an open rupture with the northern ally was at hand; Austria pushed preparations to fight, enlarging garrisons and strengthening defenses in the Tyrol.

It was no contribution to international good will that when King Victor Emmanuel toured the capitals of Europe in 1902 he omitted Vienna from his itinerary, avowedly because Francis Joseph would not pay a courtesy call in Rome. Austrian diplomatists repeatedly begged the emperor to visit the Holy City, but the old stickler for form and devout Catholic declined, knowing full well that his presence in Rome would enrage "the prisoner of the Vatican." Even though the gap between Austria and Italy was perceptibly widening, the Triple Alliance in its fourth version was renewed in 1902; in a postscript to the treaty, Austria bound herself not to interfere with Italian ambitions in Tripoli and arrangements were effected to lower tariffs on imports from Italy.

These were surface manifestations of friendliness. More truly indicative of Italian sentiments were recurrent anti-Austrian outbursts, as in 1905 when M. Marcora, president of the chamber of deputies, alluded to "our Trieste and our Trentino." Austria's demand for an apology was answered by a perfunctory expression of regret. Italian candidates for municipal office in Trieste benefited from funds supplied by Irredentists in the kingdom which helped them triumph over Slovene opponents who had the undercover backing of Austrian officialdom. Membership in hate-spewing, anti-Hapsburg societies swelled and tendentious Irredentist literature, both learned and popular, increased in volume and asperity.[7]

A stirring drama from the pen of Gerolamo Rovetto, entitled *Romanticismo,* which glorified Italian conspirators and revolutionaries against Austrian rule in Lombardy before 1859 and preached hatred of the Hapsburgs, was rapturously applauded by Italian theatergoers. Caustic allusions to Austria evoked cries of *Pfui* and audiences retired from theaters lustily yelling: "Long live Italy! Long live Trentino and Trieste!" The Italian government would scarcely have allowed such spectacles had it been genuinely desirous of retaining the friendship of the Austrian ally.

On "the other shore" of the Adriatic, in Montenegro and the district of Albania, Italian activity, growing after 1900, envenomed relations with Austria, which conceived of the western Balkans as her peculiar and legitimate sphere of influence.[8] It was asserted in *Mare Nostro,* the organ of the Italian navy league, that the Adriatic must become an Italian lake, and Gabriele D'Annunzio's sensational play *La Nave* taught a similar doctrine and had a quickening influence upon anti-Austrian sentiments. Some Italian expansionists, however, fastened their eyes on Valona, a splendid harbor commanding the eastern approach to the Adriatic, the "Calais," in fact to the Italian "Dover," Brindisi.

If Italy gained control of Valona, both sides of the entrance to the Adriatic would have been in the hands of a single power for the first time since the disintegration of the Roman empire. Italy could then have effectively blocked Austrian shipping in the event of war and Hapsburg sea forces could have proceeded into the Mediterranean only at great risk. From Valona, moreover, Italians might build railways into the western Balkans for commercial and strategic purposes. All in all, for Austria the exclusion of Italy from anything like a monopolistic position on the eastern side of the Adriatic was a matter of vital interest, a question of life or death, some diplomatists and publicists were wont to say.

Into Albania aggressive Italian enterprise peacefully penetrated to the detriment of established Austrian interests. Under agreement with Turkey, Austria was the official guardian of the Albanian Roman Catholic minority, fully two hundred thousand, and Austrian funds had erected churches and schools. For centuries, on the other hand, the Italian language had served as a sort of lingua franca among Albanians and was long spoken even in Austrian-sponsored institutions of learning. But when Italian operations grew sharply competitive, the Albanian tongue was introduced into the schools and Italian-speaking clergymen were replaced by natives.

Agents of Italy then set up schools in which pro-Italian sympathies were cultivated; pupils were taught Italian national anthems and how to shout "Long live Italy." At Scutari, key town of northern Albania, a kindergarten, elementary schools for boys and girls, and a commercial technical institute were operated under Italian auspices; and by royal order a chair of Albanian literature was created in the *Istituto Orientale* at Naples. Schools to train priests and teachers for Albania were also established on Italian soil. Clubs and popular literature of a propagandist character stimulated Italian interest in Albania, and Italian business concerns were energetically at work. From Albania, Italian commerce reached into Macedonia, everywhere to the disadvantage of Austrian trade and traders.

In a verbal agreement of 1897, Austria had acknowledged the equality of Italian rights in Albania, and in 1900–01 the understanding was confirmed in writing. Turkish sovereignty, it was agreed, should be perpetuated "as long as circumstances permitted," but if and when changes were effected Albania should become an autonomous state, and the interests of Austria and Italy in the region should be fixed by negotiation. That statement of policy was reaffirmed in the text of the Triplice treaty as renewed in 1902. Even so, Austria was resolved, as Goluchowski phrased it in 1901, to prevent any changes in the Balkans "prejudicial to her vital interests or involving danger for her position in the future."

As in Albania, so in Montenegro, Italian influence waxed. The Montenegrin princess Helena, notoriously Austrophobe, was the wife of Italy's king, and two of her sisters, girls of Juno-like proportions, were wedded to Russian archdukes, likewise unfriendly to Austria. Italian finance, moreover, built a short railway from the port of Antivari to Virbazar, on the Montenegrin shore of Lake Scutari, and contemplated extending the line as far as the Danube; Austria possessed the right, under the Treaty of Berlin, to veto the building of this railway, but chose not to do so. At Antivari, an Italian company laid out harbor works and Italians were increasingly active in the religious and educational affairs of the tiny principality.

So long as Austria and Russia collaborated in the Balkans, the Italians could not give free rein to their aspirations. In the early phases of the acute tension over Macedonia, presently to be related, Italy coöperated helpfully with Austrian diplomacy, and on Austria's recommendation an Italian general was placed in command of an international police force organized to preserve law and order in Macedonia. With characteristic glibness, Goluchowski reported to the delegations in May of 1904, "My recent meetings with the Italian foreign minister strengthened me in the knowledge that the most authoritative circles in Rome attach no less value than we do to the cultivation of intimate and trustful relations."

This was diplomatic eyewash, for fresh Irredentist outbursts and intensifying competition in the Balkans so strained relations that Italy ostentatiously shifted part of her armed forces from the French to the Austrian borders. In response to inquiries in Rome as to whether French diplomatists had lured the kingdom away from the Triplice and were stirring up bad blood with Austria, the Italians entered strong denials, which no one in the know, however, accepted at face value.

The blunt, inescapable fact was that Hapsburg and Italian interests and ambitions in the Balkan peninsula were irreconcilable and that, combined with the prevalence of Irredentism, rendered impossible anything approaching genuine friendship. Distrust, even hatred, of Italy was the one point in public affairs on which there was almost universal concurrence in Austria. "Only a war with Italy," wrote the German ambassador at Vienna in 1906, "would be really popular in the Hapsburg Monarchy." [9]

IV

From the making of the truce in 1897 down to 1907, Austro-Russian relations were extraordinarily cordial. In 1898 Tsar Nicholas II advanced proposals for an international conference to deliberate on limitation of armaments and the setting up of machinery for the peaceful adjustment of international controversies. What on the surface appeared to be an idealistic, peace-minded project was actually motivated by starkly realistic considerations on the part of the Russians. For one thing, tsarist imperialism in the Far East had brought into the foreground the very real possibility of an armed clash with Japan, abetted perhaps by Britain; in such an eventuality it would be highly advantageous for Russia if the likelihood of war in Europe were reduced to a minimum. Moreover, Russian imperial finance was in a parlous state, unequal to equipping armies with new artillery such as Germany had just introduced and Austria might also adopt. Russian military leaders therefore recommended that an overture be addressed to Austria for an understanding binding the two countries not to purchase the new guns for ten years. But that suggestion tsarist policymakers pigeonholed in favor of an international conference on armament limitation.

Austria and the other powers endorsed the idea of a meeting and the conference convened at the Hague in 1899. Austrian delegates played only an inconspicuous role at the conference, though they joined with the representatives of other countries in accepting guarded and perfunctory resolutions concerning reduction of armaments. Not less than the Germans and the French, the Austrians could see little practical value in schemes for international arbitration. A permanent court of arbitration was indeed created, but its scope was so circumscribed that it had only limited significance.

Nevertheless, Austria's cordial response to the invitation to the conference gratified the Russians, and other marks of good will were not lacking. Grand Duke Michael, the last surviving son of Nicholas I and a confirmed partisan of Austro-Russian coöperation, was splendidly welcomed in Budapest in October 1901 by king and populace, and Archduke Francis Ferdinand, a few months later, was warmly received in St. Petersburg. Goluchowski's remarks to the delegations in May of 1902 on relations with Russia struck a highly optimistic note. The thoroughly satisfactory development of relations with Russia since the making of the entente, he observed, "may rightly be regarded as one of the most favorable phenomena of recent times, since it has checked perils which caused permanent anxiety on the continent. It may be hoped that this state of affairs will steadily improve." The most efficacious remedy for differences, he continued, was "a mutual exchange of views, sincere and without reserve."

Certain Austrians linked the entente with Russia and the Triplice as engagements of equal importance in preserving European tranquillity and the standing of the Dual Monarchy as a great power. Aehrenthal, the Austrian ambassador to Russia, urged that the entente with Russia should be elaborated, and indeed that the old *Dreikaiserbund* should be revived. Minor irritations, as for example the expression of Czechophile sympathies by prominent Russians, were officially overlooked or explained away.

More troublesome was the rumor, later known to be fact, that Russia had come to a formal diplomatic understanding with Bulgaria. Prince Ferdinand of Bulgaria, who regarded the Austro-Rumanian alliance (renewed in 1902) as directed against his principality, sought a counterweight in an arrangement with Russia. The upshot of exchanges was a very secret military convention of the spring of 1902, in which Russia promised to protect the integrity of Bulgaria against challenge from any quarter. With that treaty in the archives, the Bulgarian government felt freer to indulge in Irredentist activity in the Bulgar-inhabited areas of Turkish Macedonia, and Russian agents exerted pressure in Paris to secure a Bulgarian loan for military purposes.[10]

v

Grave disorders in Macedonia in 1903 put the Austro-Russian entente to a real test. As has previously been related, this Turkish-owned region was a theater of hot competition between Bulgars, Serbs, and Greeks, each of whom coveted slices of the area. Deeds of rival *comitadji* bands and the oppressive Turkish administration earned for Macedonia the unenviable distinction of Europe's most distracted region. Early in 1902, when a general insurrection threatened, Austrian and Russian statesmen conferred on the situation, quite in keeping with the agreement of 1897, and recommended to the sultan that administrative reforms should be promptly introduced. And Austria and Russia admonished the Balkan governments that had pretensions to Macedonia "to keep their turbulent elements in check in order not to lay themselves open to the suspicion of wanting to create complications." That warning was followed in February of 1903 by a specific schedule of reforms drawn up by the cabinets of Austria and Russia in general conformity with British suggestions, and concurred in by the Porte. But the program was a case of too little and too late. Presently Macedonia was the scene of bloody excesses, *comitadji* outrages, Turkish military brutalities against insurgents and their families, wanton destruction of life and property.

As of old time, the cry went up in Christian Europe that something effective must be done to stop the murders and rapine and to alleviate the harsh and forbidding lot of the Macedonian population. Official Britain put forth fresh schemes for administrative and judicial reform; and Austrian and Russian statesmen, in conferences at Vienna and at Mürzsteg, a dismal hunting lodge in Styria, drafted another program for Macedonia, known as the Mürzsteg Punctation. That document forbade territorial changes, formally and specifically reaffirmed Turkish sovereignty over Macedonia, and outlined administrative and judicial innovations that ought to be inaugurated. Austrian and Russian agents would participate jointly in the execution of taxation and police reforms and in the establishment and preservation of law and order; in the bedeviled region a gendarmerie would be organized, to be commanded by foreign officers. Thereafter the Macedonians would be given a share in local government, courts of law included. Villages that had been destroyed during the recent disorders would be rebuilt and refugees might freely return to their homes and hearths.

One clause in the Mürzsteg Punctation, full of ill omen, prescribed that once order and discipline had been restored Macedonia should be subdivided administratively "along lines of nationality"—that in a region where national affiliations were hopelessly confused and subject to change without notice! All the great powers, except Germany, concurred in the Mürzsteg agenda and Turkey hesitantly accepted them. It was fondly believed that Macedonia was now on the way to better and brighter days.

With the help of a gendarmerie administered by foreigners, order was partly restored in Macedonia and thousands of wrecked cottages were rebuilt. In 1905 rehabilitation of finance and taxation was begun, though not until a naval demonstration had coerced Turkey into acquiescence. Beyond that the Mürzsteg Punctation remained a dead letter. Judicial reform was entirely ignored and Christians were denied even elementary rights in the courts; Turkey adamantly resisted the participation of outsiders in the judiciary, and in that stand she had considerable backing in foreign chancelleries. Brigand bands once more ravaged and laid waste peasant communities as each of the competing nationalities strove to clinch claims to as much of Macedonia as possible, against the day when the province would be remodeled for administrative purposes. Not very much, in a word, was accomplished in bettering the wretched lot of the Macedonians.

The British foreign office at the end of 1907 therefore besought the other major nations to coöperate in forcing the sultan to remove the principal causes of misery and insecurity. To that overture Austria and Russia responded negatively, contending that the time was "singularly inopportune for advancing fresh proposals." Momentarily the Ballplatz played with the idea of an international combination, from which Britain would be excluded, to deal with the Macedonian situation; by revealing that project to London (if project it could be called) the men on the Neva caused British resentment toward Austria.[11]

Only force, as a matter of fact, could compel the Turk to rectify evils in Macedonia, and that the powers were unwilling to apply. Germany in particular was of the opinion that the use of force would set off dangerous political convulsions throughout the Ottoman empire. All plans to effect reform in Macedonia by international pressure upon the sultan were abandoned after the crack-up of the Austro-Russian entente and the Young Turk revolution of 1908.

Aggressive Muscovite maneuvers in eastern Asia, in the meantime, had brought on war with Japan, resounding Russian military disasters, and revolution inside the tsardom. Instead of exploiting Russian perplexities to her own advantage, Vienna entered into a secret neutrality treaty with St. Petersburg, while the Japanese conflict was on, as "a mark of friendship and reciprocal confidence." [12] Unquestionably the Austrian course was dictated, up to a point, by the grave constitutional struggle between the crown and the Magyar dissidents then under way; political strife inside the Monarchy made passive diplomacy a virtue.

Magyar sympathies for the little yellow men of the East were candidly expressed. But, on the other side, Slavs in the Dual Monarchy, apart from the Poles, favored Russia, as did the Pan-Germans and the Jew-haters. Vast enthusiasm for the big Slav brother was exhibited in Czech quarters; the city council of Prague, for instance, amidst thunderous applause voted "that the inhabitants of Prague are animated by the sincere wish that the Almighty may bless the weapons of Russia with victory in the interest of culture and for the honor and glory of all Slavic races." And police had to be summoned to disperse angry crowds that demonstrated for Russia in front of the consulates of Great Britain and the United States in Prague.

Balked in imperialistic ambitions in the Orient, Russia now reverted with old-time fervor to the Near East, to the Balkans, where nationalism had recently undergone rapid growth. The dynamic of Pan-Slavism, which had operated potently upon tsarist foreign policy in the seventies, but which had been in eclipse for over two decades, emerged again to help shape Europe's fortunes. For the Austro-Russian armistice in the Balkans, the reorientation of Russian diplomacy proved fateful and fatal.

It has seemed to some students of very modern European diplomacy, who perhaps exaggerate the personal equation in public affairs, that Austro-Russian relations, which for years had been incredibly cordial, might have remained tranquil had not new and ambitious personalities taken charge of the foreign offices in 1906: Alexander P. Izvolsky for Russia and Baron Alois Lexa von Aehrenthal in Vienna. Certainly they were forceful, strong-willed individuals, keenly jealous of the international standing of their respective countries, and keenly desirous of raising the prestige and position of their respective monarchies in southeastern Europe.

Izvolsky personified the school of opinion which believed that Russia should press for the realization of her "historic aims in the Near East" and that operations in the Orient should be cut to a minimum. Similarly, Aehrenthal espoused a positivist Hapsburg foreign policy which would give Austria greater independence with respect to Germany and consolidate the Hapsburg place in the Balkans. He did not relish the title of "brilliant second"; his mind harked back to the heroic Hapsburg yesterdays. Cartwright, British ambassador to Vienna, shrewdly summed up Aehrenthal's prime motive as foreign secretary in this language: "It may be due to vanity on the part of Aehrenthal, or it may be due to patriotic feeling, but it is quite certain to me that he is determined to play an independent and personal role in European politics, and that nothing would be more distasteful to him than to feel himself at the mercy and dictation of Berlin." [13]

In the view of Aehrenthal, Austrian international policy as conducted by his easygoing predecessor, Goluchowski, had been too timid, too lackadaisical. It was imperative that the Monarchy's diplomatic reputation should be raised and that the energies of the heterogeneous nationalities should be diverted from petty domestic controversies to the far larger issue of the Austrian place in the constellation of great powers. Aehrenthal had faith in the durability of the monarchy, in its capacity to live, and in its destiny; once diplomatic prestige had been built up, the way would be open, he thought, for the constitutional reconstruction of the realm, possibly along the lines of trialism. The gravest perils to the future of Austria as a great power Aehrenthal believed to be Serbia and Pan-Serb zealotry.

Aehrenthal belonged to a Bohemian-German noble family, which had some Jewish connections.[14] His father had been active in public affairs as a leader of the Bohemian aristocracy; his mother was a Thun, his wife a Magyar countess, Pauline Széchényi. Reared in an atmosphere of aristocratic privilege, Aehrenthal remained to the end a believer in the efficacy of divine-right monarchy; by reason of family traditions he was reputed to be antipathetic to the Czechs and to Slavs generally.

After studying in the Universities of Prague and Bonn, Aehrenthal joined the Austrian diplomatic service in 1877 as attaché in Paris. Transferred to St. Petersburg, he won the respect of Ambassador Kálnoky, and when the latter moved to the Ballplatz, he named Aehrenthal as *chef de cabinet*. Subsequently he served as counselor of the embassy in Russia and as ambassador to Rumania, and in 1899 he was placed at the head of the Russian embassy. A career diplomatist par excellence, Aehrenthal deeply admired Kálnoky and claimed him as his idol and ideal.

While in St. Petersburg, Aehrenthal had diligently studied the language and literature of Russia and had solidly established himself in the good graces of tsarist policymakers. He acquired a thorough knowledge of currents of opinion in Russia, and learned the strong and weak points in the armor of the eastern colossus. As ambassador he recommended the making of a full-bodied Russian entente, and he liked the Bismarckian formula of

the partition of the Balkans into an Austrian and a Russian sphere. Aehrenthal rejoiced over the coöperation embodied in the Mürzsteg Punctation
and carried on the negotiations for the neutrality accord while the war with
Japan was on. Like many another influential Austrian, he cherished the
dream of resurrecting the *Dreikaiserbund*.[15]

Called from St. Petersburg in October of 1906 to preside over the Austrian foreign office, Aehrenthal discharged that responsibility through years
of unexampled stress and strain until the very eve of his death in February
1912. Goluchowski, like Kálnoky before him, was driven from the Ballplatz
by the Magyars, of whose constitutional struggle with the crown he had
spoken disparagingly. At the meeting of the delegations in June 1906, Goluchowski was spared a humiliating demonstration only by the intervention
of Prime Minister Wekerle; Magyar pressure on the crown forced him out
of office and with him passed into oblivion the joint minister of war, Pitreich.

Tall, broad-shouldered, a bit bowed, bespectacled, the new director of
Hapsburg diplomacy was extremely nearsighted; his eyes were almost
always drooping and weary looking. Nevertheless, he impressed many contemporaries as the grand seigneur, but to one commentator at least he
appeared to be more typically a German university professor than a diplomatist and statesman, a man more suited for theoretical and abstruse research
than for practical public affairs. Aehrenthal's manner of speech was monotonously precise, without any pretensions to oratory; suave he was, and
in the diplomatic art of verbal dissimulation he was an acknowledged
master. Some foreigners, and indeed some of his own countrymen, came
to think of him as the veritable spawn of Beezlebub.

Under a languid exterior Aehrenthal concealed qualities of force and
resolution which made him the most respected and most feared Austrian
foreign secretary since Andrássy. The Rumanian statesman, Take Jonescu,
assigned his quick intelligence, his capacity for adaptation, and his remarkable understanding of affairs to the Jewish strain in his ancestry; von Bülow
discovered in him the characteristic qualities of the Austrian aristocrat, not
least, "innate arrogance." Avidity for fame and pride of place were certainly
traits of Aehrenthal, as tact surely was not.

Sharing Aehrenthal's general convictions on the future and security of
the Monarchy, though differing sharply from him in the means to reach
the ends, was another "strong man," Count Conrad von Hötzendorf, who
was named chief of the Austrian general staff shortly after Aehrenthal took
over the foreign secretaryship.[16] Attached to the entourage of Francis Ferdinand, the first of his confidants, in fact, to be chosen for high office, Conrad
was widely regarded, and with sufficient reason, as the heir presumptive's
man. As an infantry officer, he had served in the Balkans, taught military
tactics in the war college, and commanded troops posted along the Italian

frontier. Conrad devoted considerable thought to international politics, developed profound distrust of Italy, and considered the South Slav question as extremely perilous for the Hapsburg Monarchy.

As chief of staff Conrad pushed through far-reaching reforms in the army for the purpose of rehabilitating morale and fighting capacity after a decade of intense domestic political discord and the laissez-faire methods of his predecessor, Beck. His exalted position afforded this blunt militarist ready access to Francis Joseph, and enabled him to exert an effective influence upon state policies.

In season and out, like Cato of old time, Conrad pleaded for a preventive war, not with Carthage but with Rome, as an imperative necessity. But that doctrine Aehrenthal resisted with dogged tenacity, and successfully. War, Conrad also believed, was the only way to settle matters with the spunky and troublesome Serbian neighbor. Of this "one-ideaed man," the British military attaché stationed in Vienna just before 1914 has written: Conrad was "a very winning and delightful little man, dapper, erect, alert, with grey hair '*à la brosse*' over a keenly intellectual and rather ascetic face. He was a man of great moral courage, frank and straightforward, but essentially a one-ideaed man . . . He was certainly the bright star in a rather dull constellation and all the foreign attachés had great regard and affection for him." [17]

When Aehrenthal took hold of the Hapsburg diplomatic reins he was intent upon moving closer to Russia. He no doubt hoped that the old League of Three Emperors might be resurrected and that in that way the monarchical order and the peace of Europe might be preserved. [18] On the Russian side, Nicholas II and his chief minister, Stolypin, who rejoiced heartily over the promotion of Aehrenthal to the Ballplatz—not least because he superseded the Pole, Goluchowski—were inclined to see wisdom and virtue in the revival of the League.

But opposed to them was the restless and ambitious Muscovite foreign minister, Izvolsky, who frankly disapproved of greater intimacy with Vienna and believed that the tsardom should push ahead with her historic mission in the Near East. Cheek to jowl with Isvolsky stood the enlarging company of Pan-Slavs, who resented bitterly Austria's cavalier treatment of little Serbia. It was evident to Aehrenthal that the prerequisite to a peaceful future with Russia was an improvement in relations with Serbia, and on that objective he first intended to concentrate.

What then was the appearance of the diplomatic landscape from the vantage ground of Vienna when Aehrenthal stepped into the Ballplatz? With Britain, a hereditary friend, relations were deteriorating, mainly because of the growing asperity of the Anglo-German feud, partly because of unmistakable signs that Britain was seeking to arrange a diplomatic bargain with Russia. Relations with France were correct, though scarcely cordial, with Serbia exceedingly strained, with Bulgaria uncertain, with Rumania officially friendly, with Turkey none too good, directly because of Austrian interference in the Macedonian question; yet Aehrenthal proposed to hold firmly to the settled Austrian policy of preserving the territorial integrity of Turkey as long as possible.

In Berlin, Aehrenthal's appointment was received with mingled emotions, for he was looked upon as a confirmed Russophile and he never won Bülow's confidence as Goluchowski had done. It seems clear, finally, that Aehrenthal was sincerely desirous of deserving Italy's friendship.

VIII

At the time of Aehrenthal's accession, relations with Serbia could only be described as evil, and they grew much worse before they became any better. Fundamentally, the antagonism arose out of the Austrian resolution to maintain the *status quo* and the Serbian desire to change it. More specifically, the Greater Serbia party hungered for those areas in the Hapsburg realm (and in Turkey, too) which were inhabited by Yugoslavs, while Austria was intent upon thwarting that ambition at any and all costs. Austrian opposition to a united Yugoslavia was essentially analogous to her aversion to a united Italy, half a century earlier. If anything, Austria dreaded the Yugoslav ideal even more than the Italian, for in the intervening years nationalism with centrifugal tendencies had grown among other Hapsburg minorities. Should the Yugoslav-peopled districts be lost to the Monarchy, the ancient and polyglot realm would swiftly decompose and disappear, it was reasoned.

The notion that the kingdom of Serbia should serve as the Piedmont of a united Yugoslavia had nothing of novelty about it, or rather, the only new element was the intensification of the belief. That was a perfectly natural development, reflecting one of the master trends of the age in Europe and the wider world. The Radical party of Serbia cherished the political unification of the Yugoslavs as their supreme and consuming objective. Through the eighties and the nineties Austria had exercised considerable control over the politics of Serbia, by reason of the bonds of intimacy with the Obrenovitch dynasts who sat uneasily on a volcanic throne. Still, ugly and disturbing incidents now and again popped up, as in 1896 when a Belgrade mob burned a Hungarian flag and the official apology was merely perfunctory in content. Premier Bánffy at the time decried Serbian conduct as "not simply unfriendly but also discourteous," adding that "the Serbian government lacked the courage to withstand the pressure exerted upon public opinion by certain extreme parties." In 1900 the Belgrade government again caused ill will by imposing a ban on the purchase of Austrian manufactures to fulfill government contracts.

Relations took a decided turn for the worse in 1903. A conspiratorial band of Serbian army officers and ordinary cutthroats barbarously murdered the unpopular King Alexander Obrenovitch and his wife; and Peter, of the rival Karageorgevitch dynasty, a man of known Russophile sympathies, was seated on the throne. It was hoped, naturally, in Austria that the palace revolution would not involve diplomatic complications. "I hope," commented the Hungarian prime minister, Széll, "that it will be possible to avoid developments such as to compel Austria-Hungary to modify its Balkan policy. The age, experience, and character of the new king form some safeguard against the dangers to which a young and easily influenced ruler might be tempted." Other Hapsburg statesmen, however, were less sanguine, suspecting that King Peter would give free rein to Austrophobia in order to win political popularity.

It was the Radical party in Serbia that sponsored and benefited from the change in dynasty. From 1903 to 1918 this party, whose chief personality was Nikola Pasič, determined the course of Serbian politics without serious interruption. It aimed among other things at economic liberation from Austria, it spread separatist propaganda among Yugoslavs beyond the borders of Serbia, it preached union with Montenegro and reconciliation with the hereditary enemy, Bulgaria.[19] A government with those objectives inescapably provoked apprehension and consternation in Austria.

Serbia in 1904 negotiated a treaty of friendship with Bulgaria and drew up plans for a customs union. Mistrustful of the political implications of that scheme, Austria intervened and, arguing that a customs union would violate her most-favored-nation rights, compelled the two states to abandon the project. Another and much more serious strain was put upon Austro-Serbian relations by another "pig war." Pigs made up Serbia's principal exports, they were the peasants' cash crop, and they were sold by the grace of Hapsburg railways in the Monarchy and beyond.[20] If Austria so decided, Serbian pigs could no longer go to market, and in 1906, Austria so decided.

Three main reasons dictated that dubious decision. First, agrarian elements in the Monarchy, especially farmers of southern Hungary whose products competed directly with the more cheaply produced Serbian swine (corn and plums, too) pressed for the curtailment if not the total stoppage of imports from the south. In the second place, through her commercial policy Austria intended to coerce Serbia into buying military supplies from the Škoda armament firm, as had been the custom, instead of placing orders in France as was contemplated in Belgrade. Finally, it was calculated that economic pressure would compel Serbia to return to an Austrophile orientation in foreign policy. Economics, in other words, would be invoked to keep Serbia politically subservient to the great northern power.

So early as 1903 protests began against the renewal of the trade treaty with Serbia, which was not due to expire until 1906. Serbian dickerings with Bulgaria lent impetus to the agitation. Austria, accordingly, refused to renew the treaty, virtually closed the doors to Serbian goods, and forced Serb dealers to return pigs to the place of origin. Serbia retaliated by raising duties on Austrian products; exchange of goods dropped perpendicularly; in 1907 Serbia sold only about 16 per cent of her exports in Austria and bought from her only 36 per cent of imports.

While housewives of Vienna bewailed the high cost of meat, Belgrade officials cast about for new markets over new routes and found them in western Europe principally. Under cover of darkness some swine were smuggled into Austrian territory. King Peter, himself the descendant of a swineherd, encouraged the building of slaughter houses and packing plants in Serbia. Sufficient credits were obtained from sales abroad to pay for military supplies in France, but the volume of exports was not so large as before the dispute with Austria, and injured Serb peasants who previously had taken little interest in international politics turned violently against their northern neighbor. Moreover, official Serbian detestation of Austria exceeded all precedent, and the government was more desirous than ever of establishing direct rail communication with the Adriatic which would release the kingdom from dependence upon Austrian transportation facilities. Certain Yugoslav partisans within the Dual Monarchy and Russian Pan-Slavs too resented the hardships which Austrian policy imposed upon Serbia.

The "pig war" was still being waged when Aehrenthal arrived at the Ballplatz. Alert to the harmful effects the quarrel was causing in relations with Russia, Aehrenthal was concerned to bring the dispute to an end. That objective he repeatedly expressed in private, and the very month after becoming foreign secretary he told the delegations that he hoped normal relations with Serbia might soon be restored. Beyond question, Aehrenthal at this time considered it possible, or at least desirable, to attract the Serbs into the Hapsburg orbit.[21]

Conversations with Belgrade were initiated, which in time resulted in a provisional trade treaty, admitting a fixed quota of Serb pork products into the Monarchy. That accommodation irritated Austro-Hungarian agrarians and failed to satisfy Serb interests, though Premier Pasič expressed personal gratitude. He felt that the commercial settlement would smooth the way to better feelings between the two cabinets, as assuredly it did. It can hardly be doubted that in the first phase of his tenure at the Ballplatz Aehrenthal worked to mitigate the Serbian animosities that he had inherited.[22]

IX

Before the armistice in the "pig war" had been negotiated, Aehrenthal surprised the European public, though scarcely the governments, by revealing in January 1908 that a deal had been perfected with Turkey for the survey of a railway line across the Sanjak of Novibazar.[23] This track, which had been contemplated in the original program for railways linking the Ottoman empire with the rest of Europe, would give Austria a new commercial outlet at Salonika and would have strategic implications, too. But the Ballplatz was more interested in the political aspects of the enterprise—the effects the announcement of the plan would have upon Hapsburg patriotism and Austrian international prestige—than in the commercial or strategic importance of the road. Though small in itself, the presentation of the Novibazar scheme heralded the revival of the perennial Austro-Russian rivalry over the Near East in an acute form, sharpened international animosities generally, strengthened latent dreads that the Austro-German coalition aspired to hegemony over the Balkans, and gave an impetus to a plethora of competing railway projects.

Before revealing his railway plan to the world, Aehrenthal had informed the other major European governments of his intentions. None protested. And Austria secured from Turkey permission to undertake the necessary surveys. The scheme was publicly disclosed by Aehrenthal in a flamboyant speech which startled Europe less because of the railway project itself than for the manifestation that the traditional Austrian foreign policy of *quieta non movere* had been jettisoned in favor of a forward course reminiscent of the administration of Andrássy. Europe was brought suddenly to the realization that a strong hand had grasped the Hapsburg diplomatic tiller.

Abroad, Aehrenthal's success in obtaining the sanction of the sultan for preliminary surveys for a relatively insignificant railway in a forgotten corner of the Balkans provoked a tremendous uproar. In Russia the fury attained sensational dimensions as the press, particularly the Pan-Slav section, demanded that the entente with Austria should be canceled and that Russia should revert to the historic anti-Austrian policy; upon Germany was saddled prime responsibility for Austria's action. Izvolsky, Russian foreign minister, who earlier had tacitly approved the Sanjak project, bent before the journalistic storm and not improbably would have taken strong measures to thwart the execution of the Austrian scheme had Russian fighting services been in better shape. He did not share the prevalent opinion that Germany had inspired the Novibazar undertaking, and tardily took steps which quieted the anti-Teutonic tempest in the Russian journalistic teapot. Russia, moreover, gave its blessing to a railway to be built from the Danube to the Adriatic, a line much desired by Serbia.

In Serbia old resentments against Austria flared up afresh. The press unanimously denounced the Sanjak scheme as an Austrian stratagem, backed by Germany, to dominate the Balkans. The Serbian government, however, preferred to exploit the opportunity to secure international backing for a railway from the Danube to the Adriatic. Elsewhere, in Italy, in France, in Great Britain, criticism of Austria was vehement, though emotions subsided after the Russian tone was modified and Aehrenthal indicated approval for surveys to build a Danube-Adriatic railway. Imperial Germany, though guiltless of the allegation that it had prompted the Sanjak plan, loyally stood by her Austrian ally in a manner that became almost a habit in the years that followed. Nothing that statesmen in Berlin or Vienna did or said could shake the conviction held in other capitals that Austria was merely the cat's-paw of her powerful ally.

Although in October of 1908 Austria announced that troops stationed in the Sanjak under the Berlin Treaty would be evacuated, Vienna did not immediately renounce the railway project. Surveys for the road were carried through but no decisions were reached on the financing of the line, and in 1909 the whole plan was put in cold storage.

Aehrenthal had accomplished his central purpose of making Europe aware that the Hapsburg Monarchy, regardless of internal convulsions, had vitality and intended to play the game of power politics as a great and independent state. But in scoring a technical victory in the Balkans he had damaged Austrian relations with the members of the Triple Entente, with the nominal ally, Italy, and with Serbia. Appetite grew with eating; success in the Sanjak gamble inspirited Aehrenthal to make a much more adventuresome move: the conversion of Bosnia, under Hapsburg occupancy since 1878, into an integral part of the Danube Monarchy.

CHAPTER EIGHTEEN

THE BOSNIAN CRISIS

AFTER 1875, THE LEADING NATIONS OF EUROPE INDULGED IN a furious scramble for colonies and special privileges in the economically backward areas of the globe. In that competition the Hapsburg Monarchy had no part. More than once it was hinted in the Austrian half of the realm that colonies ought to be acquired, but Magyar leaders were intransigently opposed to colonialism, and extra-European commercial operations were not in the Austrian tradition. True, an Austrian East India company had founded trading stations in the East Indies and Emperor Joseph II tenuously held the Nicobar Islands in the Bay of Bengal. But these colonial ventures were short-lived.

At the end of the nineteenth century, when spheres of European interest were being carved out in the crumbling Manchu empire of China, it was reported that Austria contemplated the occupation of a coastal section of the Celestial empire. Italian pretensions to a share of the Chinese spoils stimulated spokesmen for Austrian business interests and naval men to claim like concessions. But energetic participation in overseas imperialism was really out of the question unless the Dual Monarchy was prepared to build large naval forces, and that it could not afford to do. Hungary, which had almost no interest in extra-European markets, steadfastly resisted any considerable expansion of sea power and therewith overseas adventures. Only two Austrian firms had branches in China, Austrian shipping handled only one-third of 1 per cent of China's trade, and not more than twenty Hapsburg subjects were missionaries in China and even they were under the guardianship of other countries. A mere handful of Austrian troops marched in the international army which suppressed the murderous Boxer fanaticism.

Such colonial enterprise as the Danube Monarchy manifested was confined to Bosnia-Herzegovina. After 1878 when Austria occupied and undertook the administration of the region, economic and cultural affairs experienced a distinct, one might almost say a phenomenal, improvement.[1] Prosperity such as was not surpassed elsewhere in the Balkans, if indeed it was equaled, replaced the anarchy and devastation that had filled the long centuries of Turkish governance. Even a severe British critic of the Monarchy in general saw fit to write in 1908 that "the transformation wrought in Bosnia and Herzegovina by the Danube Monarchy, though naturally distasteful to Belgrade and Cettinje, has no modern parallel, save in the Egypt of Lord Cromer."[2]

An official survey of Bosnia,[3] carried out in 1906, revealed a great deal concerning the Hapsburg stewardship. Population had grown by more than half since Austria assumed charge—mute testimony in itself to the peace and order that prevailed. And whereas in 1878 there had been less than 600 miles of roads and only the faintest beginning of a railway system, by 1905 there were fully 4,000 miles of highways and 900 miles of railways, and the trackage would have been even greater had not Hungary raised objections to expansion. Native Bosnian spokesmen, it is true, contended that strategic interests of the Monarchy rather than commercial usefulness had largely determined the routes of transportation.

Bosnian industry, especially carpetmaking and the working of metals, had grown even in the face of stiff competition from machine-made wares in the Monarchy proper. With mixed success, the Bosnian government operated mines, and beginnings were made in the efficient exploitation of the forests that covered over half the province. Public revenues had risen prodigiously, partly because of more efficiency in the collection of taxes. Schooling facilities had been considerably extended; primary education was furnished by the government, which also subsidized schools conducted by religious bodies, but attendance was not compulsory. Specially talented Bosnian students were taken to Vienna on scholarships, which might, however, be revoked if the holders engaged in political activities; some students preferred Belgrade to Vienna, where they divided their time between study, idle vagabonding, and participation in the doings of Serbian political societies.

Under government auspices a few specialized agricultural schools, model farms, and breeding studs were established. In places excellent irrigation and water-supply systems were built, and the state furnished physicians and hospitals; medical and hygienic improvements indeed were noteworthy achievements of Austrian administration. Plain but comfortable hotels were built to attract tourists; Ilidže, an ancient watering place near Sarajevo, was converted into an attractive health resort and vacation spot.

The admirable Austrian gendarmerie, backed by a large military garrison, wrought something approaching a miracle in making life and property safe.

Violence and rapine were less common than anywhere else in the Balkans, and murders and manslaughter were even rarer than in Bavaria or East Prussia. The civil administration contained a large proportion of capable and conscientious officials; about a fourth of them were Bosnians, employed mostly, to be sure, in the lower ranks of the service. Religious creeds were treated impartially, which stirred resentment on all sides; the acutely competitive spirit of the rival sects was, however, somewhat mitigated by the compulsory tolerance enforced by the Austrian ruler. As of 1895, and ratios were little altered thereafter, about 43 per cent of the population professed the Orthodox Catholic faith, 35 per cent were Moslems, and 21 per cent Roman Catholic.

However impressive the material and social advancement which Hapsburg occupation brought, the fundamental problem of liberating the *kmets* (tenant peasants) from grasping landlords remained unsolved. The institution of primitive tenantry lay at the root of much of the discontent that existed in the provinces. For the greater part the cultivated land was worked by sharecroppers whose rights and duties were defined in a Turkish statute of 1859 which the Hapsburg administration preserved; as a rule, a tenth of the crops passed to the government, a third of the remainder to the landowner (*beg*), and the balance to the peasant cultivator.

Landlords were expected to furnish dwellings and farm buildings and keep them in repair. If they supplied seed, oxen, and farm implements they often were compensated with as much as half of the crops. A tenant, while free to move away, could not lawfully be evicted unless he failed to meet obligations or cultivated the soil in a slovenly manner; that rule prevented the rise of a class of landless peasants, such as cursed other sections of the Hapsburg realm. A tenant, moreover, had first option on the purchase of the land that he worked. Wealthy Bosnian landlords had as many as eighty *kmets* on their properties.

Endless bickering between owners and tenants over rights and rules gave rise to a profusion of lawsuits. On occasion, poverty-stricken peasants rebelled against their landlords; a rising in the Banjaluka district in 1910 threatened to develop into a general agrarian insurrection until soldiers intervened. In some places tenant lands were worked by *zádrugas* or household communities, though this custom declined under Austrian rule in favor of individual undertakings.[4]

Sharecropping was no more conducive to agricultural well-being in Bosnia than anywhere else in the world. The tenant, short on enterprise or initiative, was content to raise the minimum for personal needs; he allowed about half of the land to lie fallow, and was uninterested in more efficient techniques of farming. Soil was turned up with a *ralo,* a long wooden spike, and the peasant thought nothing of walking miles to market a few pounds of butter or a goat. Nearly all tenants were Christians, while the large landlords and almost all the peasant proprietors were Moslems, and that social cleavage aggravated the agrarian problem.

The Austrian administration hesitated to inaugurate radical innovations in the tenure of land, for the officials required the good will of the wealthy and they were concerned to prove to other Balkan Moslems that Austria could govern in an acceptable fashion. For the same reason, Moslem legal and religious customs were scrupulously respected and the faithful were even permitted to celebrate the Turkish sultan's birthday. While Benjamin Kállay was chief administrator, tenants were assisted in buying land. They could borrow up to half the purchase price from the government at 7 per cent; the rest they had to save or obtain privately at exorbitant rates. Count Stephen Burián, who succeeded Kállay in 1903, arranged with a Hungarian banking house to advance to the peasant all the money needed to purchase the land he worked. Loans would be repaid in installments, and the government assumed liability for what the peasant might fail to pay. That plan was replaced in 1911 by a government credit scheme whereby the tenant would become the owner of his holding by paying for it over a period of years. Landlords, however, were not obliged to dispose of their land, though compulsory sale was being seriously considered in official circles in 1914. Many peasants who took advantage of the government lending scheme soon found themselves hopelessly in arrears and on the outbreak of war in 1914 the whole project was abandoned.

None of the measures to convert tenants into proprietors did anything more than merely scratch the surface. In other words, the great bulk of the Bosnian landworkers remained in chains, and some of them were restless and rebellious. Popular discontent, furthermore, was encouraged by the fact that in the neighboring kingdom of Serbia, Orthodox Christians owed no payments to landlords, but owned their own land. In June 1914, a Serb deputy in the Bosnian diet exclaimed, "The government is always promising the solution of this [land] question, and always leading us astray. I tell you the guns, which will solve the question, are ready and waiting."

Failure of the Austrian administration to solve the land problem was only one of the deep grievances of the Orthodox (generally Serb) population of Bosnia. Intensely conservative, this element resented most of the social and political changes that had been introduced by the alien "Schwabs." They protested increases in taxation, prohibitions on the carrying of arms and of massacring Moslems, and forestry regulations, which restricted hunting, fishing, and the cutting of timber. And they complained bitterly against compulsory military service, exacted of all young men, and the sending of recruits outside of Bosnia for their training, as was generally done.

Orthodox Serb intellectuals, moreover, heatedly inveighed against limitations on civil freedoms, charged that their churches and schools were given less financial assistance than Roman Catholic institutions, and complained that commercial concessions and government contracts were granted only to Roman Catholics and to foreigners. There was yet another source of dissatisfaction among the politically articulate: the limited rights allowed natives in government. True, a consultative assembly composed of Bosnian high churchmen and a dozen laymen had been created to tender advice to the Austrian viceroy, and the larger towns had certain rights of home rule, but native politicians desired an elective legislature which would have authority over purely provincial affairs. Governor Burián acknowledged the validity of that claim and recommended in 1907 that a local assembly of some sort should be established.

II

Active discontent with things as they were facilitated the growth of Pan-Serb enthusiasms. Christmas issues of Serbophile newspapers in 1907, for instance, summoned readers to rebel and strike off the yoke of foreign oppression; "Now is the time to die for the holy cause of liberty," a popular local poet, Skrgo, sang in his Christmas carol. The newspaper *Srpska Ryeč* of Sarajevo, which was believed to be subsidized by the Serbian government, was confiscated on at least seventy occasions for vitriolic attacks upon the Austrian administration, and many political tracts for the time, teaching sedition and revolt, were in circulation.

Without help from Serbia it may well be doubted whether anti-Austrian sentiments in Bosnia would have had very extensive currency. How the partisans of Greater Serbia felt about Bosnia was recounted by Miroslav Spalajkovič in *La Bosnie et l'Hercegovine* (1899), a study that was crowned with a prize by the Parisian institution in which it was written. The population of the provinces, the book argued, was entirely Serb, the best part of the Serb "race" in fact, and to annex the region should be and actually was the supreme ambition of Serbia and Montenegro; Austria could be and would be shoved aside. Spalajkovič, who secured an important position in the Serbian foreign office, married a Bosnian Serb and promoted anti-Hapsburg feelings in the province.

A band of agitators, furthermore, from Serbia roved over Bosnia, preaching sedition. And willingness to appeal to arms if necessary to achieve the goal of Greater Serbia was not restricted to professional revolutionaries and everyday desperadoes; the bishop of Serbian Nish, indeed, exclaimed to an English visitor in 1905: "Don't send us Bibles, we don't need them; send us weapons and cannon." Obviously Austria could not remain indifferent to the Serbophile propaganda, so much of which had an anti-Hapsburg cutting edge.

Unlike run-of-the-mill politicians of Austria, Joseph M. Baernreither, a far-sighted and broad-gauged Bohemian German, displayed a keen interest in the people and problems of Bosnia and in the wider Yugoslav question. Repeated journeys to Bosnia, personal acquaintance with local leaders of thought and opinion, and sustained study qualified Baernreither to speak and write on the province with the voice of authority. Early in the twentieth century he candidly reported that unrest and dissatisfaction with Hapsburg rule were surprisingly widespread, and he deplored the failure of the administration to win the loyalty of Bosnian opinion makers. Moslems, he found, cherished strong sympathies for Turkey and had no desire to see their homeland incorporated in the Danube Monarchy; Roman Catholics, on the other hand, inclined toward Croatia, and the influential archbishop of that faith in Sarajevo frankly preached political union with Croatia.

It was Baernreither's judgment that Orthodox Serb leaders in the main desired home rule under a constitution and frowned upon the idea of annexation to the Hapsburg Monarchy. But certain influential Serb journalists in the province openly espoused union with the kingdom of Serbia. Mostar's *Narod,* for example, declared in April of 1907 that unless the Hapsburg forces of occupation were evacuated violent revolution would ensue, in which Austria would be wrecked as easily as a bomb destroys a house. Such doctrine was the conviction of a town-dwelling fringe; it had not taken root in the rustic population, Baernreither reported. Balancing conflicting interests and currents as maturely as he could, Baernreither concluded that Bosnia ought to be annexed to the Dual Monarchy and that steps should be taken to organize a third Hapsburg state, containing South Slav subjects, to which the kingdom of Serbia would be drawn like a filing to a magnet.[5]

Europe in general cared little and knew less about Bosnia. An English traveler to the province in the late eighties remarked in a fashionable London drawing room that he had just been in Sarajevo. "Oh, do tell us," begged one of the company, "the latest news of Stanley then. You must have seen him quite lately!" An announcement in October of 1908 that Austria had annexed Bosnia brought the forgotten province into the very spotlight of European high politics.

III

Bosnia's constitutional status resembled that of Egypt, for while legally it belonged to Turkey, it was administratively Austrian. Outright annexation had frequently been discussed in high Austrian circles and had indeed been approved by foreign powers, Russia conspicuously.[6] The growth of Pan-Serb sentiments in the province unquestionably influenced Aehrenthal to decide that the time for annexation had now arrived. Such a move would be a pointed blow to the Greater Serb agitation, would attest anew the virility of the Monarchy and enhance its prestige, which the foreign secretary felt had already benefited by his boldness and resolution in the Novibazar railway affair. Furthermore, if Austria had full sovereign jurisdiction it could proceed to reform the governmental institutions of Bosnia and introduce some sort of representative assembly. The decision to act rapidly was taken after a successful Young Turk revolution in July 1908; Turkey's new leaders might well try to put an end to Hapsburg administration, unless Bosnia became wholly Austrian.

Aehrenthal appreciated, of course, that annexation would contravene the strict letter of the Treaty of Berlin, but revisions in that document had repeatedly been made before. He foresaw that there would be resistance from Turkey, the nominal sovereign, and from Serbia, because of the Yugoslav population in Bosnia, but they could be dealt with if the great powers would concur and there was valid reason for supposing that they would. Italy would probably cause no serious trouble, for she had forsworn in diplomatic instruments any claim to compensation if Austria should take over Bosnia; France at the moment was immersed in another controversy with Germany over Morocco; Britain, which had backed Austria's Bosnian pretensions in 1878, would probably content herself with a mild legalistic protest. Germany was a faithful friend who would support Austria in order to retain her only reliable ally, if for no other reason.

What, then, of Russia, the ancient competitor in the Balkans, the defender and champion of the interests of the Balkan Slavs? When entering the *Dreikaiserbund* with Russia in 1881, Austria, it may be recalled, had reserved the privilege of possessing Bosnia whenever she saw fit, but in the Austro-Russian conversations of 1897, Russia asserted that annexation was still an open question which would require special examination at the appropriate time. Russia, after the Japanese war, was militarily weak, but she had ambitions and keen interest in prestige. Wherefore, it would be politic for Austria to strike a new, mutually profitable, bargain with the men on the Neva as the preface to annexation of Bosnia.

During an interview with Aehrenthal in October 1907, the mercurial Russian foreign secretary, Izvolsky, intimated that Russia contemplated seeking international sanction for the passage of her battleships through the Straits. By international treaties the Straits were barred to all foreign men-of-war, and what Izvolsky desired was the revocation of closure in the case of Russia but the maintenance of the barricade so far as other countries were concerned. Regulations on the use of the Straits were not alone humiliating to Russian national pride, but a positive strategic handicap, as had been recently demonstrated in the war with Japan, when battleships could not be moved out of the Black Sea. More than once, in the negotiations which culminated in the Anglo-Russian entente of 1907, representatives of

Nicholas II had broached the subject of the opening of the Straits but they found the British hesitant, evasive.

When Izvolsky raised the Straits question with Aehrenthal, the Austrian murmured something about the immensely involved nature of the problem and avoided committing himself. The Russian ministerial council informed Izvolsky that the country was physically incapable of risking a war to secure revision at the Straits, so, perforce, Izvolsky was obliged to turn again to the stratagems of diplomacy to reach his objective. He blandly assumed that Britain and France would assent because of their diplomatic friendship, and Germany had intimated approval more than once. Only Austria had to be won over.

Just as Izvolsky desired Austrian approval of revision in the Straits treaties, so Aehrenthal was eager to have Russian blessing for the annexation of Bosnia. Here were materials for a grand international deal, promising advantages to both parties. Izvolsky in July of 1908 confided to the Ballplatz that he was ready to discuss the future of Bosnia, of the Sanjak of Novibazar, and of the Straits, "dans un esprit d'amicale reciprocité." In view of the recent Young Turk revolution, Aehrenthal had decided that Austria must annex Bosnia and clear out of the Sanjak.

If Serbia caused trouble over Bosnia, the kingdom would be sponged off the map. Part of Serbia would be awarded to Bulgaria, which would consolidate Bulgarian friendship with Austria, and what remained would be merged in the realm of the Hapsburgs. That line of reasoning diverged radically from the attitude toward Serbia that Aehrenthal had adopted upon his accession to the Ballplatz two years before. Serbian promotion of disaffection and separatist feelings in the Dual Monarchy, Serbian resistance to the Sanjak railway project, and the counsels of Magyar statesmen who detested and dreaded the Pan-Serb agitation seem to have been the influences that caused the foreign minister to change his mind.

Before responding to Izvolsky's initiative, Aehrenthal laid his diplomatic logic before a Hapsburg crown council. The Monarchy, he explained, ought to annex Bosnia and give up treaty rights in Novibazar, a gesture, he reasoned, that should appease the Turks for the loss of sovereignty in Bosnia and ought to puncture the prevalent myth that Austria nurtured designs of territorial aggrandizement in the lower Balkans. For the council the foreign minister sketched the manner in which he expected the European cabinets to react to a declaration of annexation.

At a second conference early in September of 1908, Aehrenthal reviewed the whole Bosnian situation afresh and assured his colleagues that Russia would approve annexation. The Hungarian premier, Wekerle, expressed doubt and misgivings, and Beck, his Austrian counterpart, thought nothing should be attempted without a full understanding with the major powers.

But Francis Joseph, persuaded that annexation would not produce warlike complications, gave the plan his blessing and the council finally endorsed it.

Already at the end of August, Aehrenthal had informed Izvolsky that if Russia would consent to the annexation of Bosnia, Austria would "exchange views" on the Straits question and would evacuate her soldiers from Novibazar. And on September 15–16, 1908, the two statesmen held lengthy exchanges at Buchlau, the Moravian country seat of Count Leopold von Berchtold, Hapsburg ambassador to Russia.

Precisely what was said and understood at Buchlau may never be known. Only Aehrenthal and Izvolsky conferred, nothing was set down on paper, and subsequently each minister drew up a personal version of what had actually transpired, accounts that by no means tallied. An acrid and by now rather arid controversy has raged over the elements of truth, falsehood, and misunderstanding in the two "cases"; since Izvolsky claimed that he had been crudely tricked by the Austrian in the Sanjak railway affair, it is a sign either of incredible incompetence or of singular obtuseness that at Buchlau he neglected to nail Aehrenthal down to a black-and-white understanding.

Surely Izvolsky agreed to the annexation of Bosnia; surely Aehrenthal agreed that the Straits should be opened to Russian warcraft—though he probably never intended that this should happen—and he promised that Austria would clear out of Novibazar. It would seem that Izvolsky insisted that the signatories of the Berlin Treaty would have to concur in these arrangements and that Aehrenthal was sympathetic to an international conference to ratify the contemplated changes, without, however, debating them. No one knows what was said at Buchlau concerning the time when the changes would be effected.

According to Aehrenthal's version, he told the Russian that the annexation of Bosnia would very probably be divulged before the Hapsburg delegations assembled early in October; he would communicate the precise date to Izvolsky at the earliest practicable moment. On the other hand, there were grounds for Izvolsky's assumption that Austria would not act before the Buchlau conversations were exchanged in writing. At any rate, Izvolsky set off from the parley with Aehrenthal to solicit the backing of France and Britain for a new deal at the Straits. Upon his arrival in Paris, Izvolsky learned by a note from Aehrenthal that annexation of Bosnia would be proclaimed in the very near future.

IV

Prior to his conference with Izvolsky, Aehrenthal had divulged the secrets of his heart—though not the innermost ones—to his Triplice partners. Without giving details, he apprised Italy of the prospective annexation and promised, as a kind of compensation, though Italy asked for none, to back an Italian-favored project for a railway from the Adriatic to the Danube. Italy's sympathetic response confirmed Aehrenthal in the hypothesis that annexation would occasion no difficulty in that quarter.

Aehrenthal's disclosures to Berlin were hardly more precise than those to Rome. He was convinced that Germany, friendless save for Austria and keenly aware of her predicament, would support him. When communicating his plans to the Wilhelmstrasse—the substance of the Buchlau bargain—he neglected to mention the time when annexation would be declared. As had been calculated, the Germans in no wise applied the brake to the Austrian chariot. Nothing of what was afoot was vouchsafed to the other European cabinets until they were officially notified that annexation had taken place, though the Viennese press hinted days in advance of the impending event and foreign newspapers reproduced the reports.

Bulgaria, in the meantime, had come into the orbit of Aehrenthal's calculations. After the Young Turk revolution, wily Prince Ferdinand thought that the time had arrived to strike off the remaining vestiges of Turkish sovereignty, to declare Bulgaria's complete independence. Aehrenthal, who regarded Bulgaria, a country without pretensions to Austrian territory, as a useful counterweight to Serbia, was sympathetic to Bulgarian independence, and told Ferdinand as much late in September. But that Aehrenthal spurred the prince to act is far from clear; certainly no formal secret pact was signed.

It was the intention of Aehrenthal to proclaim the annexation of Bosnia before Ferdinand moved, but the prince beat the diplomatist to the draw by a day. Despite Aehrenthal's disclaimers, it was believed in foreign chancelleries that the two men had conspired to make the changes in which each was interested. Actually, the real game of Ferdinand, and he played it with consummate skill, was to oscillate between Austria and Russia, without becoming the pawn of either.[7]

On October 6, 1908, an imperial Austrian rescript notified the world that, in order to raise Bosnia "to a higher level of political life," parliamentary institutions would be set up, which would "take account of prevailing conditions and general interests." Bosnians would be given "a voice when decisions are taken concerning their native land, which, as hitherto, will have a separate administration." To carry out these reforms "a clear and unambiguous juridical position" was required in Bosnia, the note explained; wherefore, Bosnia was annexed to Austria. Simultaneously it was disclosed that Francis Joseph had ordered his troops to evacuate Novibazar.

To the delegations Aehrenthal reported that annexation had been decided upon because Bosnia could no longer be denied a constitution now that the Young Turks had given Turkey one, and that necessitated bringing the province entirely under Hapsburg sovereignty. The delegations overwhelmingly ratified annexation, though certain critics complained about the withdrawal from Novibazar.

Articulate opinion within the Danube Monarchy largely, though by no means wholly, approved the annexation of Bosnia. Many Croat and Slovene politicians, for example, rejoiced because they interpreted the move as a step toward the creation of a South Slav state within the Hapsburg framework. Out of loyalty, Polish leaders and some Czechs accepted the annexation as a *fait accompli,* though they expressed misgivings as to manner and time at which it was declared. Even the Young Czech firebrand Kramář approved at first, though he changed his tune after Russia raised a hue and cry.

Hostility to annexation was popularly reflected by demonstrators who paraded through Prague shouting "Long live Serbia"; outrageous assaults were made upon German students, and the imperial flag was trampled upon. So serious, in fact, did disorders grow in Prague—observers likened the tumult to that which prevailed when the Badeni ministry had been dismissed eleven years earlier—that in December of 1908, on the very day that Francis Joseph celebrated the sixtieth anniversary of his accession to the throne, the Czech capital was once more placed under martial law. Masaryk in parliament thundered against Aehrenthal's course and pilloried the foreign secretary as "Annexander the Great."

Austro-Germans in the main applauded the alteration in the status of Bosnia. The influential press of Vienna performed yeoman service in combatting foreign criticisms and generally upheld the Aehrenthal course. Professor Joseph Redlich and his friend, Baernreither, brilliantly defended the annexation, and Baernreither begged the government to inaugurate far-reaching reforms in Bosnia and to pursue a Yugoslav policy that would appease Yugoslavs within and without the Monarchy. But the Austro-German chorus on annexation was not unanimous; Socialist newspapers, for instance, and the independent and liberal *Die Zeit,* hotly condemned Aehrenthal's diplomacy, and Prime Minister Beck thought it extremely imprudent, as did the veteran Liberal statesman, Ernst von Plener.

Within the Hungarian cabinet the ministers debated earnestly the wisdom of changing the status of Bosnia. Andrássy the Younger and Apponyi strongly opposed any alteration and the ministry as a whole only reluctantly went along with Aehrenthal, on whom was placed full responsibility for what was done. Hungary's press and parliament, without important dissent, rallied behind the foreign office. Some responsible spokesmen even advocated that Bosnia should be incorporated bodily in the kingdom of the Magyars.

v

After annexation was announced, involving revision in the form, not the substance, of the Austrian position in Bosnia, that diplomatic volcano which was twentieth-century Europe, ever in a state of latent eruption, belched forth fire, flame, and lava. Izvolsky professed to be grievously shocked by what he termed Aehrenthal's treachery in confronting him with a *fait accompli* and in violating his pledge to inform him in good time. Moreover, he found the French cold to his request that the Straits be opened to Russian warships; and Britain too, aghast at the Buchlau bargain, assumed a noncommittal attitude on the Straits question, holding that Turkey would have to consent to any revision.

Russian Pan-Slav circles, already exasperated by the Austrian success in the trifling Sanjak railway issue, indignantly denounced the annexation, upbraided Germany as the real instigator of the move, and turned savagely upon Izvolsky after news of the dickerings at Buchlau leaked out. The foreign secretary, it was charged, had criminally sold the Yugoslavs of Bosnia down the river; the powerful Stolypin was so angry that he even threatened to quit as first minister. No man, however strong, could stand up against such criticism, especially since there was almost no likelihood that Britain and France would agree to revision of the Straits regime. Cornered and forsaken by his ministerial colleagues, Izvolsky indulged in wild, ill-grounded allegations of Austrian perfidy; he murmured about justice for Serbia and solicited Anglo-French backing for a conference of the Berlin Treaty powers in which the future of Bosnia should be decided.

Much to Aehrenthal's surprise, opinion in Italy reacted unsympathetically to the declaration of annexation. Mass demonstrations of protest were staged in front of the Hapsburg embassy in Rome, and the chamber of deputies heartily applauded an address of former premier Fortis denouncing annexation and warning that the recent military expansion of Austria brought up the possibility "that we must war upon an Allied power." But just when popular excitement was at a high point Italy was upset by a terrible earthquake in Sicily, which temporarily diverted attention to the home scene. Throughout the diplomatic crisis over Bosnia, the Italian ministry, badgered behind and before, pursued a vacillating, irresolute course. Foreign Minister Tittoni tried to capitalize on the situation by seeking a pledge from Austria to establish a university for Austro-Italians at Trieste, but Aehrenthal was of no mind to bargain.

Aside from Chancellor von Bülow, statesmen in Germany were appalled at the swiftness with which Aehrenthal had acted. William II, who learned of the Austrian intention only on the day of the public proclamation, boiled over with indignation. The Austrian move, he declared, would jeopardize the prestige and prospects of Germany in Turkey and would deepen British suspicion of the Central Powers. It was his initial judgment that Austria should be urged to disavow Aehrenthal's policy and to dismiss him—as was in fact urged by the German ambassador in Vienna—even though that should cost Germany her only reliable ally; similar recommendations were made by the more sober sections of the German press. Yet Bülow's reasoning, that unless Austria were firmly supported Germany would lose her friendship and stand isolated, eventually carried the day in the Wilhelmstrasse. So, without reservations, Germany promised to stand by her ally, but urged Austria to conciliate Turkey quickly. By handing Vienna a blank check, Berlin encouraged Austrian obduracy in the diplomatic crisis that ensued.

On the other side of the North Sea, the British press poured out a cataract of condemnation on Austrian "brigandage." The foreign office vigorously protested against the annexation—and against the Bulgarian declaration of independence—because of the unfortunate repercussions it would have upon the infant constitutional regime of the Young Turks. Much play was made with the immorality of revising an international treaty by unilateral action; formal British representations in that vein were dispatched to Austria and Bulgaria, and Britain endorsed Izvolsky's demand for an international conference on Bosnia. And just as German support enheartened Austria, so the British stand stiffened the Russians, the Serbs, and the Turks in resistance to annexation.

Britain's point of view represented a departure from her historic relationship with Austria, her traditional associate in blocking Russian progress toward Turkey. The key to the British attitude is to be found in the mounting tension with Germany, Austria's ally. For official Britain, it had become a conviction, if not quite an obsession, that Austrian policy was really determined in the Wilhelmstrasse and that the Hohenzollerns were leading the Hapsburgs round by the nose. Thus was explained the origin of the Sanjak railway scheme, thus was explained Austrian diffidence in the matter of judicial reforms in Macedonia, thus was explained the Bosnian annexation.

Austria, on its side, was equally convinced that the recent British *rapprochement* with Russia boded ill for the Dual Monarchy. With British sympathy, Russia might proceed to carry out her Balkan pretensions, which could scarcely fail to damage Austrian interests, and might conceivably challenge her position as a great power. In mid-August of 1908, Francis Joseph had entertained Edward VII at Ischl, as often he had done before, and statesmen of the two countries exchanged views on European issues during the visit, without accomplishing anything in the way of bettering Austro-British relations.

The press of France adopted a strongly bellicose tone on the Austrian course in Bosnia, but the ministry, deeply involved as it was in a quarrel with Germany over Morocco, contented itself with formal protestations. The pacific tenor of French diplomacy exercised a certain restraint upon the Russian ally.

In Turkey the outcry against Austria was loud and vehement. A boycott was declared on Austrian goods and shipping, infuriated mobs demonstrated before the Hapsburg embassy in Constantinople, Austrian-owned shops were stormed, and troops were mobilized. Not for nothing would the Young Turks sacrifice sovereign rights in Bosnia and lose face thereby.

VI

Greater fury and popular commotion were conjured up in Serbia than anywhere else, and that country was directly responsible for the magnitude of the diplomatic crisis that developed. The point was that if Austria annexed Bosnia, the prospect of adding that coveted area to Serbia would become even more remote; Serb hotheads, in fact, and some cooler ones, clamored for war on the House of Hapsburg, without or with the assistance of the big Slav brother, Russia. With a view to preventing annexation by main force, a national defense society (*Narodna Odbrana*) was founded by prominent citizens of Serbia; guerrilla bands were fitted out, evangelists of revolt hurried into Bosnia, and an effective boycott on Austrian goods was organized. Parliament, quickly convoked, reviled the annexation and voted preparatory measures of war such as massing troops along the Bosnian border. And Premier Pasič rushed to St. Petersburg to seek assurances of help, while his foreign minister set off on a similar errand to other major capitals. Even stanch admirers of the Serbs in western Europe complained of the intemperate character of the national convulsion.

What the Serbs desired above all was an autonomous Bosnia, or, failing that, territorial compensation for the Austrian annexation, possibly in the form of a slice of the Sanjak of Novibazar. But to the dismay and grief of the Serbs no country was prepared to back their pretensions wholeheartedly; Izvolsky, for instance, admonished the impetuous Serbs to avoid any act that would supply Austria with a pretext for military operations, though he thought simple justice required that Serbia should be given compensation, a fragment of Bosnia or a commercial outlet on the Adriatic, perhaps. Austrian annexation of Bosnia, the Serbs were told, need not be considered something fixed and final forever.

Aehrenthal, while prepared for the Turkish and Serbian response to annexation, was astonished at the reaction in Italy and in Britain, and angry at the manner in which Izvolsky had repudiated the Buchlau arrangement —or rather Aehrenthal's understanding of it. Nevertheless, the Austrian was resolved to follow to the end the trail along which he had started. Montenegro, whose prince had protested the annexation, might be placated with gold, but Serbia, whose hysteria was particularly exasperating to Aehrenthal, would get nothing, exactly nothing. Russian advocacy of a reward to Serbia encouraged Serbian lust, Aehrenthal thought, and was unwarrantable interference in the Austrian side of the Balkans; if Russia won a point now, what next in the way of Hapsburg territory might it seek?

Austria flatly warned Serbia that "we are not inclined to pursue a policy of patience and long suffering ad infinitum." Aehrenthal, in a word, would not stoop to conquer. As for the conference idea raised by Russia and seconded by Britain, that Austria would accept provided the right of annexation was not called into question. Aehrenthal even threatened to publish an account of the Buchlau conversations if Izvolsky did not cease spreading false and malicious accusations; that threat caused cold shivers to run down the Russian's spine.

Germany let it be known that it would favor a conference only on such conditions as Austria might prescribe. It was realized by Izvolsky that if he persisted in the demand for a conference war would be the sequel, and Russia was not in shape for that. Nor could Russia count on French aid, for French hands were tied in Morocco, and France had no stomach to fight at this time directly because of Muscovite interests in the Balkans; and the same held good for Britain. Russia, in short, was isolated; hence the counsels of sobriety which Izvolsky transmitted to the Serbian war hawks.

Heedless of this sage advice, militant Serbs, outside the Danube Monarchy and within, kept up their impassioned denunciations of Austria. And Hapsburg subjects charged with treasonable trafficking with Serbia were arrested in droves, as the prelude to the notorious Agram and Friedjung trials. It seemed prudent, too, to call up part of the Austrian troops and post them along the Serbian frontier. Since Serbia had already mobilized, Europe might have been enveloped in a general conflagration, if Russia had been minded to back Serbia to the limit.

Uncertain as to what Russia would do if the sword were unsheathed against Serbia, Aehrenthal proposed that the Austrian and German general staffs should put into writing their plans for joint military operations, which would be invoked if Russia interfered. To that Germany assented, and letters were exchanged between the two general staffs, which somewhat modified the purely defensive character of the Austro-German alliance of 1879; the Germans, in effect, promised that if Austria made war on Serbia and Russia came in, Germany too would fight. By pledging to help Austria in this wise, the successors of Bismarck departed radically from the old master's version of the duty of Germany to her ally. Thus fortified, Austria could deal more confidently, more stubbornly, with Serbia and with Russia.

Aehrenthal, meanwhile, had reluctantly agreed to appease the Turks, as Germany and Britain and Austrian business houses with interests in

Turkey had urged. The Turkish government was quite ready to barter away the ancient rights in Bosnia for cold cash, but Austrian crown councilors, holding that "purchase" of Bosnia would be incompatible with Hapsburg honor, balked at paying anything except for Turkish-owned public lands in the province. Conversations were undertaken which the Turks dragged out while waiting to see whether any power intended to prevent the Bosnian annexation by force of arms. Aehrenthal ascribed the Fabianism of Turkey to British diplomatic maneuvers in Constantinople. But at length, in February of 1909, when the likelihood of armed interference with Austrian designs appeared exceedingly improbable, Turkey abandoned claims to Bosnia in exchange for about ten million dollars, nominally compensation for public lands in the lost province. And the Turks were assured that the religious rights of Moslems in Bosnia would not be impaired.

By a similar deal Turkey acknowledged Bulgarian independence. Yet dickering over the sum to be remitted by Bulgaria caused complications and both countries enlarged their armies. Austria backed Bulgaria under cover, calculating thus to reinforce the bonds of friendship and to safeguard Austrian railway interests. Russia, however, turned the tables by promising to loan Bulgaria the funds that were needed to satisfy the Turks. In April 1909 a Turko-Bulgar contract was completed, and the great powers officially recognized Bulgarian freedom. Russia seemed to have strengthened her influence in Bulgaria, to the discomfiture of the Ballplatz.

VII

Within Austria, powerful forces pressed for a preventive war upon pestiferous Serbia. It was extremely humiliating, damaging to prestige, for a great power to be overtly challenged by a puny Balkan powerlet, and the crisis involved expenditures that the straitened monarchical exchequer could ill afford to bear. Conrad, the mouthpiece of the war party, argued that the moment had come to remove Serbia from the map, annex most of the kingdom, and award the balance to Bulgaria; in that manner the Yugoslav peril would be permanently liquidated. No need to dread a general war, Conrad reasoned, for Britain and France would not fight and Russia and Italy could not. If the present opportunity were not seized, Serbia's friends might grow stronger, Russia surely would, and then Austria would be confronted by an even more dangerous menace.

Opposed to the logic of the Austrian war hawks were the aged and infirm Francis Joseph, Francis Ferdinand,[8] the heir presumptive, and for a time Aehrenthal also, for he then calculated that a grateful Bulgaria would serve as a sufficient counterpoise to Serbia in the future. But, as the crisis lengthened, the doctrine of preventive war found ever wider acceptance. Aehrenthal decided that Serbian preparations to fight must cease, would cease if Russia so commanded, and could be made to cease by strong military gestures by Austria; and simultaneously Serbia could be forced to recognize the Bosnian annexation. Wherefore, in mid-March of 1909, troops along the Serbian border were increased and the Austrian flotilla on the Danube was prepared for combat. Serbia boldly countered by summoning all her reserves to the colors. It looked as though an armed Austro-Serb clash were imminent and inescapable.

At that critical juncture, with war fever mounting in Austria and Serbia, with Russian Pan-Slavs hurling verbal threats at the Central Powers and the Russian ministry still uncommitted to the annexation of Bosnia, Germany resolved to step in and compel a quick termination of the tension. A plan of accommodation was drawn up which, while satisfying Austria, would likewise be of service to the harassed Izvolsky. Concretely, Germany proposed that Austria should be requested to invite the signers of the Treaty of Berlin to ratify the Bosnian annexation on the assumption that Russia would pledge acquiescence in advance; no "compensation" would be granted to Serbia. Izvolsky, averse to sacrificing the "free" conference principle on which he had staked his grievously impaired reputation, answered evasively, though he seemed to be yielding.

Thereupon the Wilhelmstrasse, in a momentous dispatch of March 21, 1909, insisted upon a Russian reply devoid of conditions or ambiguity. Should Russia refuse to comply, the German telegram continued, "we should then draw back and allow matters to take their course." Very likely the sequel to an unacceptable Russian answer would have been the invasion of Serbia by Hapsburg forces and, if Russia had taken up arms on Serbia's behalf, Germany would have stood faithfully behind her Austrian ally. For the men on the Neva every prospect on the international horizon was displeasing, war with the Central Powers most of all. So Izvolsky surrendered without reservation and assented to annexation, as did the other Berlin Treaty powers. Nothing more was heard of a conference and the Straits, of course, remained bolted and barred as tightly as ever. Serbia in the circumstances had no feasible alternative except to capitulate, though only after a sharp exchange between Austria and Britain over the terms of surrender. The dark clouds of war which had hung perilously low over Europe for six months lifted.

VIII

How then may the consequences of this grave Bosnian quarrel, sometimes saluted as the dress rehearsal for the greater diplomatic crisis of 1914, be evaluated?

In a formal renunciation of ambitions and a confession of purpose, dated March 31, 1909 and addressed to Austria, Serbia acknowledged that her rights had not been injured by the alteration in Bosnia's status. Serbia likewise promised to pursue the way of the good neighbor in future dealings with Austria, and to cut her military services to a normal peacetime basis. Crown Prince George, one of the most fervent apostles of war, renounced his claim to the Serbian throne, a gesture with only surface diplomatic significance since his scandalous life made it unlikely that the nation would ever permit him to become king.

From the nerve-wracking crisis Austria emerged with sovereign authority over Bosnia, with Germany more closely bound to her, and with Serbia and her Russian patron ingloriously humiliated. No one could doubt that the seemingly decrepit Hapsburg Monarchy still possessed considerable vigor and resolution in international affairs. On the other hand, what remained of the Austro-Russian entente of 1897 after the Sanjak railway imbroglio had vanished into the mists of history, and Izvolsky's hatred for the crafty Aehrenthal knew no bounds.

Turkey had regained untrammeled jurisdiction over the Novibazar district and had secured modest cash compensation for the loss of position in Bosnia. Montenegro likewise made minor, very minor, gains, but Serbia obtained precisely nothing, and hatred of the colossus to the north burned more fiercely and ominously than ever, regardless of what the Belgrade cabinet had promised on paper. Instead of dampening the zeal of the Pan-Serbs the Bosnian affair whetted it; instead of stopping subversive and incendiary Pan-Serb propaganda in the Danube Monarchy, Aehrenthal's diplomacy actually stimulated its dissemination.

The humiliated Serbs were consoled by assurances from highly placed Russians, Izvolsky among them, that Bosnia had not been irretrievably lost, that in due time "days of joy would come." A Pan-Slav gathering at St. Petersburg published a circular to the Balkan Slavs, counseling prudence and patience until Muscovite military power was stronger and then Russia would stand forth anew and unafraid "as protectress of the Slav world."

By unswerving support of the Ballplatz in the delicate Bosnian months, Germany made possible the glittering diplomatic triumph of the Central Powers. But, as the future was to demonstrate, it was a victory of Pyrrhic quality. The men on the Neva nursed bitter memories of their spectacular humiliation; for many of them Germany's terse wire of March 21 was an ultimatum, a peremptory challenge to beat a hasty retreat or to fight. It is, however, significant that Izvolsky himself did not place that interpretation upon the German move; rather he considered the diplomacy of Berlin well-intentioned, offering an escape from whatever probability of international war there may have been.[9]

Astride Austria, spurring her on, the malevolent instigator of the Bosnian enterprise, it was believed in foreign chancelleries and press, was the ambitious, restless German empire, clad "in shining armor," in the inept phrase of William II. That conviction deepened the estrangement between Russia and Germany, and between Britain and Germany. Against the day of another test on the diplomatic dueling ground Russia pressed ahead energetically in the upbuilding of her fighting services.

IX

Austria's Bosnian adventure set rolling a new wave of Irredentism in Italy, attended by a characteristic spate of polemical tracts against the "robber" Monarchy. The Italian government, in order to protect and promote national interests in the Balkans, drew alongside of Russia. In October of 1909, a very secret understanding, known as the Racconigi pact and largely the handiwork of the vengeful Izvolsky, provided for Russo-Italian collaboration to hold Austria in check. Together the powers would work to preserve the *status quo* in the Balkans, but if and when changes became unavoidable they would favor the distribution of Turkish territory on the basis of national self-determination. Italy, moreover, committed herself to benevolence on the Russian ambition anent the Straits, and Russia gave a reciprocal pledge concerning Italian pretensions to Tripoli. By this arrangement with Russia, Italy became more intimately linked to the Triple Entente and by the same token moved farther away from the Triplice fellowship.

One clause in the Racconigi pact bound Italy not to enter into a Balkan understanding with a third power without Russian assent. That pledge did not, however, deter Italian statesmen from making an accord with Vienna promising "not to conclude agreements with Russia" unless Austria participated. Austria agreed not to seek to recover the rights she had just renounced in Novibazar without a previous understanding with Italy, assuring her of compensation.

In spite of Italy's soft words and solemn pledges, the confirmed Austrian enemies of Italy had small confidence in her sincerity. Aehrenthal had grown extremely skeptical of her value as an ally, though he, of course, had no knowledge of the Racconigi pact. That Italy was the most dangerous foe of Austria seemed to be verified by preparations being made on land and sea for war against the Monarchy; frontier defenses were improved, strategic railways were laid down, and a new naval base was constructed. Conrad pleaded earnestly for the strengthening of Austria's southern ramparts, but Aehrenthal, unwilling to admit that Italy had been wholly lost to the Triplice, interposed a veto, and when the Italian ambassador expressed displeasure over the presentation of a drama entitled *The Battle of Lissa*—the Austrian naval triumph over Italians in 1866—the foreign secretary forced the title to be changed to an anonymous sea engagement.

Like Italy, Rumania was aggrieved by Aehrenthal's large policy in the

Balkans. It was feared in Bucharest that the annexation of Bosnia would be the prelude to the march of Austria deeper into the Balkan peninsula. And good relations were further impaired by commercial controversy. Two years, in fact, were required to work out a trade treaty, and even then Rumanian live cattle, owing to the pressure of Austro-Hungarian agrarian interests, were wholly debarred from the Hapsburg market.

If it is impossible to accept unreservedly Baernreither's conclusion that throughout the Bosnian crisis Aehrenthal displayed "a combination of firmness of will and clarity of purpose with real acumen in handling complex issues," it is undeniable that he had enhanced the diplomatic prestige of the Monarchy. Admirers, with dubious propriety, labeled him the "Austrian Bismarck," and Francis Joseph honored him with the title of count. Yet the Machiavellian strain in Aehrenthal's make-up had roused heartburnings even in Austria's own diplomatic service; the more farsighted reasoned that Serbia had simply been slapped on the wrist, not soundly chastised, and that Russia had been alienated against reconciliation this side of war. Aehrenthal, in the Bosnian affair, had won the round, but the bout as a whole was to end with a knockout for the Austrian pugilist.[10]

‡ CHAPTER NINETEEN ‡

AUSTRIA ON THE EVE

From the end of 1908 to the outbreak of war in 1914, three ministries were charged with the conduct of Austrian affairs, each presided over by weak, incompetent chiefs, each constantly harassed by sharpening nationalistic antagonisms which lacerated the country at a time when the Monarchy's international position was perilously endangered. Democratization of the suffrage had not proved to be a panacea for the political and spiritual maladies of the empire, as exponents had confidently hoped.

Baron von Bienerth, who followed Beck as prime minister, owed his appointment to his patron, Francis Ferdinand, and to the foreign minister, Aehrenthal, who anxiously desired a premier sympathetic with the diplomacy he had in hand. Without creative talent, Bienerth's political strategy was to blunder along as best he could, while national convulsions became progressively more distressing.

When the diplomatic crisis over Bosnia was at its peak, Czechs in Prague, as has been noted, organized antidynastic demonstrations. Crowds paraded through the streets shouting "Long live Serbia!" "Down with Austria!" and cheering for England and flaunting the Union Jack. On the day marking the sixtieth anniversary of Francis Joseph's accession to the throne, martial law of the most stringent character was laid upon the Czech metropolis and enforced for twelve days. Czechs in parliament retorted with a raucous cacophony, and free-for-all fights with Germans ensued, until the ministry ordered the deputies to go to their homes; in an hour when the Monarchy seemed on the verge of international war, politicians jubilantly retired from the legislative chamber chanting their respective national anthems. Germans in the Bohemian assembly invoked obstruction again, producing another deadlock; renewed conversations for a settlement of the Bohemian strife ran into sand.

Carniola likewise was the scene of disorders. Quarreling between Slovenes and Germans in Laibach led to the intervention of troops who killed two citizens and wounded several more. The assembly was thrown into confusion and soon prorogued when anticlerical deputies hurled bombs filled with hydrogen sulfide at their Clerical opponents; and the emperor refused to approve as mayor of Laibach the Slovene leader, Dr. Hribar, distrusted for his Pan-Slav proclivities, even though he was five times elected to the office.

In the Italian-inhabited areas the forces of separatism were on the march. When the Bienerth cabinet announced that it intended to set up a law faculty for Italians in Vienna, rioting occurred in the imperial capital in which revolvers were brought into play. Still the ministry was not deterred, though it revealed that the institution in Vienna would be only a temporary expedient and that eventually the law school would be transferred to a community in the Italian section of the empire. Promises of that sort found no favor with Italian zealots, and protesting students marched through Vienna singing an Irredentist Dante song and shouting for an Italian university at once.

Effervescent student disturbances could perhaps be overlooked by time-hardened bureaucrats, but there were more ominous symptoms of resurgent Irredentism. For instance, the funeral of the mother of Oberdank, who had been executed in 1882 for conspiring against the life of Francis Joseph, was converted into a solemn patriotic celebration, and a municipal officer of Pola carried a wreath to Trieste in honor of the son of the deceased woman. At Trient an Irredentist mob tried to prevent Austrophile deputies from entraining for Innsbruck to take part in a centennial jubilee for Andreas Hofer, the Tyrolese patriot of 1809; hooligans smeared paint over the imperial coat of arms on public buildings and draped an effigy of Hofer on a statue of Dante.

It was alleged by Austrian police that papers had been uncovered which proved that Irredentist fanatics were plotting to dynamite state buildings. Arrests were made wholesale and patriotic student clubs were broken up. When in 1909 Francis Ferdinand journeyed to Trieste for the formal opening of a newly constructed railway, conspirators tried to blow up the train on which he was traveling; and in Trieste the heir presumptive listened to unfriendly crowds singing Irredentist tunes and yelling, "Down with Austria! Down with the Hapsburgs! Down with the Prince!"

When Irredentist insolence verged on treason, the Austrian authorities intervened with a heavy hand. Press censorship was tightened, fines and prison sentences were imposed upon ringleaders. Italian emotions were cut to the quick by an order of Trieste's governor, Hohenlohe, in 1913, depriving

Italians from the kingdom (*regnicoli* they were called) of positions in the public service. But thanks to the intervention of the Italian ambassador in Vienna, the phraseology of the order was modified so as to debar all foreigners from employment in the government of Trieste, though it was obvious that the measure was directed against the *regnicoli* alone. Early in 1914, Trieste witnessed a recurrence of street fighting between Italian and Slovene residents.

Only the Bucovina provided a patch of blue in the beclouded nationality sky of Austria. In that backward province, peopled by four national groupings, Ruthenians and Rumanians predominating, the electoral law for the assembly was altered along the lines of the Moravian compromise of 1905, and an enlightened adjustment was hammered out on the language of instruction in the state schools. As of 1911, 531 elementary schools were operating in the Bucovina; in 216, the Ukrainian tongue was spoken; Rumanian in 172; German in 82; and in the remainder, teachers used at least two languages.

German, however, continued to serve as the lingua franca of the Bucovina, even in the assembly. Czernowitz, the capital, which contained a very mixed population, and the Francis Joseph University there preserved their essentially German character. At the university there were five Ruthenian chairs, and the province boasted five secondary schools and two teacher-training institutions for Ruthenians. Rumanians, little affected by the Irredentism which had captured some of their kinsmen in Hungary, battled valiantly to keep the Ruthene element from becoming too powerful in the Bucovina.

For a short span the Bienerth ministry checked filibustering in the reichsrat by a change in procedure that authorized the presiding officer to decline to entertain motions, though only after much travail were the annual budget and the military-recruit bills passed into law. Under Czech guidance, Slav deputies, apart from the Poles, organized a weak coalition of parties to protect and promote the welfare of the Slav groups, and several German-bourgeois factions merged in a *Nationalverband* to look after German interests.

What the Slav bloc aimed at was disclosed by a Czech agrarian leader, Udrzal, in an address to parliament. "We wish to save the Austrian parliament," he said, "from utter ruin, but we wish to save it for the Slavs of Austria, who form two-thirds of the population. The empire is ours by right. The Slav question must be solved in favor of the Slavs in the north, in the south, and in the east of the empire. The present system of government must be done away with." Polish support of the ministry was purchased by promises of funds for the construction of canals in Galicia. Presently Czech and Social Democratic mischief-makers paralyzed deliberations, once again the legislature was dissolved, and new elections were ordered. Essential legislation was decreed under the obnoxious paragraph fourteen, which had not been invoked for six years.

II

In the imperial election of 1911, the last before World War I, 2,987 candidates representing over fifty political groupings campaigned for the 516 seats. Ministerial parties, the Christian Socialists and the Polish club, sustained heavy losses. Christian Socialism had been weakened by the death of Lueger, whose strong personality had held disparate factions together, and by charges of corruption on the part of party chiefs; in Vienna, their stronghold, the Christian Socialists returned only three of the thirty-three deputies, a loss of seventeen seats. The parties arrayed in the German *Nationalverband* scored the largest gains. Although the Social Democrats elected a majority of the deputies from Vienna, in the empire as a whole the party was lamed by nationalist antipathies.

These cleavages were ventilated at congresses of the second Socialist International. At Copenhagen in 1910, for instance, Czech Socialists declared their complete independence of Viennese leadership, and the larger Czech wing identified itself with the militant branch of Czech patriotism. Polish and Ukrainian Socialists, too, subordinated the ideal of international fraternity of workers to the political interests of their particular nationalities. Critics of the Socialist creed did not neglect to point up the lesson that secular divergencies proved that blood was thicker than doctrine.

Unable to command a majority in parliament, Bienerth retired in favor of that hardy perennial Baron Gautsch, whom Francis Joseph had twice before produced like a rabbit from his hat. The new parliament was opened with a stereotyped exhortation to the deputies to place the welfare of the empire above and beyond nationalist concerns; it was imperative, the speech from the throne asserted, that legislation to strengthen the armed services be enacted.

Before the chamber got down to business, Socialists of Vienna instigated a "small-scale revolution" in protest against intolerable housing congestion and the high cost of living in general. Among the seditious cries heard was "Hurrah for Portugal!" which had just set up a republic by revolutionary processes; somehow or other the dissidents identified higher standards of comfort with republicanism. Encounters between police and demonstrators cost several lives; martial law was proclaimed and that, combined with promises from the ministry that tariffs on foodstuffs would be scaled down, brought peace to the imperial capital. During debate in parliament on the Vienna disturbances a young Social Democrat in the gallery whipped out a revolver and fired five times at the minister of justice, who had approved sentences meted out to ringleaders in the rioting.

Once more—and for the last time—the Bohemian problem brought about the downfall of an Austrian ministry. Premier Gautsch seems to have shared the optimistic faith of Prince Francis Thun, recently reappointed as governor of Bohemia, that a solution of the vexing conflict in Bohemia could be found. Thun brought rival partisans together in conferences and appointed committees to explore delicate phases of the agelong Czech-German controversies. It appeared that progress in the direction of compromise was being made when, true to pattern, extremists on both sides fell afoul of one another. The language question became hopelessly entangled with social and economic disputes and the deliberations were brought to a standstill. Czech deputies in parliament exploded because a Czech school in Vienna was closed; and Czech mothers and children who attended parliament to protest combined forces with deputies in doing battle with German deputies. The dream of Czech-German reconciliation shattered, the Gautsch cabinet gave way to a ministry headed by Count Karl Stürgkh, sometime minister of education.

III

Stürgkh, who belonged to an impoverished noble family, contrived to hang on to the premiership until removed by an assassin's bullet in October of 1916. His philosophy and practice of government harked back to the era of Count Taaffe, and he felt it his duty to shield the aged emperor from public problems and to spare him from political innovations. Known as an ultraconservative and a clerical who had stubbornly resisted the suffrage reforms of 1907, Stürgkh was caricatured by unfriendly cartoonists in a priest's surplice. He was essentially a schoolman, an acknowledged expert on secondary schools, who was hoisted by luck and ambition into the prime minister's chair. His initial successes as premier in obtaining parliamentary ratification of military bills consolidated his position with weight-carrying personalities of the empire.

Owing to the ever graver international tension, Austria, like other European countries, took steps to improve its capacity for war. An army law of 1912, though it reduced the term of training for conscripts, raised the annual contingent of recruits from 103,100 to 159,500 (for Austria and Hungary) and increased the size of the *Landwehr* of the two partners; in this way the war footing of the Monarchy would reach 1,500,000 men, as against 900,000 previously. An interesting feature of the bill softened the military penal code which had stood unaltered for a century.

Under the War Service Act of 1913, civilians could be compelled to supply manufactures and agricultural products for army needs or could be drafted for labor in industry. The ministry, moreover, might commandeer the entire equipment and military resources of the country; the bill, in other words, contemplated a rigid military dictatorship in wartime. Only over vigorous resistance was this law pushed through the reichsrat, and a measure of similar content was passed in Hungary and ordained by the monarch for Bosnia-Herzegovina.

The Hapsburg military machine was comprehensively overhauled, time-tables to accelerate the mobilization of troops were matured, and, when dynastic loyalties were running high because of the centennial celebration of the Allied victory over Napoleon at Leipzig in 1813, the term of the conscript was raised from two to three years. Greatly enlarged armament appropriations, recurrent deficits on the state railways, and unending parliamentary crises entailed progressive deterioration in state finances; it was officially reported that the empire had for a decade been going into debt at the rate of $200,000 a day. Austrian bankers mainly, but Germans and Dutchmen too, bought up state loans, and in 1912, after vainly trying to float a bond issue in Paris, Austria borrowed for the first time in the costly New York money market.

No more than other ministries could the Stürgkh cabinet control the centrifugal forces of nationalism; rather they grew in volume and in menace to the stability of the empire. National consciousness among the Poles was quickened in 1910 by the five-hundredth anniversary of the Slav victory over the Teutonic Knights at Grünwald (Tannenberg). And at the unveiling of a symbolic monument in Cracow, commemorating the triumph of 1410, hallowed memories of the ancient grandeur of independent Poland were recalled in a patriotic address by the famous musician, Ignace Paderewski, a Russian Pole, who on this occasion made his debut in politics. "The work of art," he said, "which you gaze upon did not arise from hate. It was born of a deep love of the fatherland . . . and [confidence] in its certain future power."

Uneasiness in Polish circles and to a degree in the government at Vienna was occasioned by the unmistakable growth of national feeling among the Ruthenians and the secession of some Ruthenian Uniats to the Orthodox Church. By recourse to noisy obstructionism in parliament and in the Galician assembly, the Ruthenians managed to extract promises of electoral reform for the assembly and of an independent university. Plans to implement these pledges in a manner gratifying to the Ukrainophile wing of the Ruthenian population were perfected, but the outbreak of war in 1914 obliged the authorities to put the schemes in cold storage.[1]

Russophile emotions in Ruthenian districts seem to have increased early in the twentieth century, even though not reflected in election returns. Agents from imperial Russia worked with local politicians in stirring up peasant passions against Polish landlords and in giving assurances that in the not distant future great and holy Russia would liberate the Ruthenians from the thralldom of Pole and Hapsburg alike. Propagandistic literature from Russia, newspapers, books, even small libraries were circulated in the areas of Ruthenian residence.[2] Certain Ruthenian priests, barely superior to medicine men, persuaded their flocks to secede from the Uniat communion and affiliate with the Orthodox Church, as the prelude to the merger of the Ruthene-peopled districts of the Dual Monarchy with imperial Russia. Young men passed to Russia to be trained for the priesthood and promises were made that funds would be supplied from Russian sources to erect Orthodox churches.

However much individual Ruthenian clergymen may have inclined Russiaward for political reasons or because of "rolling Russian rubles," the point of view of parishioners was much more affected by efforts of the Uniat hierarchy under Polish Catholic pressure to have the services of public worship performed in Latin. Back in the sixteenth century, when Ruthenian bishops broke away from Orthodoxy and acknowledged the spiritual headship of the Pope, the changeover had made extremely little impression upon the humble peasantry; except for the organic bond with Rome, the Uniat faith and Orthodoxy had much in common: the same liturgy, the same ceremonial, the same old Slavonic language in public worship. Uniat worshipers murmured the conventional Orthodox prayers, witnessed the traditional Orthodox rites in services, and bothered not at all about the name attached to their creed.

It was another story, however, when Uniat officialdom had the temerity to modify the ecclesiastical conventions. Then devout peasants turned resentful, cast their eyes eastward, were eager to reënter the Orthodox fold. Polish authorities, try as they would, were unable to check the trend to Orthodoxy, and the contagion spread incidentally to Ruthenian settlers in the United States, fully forty thousand of whom seceded from the Uniat religion to Orthodoxy. A learned English student of the Orthodox Church, W. J. Birkbeck, who investigated the religious situation in Galicia in 1912, reported: "Whole villages have declared themselves Orthodox and though they can't get Orthodox priests they won't have anything to do with the Uniats, and are actually burying their dead without any funeral rites rather than have anything to do with their former Uniat clergy."[3]

Birkbeck recounted the persecution to which the seceders were subjected, but doubted whether the movement had political implications, not at least in the sense that the peasantry preferred the flag of the Romanovs to the flag of the Hapsburgs. When he inquired of peasants whether Russian agents had bribed them to change their religion: "Men clenched their fists, women burst into tears . . . 'We have never seen a single ruble in our lives.'" They professed allegiance to the Hapsburg sovereign. "If our Tsizar [emperor] knew what was going on he would soon put matters right," the countryfolk told Birkbeck.

At St. Petersburg in 1913, the Galician Benevolent Society, founded to propagate Russophilism in Galicia, held a conference, with Russian prelates and both Russian and Ruthenian politicians and intellectuals in attendance. Count Vladimir Bobrinsky, the director of the society, welcomed the Ruthenians as brothers and lauded them for their constancy and fortitude in the face of severe oppression and persecution. "We Russians," he exclaimed, "can profit by the example you are setting in your fierce struggle for the Orthodox faith and Russian culture." Asserting that the society pursued only cultural and not political aims, Bobrinsky appealed for closer ties between Ruthenians and Russians, a plea to which the delegates from the Hapsburg Monarchy heartily assented. A chorus entertained the delegates with a prayer to St. Peter imploring him to release Galicia from the alien yoke. And a few months later Russophile Ruthenians at a meeting in Lemberg adopted resolutions of gratitude to Russia for solicitude on behalf of the poor brothers in the realm of the Hapsburgs.

Not long afterward Austrian and Hungarian police arrested scores of Russophile Ruthenians, priests and peasants, on charges of high treason, of conspiring to unite the Ruthenian areas to Russia. All the accused who were Austrian subjects were acquitted, but thirty-two of their fellows in Hungary were fined and imprisoned; Austrian officialdom, it was clear, regarded Russophilism as much less a menace than it was considered in Hungary. Yet the authorities flared up when Sazonov, the Russian foreign minister, in the spring of 1914, spoke in a threatening tone concerning human conditions in eastern Galicia; the cabinet in Vienna declared that it would brook no external interference in domestic affairs and that the government was concerned to better the lot of the Ruthenians.

IV

Among Austrian Slavs, in the meantime, a new version of Slav fraternity along cultural and economic lines had come into being, under the title of Neo-Slavism. Sponsored in particular by the Czech Kramář, the movement was taken up and popularized by other Slav politicians and intellectuals. Kramář proposed that economic bonds between Austrian Slavs should be knit more closely, that a Slav bank should be organized, that a Slav commercial fair should be established to promote the sale of Slav-made products, and that transportation facilities with Russia should be improved. With other Austro-Slav deputies he visited St. Petersburg early in 1908 to confer on the material and cultural interests of Slavdom with prominent Russians and other Slavs. Hearty approval of the ideals of Neo-Slavism was expressed at a banquet in honor of the Austrian guests, attended by the ministers of Tsar Nicholas II. Publicists of the day remarked that the spirit of Slav brotherhood had never been so real or so deep.

At Prague in July of 1908, representative public men and writers from all branches of Slavdom, except the Ukrainians but including Poles, assembled for the first of a series of annual Neo-Slav conferences. Discussions and resolutions dealt with Kramář's economic schemes, the exchange of visits between Slavs of different countries, and the formation of a permanent international Slav committee. Efforts were made to foster better feelings between the Czechs and the Austrian Poles and to heal the old feud between Poles and Russians, without however producing anything concrete. It is claimed that in secret sessions the avowed objectives of the Neo-Slav conference were jettisoned in favor of purely political aims, that it was decided that the Austrian Slavs should coöperate to achieve Slav dominance in the Hapsburg Monarchy, and that in the event of a general European war the Slavs should rebel against the Triple Alliance.[4]

The inability of Russia to block the Austrian annexation of Bosnia and the studied repression of Polish subjects persuaded Kramář that the Austrian Slavs must take leadership in Slavdom. That theme he expounded in a reichsrat address, remarking that "it is lucky that Russia can find in the West a bulwark of Slavdom" against the German menace. At another conclave of Neo-Slavism, held at Sofia in 1910, Balkan political questions were canvassed in secret and a common Slav policy was considered, though probably not actually agreed upon.[5]

Thousands of Slav gymnasts participated in an international Sokol carnival at Prague in 1912. Disapproval of Hapsburg foreign policies and fraternal sympathy for the Yugoslavs were freely expressed. Athletes and spectators joined lustily in an Inter-Slavonic anthem, *Hei Slovane,* which contained such sentiments as "Thunder and lightning, thunder and lightning, the Russians are with us, and those who withstand them, the French will sweep away," and "The Slavs shall never perish even though the number of Germans equals the number of souls in hell." To Kramář an English journalist commented: "These are not gymnasts; they are an army." "Yes," the Czech chieftain responded, "with proper weapons they would count in a European war."[6] That cultural Neo-Slavism was a sort of veneer on old-fashioned political Pan-Slavism was suggested in 1914 when Kramář proposed to Nicholas II that the kingdoms of Bohemia and Poland should be governed by Russian grand dukes as parts of a huge Slav state.[7]

In Bohemia, meanwhile, an authoritarian regime had been set up to administer provincial affairs. Since the storms of 1908 the assembly had been wholly ineffectual, owing to German filibustering; local finance had become chaotic, and the provincial scene was darkened by unemployment and industrial warfare. By a *coup d'état* in 1913 the Stürgkh ministry dissolved the assembly and appointed an imperial committee with representatives of both nationalities to look after affairs until conditions were propitious for an election. Czech and German spokesmen alike berated Stürgkh for arbitrarily shelving the legislature.

The final proposals to reach a compromise settlement in Bohemia were brought forward early in 1914. The distinguished Austro-German historian and publicist, Heinrich Friedjung, recommended that members of the law faculties of the two universities in Prague should be given a chance to formulate an acceptable plan. But that idea, full of promise though it was, was scorned in influential quarters as doctrinaire, and Count Ottokar Czernin, speaking, no doubt, as the mouthpiece of Francis Ferdinand, bluntly declared that the national question in Bohemia could be solved only by the dictatorial intervention of the crown. Nevertheless, another conference of Bohemian leaders was brought together, whose deliberations dragged along without yielding a settlement.

Upon the convocation of the reichsrat in March of 1914 Czech deputies engaged in the familiar tactics of obstruction in retaliation for the ministry's unwillingness to order new elections for the Bohemian assembly. "Ohne Landtag, kein Reichsrat" was their battle cry. So thoroughly was the conduct of business interrupted that the ministry soon dismissed the parliament and proceeded to govern the empire under the notorious article fourteen of the constitution.

Just before the tocsin of World War I sounded, the reichsrat and the provincial assemblies, too, were formally dissolved by imperial edict, and administration was entrusted to officials responsible exclusively to the emperor. Francis Joseph's long reign, which had been inaugurated with the dictatorial rule of Schwarzenberg and Bach, closed with the authoritarianism of Stürgkh—and of Stephen Tisza.

v

On the eve of World War I, after almost half a century of checkered and confused parliamentarianism, of awakening nationalisms, and of modest economic advance, the status of the national groups in the Austrian empire may be sketched as follows. Out of a population of 28,324,940, 9,950,266 or 35.58 per cent were listed as Germans.[8] They were concentrated in the heart of the empire—in the area embraced in the Austrian Republic as it existed from 1919 to 1938—along the southern and western rims of Bohemia, and were also found in islets scattered indiscriminately all over the state, more particularly in the commercial centers. German culture still held first place, however much its absolute importance had been impaired by the cultural progress of other nationalities. And Germans, with whom Jews were generally included, were more prominent in the intellectual and economic affairs of the empire than all other nationalities taken together. For example, well over half of the newspapers and periodicals of Austria were printed in the German language.[9] The comparative prosperity of the German-speaking group was illustrated by the tax returns; a German paid on the average twice as much in taxes as a Czech or an Italian, four and a half times as much as a Pole, and seven times as much as a Yugoslav.[10] And Austro-Germans filled most of the important places in the public services, even though their relative position in the bureaucracy as a whole had declined.

In large majority the Austro-Germans were *Hapsburgtreue,* though many were inclined to favor reorganization of constitutional institutions in the direction of federalism. That tendency was probably more prevalent among Bohemian Germans than among inhabitants of the Alpine provinces, and both the Christian Socialists and the Social Democrats had put on record their desire for constitutional reconstruction. One German faction had agitated continuously since the seventies for the union of the German-peopled districts with Germany, and at times, as in 1897, the agitation had seemed really formidable. Yet, even though the Pan-Germans enlarged their parliamentary delegation in 1911, converts to the cause were not overnumerous and, as of 1914, the prospects of *Anschluss* appeared extremely dim and the idea visionary.

Next to the Germans, the Poles, enumerated at 4,967,984 (17.77 per cent) were least unhappy with the prevailing scheme of things. Dominated by the landed nobility and the clergy and beneficiaries of privileges including considerable autonomy which gave them mastery over Galicia, the Austrian Poles were better off politically than their brethren in Prussia and Russia—and their politicians knew it. Their kinsmen in the neighboring empires looked upon Galicia as a haven of refuge, a kind of political and intellectual paradise.

Polish loyalty to the Hapsburg state was general and Pan-Slav seed fell on stony ground in Polish Galicia. As a rule, the Poles shunned international Slav conferences and even eschewed an enduring alliance with fellow Slavs in the parliament at Vienna; for them, or most of them, Slavdom began and ended with Polonism. Declared Deputy R. Jendrezejowicz in an address before the Austrian delegation in 1910: "It is utopian to anticipate a close union of all Slavs . . . The gentlemen who foster Neo-Slavism forget the history of the several Slav peoples, the differences in culture and religion which separate them. Old memories which are painful to us cannot be erased by theories." Particularly the speaker had in mind, of course, the oppressive Russian treatment of Slav cousins. Secretly, Joseph Pilsudski, who was to dominate Polish politics for a time after the war, organized fighting

units at Lemberg for operations against Russia in case of a European con
flict. They were subsequently superseded by open societies which secured
weapons and ammunition with the help of Austrian army authorities, and
Pilsudski even set up a miniature military staff college at Cracow.

The idea of resurrecting an independent Poland, while not without
fervent partisans in the Galician middle class, intellectual circles and town
workpeople, had small practical importance and was looked upon by the
realistically minded as something fantastic and remote. Polish landed magnates and the bulk of the clergy and the professional politicians were stanchly
Austrophile, *Hapsburgtreue*.

According to Ruthenian nationalists, Austrian census takers willfully
garbled the figures on population so that though Ruthenians were an actual
majority in Galicia (and the largest grouping in the Bucovina) they were
reported as only 3,518,854 (12.58 per cent of the empire). For the most part
toilers on the estates of Polish landlords, victims of discrimination and repression, the Ruthenians had few opportunities for economic or cultural improvement. Nonetheless, a small but active intelligentsia had emerged which
was militantly resentful of Polish dominance. For two generations the politically articulate among the Ruthenians had been split into conflicting factions.
The largest one, the Ukrainophiles, though professing allegiance to Austria,
dreamed long dreams of a free and independent Ukrainia extending deep
into the Russian empire; the competing Russophile party, on the other hand,
cherished strong sympathies for Russia and longed for the day when the
flag of the Hapsburgs would be superseded by the flag of the Romanov
dynasty.

Czechs and Austrian Slovaks, remarkably well unified in political outlook by 1914, numbered 6,435,983 or 23.02 per cent of the entire Austrian
population. No nationality in the empire had progressed culturally, economically, or in national consciousness so rapidly as the Czechs in the preceding
half century; they justly deserved the title of the most advanced member of
the Slav family. Although concentrated principally in the area once embraced in the ancient kingdom of Bohemia, Czechs also lived in large
numbers in Vienna and other cities outside of Bohemia. Whether bourgeois
or Socialist, Czechs in overwhelming majority were heartily dissatisfied with
the existing political arrangements, and some of the large landlords shared
that discontent.

What Czech patriotism in the main desired—and the aim had not
changed since 1867, it had only become more popular—was home rule for
the territory of the ancient kingdom of St. Wenceslaus, within the framework of the Hapsburg Monarchy. They desired, in other words, the same
measure of autonomy that had been awarded to the Magyars in 1867, nothing
less than that. Had that demand been granted without qualification, the

large German minority in the Bohemian region would have been subordinated, of course, to the Czech majority and that prospect was the insuperable obstacle to a settlement of the Bohemian problem. Year after year leaders of good will—and others—had deliberated on ways and means of reconciling Czech claims with the interests of the Bohemian Germans, but every project had come to grief.

Among Czech politicians differences on constitutional matters were essentially differences in detail or in tactics; all or almost all of them set Bohemian self-government as their goal. Before World War I the idea of cutting loose from the Hapsburg empire and of establishing a separate state had small political importance. Eduard Beneš, Masaryk's principal colleague in the founding of the Czechoslovak Republic, closed his doctoral dissertation (1908) with these words: "People have often spoken of the dissolution of Austria. I do not believe in it. The historic and economic ties which bind the Austrian nations to one another are too powerful to let such a thing happen." [11] Czech sentiment favorable to full separation from Austria was scattered, sporadic, confined to extremists, and without significant bearing upon practical politics.

The South Slavs, or Yugoslavs of Austria, were listed in 1910 as 1,252,940 Slovenes (4.48 per cent) and 783,334 (2.8 per cent) Serbs and Croats. Both these groups had been historically and proverbially Austrophile, though a change had come over some of their political spokesmen in the twentieth century, Serbo-Croats more than Slovenes, for the latter with a few notable exceptions had as yet little consciousness of community with their linguistic cousins to the south. One Yugoslav faction, the larger doubtless, desired the creation of a Yugoslav unit, embracing all the Yugoslavs of the Dual Monarchy, which would have parity with Austria and Hungary. This was the familiar "trialistic" solution of the Hapsburg constitutional problem. A less numerous party among the Yugoslavs frankly preferred to break away from the Monarchy and to merge with Serbs and Croats in adjacent areas to form a large, independent Yugoslav state.

According to the Austrian census report of 1910, 768,422 (2.75 per cent) Italian-speaking people resided in the empire. They lived in the southern reaches of the Tyrol, in Gorizia, Istria, and Trieste, the moral capital of Italia Irredenta, where they were intermingled with large Yugoslav minorities (Slovenes and Croats), and tiny Italian islets existed in northern Dalmatia, almost drowned, however, in the Slav sea. These Italian folk had importance not by reason of their numbers but because of their conationals in the kingdom of Italy who yearned to redeem their brethren, even as half a century earlier Lombardy and Venetia had been wrested from Hapsburg lordship. That the Italian minority had legitimate grievances against Austrian rule was candidly recognized by so devoted a servant of imperial interests as Count Aehrenthal, who said, "Were I to admit that I believe this, I should be taken for a madman." [12]

The politically conscious among the Austro-Italians, the cultivated classes, with the exception, apparently, of most of the Catholic clergy, were quite unreconciled to Hapsburg dominion and passionately desired, as had their fathers before them, to belong to the Italian kingdom. Even among Socialists, Irredentism crowded aside international doctrines and the Socialist chief of Trentino, Cesare Battisti, fled over the border when fighting began in 1914 and begged Italy to enter the conflict in order to liberate his homeland. Enlisting in the Italian army, Battisti was captured by Austrian troops and executed as a traitor; thus another name was added to the long roll of Italian patriotic martyrs who perished by the Hapsburg sword.

No other national group in the Hapsburg Monarchy, not even the Rumanians of Hungary, so earnestly desired to secede as did the Italians. Only those peasants who profited materially from citizenship in the Austrian state or who were influenced by their spiritual shepherds, and most of the clergy, were Austrophile. On the banners of Austro-Italian politicians was inscribed the word autonomy. Yet it was unquestionably true that their real goal was not home rule, but complete separation from Austria and union with Italy.

‡ CHAPTER TWENTY ‡

HUNGARY MILITANT

In January of 1910, a "caretaker" ministry headed by Khuen-Héderváry, hand-picked by the crown, assumed the management of Hungary. Parliament greeted this unconstitutional cabinet with a most unflattering welcome. Militant deputies of the Independence party indulged in shameless excesses, hurling anything they could lay their hands on at the ministerial benches. Hit several times, the premier bled profusely, while several of his colleagues suffered minor injuries. By an immense majority the chamber voted lack of confidence in the ministry, whereupon the legislature was dissolved. The crisis in dualism remained critical.

Preliminary to a fresh appeal to the electorate, the Liberal party, which had been disastrously routed in 1905, was rehabilitated as the party of National Work (*Munka*). Count Stephen Tisza reëntered the political arena as the directing genius of the party. In retirement Tisza had grown more and more convinced that the agitation of partisans of independence imperiled the safety of the kingdom and that national salvation demanded the preservation of the partnership with Austria. With clouds on the international horizon growing progressively darker, he kept repeating: "The Slavs are our danger, the Germans our shield and buckler."

For Tisza and his allies the election of 1910 was of crucial importance, for if the friends of independence triumphed they would immediately push for complete separation from Austria, with an independent bank as the first item on the agenda. Reinforcing argument with unexampled bribery and violence, the party of National Work swept the boards; independence factions lost many seats and non-Magyar deputies dwindled to a mere eight, five Rumanians and three Slovaks.

Thrilled by the results, Tisza gave utterance to his satisfaction in an address to the chamber. All must welcome "with patriotic joy," he remarked, the outcome of an election that had virtually "wiped the nationalist agitators out of public life . . . Our non-Magyar fellow citizens must first of all reconcile themselves to the fact that they belong to a national state which is not a conglomerate of different races, but which one nation has conquered and founded, upon which one nation has stamped the ineradicable impress of its individuality." Nationalistic agitators would be treated with "pitiless severity," Tisza said, but "the fullest brotherly fairness" would be shown to the rank and file of the minority groups.

From 1910 to the coming of war in 1914, the paramount issues in Hungarian domestic politics were the joint-bank question, army affairs, and suffrage reform. Austria promptly renewed the charter of the joint bank, but Magyar separatists brought up their old demand for an independent Hungarian bank, coupling with that the slogan of economic freedom from Austria. *Munka* was, however, too strong and the life of the joint bank was prolonged to 1917, the year in which the customs union would likewise come up for review.

The dynamite-laden subject of the common army was revived when the Hapsburg High Command requested that the crown be authorized to call out reserves and to keep under arms men who were already in service, if parliament should decline to vote the annual contingent of troops. The Hungarian ministry requested small concessions as the prerequisite to assenting to the military proposals, but these the crown would not grant.

Unable to secure majority support for the army laws and plagued by a fresh spasm of filibustering, Khuen-Héderváry gave way in 1912 to a cabinet headed by Ladislaus Lukács, with Tisza as president of the lower house. As he had attempted a decade earlier, Tisza undertook to conquer obstruction by revising the rules of parliamentary procedure, imposing a gag on debate, and authorizing gendarmes to eject deputies who provoked disturbances. This time Tisza carried the day; filibustering was effectively throttled and the military bills were passed into law. Thenceforth Tisza for practical purposes was the dictator of the kingdom, Hungary's unofficial, uncrowned king. His parliamentary enemies, not numerous but determined, savagely attacked him for arbitrary conduct and an irate deputy attempted to kill Tisza in the chamber, but he proceeded to carry on business as though nothing had happened. At one point Independence deputies interrupted deliberations by blowing horns and hooters, singing a Kossuth anthem, and engaging in hand-to-hand encounters with henchmen of Tisza; still fighting, the Kossuthists were forcibly ousted by police.

In June of 1913 Tisza became in title as he had been in fact the first minister of Hungary, replacing Lukács. The latter was charged with obtaining funds for party ends from financial interests in exchange for special favors and of exploiting his public position to fatten his own pocketbook. Lukács sued his accuser for libel but he was acquitted, and thereupon Lukács quit the premiership.

Tisza managed to get constructive legislation adopted. Dissenting deputies, even such prominent personages as Counts Andrássy and Aládar Zichy, were removed by physical force from the chamber. The premier was branded a bloodthirsty tyrant and obliged to fight several saber duels. But laws on labor welfare, social insurance, increases in the salary of civil servants, and enlargement of the fighting services were enacted; the state budget was balanced by borrowing—from German financial houses when Hungarian capital resources dried up.

On the last day of 1912 a bill to extend the franchise privilege, without disturbing Magyar hegemony, was presented to parliament. Educational, property, or occupational requirements in the act excluded large sections of the population from voting rights; illiterates over thirty, for instance, might vote only if they paid the equivalent of about $8.50 in taxes or owned seventeen acres of land. That clause in the proposed bill would deny the franchise to virtually all the propertyless laborers, over half the farm owners, artisans, and civil servants, and almost half the tradesmen.

II

The political situation in autonomous Croatia, after improving slightly, deteriorated seriously in 1912-13 as the elements hostile to Magyar overlordship turned more militant; and yet by 1914 the barometer stood again at fair and clear. Dr. Tomásič, a Magyarone who had replaced the discredited Rauch as viceroy in 1910, courted the support of the Serbo-Croat bloc of deputies by promising revision of the electoral laws and the revocation of the unpopular Railway Servants Act of 1907. In keeping with the first of these pledges, a new suffrage bill was offered to the assembly and passed. Although the inequitable manner in which seats were distributed was not significantly altered, property qualifications for the right to vote were lowered, increasing the electorate fivefold. In the balloting under the new franchise only eighteen of the eighty-eight constituencies returned representatives who were loyal supporters of the *status quo*. And when the executive temporized on the railway servants' issue, opposition deputies paralyzed the assembly by obstruction.

The sequel repeated the monotonously familiar pattern in the Hapsburg realm; the assembly was dismissed and the electorate invited to choose another set of deputies. As a preface to the voting a furious campaign, which had the quality of a crusade, was directed against the enemies of the viceroy. Hostile newspapers were confiscated time and again and their editors thrown into jail; electors were threatened with dire punishment if they did not vote "right," and actual deeds of violence were committed. But this was all to little avail, for two-thirds of the seats were won by antiadministration candidates.

Thereupon Edward von Cuvaj, an understudy of former Governor Rauch, stepped into the viceroy's chair. Again the assembly was disbanded and police broke up a meeting to protest against dissolution, wounding seventeen participants. Doors of the University of Agram, a hotbed of anti-Magyar agitation, were bolted and barred, and in April 1912 the constitution of Croatia was suspended and Cuvaj ruled as royal commissioner. In some quarters it was charged that the repressive policy was intended to goad Croatian politicians into an insurrection which would be crushed without ruth.

Extremists plotted to rid the land of the dictator in their own distinctive way. A young Bosnian who was studying in Agram fired at Cuvaj, wounding a companion of the governor, and killing a police official outright. The assassin, Tukič, was a tool of the notorious Serbian "Black Hand" society of Belgrade, a city he had visited a month before the crime. He and more than fifty accomplices were arrested, and eight of them, Tukič included, were sentenced to jail. Nevertheless, Tukič was lauded by admirers as a martyr to the cause of Greater Serbia, and on the anniversary of his attempt to murder Cuvaj a Belgrade newspaper, *Pravda* (Truth), exulted: "We have ten million Tukičs now. We are firmly convinced that through his prison window he will see the final shot for freedom."[1] A Croatian student, too, tried to kill Cuvaj and then committed suicide.

Absolutism in Croatia undoubtedly strengthened sentiments favorable to the merger of Croatia with the kingdom of Serbia. A band of Agram students on a visit to Belgrade, where they were regally entertained, shouted to King Peter, "Long live our King." The warmth of the welcome accorded the students went not unmarked in Croatian, in Hungarian, and in Hapsburg circles. And upon the outbreak of the Balkan war of 1912 Croatian youths streamed into Serbia to fight in King Peter's army.

After Tisza became Hungarian premier, steps were taken to appease the Croatian dissidents. The detested Cuvaj was supplanted as royal commissioner by Baron Ivan Skerlecz, who had a reputation for liberalism, and assurances were given that authoritarian rule would soon be abandoned. Scarcely had the new administrator reached his post when he was shot and gravely wounded; the would-be assassin said that he had come to Agram from Chicago for the sole purpose of murder. Yet by minor concessions to Croatian moderates Skerlecz managed to bring a semblance of order and peace to the distraught province. In October of 1913 constitutional government was restored (with Skerlecz as ban) and a compromise was worked out on the language of railway servants, the immediate source of the Croatian turbulence. Railway employees and officials who came in contact with the public would have to be able to speak Croatian, while office workers had to have a knowledge of Magyar.

At the end of 1913 another election for the assembly was held. It resulted in a new victory for the Serbo-Croat federation, and the assembly was convened after a two-year interlude. Premier Tisza on a trip to Agram commented upon the contentment which the restitution of normal constitutionalism had produced. Although another attempt was made to slay Skerlecz—this time by a Bosnian student who was in touch with a Belgrade secret society—the political atmosphere in the province was more composed in the spring of 1914 than it had been for some time.

Separatist tendencies among politically conscious Ruthenians and Rumanians in the eastern reaches of Hungary caused anxiety at Budapest in the years just before the war. Russophile emissaries working in the Ruthenian areas converted a few thousand Uniat believers to the Orthodox creed; their propaganda, though nominally religious, and no doubt so regarded by converts, had as its hidden purpose the union of the Ruthene-peopled districts with imperial Russia. Scores of clergy and peasants, all Hungarian citizens, were arrested on charges of treasonable trafficking with Russians.

At the trial in 1914 it was brought out that the accused had been suborned by Muscovite gold or promises of it and that the urge for secession was in no wise spontaneous but fostered in fact by propagandists from Russia. Thirty-two of the Ruthenian ringleaders were fined and imprisoned for short terms. It was claimed in Czech and other quarters that the trial was conducted as unfairly as that at Agram in 1909, and credence was lent to that charge by the fact that Ruthenians arrested on similar grounds who were Austrian subjects were set free.

That Magyar treatment of the Rumanian minority was largely responsible for the lukewarmness of the kingdom of Rumania toward the alliance with the Central Powers was fully appreciated by German and Austrian statesmen. Time and time again the men of Berlin implored Hapsburg leaders to make concessions to the Rumanians; William II, for example, discussed the problem at full length with Francis Ferdinand and begged him to do something to mitigate the dangerous tension. Such counsel the heir presumptive really did not require, for he had long been sympathetic toward Rumanians on both sides of the Carpathians and he had not concealed his friendly disposition nor his detestation of the denationalizing tactics of the Magyars.

On the way to visit Rumania in 1909, the Archduke was lustily cheered by Transylvanian Rumanians who lined the railway track and in Bucharest he freely declared his disapprobation of Magyar oppression of Rumanians. Francis Ferdinand derived real pleasure from the fact that Magyar politicians were irritated over the visit. In conversation with the German emperor, the Archduke upbraided Tisza for neglecting to conciliate the Rumanians and begged William II to exert influence on the Magyar statesman; instructions in that vein were actually dispatched to the German ambassador in Vienna.

Count Tisza, it is true, made an effort that was far less than halfhearted to placate the Rumanian minority. During the winter of 1913–14, he held a series of private conferences with representatives of the Rumanian National party who had no hesitancy in listing their grievances and asking for appeasing concessions. Their demands included the use of the Rumanian tongue in schools attended by Rumanians, the appointment of judges in Rumanian districts who spoke the local language, greater freedom of press and assembly, and state financial assistance for Rumanian self-help economic societies.

For all his well-known antipathy toward Rumanians, Tisza is said to have admitted the justice of certain of these demands, yet he felt (or said he felt) that Magyar politicians could not be brought around to make concessions.[2] The nub of the matter was that Magyar chauvinists, stubborn, arrogant, prejudiced, looked upon the Rumanians, as indeed upon other minority stocks, as an inferior breed of humanity, whom it was a tradition to despise and a duty to Magyarize. By refusing to exert his great personal prestige to persuade his fellows to satisfy Rumanian expectations, at least in part, Tisza muffed an opportunity for which he, his Hungary, and the Dual Monarchy would one day pay the penalty.[3]

Trials of Rumanian journalists continued to be frequent and punishments heavy. And petty incidents constantly bobbed up to envenom the Magyar-Rumanian feud. For example, in order to extend the area of Magyar speech, the cabinet at Budapest secured papal sanction for the transfer of several Uniat parishes to the jurisdiction of the Magyar bishop in Debreczen and for the use of Magyar as the liturgical language in these churches. The Rumanian population that was affected by this dubious deal protested vehemently, the life of the bishop was threatened, and early in 1914 a bomb actually exploded in the episcopal office, killing the vicar and two others and wrecking the building. Possibly this crime was intended to be a signal for a general rising in Transylvania against the lordship of the Magyars.[4] The culprits escaped abroad, evidently to Rumania. A Uniat priest and several of his parishioners were imprisoned for inveighing against the use of the Magyar tongue in religious services.

Across the border, in the kingdom of Rumania, anti-Hapsburg antipathies were rising, which augured ill for the security of Hungary and for Rumanian faithfulness to diplomatic commitments to the Dual Monarchy. Societies and individuals persisted in their clamor against the restraints imposed upon their conationals on the nether side of the Carpathians, and they whipped up popular hatred of the Hapsburg Monarchy. The League of Culture, which counted Transylvanians among its members and was presided over by the respected and respectable historian, Nicholas Jorga, propagated Irredentist doctrines among Hungarian Rumanians. A stirring anti-Hapsburg drama presented on the stage of the national theater at Bucharest set off mass demonstrations, and prominent Rumanian army officials publicly pleaded for armed invasion of Hungary. Of all this Magyar and Austrian statesmen were, of course, not ignorant.

III

The course of Hungarian domestic history to 1914 may appropriately be rounded off with a survey of the several national groupings at that point.[5] According to the official census of 1910, 9,944,267 Magyars lived in Hungary proper, or just under 55 per cent of all inhabitants. In that figure were included half a million Jewish Magyarones, for the official test of nationality was "maternal tongue," defined as "the language which a person speaks best and most readily." If the kingdom of Croatia is taken into account, the proportion of Magyars in Hungary entire stood at almost exactly 48 per cent.

Magyars in 1914 comprised a smaller fraction of the population of the kingdom than was the case before Turkish invasion in the fifteenth century, when it was approximately 80 per cent On the other hand, the proportion of Magyars was substantially higher than in the eighteenth century, after generations of warfare and Turkish rule had reduced the Magyar element to less than 40 per cent. The situation as of 1914 was a far cry indeed from 1849, when several of the members of the revolutionary cabinet of Kossuth were unable to speak a dozen words in the national idiom.

Magyars predominated in the central plain of Hungary, though fragments of minorities were there interspersed with them, and close to the Balkan frontier minority groups actually outnumbered Magyars. In the extreme eastern section of Transylvania, Magyars (the Szeklers) [6] formed a solid body of half a million, and compact communities of Magyars were found in other parts of this province. Landlords the kingdom over were as a rule Magyars, and the middle class, owing to half a century of resourceful and systematic Magyarization, was overwhelmingly Magyar in speech. Yet many who spoke Magyar were descended from other national stocks and not all of them were Magyar in political (national) feeling. It was estimated that Magyar speakers made up between 80 and 95 per cent of the members of the learned professions, except in the case of the clergy, where the percentage dropped to 63; 90 per cent of the students in institutions of higher learning claimed to be Magyar in nationality.[7] The commercial and industrial classes, the skilled artisans, and the great majority of civil servants spoke Magyar and no doubt thought of themselves as Magyars.

It was, therefore, entirely understandable why a foreigner casually traveling in Hungary should carry away the impression that Magyar and Hungarian were identical. But cold facts, even those collected by Magyar census takers, revealed the inaccuracy and superficiality of such a judgment. In a broad belt of territory encircling the central plain, the language of one or more of the minority groups was in the ascendant, despite the zeal which the official world had shown in encouraging or forcing the use of the Magyar tongue.

In sections of the kingdom, the linguistic diversity, traceable in part to immigration from the middle of the seventeenth century onward, was not less bewildering than in the heart of the Balkan peninsula.[8] As in language, so in customs and costumes, there was endless and refreshing variety; for instance, the peasants seldom changed the slightest detail of their headgear. Not altogether untypical was the town of Eperjes, a community of about 12,000, in a lovely valley on the Galician border, where the inhabitants were accustomed to speak and hear six different languages and several dialects. It was not uncommon to find in a well-to-do household a Slovak man-servant, a Magyar coachman, a German cook, and a Polish chambermaid, and each layer of society clung tenaciously to its own language.

Germans were the most widely dispersed of the Hungarian minority stocks. As of 1910, 1,903,357 German speakers resided in Hungary proper, many of them Jews who because of their Yiddish speech were officially classified as Germans; at that time Germans represented over 10 per cent of the population, less by 3 per cent than in 1880. The German element was found in substantial numbers in the extreme west—the Burgenland—in the south (Swabians), in Transylvania ("Saxons"), and in urban communities; "peaceful propagation of Magyar culture" over the years had notably diminished German speech and sentiments. The Roman Catholic Swabians had rather generally turned Magyarone in spirit, though the "Saxon" Lutherans struggled manfully to preserve their German heritage; by means of electoral geometry the voice of the "Saxons" in politics was kept at a minimum. Resentment over Magyarization had been lively among the "Saxons," though many of them were quite pro-Magyar in outlook and willing, in fact, to ally with the dominant nationality against the numerically preponderant though culturally backward Rumanian and other groupings.

The Slovak language was spoken in 1910 by 1,946,357 persons, a falling off of about 3 per cent since 1880, and almost all of them were poor in purse and spirit. The cult of the Magyar language applied to the educational facilities in the Slovak districts had performed its appointed task remarkably well. As of 1914, teachers of elementary schools in the area who spoke Magyar exceeded the Slovak speakers fourteen to one, and the ratio was still higher among civil servants. Many a Slovak, alert to the social or pecuniary advantages of membership in the Magyar nationality, professed conversion, following the example set by Louis Kossuth, the Magyar national hero par excellence, a Slovak by birth, and by Petöfi, "the incarnation of Hungary's poetic genius," who started life with the unmistakably Slav name of Petrovich.

The trend in the early twentieth century pointed toward the eventual extinction of the Slovak language by the Magyar. In the plain districts of the south even Slovak laborers on the soil and in the workshop had turned Magyar in speech, and possibly in feeling as well. Inasmuch as most of the Slovaks were Roman Catholics, there was no religious barrier to assimilation with the Magyars as in the case of the Orthodox Rumanians and Serbs. In spite of such episodes as the Csernova tragedy, recounted earlier, it does not appear that the mass of the Slovak population, simple peasants, was resentful of the relentless efforts to fuse them with the dominant Magyar society.

Consciousness of Slovak nationality or of partnership in the broader Czechoslovak family was confined to a thin layer of the population, intellectuals and clergymen principally. Stated otherwise, Slovak nationalism was a militant faith for only a chosen few; it has been proposed that the politically active hardly exceeded a thousand and in no sense could they be regarded as a danger to the integrity of the kingdom of St. Stephen. If World War I had not intervened, it is quite probable that within a generation or two the Slovaks would have been fully merged with the Magyars in tongue and national sympathies.

The small, poor, illiterate, and downtrodden Ruthenian group (464,270) possessed even less national feeling than the Slovaks. Geography, poverty, and processes of Magyarization largely immunized this minority from the stirrings and aspirations that animated some of their "racial" brethren in the Austrian empire. Magyar was the language of almost all schools in the Ruthenian districts, though in a very few Ukrainian was also spoken. In Hungary entire only a few hundred Ruthenian professional folk, priests mainly, had thorough command of the "mother tongue." Clergy of the Uniat church, to which a majority of the Ruthenians adhered, were largely Magyarones and as such a valuable asset for the *status quo*. Except for a handful of messianic Russophiles, Hungarian Ruthenians were blissfully uninterested in public affairs, and the prospect was that the entire group would be absorbed in the Magyar nationality within a short time.[9]

Yugoslavs in Hungary proper were enumerated in 1910 as 416,516 Serbs, 194,808 Croats, and splinter groups variously described, altogether a slightly smaller percentage than in 1880. Concentrated in the extreme west and south of the state, the Yugoslavs had preserved their national character extraordinarily well, in the countryside at least, being helped by a fairly extensive network of primary confessional schools and a few higher schools. The kingdom of Croatia, or more precisely Croatia-Slavonia, was reported to contain 1,630,354 Croats and 644,955 Serbs, together 90 per cent of the total. Almost all the Magyar speakers there were relatively recent immigrants or late "converts" to the ruling nationality; Magyarization had scored only very limited successes among the Yugoslav population. Croats had a well-developed national consciousness, which underlay the drive for liberation from Magyar control, and that was true, though perhaps less conspicuously, of the rank and file of the Serbs.

The nationality complexion of Fiume in 1910 bore little resemblance to that of half a century earlier. What had been almost wholly a Croat village had been transformed into a preponderantly Italian seaport, and the Slavs were by way of being assimilated with the Italian group. Hungarian officials had deliberately welcomed Italian settlers as allies against the Croats, and had not permitted any Croat schools; signs and inscriptions, for instance, were written in the Italian tongue and that was the language of administrative officials. In the twentieth century, to be sure, the government at Budapest tried to foster the use of Magyar, directly through the schools, but by then Italian was too deeply entrenched. Among the Italians of Fiume the desire to unite with the kingdom of Italy was not active; commercial interests bound the community intimately to Hungary and tended to make the population pro-Magyar in feeling.

Of all the minorities in Hungary the Rumanians had certainly been most effective in combatting denationalization by the Magyars. Their leaders were ever on guard lest the Magyars rob them of their heritage of language, customs, and religion, or impair the legend that they were the lineal descendants of ancient Roman legionnaires. It used to be said that the Hungarian Rumanians even surpassed the citizens of the kingdom itself in national patriotism. Rumanians numbered in 1910 just under three millions and dwelt principally in Transylvania, but in southern Hungary too. Yet the administrative and judicial institutions in Rumanian areas were monopolized by Magyars or Magyarones and Magyarization had deeply invaded the educational facilities.

In Transylvania the Magyar language was used ever more extensively, much more so by minorities other than Rumanian, for Rumanian speakers fell off only fractionally in half a century. Seldom did Rumanians marry persons of other national groupings. Many Rumanian youths studied in Magyar institutions of higher learning without becoming imbued with the Magyar outlook, and the clergy, both Uniat and Orthodox, held steadfastly to the Rumanian language and customs. They far exceeded in numbers and influence the militantly pro-Magyar Roman Catholic clergy.

Articulate Rumanians, for the most part, detested Magyar rule and longed to be politically united with their fellows in the kingdom of Rumania. Spokesmen unceasingly declaimed against discriminations in schools and courts and electoral arrangements which made it impossible for Rumanians to secure anything like equitable representation in parliament. And they cried aloud about discriminations against Rumanian workers; in 1914 a contract negotiated with a British mining firm to exploit the state gold mines prescribed that all executives employed should be Magyars, or at least not Rumanians. It has been correctly said that "in 1914 Transylvania was ruled by and for the Magyar, without and largely against the Rumanians." [10]

Yet it must not be assumed that opinion among Transylvanian Rumanians was universally sympathetic to union with Rumania. So distinguished a Transylvanian politician as Dr. Alexander Vaida-Voivod, sometime a personal adviser of Francis Ferdinand, and the prime minister of Greater Rumania in 1919, saw fit to write in 1916: "In our people and in our intellectuals there is a deep conviction that we owe our culture and our progress to the House of Hapsburg. It is deeply realized further that the political struggle between Magyars and Roumanians can only be considered as a dissension among brothers, all the more so since in view of the common danger of annihilation by Russia both peoples are welded into one by the unbreakable ties of common vital interests, now and evermore." [11]

Rumanians inhabiting the southern provinces of Hungary preserved their national characteristics. But contacts with their conationals in Transylvania were limited and few among them manifested much interest in the Irredentist cause and its political objectives.

CHAPTER TWENTY-ONE

BEFORE THE WAR

FROM 1909 TO HIS DEATH IN 1912, THE DIPLOMACY OF Aehrenthal had an essentially negative character. Anything savoring of a forward policy, he reasoned, would inescapably provoke fresh war scares involving Russia. Wherefore the true course for the Hapsburg Monarchy was to eschew foreign adventure, wait watchfully in the Balkans, and concern itself with internal reorganization in a manner that might conciliate the Yugoslav minorities.

Aehrenthal's logic and line of policy were attuned to the wishes of the aged Francis Joseph, but ran diametrically counter to the convictions of the Austrian war party, headed by General Conrad, which believed that the military humiliation of Serbia or Italy or both could alone save the realm of the Hapsburgs from a fearful end. But Aehrenthal resourcefully and courageously combatted that philosophy, and so long as he directed the Ballplatz the apostles of salvation by the sword were voices in the wilderness.

At the meeting of the delegations in the fall of 1910, opened by Francis Ferdinand for the first time, Aehrenthal ably defended his Balkan policy. He expressed gratification over improvements that the Young Turks were introducing in Turkey. They relieved the great powers of "the anxiety and the danger of concerning themselves with the internal affairs of the Ottoman empire." "Austria," he declared, "desires peace and the maintenance of equilibrium," and he meant it. So far as relations with Russia were concerned, Aehrenthal observed that the entente of 1897 had disappeared, having lost its *raison d'être*, when constitutionalism, which promised humane and progressive administration, was inaugurated in Turkey. "There is," he went on, "no conflict of aims between ourselves and Russia in the Balkans.

We are striving for the maintenance of peace and the *status quo* in the peninsula and the development of the Balkan states."

Kramář, the Young Czech enthusiast, struck a sourly cacophonous note in the delegation meeting by condemning the annexation of Bosnia, which once he had favored, in scalding language. That adventure had ruined good relations with Russia and converted the Monarchy into the merest slave of Germany, chained to the chariot wheel of *Weltpolitik*—an interpretation widely shared in foreign capitals. Aehrenthal, he complained, had gone in for "theatrical methods," and his intransigence on Izvolsky's plan for a "free" conference on Bosnia was responsible for the war scare, and injured the Monarchy's finances and international reputation. As the utterance of a Slav evangelist, Kramář's words were properly discounted; they might better have been spoken in the Russian Duma or the Serbian Skuptschina, one critic remarked.

After 1909 the Hapsburg Monarchy belatedly undertook to build up its sea power, half in response to the challenging rivalry of Italy in the Adriatic, half in the name of imperial defense, related to the alliance with Germany. Francis Ferdinand, the first member of the House of Hapsburg to associate himself actively with the fleet—of which he was an admiral—understood, as did his friend William II, the values in sea power; the importance of the navy had been impressed upon him during the world tour that he made in the early nineties. True to form, Francis Joseph relied for security upon land power and took little interest in the newfangled leviathans of the sea. But the Crown Prince lent his weighty support to the doctrine that the fleet must be strong enough for attack instead of merely a coastal defense force, as was the Austrian tradition.

Although the Austrian navy had gained prestige by Admiral Tegethoff's victory over the Italians off the island of Lissa in 1866, it had been neglected in the decades that followed. Appropriations were small—between 1871 and 1897 they increased only from eleven to fifteen million guilders a year—and politicians and naval men alike were wedded to the idea that an adequate fleet meant merely a force capable of protecting the relatively short coast line. With the armies devouring huge sums and the implications of sea power little appreciated, the navy was looked upon as a costly and superfluous luxury. And Vienna's great newspapers, which cherished antimilitary traditions stemming from the revolutionary ideology of 1848, rather generally and obstinately preached niggardliness in naval appropriations. As late as the nineties Austrian warships, even armored ones, depended upon sail rather than steam, and vessels were built in foreign yards, German and English.

The Austrian Naval College near Fiume provided rigorous training along rather antiquated lines, and instilled into potential officers the implications of the motto, *"Höher als das Leben steht die Pflicht"* (Duty outweighs life itself). Officers, chosen from the German aristocracy for the greater part, but including a few Magyars, were required to speak Italian and Croatian as well as German, for most of the able seamen were recruited from the Adriatic provinces. While all nationalities were represented in the navy, nationalist emotions were conspicuously absent from the service until a great mutiny in the fleet in February 1918.

Superb sea bases the Hapsburg Monarchy had at Pola, on the southern tip of the Istrian peninsula, a large and landlocked harbor, and in the Gulf of Cattaro at the southern end of Dalmatia, one of the most splendid and most easily protected anchorages, or series of them, in the world. Mount Lovčen, towering over the principal harbor, was studded with Montenegrin forts which impaired somewhat the security of Cattaro.

Beginnings in the expansion of Austrian sea power were made under the commander in chief, Baron von Spaun, who was appointed in 1897, the very year that von Tirpitz became secretary of state for naval affairs in Germany. His policy was elaborated by his successor, Count Montecuccoli, sometimes called the father of the Hapsburg navy. Against the advice of Aehrenthal, who feared the effects of naval expansion upon relations with Italy, an expensive program of construction, which called for four dreadnoughts to be built in as many years, was published in 1909.[1] But not until 1911 were the delegations willing to vote the necessary funds for the ships. Money for two had, however, already been advanced by Albert Rothschild after a personal appeal by Francis Ferdinand, it is said; shares of the Škoda company, with which Rothschild had financial connections, doubled in price in two weeks.

The prospect of an Austrian navy capable of operations in the Mediterranean in case of war excited dark suspicions in London. And fears were not at all softened by Austrian assurances that the sole purpose of fleet expansion was to prevent the Adriatic from becoming the *mare nostro* of Italian patriotic dreams.

As of 1911, the fighting capacity of the Austrian navy was probably not half so strong as the Italian, but by 1914 the gap had been somewhat narrowed, though Italy still remained superior. When war actually came, Austria had no plans for naval operations outside of the Adriatic and only two warships and two or three submarines were equipped for battle in the Mediterranean. The flagship, *Viribus Unitis,* the first Austrian dreadnought put into service, carried the bodies of Francis Ferdinand and his wife up the Adriatic after the murders at Sarajevo. Assigned to the Yugoslavs at the end of the war, the ship was maliciously torpedoed and sunk by Italian naval men.

II

Reconciliation with Serbia Aehrenthal apparently hoped would be the prelude to the union of that kingdom with Austria in some fashion—an idea which was not without support in Serbia itself.[2] In August of 1910, the Serb foreign minister, Milanovič, who had displayed uncommon sobriety during the furore over Bosnia and was favorably regarded in the Ballplatz, confided to Aehrenthal that Serbia desired Austrian friendship. Agitation against Austria (and Turkey too) the Serbian government was resolved to suppress, and it wanted the territorial integrity of Turkey maintained. All of this was sweet music to Aehrenthal's ears, but when the Serb hinted that some day his country might be obliged to annex the Sanjak of Novibazar the Austrian drew into his shell. That the Serb attitude toward the Monarchy appeared to be more cordial was suggested by the tepid reaction in the kingdom to the Friedjung libel trial, which kicked up only a small-scale newspaper campaign against the Monarchy.

One school of Austrian thought held to the thesis that the surest way to the Serbian heart was through the stomach, and pressed for the restoration of ordinary commercial dealings. During the Bosnian crisis the temporary trade treaty had lapsed and exchange of goods had practically ceased, to the detriment of exporters in both countries. Certain Austrian politicians reviled Hungarian agrarians for opposition to trade with Serbia, harping upon the melancholy political consequences of this folly. Aehrenthal managed to arrange a commercial treaty in 1911 which was in the nature of a compromise; under its terms Austrian manufacturers regained much of their former business in the Serbian market but the Hapsburg door was kept closed to the live swine of the little kingdom. Austrian advocates of full and unrestricted trade with the Serbs were unable to overcome the resistance of powerful Magyar agricultural interests, which complained that disease was prevalent among Serbian pigs.

As a gesture of good will and the desire for better relations, the Serbian cabinet proposed in 1911 that King Peter should pay a courtesy call in Budapest. Austrophobe newspapers in Serbia branded the projected journey as a national humiliation. Pasič raised his influential voice in protest, and a section of the Magyar press let it be known that the king would not be a welcome guest. It was therefore a great relief for Peter to learn that Francis Joseph was "too ill" to receive him. The episode showed that, however well-intentioned the cabinets may have been, articulate opinion was too embittered for reconciliation.

After the fiercer fires of Russian resentment over the annexation of Bosnia had burned down, Aehrenthal cast about for means of bettering feelings. If Russia could be appeased, Austria would be less dependent than ever on Germany; Aehrenthal, it may be, reverted to his earlier idea of resurrecting the entente of 1897. But if that was Aehrenthal's vision it was frustrated by the sleepless enmity of Izvolsky and his intrigues in the Balkan capitals for a league of nations, without or with Turkey, which could be pointed against Austria. Diplomatic exchanges revealed that the gulf between the two eastern monarchies was too wide to be bridged.

Izvolsky tried to stir up bad blood between Berlin and Vienna by reporting to the Germans that Aehrenthal was angling for a secret treaty with Russia, to which Britain and France would be parties, for the purpose of preserving the Balkan *status quo*. That was sheer fabrication, but it accentuated the distrust of the Ballplatz in Berlin. A superficial Austro-Russian understanding of 1910 outwardly restored normal diplomatic relations and no one rejoiced more than Aehrenthal when Izvolsky, his discomfited rival, was transferred in September 1910 from the office of foreign minister to the Russian embassy in Paris.

However friendly and fulsome the public expressions of cordiality, Austria and Germany did not always see eye to eye on diplomatic policies. Aehrenthal, for example, reacted violently to a report that Berlin, seeking to detach Russia from Britain, had promised not to back Austria in any way if she should seek to enlarge her position in the Balkans. In itself the report reflected the shift in thought that came over the Wilhelmstrasse after von Bülow resigned as chancellor in 1909. His successors at the foreign office— the guiding spirit was Kiderlen-Wächter, minister to Rumania and later foreign secretary—disapproved of von Bülow's unqualified reinforcement of Austria in the Balkans and reverted to the Bismarckian theme of the division of the peninsula into an Austrian and a Russian sphere of influence. Von Bülow's Austrophile course, it was contended, had grievously disturbed German relations with the eastern colossus.

Pan-Slav zealotry and maneuvers of British diplomacy persuaded the directors of Russian policy to reject the Berlin initiative, and the Germans had to be content with a less far-reaching understanding concerning Persia and the Bagdad Railway. The very fact, however, that Berlin had unilaterally undertaken overtures to the men on the Neva annoyed Aehrenthal. Furious press criticism of Germany because of inconsiderate treatment of seasonal workers from Austria, Slavs mostly, and the sudden cancellation of a visit which the Kaiser had planned to Vienna produced real tension between the cabinets of the two allied powers.

At the outset of the next—and the last—imbroglio over Morocco, in 1911, Berlin discovered that Aehrenthal was diffident about identifying Austria with the ambitions and interests of her ally.[3] As had been the case in 1905, Hapsburg civilian authorities preferred not to become embroiled in a dispute in which the Monarchy had no direct interests and they had the backing of the press. The Hungarian premier, Khuen-Héderváry, baldly declared that the Moroccan controversy lay outside the sphere of the alliance with Germany. When Berlin complained over that utterance, Aehrenthal retorted with an unveiled rebuke. But, in contrast to civilian officials, military men urged that Austria should back the Germans in Morocco, just as Austria had been supported in the quarrel growing out of the annexation of Bosnia.

After Britain intervened flatly in the Moroccan dispute on the side of France, the Viennese press adopted a somewhat more sympathetic tone regarding Germany. The foreign office supported Germany reservedly when new disturbances in the Balkans made it seem probable that Berlin's cooperation would be essential there. The failure of Austria to side unequivocally with Germany in the controversy over Morocco was deeply resented by the policy makers in the Wilhelmstrasse. As this episode amply shows, it is sheer mythology to imagine that the two cabinets worked hand in hand whenever an international quarrel arose.

The divergence between Vienna and Berlin was again exhibited when Russia, seizing a moment when Turkey was at war with Italy, informally renewed the effort to secure international consent for the passage of Russian warcraft through the straits. Aehrenthal not only rejected the Russian request, but promised to stand by Turkey in resisting any change. Contrary to Aehrenthal's assumption, the Germans were by no means happy over the decision, for they were unwilling that Austria should unilaterally determine the policy of the alliance in southeastern Europe. Only if Britain failed to resist Russian pretensions would Germany intervene, and then surely not as the bow to Aehrenthal's fiddle. Austria was frankly notified that it could not rely upon unqualified German backing in the Balkans.

III

Only the credulous or the hyperoptimistic could have supposed that the Austrian alliance with Italy was anything more than farcical, a Potemkin village. Aehrenthal, however, would not concede that the bond with Italy was worthless; after a conference with Aehrenthal at Salzburg in the summer of 1910 the Italian foreign minister announced that the two cabinets were at one on Balkan questions and would preserve the Triplice in full vigor. But the alliance was subjected to severe strains when Italy in 1911 suddenly took up arms against Turkey for the purpose of acquiring Tripoli. Austria, it is true, along with the other great powers, had bestowed its blessing on the Italian ambitions in Tripoli. But would Italy's appetite be sated with African territory? Or would that be merely breakfast? And would Italy lunch on European Turkey? And what about dinner?

Apprehensive lest the conflict between Italy and Turkey might set the entire Balkans in flame, Aehrenthal, on the war's eve, strove to avert recourse to arms. He implored Turkey "to meet as far as possible" the economic claims of Italy, but to no avail, for when Turkey rejected the Italian demand for control over Tripoli fighting started. Somewhat reassuring to Austria was Italy's promise to exclude the Adriatic territory of Turkey from the sphere of military operations.

If the war should burn itself out in Africa, well and good, Aehrenthal thought, for popular Italian covetousness would be diverted from the "unredeemed" lands, but if the struggle should reach into European Turkey, Austrian interests would be vitally affected. Wisdom dictated, therefore, that the Ballplatz should work to preserve amity with both belligerents and to keep the fighting out of Europe.

On the other hand, Conrad, speaking the mind of the Hapsburg war hawks, inquired whether the march of events had not presented a unique opportunity to settle old scores with Italy and strengthen Austrian influence in the Balkans. Bluntly and categorically Aehrenthal replied in the negative, for it is almost certain that he intended to use the embarrassment of Italy in the war to bind the southern ally closer to Vienna. These two Hapsburg policy makers had grown to dislike one another bitterly; Aehrenthal felt that the military man was encroaching upon the private domain of the foreign office. The quarrel over Italian policy attained fierce dimensions. Cherishing no illusions on Italian fidelity to the Triplice, Conrad recommended as a minimum that preparations to fight Italy should be hurried along. Much of what he thought and said reflected the convictions of the Crown Prince, Francis Ferdinand, but Aehrenthal stubbornly resisted counsels of force.

Obliged to choose between the two points of view, Francis Joseph sided with the foreign minister. Conrad turned in his resignation, which represented an unmistakable moral setback for his sponsor, Francis Ferdinand. He resolved to drive Aehrenthal from the Ballplatz and in that course he had the backing of the more influential Viennese newspapers, which had commented wryly upon the withdrawal of Conrad, without, of course, knowing the immediate antecedents. Another satellite of the heir presumptive, Count Blasius Scheuma, was named chief of staff, a far less capable man but more suave and tactful.

Austria meantime brought forth proposals to halt the Tripolitan war by international mediation, but the other cabinets spurned the idea as impracticable. Aehrenthal then warned Italy that the extension of military operations into European Turkey would infringe the Triplice. Count Berchtold, who succeeded to the Ballplatz in February of 1912, hewed to the diplomatic course that had been marked out; the veto on hostilities in Europe was reasserted, to the indignation of Italians who knew that limitation would prolong the war. And the evil habit of the Vienna press of twitting Italy over military perplexities and magnifying minor Turkish successes fed resentment south of the border.

On urgings from Berlin, Austria eventually agreed that Italy might occupy Turkish Rhodes and a few adjacent islets. But instead of stopping there the Italians landed troops at other points in the Aegean and even bombarded forts that guarded the Dardanelles. It was feared in Vienna that these aggressive gestures might incite the Balkan Christian powerlets to pounce upon Macedonia—a hypothesis not endorsed in Berlin. If the Balkan states acted, Austria might be drawn into the struggle; wherefore Berchtold insisted that the monarchical fighting machine should be toned up.

With Bulgaria Berchtold curried favor, as Aehrenthal had attempted with mixed results, hoping that if Austrian interests required it Bulgaria could be turned against Serbia. Berchtold imagined, however, that strife in the Balkans might be avoided if Turkey overhauled her administration in Macedonia. A rather vague proposal which Austria offered to the powers, for joint representations to Turkey for reforms, elicited little enthusiasm and was quickly cast aside; the march of events presently "solved" the question of Macedonia in another way, in a way that appeared injurious to Austrian interests. Owing to mounting troubles in her European provinces, Turkey, beaten on every hand, consented to an armistice with Italy, and on October 18, 1912 a treaty of peace was signed.

Before the outbreak of the struggle with Turkey, Italy broached the renewal of the Triplice treaty, which was not due to expire until 1914. But Aehrenthal temporized and the coming of war postponed negotiations. Even though Germany, as well as Austria, was scarcely friendly during the hostilities, the Italian cabinet calculated that it was worth while to preserve the alliance, and at end of 1912 the treaty was renewed without alteration, to run until 1920.

IV

In February of 1912, Aehrenthal, the most effective and forceful man at the Ballplatz since Andrássy, if not in fact since Prince Metternich himself, passed away after a long illness. A matter of hours before his death, Francis Joseph conferred upon him the highest Hapsburg honor, the Grand Cross of St. Stephen with brilliants. That token of esteem may have consoled the dying man for captious press criticisms of his policies.

Aehrenthal had managed famously to raise the drooping prestige of the Danube Monarchy, notably by the annexation of Bosnia. The British ambassador, Cartwright, declared that he "had raised high the banner of the Hapsburg Monarchy which he found almost ignored by the other European powers when he came into office." And he had transformed the German alliance into a partnership of equals, at least. On the other side of the ledger, Serbian hatred of the House of Hapsburg had intensified, and behind Serbia loomed the frightening specter of Russian Pan-Slavism; the appeasement of the Yugoslavs inside the Monarchy had not been achieved either. With the wisdom that time and perspective have brought it is arguable indeed that Aehrenthal blundered in vetoing the counsels of the Austrian war party for the military chastisement of Serbia in 1909.

Great Britain, moreover, historically the friend of Austria, had openly ranged herself in the camp of the opponents during the tenure of Aehrenthal, while Italy, a traditional enemy, though an ally on paper, had returned to her ancient mooring, for most practical purposes. The success of Aehrenthal in improving the position of his country in the councils of Europe had been bought at a heavy price.

As Aehrenthal recommended, Francis Joseph installed Count Leopold Berchtold at the foreign office, where he remained until January of 1915. Berchtold has been charged, both popularly and by learned scholars, with unique responsibility for the coming of World War I and reviled as woefully incompetent to bear the diplomatic burden laid upon his shoulders. In the ungenerous judgment of the foremost Briton of the twentieth century, "Berchtold is the epitome of this age, when the affairs of Brobdingnag are managed by the Lilliputians." [4] On the other hand, fuller acquaintance with the thinking and action of Berchtold, revealed in the rich Hapsburg archives, has tempered early estimates of the man. That learned and balanced British judge, Professor G. P. Gooch, doubts whether any other Austrian statesman could have managed better than Berchtold.[5] Like an able mariner he knew whither he desired to sail, and to reach port he repeatedly changed his tack in response to shifts in the wind.

It was the familiarity of Berchtold with Russia that dictated his selection as Austrian helmsman. Perhaps he could improve feelings, lessen animosities between the two eastern monarchies. For five years he had represented Vienna in St. Petersburg, and like Aehrenthal before him he had intimate associates in the policy-making elements of Russian society. His well-wrought and informing dispatches from Russia distinguished him as a superior craftsman. At his own request, in 1911, he had withdrawn from the foreign service, after twenty-eight years of experience.

By the test of lineage Berchtold was a capital choice for the Austrian foreign office, for in his veins flowed the blood of Magyars, Poles, Czechs, Italians, Ruthenians, Yugoslavs, and Austro-Germans; a nimble student of such matters discovered, in fact, that he was related to Francis Joseph, William II, and Nicholas II. His landed estates were so numerous that it was humorously reported that he had never visited them all. Something of a dandy, an enthusiastic turfman and patron of motorcar and aviation competitions, he was regarded by contemporaries—or some of them—as a trivial and leisurely lightweight, albeit an admirable conversationalist.

Berchtold had no hankering to preside over the Ballplatz and often begged permission to resign. His health was poor, his acquaintance with the complexities of the internal politics of the Monarchy was limited, and he lacked experience as a public speaker, all of which made him hesitate to take office, but a strong sense of duty eventually led him to accept, though with extreme reluctance. He once likened his career at the Ballplatz to martyrdom.[6]

Highly placed Russians hailed the appointment of Berchtold with transports of delight. Nicholas II believed that the new statesman would obediently follow the lead of Germany in foreign policy; under his guidance Vienna might seek to resurrect the old League of Three Emperors. The Wilhelmstrasse, in contrast, regretted the choice of Berchtold, who had never served in Berlin and who was credited with being "soaked in Russian ideas and sympathies." It was not long before Berchtold let the Germans know that he was a man of an independent cast of mind, no less than Aehrenthal.

Berchtold took up his duties at the Ballplatz without detailed knowledge of the intricacies of the Balkan problems. His understanding of the perilous Yugoslav question, for instance, was rather superficial, though he learned fast. Broadly regarded, his central convictions on foreign policy paralleled Aehrenthal's: no territorial aggrandizement, for that would increase the already unwieldy Slav population of the Monarchy and might precipitate war with Russia; diminish, if possible, the antipathy of Serbia; preserve, if possible, the *status quo* in the Balkans. If, however, Turkey could not be kept intact, Serbia must not be permitted to grow too big; rather Bulgaria, her hereditary rival, should be allowed to expand, and an autonomous Albania should be laid out, which would at once block Serbia from the Adriatic Sea and checkmate Italian pretensions in the western Balkans.

In his initial address to the delegations Berchtold affirmed the allegiance of the Monarchy to the Triple Alliance in letter and in spirit. "Our policy," he said, "is a policy of stability and peace framed to protect our legitimate interests at all times and places. We pursue . . . no aggressive tendencies, no ideas of expansion." And yet, he warned, "We are situated geographically in the midst of military states, which ceaselessly increase their defensive strength."

v

With the Near Eastern question, whose essential core was the destiny of European Turkey, Old World diplomacy had wrestled for generations with no more apparent success than Jacob with temptation in Holy Writ. A happier era seemed to have dawned after the revolution of the Young Turks in 1908, but the bright promise was not fulfilled. Instead of treating Macedonia and Albania with enlightened humanity, the regime of the Young Turks weighed more grievously upon minorities than the rule of Sultan Abdul Hamid. Goaded to fury, Albanian chieftains unfurled the standard of revolt in 1910 and the insurrection swept across into Macedonia. Immediately the great powers were on the alert, resolved to prevent if possible any territorial changes in the Balkans that would adversely affect their interests; immediately the Balkan Christian states were on the alert, resolved to benefit as fully as possible if the long-heralded dissolution of the Ottoman state came to pass.

As early as 1909, on the morrow of the humiliating capitulation in the Bosnian controversy, Russian diplomacy had taken up the idea of forming a Balkan league of nations as a bulwark against further extension of Hapsburg power in the peninsula. To that purpose the men on the Neva subsequently added the aim of expelling the Turk from Europe. Tsarist diplomatists promoted the league notion in the Balkan capitals, most energetically and most fruitfully in Belgrade and Sofia.[7]

Convinced by Russian persuasions that national aspirations would best be served by a united front, Serbia and Bulgaria, hereditary enemies, agreed to bury the hatchet, though not too deeply, and to enter into an alliance. Rumors of a pact got abroad, but St. Petersburg denied them and the men in the Ballplatz scouted their validity. Nevertheless, in the spring of 1912 Serbia and Bulgaria concluded a treaty, and so did Greece and Bulgaria; both documents were supplemented by military accords pointed potentially against Turkey and the Danube Monarchy. In the Serbo-Bulgar treaty, the allotment of Ottoman territory each party should have in the event of war and victory was outlined, but the Greco-Bulgar pact contained no parallel arrangement; rather the division of the Ottoman spoils would depend upon circumstances at the end of hostilities. Montenegro, too, was bound informally to Serbia and verbally promised to work hand in glove with Bulgaria.

In spite of the ostensibly defensive character of the Balkan league of Christians, the combination might in fact be directed against Turkey—or Austria. Fortified by the patronage of Russia, the Balkan allies contemplated radical changes in the territories of European Turkey. It was a master diplomatic coup for Russia, and the implications excited genuine alarm in the Wilhelmstrasse, not least because of apprehension that the Ballplatz would attempt to disrupt the Balkan partnership and confront Germany with a *fait accompli.*

As the Tripolitan struggle moved to its close, and convulsions in Albania and Macedonia grew more serious, statesmen in Balkan capitals talked freely of launching an attack upon the Turk. Such murmurings annoyed the men of the Neva, but they were incapable of fastening gags on the mouths of their spirited little protégés. Thoroughly aware·of the international reverberations that a war in the Balkans would unloose, the great powers tardily acted to keep the peace. They promised to compel Turkey to improve administration in Albania and Macedonia and they admonished the Balkan powerlets, in tones intended to convey finality, that even if they fought Turkey and won, no changes in the Balkan map would be tolerated.

That pronouncement of purpose, however, exerted no positive influence on the march of events.[8] On October 8, 1912, the very day after the declaration of the great powers was published, pugnacious Montenegro, egged on by her neighbors, opened fire upon Turkey, and the Balkan allies followed along afterward.

At the start of hostilities, it was widely assumed that Austrian forces would reoccupy Novibazar so as to keep Serbia and Montenegro out. If that had happened Serbia and Bulgaria might very well have turned their guns against the Hapsburg power. Certainly the desirability of reoccupying Novibazar was debated in the Ballplatz, but it was ruled out by the arguments that Italy would demand compensation, that the military services were unprepared, and that the German ally would not countenance it.

To the amazement of Europe in general, and to the consternation of Austria in particular, the armies of the Balkan league rapidly smashed the Ottoman forces and pressed enthusiastically into coveted lands. According to the calculations of pundits in Vienna, the struggle would be drawn out; Turkey in the end would be defeated but all belligerents would be exhausted. Instead, the allies had quickly triumphed and they were satellites of Russia! Even the veriest tyro in diplomacy realized that the great powers could not force the maintenance of the territorial *status quo ante bellum*.

In the light of stark and unpalatable facts, the Ballplatz mapped out anew the specifics of Austrian diplomacy in the Balkans. The economic interests of the Hapsburg Moñarchy must be safeguarded; strict limits must be set to the expansion of Serbia; a large and independent Albania and a big Bulgaria must be created; and Bulgaria must cede territory to Rumania, ally of Austria and the barrier to Muscovite pressure into the Balkan peninsula overland. Once they were decided upon, Berchtold held to these particulars of policy with uncommon tenacity.

An exceedingly grave controversy arose over the fate of Albania. Native chieftains had proclaimed independence of Turkey, but Serbian troops had partly occupied the region, and the government in Belgrade intended to annex the northern fringe fronting on the Adriatic Sea. For a time the Russians supported the ambitions of Serbia. On the other hand, Austria and Italy, though not for precisely identical reasons, were determined that an independent Albania should be set up embracing the entire Adriatic littoral of Turkey. Austria, it is true, was amenable to a Serbian railway across Albania to the sea, but not to political sovereignty; Serbian ports on the Adriatic, for one thing, might be loaned or leased to Russia for naval purposes. And Austria was prepared to see the Serb kingdom expand into areas of Macedonia peopled by Serb-feeling folk.

To the Russian contention that, if Serbia were allowed frontage on the Adriatic, the national appetite would be satiated, the Ballplatz, in view of the powerful and well-known agitation for Greater Serbia, strongly dissented. Wherefore the ancient Austro-Russian antagonism flared up again in a serious way. Tension indeed reached such a peak that Berchtold remarked that an armed clash with Russia was not impossible. Already Austria had taken preparatory steps to fight Serbia and was also massing troops near the Russian frontier; every bridge and tunnel in the Monarchy was placed under guard. The bellicose Conrad, who was now recalled to the office of chief of staff, resumed his warnings against Serbia and pleaded for an immediate attack.

The Austrian public was inflamed to war fury by stories that the Austrian consul in the town of Prizren, one Prochaska, had been emasculated or killed by Serb soldiers. Actually no physical harm befell Prochaska, though he was kept under close surveillance; he later acknowledged that the reports of mutilation were a fake, and made light of them. Whether the affair was deliberately fabricated in the Ballplatz in order to whip up popular passions against Serbia has not been, perhaps cannot be, conclusively proved. Propaganda or not, the Prochaska episode roused feelings against the Serbs; and when Serb students in Vienna indulged in a street celebration after attending a thanksgiving service for the recent military victories of their countrymen, Viennese set upon them and thrashed them soundly. Restaurants and beer halls in Vienna resounded with the *Prince Eugen Lied* or the *Radetsky Marsch,* which, with *Gott erhalte,* the imperial anthem, formed for weeks the favorite items of the musical repertoire. Even grocers were heard to protest indignantly against Serbian arrogance and inquired when the fighting was going to begin.

Mobilization of troops, as always, involved financial losses for the men called to the colors and upset Austrian economic life, which had already been adversely affected by the disruption of commerce with the Balkans. The popular belief that war was imminent stimulated emigration, peasants eagerly sacrificing their parcels of land for enough to pay transportation costs overseas. Nonetheless, outside of the officer corps, no one of consequence endorsed Conrad's dictum that a preventive war should be initiated. Russia, on her part, commenced mobilizing along the Austrian borders, which had similar repercussions upon the internal affairs of the tsardom.

An armistice in the meantime had called a halt to the Balkan fighting and the belligerents were instructed to negotiate a settlement at London under the watchful surveillance of the ambassadors of the great powers. At that point the Serbian cabinet attempted to strike a secret bargain with Austria, employing the distinguished Czech savant, Professor Masaryk, as confidential intermediary. If Serbia were granted sovereign control over an Adriatic harbor and a broad railway corridor down to it, then the Belgrade government would guarantee neither to fortify the port nor to place it at the disposal of a third power, and would, moreover, confer special commercial privileges upon Austria. Should Vienna, however, scorn these proposals, Serbia would align herself more closely with the Balkan allies and would impose a boycott on Austrian wares. Reject the overture Berchtold did; publicly on the ground that a Serbian port and corridor would do violence to Albanian national rights, privately because he had no faith in Serbian promises and envisaged a Serbian harbor as a potential Muscovite outpost. Masaryk he maliciously accused of seeking "to earn a commission" by acting as go-between.[9]

With Austria and Russia at loggerheads and the peril of an armed clash dangerously real, the British and German governments intervened, and persuaded the disputants to take part in a conference of ambassadors at London to iron out the perplexities which the defeat of Turkey had brought to the fore. In the course of the winter of 1912–13, the London conference decided that a relatively large and fully independent Albania should be blocked out, the precise boundaries to be settled later. By that decision Serbia of course was denied an Adriatic harbor, but she was assured of a railway connection across Albania to the sea. Russia, after championing Serb aspirations, drew back when it seemed that persistence would mean war, for which the tsardom was still unready.

Once the Adriatic littoral had been wholly assigned to Albania, Austria and Russia quarreled over the future of the key town of Scutari and after that over the eastern frontier of Albania, Austria working to get the maximum for Albania, Russia standing firm on the pretensions of Serbia and Montenegro. In the end, however, Austria gave way on the eastern border in return for an understanding that Scutari should belong to Albania and that Serbian and Montenegrin troops should promptly be evacuated from Albanian soil. That accommodation represented a decent compromise without loss of face for either Austria or Russia; and yet chauvinistic Austrian elements assailed the Ballplatz for yielding on the eastern boundary of Albania.

Still the Balkan crisis was not entirely over, for Montenegro obstinately refused to abandon its claim to Scutari, even though counseled by Russia to do so. Russia, not yet prepared to fight and uncertain whether Britain would stand by her in case of a general struggle, was no more inclined to aid Montenegro on the Scutari issue than she had been to back Serbia to the limit on the Adriatic littoral. Austria in fact threatened to invoke force to keep Montenegro out of Scutari, but finally united with the other great powers in a coercive naval blockade of the little country. Nonetheless, Montenegrin soldiers marched into Scutari in April 1913, and the occupation of the community was jubilantly celebrated in Balkan towns and in Russia. At Cetinje, the idyllic, primitive capital of Montenegro, a victory parade was featured by a royal ass, draped in black and bearing a huge placard vilifying the Hapsburg Monarchy!

The advance of Montenegro into Scutari thoroughly enflamed the men in Vienna. At a crown council the advisability of applying force upon Montenegro was debated, with Hungarian spokesmen dissenting on financial and diplomatic grounds. It was announced, however, that unless Montenegro withdrew her soldiers Austria would drive them out, and Germany identified herself with that stern warning. Had Montenegro proved obdurate and Austria gone to war, Russia might have joined in, thus setting Europe ablaze. Happily, Montenegro evacuated Scutari. Austria won its point; it seemed as though the Albanian problem had been durably solved. International tension subsided, and the armed services of the Monarchy reverted to a more normal basis.

Throughout the desperate tussle over Albania the Wilhelmstrasse consistently stood by the Austrian ally, though with considerable misgiving, half because of skepticism on the ability of Albania to lead a separate national existence, half because of the acute tension that the course of Austrian diplomacy helped to create. It is reasonably clear that Berlin was far less apprehensive of Pan-Serb ambitions than Vienna and urged conciliatory concessions to the spunky Serb state; William II, for instance, repeatedly implored the Ballplatz to appease the Serbs. On the other side, the fidelity of Germany to the Austrian alliance was made plain beyond peradventure of a doubt.

VI

In February 1913, while the diplomatists were bargaining in London, a successful *coup d'état* was staged in Turkey, and the rebels reopened the war against the Balkan alliance. Once more the Turks were decisively beaten and agreed to a second armistice; and in May 1913 Turkey signed a "peace" with the victors at London, renouncing all European holdings except a small area round about Constantinople and the Straits. Already, however, the victor states had fallen to quarreling over the distribution of the conquered territory and Rumania put in a claim for compensation as a reward for standing on the sidelines. What had started as a war of liberation from the infidel

Turk swiftly degenerated into a war of extermination among the Christian powers.

Denied frontage on the Adriatic by reason of the creation of a big Albania, Serbia demanded a section of western Macedonia, which in the secret treaty of 1912 had been assigned to Bulgaria. Intoxicated by the champagne of military victories over Turkey, Bulgaria would not comply with the Serb demand. Beyond that, Bulgaria laid claim to Salonika, best of Aegean ports, which Greek soldiers had occupied during the fighting. And Rumania, jealous of the enlarged Bulgaria, demanded that the southern Dobrudja should be handed over to her. Since no amicable adjustment of claims and counterclaims could be worked out, the Balkan nations turned their swords at one another's throats. On June 29, the Bulgars treacherously fell upon the soldiers of Serbia and Greece in Macedonia; Rumania entered the lists against Bulgaria, and Turkey, down but not out, joined in the melee.

During the acute controversy among the Balkan states, Austrian diplomacy was guided, as earlier, by four positive objectives: the disruption of the Balkan alliance, prevention of too great expansion of Serbia, assistance to Bulgaria, and compensation for Rumania.[10] Austria recommended that Bulgaria should transfer all of southern Dobrudja to Rumania in exchange for Salonika, but the Greeks had no intention of quitting the "pearl of the Aegean"; in that stand they were abetted by Germany which preferred to court the sympathy of Greece rather than of Bulgaria. Austrian attempts to placate Rumania with less than all of southern Dobrudja proved futile.

As patron of the Balkan league, Russia begged Bulgaria and Serbia to allow the tsar to arbitrate their dispute, but the appeal fell on Bulgarian ears that were deaf. While the Ballplatz did not encourage Bulgaria to go to war against Serbia, much less goad her on as was once confidently believed, it nonetheless preferred—much preferred—a Bulgarian to a Serbian victory, for new Serbian triumphs would surely quicken Yugoslav appetites respecting Hapsburg territory. Decisive in this renewal of Balkan war was the intervention of Rumania; if Rumania had stood aside, Bulgaria might well have vanquished her Serb, Greek, and Turkish adversaries.

As things turned out, Bulgaria was compelled to sue for peace after a month of fighting. Austria, alarmed by the military triumphs of Serbia and the prospective access of territory at Bulgaria's expense, contemplated military action against Serbia. Before moving, Berchtold applied in Berlin and Rome for pledges of aid, should Russia rally to Serbia's assistance. But both cabinets, the German in stern language, vetoed the Austrian plan, holding that it would involve all Europe in war. That and the consideration that war with Serbia would almost certainly entail fighting with Rumania knocked the Austrian design into a cocked hat.

When defeat appeared imminent, Bulgaria applied to Austria for an alliance to which Rumania would also be party, it was hoped. Berchtold's response was cordial enough, but he insisted that the allies of Austria must first be sounded out on the proposition. In a strongly worded note Berchtold besought German support for Bulgaria, as a means of neutralizing the Serb menace to Austria; but the Germans held resolutely to the thesis that the Austrians grossly exaggerated the potential challenge of Serbia to the security and integrity of the Dual Monarchy.

Defeated Bulgaria submitted to the Treaty of Bucharest in August of 1913. Thereby Bulgaria was deprived of western Macedonia and the southern Dobrudja, and abandoned its wider aspirations at the head of the Aegean. Serbia, on the other hand, reached its territorial objectives in Macedonia and by reason of acquisitions in the central Balkans bestrode the routes from Austria to Salonika. Berchtold, arguing that Serbian expansion jeopardized the future of Austria, considered seeking revision of the Bucharest settlement in a way that would benefit Bulgaria to Serbia's detriment, but neither Berlin nor any other cabinet responded sympathetically and the project was tucked away in the spacious Hapsburg archives.

Great was the joy in Serbia over the gains that had been won. The Greater Serbian dream as it affected Turkey had come true, except in Albania. Premier Pasič exuberantly exulted: "The first round is won; now we must prepare for the second, against Austria." Cheered by the gains to the south, the apostles of Greater Serbia, within the Hapsburg Monarchy and without, grew more audacious, more impatient, more impetuous.

For Austrian diplomacy the outcome of the Balkan struggles, above all the aggrandizement of Serbia, involved a stinging setback, and the foreign minister was bitterly flayed for supineness and incompetence. At the meeting of the delegations in November of 1913, Berchtold delivered a misleading apologia, or part of one, telling his auditors that in the critical phases of the recent Balkan controversy Germany and Italy had acted as faithful allies and that relations with Russia were correct and friendly. Many points on which the delegates desired information were skillfully glossed over or entirely omitted, and the address as a whole was received coldly. "In matters where he had not scored successes," commented the Magyar leader, Count Julius Andrássy, "Berchtold was silent"; lively dissatisfaction with the handling of foreign policy was freely voiced by spokesmen of almost all national groupings. Still Berchtold's diplomacy had the approval of Francis Joseph, and that was sufficient to keep him in office.

The Ballplatz, the pronouncement of Berchtold aside, was sorely aggrieved over the German refusal to go along wholeheartedly with Austrian plans in the Balkans. Whereas Austria had stood forth as the champion of Bulgaria, Germany had cordially befriended Greece and Rumania, which in the interpretation of Vienna was tantamount to abetting Serbia and that was disloyalty capitalized; the Kaiser in fact during the second Balkan war had expressed the wish that Bulgaria would be roundly chastised. Policy makers in Berlin regarded the Austrian bill of indictment against Serbia and Pan-Serbism as weak and unconvincing. On the morrow of the Bucharest peace Austria and Germany were each profoundly disappointed with the attitude and the action of the other. "Certain it is," writes Wedel, "that the Central Powers were completely at loggerheads with each other and only sheer inertia was holding them together . . . Had the World War not come when it did, some kind of readjustment must have taken place." [11]

It was generally assumed in diplomatic quarters that the Bucharest peace represented merely a truce in the Balkan turbulence. Bulgarians had no intention of renouncing forever their pretensions to "Serbian Macedonia," and they cast about for an ally which would be useful in another contest with Serbia. Mistrust and hatred of Serbia created a common bond between Austria and Bulgaria, but the frigid attitude of Germany made Austria hesitate to seek an alliance with Sofia. Elsewhere in the Balkans the wars of 1912-13 had brought not peace but the sword; for instance, the new creation, Albania, floundered hopelessly, while her neighbors prepared to despoil her. And Greeks and Turks disputed acrimoniously over the ownership of Aegean islands.

Albania in October of 1913 caused another sharp diplomatic passage between Austria and Serbia, which involved the other powers. Serbian soldiers frequently interfered with commissions that were laying out the Albanian eastern boundary, and, in a fight with natives, Serb troops were routed. Whereupon the press of Serbia set up clamor for revision of the Albanian frontiers, and a section of the army was mobilized and moved into Albania for the avowed purpose of restoring order. The Belgrade cabinet informed Vienna that the soldiers would not remain on Albanian soil, but the Ballplatz had no faith whatsoever in that assurance—and with reason, for Serbia was actually angling for international sanction to take part of the land that had been allotted to Albania. [12]

At a Hapsburg crown council Berchtold argued that the Serbs would stay in Albania unless expelled by Austria. Conrad expounded his familiar thesis of war upon Serbia to put an end to the incessant controversies. Tisza, on the other hand, preferred that diplomacy should be employed to get the Serbs to withdraw, with military force to be invoked if necessary. But he was adamantly opposed to adding any Serb territory to the Monarchy, as Conrad was recommending.

On October 14, Serbian troops having marched deeper into Albania, and the London conference powers having refused an Austrian request for joint action against the Serbs, the Ballplatz formally asked Serbia to call back its troops. Serbia's reply was evasive, ascribable, Vienna thought, to advice from

Russian sources. Wherefore, without consulting Berlin, Vienna dispatched a peremptory ultimatum to Belgrade, threatening to invoke "proper measures" if Serbian soldiers were not evacuated within eight days. Here indeed was concrete testimony that Berchtold had ceased believing in a pacific solution of the Serb problem and was ready to appeal to the sword. Copies of the document were handed to the great powers along with a recital of Serbian stubbornness and Austrian patience. With reluctance Germany endorsed what her ally had done and, after momentary hesitation, the other great powers, Russia among them, convinced that Austria really meant business, strongly urged the Serbs to clear out of Albania. And they did so—grudgingly, but on time.

In this obscure debate that was elevated to the dignity of a question of national prestige and honor, Austria had scored handsomely over Serbia and her imperial friend, Russia. The pattern of events engraved itself upon the memory of the Ballplatz. In a quarrel with Serbia, in which Russia was a silent partner, Serbia had not yielded until Austria launched an ultimatum, then, bereft of international support, Serbia gave way. Germany had backed Austria, albeit reluctantly.

Perhaps that sequence would be repeated in the event of an analogous controversy. And William II presently enheartened the Austrians by melodramatically underscoring the solidarity of the alliance in conversations with Austrian policy makers. "If His Majesty the Emperor Francis Joseph makes a demand, the Serbian government must obey. If not, Belgrade must be bombarded and occupied till his wish is fulfilled," the emperor went on, "and rest assured that I am behind you and am ready to draw the sword whenever your action requires." [13] The Kaiser at least among German statesmen had come to appreciate that Serbia was a real menace to Austrian welfare.

After the Serbian withdrawal from Albania relations with Austria were as strained as possible and the press of both countries harped upon the "inevitable war." Serbian Irredentism was Austria's supreme nightmare and the march of events had converted many sober minds to the doctrine of a preventive war against the annoying southern neighbor. Berchtold himself concluded in November 1913 that "in view of the tenacity and confidence with which Serbia is pursuing the idea of a greater Serbia" the problem could be settled only by force. Recourse to arms would "either completely destroy the present state of Serbia or shake Austria-Hungary to its foundations." [14] From that conviction Berchtold never thereafter swerved. Essentially, Austrian policy with respect to Serbia was defensive, directed to the maintenance of the *status quo,* though many a foreigner believed—and many still do—that the Ballplatz cherished expansionist designs at Serbian expense. True, a segment of Austrian opinion was of that view, but it was a small, if noisy, minority; most of the responsible Hapsburg policy makers had no desire to acquire more Slavs, indigestible Orthodox Slavs at that.

Serbia, having achieved its territorial ambitions against Turkey, could—and did—concentrate its energies on the Yugoslav-inhabited areas in the realm of the Hapsburgs. For the Serbs the supreme goal was the political unification of the Yugoslavs—an objective easily understood in a Europe that had long since grown accustomed to the dynamic of the national process.

Anti-Austrianism, pushed by Serbia with unprecedented vigor, intensified discontent and unrest in the Monarchy, in Bosnia and elsewhere. The Serbian government was either unwilling or unable to curb this disruptive and incendiary agitation, as it had solemnly promised to do in 1909. Rumors of an impending merger between Serbia and Montenegro contributed to the growing anxiety in Vienna; and suspicions of the darkest hue seemed to be confirmed by a visit of Premier Pašič to St. Petersburg in January 1914. At the Russian capital the Serbian chief alluded to the eventual unification of the Yugoslavs and heard encouraging words from highly placed tsarist officials.[15] One day, Pašič was assured, Serbia might come into possession of Bosnia. That was his high ambition; only shrewd patience, he once explained, had restrained him from precipitating a general war during the first Balkan struggle, so that Serbia might obtain Bosnia. Bosnia could wait, however, until Serbian claims upon Turkey had been liquidated, an objective which the Balkan wars had now accomplished.

The Russians, meantime, were feverishly working to resuscitate the Balkan league of nations, as a barrier to Austrian (and German) pressure into the Balkans. They besought the Serbs to effect a reconciliation with Bulgaria. Austrian soil to be acquired in the future would compensate for the cession to Bulgaria of "Serbian Macedonia," but the Serbs knew well the ancient maxim about a bird in the hand. And unless Bulgaria secured the coveted Macedonia area the chances of her entering a league with Serbia were precisely zero.

Serbia had a dual community of interest with Rumania, distrust of Bulgaria and Irredentist claims upon the Dual Monarchy, overlapping though the claims were in places. Russia, soliciting Rumanian membership in a new league, dangled parcels of Hapsburg territory before her eyes. Hatred of Bulgaria gave Greece, too, a common bond with Serbia. Early in 1914, owing in large measure to Russian diplomatic manipulations, Serbia, Rumania, and Greece actually united in a new diplomatic partnership.

VII

Next to Serbia, Rumania was the source of greatest direct concern to the Ballplatz. Although the alliance was renewed in February 1913, Rumanian Irredentist passions together with pro-Bulgar sympathies in Vienna had robbed the treaty of effective value. Moreover, Austrian feelers for revision of the Peace of Bucharest inescapably antagonized Rumanian policy makers, and the unmistakable cordiality of the latter toward Serbia excited angry reactions in Vienna.

On the other hand, a conservative faction in Rumania, which conceived of Russia as the supreme and everlasting national enemy, argued for a strongly Austrophile policy. The kingdom's war minister, Nicolas Filipescu, an influential exponent of that school of logic, dusted off in 1913 an old plan whereby Hungary would cede Transylvania to Rumania and the enlarged kingdom would then be incorporated in the realm of the Hapsburgs; Rumania's position in the new structure would correspond broadly to that of Bavaria in the German federal empire. Certainly few of the Rumanian politicians thought Filipescu's project desirable, and not less certainly the Magyars would have refused to part with Transylvania, so that the plan of union, had it been brought into the open, would surely have come to grief.

It is extremely doubtful whether concessions to the Rumanians in Hungary would have appeased Rumanian Irredentists. So strong indeed had the spirit of secession grown in Transylvania that it was remarked that Hungarian Rumanians were more nationalistic than their fellows in Rumania itself. And in the Regat, hatred of Hungary had largely supplanted the deeply rooted distrust of Russia, precisely as Aehrenthal had warned would happen when he was stationed in Bucharest. To many of the politically active it appeared that Transylvania could be acquired more easily from the supposedly feeble Dual Monarchy than Bessarabia could be recovered from Russia.

Was it at all possible for the Hapsburg Monarchy to recapture the favor of Rumania? To study that problem and suggest an answer, Count Ottokar Czernin, Francis Ferdinand's most trusted adviser on foreign affairs, was dispatched to Bucharest as ambassador in November of 1913. Czernin, like his sponsor, was known to be sympathetic toward the Hungarian Rumanians and in an acid pamphlet he had roughly criticized Magyarization. Magyar politicians angrily declaimed against his appointment to the embassy in Rumania.

Formally Czernin was instructed to seek to restore good relations by explaining Austrian motives during the Balkan wars, to try to separate Rumania from Serbia, and to ascertain the probabilities of Rumanian diplomacy. If the Rumanians desired political intimacy with Austria, then they should agree to the publication of the treaty of alliance, which at the time was known only to a handful of public men.

From Bucharest Czernin dispatched to Vienna illuminating reports on the currents of opinion in the kingdom and sketched the alternatives that confronted the Ballplatz. Very properly he dwelt upon the evil consequences of the inconsiderate Magyar treatment of Rumanians and the necessity of far-reaching reform. Rumanian politicians, he was convinced, were actively promoting hatred of the Monarchy; King Carol regretfully confided to Czernin that if Austria became involved in a conflict with Russia in the immediate future, Rumania would not line up with her ally. Czernin's broad and sound conclusion was that, as matters stood, the Austro-Rumanian treaty had no more value than a scrap of paper. General Conrad recommended that the defenses along the Rumanian frontier should be reinforced, but the civilian authorities, unwilling to aggravate Rumanian hostility, imposed a veto.

The inclination of Rumania toward Russia was openly trumpeted abroad in the spring of 1914, by an exchange of royal visits. Rumania's crown prince, Ferdinand, and his wife spent three weeks in the tsardom for the official purpose of arranging a match between their son, Carol, and a Russian lady, but none of the eligibles had photogenic qualities sufficiently appealing to the epicurean prince. So the attempt to draw the two countries together by means of a royal marriage fell flat. Presently Tsar Nicholas II appeared in Bucharest, bringing Foreign Minister Sazonov with him. As noted above, Russian diplomacy had been working to organize a new Balkan league, which, while nominally a coalition to preserve tranquillity in the Balkans, would be serviceable to Russia in the event of a European war. That initiative had not been fruitless, for Rumania had agreed with Serbia and Greece on the policy to be pursued should an attempt be made to revise the Treaty of Bucharest by force.

Sazonov and Bratianu, the Rumanian premier, held long and secret conversations, and the two statesmen took a journey into Transylvania which naturally provoked shrill outcries in the Magyar press and seriously annoyed the Ballplatz. Newspapers speculated at length on the probability of Russo-Rumanian collaboration and doubted whether it would be confined merely to upholding the Bucharest settlement. Though no formal understanding was signed, Sazonov promised Transylvania to Bratianu if Rumania would align itself with Russia, and he returned to St. Petersburg with the conviction that if a Russo-Austrian war came Rumania would side with the belligerent that seemed likely to be the victor and promised her the larger territorial advantages. At the very time that the Russians were ardently wooing Rumania, French publicists, André Tardieu for one, were busy in Bucharest cultivating pro-Entente sympathies. Time and again popular demonstrations expressed affection for Russia and hatred for the Dual Monarchy.

Statesmen in Berlin recognized that the new orientation in Rumanian foreign policy was chiefly due to Magyar treatment of Rumanians in Hungary and they applied pressure in Budapest to secure a modification of policy. Still the Wilhelmstrasse believed that in case of war the worst that Rumania would do would be to remain neutral; active military cooperation with Russia seemed beyond the range of probability.

As a natural and adequate counterpoise to the set of Balkan states that had gravitated into the Russian orbit, Austria strove to build up a Bulgar-Turkish coalition. Bulgaria, however, despite bitterness toward her neighbors, drew back, afraid of being implicated in a grave Turkish dispute with Greece over certain Aegean isles. Vienna pressed upon Berlin the value of an alliance with Bulgaria, but the Germans could not be moved, holding that such an alignment would irretrievably alienate Rumania from the Triplice. As the Austrians saw it, Rumania had for practical purposes already passed into the camp of the common enemy and Bulgaria, as an ally, would compensate for that perfidy. But only after the beginning of war in 1914 and the Rumanian declaration of neutrality did the Germans veer round to the Austrian views concerning Bulgaria.

VIII

No one in the Ballplatz doubted that the ultimate cause of anxiety over the Balkans was Russia. The tsardom was the guardian angel of the Serbs and utterly distrusted the objectives of Hapsburg diplomacy, refusing to believe that Austria was a satiated state without territorial ambitions. In the winter of 1913 a Russian quarrel with Germany over the sending of a military mission to Constantinople momentarily diverted Muscovite hostility from Vienna to Berlin, for it was suspected that Germany was angling to obtain mastery at the Straits and thus forestall Russian aspirations in that area.

Stories in the Pan-Slav press of Russia on the formation of the new Balkan league excited grave disquiet in Austria, and journalists shouted violently about "the Russian peril." Russian Pan-Slavism, commented the influential *Neue Freie Presse,* constantly endangered the peace of Europe and was moving heaven and earth to make Russia the patron and protector in one form or another of every Balkan country. Austrian mistrust of Russia was not restricted to the doings of Muscovite diplomatists in the Balkans. Mischief-making propagandists were sleeplessly at work in the Slav provinces of the Monarchy, particularly among the Ruthenians, sowing seeds of dissension; but the cabinet of Vienna preferred not to complain over incidents lest tension be heightened to no good purpose. Almost daily, episodes along the border of Galicia provoked acrid press comment, and animus toward Russia grew with the arrest of Hapsburg subjects who allegedly were tools of the tsardom. Keen apprehension was aroused by the expansion of Russian armaments, by preparations for war along the frontiers of the

Monarchy and of Germany, and by the blatant boasting of certain Muscovite military chieftains.[16]

With Italy, Austrian relations grew so strained in the spring of 1914 that responsible German statesmen expected an armed clash. Each cabinet suspected that the other had predatory designs upon the new creation, Albania; rival financial houses competed for the dubious privilege of equipping the little country with a national bank. Sharp cleavages of opinion developed over the Austrian claim to a protectorate over the Catholic population and over the actual prerogatives of the ruler, Prince William of Wied, a German prince and a captain in the German army.

Ignorant of Albania and the people, unschooled in the devious arts of diplomacy, the Prince had only grudgingly accepted the crown at the request of Austria and Italy. His state had no army, no administrative system, no treasury, a superabundance of politicians, and a band of emigrants returned from the United States with acquired notions as to how an up-and-coming country should be governed. Shortly after the Prince landed in his adopted country he was confronted by a nativist rebellion. In June of 1914 the "great press" of Vienna teemed with stories of anarchy in Albania and with earnest appeals to the powers to intervene and restore discipline, for disturbances anywhere in the Balkans had a nasty habit of inspiring convulsions elsewhere. For Austria and Italy, in short, Albania was another Schleswig-Holstein; each foreign office jealously and suspiciously watched every move the other made and took appropriate countermeasures.

Yet, despite the cleavage, the cabinets kept up the pretense of solidarity. At the conclusion of a conference in April 1914, the two foreign ministers issued a joint communiqué affirming their devotion to the Triplice and stating that both governments held identical views on international questions.[17]

It was not possible in Austria to reconcile formal, official assertions of friendship with fervent anti-Hapsburg outbursts in the Italian press, in patriotic societies, and in the broad mass of the population. Well has it been said that "every Italian carried in his heart a seed of Irredentism."

Considerations of prestige and security impelled Austria and Germany to hang together regardless of differences on particular points. For them, as for the nations arrayed in the Triple Entente, union brought strength, disunity would invite destruction. On specific Balkan items Vienna and Berlin stood leagues apart; the desire of Austria, for example, to attract Bulgaria into the Triplice fellowship was resisted by the Wilhelmstrasse. And, although Germany regarded Greece as a valuable candidate for admission to the Triplice, the Ballplatz distrusted Greece because it coquetted with Serbia.

Hesitantly Berlin had come round to the thinking of Vienna with regard to the menace of the Greater Serb idea to the Hapsburg Monarchy. It was understood that provocative behavior by Serbia in the future would be severely punished. The two cabinets likewise agreed that the ambitions of imperial Russia were dangerous for both countries. Yet at a conference in March of 1914 Francis Joseph and William II professed to see no clouds on the horizon that could not be dissipated by the procedures of diplomacy.

At the final meeting of the delegations before the war—in April 1914—the Austrian international situation was discussed with remarkable calm and sobriety. Berchtold noted "a certain slackening of the tension" between the Triple Alliance and the Triple Entente, which he ascribed to the diplomacy of Great Britain; he ventured the hope that relations with Russia would grow more cordial. With regard to the Balkans, he referred especially to the desire for closer trade ties with Bulgaria, to railway negotiations with Serbia, to a recent mission of good will of Venizelos, prime minister of Greece, and to the political and economic interests of the Hapsburg Monarchy in Turkey. He even thought, or so he said, that Rumania would not risk losing the advantages that the alliance with Austria afforded.

Delegates and press criticized Berchtold's exposition as incomplete and unduly optimistic. Twelve lines were devoted to the riches Austria might gain in the Turkish province of Cilicia, bemoaned the *Neue Freie Presse,* while relations with Russia, the main cause of the staggering tax burden, were disposed of in seven! The president of the Austrian delegation expressed the hope that "steps might be taken to put a decisive check upon the anti-Hapsburg propaganda carried on in the frontier districts." A hot-blooded and temperamental Magyar delegate, Count Michael Károlyi, charged that the alliance with Germany was responsible for the unhappy state of tension with Russia; perhaps he intended by this utterance to embarrass his arch-enemy the Hungarian premier, Tisza, who was a warm partisan of the German alliance.

The diplomatic posture of the Hapsburg Monarchy in the late spring of 1914 was scarcely calculated to excite envy. Serbia had grown bigger, more self-assured, and more exasperating; and it had already been decided in the Ballplatz that the next serious controversy with Serbia must be settled not by orderly processes of diplomacy, but by drastic military punishment. Austrian patience, rightly or wrongly, had reached the breaking point. Rumania, moreover, had been estranged from Vienna chiefly by the rising desire to obtain the Rumanian-inhabited areas of Hungary, and no Balkan ally had been secured to take its place; yet Bulgaria was in the market and by proper handling might be induced to cast in her lot with the Hapsburgs. Turkey, the only reliable friend of the Central Powers in southeastern Europe, had been reduced territorially and militarily humiliated; negotiations for an alliance might, however, bear useful fruit. Distraught Albania, too, might be drawn or dragooned into the Austrian orbit.

Russia's age-old ambitions in the Near East, the longing to be the dominant force in that part of the world, together with the doings of Pan-Slavs and Russophiles within the borders of the Danube Monarchy, portended no good for Austria's standing as a great power. Great Britain, once the Austrian champion in tussles with Russia, had wandered far afield, and looked upon the Monarchy as so much pliant putty in the hands of an assertive Germany. As for Italy irreconcilable differences, however glossed over, ruled out anything like genuine fraternity; the treaty of alliance was of scarcely more value than the wax and parchment of which it was made. Beyond and above all, however, there was great and powerful Germany, and upon the Nibelung loyalty of that ally the men at the Ballplatz reckoned with full confidence.

That faith was shown not to have been misplaced during the terrible diplomatic crisis that followed the murders of the Austrian heir presumptive, Francis Ferdinand and his wife, by a fanatical and patriotic Pan-Serb on the streets of Sarajevo, the capital of Bosnia, on June 28, 1914.

SCHEMES FOR REFORMATION AND
SOURCES OF STRENGTH

FROM THE BIRTH OF THE DUALISTIC COMPROMISE UNTIL THE resounding downfall of the ramified Hapsburg structure in 1918, the impending dissolution of the realm was freely and frequently predicted in responsible quarters and others. Naturally the intensity of the belief that the Monarchy was doomed to destruction varied, but from 1895 on, as the feud between German and Czech waxed hotter, as the struggle between the crown and the Magyars attained dangerous dimensions—developments that stimulated nationalistic agitation among other groups in the realm—and as the Hapsburg quarrel with Serbia was only superficially adjusted, the conviction deepened that the Monarchy had taken a bed alongside Turkey in the hospital of the dying. Diplomatic reports that emanated from Vienna just before 1914 were peppered with prognostications of the imminent disruption of the Monarchy and with speculations on the political and strategic changes that would follow.

In an epoch of emergent and jealous nationalisms it seemed hard to believe that the multinationality Hapsburg realm could much longer endure. Yet, as has earlier been explained, the potency of the nationalisms within the Monarchy in so far as they had separatist, secessionist implications may easily be exaggerated. Among wide masses of the rural minority populations, national consciousness was only feebly awakened, and even among those elements of the citizenry in which nationalism was mature, among the intelligentsia and other sections of the bourgeoisie, advocacy of independence and the disruption of the venerable Monarchy was exceptional rather than representative.

It must be said, and said again, that nowhere in continental Europe, except in Switzerland, were the peculiar interests of national minorities given more protection and consideration, unsatisfactory though they were, than in the Austrian half of the Dual Monarchy. It was possible for a Rumanian to write with perfect candor that Austria had "organized and civilized, rather than Germanized, her peoples." [1] And nowhere as much as in the Austrian empire were the tangled problems of national minorities subjected to more thorough or competent analysis; literally scores of studies on the subject, learned and polemical, were published. It was, however, another story in Hungary where, in striking contrast, the settled policy of Magyarizing minorities was sedulously, and to a remarkable extent successfully, pursued.

Plans were not wanting for the abandonment of the dualistic regime, considered by a host of thoughtful observers as the largest source of political evil in the Hapsburg state, and for the constitutional reordering of the dominions. Indeed, attached to the office of the Austrian prime minister was a special department for the revision of the constitution, presided over by a Professor von Hold, which reviewed various proposals for the transformation of the monarchy and prepared patterns of its own.[2]

Public men, scholars, and publicists at home and abroad concerned themselves in the main with two broad types of program for reconstruction. One called for the organization of a third unit of the realm containing the Yugoslav subjects of the Hapsburgs; the other, more far-reaching, the conversion of the Monarchy into a "monarchical Switzerland," in which each nationality would have considerable control over local affairs but the economic solidarity of the realm would be preserved and the federalized state would present a united front in its dealing with foreign powers.

The more modest of the programs for constitutional reformation contemplated the establishment of a third autonomous unit in the Monarchy, comprising Yugoslavs, and possessing identical political rights with the empire of Austria and the kingdom of Hungary. For dualism, in other words, trialism would be substituted. Conceptions of the territorial limits of the third state varied, but all plans of importance assumed that it would include Croatia, Dalmatia, and Bosnia; some schemes added the Slovene districts, and others Trieste, Istria, and Fiume. Croatia in any case would have been the core of the Yugoslav unit and Agram the political and cultural capital.

In essence, the idea of a state of Yugoslavs within the Hapsburg fold reached back to the province of Illyria, covering Dalmatia, Fiume, Istria, Görz and Gradisca, Carniola, and portions of Croatia and Carinthia, which Napoleon had set up in 1809. French administrators at the time radically improved administration, promoted material betterment, and fostered national sentiments among the inhabitants, seeking to have Illyria as a strategic

French outpost at the head of the Adriatic. If French authority had lasted longer it is reasonable to imagine that Illyria might have become the center round which all Yugoslavs would have rallied, but when Bonaparte's power faltered the region reverted to the House of Hapsburg. Still the memory of the French epoch and of the partial Yugoslav unity that then prevailed lingered on; the "Illyrist" dream, as has earlier been recounted, experienced checkered fortunes in the nineteenth century, whether in the form of Great Croatia or in the more grandiose program of Bishop Strossmayer.[3]

Croat politicians long gloried in their Austrophile outlook, even though Viennese policy was repeatedly and cruelly disappointing, and even men of the Great Croatian persuasion were usually partisans of trialism. And in the twentieth century the Austrian Christian Socialists, Hapsburg loyalists and Catholics like the Croats, and individual Austro-Germans of prominence and influence looked with sympathy upon a trialistic reorganization of the Monarchy. Foreign Secretary Aehrenthal, for example, toyed with that idea as a sequel to the establishment of untrammeled Hapsburg sovereignty over Bosnia. It is not impossible that if Francis Ferdinand, who, like Crown Prince Rudolph before him, was kindly disposed toward the Croats, and firmly resolved to whittle down Magyar power, had acceded to the throne, he would have striven to create a Yugoslav unit alongside the Austrian and the Hungarian. That this was the Archduke's certain intention has been argued by Ernst Klein, an ardent Austrian monarchist and international journalist.[4]

On behalf of trialism it was urged that this plan would solve the Yugoslav problem within the framework of the Hapsburg Monarchy and would placate the Croats and possibly the Hapsburg Serbs, and that, conceivably, a trialistic state would in time attract the kingdom of Serbia into the Hapsburg circle. Certainly a section of opinion in Serbia thought of union with the Hapsburgs as desirable and mutually profitable; King Milan in the eighties was sympathetic to the idea and in 1892 M. Pirostchanaz, sometime Serbian prime minister, published a little-known brochure in which he frankly proposed the merger of the Balkan states in a federalized Hapsburg Monarchy. "This federal union," he declared, "is an historical and geographical necessity for the peoples of southeastern Europe. Where so many separate nationalities exist, mixed with each other, no other political system is practicable."[5]

Yet because of the momentum which the Greater Serb concept attained in the twentieth century it is very doubtful whether trialism would have eliminated the Pan-Serb challenge to the integrity of the Dual Monarchy. It was also argued by Austrian proponents of trialism that such an arrangement would undermine the powerful position that Hungary held in the common affairs of the Monarchy, for whenever differences arose, Austria, if supported by a third partner, would be able to carry the day against the Magyars. Friends of trialism—some of them—who cherished dreams of evolutionary federalism contended that their plan would be the prelude to the recognition of an autonomous Czech state (quadrilism), and so on to other national groupings until a Hapsburg union of free peoples had come into being.

But the arguments on trialism were not all on one side. Trialism found no support in the ruling classes of Hungary, for a third state would surely lessen the importance and weight of Hungary in the common affairs of the Monarchy; and trialism would entail the loss of Croatia and probably of Fiume, and the renunciation of claims to Dalmatia, which would deprive Hungary of access to the sea—and that when the belief was gaining ground that the future of the kingdom lay upon the water. A Yugoslav unit in the Monarchy would, moreover, exercise a disturbing influence upon the Serbs of southern Hungary and its establishment would tend to strengthen autonomist, if not, indeed, secessionist sentiments among the Rumanians. As for enticing the kingdom of Serbia into the Hapsburg orbit, it was the dominant Magyar opinion that already the Monarchy contained too many Slavs for comfort.

And in Austria weighty arguments against a triune partnership were raised, for Austria would lose direct authority over Dalmatia with its ports and naval stations, and Trieste and the Slovene areas, too, might be embraced in the Yugoslav unit. Were such a state formed, furthermore, it might conceivably coöperate with the Magyars against the crown as the Croat-Serb coalition of deputies had done temporarily during the constitutional conflict of 1905-06. Or, even more dangerous, a Yugoslav state might gravitate toward Belgrade and seek to unite with the kingdom of Serbia.

II

More sweeping and more difficult of practical application than trialism were diverse projects to convert the Dual Monarchy into a really federal association of equal nationalities, each possessing a wide measure of autonomy. Even before the experiment with dualism had begun, active groups and individuals had pleaded and worked for the organization of the Monarchy on federal principles. Responsible leaders of smaller nationalities were consistent exponents of a federalistic reordering of the government; from Palacký through Rieger to Masaryk the line of Czech political thinking, for example, ran straight. And many forward-looking, statesmanlike Austro-Germans, from Adolf Fischhof to Joseph Baernreither and Professor Joseph Redlich, believed that federalism would go far to allay the convulsive nationalistic antagonisms that imperiled the Hapsburg structure. With the approval of Francis Joseph, the Hohenwart ministry, it may be recalled, at the very outset of the seventies was preparing the way for federalism in Austria, but when the emperor, under pressure of events, changed his mind the plan was put into cold storage.

Constitutional reform which would convert the Dual Monarchy into some kind of a federal union was advocated and explained in a spate of books that appeared in the last twenty years of the Monarchy's existence.[6] It was entirely logical that the Austrian Socialists, in keeping with the international orientation of their creed, should formulate and espouse programs for the solution of minority problems by the creation of a supranationality state. Thus at the party congress of 1899, held in the Moravian capital of Brünn, the Social Democrats formally declared themselves, it may again be emphasized, in favor of democratic federalism; instead of the historic Austrian provinces, the empire should be made over into a set of territorial units on a nationality basis. So far as purely national interests were concerned, each unit would have the right of decision, and special provision would be made to safeguard the cultural interests of minorities in districts of mixed nationality. All units, the Socialist resolution affirmed, would participate in a federal government to transact affairs of general concern, and in administration one language, German, would be employed.

Quite in harmony with this viewpoint, individual Socialist thinkers elaborated and refined the party doctrine of cultural autonomy for nationalities. Not that this idea had originated in the brains of Marxists; it had as a matter of fact been worked out with considerable astuteness and reference to realities in middle-class academic circles of the University of Vienna. Socialist writers seized upon the theory and gave it a Marxist slant. One of them was Otto Bauer, a gifted expositor of strait-laced Marxism, who was convinced that nationalist quarrels were simply a manifestation of economic class struggles; in a ponderous but invaluable volume—*Die Nationalitätenfrage und die Sozialdemokratie* (1907)—Bauer elucidated the whole nationality problem with rich historical perspective and summoned Socialists to bend their energies to its solution.

Less doctrinaire, more compelling were the writings of the Moravian-born Socialist leader, Karl Renner, chancellor of the Austrian Republic in 1919 and again in 1945, who, under a variety of pseudonyms, Rudolph Springer for one, argued for federalism as the way out of the nationality perplexities of the Monarchy. Renner was firmly convinced that it was desirable for all concerned that the Danube Monarchy should be preserved and equally persuaded that fundamental revision of the constitution was the only method of salvation. His scheme of reform was set forth, for example, in a weighty book entitled *Grundlagen und Entwicklungsziele der Oesterreichischen-ungarischen Monarchie* (1906). After cleverly criticizing the character of the dualistic regime and pointing up its flaws and frailties,

Renner sketched a wide-ranging, clear-visioned plan for the federalization of Austria, which he felt Hungary, in the name of security and integrity, would be compelled to imitate.

Renner's central theme—the personality principle of national rights—contemplated that all adherents of a given nationality, wherever they lived in the empire, would be organized in a "national association," to which would be entrusted authority over all nationality interests of an unmistakably cultural nature. Put otherwise, each distinct nationality would be organized on much the same terms as were religious confessions, and every citizen might freely register allegiance to the nationality of his choice. Each "national association" would have jurisdiction over the schools and education, for instance, of its particular grouping, and no outsider might interfere with the purely cultural affairs of another nationality. A supreme court of arbitration would smooth out jurisdictional or other controversies between "national associations." It was Renner's confident belief that the application of this scheme of national cultural autonomy would go far to mitigate the perpetual conflicts that envenomed human relations in Austria.

Renner's thinking and program ranged beyond the cultural sphere. Existing provinces would be abolished and Austria would be partitioned, for purposes of local self-government into territorial units (*Kreise*), based on nationality as far as practicable. If a unit contained members of only one nationality, the local government would have competence over cultural as well as administrative matters, but if more than one nationality were present it would have merely administrative responsibilities, cultural affairs being regulated by the "national associations." The several territorial units would in turn send representatives to a federal parliament to deal with matters of concern to the whole Monarchy. In that fashion Austria would be converted into a "democratic Switzerland with a monarchical apex"; Hungary would follow along afterward. Some partisans of the Renner scheme were of the opinion that if Austria were transformed as he recommended the neighboring countries of Rumania and Serbia could be drawn into the Hapsburg union.

For all their attractiveness, the theories of these Socialists were never put to demonstration. Yet they had considerable influence upon subsequent thinking on minority rights and guarantees to safeguard them, not in Austria alone but in Europe entire.

Rather more acceptable to the ruling authorities than the formulations of the Socialists was the federalistic scheme broached by Aurel Popovici in *Die Vereinigten Staaten von Gross Oesterreich* (1906). The author, a Hungarian Rumanian intellectual, who had been active on behalf of his fellow nationals, composed the book in foreign exile. His conception of federalism, which was patterned more or less upon the governmental institutions of the

United States of America, exalted the principle of the integrity of the Hapsburg lands; in his judgment, Magyar separatism and oppression of non-
Magyars were driving the Danube Monarchy onto the rocks of destruction.

Popovici believed that the Monarchy had a vital mission to perform
in the valley of the Danube and in the Balkans. "All the peoples concerned
are at bottom devoted to the Austrian idea," he declared, "for between all of
them there exists an inner community of interest . . . A Great Austria which
would do justice . . . to all her peoples would have a special mission beyond
her own frontiers in eastern Europe, and by fulfilling it would render her
own future secure." He likened the Monarchy as it stood to a great house
chock-full of quarrelsome families; the house required to be modernized and
divided into apartments.

Popovici's project for "doing justice" to the several nationalities called for
the organization of the Hapsburg realm into fifteen autonomous units: three
German, three Yugoslav, two Magyar, two Italian, one Polish, one Ruthenian,
one Czech, one Slovak, and one Rumanian. Each unit would have a legislature of its own to decide purely local matters and all would send delegates
to a central parliament.[7] The federal government, to be called "the United
States of Great Austria," and defined as a constitutional monarchy, with
headquarters at Vienna, would have jurisdiction over foreign affairs and the
fighting services and would legislate on matters of concern to all nationalities
such as jurisprudence, tariffs, trade and coinage, railways, and sanitation.
Member states in "Great Austria" would enjoy home rule, exercised through
local parliaments and responsible ministries, in all spheres not specifically assigned to the jurisdiction of the federal government, and disputes between
member states would be adjusted by a federal supreme court. While each
autonomous unit would choose its own official language, German would
serve as the *lingua franca* in the fighting forces, in the bureaus of the central
government, and in transactions between the several autonomous units.

Popovici was aware of the points at which his proposals would be attacked
and endeavored to counteract all possible adverse arguments in advance. He
realized, too, that the transformation he was advocating could not be brought
to pass by processes of parliamentary decision; wherefore, he recommended
that the change-over should be accomplished by the arbitrary act of the
crown.

Some leaders of minority fragments in Hungary, Austrian Christian
Socialists, certain Bohemian Germans of weight, and Roman Catholic Yugoslavs responded sympathetically to the broad outlines of Popovici's scheme,
though it was felt that modification and refinement in details would be
necessary. Certain Rumanian and Slovak critics, for instance, thought too
much authority was assigned to the central government; yet Slovak politicians were ready to discuss the plan as the prelude to a "Danubian Com-

monwealth of Nations." [8] And Francis Ferdinand looked upon the Great Austrian project with no little favor, for it may have paralleled his personal conclusions on the manner in which a united monarchy with a strong ruler could be ensured.[9]

Czech and Polish spokesmen, on the other hand, were hostile to the projected partition of Bohemia and Galicia, a large share of the influential Vienna press poured cold water on the plan, and Magyars were positively infuriated and registered Popovici's work on the Index of Forbidden Books.[10]

Without conspicuous exceptions, the Magyar governing caste was adamantly and obtusely opposed to any remodeling of the constitutional structure that would in any wise impair the integrity of the Hungarian kingdom. If the dualistic regime were reconstructed, many a Magyar politician thought, the revision should take the form of a reduction of the Hungarian bond with Austria to the mere person of the sovereign, leaving the Magyars even wider authority in public affairs than they had.

Another current of Magyar thought cherished fantastic visions of a Greater Hungary and argued that Austria must inevitably become a mere annex of the Hungarian state. "The more quickly the gentlemen in Vienna grasp that truth the better for all concerned," one Magyar extremist blandly remarked.[11] Budapest in this view was destined to become the center of political gravity not alone for the Hapsburg peoples but for the Balkans. Count Stephen Tisza was the most prominent upholder of this concept in the twentieth century.

Profoundly disgusted with the confusion that reigned in the snarling Austrian parliament, Tisza thought that the realm of the Hapsburgs could be spared from destruction only if Hungary were indisputably paramount. Devout Calvinist that he was, Tisza believed that he personally had been invested by Providence with the holy mission of keeping the Monarchy intact, and to succeed in that task he was willing to suffer any ignominy. In a letter to his friend, Baron Burián, Tisza voiced, in unequivocal language, antipathy to any constitutional reform that would lessen the power of the Magyars.

"The Hungarian nation," he wrote, "cannot abandon its right to stand on equal terms with all the other states united under the scepter of the common sovereign, and it cannot allow itself to be placed in a position to be outvoted by the others. It cannot surrender the constitutional rights which it has acquired at the cost of centuries filled with bloody combats; and it cannot permit itself to sink to the status of a province in an enlarged empire which would wield the supreme authority." [12] It is as plain as a pikestaff that changes in existing constitutional institutions, whether along trialistic or federalistic lines, would have had to be effected over the prostrate forms of Magyar politicians.[13]

Furthermore, no scheme of constitutional revision that promised to subordinate Germans to Czechs in Bohemia or to put Ruthenians on a parity with Poles would have the support of Austro-German or Polish public men. And the thought was never out of the mind of Hapsburg policy makers that federalization might stimulate secessionist tendencies among Italians, Rumanians, and Yugoslavs, at least, perhaps among Austro-Germans as well.

Francis Joseph was not concerned in his later years with questions of internal reconstruction, but Francis Ferdinand, as has been indicated, was known to desire thoroughgoing changes, though in precisely what direction must remain conjectural until his private papers are available for scholarly scrutiny. It is almost certain, however, that he intended to postpone his coronation as king of Hungary until the constitution had been remodeled. Yet many Austrians who worked with him have doubted whether he possessed the resolution to carry out his intentions in the teeth of the certain resistance of the Magyars, particularly if the authorities in Berlin abetted them. In any case, the murder of the Archduke at Sarajevo in June of 1914 dealt a staggering blow to those who anticipated that his accession to the throne would be followed by a "new constitutional deal" in the old Monarchy.

III

Whether without the intervention of World War I the Hapsburg Monarchy would have endured much longer must always remain, as it has already been, a subject of lively academic speculation. The Hapsburg institution, like others, carried within it the seeds of its own destruction. Nonetheless, four terribly wasting years of war, crowned by catastrophic military defeat and accompanied by cruel human suffering and militant separatist propaganda, were required to bring about the actual dissolution of the realm. That record in itself proves that the seemingly "unworkable anachronism" of the Hapsburgs possessed elements of toughness and vitality which the clashing national disharmonies tended to conceal or smother. What indeed were the sources of strength of the venerable Hapsburg state, what the forces that combined to hold the congeries of Irelands which was Austria-Hungary together?

Palacký's oft-quoted utterance that if Austria had not existed it would have been necessary to create her applied with peculiar force in the economic sphere.[14] In greater or lesser degree, all Hapsburg citizens benefited from living in the largest free-trade area in Europe outside of Russia, and tariff protection shielded manufacturers from the superior industrial establishments of Germany and Britain and guarded agricultural producers from transatlantic, Russian, and Balkan competition. The maintenance of economic unity under dualism was possible because when the customs union was from time to time prolonged Austria almost invariably made concessions to Hungary—concessions which tended to work to the injury of Austrian manufactures and were of advantage to Hungarian agriculture and industry. At the renewal in 1907, the customs union was for the first time defined as a treaty, an arrangement which underscored the fact that the economic partnership was wearing thin and suggested that when the treaty expired in 1917 the Magyars might be content with nothing short of full economic independence. Roseate Hungarian plans for industrial progress looked, in fact, to the time when the kingdom would be essentially self-sufficient in manufactured goods.

Across the generations of political unity the economy of the Hapsburg peoples and provinces had become integrated, though huge disparities existed between west and east in material development and standards of comfort. A kind of rudimentary division of labor had evolved, with the productions of one region complementing those of another. Greater specialization was handicapped by traditional differences in customs and costumes, in the methods of farming, by the hindrance which linguistic differences imposed, and by the low purchasing ability of the mass of the population. But with the passing of time a delicate economic balance had emerged, production and consumption within the borders of the Monarchy were fairly matched, and, except for rubber, cotton, nickel, copper, and wool, the Hapsburg dominions were virtually self-sustaining.

Surpluses of wheat and corn and livestock raised on the plains of Hungary and Galicia were advantageously marketed in the industrialized areas of Austria. And Italian winegrowers had more profitable outlets than would have been theirs if they had been citizens of the kingdom of Italy. The timber of the Alpine provinces and of the northern reaches of Hungary, the coal of Bohemia and Moravia, the iron ore and magnesite of Styria, the oil of Galicia—these resources met the requirements of other sections of the sprawling realm remarkably well. Moreover, large-scale industries in Bohemia, in the Vienna area, in Styria, in parts of Hungary, all of which expanded phenomenally in the decade before 1914, went far to satisfy the rising though still relatively limited demands for finished textiles and other manufactures; and Vienna was the financial and commercial heart of the realm, with arteries running off in every direction.

True, competitive nationalisms generated friction in the economic sphere in the form of local boycotts and the like. Yet the material advantages of the Hapsburg union were pretty generally recognized, save in extreme secessionist circles. Representative Czech, Magyar, Slovak, and Slovene spokesmen acknowledged that their nationalities were too small to form viable independent states in an age of mass production demanding broad markets.

Integration of trade and exchange was matched and promoted by the transportation facilities of the Dual Monarchy. The great Danube and her tributaries tied the realm together except for the provinces of Galicia, the Bucovina, Dalmatia, and Vorarlberg. The Danube was the natural highway for internal commerce, though as a means of world trade the river had two major drawbacks: the haul to the principal markets of western Europe was circuitous and long; and traders had always to reckon with possible political complications at the lower end of the river and in the Turkish-ruled zone of the Straits.

Railways that discharged their burdens at Trieste or Fiume afforded better communication to the west than the Danube, and trackage into the Balkans facilitated business to the southeast. After 1890, the international trade of the Monarchy actually advanced more rapidly than exchange between Austria and Hungary. Internal commerce profited enormously from the network of railways; as a rule, lines followed historic trade routes linking the different sections of the Monarchy in economic interdependence to a degree that had not been true when the Danube and roads had been the sole ways of travel. Uniformity of gauge prevailed on the principal railways, though there was no uniformity in rates, since both Austria and Hungary—the latter more energetically than her partner—manipulated charges so as to foster their respective economies rather than to promote the common welfare of the realm.

So long as the Monarchy remained intact, it would confer material blessings on all national groupings; in union there was economic strength. Dissolution, likely enough, would bring lowered standards of comfort, already exceedingly low in the more backward and unprogressive sections. Logic of this order (or something like this) proved a potent force in holding the supranational state together.

The heritage of political traditions and of a common dynasty was another substantial unifying bond in the Dual Monarchy. For many generations the Hapsburg family had been the connecting link between the motley complex of peoples and provinces of the realm. Conservatism, the force of inertia, the dead hand of the past were themselves subtle bonds of solidarity.

Through the churches, particularly the Roman Catholic, through the fighting services, and partly through the press and schools, loyalty to the ruling house was inculcated. Roman Catholic clergymen, conservative for the most part, were notably *Hapsburgtreue,* allied with the dynasty for mutual self-perpetuation, and their sway over parishioners carried all the weight of centuries of hallowed acceptance. Some divines, to be sure, enlisted in national movements with centrifugal tendencies, but they were distinctly in a minority, and seldom were national patriots found in the higher, more influential offices of the Church. Of the value of Catholicism as an agency in holding the disparate peoples together, Hapsburg statesmen were fully aware; and in different ways and words many a leader gave voice to the conviction ascribed to

Bach in the fifties: "The only sound internal policy for Austria is one which is favorable to Catholicism. The Monarchy has really only two sound bases for its unity: the dynasty and religion." [15]

It was the considered judgment of the distinguished British Catholic historian, Lord Acton, that the Dual Monarchy was the perfect exemplar of Christian polity because it bound together a large number of distinctive nationalities by common attachment to Church and Crown.

In the rural districts especially, the sentiment of dynastic patriotism was strong and real, and the circumstance that Francis Joseph had reigned so long and refused to die tightened that sentimental and moral bond. No other monarch of Europe in all probability was so popular nor so beloved by his subjects as the old Hapsburger, who posed as mediator, as it were, between the jarring sections and nationalities, the guardian of monarchical unity. It was often prophesied that his departure would remove one of the stoutest pillars of the state, unless his successor possessed personal qualities and a political outlook that were almost universally appealing.

A consideration of a negative sort that contributed to the perdurance of the Dual Monarchy was the inability or unwillingness of the politicians of the lesser nationalities to join forces for simultaneous or sustained action against the *status quo*. Austrian Slavs, despite the untiring efforts of men like Masaryk, were more generally at odds with one another than coöperative for common ends; seldom did Poles in particular see eye to eye with Czechs and Yugoslavs. And rarely was coöperation among the chiefs of the Hungarian minorities anything more than sporadic or halfhearted; and, of course, Magyar policies were emphatically calculated to prevent the formation of a united front.

Moreover, the government at Vienna had traditionally fostered ill will between the various nationalities on the assumption that if they fought with one another they could the more readily be governed. Shrewd observations of Emperor Francis I to the French ambassador at his court possessed a certain enduring validity. "My peoples," he said, "are strangers to one another; so much the better. They do not take the same diseases at the same time. In France, when the fever comes, it seizes you all on the same day. I place Hungarians in Italy, Italians in Hungary, each guards his neighbor. They do not understand each other and they detest each other. From antipathies is born order and from their reciprocal hates general peace." [16] Count Taaffe, we are told, boasted that as prime minister he contrived to govern Austria "by keeping all the nationalities in a state of uniform, nicely tempered discontent." [17]

And yet it is defiance of fact to accept without reservation the assertion sometimes met with that in the dualistic era the ruling class elevated the principle of "divide and rule" into a deliberate and consistent doctrine of public policy. In many parts of the dominions it was unnecessary indeed for the Hapsburg to stir up national discontents, for local political and social differences, fostered by intensifying nationalisms, taught Croats and Slovenes to hate Italians, Poles to despise Ruthenians and vice versa, the Magyars to look down upon all Hungarian minorities, Czechs and Germans to engage in mutual recriminations, and so forth. National prejudices and jealousies required no subtle stimulation from on high and got relatively little in the age of dualism. The aphorism that "the Hapsburgs ruled their dominions by a judicious distribution of discontent," like many another clever epigram, carries more journalistic color than historical validity.

Historically, the Hapsburg official world, the bureaucracy, both civilian and military, had been a unifying and consolidating institution of considerable significance, and that continued to be true in large measure to the very end of the life of the Dual Monarchy. Bureaucratic conventions reaching back to the eighteenth century and reinforced in the age of Metternich lingered on without radical modification, though, in consequence of the rapid expansion of the bureaucracy in the dualistic period, *esprit* appears to have deteriorated; new recruits failed to measure up to traditional standards of diligence and service.[18] Civil servants were greatly increased as social-welfare legislation was extended and government took over the management of railways and other services. It was frequently charged, in Hungary especially but in Austria as well, that there were altogether too many officials for the work that had to be done.

Public servants were modestly compensated, assured of pensions in the eventide of life, and enjoyed a certain social prestige. Many of the lower positions were filled by former noncommissioned officers in the army while the more responsible offices were reserved for technically trained experts or the socially accomplished. The various grades of the bureaucracy formed almost exclusive castes and it was not easy to attain a higher rank, unless one were the favorite of an official well up in the hierarchy. Though the real makers of policy were drawn heavily from the German and Magyar nationalities, the central administration was a supranational body, with a growing representation of Slavs after, say, 1880. Mutual "racial" antagonisms in Austria made it impolitic to transfer local officials from one area to another. Rigorous, almost military, discipline prevailed in the bureaus, with their heads exercising tyrannical authority over their subordinates. Ministries rose and ministries fell but the bureaucracy plodded on with dogged persistency.

The standard frailties of bureaucracy were amply exhibited in the Monarchy of Francis Joseph. Civilian officials behaved officially. Bound by rules and red tape, they seemed more concerned with the machinery than with the service they were expected to perform. Energies were consumed by the *paperasserie* of the hour, so that officials seldom looked forward. They were not accustomed to make quick decisions in unusual situations requiring original treatment and they were not given to knot-cutting expedients. Civil servants, in other words, were efficient in a routineering sort of way, cautious, unimaginative, servile toward superiors, surly and even rough in dealing with ordinary citizens. Venality and corruption, on the other side, were minor evils in the bureaucracy of the Hapsburg Monarchy.

An incident involving an English traveler to Vienna tells much about the bureaucracy and its limitations. This gentleman, who was in a great hurry to execute a business transaction, was arrested for alighting from a train a few seconds before the other passengers. Admitting the charge of wrongdoing, he pleaded ignorance of the regulations and declared his willingness to pay the legal fine. But he was bluntly informed that customary legal formalities would have to be observed and he was haled before a police official. At an interview consuming more than an hour, the culprit had to answer questions concerning his place of birth, the Christian name of his wife, his religious affiliation, and whether a nonconformist could not be described as a member of the Church of England. That completed satisfactorily, he was allowed to pay the small fine and at last released.

Close surveillance by police officials over the goings and comings of citizens was accounted another shortcoming of the Hapsburg bureaucracy. Every man habitually carried on his person an official certificate of his identity and good standing, just as a vessel on the high seas carried her papers. Supervision over the press and societies of all sorts was vigilant and inquisitorial.

Loyalty to the Monarchy and the established order were surely traits of the Hapsburg bureaucracy. Among lesser officials in Austria, evidence of separatist feeling was not unknown, but it was never pronounced, while in Hungary civil servants were uniformly Magyar or Magyarone. Men drawn into the joint ministries seldom showed national sentiments. Officials in the foreign office were exceptionally harmonious; one who served there for fourteen years knew of only a single dispute caused by differences in nationality.[19]

As a rule, the higher Hapsburg officials were recruited from families in which service to the dynasty was a settled tradition. For them devotion to monarchical interests transcended all considerations of nationality. Officers in the fighting services, too, displayed that sense of loyalty which was characteristic of their profession the world around. Aristocratic and well-to-do elements of the Monarchy, more so perhaps in Austria than in Hungary, were, speaking generally, *Hapsburgtreue,* if for no other reason because they feared that radical political change would be accompanied by social upheaval. These classes constituted a mighty pillar of the *status quo.*

And dread of the consequences of disintegration effectively operated to keep Hungary and Austria from flying apart. "Nothing holds Austria and

Hungary together," wrote the American minister to Vienna in 1895, "but the fear of the result of separation and the great personal influence of Francis Joseph. Separation means disintegration; it means the creation of two or more smaller states, the loss of prestige which the nation has held so long in the affairs of Europe: its erasure from the list of the Great Powers and the degradation of each to the place occupied by the smaller and dependent nations. It means more, it means subjection to the great nations which make and unmake the map of Europe as well as shape the policy of other continents. Hungary would at once become the prey of the Slavs by which she is surrounded, while Austria would become bound to Germany." [20]

Common international interests and mutual concern for the security and integrity of their respective states helped to keep the dominant Austro-Germans and the Magyars together; for defense, as in trade, they realized their interdependence. Overriding the endless bickerings and dissensions between these two groups was the conviction that unless they presented a common front in foreign affairs both would go down in common ruin. Only the more extreme and turbulent of the Magyar chauvinists ignored this truth.

Austro-German, Magyar, and Pole distrusted the ambitions and power of Russia, real or fancied, and feared the spread of corrosive Pan-Slav propaganda and the vaunted aspirations of the Great Serb propaganda. Mistrust and hatred of Italy were almost universal in the Monarchy; even dissidents among the Yugoslavs cherished that emotion. By reason of their apprehensions, Austro-German and Magyar at least looked upon the alliance with Germany as their shield and buckler; and the influence of Germany upon the Monarchy was in itself a not inconsiderable unifying force.

The fighting services, finally, raised on the principle of manhood liability, infused vitality into the monarchical regime. However deficient the army may have been in capacity for war as compared with the great German or French military machines, it was at once a visible symbol of the unity of the Monarchy and an earnest of the intention to perpetuate the state. Until the very smash-up of the realm the paean of Grillparzer to the Hapsburg army, "In deinem Lager ist Oesterreich," rang true. Francis Joseph, it has already been emphasized, would brook no compromise on any proposal that threatened to impair the solidarity of the armed forces; he never forgot that the sword had saved the dynasty in 1848 and he consistently balked Magyar pressures for an independent Hungarian army.

The medley of tongues in the armed services, as in other phases of life, created everlasting difficulties. German served as the official language and commands were given in German, but few noncommissioned officers spoke German except men from German districts, and fewer could read and write the army language. Officers were expected to be familiar with the language or languages of their men, but since such linguistic attainments were rare a synthetic tongue called "horse German" was spoken in Slav regiments.

An observer who watched military maneuvers turned humorist in describing the linguistic trials of officers. While he talked with a battery commander, a cavalry patrol pulled up "and the leader . . . reported something in Czech. The captain, not conversant with the language . . . questioned him in German but could get no other answer but '*Nerozumin*' (I do not understand). While the captain was giving orders to a lieutenant to go reconnoitering with a dozen men a second patrol . . . arrived. The excited leader spoke very rapidly and sonorously in Magyar. Every question of the captain was answered monotonously with '*Nemtudom*' (I do not understand) . . . Then a panting sergeant . . . gabbled most furiously in Polish and to the captain's eager query, 'Can you not speak German?' he had but one answer: '*Neznam*' (I do not understand)." [21]

Owing to the polyglot composition of the army it is not surprising that there was lively skepticism, both within the Monarchy and outside, as to the fighting and staying qualities of the forces in the event of war. To cite but a single illustration, Governor Casimir Badeni of Galicia, who had won the plaudits of the authorities in Vienna for the manner in which he had kept the province steady during the grave Russian war scares of 1886–87, remarked in 1895, "Every war [is] an impossibility for Austria. Should we be attacked, we must accept the situation with God's help . . . A State of nationalities can make no war without danger to itself. Among a conglomeration of nations victory or defeat causes almost equal difficulty." [22]

Nonetheless, out of the babel of tongues a manageable army was fashioned by the professional officers' corps, who were recruited largely from the German and Magyar elements in the Monarchy. In their first lessons these professional soldiers were indoctrinated with the idea that they formed a military brotherhood with the sacrosanct monarch as their grand master and all were obliged to swear personal fealty to the crown. Within the officers corps a spirit of camaraderie tended to blot out national heritages and distinctions. Bismarck's reflection that "in Bohemia the antagonism between Germans and Czechs has in some places penetrated so deeply into the army that the officers of the two nationalities in certain regiments hold aloof from one another even to the degree that they will not eat at mess," [23] contains more than a kernel of truth, but gives a somewhat distorted impression of the general situation in the Hapsburg officers' corps.

Raw conscripts drawn into the military service were inculcated with some kind of dynastic sentiment and discipline which counteracted, or tended to counteract, the particular national patriotism that had touched them in their boyhood environments. The Hapsburg army was, in fact, a veritable monarchical melting pot, a school of the civic virtues of devotion and discipline. At induction, soldiers swore a "solemn oath to God Almighty, of loyalty and obedience to His Majesty, our exalted Prince and Master, Francis Joseph, Emperor of Austria, King of Hungary . . . Also to obey his generals, to follow their orders against every enemy whatever . . . at all times, in all places, and on all occasions, to fight manfully and bravely, and in this way to live and die in honor. So help us God! Amen!" Aside from dynastic feelings, the great majority of the soldiers were united by their common Catholicism, of which the troops were constantly reminded by the image of the Madonna that figured on the Hapsburg banners and by the mass celebrated by the chaplain.

Disaffection and discontent among the rank and file, inspired by considerations of nationality, were by no means unheard of, and that was unquestionably a weak link in the monarchical armor. And yet, except among some of the Slav soldiers, Czechs notably, who threw down their arms when ordered against Russia, months elapsed after the cannon began to boom in 1914 before national antagonisms or ideological cleavages seriously affected the prosecution of the war. And the spirit of monarchical patriotism was conspicuously fervent in the naval services of the House of Hapsburg.

IV

Once upon a time the Hapsburg mission in central Europe had been to stem and then to hurl back the onrushing forces of the Turk and to preserve and extend western European civilization along the great Danube reaching from the Black Forest to the Black Sea. In very modern times the task of the Dual Monarchy was to maintain in a single political community an array of discordant, more or less nationalistically intoxicated peoples. Economic traditions and conditions, the historical and dynastic heritage, the wide popularity of Francis Joseph, the absence of concord among the smaller national groupings, the monarchical patriotism of the official, conservative, aristocratic, and well-to-do classes, and the menace of external dangers—these circumstances enabled the ancient realm of the Hapsburgs to maintain its standing as one of Europe's great powers.

And many months of extraordinary strain and war stress were required to bring the old structure tumbling to the ground. After the collapse, a wise wit likened the Danube Monarchy to a beautiful old vase whose value was depreciated until it fell to the floor and shivered into fragments.

Notes

Bibliography

NOTES

I · THE REALM OF THE HAPSBURGS

1. A concise and lucid survey of Austria's early history in all its aspects is available in F. M. Mayer, R. F. Kaindl, and Hans Pirchegger, *Geschichte und Kulturleben Deutschösterreichs*, 3 vols. (Vienna, 1929–1937). It contains copious notes on scholarly contributions to Austrian history, and I have confined my references to works of merit, more particularly in the English language, not therein noted.

2. A. W. A. Leeper, *A History of Medieval Austria* (New York: Oxford University Press, 1941).

3. Oswald Redlich, *Rudolf von Habsburg* (Innsbruck, 1903).

4. R. W. Seton-Watson, *Maximilian I* (London, 1902).

5. Jan Herben, *John Huss and His Followers* (London, 1926).

6. C. A. Macartney, *Magyars in the Ninth Century* (Cambridge, 1930).

7. Ruthene, which is derived from the medieval Latin Ruthenus, meaning Russian, was a term commonly used for the Ukrainians of the Hapsburg realm.

8. Wilhelm Fráknoi, *König Matthias Hunyádi* (Freiburg: 1891).

9. R. B. Merriman, *Suleiman the Magnificent* (Cambridge: Harvard University Press, 1944), esp. chapter iv, "Mohács."

10. Henry Marczali, *Hungary in the Eighteenth Century* (Cambridge, 1910).

11. R. J. Kerner, *Bohemia in the Eighteenth Century* (New York: Macmillan, 1932).

12. S. K. Padover, *The Revolutionary Emperor, Joseph the Second* (New York: Ballou, 1934).

13. Francis II, the last Holy Roman Emperor; Francis I, first emperor of Austria.

14. On the Vienna meetings, consult the lucid and brilliant study by Harold Nicolson, *The Congress of Vienna* (London: Constable, 1946). Metternich was made a prince in 1825.

15. R. J. Rath, "Training for Citizenship in the Austrian Elementary Schools During the Reign of Francis I," *Journal of Central European Affairs*, IV (1944), 145–164.

16. Helene du Coudray, *Metternich* (New Haven: Yale University Press, 1936) and Peter Viereck, *Conservatism Revisited, the Revolt against Revolt, 1815–1849* (New York: Scribner, 1949).

17. Jerome Blum, *Noble Landowners and Agriculture in Austria, 1815–1848* (Baltimore: Johns Hopkins Press, 1948).

18. Kossuth, who came of minor noble stock, Lutheran in faith, earned a degree in law and served as a local administrator before being sent to the Hungarian assembly. Although his parents were Slovaks, he stood forth as an ardent Magyar partisan, one of many intellectual apostates of the Slovak nationality. He was a compelling speaker, and his intemperate criticism of Austrian policies led to his imprisonment for three years.

19. For a succinct estimate of Palacký and his meaning for the Czech nationality, consult Hans Kohn, *Not by Arms Alone* (Cambridge: Harvard University Press, 1940), pp. 69–83.

20. For a careful, brief study of the upheaval in the Danube monarchy, consult Veit Valentin, *Geschichte der deutschen Revolution von 1848–49* (Berlin: 1930–31), vol. I, chaps. i, vi, vii; vol. II, chaps. ii, iv. Cf. A. J. May, *Contemporary American Opinion of the Mid-Century Revolutions in Central Europe* (Philadelphia, 1927), chaps. iii, iv; Roy Pascal, "The Frankfort Parliament, 1848, and the Drang nach Osten," *Journal of Modern History*, XVIII (1946), 108–122.

21. Adolph Schwarzenberg, *Prince Felix zu Schwarzenberg, Prime Minister of Austria* (New York: Columbia University Press, 1946), a short and incomplete sketch by a great-grandnephew.

22. Between 1848 and 1866 the monarchi-

cal debt almost doubled and outlays for service of the debt consumed a larger part of the revenues than any other appropriation. Since 1789, in fact, Austrian public income had never matched expenditures and all manner of fiscal expedients were resorted to to cover deficits.

II · GOVERNMENTS OF THE DUAL MONARCHY

1. C. W. Clark, *Franz Joseph and Bismarck* (Cambridge: Harvard University Press, 1934).

2. *Memoirs of Friedrich Ferdinand Count von Beust*, 2 vols. (London, 1887), pp. iv–v.

III · GERMAN LIBERAL PREDOMINANCE IN AUSTRIA

1. Bonar to Stanley, Dec. 31, 1867, Public Record Office, London, MSS, Foreign Office, *Austria*, 7/728.

2. Jay to Fish, June 22, 1869, U. S. National Archives, Dept. of State, MSS, *Austria*, Despatches, VIII.

3. Jay to Fish, June 22, 1869, U. S. National Archives, Dept. of State, MSS, *Austria*, Despatches, VIII.

4. S. P. Mizwa, ed., *Great Men and Women of Poland* (New York: Macmillan, 1942), chap. xxx.

5. Mizwa, *Great Men and Women of Poland*, chap. xix.

6. It seemed to the United States minister resident in Vienna at the time that the idea of a "Federative system somewhat resembling our own" which would "reconcile the conflicting requirements of the monarchy and the nationalities and combine as in America national strength with local self-government" was gaining in popularity. "The thought," he continued, "that America has had the Orleans territory with a French population, Florida with the Spaniards, a yearly invasion of Germans and Irish, and four million negroes is not forgotten by the Austrian advocates of a Federation. The greatest difference in the two countries," he thought, "is in the far lower tone of the masses of the people as regards morals, education, intelligence, Christianity and civilization." Jay to Fish, April 2, 1870,

April 8, 1870, U. S. National Archives, Dept. of State, MSS, *Austria*, Despatches, IX.

7. Bloomfield to Clarendon, February 1, 1870, Public Record Office, London, MSS, Foreign Office, *Austria*, 7/764.

8. For the composition of the Austrian parliament in 1871, see Eric Fischer, "The Negotiations for a National Ausgleich in Austria in 1871," *Journal of Central European Affairs*, II (1942), 134–145.

9. Consult for these exchanges A. E. F. Schäffle, *Aus meinen Leben*, 2 vols. (Berlin, 1905).

10. The concept of democratic equality was, of course, alien to Austrian political thought. Nineteen electors on the average would elect a deputy from the Bohemian landlord curia, while at the other extreme fully a million peasants would choose the 131 deputies allotted to their class. Women, curiously, were eligible to vote in the large-proprietor curia.

11. Cölestin Wolfsgruber, *Cardinal Rauscher* (Freiburg, 1888), pp. 210 ff.

12. Jerome Blum, "Transportation and Industry in Austria, 1815–1848," *Journal of Modern History*, XV (1943), 24–38.

13. Max Wirth, *Geschichte der Handelkrisen* (Frankfurt, 1885).

14. Hans Rosenberg: "Political and Social Consequences of the Great Depression of 1873–1896 in Central Europe," *Economic History Review*, XIII (1943), 58–73.

IV · AUTONOMOUS HUNGARY
1867–1875

1. The trends and tides of parliamentary representation in the period 1867–1915, as well as a concise characterization of each political party, is graphically depicted in *Hungarian Peace Negotiations* 3 vols. in 4 (Budapest, 1920–1922), vol. IIIb, p. vii.

2. Béla Menczer, "Joseph Eötvös and Hungarian Liberalism," *Slavonic Review*, XVII (1938–39), pp. 527–538.

3. On Strossmayer, see R. W. Seton-Watson, *The Southern Slav Question and the Hapsburg Monarchy* (London, 1911), chap. vi; Charles

Loiseau, "Strossmayer, son époque et son oeuvre," *Le monde slave,* XIV (1937), pp. 423–450; Adrian Fortescue, "A Slav Bishop: Joseph George Strossmayer," *Dublin Review,* CLXIII (1918), pp. 234–257.

4. Originally Croatia was allotted twenty-nine deputies, but the number was subsequently raised to forty and Croatia was given three seats in the house of magnates.

5. Hermann Wendel, *Aus dem südslawischen Risorgimento* (Gotha, 1921).

6. L. H. Lehmann, ed., *Bishop Strossmayer's Speech in the Vatican Council of 1870* (New York: Agora Publishing Co., 1941).

7. Vladimir Zagorsky, *François Rački et la renaissance scientifique et politique de la Croatie (1828–1894)* (Paris, 1909).

8. M. I. Pupin, *From Immigrant to Inventor* (New York, 1929), pp. 7–9.

9. Vasa Stajić, "Svetozar Miletić," *Slavonic Review,* v (1926), pp. 106–113.

10. Pupin, *From Immigrant to Inventor,* pp. 154–156.

11. Owing to the electoral laws, only in the Saxon areas were non-Magyars sufficiently strong to force the use of a tongue other than Magyar in the assembly records.

12. As late as 1910, churches operated over two-thirds of the Hungarian schools.

V · THE GREAT RENUNCIATION

1. Andrássy to Beust, June 22, 1877, *Slavonic Review,* X (1931), pp. 449–450.

2. The idea that the Austro-German alliance was "a form of annexation on the part of the Hohenzollern empire" long haunted imaginative minds. See, for example, André Géraud, "The Anglo-French Alliance," *Foreign Affairs,* XVIII (1940), p. 601.

3. Stephen Burián, *Austria in Dissolution,* English trans. (London, 1925), p. 245.

4. Quoted in Antoine Guilland, *Modern Germany and Her Historians,* English trans. (London, 1915), p. 287.

5. H. W. Steed, *The Hapsburg Monarchy* (London, 1913), p. 187.

6. Cf. Steed, *The Hapsburg Monarchy,* pp. 194–201.

7. Theodore v. Sosnosky, *Die Balkanpolitik Oesterreich Ungarns seit 1866,* 2 vols. (Stuttgart, 1913–1914), vol. I, p. 95.

8. Alfred Fischel, *Der Panslawismus bis zum Weltkriege* (Stuttgart, 1919), pp. 395–399.

9. *Ibid.,* pp. 400–404.

10. R. W. Seton-Watson, "Les Relations de l'Autriche et de la Serbie entre 1868 et 1874 . . . ," *Le Monde Slave,* I (1926), 210–30; II (1926), 186–204, 273–288.

11. Lord Newton, *Lord Lyons,* 2 vols. (London, 1913), vol. I, p. 162. See G. W. Prange, "Beust's Appointment as Austrian Foreign Minister," *University of Iowa Studies in the Social Sciences,* XI (1941), 221–223.

12. Loftus to Stanley, January 18, 1868, Veit Valentin, *Bismarcks Reichsgründung im Urteil englishcher Diplomaten* (Amsterdam: Elsevier, 1937), pp. 535–537.

13. Walter Platzhoff, "Die Anfänge des Dreikaiserbundes (1867–1871)," *Preussische Jahrbücher,* CLXXXVIII (1922), 283–306, 286, 304.

14. K. A. Schierenberg, *Die deutschefranzösische Auseinandersetzung und die Luxemburger Frage . . .* (Luxemburg: Beffort, 1933).

15. For a careful study of the voluminous literature on Napoleon's diplomatic maneuvers involving Austria, consult Anton Lamberti, *Die Bündnisverhandlungen Napoleons III gegen Preussen in den Jahren vor 1870* (Würzburg: Triltsch Verlag, 1939).

16. Beust to Metternich, April 27, 1867, Hermann Oncken, *Die Rheinpolitik Kaiser Napoleons III von 1863 bis 1870 . . . ,* 3 vols. (Stuttgart, 1926), vol. II, pp. 361–365.

17. Oncken, *Die Rheinpolitik Kaiser Napoleons III,* vol. II, pp. 454–458; Valentin, *Bismarcks Reichsgründung,* pp. 365–366.

18. Metternich to Beust, Sept. 14, 1868, Oncken, *Die Rheinpolitik Kaiser Napoleons III,* vol. III, pp. 23–26.

19. Metternich to Beust, Oct. 28, 1868, *ibid.,* pp. 53–56. Somewhat later, Clarendon advanced "disarmament" proposals to Bismarck, who haughtily rejected them. Lord Newton, *Lord Stanley,* vol. I, chaps. vi and vii.

20. The treaty is conveniently available in Oncken, *Die Rheinpolitik Kaiser Napoleons III,* vol. III, pp. 186–188.

21. The thesis that Napoleon III was utterly stupid in not purchasing Italian adhesion to the alliance by evacuating Rome is argued by Emile Bourgeois and Emile Clermont, *Rome et Napoleon III* (Paris, 1907), pp. 231–235.

22. Napoleon to Francis Joseph, Sept. 24, 1869, Oncken, *Die Rheinpolitik Kaiser Napoleons III*, vol. III, pp. 235–236.

23. Vitzthum to Beust, Oct. 7, 1869, *ibid.*, pp. 250–252. Remarked Napoleon III, "Je considère nos conventions comme moralement signées . . . L'alliance autrichienne forme donc le pivot de ma politique."

24. Valentin, *Bismarcks Reichsgründung*, pp. 388–389.

25. Lamberti, *Die Bündnisverhandlungen Napoleons III*, pp. 71–74; J. Tassier, *Le Plan de l'archiduc Albert* (Caen, 1903).

26. Lamberti, *Die Bündnisverhandlungen Napoleons III*, pp. 74–75.

27. Beust to Metternich, July 11, 1870, Oncken, *Die Rheinpolitik Kaiser Napoleons III*, vol. III, pp. 421–427.

28. Anonymous, "Count Beust," *Living Age*, CLXXV (1887), p. 657.

29. R. H. Lord, *The Origins of the War of 1870* (Cambridge, 1924), p. 94.

30. Platzhoff, *Die Anfänge des Dreikaiserbundes*, p. 299.

31. Bernhard von Bülow, *Denkwürdigkeiten*, 4 vols. (Berlin, 1930–31), vol. IV, pp. 164–165. The course of Hapsburg diplomacy of the time is learnedly discussed by Friedrich Engel-Janosi, "Austria in the Summer of 1870," *Journal of Central European Affairs*, V (1945–46), 335–353.

32. Bülow, *Denkwürdigkeiten*, vol. IV, p. 163.

33. Oncken, *Die Rheinpolitik Kaiser Napoleons III*, vol. III, pp. 488–489, 515–516.

34. G. H. Rupp, *A Wavering Friendship: Russia and Austria, 1876–1878* (Cambridge: Harvard University Press, 1941), p. 27.

35. Heinrich Mertz, *Die Schwarze-Meer Konferenz von 1871* (Stuttgart, 1927).

36. Actually, little was done in the way of building a Black Sea fleet and in the War of 1877 the tsar's sea force was no match for the sultan's.

37. Heinrich von Treitschke, *His Doctrine of German Destiny and International Relations* (New York, 1914), p. 244.

38. Egon Corti, *Elizabeth, Empress of Austria*, English ed. (New Haven: Yale University Press, 1936), pp. 142, 202.

39. See R. B. Mowat, "Beust," *Hungarian Quarterly*, IV (1938), 247–254.

40. Lytton to Granville, Nov. 23, 1871, Public Record Office MSS, Foreign Office, Austria, 7/791.

41. Fritz Leidner, *Die Aussenpolitik Oesterreich-Ungarns vom Deutsch-Französischen Kriege bis zum Deutsch-Oesterreichischen Bündnis, 1870–1879* (Halle: Akademischer Verlag, 1936), pp. 14–20.

42. B. H. Sumner, *Russia and the Balkans, 1870–1880* (Oxford: Clarendon Press, 1937), p. 86.

43. Cf. W. N. Medlicott, *The Congress of Berlin and After* (London: Methuen, 1938), p. 367.

44. Leidner, *Die Aussenpolitik Oesterreich-Ungarns*, p. 35.

45. Walter Schinner, *Der Oesterreichische-Italienische Gegensatz auf der Balkan und der Adria, 1875–96* (Stuttgart: Kohlhammer, 1936), pp. 8–9.

46. Leidner, *Die Aussenpolitik Oesterreich-Ungarns*, p. 42.

VI · THE NEAR EAST AND THE GERMAN ALLIANCE

1. A. J. Evans, *Through Bosnia and Herzegovina on Foot During the Insurrection . . .* , second ed., enlarged (London, 1877); Joan Evans, *Time and Chance: The Story of Arthur Evans* (London: Longmans, 1943); Charles Yriarte, *Bosnie et Herzegovine* (Paris, 1876).

2. H. W. V. Temperley, *The Bulgarian and Other Atrocities, 1875–8 . . .* (London: Milford, 1931), pp. 4–7.

3. Theodor Sosnosky, *Die Balkanpolitik Oesterreich-Ungarns seit 1866*, 2 vols. (Stuttgart, 1913–14), vol. I, p. 194.

4. David Harris, *A Diplomatic History of the Balkan Crisis of 1875–1878, The First Year* (Stanford: Stanford University Press, 1936), pp. 31–33.

5. G. H. Rupp, *A Wavering Friendship* (Cambridge: Harvard University Press, 1941), pp. 78, 80.

6. Rupp, *A Wavering Friendship*, pp. 96ff.

7. Alois Hajek, *Bulgarien unter der Turkenschaft* (Stuttgart: 1925), pp. 252–293; David Harris, *Britain and the Bulgarian Horrors of 1876* (Chicago: University of Chicago Press, 1939).

8. G. H. Rupp, "The Reichstadt Agreement," *American Historical Review*, XXX (1925), 503–510; *A Wavering Friendship*, pp. 134–151.

9. Bülow, *Denkwürdigkeiten*, vol. IV, p. 397.

10. Rupp, *A Wavering Friendship*, chap. viii.

11. Fischel, *Der Panslawismus*, p. 418.

12. See, for example, Andrássy to Beust, May 29, 1877, *Slavonic Review*, X (1931–32), 191–195.

13. See E. Hertslet, *The Map of Europe by Treaty*, 4 vols. (London, 1875–1891), vol. IV, pp. 2672–2696.

14. Rupp, *A Wavering Friendship*, chap. xiv.

15. Viktor Bibl, *Der Zerfall Oesterreichs*, 2 vols. (Vienna, 1924), vol. II, p. 357.

16. Medlicott, *The Congress of Berlin*, p. 27.

17. D. E. Lee, *Great Britain and the Cyprus Convention Policy of 1878* (Cambridge: Harvard University Press, 1934).

18. Bülow, *Denkwürdigkeiten*, vol. IV, p. 446.

19. By a special Austro-Russian convention Austria might, under certain circumstances undertake the administration of the Sanjak district.

20. H. W. V. Temperley, *Research and Modern History* (London, 1930), p. 16.

21. Gyula Andrássy, *Ungarns Ausgleich mit Oesterreich* (Leipzig, 1897), p. 164.

22. Karl Tschuppik, *Francis Joseph I*, English ed. (New York, 1930), pp. 250–251.

23. C. G. Haines, "Italian Irredentism during the Near Eastern Crisis, 1875–78," *Journal of Modern History*, IX (1937), 23–47.

24. W. K. Wallace, *Greater Italy* (New York, 1917), p. 25.

25. Schinner, *Der Oesterreichische-Italienische Gegensatz*, pp. 9–13.

26. *Ibid.*, p. 53.

27. Alois von Haymerle, *Italicae res* (Vienna, 1878).

28. A. F. Pribram, *The Secret Treaties of Austria-Hungary, 1879–1914*, 2 vols., English ed. (Cambridge, 1920–1922), vol. I, pp. 6–9.

29. S. B. Fay, *The Origins of the World War*, 2 vols., new ed. (New York, 1930), vol. I, pp. 343–344.

VII · THE HAPSBURGS AND THE AUSTRIAN ARISTOCRACY

1. H. W. Steed, *The Doom of the Hapsburgs* (London: Arrowsmith, 1937), p. 24.

2. Eduard Heller, *Kaiser Franzis Joseph I* (Vienna: Schubert, 1934); Eduard von Steinitz, ed., *Erinnerungen an Franz Joseph I* (Berlin: Verlag für Kulturpolitik, 1931), a set of twenty-five valuable sketches, many of them based upon personal association with the emperor-king.

3. Otto Ernst, ed., *Francis Joseph as Revealed by His Letters* (New York, 1927), p. 35.

4. Cf. Stephen Bonsal, *Unfinished Business* (New York: Doubleday, Doran, 1944), pp. 111–114.

5. Rudolph Sieghart, *Die letzten Jahrzehnte einer Grossmacht . . .* (Berlin: Ullstein, 1932), p. 274.

6. Austria, historically, was one of the Catholic powers that could veto any candidate regarded as unfit to become Pope. The right fell into desuetude, and had become something of an anachronism since the Pope was no longer a temporal sovereign. Cardinals protested against Austrian intervention in 1903, but Francis Joseph's act seems to have carried great weight in the Sacred Conclave. Until Austria acted, Rampolla stood first in the balloting, lacking only three votes of election. H. W. Steed, *Through Thirty Years, 1892–1922*, 2 vols. (London, 1924), vol. I, p. 256.

7. Bülow, *Denkwürdigkeiten*, vol. I, p. 159; vol. III, pp. 228–229.

8. Miss Schratt, whose married name was Maria Katharina Kiss de Ittebe, died in 1940, without opening to the public the storehouse of memories in her possession (*New York Times*, April 19, 1940).

9. Ernst, *Francis Joseph As Revealed by His Letters*, p. 227.

10. Oscar Jászi, *The Dissolution of the Habsburg Monarchy* (Chicago, 1929), p. 447.

11. Roosevelt, while in the White House, astonished two Austrian visitors by the knowledge and understanding of the Monarchy's affairs that he possessed. J. M. Baernreither, *Der Verfall des Habsburgerreiches und die Deutschen* (Vienna: Holzhausen, 1939), pp. 141–144.

12. J. B. Bishop, *Theodore Roosevelt and His Time*, 2 vols. (New York, 1920), vol. II, p. 216.

13. S. S. and J. Mildmay and H. St. John, eds., *John Lothrop Motley and His Family* (Boston: 1910), p. 149.

14. Countess Marie Larisch, *Her Majesty Elizabeth* (New York: Doubleday, 1934), pp. 210–212.

15. Bülow, *Denkwürdigkeiten*, vol. I, p. 239.

16. *Eine Orientreise*, 2 vols. (Vienna, 1881); English ed., *Travels in the East* (London, 1884).

17. *Die Oesterreichische-Ungarische Monarchie in Wort und Bild* (Vienna, 1886–1902).

18. Oscar von Mitis, *Das Leben des Kronprinzen Rudolf* (Leipzig, 1928), p. 169.

19. B. S. Zuckerkandl, *My Life and History* (New York: Knopf, 1939), p. 133.

20. Von Mitis, *Das Leben des Kronprinzen Rudolf*, pp. 194–246. See also, for example, Carl Lonyay, *Rudolph, the Tragedy of Mayerling* (New York: Scribner, 1949).

21. As of 1870 the male Austrian nobility of various grades exceeded 87,000, with well over a quarter of them residing in Galicia. Bohemia had only 2,260 nobles, of whom fourteen were princes, 172 counts, and 80 barons.

22. It was the hope of Prince Francis Liechtenstein, sometime Hapsburg ambassador to Russia, that political relations with the tsardom might be bettered by the marriage of the heir presumptive to a Russian archduchess. Francis Ferdinand declined to warm up to the proposal. Von Steinitz, *Erinnerungen an Franz Joseph I*, p. 243.

23. See A. J. May, "The Archduke Francis Ferdinand in the United States," *Journal of the Illinois State Historical Society*, XXXIX (1946), 333–344.

24. Bülow, *Denkwürdigkeiten*, vol. I, p. 184.

25. Rebecca West, *Black Lamb and Grey Falcon*, 2 vols. (New York: Viking, 1941), vol. I, p. 337.

26. By preference, the nobility chose the cavalry; few served in the artillery or as engineers or in other newer and less glamorous branches of the military service.

27. See A. F. Seligmann, "Fürstin Pauline Metternich," *Neue Oesterreichische Biographie*, 8 vols. (Vienna, 1923–1935), vol. III, pp. 43–52.

28. *Der österreichische Adel und sein konstitutioneller Beruf. Mahnruf an die aristokratische Jugend von einem Österreichen* (Munich, 1878).

29. S. K. Padover, *The Revolutionary Emperor, Joseph II* (New York: Ballou, 1934), p. 9.

30. See August Sauer, "Marie Freifrau von Ebner-Eschenbach," *Neue Österreichische Biographie*, vol. I, pp. 146–157.

VIII · THE AUSTRIAN "OTHER HALF"

1. In the archduchy of Austria this practice was abolished in 1868.

2. James Howard, *Continental Farming* (London, 1870), p. 25.

3. For valuable insights into peasant life and labor, see Jan Slomka, *From Serfdom to Self-government . . . 1842–1927* (London: Minerva, 1941).

4. Standard works on Vienna's Jewry are Sigmund Mayer, *Die Wiener Juden . . . 1700–1900* (Vienna, 1917); Max Grunwald, *History of Jews in Vienna* (Philadelphia: Jewish Publication Society, 1936).

5. See Chapter XIII.

6. Count J. N. Wilczek, *Happy Retrospect* (London: Bell, 1934), pp. 40, 242.

7. Census returns of 1910 showed 78.8 per cent Roman Catholic; 12 per cent Uniat, 2.3 per cent Orthodox Catholic; 2.1 per cent Protestant; 4.6 per cent Hebrew. *Statesman's Year Book* (London, 1913), p. 686.

8. Franz Borkenau, *Austria and After* (London: Faber and Faber, 1938), p. 122.

9. See Chapter III.

10. Gaudens Megaro, *Mussolini in the Making* (Boston: Houghton Mifflin, 1938), pp. 165–175.

11. Arthur Chervin, *L'Autriche et la Hongrie de demain* (Paris, 1915), p. 97.

12. The standard work is Georg Loesche, *Geschichte des Protestantismus in Oesterreich*, third ed. (Vienna, 1930).

13. J. Bodmer, "Edward Beneš, the Man," *Contemporary Review*, CLXI (1942), 82–86.

IX · TAAFFE'S IRON RING
1879–1893

1. *United States Consular Reports*, XIX (1886), No. 63, pp. 3ff.

2. A Czech representative at a great student gathering in French Nancy on the edge of Alsace-Lorraine declared in 1892: "We extend to you our hands, close to the bleeding frontier, created by the cruel policy of a brutal power. Our enemies are your enemies, your enemies are ours. No power can keep us apart. Long live France." Certain Russian newspapers frankly identified themselves with the Young Czech policy, which lent color to the hypothesis held in German quarters that if an autonomous Bohemia were created it would be little more than a Muscovite outpost.

3. Thomas Čapek, "Sociological Factors in Czech Immigration," *Slavonic Review*, XXII (1944), 93–98. For a revealing account of Czech immigrants of the Jewish tradition, see Guido Kisch, *In Search of Freedom* (London: Goldston, 1949).

4. Ladislas Jandásek, "The Sokol Movement in Czechoslovakia," *Slavonic Review*, XI (1932), 65–80.

5. Josef Pfitzner, "Die Geschichtsbetrachtung der Tschechen und Deutschen in den Sudetenländern," *Historische Zeitschrift*, CXLVI (1932), 71–85.

6. Anonymous, "Political and Social Poetry among the Czechs," *Review of Reviews*, XLVII (1913), 358–359.

7. Part of the fame of Dvořák was due to gifted pupils. Joseph Suk, who married Dvořák's daughter, faithfully imitated the master's style; his compositions were unmistakably Czech in inspiration, without, however, being stridently nationalistic.

8. According to *Mein Kampf*, Hitler analytically studied Schönerer's technique and later put into practice some of his ideas; appropriately, after National Socialism seized Austria (1938), a prominent Vienna street, which bore the name of the distinguished Jewish poet, Heinrich Heine, was renamed Schönerer.

9. Vogelsang's career and achievements have been extolled by his son-in-law, Wiard Klopp, *Leben und Wirken des Sozialpolitikers Freiherr von Vogelsang* (Vienna, 1930).

10. Consult Rudolf Kuppe, *Karl Lueger und seine Zeit* (Vienna: Oesterreichische Volksschriften, 1933); Eugen Mack, *Karl Lueger, Der Burgermeister von Wien* (Rottenburg, 1910).

11. Dmitro Doroshenko, "Dragomanov and the Ukrainian National Movement," *Slavonic Review*, XVI (1937–38), 654–666; Nicholas Andrusiak, "The Ukrainian Movement in Galicia," *Slavonic Review*, XIV (1935), 162–175, 372–379.

12. Julian Romanczuk, *Die Ruthenen und ihre Gegner in Galizien* (Vienna, 1902).

13. A. J. Klančar, "Josip Jurčič, the Slovene Scott," *American Slavic and East European Review*, V (1945–46), 19–33; W. S. Vucinich, "Modern Yugoslav Drama," *ibid.*, 1–18.

14. Human conditions in Vienna are discussed in Chapter XIII.

15. Glaring inequalities existed in the electoral constituencies of Bohemia. Parchen and Schoenfeld, for instance, German towns with about a thousand residents, each chose a deputy, while the heavily Czech communities of Vinobrady, with 35,000 inhabitants, and Zizkov, with 41,000, were quite unrepresented.

X · THE SOCIAL AND ECONOMIC STRUCTURE OF ROYAL HUNGARY

1. J. B. Bishop, *Theodore Roosevelt and His Time*, 2 vols. (New York, 1920), vol. II, p. 224.

2. Big entailed estates doubled after 1867. Just before 1914, the properties of the Esterházy family totaled 695,000 acres; of the Schönborn, 300,000; of the Károlyi, 218,000;

of the Pállfy, 130,000. Other great landed families were the Pallavicini, Kohary, Barkoczy, Almássy, Festetics, Batthyány, Széchényi, Wenckheim, Dessewffy, Andrássy; in Transylvania, the great magnates included the Bethlens, Telekis, Josikas, and Bánffy.

3. Another aristocrat of competence, Prince

Tassilo Festetics, is described by Zsolt Harsányi, "A Hungarian Magnate," *Hungarian Quarterly*, V (1939), 90–98.

4. Harold Nicolson, *Portrait of a Diplomatist* (Boston, 1930), pp. 58–59.

5. Rather a sport in the aristocratic caste was Count Michael Károlyi, who took up with Socialism, and preached manhood suffrage and dismemberment of the landed properties of the grandees. For his own side of the case, see Michael Károlyi, *Fighting the World* (New York, 1925).

6. C. A. Macartney, *Hungary* (London: Benn, 1934), p. 188.

7. Such a collectivist community of Slovaks in the eighties, which may be taken as reasonably characteristic of similar institutions among Europe's Slavs, was described in this way: "The houses are ranged on both sides of a road some four or five kilometers long. The cultivated lands belonging to each dwelling stretch behind it in an unending strip. The houses of the family communities are distinguished by their vast proportions. Some of them can hold as many as seventy persons. Usually they are two-storied. On the ground floor are a kitchen and a large room in which the old men, the lads and the children sleep. Each married couple has its own room on the first story. All the chattels and real estate form an indivisible collective property, transmitted undivided from generation to generation. The head of the family, the *Wirth,* generally the eldest man, regulates each person's work, but consults the grown members of the community when important decisions are to be taken . . . Everyone puts his earnings, even his earnings outside the family land, into a common till. But everyone also has his private purse; sometimes he distills a certain quantity of grain, sometimes he fattens a calf or pig. The *Wirth's* wife is housekeeper. Meals are taken in common, all helping themselves from one great dish in the center of the table, unless there is meat when the *Wirth* cuts it up and gives each one his share . . . When a member of the household breaks its order or will not obey the *Wirth,* he is expelled with a gift of two florins to help him find work elsewhere. When a girl marries she is given a cow, a bed with its bedding, and a chest." Emile de Laveleye, *Les Communautés de famille et de village,* quoted in H. D. Irvine, *The Making of Rural Europe* (New York, 1923), pp. 38–39.

8. In 1910, 4,580,485 were actually employed in agriculture; 1,622,857 were inde-

pendent proprietors, of whom 1,353,875 averaged a little more than two and a half acres. Over two-thirds of the rural workers had no land and the proportion was higher in northern Hungary. Consult Stephen Jansák, "The Land Question in Slovakia," *Slavonic Review,* VIII (1929), 612–626.

9. Bread made of rye was coarse, almost black in northern Hungary; on festive occasions the peasant ate wheat-flour bread, called in the vernacular *Kalacs* (cake). The Rumanian peasants depended upon corn bread for the most part. Insufficient or improper food laid the poorer peasantry open to the ravages of pellagra, trachoma, and hunger typhus.

10. Beale to Fish, January 30, 1877, U. S. National Archives, Dept. of State, MSS., *Austria,* Despatches, XXIV.

11. Joseph Black to Rives, September 4, 1888, U. S. National Archives, Dept. of State, MSS., Consular Letters, *Budapest,* II.

12. See Chapter XIV.

13. For enlightening details on the movement to Canada, consult A. A. Marchbin, "Early Emigration from Hungary to Canada," *Slavonic Review,* XIII (1934), 126–139.

14. M. I. Pupin, *From Immigrant to Inventor* (New York, 1929), pp. 152ff.

15. 61st Cong., 3rd Session, *Senate Documents,* vol. 12, serial no. 5870 (1911), "The Emigration Situation in Austria-Hungary," p. 388.

16. In his memoirs, Count Dumba, Hapsburg ambassador to the United States from 1913 to 1915, tells us: "A great many Magyars even from the fertile Alföld emigrated to America. These people . . . mainly adherents of the 1848 party, later returned to their home, professed Republicans, to strengthen the extreme radical movement. Mill managers found workers who had been tractable before they left hard to manage on their return; they ascribed the spread of unionism to the American influence." Constantin Dumba, *Memoirs of a Diplomat* (Boston: Little, Brown, 1932), pp. 157–158; a slightly abridged edition of *Dreibund- und Entente-Politik in der alten und neuen Welt* (Vienna, 1931).

17. R. E. Park, *The Immigrant Press and Its Control* (New York, 1922), pp. 417–420.

18. Lajós Hatvány, *Bondy Jr.* (London: Hutchinson, 1932).

19. For a charming account of the emergence and character of a Jewish intellectual, consult the memoirs of the famous Orientalist,

Armin Vambéry, *The Story of My Struggles* (London, 1905).

20. Samuel Gompers, *Labor in Europe and America* (New York, 1910), p. 226.

21. The distribution in the Slovak counties in 1913 is illustrative. That region had 1,631 Roman Catholic schools, 284 Uniat, 474 Lutheran, 221 Calvinist, and 110 Jewish. Along-side them were 712 state schools, 116 communal, and 51 conducted by private societies. Consult Anton Stefánek, "Education in Slovakia," *Slavonic Review* II (1923), 309–329.

22. For an authoritative exposition of the character of Hungarian education, consult Oscar Jászi, *The Dissolution of the Habsburg Monarchy* (Chicago, 1929), pp. 440ff.

XI · THE REIGN OF COLOMAN TISZA

1. Johann von Bazant, *Die Handelspolitik Oesterreich-Ungarns 1875 bis 1892* (Leipzig, 1894).

2. Germany in 1877 adopted stringent measures against the importation of horned cattle and swine from the Dual Monarchy, with the result that exports dropped to a mere fraction of what they had been. It was asserted that Germany's purpose was protection against epidemic disease, but the larger consideration was protection against competition.

3. The expansion of railways as well as many other useful data on Hungarian economic affairs is shown on the maps contained in *The Hungarian Peace Negotiations* (Budapest, 1921), vol. IIIB.

4. Alexandre de Hollán, "The Results of the Measures Taken in Hungary for the Development of Industry," *Economic Journal*, XXI (1911), 137–152.

5. A collection of maps exhibiting the outcome of Hungarian elections, 1866–1915, may be found in *The Hungarian Peace Negotiations* (Budapest, 1921), vol. IIIB.

6. The three Slovak secondary schools had been closed in 1874 and their funds appropriated by the state.

7. Some evidence suggests that this program actually originated in Irredentist circles in Rumania. See Eugene Horváth, *Transylvania and the History of the Roumanians* (Budapest: Sárkány, 1935), pp. 75–76.

8. The editor of the Serb newspaper in Agram, Paul Jovanovič, was nicknamed Dinarič, because he was the recipient of cash (dinars) from Belgrade.

9. Much of value on the involved politics of Croatia may be found in Oskar Mitis, "Crown Prince Rudolf and the Croats," *Slavonic Review*, V (1926–27), 580–593.

10. This demand, which was to envenom political affairs for a generation was, of course, only an aspect of the movement for the independence of Hungary, or at any rate for more complete autonomy. The superficiality of the demand was shown by the fact that fewer than a hundred words were used in commanding troops.

XII · THE TRIPLE ALLIANCE
1880–1897

1. Alfred Arneth, *Heinrich Freiherr von Haymerle* (Berlin, 1882).

2. Bülow, *Denkwürdigkeiten,* vol. IV, p. 573.

3. See John Morley, *The Life of W. E. Gladstone*, 3 vols. (London, 1903), vol. III, p. 8; "Correspondence between Count Károlyi and Mr. Gladstone," *British Documents on the Origins of the War*, IX, part I (London: His Majesty's Stationery Office, 1933), 773–774.

4. Bosnian history under Austrian administration is considered in greater detail in Chapter XVII.

5. Ernst, *Francis Joseph as Revealed by His Letters*, p. 168.

6. Austria failed to secure Russian consent to the annexation of the Sanjak of Novibazar at some future date.

7. Heinrich Friedjung, "Graf Gustav von Kálnoky," *Historische Aufsätze* (Stuttgart, 1910), pp. 327–361. Andrássy expected to be recalled to the Ballplatz at this time, but the ruler passed him over with the comment that he was an admirable person for cutting through diplomatic knots but that Kálnoky was more capable of untying them. Andrássy's disappointment was the keener because he disliked Kálnoky personally and thought him too considerate of Russia.

8. W. L. Langer, *Alliances and Alignments* (New York: Knopf, 1931), p. 229.

9. How little was known of the actual character of the treaty is suggested in a dispatch sent to Washington by the American minister in Vienna, three years later: "With Italy, the Austrian government is on fairly amicable terms, but nothing more . . . The fact is no alliance, not even what in modern European diplomatic phraseology is called an entente, has been concluded. [During the royal visit to Vienna in 1881] there were conversations but no understanding . . . the question of an alliance was not mooted." Francis to Bayard, March 28, 1885, U. S. National Archives, Dept. of State, MSS., *Austria*, Despatches, XXXIV.

10. Michael Mayr, *Der italienische Irredentismus*, new ed. (Innsbruck, 1917), p. 291.

11. Rumania's case was legalistically argued by F. H. Geffcken, *La Question du Danube* (Berlin, 1883) and rebutted for Austria by Georg Jellinek, *Oesterreich-Ungarn und Rumänien in der Donaufrage* (Vienna, 1884). Consult J. P. Chamberlain, *The Regime of the International Rivers: Danube and Rhine* (New York, 1923), pp. 70–90.

12. Joseph Grunzel, *Die Handelsbeziehungen Oesterreich-Ungarns zu den Balkanländern* (Vienna, 1892).

13. Alois Hajek, *Bulgariens Befreiung und staatliche Entwicklung unter seinem ersten Fürsten* (Munich: Oldenbourg, 1939), especially chap. 7; C. E. Black, *The Establishment of Constitutional Government in Bulgaria* (Princeton: Princeton University Press, 1943).

14. See L. B. Packard, "Russia and the Dual Alliance," *American Historical Review*, XXV (1919–20), 391–410.

15. Carlo Sforza, *Fifty Years of War and Diplomacy in the Balkans* (New York: Columbia University Press, 1940), chap. iv.

16. How a Serbian antiroyal revolution would affect Austria was thoroughly understood in official circles in Vienna. The American minister stationed there wrote: "The elements of danger are so great to her [Austria] should she fail to secure for Serbia some territorial compensation that I am almost in-

clined to believe that she will sacrifice part of Bosnia to her friend rather than permit a revolution which . . . would certainly recall to the portfolio of Foreign Affairs, Mr. Ristics who heads the Russian party." Lee to Bayard, Oct. 15, 1885, U. S. National Archives, Dept. of State, MSS., *Austria*, Despatches, XXXIII.

17. Ernst, *Francis Joseph as Revealed by His Letters*, p. 169.

18. Langer, *Alliances and Alignments*, p. 423.

19. See correspondence between Berlin and Vienna, *Die Grosse Politik*, VI (Berlin, 1922), pp. 82–87.

20. That Bismarck committed a grievous error in not siding with Austria in striking down Russia at this time is the theme of Ulrich Noack in *Bismarck's Friedenpolitik und das Problem des deutschen Machtverfalls* (Leipzig, 1928). If Russia had been humiliated, Noack contends, the reconstruction of Slavic Europe could have been undertaken along lines which would have "permanently" eliminated the Slav danger to *Deutschtum*.

21. Bülow, *Denkwürdigkeiten*, vol. I. p. 189.

22. Hans Rosenberg, "The Struggle for a German-Austrian Customs Union (1815–1931)," *Slavonic Review*, XIV (1935–36), 332–342.

23. W. L. Langer, *The Franco-Russian Alliance, 1890–1894* (Cambridge, 1929), pp. 275–284.

24. W. L. Langer, *The Diplomacy of Imperialism, 1890–1902*, 2 vols. (New York: Knopf, 1935), vol. I, pp. 52–54.

25. H. W. V. Temperley, *History of Serbia* (London, 1917), p. 309.

26. Eulenburg to von Hohenlohe, March 6, 1896, *Die Grosse Politik*, XI (Berlin, 1923), pp. 126–129.

27. A. F. Pribram, *England and the International Policy of the European Great Powers* (Oxford: Clarendon Press, 1931), p. 67.

28. Consult Alexander Hoyos, *Der deutschenglische Gegensatz und sein Einfluss auf die Balkanpolitik Oesterreich-Ungarns* (Berlin, 1922).

XIII · AUSTRIA: *KULTUR UND STURM*
1893–1899

1. Strictly speaking, metropolitan Vienna is not really on the Danube, but a canal winds through the city connecting with the river be-

low the Prater, the famous playground of Vienna.

2. Lytton to Bloomfield, December 31,

1869, P.R.O. MSS. F.O., *Austria*, 7/770.

3. Anonymous, "Vienna and Viennese Life," *Blackwood's Magazine*, CXXIII (1878), p. 618.

4. Much quoted to demonstrate the absence of seriousness among the Viennese was a fragment from one of their songs; "Verkauft mein Gewand, ich fahr in Himmel" (Sell my clothes, I am going to heaven), the equivalent, no doubt, of the American "ish ke bibble."

5. Adolf Hitler, *Mein Kampf* (New York: Stackpole, 1939), pp. 72, 88.

6. Sol Liptzin, *Arthur Schnitzler* (New York: Prentice-Hall, 1932), p. 274.

7. See Jakob Minor, *Ferdinand von Saar* (Vienna, 1898).

8. In another connection, attention is called to novels on the Austrian aristocracy by Ebner-Eschenbach, who was born in Moravia, but educated in Vienna. See Chapter VII.

9. Alfred von Arneth, *Aus meinem Leben*, 2 vols. (Vienna, 1891–1892).

10. Consult W. A. Scott, *The Development of Economics* (New York: Century, 1933), chaps. xx–xxiv, for a brief exposition and critical analysis of the teachings of the Austrian school of economists.

11. Graz, Innsbruck, Czernowitz, the German institution at Prague and the other German universities in Austria, had little more than local importance, though the medical faculty at Graz attracted students from the Near East.

12. It was at once pointed out that if this bill became law, 1,299,845 voters would elect the thirteen workers' representatives, 1,167,-357 of the smallest taxpayers would choose the other thirty-four deputies of the fifth curia, while 1,984,628 citizens would continue to choose the 353 deputies assigned to the existing four "spheres."

13. According to the census of 1890, Czechs comprised 60 per cent of Bohemia's popula-

tion, though in seventy-two administrative divisions the Czech element formed only 1 per cent. In Moravia the Czech proportion was somewhat heavier, but even there in ten districts almost no Czechs were to be found, except for seasonal laborers in harvest time.

14. To this intemperate utterance the Czech poet, Sova, retorted,

. . . Overweening spokesman of slavery!
Do you behold naught else but the blossoming peaks of your country,
And all beyond would you leeringly crunch
Beneath war-chariots of conquerors
And their uncouth tread?

Quoted in Paul Selver, *Masaryk* (London: Joseph, 1940), pp. 194–195.

15. A Pan-German brochure, bearing a Munich imprint, angrily recommended that German troops should occupy Bohemia and Upper Austria, that the Hapsburg crown should be transferred to the Hohenzollerns, that Schönerer and Wolf should be appointed viceroys, and that Austria should be ruthlessly Germanized, except for the Czech areas, which should be converted into a sort of concentration camp.

For lists of German chauvinistic literature relating to Austria-Hungary, see S. Wertheimer, *The Pan-German League* (New York, 1924), p. 241, and Lothar Werner, *Der alldeutsche Verband* (Berlin: Ebering, 1935), pp. 288ff.

16. On more than seventy occasions between 1897 and 1904, imperial decrees were published and eventually validated by parliament.

17. Hungary held aloof from the jubilee celebration, for there the reign was regarded as starting with the royal coronation of 1867.

18. Irvin Abrams, "The Austrian Question at the Turn of the Twentieth Century," *Journal of Central European Affairs*, IV (1944), 186–201.

XIV · A LEAP IN THE DARK

1. Typical of the Pan-German election propaganda was this morsel from a campaign document: "Our motto can be nothing but purely German, Pan-German, undivided! The Germans in Bohemia must decide whether they wish to become Slavs, or whether, in accordance with their destiny, they will German-

ize. A third possibility does not exist." Elizabeth Wiskeman, *Czechs and Germans* (New York: Oxford University Press, 1938), p. 66, note 3.

2. For a learned analysis of Socialist thinking on the reconstruction of Austria, consult A. G. Kogan, "The Social Democrats and the

Conflict of Nationalities in the Habsburg Monarchy," *Journal of Modern History,* XXI (1949), 204–217; Rudolf Schlesinger, *Federalism in Central and Eastern Europe* (London: Kegan Paul, Trench, Trubner, 1945), pp. 210–247.

3. A misguided statistician counted 1,763 abusive epithets, ranging from "ass" to "zebra," with which deputies insulted one another.

4. Consult, for instance, Karl Renner, *Der Kampf der österreichischen Nationen um den Staat* (Vienna, 1902).

5. Socialist pressure persisted until the electoral laws were revised; at one point leaders threatened a general strike to compel action. See S. W. Page, "The Russian Proletariat and World Revolution: Lenin's Views to 1914," *The American Slavic and East European Review,* X (1951), 6–7.

6. Germans comprised 35.8 per cent of the population, but paid 63.4 per cent of the direct taxes and were given 45.1 per cent of the seats; at the other extreme, the Ruthenians forming 13.2 per cent of the population, paid only 3.6 per cent of the taxes, and were allowed 6.3 per cent of the deputies. An interesting feature of the law authorized provincial assemblies to decide whether voting should be compulsory; five of them imposed fines on voters who neglected to vote without good and sufficient cause. Consult Heinrich Rauchberg, *Die statistischen Unterlagen der österreichischen Wahlreform* (Vienna, 1907).

7. The essential principles of the arrangement in Moravia were subsequently applied in Bucovina and in Bosnia-Herzegovina.

8. Nicholas Andrusiak, "The Ukrainian Movement in Galicia," *Slavonic Review,* XIV (1935), 372–379; the University of Rochester *Alumni Review,* IX (1930), 87–89.

XV · DUALISM IN CRISIS: HUNGARY
1890–1910

1. For a Catholic version of the secularization campaign and the Agliardi episode, consult Alphonse Kannengieser, *Juifs et Catholiques en Autriche-Hongrie* (Paris, 1896), pp. 260–359.

2. Franz Ninold, *Der Kossuthcultus in Ungarn* (Linz, 1907). Drawing upon memoirs from the revolutionary period, Ninold, in this "debunking" brochure, stripped bare the Kossuth legend, showed how highly embroidered it was, and disputed Kossuth's claims to eminence either as patriot or as statesman. And yet so deep was affection for Kossuth that toward the end of World War I peasants in one constituency cast 180 votes for the national demigod!

3. The election of 1901 usefully illustrates the undemocratic character of the Hungarian franchise. Almost a third of the deputies were returned by constituencies with fewer than a hundred voters; over nine-tenths were elected in constituencies with under fifteen hundred voters; only in eleven did the electors exceed two thousand.

4. Stephen Burián, *Austria in Dissolution,* English trans. (London, 1925), pp. 247–248.

5. David Angyal, "Stephen Tisza," *Neue Österreichische Biographie, 1815–1918,* 8 vols. (Vienna, 1923–1935), vol. I, pp. 55–69.

6. A. B. Yolland, *The Hungarian Diet of 1905* (Budapest, 1905), largely translations of Magyar documents.

7. H. W. Steed, *Through Thirty Years,* 2 vols. (London, 1924), vol. I, p. 223.

8. Arthur Polzer-Hoditz, *The Emperor Karl,* English trans. (New York, 1930), p. 71.

9. The publicist, Emil Reich, ingeniously argued that universal suffrage would not imperil the hegemony of the Magyars. Just as in the multinationality United States, the British element, men of English and Irish stock, really dominated because of their intellectual superiority, so in a democratized Hungary the politically abler Magyars would stay on the top of the heap. Reich's reasoning carried little conviction in Magyar ruling circles. Emil Reich, "The Crisis in Hungary," *Contemporary Review,* LXXXVIII (1905), 647.

10. A cartoon in an Amsterdam journal depicted Premier Féjerváry offering the aged king, as he sat forlornly in a chair, a glass of medicine, the universal suffrage tonic, and saying, "Yes, Your Majesty, it is a bitter dose but our last remedy."

XVI · MAGYAR CULTURE AND THE MINORITIES

1. H. W. V. Temperley, "Maurus Jókai and the Historical Novel," *Contemporary Review*, LXXXVI (1904), 107–115.

2. Adam Hegedüs, "Studies in Modern Hungarian Literature," *Slavonic Review*, X (1931–32), 293–300.

3. Watson Kirkconnell, "The Poetry of Ady," *Hungarian Quarterly*, III (1937), 501–514; Joseph Reményi, "Endre Ady, Hungary's Apocalyptic Poet," *Slavonic Review*, XXII (1944), 84–105; Joseph Reményi, "Mihaly Babits, Hungarian *Poeta Doctus*," *ibid.*, 111–120.

4. Zoltán Kodály, "What is Hungarian in Music?", *Hungarian Quarterly*, V (1939), 474–481.

5. Two composers of Hungarian origins who won renown in Vienna were Karl Goldmark and Francis Lehár.

6. Wilhelm Offergeld, *Grundlagen und Ursachen der industrielle Entwicklung Ungarns* (Jena, 1914).

7. Whitehead bought in 1872 the *Stabilimento Tecnico Fiumano*, in which he had been interested for some years, and concentrated on making torpedoes and torpedo appliances; in 1898 the plant at Fiume was greatly enlarged.

8. Anarchism of the Tolstoyan variety attracted a handful of Hungarian aristocratic and bourgeois disciples, Count Ervin Batthyány among them; it published a weekly journal and patronized a school for instruction in philosophical anarchism.

9. As of 1914, in 3,320 primary schools instruction was given in non-Magyar languages, Rumanian and Slovak largely, and fully three-fifths of these schools were beneficiaries of state aid and so subject to the Apponyi legislation. It is worthy of note that literacy was higher among the Rumanians and Serbs of Hungary than among their national brethren in Rumania or Serbia. Paul Teleki, *The Evolution of Hungary* (New York, 1923), pp. 157ff.

10. R. W. Seton-Watson, *Racial Problems in Hungary* (London, 1908), pp. 274ff.

11. His son, Vladimir Hurban, as a young man engaged in the Slovak struggle against the Magyars and was several times imprisoned. Entering the employ of the Russian General Staff, he taught officers in preparation for war with the Hapsburg Monarchy. From 1936 to 1946, Hurban represented Czechoslovakia in the United States.

12. Milan Hodža, *Federation in Central Europe* (London: Jarrolds, 1942), chap. i.

13. "Whether the Magyars like it or not, the fact remains that the Slovaks and Czechs form but one race, one civilization, and one nation," Hlinka is reported to have remarked in 1908. Vladimir Nosek, *The Spirit of Bohemia* (London, 1926), p. 300.

14. R. W. Seton-Watson, *Slovak Peasant Art and Industries* (London, 1911).

15. Father Hlinka himself spent three years in prison, where he translated the Old Testament from Latin into Slovak. After World War I, and the establishment of the Czechoslovak Republic, he was the principal leader of the Slovak autonomist party. In 1926 he toured the United States to raise funds for the autonomist cause and to attend a Eucharistic Congress in Chicago. On the eve of the destruction of the Czechoslovak state, in August 1938, Hlinka passed away, worshiped by friends and respected by enemies; a handful of earth from his grave was placed in a golden urn to be shipped to Slovaks residing in the United States.

16. Seton-Watson's *Racial Problems in Hungary* caused an immense sensation when it appeared and ever since has been a standard volume on its subject.

17. For a typical example of the Magyar defense, consult Joseph Mailáth, "Racial Strife in Hungary: A Reply," *Westminster Review*, CLXX (1908), 28–31.

18. Representative specimens of the controversial literature on the Germans in Hungary are F. G. Schultheiss, *Deutschthum und Magyarisierung in Ungarn* (Munich, 1898), and S. Rado, *Das Deutschthum in Ungarn* (Berlin, 1903).

19. Raymond Recouly, *Le Pays Magyar* (Paris, 1903), chap. xx.

20. Quoted in Paul Selver, *Masaryk* (London: Joseph, 1940), p. 166.

21. Supilo, a huge creature, was the son of a mason from Ragusa. Expelled from school for trampling upon the Austrian flag, he managed to learn five languages and drank deeply at the intellectual wells of Mazzini. Carlo Sforza, *Fifty Years of War and Diplomacy in the Balkans* (New York: Columbia University Press, 1940), pp. 107ff.

22. Few Croats were well acquainted with Magyar; of the forty Croatian deputies in the Hungarian parliament at the time, only one spoke Magyar fluently.

23. For an interesting, though incomplete, estimate of Aehrenthal's connection with the forged documents, see Cartwright to Grey, January 4, 1911, *British Documents*, IX, Part I (1933), 243–245.

XVII · THE HAPSBURG MONARCHY AND EUROPE
1897–1908

1. Bülow to Alvensleben, Feb. 15, 1905, *Die Grosse Politik*, XXII (1925), 11–12.

2. C. W. Porter, *The Career of Théophile Delcassé* (Philadelphia: University of Pennsylvania Press, 1936), pp. 140–144.

3. Bülow to Schlözer, June 25, 1908, *Die Grosse Politik*, XXV (1925), 474–479.

4. Austria's not unsympathetic attitude toward French ambitions in the Moroccan dispute may well have been related to the desire to obtain admission for Austrian industrial and government bonds to the Paris Bourse. See Herbert Feis, *Europe, the World's Banker* (New Haven, 1930), pp. 202–203.

5. Oswald Wedel, *Austro-German Diplomatic Relations, 1908–1914* (Stanford: Stanford University Press, 1932), p. 37.

6. Italicus, *Italiens Dreibundpolitik, 1870–1896* (Munich, 1928).

7. Certain Italian publicists, L. Magrioni, for example, in *Il pericolo tedesco* (1907), lashed out against Germany as the real barrier to the realization of the Irredentist goals and pleaded for secession from the Triplice and an alignment with Slavic Europe.

8. On this phase of the Austro-Italian antagonism, consult Leopold von Chlumecky, *Oesterreich-Ungarn und Italien*, second ed. (Leipzig, 1907), a detailed, lopsided narrative.

9. Wedel to Bülow, February 12, 1906, *Die Grosse Politik*, XXI (1925), 157–159.

10. E. C. Helmreich and C. E. Black, "The Russo-Bulgarian Military Convention of 1902," *Journal of Modern History*, IX (1937), 471–482.

11. H. W. Steed, *Through Thirty Years*, 2 vols. (New York, 1924), vol. I, pp. 248–254.

12. A. F. Pribram, *The Secret Treaties of Austria-Hungary, 1879–1914*, 2 vols. (Cambridge, 1920–1922), vol. I, pp. 236–239.

13. Cartwright to Grey, Sept. 28, 1910, *British Documents*, V (1928), 814–815.

14. His grandfather, an enterprising Jewish grain merchant of Prague, had taken the name of Aehrenthal, meaning "corn valley," at the time he was ennobled; the diplomatist was not proud of his Jewish lineage.

15. Berthold Molden, *Alois Graf Aehrenthal* (Stuttgart, 1917): Bülow to William II, May 31, 1906, *Die Grosse Politik*, XXI (1925), 360–362.

16. Conrad's massive memoirs, *Aus meiner Dientszeit, 1906–18*, 5 vols. (Vienna, 1921–1925), are an indispensable quarry of information. Original documents therein refute a good deal of the mythology that was fabricated about Hapsburg diplomatic principles and practices.

17. Thomas Montgomery-Cuninghame, *Dusty Measure* (London: Murray, 1939), p. 116.

18. Schoen to Bülow, July 18, 1908, *Die Grosse Politik*, XXII (1925), 26–29.

19. Leopold Mandl, *Die Habsburger und die Serbische Frage* (Vienna, 1918), p. 62.

20. Fully 90 per cent of Serbia's exports passed to the Danube Monarchy, and it was the source of about 70 per cent of the imports, manufactures chiefly, with textiles in first place, but including everything from scientific instruments to burlap bags. All told, the business was worth about $18,000,000 annually.

21. J. M. Baernreither, *Fragments of a Political Diary* (London, 1930), p. 36.

22. Goschen to Grey, May 11, 1908, *British Documents*, V (1928), 166–167.

23. A. J. May, "The Novibazar Railway Project," *Journal of Modern History*, X (1938), 496–527.

XVIII · THE BOSNIAN CRISIS

1. Ferdinand Schmid, *Bosnien und die Herzegovina, unter der Verwaltung Oesterreich-Ungarns* (Leipzig, 1914), relates the Austrian accomplishments in lavish detail.

2. Scotus Viator, "Austria-Hungary, Italy, and the West Balkans," *Contemporary Review*, XCIII (1908), 347.

3. Throughout this chapter, "Bosnia" is

substituted for the more cumbrous "Bosnia-Herzegovina."

4. An English traveler happened upon a *zádruga*, when the family of about fifty were at the morning meal. The men—five brothers, their sons, and oldest grandsons—surrounded one table, the younger boys sat at a second, babies sprawled round a third. As soon as breakfast was over the men set off for the fields and three of the boys started for school, two hours' journey away. The women, having fed the men, ate their own meal, which consisted of a paste of corn flour, dunked into a common bowl of boiled leeks. After breakfast the women started to work with needles and looms or made cheese. This particular *zádruga* contained several one-room, gray shingled huts, dark and not especially clean, and as many sheds or barns. E. F. B. Thompson, "A Ride Through Bosnia and the Hercegovina," *Nineteenth Century*, LXI (1907), pp. 692–693.

5. Baernreither, *Fragments of a Political Diary*, pp. 19–32. A fine sketch of Baern-

reither's career and ideas forms the preface of the book.

6. For scholarly detailed studies of the Bosnian annexation and its direct antecedents, consult B. E. Schmitt, *The Annexation of Bosnia, 1908–09* (Cambridge: University Press, 1937), and Momtchilo Nintchitch, *La Crise bosniaque et les puissances européennes*, 2 vols. (Paris: Alfred Costes, 1937).

7. Cemal Tuken, *Die politischen Beziehungen zwischen Oesterreich-Ungarn und Bulgarien von 1908 bis zum Bukaresten Frieden* (Hamburg: Christians, 1936).

8. Later Francis Ferdinand remarked, "Serbia may thank *me* for her escape from annihilation in 1909." Sforza, *Fifty Years of War and Diplomacy in the Balkans*, p. 74.

9. For a masterly analysis of this crucial dispatch and divergent interpretations of it, consult Schmitt, *The Annexation of Bosnia*, pp. 194ff.

10. For a penetrating critique of Aehrenthal's diplomacy, see Wedel, *Austro-German Diplomatic Relations*, pp. 102–103.

XIX · AUSTRIA ON THE EVE

1. The tangled strands of Galician parties and politics are skillfully unraveled by Georges Bienaimé, *La Diète de Galicie: ses tendances autonomiques* (Paris, 1910).

2. See Alexander Pelipenko, "Die politische Propaganda der russischen Heilige Synod in Galizien vor dem Kriege," *Berliner Monatshefte*, XII, 2 (1934), 825–838.

3. R. K. Birkbeck, *Life and Letters of W. J. Birkbeck* (London, 1922), p. 282.

4. Alfred Fischel, *Der Panslawismus bis zum Weltkriege* (Berlin, 1919), p. 538.

5. *Ibid.*, pp. 560–570.

6. H. W. Steed, *Through Thirty Years*, 2 vols. (New York, 1924), vol. I, p. 359.

7. Wolfgang Leppman, "Russland und die tschechischen Autonomie—Bestrebungen vor dem Weltkriege," *Berliner Monatshefte*, XII, (1934), 1008–1022. Actually the men on the Neva exhibited small interest in the Czech strivings for home rule.

8. The statistics come from the census of 1910. Nationality was determined by the language that a citizen customarily used. The relative percentages of the various nationalities

had changed only fractionally since 1880. A. Chervin, *L'Autriche et la Hongrie de demain* (Paris, 1915).

9. The progress of the press is shown by figures from the official publication, *Statistische Rückblicke auf Oesterreich* for 1913; newspapers and magazines included.

	German	Czech	Polish	Ruthenian
1882	912	176	89	24
1912	2492	1209	389	65

	Slovene	Italian	Misc.	Total non-German
1882	27	85	65	466
1912	96	130	193	2042

The astonishing increase in Czech publications showed in one way the growth of national feeling.

10. Oscar Jászi, *The Dissolution of the Habsburg Monarchy* (Chicago, 1929), p. 278.

11. Eduard Beneš, *Le Problème autrichien et la Question tchèque* (Paris, 1908), p. 307.

12. Carlo Sforza, *Makers of Modern Europe* (Indianapolis, 1930), p. 65.

XX · HUNGARY MILITANT

1. Viktor Bibl, *Der Zerfall Oesterreichs,* 2 vols. (Vienna, 1924), vol. II, p. 475.

2. Eugene Horváth in *Transylvania and the History of the Roumanians* (Budapest: Sárkány, 1935), p. 81, argues that the Archduke Francis Ferdinand was really responsible for the breakdown of these conversations. He is not convincing.

3. Eduard Treumund, "Tisza und die Rumänen," *Oesterreichische Rundschau,* XXXVIII (1914), 205–212.

4. Horváth, *Transylvania and the History of the Roumanians,* p. 82.

5. The indispensable study in this connection is C. A. Macartney, *Hungary and Her Successors, 1919–1937* (New York: Oxford University Press, 1937), a perfect mine of information by a judicious and learned scholar.

6. Literally, Szeklers means "frontiersmen," and they probably were descendants of medieval Magyar colonists sent to the east as permanent military garrisons, though another theory, which has been championed by learned controversialists, claims them as descendants of Attila's Huns. Rumanian publicists held them to be their very own national brethren, polluted by Magyar ways and manners. The Szeklers led a hard and frugal existence in their mountain fastnesses and preserved unimpaired many of their ancient customs and beliefs.

7. Oscar Jászi, *The Dissolution of the Habsburg Monarchy* (Chicago, 1929), p. 278.

8. The linguistic confusion was well exhibited in the make-up of the electoral constituencies. Magyars lived in every one of the 413 districts; Germans in all but 37; Slovaks in 202; Rumanians in 178; Croats in 69; Serbs in 62; and Ruthenians in 57. See C. M. Knatchbull-Hugessen, *The Political Evolution of the Hungarian Nation,* 2 vols. (London, 1908); vol. II, chap. xx.

9. For another estimate of national sentiments among the Ruthenians, consult Kamil Krofta, "Ruthenes, Czechs, and Slovaks," *Slavonic Review,* XIII (1934), 611–626.

10. Macartney, *Hungary and Her Successors,* p. 348.

11. Quoted in Paul Teleki, *The Evolution of Hungary* (New York, 1923), pp. 153–154.

XXI · BEFORE THE WAR

1. The inability of Austria to prevent Turkish attacks upon citizens and their property during the Bosnian imbroglio was a minor factor influencing naval expansion.

2. Gerhard Hiller, *Die Entwicklung des österreichisch-serbischen Gegensatzes, 1908–14* (Halle: Akademischer Verlag, 1934).

3. In some measure Aehrenthal's coolness toward Germany was bound up with his desire to have French moneybags opened to the Dual Monarchy. More than once in the course of the Moroccan crisis the French cabinet expressed gratitude for Austria's attitude, but it would not permit the flotation of loans, for that would have been resented in Russia. Other attempts of Austria to borrow in France in connection with a scheme to place Balkan railways under international control were equally fruitless. Feis, *Europe, the World's Banker,* pp. 206ff. Cf. I. C. Barlow, *The Agadir Crisis* (Chapel Hill: University of North Carolina Press, 1940).

4. W. S. Churchill, *The World Crisis,* 6 vols. (New York, 1923–1931), vol. VI, pp. 53–54.

5. G. P. Gooch, *Before the War,* 2 vols. (London: Longmans, 1936–1938), vol. II, p. 374.

6. Francis Joseph meditated on inviting Stephen Tisza, Magyar strong man, to the foreign office but he was unacceptable to Francis Ferdinand, who urged the appointment of his valued counselor, Count Ottokar Czernin, no friend of the Magyars. At this time, the Pole, Bilinski, superseded Burián, a Magyar, as common minister of finance.

7. P. E. Mosely, "Russian Policy in 1911–12," *Journal of Modern History,* XII (1940), 69–86.

8. For a sure-footed guide through the tangled diplomatic jungle of the time, consult E. C. Helmreich, *The Diplomacy of the Balkan Wars, 1912–13* (Cambidge: Harvard University Press, 1938).

9. Hiller, *Die Entwicklung des österreichisch-serbischen Gegensatzes,* pp. 58ff.

10. M. A. Faissler, "Austria-Hungary and the Disruption of the Balkan League," *Slavonic Review,* XIX (1940), 141–157.

11. Wedel, *Austro-German Diplomatic Re-*

lations, p. 200; cf. E. C. Helmreich, "The Conflict Between Germany and Austria over Balkan Policy, 1913–1914," in D. C. McKay, ed., *Essays on the History of Modern Europe* (New York: Harper, 1936), pp. 130–148.

12. Wedel, *Austro-German Diplomatic Relations*, p. 208.

13. Gooch, *Before the War*, vol. II, pp. 424–425.

14. Berchtold to Czernin, November 26, 1913, *Oesterreich-Ungarns Aussenpolitik*, VII (1930). 588–594.

15. "For Serbia we shall do everything,"

the tsar of all the Russias confided to Pašič. Quoted in S. B. Fay, *The Origins of the World War*, new ed. (New York, 1930), vol. I, p. 485.

16. See, for example, Bunsen to Grey, March 6, 1914, *British Documents*, X, Part II (1938), 756–757.

17. In a dispatch to the German chancellor, the two diplomatists declared: "In unserer Unterredungen über die uns interessierenden Fragen haben wir abermals die vollkommene Uebereinstimmung der Ainschten der drei verbündeten Mächte festgestellt."

EPILOGUE · SCHEMES FOR REFORMATION AND SOURCES OF STRENGTH

1. Quoted in David Mitrany, *The Effect of the War in Southeastern Europe* (New Haven: Yale University Press, 1936), p. 238.

2. Arthur Polzer-Hoditz, *Life of Emperor Karl*, English ed. (New York, 1930), p. 26.

3. René Gonnard, *Entre Drave et Save* (Paris, 1911), pp. 87–113.

4. Ernst Klein, *The Road to Disaster* (London: Allen and Unwin, 1940).

5. Quoted in Mitrany, *The Effect of the War in Southeastern Europe*, p. 228.

6. For a partial, highly selective list of these writings, see Viktor Bibl, *Der Zerfall Oesterreichs*, 2 vols. (Vienna, 1924), vol. II, p. 409.

7. Seats in the projected federal parliament would be distributed as follows: Germans, ten; Yugoslavs, five; Magyars, eight; Italians, two; Poles and Ruthenians, three each; Czechs, five; Slovaks, two; and Rumanians, four; deputies would be chosen by universal manhood suffrage with direct and secret balloting.

8. Consult Milan Hodža, *Federation in Central Europe* (London: Jarrolds, 1942), pp. 26–30, 37.

9. *Ibid.*, p. 51.

10. C. M. Danzer, in *Das neue Oesterreich. Eine politische Rundfrage* (Vienna, 1908), studied the response to Popovici's book by use of the questionnaire technique.

11. Emil Reich, "The Crisis in Hungary," *Contemporary Review*, LXXXVIII (1905), 524.

12. Quoted by I. F. D. Morrow, "The Last Days of the Habsburg Empire," *Edinburgh Review*, CCL (1929), 361.

13. A project for a Danubian Confederation under Magyar hegemony, drafted by

Louis Kossuth after the collapse of the revolution in 1849, seems not to have attracted much attention or support in Hungary just before 1914. The idea had momentary resurrection, however, in the wake of the split-up of the Monarchy in 1918.

14. For a suggestive survey of these matters, consult Antonín Basch, *The Danube Basin and the German Economic Sphere* (New York: Columbia University Press, 1943), pp. 5–10.

15. Quoted in S. H. Thomson, *Czechoslovakia in European History* (Princeton: Princeton University Press, 1943), p. 134.

16. Quoted in Jay to Fish, October 17, 1870, U. S. National Archives, Dept. of State, MSS., *Austria*, Despatches, X.

17. C. A. Macartney, *National States and National Minorities* (London: Oxford University Press, 1934), p. 145.

18. Joseph Redlich, *Zustand und Reform der oesterreichischen Verwaltung* (Vienna, 1911).

19. Alexander Musulin, *Das Haus am Ballplatz* (Munich, 1924), p. 136.

20. Tripp to Gresham, May 20, 1895, U. S. National Archives, Dept. of State, MSS., *Austria*, Despatches, 41.

21. Anonymous, "The Future of Austria-Hungary," *Review of Reviews*, XVII (1898), 33.

22. Quoted in Alfred Vagts, *A History of Militarism* (New York: Norton, 1937), p. 273.

23. O. Bismarck, *Reflections and Reminiscences*, 2 vols.; English ed. (London, 1898), vol. II, p. 275.

BIBLIOGRAPHY

As indicated in the preface, this bibliography is sharply selective. It may seem a rather arbitrary choice, in some cases at any rate, of works that have impressed me as particularly interesting and important. As a rule, studies already cited in the notes are not repeated here.

BIBLIOGRAPHICAL GUIDES

Bestaux, Eugène, *Bibliographie tchèque, contenant un certain nombre d'ouvrages sur la tchèco-slovaquie* (Prague, 1920).

Bibliographia Hungariae, 3 vols. (Berlin, 1923–1928).

Čapek, Thomas and A. V., *Bohemian, Czech Bibliography* (New York, 1918).

Gunzenhäuser, Max, *Bibliographie zur geschichte Oesterreich-Ungarns, 1848–1914* (Stuttgart: Weltkriegsbücherei, 1935).

Kerner, R. J., *Slavic Europe, A Selected Bibliography* (Cambridge, 1918).

Kertérz, Johann, *Bibliographie der Habsburgliteratur, 1218–1934* (Budapest: Gergely, 1934).

Kont, Jules, *Bibliographie française de la Hongrie, 1521–1910* (Paris, 1913).

Krones, Franz, *Grundriss der österreichischen Geschichte mit besonderer Rücksicht auf quellen-und Literaturkunde* (Vienna, 1882).

Wegerer, Alfred von, *Bibliographie zur Vorgeschichte des Weltkrieges* (Berlin: Quaderverlag, 1934).

LARGER WORKS

Adler, Viktor, *Aufsätze, Reden und Briefe,* 5 vols. (Vienna, 1922–1925). Literary pieces by the leading Viennese Social Democrat.

Adrássy, Julius, *Bismarck, Andrássy, and Their Successors* (Boston, 1927). A filial apologia.

—— *Ungarns Ausgleich mit Oesterreich* (Leipzig, 1897). Invaluable exposition of the subject.

Arneth, Alfred von, *Aus meinem Leben,* 2 vols. (Vienna, 1891–92). By the official archivist. Sidelights on public leaders and policy makers.

Auerbach, Bertrand, *Les Races et les Nationalités en Autriche-Hongrie,* second ed. (Paris, 1917). A quarry of useful information.

Baernreither, J. M., *Fragmente eines politischen Tagebuches* (Berlin, 1928). Broad-gauged German Bohemian. Valuable on Yugoslav questions.

—— *Der Verfall des Habsburgerreiches und die Deutschen* (Vienna: Holzhausen, 1939). A generation of enlightened and enlightening reminiscences.

Bauer, Otto, *Die Nationalitätenfrage und die Sozialdemokratie,* second ed. (Vienna, 1924). Authoritative and elaborate interpretation by a spokesman of democratic socialism.

Bazant, Johann, *Die Handelspolitik Oesterreich-Ungarns 1875 bis 1892* (Leipzig, 1894). By a leading bureaucrat. Substantial.

Beer, Adolf, *Die orientalische Politik Oesterreichs seit 1774* (Prague, 1883). Fairly detailed with some study of archives.

—— *Die österreichische Handelspolitik im neunzehnten Jahrhundert* (Vienna, 1891). An original study, using official information.

Bernatzik, Edmund, *Die österreichischen Verfassungsgesetze,* second ed. (Vienna, 1911). Standard.

Bertha, Sándor de, *La Hongrie moderne* (Paris, 1901). Useful, sympathetic survey.

—— *Magyars et Roumains devant l'histoire* (Paris, 1899). Definitely pro-Magyar. Better had it been shortened.

Bettelheim, Anton, ed., *Neue österreichische Biographie,* 8 vols. (Vienna: Wienerdrucke, 1923–1935). Invaluable, with fine bibliographies.

Beust, F. F. Graf von, *Aus dreiviertel Jahrhunderten,* 2 vols. (Stuttgart, 1887). The second volume relates to the years 1866 to 1885.

Bezecny, Anton, ed., *Die Thronreden seiner Majestät des Kaisers Franz Josef I,* second ed. (Vienna, 1912).

Bibl, Viktor, *Der Zerfall Oesterreichs,* 2 vols. (Vienna, 1922–1924). Clearly written general account.

Bittner, Ludwig, *et. al.,* eds., *Oesterreich-Ungarns Aussenpolitik von der bosnischen Krise 1908 bis zum Kriegsausbruch 1914,* 9 vols. (Vienna, 1930).

Boghitchevic, Milosch, *Die auswärtige Politik Serbiens, 1903–1914,* 3 vols. (Berlin, 1928–1931). Documents and a narrative interpretation.

Brandl, Franz, *Kaiser, Politiker, und Menschen* (Leipzig: Günther, 1936). Interesting recollections by a head of Vienna police.

Braunthal, Julius, *In Search of the Millenium* (London: Gollancz, 1945). Revealing report on Austrian Socialism by one on the inside.

Brote, Eugen, *Die rumänische Frage in Siebenbürgen und Ungarn* (Berlin, 1895). A strongly Rumanian exposition, with pertinent documents.

Brügel, Ludwig, *Geschichte der österreichischen Sozialdemokratie,* 5 vols. (Vienna, 1922–1925). Sympathetic. Documents.

Charmatz, Richard, *Adolf Fischhof, das Lebensbild eines österreichischen Politikers* (Stuttgart, 1910). Portrait of a Viennese liberal.

Chervin, Arthur, *L'Autriche et la Hongrie de demain* (Paris, 1915). Statistical data on nationalities.

Chlumecky, Leopold von, *Erzherzog Franz Ferdinands Wirken und Wollen* (Berlin, 1929). By a confidant of the Archduke.

Corti, Egon, *Elizabeth, Empress of Austria* (New Haven: Yale University Press, 1936). Sympathetic picture.

Czedik, Alois Freiherr von, *Zur Geschichte der K.-K. österreichischen Ministerien, 1861–1916,* 4 vols. (Vienna, 1917–1920).

Denis, Ernest, *La Bohême depuis la montagne-blanche,* 2 vols. (Paris, 1903). Friendly toward the Czechs.

Deutsch, Julius, *Geschichte der deutsch-österreichischen Arbeiterbewegung* (Vienna, 1922). Short.

Drage, Geoffrey, *Austria-Hungary* (London, 1909). A storehouse of background information.

Eisenmann, Louis, *Le Compromis Austro-Hongrois de 1867* (Paris, 1904). A classic study with lively interpretations.

Erényi, Gustav, *Graf Stephen Tisza* (Vienna: Tal, 1935). Flattering portrait.

Evans, A. J., *Through Bosnia and Herzegovina During the Insurrection of 1875* (London, 1876). Colorful travelogue.

Fay, S. B., *The Origins of the World War,* second ed. (New York, 1930). A book of extraordinary and dispassionate learning. Charmingly written.

Fischel, Alfred, *Das österreichische Sprachenwelt,* second ed. (Brunn, 1909). Documented work of a lawyer.

—— *Der Panslawismus bis zum Weltkrieg* (Stuttgart, 1919). Authoritative. Thin on twentieth century.

Fournier, August, *Oesterreich-Ungarns Neubau unter Kaiser Franz Josef I* (Berlin, 1917). A crisp, informed, wartime product.

Friedjung, Heinrich, *Historische Aufsätze* (Stuttgart, 1919). A collection of miscellaneous pieces. Several able biographical sketches.

—— *Der Kampf um die Vorherrschaft in Deutschland, 1859 bis 1866,* tenth ed., 2 vols. (Stuttgart, 1916–1917). Standard.

Gayda, Virginio, *Modern Austria* (New York, 1915). Suggestive on Italian Irredentism.

Giesl, Wilhelm, *Zwei Jahrzehnte im nahen Orient* (Berlin, 1927). By a diplomatist. Solidly grounded.

Glaise-Horstenau, Edmund von, *Franz Josefs Weggefährte. Das Leben des Generalstabchefs Grafen Beck* (Vienna, 1930). Revealing and of great interest.

Gonnard, René, *Entre Drave et Save* (Paris, 1911). Picturesque narrative.

—— *La Hongrie au XXᵉ siècle* (Paris, 1908). On rural life and conditions.

Gooch, G. P., *Before the War,* 2 vols. (New York: Longmans, 1936–1938). Diplomatic studies centered upon decisive personalities. By a master craftsman.

Grunwald, Max, *Jews in Vienna* (Philadelphia: Jewish Publication Society, 1936). Broad study.

Henderson, P. E., *A British Officer in the Balkans* (London, 1909). Delightful descriptions of southern Austria and Bosnia.

Henry, René, *Questions d'Autriche-Hongrie et question d'Orient,* third ed. (Paris, 1908). Elementary but suggestive treatise by a publicist.

Herbst, Eduard, *Das deutsche Sprachgebiet in Böhmen* (Prague, 1887). Detailed analysis based on the census of 1880.

Hertz, F. O., *Die Produktions-grundlagen der österreichischen Industrie vor und nach dem Kriege* (Vienna, 1917). Reliable.

Hickmann, A. L., *Geographisch-statistischer Taschenatlas von Oesterreich-Ungarn* (Vienna, 1913). Statistical data.

Hötzendorf, Conrad von, *Aus meiner Dientszeit, 1906–18,* 5 vols. (Vienna, 1921–1925). Invaluable papers and recollections of the chief of the Hapsburg General Staff.

Horn, E. M., *Le Christianisme en Hongrie,* second ed. (Paris, 1905). Informing.

Horn, Gustave, *Le Compromis de 1868 entre la Hongrie et la Croatie et celui de 1867 entre l'Autriche et la Hongrie* (Paris, 1907). Closely reasoned. Sympathetic to Croat claims.

Horváth, Eugene, *Modern Hungary 1660–1920* (Budapest, 1922). Concise. Difficult to read. Suggestive.

Hugelmann, K. G., ed., *Das Nationalitätenrecht des alten Oesterreich* (Vienna: Braumüller, 1934). Encyclopedic. Authoritative.

Italicus, *Italiens Dreibundpolitik 1870–96* (Munich, 1928). Thorough.

Jászi, Oscar, *The Dissolution of the Habsburg Monarchy* (Chicago, 1929). Contains a wealth of information. Poorly organized. Cumbrous style.

Jonescu, Take, *Some Personal Impressions* (London, 1919). Sketches of several Hapsburg political figures.

Jorga, Nicholas, *Histoire des Roumains de Transylvanie et la Hongrie,* 2 vols. (Bucharest, 1916). By a leading Rumanian historian. Presents Rumanian case most favorably.

Kaindl, R. F., *Geschichte der Deutschen in den Karpathenländern,* 3 vols. (Gotha, 1907–1911). Definitive.

Kannengiesser, A., *Juifs et catholiques en Autriche-Hongrie* (Paris, 1896). Critical of the Jews.

Katona, Béla, *Die Volkwirtschaft Ungarns* (Budapest, 1913). Very good introduction to the subject.

Klopp, Wiard von, *Leben und Wirken des Sozialpolitikers Karl Freiherrn von Vogelsang* (Vienna, 1930). Sympathetic approach.

Knatchbull-Hugessen, C. M., *The Political Evolution of the Hungarian Nation,* 2 vols. (London, 1908). Warmly pro-Magyar. Indispensable.

Kolmer, Gustav, ed., *Parlament und Verfassung in Oesterreich* (8 vols., Vienna, 1902–14). Very useful on constitutional matters.

Krebs, Hans, *Kampf in Böhmen* (Berlin: Volk und Reich, 1936). Strongly German emphasis.

Kuppe, Rudolph, *Karl Lueger und seine Zeit* (Vienna: Oesterreichische Volkschriften, 1933). Pleasant and diverting glimpses.

Lammasch, Marga and S. H., eds., *Heinrich Lammasch, seine Aufzeichnungen, sein Wirken und seine Politik* (Vienna, 1922). Selections from the career of a Viennese scholar and statesman.

Lang, Lajos, *Hundert Jahre Zollpolitik (1805–1905)* (Vienna, 1906). Mainly on Hapsburg monarchy. Clear survey.

Langer, William L., *The Diplomacy of Imperialism,* 2 vols. (New York: Knopf, 1935). Combines industry with insight. Basic.

—— *European Alliances and Alignments, 1871–1890* (New York: Knopf, 1931). Forerunner of preceding book.

Leger, L. P. M., *Histoire de l'Autriche Hongrie jusqu'an 1918,* second ed. (Paris, 1920). Comprehensive. Slavophile leanings.

—— *La renaissance Tchèque au XIX siècle* (Paris, 1911). Interesting biographical portraits.

Liptzin, Sol, *Arthur Schnitzler* (New York: Prentice-Hall, 1932). Well-informed and instructive.

Loiseau, Charles, *L'Equilibre Adriatique* (Paris, 1901). Journalistic. Knew Croats well.

Lončarević, Dušan A., *Jugoslaviens Entstehung* (Vienna, 1929). A sparkling account by a publicist.

Lonyay, Count Carl, *Rudolph, the Tragedy of Mayerling* (New York: Scribner, 1949). Interesting. Fresh evidence but fails to solve the mystery.

Louis-Jaray, Gabriel, *La Question social et le Socialisme en Hongrie* (Paris, 1909). Written with authority on workers, urban and rural.

Luschin von Ebengreuth, Arnold, *Grundriss der österreischischen Reichgeschichte*, second ed. (Vienna, 1918). Elementary treatment of constitutional questions.

Macartney, C. A., *Hungary and Her Successors, 1919–1937* (New York: Oxford University Press, 1937). Masterly analysis. Eminently readable.

—— *National States and National Minorities* (London: Oxford University Press, 1934). Delightfully provocative and informing.

Marczali, Heinrich, *Ungarische Verfassungs-geschichte* (Tubingen, 1910). Concise guide by a leading Hungarian scholar.

Margutti, Albert, *Emperor Francis Joseph and His Times* (London, 1921). Arouses more interest than it satisfies.

Matlekovits, Alexander, and Gelleri, Moriz, *Die Entwicklung der ungarischen Industrie* (Vienna, 1902). First-class book.

Mayer, F. M., Kaindl, R. F., Pirchegger, Hans, *Geschichte und Kulturleben Deutschösterreichs*, 3 vols. (Vienna: Braumüller, 1929–1937). Third volume treats the period after 1792. A learned, reliable, and penetrating work.

Mayer, Sigmund, *Die Wiener Juden, Commerz, Kultur, Politik* (Vienna, 1917). Authoritative.

Medlicott, W. N., *The Congress of Berlin and After* (London: Methuen, 1938). Excellent. Detailed.

Meister, Richard, *Geschichte der Wiener Universität* (Vienna: Auer, 1934). Admirably comprehensive and clear guide.

Mitis, Oskar von, *Das Leben des Kronprinzen* (Leipzig, 1928). Standard. Superb bibliography.

Molden, Berthold, *Alois Graf Aehrenthal* (Stuttgart, 1917). A noteworthy appreciation.

Molisch, Paul, *Geschichte der deutschnationalen Bewegung in Oesterreich* (Jena, 1926). An impeccable record.

Nadler, Joseph, and Srbik, Heinrich von, *Oesterreich, Erbe und Sendung im deutschen Raum* (Salzburg: Pustet, 1936). Compact and agreeable essays. Pan-German tone.

Návay de Földeák, A. de, *La Hongrie, son rôle économique* (Paris, 1911). Encyclopedic. Dull.

Ninold, Francis, *Der Kossuth Kultus in Ungarn* (Linz, 1907). A debunking brochure.

Nintchitch, Momtchilo, *La Crise bosniaque, 1908, et les Puissances européennes*, 2 vols. (Paris: Alfred Costes, 1937). Full-bodied scholarship.

Offergeld, Wilhelm, *Grundlagen und Ursachen der industriellen Entwicklung Ungarns* (Jena, 1914). Thorough and careful presentation.

Palmer, Francis, H. E., *Austro-Hungarian Life in Town and Country* (New York, 1903). Popular sketches.

Partsch, Joseph, *Mitteleuropa* (Gotha, 1904). Influential work.

Pfitzner, Josef, *Das Sudetendeutschthum* (Cologne, 1928). Militant German emphasis.

Plener, Ernst von, *Erinnerungen*, 3 vols. (Stuttgart, 1911–1921). Valuable and informative. Good portraits of political personalities.

Pribram, Alfred F., *Austrian Foreign Policy, 1908–18* (London, 1923). A memorable summary.

—— *The Secret Treaties of Austria-Hungary, 1879–1914*, 2 vols. (Cambridge, 1920–1922). Invaluable, original documents.

Przibram, Ludwig von, *Erinnerungen eines alten Oesterreichers*, 2 vols. (Stuttgart, 1910–1912). Second volume begins at 1866. Diplomatic journalist with a wide circle of acquaintances.

Rádl, Emanuel, *Der Kampf zwischen Tschechen und Deutschen* (Reichenberg, 1928). Notable contribution to the subject. Czechophile.

Redlich, Joseph, *Emperor Francis Joseph of Austria* (New York, 1929). First-rate portrait.

Rogge, Walter, *Oesterreich seit der Katastrophe Hohenwart-Beust*, 2 vols. (Leipzig, 1879). Detailed piece of journalism. Germanophile.

Salomon, Henry, *L'Ambassade de Richard de Metternich à Paris* (Paris: Firmin Didot, 1931). Slight. Dealing with period of Napoleon III.

Samassa, Paul, *Der Völkerstreit im Habsburgerstaat* (Leipzig, 1910). Shrewd, interpretative essays.

Schäffle, Albert E. F., *Aus meinem Leben*, 2 vols. (Berlin, 1905). An enlightening personal record by a minister of the 1870's.

Schenk, Josef, *Julian von Dunajewski, ein österreichischen Finanzminister* (Vienna: Oesterreichischer Bundesverlag, 1934). Brief, but informing.

Schmid, Ferdinand, *Bosnien und die Herzegovina, unter der Verwaltung Oesterreich-Ungarns* (Leipzig, 1914). Massive. Indispensable.

Schmitt, Bernadotte E., *The Annexation of Bosnia, 1908–1909* (Cambridge: University Press, 1937). Learned analysis of the diplomatic records.

Schnee, Heinrich, *Burgermeister Karl Lueger* (Paderborn: Schöningh, 1936). Elementary. Colorful.

Schweinitz, Wilhelm, ed., *Denkwürdigkeiten des Botschafters General von Schweinitz*, 2 vols. (Berlin, 1927). Many useful data on 1870's.

Selver, Paul, *Masaryk* (London: Joseph, 1940). Excellent.

Seton-Watson, R. W., *Absolutism in Croatia* (London, 1912). Contemporary appraisal.

—— *Corruption and Reform in Hungary* (London, 1911).

—— *Racial Problems in Hungary* (London, 1908). Elaborate and illuminating exposé of Magyarization.

—— *Slovak Peasant Art and Industries* (London, 1911).

—— *The Southern Slav Question and the Hapsburg Monarchy* (London, 1911). Another singularly valuable study.

Sieghart, Rudolph, *Die letzten Jahrzehnte einer Grossmacht* (Berlin: Ullstein, 1932). Vivid picture by an influential bureaucrat.

Skedl, Arthur, *Der politische Nachlass des Grafen Eduard Taaffe* (Vienna, 1922). Voluminous sheaf of letters and state papers.

Sosnosky, Theodor von, *Die Balkanpolitik Oesterreich-Ungarns seit 1866*, 2 vols. (Stuttgart, 1913–1914). Full-length study, now antiquated.

―――― *Die Politik im Habsburgerreiche*, 2 vols. (Berlin, 1912–1913). Based upon press materials largely.

Steed, H. W., *The Hapsburg Monarchy*, second ed. (London, 1919). By a distinguished British journalist, antipathetic to Germans.

Steinitz, Eduard, ed., *Erinnerungen an Franz Joseph I* (Berlin: Verlag für Kulturpolitik, 1931). Fine estimates of ruler from diverse viewpoints.

Sumner, B. H., *Russia and the Balkans 1870–1880* (Oxford: Clarendon Press, 1937). Invaluable. Careful and reliable scholarship.

Taylor, A. J. P., *The Habsburg Monarchy, 1815–1918*, rev. ed. (London: Hamish Hamilton, 1949). Superior to any other general study. Accent on internal politics. Skillful exposition. Somewhat opinionated.

Teleki, Paul, *The Evolution of Hungary* (New York, 1923). Introductory. Long booklist.

Thomson, S. H., *Czechoslovakia in European History* (Princeton: Princeton University Press, 1943). Admirably comprehensive. Nicely proportioned.

Völker, Karl, *Die Entwicklung der Protestantismus in Oesterreich* (Leipzig, 1917). Original materials.

Wendel, Hermann, *Aus dem südslawischen Risorgimento* (Gotha, 1921). Eloquent essays on cultural leaders.

Wertheimer, Eduard von, *Graf Julius Andrássy*, 3 vols. (Stuttgart, 1910–1913). Indispensable, though later studies have forced many revisions in emphases.

Wilczek, J. N., *Happy Retrospect, 1837–1922* (London: Bell, 1934). Charming sidelights on the more enlightened aristocracy.

Wiskemann, Elizabeth, *Czechs and Germans* (New York: Oxford University Press, 1938). Uniquely authoritative summary.

Wolfsgruber, Cölestin, *Joseph Othmar Cardinal Rauscher* (Freiburg, 1888). Easygoing study of the prelate. Many original data.

Zagorsky, Vladimir, *François Rački et la Renaissance scientifique et politique de la Croatie, 1828–94* (Paris, 1909). A first-rate dissertation. Elaborate bibliography.

Žolger, Ivan, *Der staatsrechtliche Ausgleich zwischen Oesterreich und Ungarn* (Munich, 1911). Highly detailed analysis.

Zuckerkandl, B. S., *My Life and History* (New York: Knopf, 1939). Interesting reminiscences from the world of journalism.

MONOGRAPHIC STUDIES

Abrams, Irwin, "The Austrian Question at the Turn of the Twentieth Century," *Journal of Central European Affairs*, IV (1944–45), 186–201.

Adler, Sigmund, *Zur Rechtsgeschichte des adeligen Grundbesitzes in Oesterreich-Ungarn* (Leipzig, 1902). Brief analysis.

Arneth, Alfred von, *Heinrich Freiherr von Haymerle* (Berlin, 1882). Thin, uncritical, disappointing.

Arnold-Forster, Florence, *Francis Deák* (London, 1880). Laudatory estimate.

Askew, W. C., *Europe and Italy's Acquisition of Libya, 1911–12* (Durham: Duke University Press, 1942). Definitive.

Behrendt, Johannes, *Die polnische Frage und das österreichische-deutsche Bündnis, 1885 bis 1887* (Berlin, 1927). An excellent dissertation.

Beneš, Eduard, *Le Problème autrichien et la Question tchèque* (Paris, 1908). No suggestion of solution of Austrian problems by dissolution of the Monarchy.

Benzion, Eugen, *Die Ausgleichskämpfe Oesterreich-Ungarns als eine der Ursache des Weltkrieges* (Vienna, 1915). Interesting but unconvincing.

Berger, E. E., *Italiens Dreibundpolitik, 1870–1896* (Freiburg, 1928). Critical of Italy.

Brügel, Ludwig, *Soziale Gesetzgebung in Oesterreich von 1848 bis 1918* (Vienna, 1919). Authoritative.

Bunzel, Julius, *Studien zur Social- und Wirtschaftspolitik Ungarns* (Leipzig, 1902).

Čapek, Thomas, *The Slovaks of Hungary* (New York, 1906). Partisan. Informed.

Engel-Jánosi, Friedrich, "Austria in the Summer of 1870," *Journal of Central European Affairs,* V (1945–46), 335–353.

Erichsen, Ernst, *Die deutschen Politik des Grafen Beust im Jahre 1870* (Kiel, 1927). Detailed. Readable.

Förster, Leo, *Das Bundesverhältnis Deutschlands zu Oesterreich-Ungarns in der Epoche Aehrenthal* (Freiburg: Gatzer, 1934). Exhaustive.

Fournier, August, *Wie wir zu Bosnien kamen* (Vienna, 1909). By a respected historian.

Gargas, Sigismond, *Le Problème du Fédéralisme en Autriche-Hongrie* (Paris, 1927). Interpretative essay.

Giesche, Richard, *Der serbische Zugang zum Meer und die europäische Krise 1912* (Stuttgart: Kohlhammer, 1932). Thoroughly documented.

Granner, Wilhelm, *Franz Ferdinand, seine Entwicklung und seine politischen Ideen* (Vienna, 1942). An ambitious but disappointing investigation.

Grunzel, Joseph, *Die Handelsbeziehungen Oesterreich-Ungarns zu den Balkan Länder* (Vienna, 1892). Good.

—— *Handelspolitik und Ausgleich in Oesterreich-Ungarn* (Vienna, 1912).

Harris, David, *A Diplomatic History of the Balkan Crisis of 1875–1878. The First Year* (Stanford: Stanford University Press, 1936). Complete and absorbing study.

Heller, Eduard, *Das deutsch-österreichisch-ungarische Bündnis in Bismarcks Aussenpolitik* (Berlin, 1925). Certain sections have been modified by later studies.

Helmreich, E. C., *The Diplomacy of the Balkan Wars, 1912–13* (Cambridge: Harvard University Press, 1938). A sure-footed guide through a diplomatic jungle. Full bibliography.

Hiller, Gerhard, *Die Entwicklung des österreichisch-serbischen Gegensatzes 1908–14* (Halle: Akademischer Verlag, 1934). Shrill indictment of Pan-Serb zealotry.

Hoyos, Graf Alexander, *Der deutsche-englische Gegensatz und sein Einfluss auf die Balkanpolitik Oesterreich-Ungarns* (Berlin, 1922). A pathbreaking study by an Austrian diplomatist.

Janossy, Dionys, *Der handelspolitische Konflict zwischen der österreichisch-ungarische Monarchie und Serbien, 1904–1910* (Vienna: privately published, 1932). Complete. Scholarly.

Jellinek, Georg, *Oesterreich-Ungarn und Rümanen in der Donaufrage* (Vienna, 1884). A brochure presenting the case for Austria.

Klepetař, Harry, *Der Sprachenkampf in den Sudetenländern* (Prague: Strache, 1932). Brief. Clear. Thoughtful.

Kogan, A. G., "The Social Democrats and the Conflict of Nationalities in the Habsburg Monarchy," *Journal of Modern History*, XXI (1949), 204–217.

Kuehnelt-Leddihn, E. R. von, "The Bohemian Background of German National Socialism," *Journal of the History of Ideas*, IX (1948), 339–371.

Leidner, Fritz, *Die aussenpolitik Oesterreich-Ungarns vom Deutsch-Französischen Kriege bis zum Deutsch-Oesterreichischen Bündnis* (Halle: Akademischer Verlag, 1936). A model dissertation. Superb bibliography.

Long, D. C., "Efforts to Secure an Austro-German Customs Union in the Nineteenth Century," in Boak, A. E. R., ed., *University of Michigan Historical Essays* (Ann Arbor, 1937), 45–74.

Mailáth, Joseph, *Hungaricae res* (Berlin, 1908). Militant apologia for Magyarization policies.

Mandl, Leopold, *Die Habsburger und die serbische Frage* (Vienna, 1918). Original, but grossly one-sided.

Markov, Walter M., *Serbien zwischen Oesterreich und Russland, 1897–1908* (Stuttgart: Kohlhammer, 1934). Important essay. Full of matter.

Mayer, Michael, *Der italienische Irredentismus*, second ed. (Innsbruck, 1917). Factual and interpretative. Sketchy after 1866.

Meyer, H. C., "Mitteleuropa in German Political Geography," *Annals of the Association of American Geographers*, XXXVI (1946), 178–194.

Miller, K. D., *The Czecho-Slovaks in America* (New York, 1922). Good.

Neugeboren, Emil, "Die Nationalitätenfrage im Ungarn der Vorkriegszeit," *Ungarische Jahrbücher*, XVIII (1938), 11–27.

Ninkov, Benno, *Die politische Anfänge Dr. Karl Luegers im Lichte der Wiener Presse* (Vienna, 1947). Illuminating thesis for the doctorate.

Oswald, Eugene, *Austria in 1868* (London, 1868). Brief, analytical survey.

Pliverič, Josef, *Beiträge zum ungarisch-kroatischen Bundesrechte* (Agram, 1886). Hard to follow, but full of interest.

Rauchberg, Heinrich, *Die statistischen Unterlagen der österreichischen Wahlreform* (Vienna, 1907). Good contemporary analysis.

Recouly, Raymond, *Le Pays Magyar* (Paris, 1903). Observations and interpretations of a journalist.

Reich, Josef, *Die Wiener Presse und der Wiener Börsenkrach von 1873 im wechselseitigen Förderungsprozess* (Vienna, 1947). Rather thin, but revealing.

Romanczuk, Julian, *Die Ruthenen und ihre Gegner in Galizien* (Vienna, 1902). Defense of Ruthenes by an able politician.

Rudert, Wolfgang, *Die Stellung des deutschen Reiches zur inner-österreichischen Lage, 1890–1900* (Leipzig: Arthur Schmidt, 1931). Unusually successful doctoral dissertation.

Rupp, G. H., *A Wavering Friendship: Russia and Austria, 1876–1878* (Cambridge: Harvard University Press, 1941). Scholarly treatise. Based upon thorough familiarity with the evidence.

Schinner, Walter, *Der österreichische-italienische Gegensatz auf der Balkan und der Adria, 1875–96* (Stuttgart: Kohlhammer, 1936). Heidelberg dissertation. Very good on Italian side.

Silber, M. H., *Der Kampf um das allgemeine Wahlrecht in Oesterreich von 1848 bis 1895 mit besonderer Berücksichtigung der Wiener Presse* (Vienna, 1933). Interesting.

Stieger, Wilhelm, *Das zweite Reich und die Innenpolitik Oesterreich-Ungarns 1871–1914* (Vienna, 1938). A well-wrought dissertation.

Thiel, H. J., *Die reichsdeutsche Presse und Publizistik und das österreichisch-ungarische Verfassungs- und Nationalitaten-problem 1903–06* (Rostock: Hinstorffs, 1936). Careful and interesting analysis.

Tukin, Cemal, *Die politischen Beziehungen zwischen Oesterreich-Ungarn und Bulgarien, 1908–13* (Hamburg: Christians, 1934). Awkwardly written. Thorough.

Walters, Eurof, "Franco-Russian Discussions on the Partition of Austria-Hungary, 1899," *Slavonic and East European Review*, XXVIII (1949–50), 184–197. With documents.

Wedel, Oswald, *Austro-German Diplomatic Relations, 1908–1914* (Stanford: Stanford University Press, 1932). Extremely useful work of painstaking and exact scholarship.

Werner, Lothar, *Der alldeutsche Verband, 1890–1918* (Berlin: Elbering, 1935). Balanced exposition.

Wichtl, Friedrich, *Dr. Karl Kramarsch, der Anstifter des Weltkrieges* (Munich, 1918). Highly tendentious. Colorful indictment.

Yolland, A. B., *The Hungarian Diet of 1905* (Budapest, 1905). Largely translations of Magyar documents.

BOOKS THAT APPEARED TOO LATE FOR STUDY

Bourgoing, Jean de, ed., *Briefe Kaiser Franz Josef an Frau Katharina Schratt* (Vienna: Ullstein, 1949).

Janetschek, Ottokar, *Kaiser Franz Joseph: Schicksale und Tragödien aus der guten alten Zeit* (Vienna: Amalthea, 1949).

Jenks, W. A., *The Austrian Electoral Reform of 1907* (New York: Columbia University Press, 1950).

Kann, R. A., *The Multinational Empire: Nationalism and National Reform in the Habsburg Monarchy 1848–1918*, 2 vols. (New York: Columbia University Press, 1950).

Srbik, Heinrich von, *Aus Oesterreichs Vergangenheit: von Prinz Eugen zu Franz Joseph* (Salzburg: Müller, 1949).

INDEX

EUROPEAN HISTORY TITLES IN
NORTON PAPERBOUND EDITIONS